Frommer's
Spain

by Patricia Harris and David Lyon

FrommerMedia LLC

Published by
Frommer Media LLC

ISBN 978-1-62887-148-7 (paper), 978-1-62887-149-4 (e-book)

Editorial Director: Pauline Frommer
Editor: Anuja Madar
Production Editor: Lynn Northrup
Cartographer: Liz Puhl
Photo Editor: Dana Davis

For information on our other products or services, see www.frommers.com.

Frommer Media LLC also publishes its books in a variety of electronic formats. Some content that appears in print may not be available in electronic formats.

Manufactured in China

5 4 3 2 1

CONTENTS

LIST OF MAPS

ABOUT THE AUTHORS

Patricia Harris and **David Lyon** have journeyed the world for American, British, Swiss, and Asian publishers to write about food, culture, art, and design. They have covered subjects as diverse as elk migrations in western Canada, the street markets of Shanghai, winter hiking on the Jungfrau, and the origins of Mesoamerican civilization in the Mexican tropics. In the name of research, they have eaten hot-pepper-toasted grasshoppers, tangles of baby eels, and roasted armadillo in banana sauce. Wherever they go, they are repeatedly drawn back to Spain for the flamenco nightlife, the Moorish architecture of Andalucía, the world-weary and lust-ridden saints of Zurbarán, and the phantasmagoric visions of El Greco. They can usually be found conversing with the locals in neighborhood bars while drinking the house wine and eating patatas bravas and grilled shrimp with garlic. They are the co-authors of *Frommer's Spain Day by Day* and *Frommer's EasyGuide to Madrid and Barcelona*.

THE BEST
OF SPAIN

We agree with the sentiment apocryphally attributed to Ernest Hemingway: "If you visit only one foreign country in your lifetime, make it Spain," Don Ernesto supposedly said. He might have added that after your first visit, you might not be tempted to go anywhere else. No other country is quite as flamboyantly romantic as Spain.

Even before Hemingway first visited in 1922 to write about trout and tuna fishing, 19th-century European writers and painters had mythologized Spain as the quintessential romantic country. It was the land of Moors and Gypsies, of swirling flamenco skirts and narrow-hipped matadors. It was the land of such legendary heroes as El Cid, such wise fools as Don Quijote, and of kings with such names as Pedro the Cruel and Alfonso the Wise. Hemingway's contribution was to give that romance both a macho gloss and an air of tragic loss.

The funny thing is that it's all still true—it's just not the whole truth. In fact, flamenco is enjoying a renaissance, and if some parts of the country have turned thumbs-down on bullfighting, many Spaniards are still obsessed with matadors. As the old *Saturday Night Live* routine goes, Franco is still dead. But Spain is very much alive. Having exported its talent during Franco's dictatorship, Spain jumped straight from the 19th century to the 21st. A flamenco beat still drives it, but Spain is now a country of high-speed trains and cutting-edge Web

ABOVE: **The Gardens of the Alhambra and Generalife in Granada.** PREVIOUS PAGE: **A horse dressed for Feria del Caballo in Jerez.**

Gaudi's Casa Mila, also known as La Pedrera.

technology, of a radical avant-garde in food and art alike, of vibrant modern metropolises like Barcelona, Bilbao, and Madrid that can hold their own on the world stage.

So Hemingway didn't get the last word. The country continues to evolve and its allures continue to multiply. Ultimately, your own experiences are the last word on Spain. Or, as a friend once said, "The sun not only rises. The moon comes out and the night is young." Here are some of what we think are highlights of Spain. Try them and see if you agree.

THE best AUTHENTIC SPANISH EXPERIENCES

o **Getting Caught Up in the Passions of Flamenco in Sevilla:** Whether you watch an artful performance at the flamenco dance museum or join the rowdier crowd in a Gypsy bar in Triana, you'll find yourself walking down the street to a syncopated beat. See p. 180.

o **Watching Children Light Up when They See Las Meninas in Madrid's Museo del Prado:** Diego Velázquez may have been the quintessential Spanish court painter, but his portrait of the Infanta Margarita and her retinue charms small children who imagine themselves in the painting. See p. 90.

o **Seeing the Homes of Moorish Royalty and Commoners in Granada:** The Alhambra palace was the crowning artistic glory of Islamic Spain. Once you've seen how the royals lived, wander the medieval warren of the Albaicín. See p. 219.

o **Joining a Tapas Crawl Around Madrid's Plaza Santa Ana:** Whole legs of air-dried mountain ham (*jamón serrano*) hang over every bar. Try it, along with bites of smoked trout, anchovies, potatoes with *bravas* sauce, or nuggets of sausage, on your evening outing. See p. 96.

o **Gaping at the Gaudís in Barcelona:** The Catalan language has the perfect verb to describe seeing the Modernisme buildings of Antoní Gaudí, including his Sagrada Familia basilica. *Badar* means "to walk around with your mouth open in amazement." See p. 355.

o **Celebrating the Basque Renaissance in Bilbao:** The bold architecture of the Guggenheim Museum set a new bar for design and sparked a chain of civic improvements. Between the new waterfront promenade and the architecture that aspires to Frank Gehry's achievement, Bilbao struts its stuff with pride. See p. 460.

o **Sunning on the Beach at the Foot of History at Tossa de Mar:** The ruins of a medieval coastal fortress crouch on one of the two headlands that bracket the sandy cove on the often-rocky Costa Brava. See p. 408.

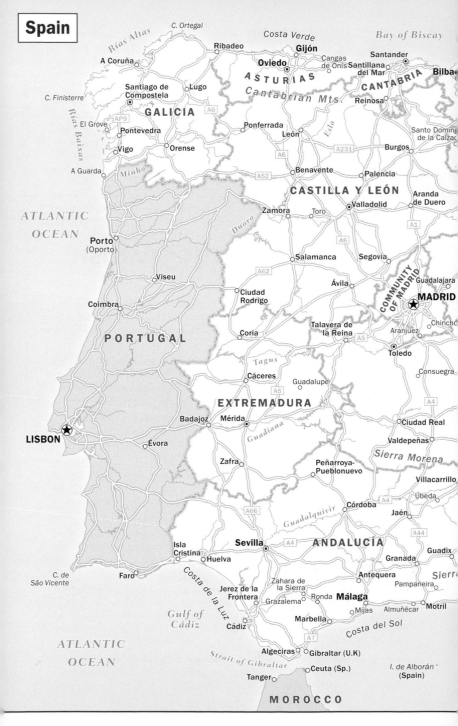

Spain

C. Ortegal
Rías Altas
Costa Verde
Bay of Biscay
Ribadeo
Gijón
A Coruña
Cangas
de Onís
Santander
Oviedo
Santillana
del Mar
A S T U R I A S
C A N T A B R I A
Bilba
Santiago de
Compostela
Lugo
Cantabrian Mts.
Reinosa
C. Finisterre
A6
Reinosa
GALICIA
Ponferrada
Santo Doming
de la Calza
Rías Baixas
El Grove
AP9
Pontevedra
León
A231
Burgos
Vigo
Orense
A6
A Guarda
Minho
Benavente
Palencia
A52
CASTILLA Y LEÓN
Aranda
de Duero
Zamora
Toro
Valladolid
ATLANTIC
Duoro
A1
OCEAN
Porto
(Oporto)
Salamanca
Segovia
A6
Viseu
A62
Ávila
Guadalajara
COMMUNITY
OF MADRID
MADRID
Ciudad
Rodrigo
Coimbra
Chinch
Coria
Talavera de
la Reina
A5
Aranjuez
PORTUGAL
Tagus
Toledo
Cáceres
Consuegra
Guadalupe
A5
A4
EXTREMADURA
Badajoz
Mérida
LISBON
Guadiana
Valdepeñas
Évora
Ciudad Real
Sierra Morena
Zafra
Villacarrillo
Peñarroya-
Pueblonuevo
Úbeda
A66
Córdoba
Guadalquivir
Jaén
Isla
Cristina
Sevilla
A4
ANDALUCÍA
Guadix
Huelva
Granada
Faro
Antequera
Sierr
C. de
São Vicente
Costa de la Luz
Zahara de
la Sierra
Pampaneira
Jerez de la
Frontera
Grazalema
Ronda
Málaga
Mijas
Almuñécar
Motril
Gulf of
Cádiz
Marbella
Costa del Sol
Cádiz
A7
ATLANTIC
Algeciras
Gibraltar (U.K)
OCEAN
Strait of Gibraltar
Ceuta (Sp.)
I. de Alborán
(Spain)
Tanger
MOROCCO

The cathedral of Santiago de Compostela.

o **Admiring the Faith of Pilgrims to Santiago de Compostela:** For nearly 10 centuries Christian pilgrims have trekked across northern Spain to the holy shrine of St. James, or Santiago. For the devout, walking into the great cathedral is an earthly taste of the gates of paradise. See p. 506.

THE best CITY AND REGIONAL EXPERIENCES

o **Driving the White Towns of the Sierra de Grazalema:** From Ronda to Arcos de la Frontera, the ancient mountain villages cling to their hilltops like a flock of nesting white birds. At the top of every town stands a medieval church built over a mosque built over a Roman temple. See p. 235.

o **Walking in Roman Footsteps in Tarragona:** The Amfiteatre Romà overlooking the ocean is a stunning reminder that Rome ruled eastern Iberia from this Costa Daurada port for more than 600 years. See p. 376.

o **Rambling the Judería of Córdoba:** Once you've seen La Mezquita, the greatest surviving medieval mosque in Europe, wander the network of narrow, shaded streets so ancient that centuries of whitewash have rounded every sharp corner of the walls. See p. 202.

o **Sampling the Future at the City of Arts & Sciences:** Few places on the planet feel as futuristic as the grand-scale buildings and plazas of Valencia's museum park. One of the buildings even winks its giant eye at you. See p. 285.

o **Surveying the Ages in Girona:** From Roman fortifications to Muslim palaces to the largest Jewish Call in Spain, Girona holds fast to its past. The ramparts above the cathedral show the whole ancient city, raised like dinosaur plates on the spine of a hill. See p. 392.

o **Seeing Rainbows While Crossing the Picos de Europa:** The abrupt limestone mountains of the Picos de Europa trap moisture flowing off the Atlantic into northern Spain. From the high mountain passes, rainbows arc across the lowlands below. See p. 482.

THE best HOTELS IN SPAIN

- **Hotel Atlántico, Parador de Cádiz:** The city of Cádiz is all about the sea and the light on the seas—and so is this hotel, where every room has a glass wall and a terrace overlooking the ocean. See p. 245.

- **Gran Hotel Domine, Bilbao:** It took a lot of architectural chutzpah to erect a contemporary design hotel right next to Frank Gehry's iconic Guggenheim Museum, but this place is up to the challenge. It's a sleek yet comfortable place to stay. See p. 463.

- **Hostal de Los Reyes Católicos, Santiago de Compostela:** Created by royal order to give comfort to pilgrims coming to Santiago, it's the most history-steeped lodging in town—or maybe in Spain. See p. 506.

- **Hotel María Cristina, San Sebastián:** Opulent in ways that only a Belle Époque hotel can be, this landmark hotel completed a tasteful renovation that makes the rooms as modern as they are luxe. See p. 448.

- **Hotel Adler, Madrid:** Rarely do luxury, grace, and decorum meet in such harmony. Perfectly reflecting its upscale neighborhood, the Adler makes its guests feel like members of the aristocracy. See p. 72.

- **Casa Fuster, Barcelona:** Modernisme's heyday lives again in this deluxe hotel designed as a private home in 1908 by Lluís Domènech i Montaner. Private balconies in many rooms open onto leafy Passeig de Gràcia. See p. 325.

- **Hostal de la Gavina, Sant Feliu de Guíxols:** This oasis amid the bustle of the Costa Brava epitomizes gracious living with a hint of Moorish style. See p. 406.

- **Hotel Marqués de Riscal, Elciego:** The Rioja wine house, Marqués de Riscal, engaged Frank Gehry to design a "City of Wine" that includes not only the production facilities, but also this striking contemporary hotel with a vast shell of anodized titanium. It's a kissing cousin to the Guggenheim in Bilbao. See p. 437.

Cordoba's La Mezquita.

○ **Las Casas de la Judería, Córdoba:** This romantic hotel with rooms carved from adjacent 17th- and 18th-century city palaces sits steps from Cordoba's famous mosque in one direction and Alcázar in the other. See p. 203.

○ **Parador Casa del Corregidor, Arcos de la Frontera:** Built for the king's magistrate in the 18th century, this palace occupies the catbird seat with commanding views of the Río Guadalete plain below. Driving here is only for the intrepid. See p. 238.

THE best TAPAS DINING

○ **Mirador de Doñana, Sanlúcar de Barrameda:** From tiny shrimp to whopping prawns, the Bahía de Cádiz off Sanlúcar has an amazing variety of sweet shrimp. Grilled, steamed, roasted, or stewed, they are perfect with a glass of the village's *manzanilla* sherry and the view of the Río Guadalquivír delta. See p. 244.

○ **Bergara Bar, San Sebastián:** San Sebastián may have more good tapas bars serving "pintxos creativos" than the rest of Spain combined, and this ultra-traditional bar that displays 60 or more tapas at a time is considered a national treasure by gastronomes and Spanish chefs alike. See p. 451.

○ **La Manzanilla, Málaga:** Daní Garcia's big city tapas bar plays the traditional dishes of the Costa del Sol against American fast food inspirations. His *raba de toro* burger tastes just like the stewed dish, while the "Pigburguer" gilds the lily of ground Iberian pork with bacon. See p. 272.

○ **Nou Manolín, Alicante:** Famous chefs from all over Spain (and even France) come on eating holidays to Alicante to treat themselves to Nou Manolín's great fish tapas. See p. 304.

○ **Estado Puro, Madrid:** Superchef Paco Roncero deconstructs the classics in post-modern tapas such as his cordial glass of liquid *tortilla Española*, or potato omelet. See p. 77.

○ **TragaTapas, Ronda:** An offshoot of the elegant Tragabuches restaurant, this tapas bar pioneered the reinvention of tapas. A single spear of grilled asparagus topped with grated cheese and accompanied by a square of quince paste is quintessentially Spanish and unlike anything you'll eat elsewhere. See p. 231.

Sampling tapas in Madrid.

○ **Tapas 24, Barcelona:** With tapas for breakfast (broken eggs over fried potatoes), lunch (grilled ham and cheese with black truffle), or dinner (hamburger with foie gras), this is chef Carles Abellean's homage to the tapas lifestyle. See p. 339.

○ **Casa Juan, Torremolinos:** Mainly a seafood restaurant, Casa Juan serves tapas between meals (i.e., between 5–9pm). It's the perfect spot for a *freidura* of mixed tiny seafood—often called "fried foam"—fried in olive oil. Eat it skin, bones, and all. See p. 267.

Suckling pig roasting in a tile oven.

o **Bodeguita Casablanca, Sevilla:** Just outside the Puerto de Jerez, this seemingly traditional bar spawns all sorts of creative twists on old-fashioned tapas, including the *tortilla al whiskey*—a *tortilla Española* with Scotch whisky sauce. See p. 190.

o **Taberna Bar Cuervo, León:** Michelin-starred chefs throughout Spain have begun to feature the air-dried beef of León on their menus. This taberna has had the best for decades, along with classic León sausages. See p. 176.

o **Taberna Casa Manteca, Cádiz:** The owners of this bullfight tavern boast the girth you might expect from "the house of lard." The tapas menu features all manner of pork dishes along with Bahía de Cadiz seafood. See p. 249.

THE best RESTAURANTS

o **Arzak, San Sebastián:** Juan Marí and Elena Arzak go into the laboratory at least 1 day a week to literally cook up something you have never tasted before. The restaurant has been a leader in avant-garde Basque cuisine for more than 4 decades. See p. 451.

o **José María Restaurante, Segovia:** Segovianos are fanatics about roast suckling pig. This restaurant is where aficionados of *cochinillo* take their families for the crispest crackling skin and the juiciest succulent meat. See p. 146.

o **Lasarte, Barcelona:** Basque chef Martín Berasategui calls San Sebastián home, but this exquisite fine dining restaurant in the foodie mecca of Barcelona reinterprets some of his greatest dishes along with innovations by his brilliant chef de cuisine. See p. 337.

o **Dani García Restaurante, Marbella:** A fixture on the Costa del Sol, star chef Dani García has a new venue where he recapitulates some of his classics such as lobster salad with "popcorn" olives (exploded with liquid nitrogen) and suckling pig with pumpkin and orange. See p. 258.

o **El Celler de Can Roca, Girona:** Roca brothers Joan (head chef), Jordi (head pastry chef), and Josep (sommelier) belie the trope about broth and too many cooks. This is Catalan home cooking with surreal twists, as if Salvador Dalí's ghost were in the kitchen. See p. 395.

○ **Viridiana, Madrid:** Chef Abraham García blogs about food online for *El Mundo* and is such a film buff that he named the restaurant after the 1961 Luis Buñuel film. Wit and wonderment abound on his menu, and many of Spain's top chefs apprenticed here. See p. 76.

○ **La Pepica, Valencia:** The Picassos of paella are the cooks in La Pepica's sprawling kitchens. This is the temple of *paella Valenciana*—and dozens of variations. See p. 291.

○ **Casa Marcial, Arriondas:** Nacho Mendez made his mark in London, but his family restaurant is where he concocts outrageous and delicious dishes such as cucumber soup over green pepper sorbet or roast woodcock with oysters and river eels. See p. 488.

○ **Solla, Pontevedra:** Pepe Solla is self-taught, so he lacks the preconceptions of a classically trained chef. He thinks nothing of pairing sea bass, for example, with braised turnip greens, Galician cabbage, and an orange-lemon sauce. See p. 516.

○ **Etxanobe, Bilbao:** Fernando Canales looks like a rock star and cooks like a genius. Always inventing new riffs on Basque cuisine, he cultivates a direct pipeline to foragers and fishermen to ensure he has the very best products of the season. See p. 464.

THE best WAYS TO SEE SPAIN LIKE A LOCAL

○ **Shop in the Fresh Food Markets of Barcelona and Valencia:** One look at the culinary riches on display in Barcelona's La Boqueria and Valencia's Mercado Central, and you'll grasp the Spanish obsession with eating. Wait till you taste that orange! See p. 342 and p. 297.

○ **Look for the Good-Luck Frog in Salamanca:** The university city has the wittiest and most phantasmagoric stone carvings in all of Spain. Students look for

Flowering patio of Cordoba.

a frog perched on a skull in the elaborate carvings around the door to the Escuelas Mayores. See p. 165.

○ **Crowd into a Bar to Root for Real Madrid:** With ticket prices for the Real Madrid football (soccer) matches as expensive as American football, most fans watch the matches on television—ideally on a *huge* screen in a bar. See p. 114.

○ **Bargain with Vendors at El Rastro:** The venerable Sunday street market in Madrid's Lavapiés district is awash with bargains, but shopping seems like even more fun when you can haggle with the vendors to get a lower price on that pashmina shawl, those silver earrings, or a leather purse. See p. 99.

o **Dance the Sardana in Barcelona:** Every Sunday people gather outside the cathedral in Barcelona for the circular folk dance known as the *sardana.* The steps are easy, and anyone is welcome. Just toss your valuables into the pile in the center, join hands, and dance. See p. 349.

o **Visit the Private Patios of Córdoba:** During the Córdoba Patio Festival in May, people open their homes so visitors can admire the flowers they grow in their interior courtyards. See p. 209.

o **Make the Evening Promenade in Marbella:** All over Spain people go out for a leisurely evening walk to show off a beau, visit with neighbors, or just enjoy the cool air. The marble sidewalks of Marbella are an elegant setting for a stroll. See p. 256.

THE best FAMILY OUTINGS

o **Talking to the Animals at the Bioparc Fuengirola:** Moats and landscape features substitute for bars and cages at this model zoo where you can see more than 140 species of animals native to three different ecosystems. See p. 263.

o **Seeing the Horses Dance in Jerez de la Frontera:** Elegant Hispano-Arab horses go through their paces every Thursday at the Escuela Andaluza del Arte Ecuestre (Andalucían School of Equestrian Art) in Jerez. They rear back and dance as part of the weekly show. See p. 243.

o **Walking on the Walls of Avila:** The 11th-century walls around Avila are some of the most intact medieval walls in Europe. Walking the ramparts gives stirring views of the countryside and puts you eye to eye with storks nesting on the city's highest buildings. See p. 151.

o **Hiking the Wind-Sculpted Hoodoos of El Torcal:** Andalucía's first natural park is a fantasia of wind-sculpted limestone boulders. Trails lead through the surreal landscape. See p. 278.

o **Taking the Tykes to Madrid's Parque del Retiro:** Madrid's families flock to the Parque del Retiro on Sundays to row around the lake in boats, catch

The Cuevas del Drach.

impromptu concerts, and let the little ones watch old-fashioned puppet shows. See p. 107.

o **Boating on the Largest Underground Lake on Mallorca:** The Cuevas del Drach (Caves of the Dragon) have concerts amid their forests of stalagmites and stalactites. Row around Lago Martel, the largest cavern lake in the world, in illuminated rowboats. See p. 537.

o **Riding the Train to the Beach in Alicante:** Hop the local light rail in downtown Alicante and arrive minutes later at the long sands of the barrier beach known as Playa San Juan (or Platja Sant Joan, in Valenciano). See p. 302.

THE best ART MUSEUMS

o **Museo del Prado, Madrid:** Created from the royal art collections, this is one of the world's greatest art museums. Its strengths are Spanish painting, beginning with anonymous Gothic masters. Diego Velázquez seems the undisputable star—until you encounter the early pastorals and late nightmares of Francisco de Goya. See p. 90.

o **Museo Nacional Centro de Arte Reína Sofía:** During the Franco dictatorship, Spain's artists fled to countries more hospitable to their modern visions. The Reina Sofía repatriates them in spades. Pablo Picasso's *Guernica,* his *cri de coeur* for the bombing of a defenseless Basque village, is the definitive antiwar piece of art. See p. 92.

o **Museo de Bellas Artes, Sevilla:** The tiled courtyards of the 1594 former convent that houses this museum almost upstage the art. Bartholomé Esteban Murillo's masterpieces painted for the convent remain in their original home, while the most haunting figures are Francisco de Zurbarán's portraits of saints. See p. 195.

o **Fundació Joan Miró, Barcelona:** More than 10,000 works by Joan Miró fill this light-filled museum atop Montjuïc in Barcelona. His surreal shapes

and dreamy spaces have a whimsy of their own, like someone telling a funny story in another language. See p. 363.

o **Teatre-Museu Dalì, Figueres:** Salvador Dalí cultivated his image as an eccentric, so it's no surprise that his final monument to himself is a former theater transformed into a non-stop sequence of visual jokes. Here it rains *inside* the car. See p. 402.

o **Museu Picasso, Barcelona:** The artist who redefined art in the 20th century was so prolific that whole museums are dedicated to him in his birthplace, Málaga, and in Paris, where he spent some of his most productive years. The Barcelona museum

The Teatre-Museu Dali in Figueres.

blossoms with his earnest early work and the joyous paintings of the 1950s and 1960s. See p. 352.

o **Museo de Santa Cruz, Toledo:** The Greek mystical painter Domenikos Theotokopoulos adopted Toledo as his home, though Toledanos always called him "the Greek," or El Greco. His passionate paintings—virtual rivers of paint on canvas, often from an angel's vantage—reside in this marvelous museum. See p. 131.

o **Museo Carmen Thyssen, Málaga:** The Baroness Carmen Thyssen (of the Thyssen-Bornemisza Museum in Madrid) endowed this institution with a sharply focused collection of Spanish paintings from 1825 to 1925 that document Spain's transition from Romantic cliché to nation with a modern sensibility. See p. 275.

o **Guggenheim Museum, Bilbao:** Frank Gehry's titanium-clad fish of a museum building was originally the institution's leading piece of art. Over time, it has accreted its own personality, with a penchant for performance pieces and sculpture (some whimsical, some not) on a gargantuan scale. See p. 466.

o **Museu Nacional d'Art de Catalunya, Barcelona:** Some of Europe's best Romanesque and early Gothic art was created for Catalan churches. Thanks to heroic rescue efforts, much of it is collected here. See p. 364.

THE best OF OUTDOOR SPAIN

o **Hiking the Alpujarra de Granada:** Ancient Moorish mountain villages southeast of Granada make for nearly ideal town-to-town hiking on exposed rocky trails. Good starter hikes begin in the outdoors outfitting center of Pampaneira. Guided hikes also can be arranged at the information center of the Parque Natural de Sierra Nevada. See p. 228.

o **Cycling to L'Albufera:** The marshlands south of Valencia's port are best explored on two wheels, and there's even a bike path much of the way. See the rice farmers toiling in the marshes, enjoy the almost deserted beaches, and stop for a great paella. See p. 301.

o **Surfing the Break in Mundaka:** The long rolling barrel curl in Mundaka on the Basque Coast is famous with surfers all over the world. It's also one of the most reliable surfing breaks in Europe. Plan on wearing a wetsuit; the Bay of Biscay can be frigid. See p. 457.

o **Exploring Parque Doñana by Boat:** One of the most important refuges for migratory birds, the Donaña marshes form part of the delta of the Río Guadalquivír as it reaches the Bahía de Cádiz. Naturalist-led boat tours leave daily from Sanlúcar de Barrameda. See p. 244.

o **Walking the Fuente Dé Ridge in the Picos de Europa:** You'll have to drive to the teleférico (cable car) station to ride up to a high ridge of Fuente Dé. Walk the ridge, visit the cafe, and marvel at the mountains. See p. 482.

A surfer tackles the barrel curl in Mundaka.

o **Visiting the Illa de Cabrera Natural Reserve off Mallorca:** Although Cabrera was a pirate base in the 13th and 14th centuries, now it is a Natural Reserve where you can see huge colonies of shearwaters and gulls as well as ospreys, falcons, and sea hawks. See p. 530.

THE best SMALL TOWNS

o **Cuenca:** With its famous *casas colgadas* ("hanging houses") cantilevered over the edge of a precipitous gorge and its three museums of contemporary art, this aerie engages the imagination even as it wins over the heart. Few villages in Spain seem so magically suspended between earth and sky. See p. 134.

o **Mijas:** Even as the countryside around it becomes a solid mass of hotels and vacation home subdivisions, tiny, whitewashed Mijas, tucked into the hills above sprawling Torremolinos, remains a quintessential Andalucian village where life revolves around ancient churches, excellent bars, and a tiny religious shrine. See p. 264.

o **Ronda:** Ronda is famed for its 150m (492-ft.) gorge of the Río Guadelevín. The Romans bridged the river at the water's edge, and Moors built homes and palaces all the way to the top. The Christians added a bullring and a belvedere. What more could you ask? See p. 229.

o **Zamora:** When the Christian kings of Castilla took back Zamora from the Moors, they made sure they could hold it by building two dozen fabulous Romanesque churches in the 12th and 13th centuries. The town fortifications have great views along the Río Duero. See p. 166.

o **Elche:** Boasting the largest palm forest in Europe and an archaeological museum devoted to the ancient Iberians, Elche also has the Pikolinos shoe

The bridge across the Jucar gorge, leading to Cuenca's hanging houses.

factory outlet at the edge of town. See p. 306.

o **Deià:** Set on the western end of Mallorca, this high-country village of stone houses draped in bougainvillea was the favored retreat of English poet and interpreter of Greek mythology, Robert Graves. It was here he wrote the enduring historical novel *I, Claudius*. See p. 532.

o **Santo Domingo de la Calzada:** Established in the 12th century as a stopover for pilgrims heading to the shrine of Santiago de Compostela, this little village in La Rioja eventually grew into a full-fledged pilgrim town where live chickens are kept in the cathedral. See p. 174.

A lively alley in Mijas.

THE best SECRET SPAIN

o **Toro:** This dusty little wine town on the Río Duero east of Zamora huddles behind medieval walls. The carvings on the main entry of its 13th-century church are some of Spain's greatest Gothic art. Most Toro shops sell wine very, very good wine. See p. 170.

o **Cadaqués:** Isolated along the coast over a steep range of mountains, Cadaqués remains the sweet fishing town that has drawn so many artists over the years. The village wraps around a half-dozen rocky coves with a stony beach better for landing small boats than sunbathing. See p. 402.

o **Poblet:** Once the greatest of Catalunya's Carthusian monasteries, Poblet has retreated to near oblivion. Yet the fortified monastery village west of Barcelona has a medieval charm, as if it were plucked directly from Umberto Eco's *Name of the Rose*. The kings of Aragon are buried beneath the church. See p. 383.

o **The Cantabrian Caves:** Whether they were painted 10,000 or 30,000 years ago, the delicate deer and hunched buffalo on the walls of Cantabria's limestone caves remain fresh and vibrant today. See p. 481.

o **Ubeda:** In an age when high-speed rail connects most Spanish cities, the elegant Renaissance burg of Ubeda stands aloof in the Andalucían highlands northeast of Granada. It is almost an open-air museum of Spanish Renaissance architecture. See p. 226.

o **Alfaro:** No one knows why, but roughly 400 pairs of white storks have adopted a single church building as their nest site in this nearly forgotten city of the Navarran countryside. Scientists flock here from February to August to observe the birds up close. See p. 436.

o **Teruel:** The Aragonese city of Teruel northwest of Valencia is a treasure trove of Mudéjar architecture—a uniquely Spanish style that came about when Christian patrons engaged Moorish architects and workmen. The synthesis of cultures yielded some of the richest design of the late Middle Ages. See p. 420.

SPAIN IN DEPTH

One of the few things that the French and English used to agree on was that "Europe ends at the Pyrenees." Those mountains kept Spain in splendid isolation, where it developed along its own path. Consequently, Spain has evolved customs, art, architecture, and even cuisine that owe as much to Islamic North Africa as to its onetime sister provinces of the Roman Empire. The country does not look like, sound like, or even taste like the rest of Europe, and nowhere else is quite as rich or demanding. When you go to Spain, you must surrender to Spain.

You must accept the rhythms of daily life—so unlike the rest of Europe—and think nothing of going to dinner after 10pm and then closing down the flamenco bar after the 3am final set. You must spend the evening in a seafront promenade, walking and talking and nodding at the other walkers and talkers. You must elbow your way to the bar, pointing at the tapas to order, and having your fill. For that matter, you must resolve to eat something new every day that you would otherwise spurn: blood sausage, roasted suckling pig, squid in its own ink. In many places, shops and museums close in the heat of the afternoon, and you must be patient and while away the hours with lunch in a cool, shady courtyard. Do all that, and you will be ready for everything Spain will throw at you.

Rest assured, it will be a lot. The cultural renaissance that followed the 1975 death of dictator Francisco Franco continues to gather steam. Madrid and Barcelona have emerged as major European artistic and intellectual centers of cinema, fashion, and gastronomy. At the same time, Bilbao has provided a blueprint to the world for using art to transform an industrial backwater into a vibrant cultural capital.

SPAIN TODAY

An international financial crisis lasting almost a decade has left Spain the equivalent of "house poor." Before the collapse began in 2007, Spain had launched some of the most audacious infrastructure improvements since Europe's recovery from World War II. New roads, high-speed rail, and new and improved airports helped knit together a physically large country. Travel times were cut to a fraction of what they once were, and relatively inaccessible parts of Spain are now a short drive or train ride away.

Barcelona's **El Prat** airport opened a new Terminal 1 in 2009, and Madrid's **Barajas** airport opened the futuristic Terminal 4 in 2006. Ironically, air traffic between Barcelona and Madrid, once one of the busiest routes in the world, slacked off considerably after the opening of high-speed rail, which covers the distance between the two cities in just 2½ hours. The first high-speed rail made Sevilla a mere 2-hour journey from Madrid, and recently expanded lines now reach from the central hub of Madrid east to Valencia, north to the edge of the Basque Country, and northwest to Santiago de Compostela.

FACING PAGE: **A bullfighter in Sevilla.**

Alas, the bills for all those infrastructure upgrades came due at the same time that the credit dried up. As a result, Spain's national economy has suffered, and inflation has turned to deflation. With one-quarter of the country's workers idle, Spain's social safety net is stretched to its limits. Tourism remains the bright spot in the economy. European visitors continue to flock to Spain's beach resorts on both the Mediterranean and Atlantic coasts, while Americans are the top visitor group to Sevilla, Madrid, and Barcelona. Spain has always been a friendly place for English speakers, and now more Spaniards than ever speak the language, often with an accent honed by American television and movies.

LOOKING BACK AT SPAIN

To understand Spain's accretion of cultures, simply look to any major religious site. The Christian cathedral is often built on the site of a Moorish mosque that had been erected on the ruins of a Visigothic church built atop the cellars of a Roman temple, which may have used the building blocks and columns from an even earlier Phoenician house of worship.

The peopling of the Iberian peninsula began around 35,000 B.C., with the arrival of Cro-Magnon refugees from the glaciation of Europe. Traces of the first settlers are scattered, and are found mainly in the sophisticated wall paintings in **Altamira** (p. 481) and other caves along the Cantabrian and Basque coasts. The **Basque Archaeological Museum** (p. 467) in Bilbao offers a good overview of what science knows about these first Spaniards.

Two Bronze Age cultures had emerged in Spain by the time other Mediterranean cultures made contact. The Iberians are perhaps best known today through a few examples of sophisticated sculpture, La Dama de Baeza and La Dama d'Elx, both seated funerary figures. The former is in the **National Archaeology Museum** in Madrid (p. 118), the latter in the **Elx Archaeology Museum.** The other culture was Celtic, and flourished around the Atlantic rim of the peninsula. One of the chief Celtic settlements, at Tartessos at the mouth of the Río Guadalquivír, became famous throughout the ancient world for its jewelry and for its dance and music. (Tartessans invented castanets.) Examples of exquisite Celtic gold work are in the **National Archaeology Museum** in Madrid (p. 118) and in the **Archaeological and Historical Museum** in A Coruña (p. 503).

Phoenician settlement began in Iberia around 1100 B.C., most notably in Málaga and in the peninsular city of Cádiz, where extraordinary Phoenician sarcophagi and some Phoenician jewelry are displayed in the **Museo de Cádiz** (p. 248). Within 200 years, Greek traders began to give the Phoenicians competition, founding the trading post at **Empuriès** (p. 405) on the Costa Brava and pushing into the Balearics and coastal Andalucía. Foreshadowing the much later invasion from North Africa, Carthaginians began colonizing Iberia in the 6th century B.C.; little remains of their material culture.

In 218 B.C., the Romans landed and changed everything. Establishing a beachhead to battle the Carthaginians in the Second Punic War, they proceeded to lay roads across Iberia and either conquer or co-opt everyone they met along the way. The Phoenicians and Greeks had already brought wine grapes and olive trees; the Romans brought wheat, law and order, a hunger for Iberian fish paste, and an insatiable need for soldiers to fight in the Roman legions. By the time of Julius Caesar, Hispania was under Roman law and began a long period of peace and prosperity.

Tarragona, a short trip south from Barcelona, became the administrative center for eastern Hispania and retains many Roman structures to this day (p. 376). The Romans were natural architects and engineers. Throughout the country, Roman roads still form the base for many highways. **Segovia,** a short trip out of Madrid, boasts one of the greatest of the Roman aqueducts (p. 143).

Iberia was thoroughly Romanized during this period, although the Basques negotiated a fragile peace with Rome that allowed them to maintain their right of self-governance. Succeeding rulers granted the Basques the same autonomy until the late 19th century. The Pax Romana prevailed throughout the peninsula, and Latin became the Iberian language.

When the Roman Empire crumbled in the 5th century A.D. Iberia was first overrun by the Vandals (northern Germans who ultimately kept going south into the mountains of North Africa) and then by the Visigoths from Eastern Europe. Rome had invited them to drive out the Vandals, but they decided to keep Iberia for themselves. Always a minority ruling class, the Visigoths left surprisingly few traces of their 200-year rule (a few country churches in northern Spain and the royal jewels and crowns, plus some of the most sophisticated gold jewelry ever fashioned, seen at **National Archaeological Museum** in Madrid (p. 118).

Centuries of Holy Wars

In A.D. 711, the game changed again. Led by the great Berber general Tariq ibn Ziyad, Moorish warriors crossed the Straits of Gibraltar from Morocco and set about conquering Iberia. Within 3 years, the Moors controlled all but the far northern fringe of the peninsula, where the Basques and the Asturian Visigoths held out in their mountain lairs.

The Iberian population had collapsed under the chaotic rule of the Visigoths, and the Moors began to repopulate their conquered land, which they called al-Andalus. While northern Europe was foundering in the Dark Ages, the Andalucían capital of Córdoba was a model of enlightenment. Religious tolerance was an official policy under the Umayyad Caliphate (A.D. 929–1031). Córdoba's **Great Mosque (La Mezquita)** (p. 202) was erected in this period, and European, North African, Near Eastern, and Jewish scholars flocked to the city. Notable advances were made in agriculture, industry, literature, philosophy, and medicine.

By the late 11th century, powerful local kingdoms had arisen in northern Spain with the single-minded goal of restoring Christian rule to Muslim Iberia. When civil war broke out in al-Andalus, the northern Christian warriors pounced. **Alfonso VI** of Castilla seized Toldeo, Madrid, and much of central Spain in 1085; the great warlord and national hero **El Cid** won back Valencia and Catalunya (including Barcelona) in 1094. By 1214, only three major powers remained in Iberia: Castilla in the north, west, and center of Spain; Aragón in northeastern Spain; and the Moorish kingdom of Granada, which would flower a century later with the supreme example of Moorish architecture and decorative arts, the **Alhambra** (p. 219).

The Castilian and Aragónese bloodlines would finally meet in Spain's first power couple, **Isabel I of Castilla and León** and **Fernando II of Aragón.** They married in 1469, bringing Toledo (and nearby Madrid) and Barcelona under the same joint rule. Isabel launched the Spanish Inquisition to ferret out heretics, and the Catholic kings (as the pope would dub them) made war on Granada and drove out its last ruler in 1492. Declaring the reconquest complete, Isabel and Fernando decreed that all Muslims and Jews must either convert to Christianity or leave the country.

Later that same year, they dispatched **Christopher Columbus** to find a westward passage to the Spice Islands of Asia, an event memorialized in statuary in the garden of Córdoba's **Alcázar** (p. 242). He sailed from the mouth of the Rio Guadalquivír in Andalucía, and, in October 1492, made landfall instead in the West Indies. His voyages of discovery laid the foundations for a far-flung empire that would bring wealth and power to Spain throughout the 16th and 17th centuries.

Imperial Spain

The grandson of Isabel and Fernando, the Habsburg king **Carlos I** became the most powerful ruler in Europe when he was crowned Holy Roman Emperor in 1519 and took the title **Carlos V.** He ruled Spain and Naples and the Holy Roman Empire and was lord of Germany, duke of Burgundy and the Netherlands, and ruler of the New World territories. His son, **Felipe II,** inherited the throne in 1556 and 5 years later moved the capital from the closed hilltop medieval city of Toledo to Madrid, where the Habsburg kings had a hunting palace.

Madrid grew quickly from dusty outpost to royal city, setting Spain on its Golden Age of arts and letters, and Madrid on its domination of the national scene. **Miguel de Cervantes** (1547–1616), a career petty bureaucrat, penned the adventures of Don Quijote and set the standard for Spanish prose. The rascal priest **Lope de Vega** (1562–1635) wrote poems and plays incessantly, redefining the Spanish theater in the company of **Calderón de la Barca** (1600–81) and **Tirso de Molina** (1579–1648).

El Greco (1541–1614) came to Toledo from Italy and brought the Italian Renaissance with him, although he could not curry favor at court and remained outside royal circles. One of his greatest works, ***The Burial of the Count of Orgaz,*** occupies a modest chapel in Toledo's **Iglesia de Santo Tomé** (p. 128). **Diego Velázquez** (1599–1660) rose to become court painter to **Felipe IV,** and the two men were bound like brothers over several decades as Velázquez chronicled the royal family. His paintings were rarely seen in his own day and became public only when the royal art collection was installed in the **Museo del Prado** (p. 90) in the 19th century.

When the crown passed from the Habsburgs to the Bourbon line in 1700, **Felipe V** revoked the autonomy of Catalunya to quash his political foes and turned to re-making Madrid as a proper capital to entertain his French cousins. His first task was to begin construction of the **Palacio Real** (p. 100). His son **Carlos III** transformed the face of Madrid with the aid of Spain's principal neoclassical architect, **Ventura Rodríguez** (1717–85), who laid out the grand boulevard of the Paseo del Prado and worked with **Juan de Villanueva** (1739–1811) on one of Spain's best neoclassical buildings, the Museo del Prado.

La Sagrada Familia.

Spain in Chaos

Napoleon Bonaparte's 1808 invasion of Spain set off 167 years of instability and political oppression. Noting that Catalunya existed because the French monarchy had created it in the 9th century as a buffer between the French and the Moors, Napoleon annexed the region (and the riches of Barcelona). The rest of Spain literally took to the hills to fight the French emperor in the War of Independence, finally driving his armies out in 1813. **Francisco de Goya** famously delineated the horrors of French occupation in a series of paintings now in the Prado.

The Catalan territory was restored to Spain, along with the Bourbon monarchy, but something in Spanish governance was irreparably broken. **Fernando VII** regained the throne but proved to be no friend of the freedom fighters and spent 2 decades putting down revolts. His arrogance and inflexibility led to the loss of Spain's most lucrative colonies in the Americas—and subsequent financial hardship for the country.

On the death of Fernando in 1833, civil war broke out between supporters of his daughter (**Isabel II**) and so-called Carlists who favored a more distant—but male—heir to the throne. Two more Carlist wars were fought, mostly in Navarra and the Basque Country, over the next 50 years, and Carlist sympathies festered into the 20th century, fueling both Franco's Falangist movement as well as the separatist sympathies among the Basques. During this period, Spain was coming apart at the seams, and nationalist fervor ran high, especially Catalunya.

Scholars began to reestablish Catalan as a language of serious letters, and the avant-garde design style known as Art Nouveau in France and Jugendstil in Austria found native expression in Barcelona in the radical architecture of **Modernisme.** The most extreme practitioner was **Antoni Gaudí** (1852–1926), who seemed as much to grow his buildings as construct them. His masterpiece **La Sagrada Familia** (p. 355) integrates the impossibly soaring arches of High Gothic with a decorative style akin to melted candle wax. Other famous practitioners of Modernisme include **Lluís Domènech i Montaner** (1850–1923), known for the **Palau de la Música Catalana** (p. 353) in Barcelona, and **Josep Puig i Cadafalch** (1867–1956), who designed the **Codorniù bodega** in Sant Sadurní de Anoia.

Isabel II ultimately was driven into exile in Paris, but the shaky monarchy was restored in 1874 when her son **Alfonso XII** became king. His sudden death in 1886 left his unborn son as monarch. The child was crowned **Alfonso XIII** at birth, but his mother, Queen María Cristina, served as regent until 1902, and her advisors botched both the Spanish economy and its international relations. During this period, Spain lost its remaining American colonies, suffering as much from the loss of national dignity as overseas riches. Although he enjoyed immense personal popularity—he was the first Spanish celebrity king—Alfonso XIII exercised little real power. His chief legacy was to adopt the **Real Madrid** football club and to create the parador hotel system. In 1923, he allowed prime minister **Primo de Rivera** to take over the country as dictator for the next 7 years.

Civil War & the Franco Years

Primo de Rivera was overthrown, and in 1931 Spain declared the Second Republic. Initially progressive and left-wing in its politics, the new government broke into ever-smaller factions. Conservative, fascist-minded parties gained ground in the elections. When a group of right-wing generals declared a coup in 1936, the Civil War began. The world took sides, with Hitler and Mussolini backing

THE SPECTACLE OF death

Whether you love or despise bullfighting, the *corrida* is impossible to ignore. In *Death in the Afternoon*, Ernest Hemingway wrote, "The bullfight is not a sport in the Anglo-Saxon sense of the word; that is, it is not an equal contest or an attempt at an equal contest between a bull and a man. Rather it is a tragedy: the death of the bull, which is played, more or less well, by the bull and the man involved and in which there is danger for the man but certain death for the bull."

We're more conflicted about bullfights than Papa was. In Spain, lithe (and, yes, sexy) matadors have all the celebrity of rock stars—and we love a good spectacle. But as animal lovers, we've never attended a bullfight in person because we know that no matter how skillful and graceful the matador, we couldn't stomach the baiting, wounding, and eventual killing of the bull. And, yes, we know that the animal is respected in death, and that some of its meat is even distributed to the poor.

Many Spaniards, including the queen, dislike (or simply have no interest) in the sport, and the autonomous region of Catalunya has banned it altogether. But the *corrida* persists as an element of Spanish identity. If you'd like to grapple with your own feelings about this confluence of culture and cruelty,

the *corrida* season lasts from early spring to around mid-October. Fights are held in a *plaza de toros* (bullring), including the oldest ring in remote Ronda and one of the most beautiful in Sevilla. Madrid's Las Ventas is arguably the most important in Spain. The best bullfighters face the best bulls here—and the fans who pack the stands are among the sport's most passionate and knowledgeable.

The corrida begins with a parade featuring all the bullfighters clad in their *trajes de luces* (suits of lights). The fight itself is divided in thirds (*tercios*). In the *tercio de capa* (cape), the matador tests the bull with passes and gets acquainted with the animal. The second portion, the *tercio de varas* (sticks), begins with the lance-carrying *picadores* on horseback, who weaken the bull by jabbing him in the shoulder area. The *picadores* are followed by the *banderilleros*, whose job it is to puncture the bull with pairs of boldly colored darts.

In the final *tercio de muleta*, the action narrows down to one lone fighter and the bull. Gone are the fancy capes. Instead, using a small red cloth (*muleta*) as a lure, the matador wraps the bull around himself in various passes. After a number of passes, the time comes for the kill, the moment of truth.

Francisco Franco, and the Nationalist generals and most of the rest of Europe nominally backing the Republicans, also known as Loyalists or the Popular Front. Germany and Italy sent weapons and military assistance to the right, while the rest of the world sent a few volunteer brigades, including the American contingent called the "Lincoln Brigade." (For those who want insight into the era, Ernest Hemingway's *For Whom the Bell Tolls* is a good read.) It took time to turn untrained militias into an army fit to battle Franco's forces, and time was something the Popular Front did not have.

In the winter of 1936–37, Franco's forces slowly began to establish power, capturing the Basque country and demonstrating his ruthlessness by calling in the German Luftwaffe to destroy the Basque town of **Gernika** (Guernica in Castilian Spanish). The horror of the scene, which became the subject of one of Picasso's most famous paintings, **_Guernica_** (p. 460), repulsed the world.

The bullfighter's greatest honor is to be awarded two *orejas*, or ears. The matador can claim the first by killing the bull with one thrust. The second is awarded by the crowd, with the consent of bullfight officials, for style and showmanship. In Madrid, those so honored are carried through the Grand Portal of Las Ventas by jubilant fans. "It opens the doors of all the bullrings in the world," a guide told us on our last tour of the bullring. A top bullfighter can earn 5–6 [euro] million a year. "It's like winning an Oscar in Hollywood— only much more dangerous."

A good alternative to attending a bullfight is to watch one in a neighborhood bar. We were once drinking happily in a small-town bar when the broadcast of a bullfight began on TV. Surrounded by intense fans, we found it impossible not to watch, and the whole event played out on the small screen and was simultaneously moving and unsettling. Then again, the best travel experiences make you think—and sometimes make you uncomfortable.

At the end of the first year of war, Franco held 35 of Spain's provincial capitals, except for Madrid and Barcelona. In 1937, the Republican forces were cut in two, and Madrid was left to fend for itself. The last great offensive of the war began on December 23, 1938, with an attack by Franco's forces on Barcelona, which fell on January 26, 1939, after a campaign of 34 days. Republican forces fled to France. On March 28, some 200,000 of Franco's troops marched into Madrid, meeting no resistance. The war was over the next day, when the rest of Republican Spain surrendered. Lasting 2 years and 254 days, the war claimed 1 million lives. Spain lay in ruins, with Franco atop the smoking pile.

Steering Spain clear of alliances, Franco continued to rule until his death in 1975. He brought order, if not freedom, but he also isolated Spain from the rest of Europe.

Democratic Spain

According to advance provisions made by Franco, **Juan Carlos de Bórbon,** the grandson of Alfonso XIII, became king when the dictator died in 1975. (Juan Carlos I remains on the throne today.) Under the terms of a 1978 constitution, Spain became a constitutional democracy with a monarch who has no role as a ruler. The constitution also devolved much of the government's centralized powers to autonomous regions, addressing long-standing calls for self-government in Catalunya and the Basque Country.

Franco's death was an equally momentous event for society as for politics. The initial giddiness of Spaniards was dubbed "La Movida" and symbolized an explosion of freedom that brought such iconoclasts as filmmaker **Pedro Almodóvar** to the fore. He broke into the art-house circuit with his 1988 *Women on the Verge of a Nervous Breakdown*—a wild comedy about Spanish women and their man problems—and promptly became the flag bearer of contemporary Spanish cinema. His work is seen by critics (and many filmgoers) as defining modern Spanish sensibilities.

Flamenco had been suppressed under Franco, but began to rise in popularity in the early 1970s just as the dictator's health declined. Young talents, such as guitarist **Paco de Lucía** and singer **Camerón de la Isla** (both deceased), fed into a popular revival of the art form, and their emergence as full-fledged international stars in the early 1980s encouraged other artists to come out of the *peñas* (private clubs for flamenco aficionados) where they had labored—some for decades—to play the bars and clubs of Madrid and the cities of Andalucía. Today, Madrid is the epicenter of flamenco, but Sevilla, Jerez, Cádiz, and Málaga remain traditional strongholds.

In a similar vein, Spanish gastronomy underwent a sea change in the mid-1970s when Basque chefs **Pedro Subijana** and **Juan Mari Arzak** applied the principles of French nouvelle cuisine to Spanish food. They in turn inspired a young Catalan cook fresh out of military service named **Ferran Adrià.** In his quest for continuous reinvention of food at his restaurant elBulli, Adrià launched a worldwide gastronomic revolution that includes but is hardly limited to the chemistry-set pyrotechnics of molecular gastronomy.

Adrià has since closed elBulli, leaving the frontiers of gastronomy to others. It is a great time to eat in Spain. Chefs have never been held in higher regard, and have finally achieved the fame and status of rock stars and star footballers. (Two-star Michelin Barcelona/Madrid chefs **Sergi Arola** and **David Muñoz** were, in fact, a rock musician and a footballer, respectively.) Yet not all the great dining in Spain costs 150€ and up—before wine. The trickle-down of culinary aspiration reaches all the way to Spain's bars, where complex and inventive tapas, called *tapas creativas,* are all the rage.

In a way, Spain's coming-out parties to the world were **Expo '92** in Sevilla and the **1992 Summer Olympics** in Barcelona. The latter spurred the transformation of its host city, completely overhauling the waterfront and heralding Barcelona's reemergence on the world stage. Spain quickly placed its cultural treasures on display as well, constructing new major museums across the country, including the Guggenheim (p. 466) in Bilbao, the City of Arts and Sciences (p. 294) in Valencia, and in Madrid the Museum Nacional Centre de Arte Riena Sofia (p. 92) and the Museo Thyssen-Bornamisza (p. 94).

The 21st century has ushered in many social changes. In March 2002, Spain officially abandoned its time-honored peseta and went under the euro umbrella, to the consternation of many Spaniards and amid widespread

TOP 10 souvenirs OF SPAIN

1. **A tin of saffron.** In most countries it is hard to find saffron in anything larger than 1-gram vials. In Spanish markets or specialty shops, you can buy it in containers of 5, 10, 20, and even 50 grams. It's still a splurge, but much less expensive than buying it at home.

2. **An embroidered shawl from Andalucía.** While you're in Sevilla, observe local women to learn how this accessory can become a major fashion statement.

3. **A Basque beret.** More structured than the French beret, a Basque beret is usually made of waterproof wool with a soft leather headband. Ideally, it should be purchased in Basque Country from a man who never takes his off.

4. **A ceramic olive serving bowl.** These bowls have a separate small compartment for placing the pits. Some also have another compartment to hold toothpicks. It will be a great conversation piece at your next dinner party.

5. **A beautiful forged kitchen knife from Toledo.** Toledo steel has been the standard to swear by since knights carried Toledo blades into battle during the Crusades. Blade makers in Toledo now make fabulous kitchen cutlery. Be sure to pack your purchase into a checked bag to fly home.

6. **A bullfight poster.** Any souvenir shop will print your name on a generic poster. Instead, go to the gift shop at a major bullring for exquisite reproductions of posters from recent seasons. A proper bullfight poster is a uniquely Spanish art genre.

7. **A Lladro porcelain figurine.** The firm is a 20th-century invention, but the style harks back to the fine workmanship of 18th-century porcelain.

8. **Canvas espadrilles with rope soles.** This summer classic never goes out of style, and Spaniards make them in both casual and high-fashion editions.

9. **Team jersey from Barcelona FC or Real Madrid.** Football (soccer) is practically a state religion, and these two teams are the most popular in Spain and among the best in the world. State your preference with your jersey.

10. **Paella pan.** It's so flat and thin that it easily slips into a suitcase. Now you can use that saffron.

complaints about price gouging. In what some Spaniards saw as an assault on their lifestyle—even their very identity—Spain came under increasing pressure to conform to short lunch breaks like those in other E.U. countries. What? No 3-hour siesta? It was heresy. Despite opposition, large companies began to cut lunch to 2 hours. Pro-siesta forces in Spain cited the American custom of "power naps" as a reason to retain their beloved afternoon break.

In April 2005, Spain became the third European country to recognize gay marriage. Contemporary Spain is an especially attractive destination for LGBT travelers, and some resort towns, such as Sitges (p. 385) on the coast south of Barcelona, are at least as gay as they are straight during the height of the tourist season. Other popular resort areas for gay travelers are Torremolinos on the Costa del Sol and the island of Ibiza.

Perhaps the most radical sign that Spain had embraced European social norms came in 2011, when, bowing to E.U. health policies, smoking was banned in all bars and restaurants throughout the country. Because Spaniards were among the heaviest smokers in Europe, observers predicted that the law was bound to fail. On the contrary, it is generally respected, as Spaniards have discovered how good food tastes without a side of secondhand smoke.

The smoking ban and the ongoing economic crisis have not diminished Spain's lively bar scene. Smokers simply pop out to the street for a smoke before coming back inside to eat and drink, and the crunch on personal income has meant a proliferation of the "especial de crisis" meal—a bargain plate for impecunious times.

WHEN TO GO

Spring and fall are ideal times to visit nearly all of Spain. The winter months can be very rainy, especially in southern Spain. In summer, it's hot, hot, and hotter still, with the cities in Castilla (Madrid, Toledo, Segovia, Avila, and Salamanca) and Andalucía (Sevilla, Córdoba, and Granada) heating up the most. Madrid has dry heat; the average temperature can hover around 84°F (29°C) in July and 75°F (24°C) in September. Sevilla has the dubious reputation of being about the hottest part of Spain in July and August, often baking under average temperatures of 93°F (34°C).

Barcelona, cooler in temperature, is often quite humid. Midsummer temperatures in Mallorca often reach 91°F (33°C). The overcrowded Costa Brava has temperatures around 81°F (27°C) in July and August. The Costa del Sol has an average of 77°F (25°C) in summer. The coolest spot in Spain is the Atlantic coast from San Sebastián to A Coruña, with temperatures in the 70s (21°C–26°C) in July and August.

August remains the major vacation month in Europe. The traffic from France, the Netherlands, and Germany to Spain becomes a veritable migration, and it may be difficult to find low-cost rooms along the coastal areas. To compound the problem, many restaurants and shops also decide it's time for a vacation, thereby limiting visitors' selections for both dining and shopping.

In winter, the Costa del Sol is the most popular, with temperatures reaching a warm 60°F to 63°F (16°–17°C). Madrid gets cold, as low as 34°F (1°C). Mallorca is warmer, usually in the 50s (low teens Celsius), but it often dips into the 40s (single digits Celsius). Some mountain resorts can experience extreme cold.

Average Daily Temperature & Monthly Rainfall for Selected Cities

BARCELONA

	JAN	FEB	MAR	APR	MAY	JUNE	JULY	AUG	SEPT	OCT	NOV	DEC
Temp. (°F)	48	49	52	55	61	68	73	73	70	63	55	50
Temp. (°C)	9	9	11	13	16	20	23	23	21	17	13	10
Rainfall (in.)	1.7	1.4	1.9	2.0	2.2	1.5	.9	1.6	3.1	3.7	2.9	2.0

BILBAO

	JAN	FEB	MAR	APR	MAY	JUNE	JULY	AUG	SEPT	OCT	NOV	DEC
Temp. (°F)	45	48	51	52	55	65	67	67	61	53	52	48
Temp. (°C)	7	9	11	11	13	18	19	19	16	12	11	9
Rainfall (in.)	.9	.8	.9	1.3	1.5	1.2	.6	.7	1.0	1.2	1.4	.8

MADRID

	JAN	FEB	MAR	APR	MAY	JUNE	JULY	AUG	SEPT	OCT	NOV	DEC
Temp. (°F)	42	45	49	53	60	69	76	75	69	58	48	43
Temp. (°C)	6	7	9	12	16	21	24	24	21	14	9	6
Rainfall (in.)	1.6	1.8	1.2	1.8	1.5	1.0	.3	.4	1.1	1.5	2.3	1.7

SEVILLA

	JAN	FEB	MAR	APR	MAY	JUNE	JULY	AUG	SEPT	OCT	NOV	DEC
Temp. (°F)	59	63	68	75	81	90	97	97	90	79	68	61
Temp. (°C)	15	17	20	24	27	32	36	36	32	26	20	16
Rainfall (in.)	2.6	2.4	3.6	2.3	1.6	.3	0	.2	.8	2.8	2.7	3.2

Holidays include January 1 (New Year's Day), January 6 (Feast of the Epiphany), March 19 (Feast of St. Joseph), Good Friday, Easter Monday, May 1 (May Day), June 10 (Corpus Christi), June 29 (Feast of the Assumption), October 12 (Spain's National Day), November 1 (All Saints' Day), December 8 (Immaculate Conception), and December 25 (Christmas). In addition, Madrid celebrates the feast of San Isidro, its patron saint, on May 15, while Barcelona holds a 4-day La Mercè festival at the beginning of the last week of September in honor of patron saint Mare de Deu de la Mercè. If a holiday falls on a Thursday or Tuesday, many Spaniards take off the weekday in between to create an extra-long weekend known as a *puente*, or bridge. Be sure to book hotels well ahead of time. You can always get money from ATMs on holidays, but intercity bus service is sometimes suspended.

Spain Calendar of Events

The dates given below are approximate and will help you start planning. Sometimes the exact days are not announced until 6 weeks before the actual festival. Check with the Tourist Office of Spain (see Chapter 20) for more information and exact dates.

JANUARY/FEBRUARY

Granada Reconquest Festival, Granada. The whole city celebrates the Christians' victory over the Moors in 1492. The highest tower at the Alhambra is open to the public on January 2. For information call © **95-824-71-46** or visit www.turgranada.es. January 2.

Día de los Reyes (Three Kings Day), throughout Spain. Parades are held around the country on the eve of the Festival of the Epiphany. Various "kings" dispense candy to all the kids. January 5–6.

Gastrofestival, Madrid. Top international chefs gather for Madrid Fusion, restaurants and tapas bars offer special menus and treats. Cooking tours and demos are held; museums and galleries host food-themed films and programs. Call ✆ **91-454-44-10** or visit www.esmadrid.com. Last week of January, first week of February.

ARCO (International Contemporary Art Fair), Madrid. One of the biggest draws on Spain's cultural calendar, this exhibit showcases the best in contemporary art from Europe, the Americas, Australia, and Asia. For more information call ✆ **91-722-30-00** or visit www.ifema.es. Dates vary, usually mid-February.

Festival de Jerez. Annual flamenco festival highlights Jerez's role in the development of the art. Performances range from intimate bars to enthusiasts' clubs to large stage shows, usually featuring major figures. Also guitar, singing, and dance workshops. Call ✆ **95-614-98-63** or visit www.turismojerez.com for tickets. Late February through early March.

Madrid Carnaval. The carnival kicks off with a parade along Paseo de la Castellana, culminating in a masked ball at the Círculo de Bellas Artes on the following night. Fancy-dress competitions last until Ash Wednesday, when the festivities end with a tear-jerking "burial of a sardine" at the Fuente de los Pajaritos in the Casa de Campo, followed by a concert in the Plaza Mayor. Call ✆ **91-454-44-10** or visit www.esmadrid.com. Just before Lent.

Barcelona Carnaval. Compared to other parts of Spain, Carnaval in Barcelona is a low-key affair. In addition to the city's main parade, stall-owners in local markets organize a competition among themselves for best costume. Just south of the city, in the seaside town of Sitges, the local gay community goes all out for Carnaval. Many Barceloneses hop the commuter rail to celebrate with them. Call ✆ **93-285-38-34** or visit www.barcelonaturisme.com. Just before Lent.

Carnavales de Cádiz. The oldest and best-attended carnival in Spain is a free-wheeling event full of costumes, parades, strolling troubadours, and drum beating.

For more information, call ✆ **62-933-28-40** or visit www.carnavaldecadiz.com. Just before Lent.

Fallas de Valencia, Valencia. Dating from the 1400s, this fiesta centers on burning gigantic papier-mâché effigies of winter demons. Burnings are preceded by bullfights, fireworks, parades, and the mascletà, a series of controlled explosions. This festival must be seen (and heard) to be believed. For information, visit www.fallasfromvalencia.com. Early to mid-March.

Semana Santa (Holy Week), throughout Spain. From Palm Sunday until Easter Sunday, a series of processions with hooded penitents moves to the piercing wail of the saeta. Heavy floats, or *pasos,* bearing the image of the Virgin or Christ are carried on the penitents' shoulders. Notable processions are held in Zamora, Cuenca, Jerez de la Frontera, Sevilla, and Madrid. Not surprisingly, Catalunya has some traditions not found in the rest of Spain. The "Mona de Pascua," a whimsical chocolate and pastry cake, is traditionally given by godparents to their

Fallas de Valencia.

Feria de Caballo.

godchildren. On Palm Sunday, palm leaves are blessed in Gaudí's Sagrada Família. Spaniards often take holidays on this week, and hotel prices soar to the highest of the year. Be sure to reserve in advance. Some restaurants and attractions curtail their hours. Unless you are interested in the religious spectacle, it's a good week to avoid. One week before Easter.

La Diada de Sant Jordi, Catalunya. St. George (Sant Jordi in Catalan) is the patron saint of Catalunya, and his feast day coincides with the deaths of Miguel de Cervantes and William Shakespeare. On this day, men traditionally give a single red rose to the significant women in their lives, and women give a book in return. This is one of the most colorful days in Catalunya, as thousands of rose-sellers take to the streets and bookshops set up open-air stalls along the major thoroughfares. April 23.

Feria de Sevilla (Sevilla Fair). This is the most celebrated week of revelry in all of Spain, with all-night flamenco dancing, entertainment booths, bullfights, horse-back riding, flower-decked coaches, and dancing in the streets. You'll need to reserve a hotel early for this one. Call 95-448-68-00 or visit www.turismo a.org. Second week after Easter.

Moros y Cristianos (Moors and Christians), Alcoy, near Alicante. For 3 days, the centuries-old battle between the Moors and the Christians is restaged with soldiers in period costumes. The Christians who drove the Moors from Spain always win. The simulated fighting takes on almost a circus-like flair, and the costumes worn by the Moors are always absurd and anachronistic. For more information, call © 96-514-34-52 or visit www.alicantecongresos.com. Late April.

MAY/JUNE

Feria del Caballo, Jerez de la Frontera. This annual livestock fair, held here since the 13th century, focuses on the famous Andalucían standard breed developed by Carthusian monks. It features 5 days of equestrian events, parades, flamenco, livestock displays, and, of course, sherry drinking. For information, call © 95-614-98-63 or visit www.turismojerez.com. Mid-May.

Festival de los Patios, Córdoba. This is a rare chance to get inside the gates to visit Córdoba's famous patios with their cascading *gitanillas* (little Gypsies), as gardeners call their geraniums. Residents decorate with flowers and welcome visitors. Visit www.amigosdelospatioscordobeses.es for more information. First 2 weeks of May.

Fiesta de San Isidro, Madrid. Madrileños run wild with a 10-day celebration honoring the city's patron saint. Food fairs, Castilian folkloric events, street parades, parties, music, dances, bullfights, and other festivities mark the occasion. Make hotel reservations early. Expect crowds and traffic. Call ✆ **91-454-44-10** or visit www.esmadrid.com. Mid-May.

Corpus Christi, all over Spain. A major holiday on the Spanish calendar, this event is marked by big processions in Madrid as well as in nearby cathedral cities, such as Toledo. In Catalunya, the streets of Sitges are carpeted in flowers. May or June, depending on liturgical calendar.

Suma Flamenca, Madrid. This month-long flamenco summit offers performances almost every night in intimate clubs and large concert halls. For information on performers and venues, see www.madrid.org/sumaflamenca. June.

Sónar, Barcelona. This international 3-day festival of advanced music and new media art has gained a reputation as one of the world's most innovative. For more information, visit http://sonar.es. Early to mid-June.

Verbena de Sant Joan, Barcelona. This traditional festival occupies all Catalans. Barcelona literally lights up, with fireworks, bonfires, and dances until dawn. The highlight of the festival is the fireworks show at Montjuïc. Call ✆ 93-285-38-34 or visit www.barcelonaturisme.com. June 23 (eve of feast of St. John).

Festival Internacional de Musica y Danza de Granada, Granada. Since 1952, Granada's prestigious program of dance and music has attracted international artists who perform at the Alhambra and other venues. It's a major event on Europe's cultural calendar. Reserve well in advance. For a complete schedule and tickets, visit www.granadafestival.org. Last week of June to first week of July.

JULY

A Rapa das Bestas (The Capture of the Beasts), San Lorenzo de Sabucedo, Galicia. Spain's greatest horse roundup

attracts equestrian lovers from throughout Europe. Horses in the verdant hills of northwestern Spain are rounded up, branded, and medically checked before being released back into the wild. Call ✆ 98-154-24-00 or visit www.turgalicia.es. First weekend in July.

Fiesta de Santiago, Santiago de Compostela. Pomp and ceremony mark this annual pilgrimage to the tomb of St. James the Apostle. Galician folklore shows, concerts, parades, and the swinging of the *botafumeiro* (a mammoth incense burner) mark the event. Call ✆ 98-154-24-00 or visit www.turgalicia.es. July 15 to 30.

Fiesta de San Fermín, Pamplona. Vividly described in Ernest Hemingway's novel *The Sun Also Rises,* the running of the bulls through the streets of Pamplona is the most popular celebration in Spain. It includes wine tasting, fireworks, and, of course, bullfights. Reserve many months in advance. Visit www.sanfermin.com. July 6 to 14.

San Sebastián Jazz Festival, San Sebastián. Celebrating its 50th year in 2015, this festival brings the jazz greats of the world together in the Kursaal. Other programs take place alfresco at the Plaza de Trinidad in the Old Quarter. For schedule and tickets, call ✆ 94-348-19-00 or visit www.heinekenjazzaldia.com. Late July.

AUGUST

Festival Internacional de Santander. The repertoire includes classical music, ballet, contemporary dance, chamber music, and recitals. Most performances are staged in the Palacio de Festivales, a centrally located auditorium custom-built for this event. Call ✆ 94-221-05-08 or visit www.festivalsantander.com. Throughout August.

Fiestas of Lavapiés and La Paloma, Madrid. Festivities begin with the Lavapiés on August 1 and continue through the hectic La Paloma celebration on August 15, the Day of the Virgen de la Paloma. During the fiestas, thousands of people race through the narrow

EL clásico

Although Spain is a nominally Roman Catholic country, church attendance has fallen off from its historic highs. The true religion of most Spaniards—and particularly of residents of Barcelona and Madrid—is fútbol (soccer). It's a red-letter day on the calendar whenever Real Madrid and FC Barcelona meet. The rivalry is known simply as "El Clásico," and fills the home stadium, while tens of millions of Spaniards tune into the matches on television. Historically, Real Madrid symbolizes the hegemony of the Castilians who have ruled the country since the 15th century, while Barcelona represents the upstart rebelliousness and nationalist yearnings of Catalunya.

streets. Apartment dwellers hurl buckets of cold water onto the crowds below to cool them off. There are children's games, floats, music, flamenco, and *zarzuelas*, along with street fairs. Call ℭ **91-454-44-10** or visit www.esmadrid.com. Two weeks in early August.

Misteri d'Elx (Mystery of Elche). This sacred drama is reenacted in the 17th-century Basilica of Santa María in Elche (near Alicante). It represents the Assumption and the Crowning of the Virgin. For tickets, call ℭ **96-665-81-96** or visit www.visitelche.com. August 11 to 15.

Feria de Málaga (Málaga Fair). One of the longest summer fairs in southern Europe (generally lasting 10 days), this celebration kicks off with fireworks displays and is highlighted by a parade of Arabian horses pulling brightly decorated carriages. Participants dress in colorful Andalucían garb, plazas rattle with castanets, and wine is dispensed by the gallon. Call ℭ **95-192-62-20** or visit www.malagaturismo.com. Weekend before August 19.

La Tomatina (Battle of the Tomatoes), Buñol (Valencia). This is one of the most photographed festivals in Spain, growing in popularity every year. Truckloads of tomatoes are shipped into Buñol, where they become vegetable missiles between warring towns and villages. Portable showers are brought in for the cleanup, followed by music for dancing and singing. Visit www.latomatina.org. Last Wednesday in August.

Fiesta de la Rosa del Azafrán (Saffron Rose Festival), Consuegra. The heart of Spain's saffron-growing region celebrates the harvest with a weekend fair featuring beauty queens, competitions to separate saffron threads from flowers, and a folk festival. A ceremonial grinding of saffron in windmills cements the friendship of Spain's chief saffron-growing villages. Visit www.turismocastillalamancha.es. Last weekend of August.

SEPTEMBER

Diada de Catalunya, Barcelona. The most significant festival in Catalunya celebrates the region's autonomy from the rest of Spain, following years of repression under the dictator Franco. Demonstrations and other flag-waving events take place. The *senyera*, the flag of Catalunya, is everywhere. Not your typical tourist fare, but interesting. For more information, visit www.gencat.net. September 11.

San Sebastián International Film Festival, San Sebastián. The premier film festival of Spain takes place in the Basque capital, often at several different theaters. Retrospectives are frequently featured, and weeklong screenings are held. Call ℭ **94-348-12-12** or visit www.sansebastianfestival.com. Second week in September.

Festa de la Mercè, Barcelona. This celebration honors Mare de Deu de la Mercè, the city's patron saint, known for her compassion for animals. Beginning after dark, and after a Mass in the Igreja de la Mercè, a procession of as many as 50 "animals" (humans dressed like tigers, lions, and horses) proceeds with lots of firecrackers and sparklers to the cathedral and then on to Plaça de Sant Jaume and eventually into Les Rambles, Plaça de Catalunya, and the harborfront. Call ✆ **93-285-38-34** or visit www.barcelona turisme.com. Mid-September.

OCTOBER/NOVEMBER

Semana de Santa Teresa, Avila. *Verbenas* (carnivals), parades, singing, and dancing honor the patron saint of this walled city. Call ✆ **92-035-40-00** or visit www. avilaturismo.com. October 8 to 15.

Feria de Otoño, Madrid. Spanish and international artists participate in this cultural program with a series of operatic, ballet, dance, music, and theatrical performances featuring companies from Strasbourg to Tokyo. This event is a premier attraction, yet tickets are reasonably priced. Make hotel reservations early. Call ✆ **91-454-44-10** or visit www.es madrid.com. Late October to late November.

All Saints' Day, throughout Spain. This public holiday is reverently celebrated, as relatives and friends lay flowers on the graves or *nichos* of the deceased. Many bars in Madrid and Barcelona hold Halloween parties the night before—an imported custom that seems to be catching on. November 1.

DECEMBER

Christmas Markets, Madrid and Barcelona. More than 100 stalls set up in Plaza Mayor in Madrid to sell handicrafts, Christmas decorations, and Nativity scenes. A similar market sets up in the plaza outside Barcelona's cathedral.

SPANISH VISIONS

Spain's artistic tradition goes back around 30,000 years if you count the magical cave paintings in the mountains above the Cantabrian coast. (Picasso himself once quipped, "After Altamira, everything is decadence.") Some of Europe's greatest masters were Spaniards or did their greatest work in Spain. Here are some not to miss—and where to see their art.

BERNAT MARTORELL (d. 1452) A painter of retables and manuscript illuminations, Martorell revolutionized Catalan painting in the second quarter of the 15th century, bringing a complexity of composition and luminous handling of color and light that drew on both the International Gothic style and Catalunya's dynamic Romanesque painting tradition. One of his greatest surviving works is the *Altarpiece of the Saints John* in the Museu Nacional d'Art de Catalunya (p. 364) in Barcelona.

EL GRECO (1540–1614) Crete-born Doménikos Theotokópoulos settled in Toledo in 1577 and spent the next 4 decades filling the city's churches with his singular style. His phantasmagoric color and action-filled application of paint made him an inspiration to 20th-century Expressionists. His work is found extensively throughout Toledo and in the Museo del Prado (p. 90).

FRANCISCO DE ZURBARÁN (1598–1664) The Spanish master of chiaroscuro concentrated on painting ascetic religious meditations for monastery walls, often using the monks as models for saints and martyrs. His forte was the struggle between passionate spirit and palpable flesh, hence his frequent rendering of St. Jeronimo. Many of his major works are in the Museo del Prado (p. 90) in Madrid, but his greatest masterworks are found in the Museo de Bellas Artes (p. 195) in Sevilla.

DIEGO VELÁZQUEZ (1599–1660) Becoming Felipe IV's court painter at age 25, Velázquez created his greatest works—mostly portraits—while in the royal employ. When the paintings were later deposited in the Museo del Prado (p. 90),

When Diego Velázquez painted *Las Meninas* in 1640, he changed the psychology of European painting. This portrait of the royal household of Felipe IV, which focuses on the Infanta Margarita and her maids, includes a reflected image of the artist. It is the star of the Museo del Prado in Madrid, and remains a touchstone of Spanish art. Pablo Picasso's obsessive reinterpretations, painted 300 years later, hang in the Museu Picasso in Barcelona.

where they occupy several galleries, his genius was rediscovered by critics and artists.

FRANCISCO DE GOYA (1746–1828) Capable of both giddy pictorialism—as in his bucolic scenes created for the tapestries hung at El Pardo—and harrowing, nightmare images, Goya stands with Velázquez and Picasso in the triumvirate of Spain's greatest artists. His late works painted during the French occupation carry a direct emotional force that was truly new in European art. The best of Goya's work is found in the Museo del Prado and in the Real Academia de Bellas Artes de San Fernando, both in Madrid.

JOAQUÍN SOROLLA (1863–1923) Born in Valencia, Sorolla was Spain's premier painter of light and saturated color. He made a career of painting nominally representational scenes that were more about the play of light than form. Adept at portraiture as well as landscape, his most heartfelt canvases depict his native Valencian shore of churning waves, sun-modeled rocks, and innocently erotic bathers. Although some of his work can be found in the Museo del Prado, the best selection fills the Museo Sorolla (p. 106) in Madrid.

PABLO PICASSO (1881–1973) The quintessential artist of the 20th century did it all, inventing new styles when he had exhausted old ones. Many of his early works as well as some seminal pieces from the 1950s are housed in Barcelona's Museu Picasso (p. 352). The Museo Nacional Centro de Arte Reina Sofía (p. 92) in Madrid also displays many Picassos, most notably the iconic *Guernica*. The Museo Picasso Málaga (p. 276) features a broad selection of his work, most of it donated by his estate in lieu of taxes.

JUAN GRIS (1887–1927) Working with a brighter palette and more mordant wit than either Picasso or Georges Braque, Gris helped pioneer Cubism. He never quit his day job drawing political satire for magazines, allowing him not to take himself too seriously. Recent reappraisals suggest that the approachable Gris influenced an entire generation of Spanish artists. The Museo Nacional Centro de Arte Reina Sofía (p. 92) in Madrid devotes a gallery to Gris and those who looked to his example.

JOAN MIRÓ (1893–1983) A poet of color and form, Miró is often categorized as a Surrealist. He did sign the Surrealist Manifesto of 1924, but his sense of form derives more from Spain's Neolithic cave paintings than the formal classicism of most Surrealism, and his lyrical celebration of color is unmatched in modern abstract art. His visionary art is best in large doses, available at the Fundació Joan Miró (p. 363) in Barcelona. Significant canvases can also be found at Madrid's Reina Sofía (p. 92).

SALVADOR DALÍ (1904–89) The clown prince of Spanish painting, Dalí defines Surrealism in popular culture. Employing a hyperrealist style to explore a world of fantasy and nightmare, he will forever be associated with limp watches. Dalí lived for a good joke, as the Teatre-Museu Dalí (p. 402) in Figueres demonstrates. Many of his works are in the Museo Nacional Centro de Arte Reina Sofia (p. 92) in Madrid.

EDUARDO CHILLIDA JUANTEGUI (1924–2002) Known mainly for his monumental abstract works in steel and stone, Chillida was born in San Sebastián and returned there from exile in 1959. His best works—such as the *Comb of the Wind* at the west end of Playa de Concha in San Sebastián—combine an abstract beauty of form with an analytical precision that makes the viewer contemplate both the object and the space it inhabits. Major collections of his sculptures are found at Reina Sofía (p. 92) and the Museo de Bellas Artes (p. 468) in Bilbao.

ANTONI TÀPIES (1923–2012) Nominally an Abstract Expressionist, the mercurial painter continuously experimented with new ideas until his death. Among the first to incorporate marble dust and gravel into his compositions, he moved on to ever-larger objects, including pieces of furniture. His works are characterized by boldly graphic composition and emotional immediacy. Many examples of his work are found in the Museo de Arte Abstracto Español (p. 140) and at the Fundación Antonio Pérez (p. 139), both in Cuenca, and in Madrid's Reina Sofia (p. 92). The best collection of his work resides in the Fundació Antoni Tàpies (p. 357) in Barcelona.

MAKING THE MOST OF MEALS

Eating and drinking are the still points around which the Spanish day revolves. The famous late Spanish dinner is an accommodation for the ferocious heat of summer. In practice, Spaniards eat four meals a day, sometimes supplemented by a sweet afternoon *merienda* (coffee break) with pastry.

Breakfast

The Spanish day starts with *desayuno*, a continental breakfast of assorted rolls, butter, and jam. Most Spaniards drink strong coffee with hot milk: either a *café con leche* (half-coffee, half-milk) or *cortado* (a shot of espresso "cut" with a dash of milk). If you find it too intense, ask for a *café Americano*, which is diluted with boiling water. Be sure to try *churros* (fried doughnut sticks) and very sweet, thick hot chocolate at least once.

Churros with chocolate.

Lunch

Typically the biggest meal of the day, the *almuerzo* can be as hearty as a farm-style midday "dinner" in the United States. Such lunches include three or four courses, beginning either with soup or hors d'oeuvres called *entremeses*. A main dish might be fish or eggs, or more likely meat with vegetables. Wine is always part of the meal. Dessert is usually pastry or flan, followed by coffee. Lunch is served from 1 to 4pm, with the busiest time at 2pm.

LOCATION, LOCATION, location

Once you've settled on a place for lunch or dinner, where you sit (or stand) will have some bearing on the final tally of your bill. Expect to pay a premium of up to 20% for outdoor dining. And even if you opt for eating indoors, sitting at a table will likely cost you 5 to 10% more than standing at the bar.

Tapas

After work or an early evening stroll, many Spaniards visit their favorite bars to drink wine or beer and eat small plates that can range from trays of olives, a few pickled anchovies, or slices of *jamón serrano* to exquisite small, composed plates that mimic fancy restaurant dishes. Usually, the convention calls for having one drink and one tapa (or a larger plate, known as a *ración*) and then moving on to the next bar for another drink and a bite. Barceloneses don't waste time walking between establishments, instead sticking to one place and staking out their patch of bar with their elbows. Granada has some of the most generous tapas (three drinks with three tapas easily substitutes for dinner). San Sebastián in Basque Country and Alicante south of Valencia have some of the most inventive tapas in Spain.

Dinner

Depending on the size of your lunch, the *cena* can also be a big meal with multiple courses. But if you've indulged in a big lunch and lots of tapas, it's quite acceptable to order a lighter meal—perhaps some cold cuts, sausage, a bowl of soup, or even a *tortilla Española* (see below). Many European and American visitors skip dinner altogether in favor of more time at the tapas bars. The chic dining hour, even in rural areas, is 10 or 10:30pm, but service usually begins by 9:30pm.

Tapas Found Throughout Spain

Tapas bars all over the country offer many of the same dishes, although *pa amb tomate* (grilled country bread rubbed with tomato, drizzled with olive oil, and dusted with salt) is a Catalan specialty. It sounds simple, but it tastes sublime. Likewise, bars along northern Spain's Atlantic coast often feature the exquisite tinned seafood of Galicia, and tiny fish fried whole are a specialty on the Andalucían coast. In addition to olives, almonds, and fresh kettle-style potato chips, standard tapas include the following:

Albóndigas   Meatballs, usually pork, served in a small casserole dish.

Chorizo   Slices of smoked pork sausage seasoned heavily with smoked paprika.

Croquetas   Small fritters of thick béchamel sauce with ham, tuna, or cod.

Gambas a la plancha   Shrimp grilled in their shells, called *gambas al ajillo* when grilled with garlic.

Jamón ibérico de bellota   Highly prized air-cured mountain ham from Iberian black pigs fed entirely on acorns; the most expensive ham in the world.

Jamón serrano   Thin slices of air-cured mountain ham.

Morcilla   Cooked slices of spicy blood sausage, served with bread.

The breadth of Spain means many regional specialty dishes, and the radical improvements in the Spanish wine industry means there are more choices than ever to drink with them. Here are some pairings of classic dishes with great Spanish wines.

Cochinillo asado (roasted suckling pig) is served all over Spain but is a specialty of old Castilla, notably Segovia. Drink a **light red from the DO Bierzo region** in northwest Castilla & León. These wines are vinted mainly from the Mencia and Garnacha Tintorera grapes.

Paella *Valenciana* is also served all over Spain, although once you get away from the coast around Valencia, it is rarely the real deal. If you find a great paella *Valenciana*, eat it accompanied by a **bracing white from the DO Valencia region** or a **Macabeo-Chardonnay white from DO Utiel-Requena.**

Bacalao al pil-pil (codfish served with pil-pil sauce, an emulsion of olive oil, fish juices, garlic, and parsley) is a quintessential Basque dish. The perfect complement is a quintessential Basque wine, the bracing and acidic *txakolí* from **DO Bizkaiko Txakolina.**

Merluza al horno (roasted hake) is another ubiquitous, reliable dish. We like to drink white wines with it, either a **DO Rueda** (preferably 100% Verdejo grape) or a brisker, more aromatic **DO Rias Baixas** based on the Albariño grape.

Pulpo Galego (octopus with boiled potatoes and paprika) is a specialty of Galicia but is popular around Spain. We find it pairs very well with a **white DOC Rioja** based on Viura and Sauvignon Blanc.

Suquet is a Catalan fish stew. Some of the best we've ever tasted came from the Empordà district on the Costa Brava, and it is delicious with a **DO Empordà white** based on the Garnacha Blanca grape.

Chuleton de buey is a whole beef rib grilled, often over an open wood flame. It is a specialty of inland Basque Country and of Galicia. The veal version, *chuleton de ternera*, is a specialty of Avila. Accompany either with an **aged red DOC Rioja,** based on Cabernet Sauvignon and Tempranillo, or with a **red DOC Priorat.**

Chuletillas de cordero are tiny baby lamb chops, a specialty of Navarra. The same region was one of Spain's first great medieval wine regions and is quickly becoming one of the 21st century's great districts. A **red DO Navarra** based on Granacha Tinta grapes, often blended with Merlot, pairs perfectly with the lamb.

Gambas al ajillo are sweet shrimp grilled in the shells with olive oil and garlic. The perfect accompaniment for this Andalucían specialty is a lightly chilled glass of **sherry from DO Manzanilla de Sanlúcar de Barrameda.**

Patatas bravas   Deep-fried potato chunks with spicy paprika aioli; invented in Madrid and available everywhere tapas are served.

Pimientos rellenos   Skinless red peppers usually stuffed with tuna or cod.

Queso manchego   Slices of the nutty sheep's-milk cheese of La Mancha.

Tortilla Española   Thick omelet with potato, usually served by the slice.

3

SUGGESTED SPAIN ITINERARIES

t would be a delight to get "lost" in Spain, wandering about at your leisure, discovering unspoiled villages off the beaten path. Indeed, we highly recommend this approach. But we also recognize that few of us have enough time (or money) for an unstructured love affair with a country. A schedule lets you get the most out of your available time, but just because you have a point of departure doesn't mean that serendipity and surprise can't intervene from time to time.

Plan on using several kinds of transportation. Because Spain is big, it's worth covering long distances either by plane or, except in the north, by high-speed train. You can take a train from Madrid to Barcelona nearly as fast as going to the airport and waiting to get through security. In practice, you'll end up using trains, planes, buses, *and* rental cars for maximum convenience and efficiency.

HIGHLIGHTS OF SPAIN IN 2 WEEKS

Spain is so large and so diverse that it's hard to think of hitting all the highlights in just 2 weeks. But this tour strikes most of the notes in the Spanish chord. And all your travel is on RENFE trains, making a Eurail Spain Pass an economical way to go.

DAY 1: Madrid ★★★: Pomp & Circumstance

Madrid was a backwater until Felipe II moved the capital here in 1561. For the next 450 years, Spain's power and glory was concentrated in the **Palacio Real** (p. 100). The current palace testifies to the ornate taste of the Bourbon kings. If kids are along, don't miss the suits of armor in the Armory. Royal males had a shot at inheriting the palace. Their sisters often took the veil, many of them at the nearby **Monasterio de las Descalzas Reales** (p. 100), and they brought their prized paintings, tapestries, and other art with them. Enjoy a late afternoon drink and people-watching on **Plaza Mayor** (p. 98).

DAY 2: Madrid ★★★: Art & Tapas

Pick up the pace today and spend the morning at the **Museo del Prado** (p. 90), one of the top museums of European art. Concentrate on Spanish masters: **Velázquez** fills Galleries 12, 14–16, and 18; Goya occupies Galleries 66–67, 85, and 90–94; and **El Greco's** works are in Galleries 9A and 10A. After a quick lunch, you're ready for modern times at the **Museo Nacional Centro de Arte Reina Sofía** (p. 92). The best works are by modern Spanish masters: Joan Miró, Salvador Dalí, Juan Gris, Antoni Tàpies, and, of course, Picasso, best represented by *Guernica*. Spend the early evening on a tapas crawl on **Plaza Santa Ana** (p. 96).

DAY 3: Segovia ★★

Swift trains let you pop into Segovia for its highlights, then keep moving. Wander over to admire the 166 arches of the **Roman Aqueduct** (p. 151), then follow the signs through the heart of the city to the fairytale-like

PREVIOUS PAGE: **The Patio de los Arrayanes at the Alhambra.**

Highlights of Spain in 2 Weeks
Bay of Biscay
FRANCE
Toulouse
Narbonne
Perpignan
ANDORRA
Figueres
CATALUNYA
Manresa
BARCELONA
Tarragona
Tortosa
Vinaròs
Balearic Sea
Lérida (Lleida)
Vielha
Gijón
Oviedo
ASTURIAS
Santander
CANTABRIA
Bilbao (Bilbo)
BASQUE COUNTRY
San Sebastián (Donostia)
Vitoria (Gasteiz)
Pamplona (Iruña)
NAVARRA
Logroño
LA RIOJA
Burgos
Lugo
GALICIA
Orense (Ourense)
Ponferrada
León
CASTILLA Y LEÓN
Zamora
Valladolid
Aranda de Duero
Soria
ARAGÓN
Zaragoza
Calatayud
Salamanca
Segovia
Ávila
COMMUNITY OF MADRID
MADRID
Guadalajara
Ciudad Rodrigo
PORTUGAL
Talavera de la Reina
Coria
Toledo
Cuenca
Monreal del Campo
Castellón de la Plana
Palma de Mallorca
Mallorca
Cáceres
Guadalupe
CASTILLA-LA MANCHA
Utiel
Valencia
BALEARIC ISLANDS
Ibiza
Formentera
EXTREMADURA
Badajoz
Mérida
Ciudad Real
Albacete
VALENCIA
Valdepeñas
Benidorm
Zafra
Peñarroya-Pueblonuevo
Alicante
Elche
Villacarrillo
Murcia
MURCIA
Córdoba
Jaén
Lorca
Cartagena
MEDITERRANEAN SEA
Isla Cristina
Huelva
Sevilla
ANDALUCÍA
Guadix
Granada
Jerez de la Frontera
Antequera
Almería
Gulf of Cádiz
Cádiz
Málaga
Motril
Marbella
Algeciras
Gibraltar (U.K)
Tanger
Ceuta (Sp.)
Oran
Melilla (Sp.)
ALGERIA
MOROCCO
0 100 mi
0 100 km
Days 1–2 Madrid
Day 3 Segovia
Day 4 Burgos
Day 5 Bilbao
Days 6–7 Barcelona
Days 8–9 Valencia
Days 10–11 Granada
Days 12–13 Sevilla
Day 14 Córdoba

Alcázar (p. 147). Have the city's signature roast suckling pig at **José María** (p. 146) before boarding the afternoon train to Burgos, where you'll have dinner and spend the night.

DAY 4: Burgos ★★ & Bilbao ★★★

The **Catedral de Santa María** (p. 173) in Burgos is a two-fer: a truly great Gothic cathedral packed with good paintings and great sculptures for art buffs, and the resting place of swashbuckling legendary hero El Cid for historians. After visiting, take the 1pm train to Bilbao.

Make your first stop the **Museo Arqueologica de Bizkaia** (p. 467) for a complicated answer to the complicated question of "Who are the Basques?" Explore the surrounding old quarter, Bilbao La Vieja (p. 469), filling up on creative pintxos in Plaza Nueva (p. 469) in lieu of a formal dinner.

The Museo del Prado in Madrid.

DAY 5: Bilbao ★★★

Last night was old Bilbao. This morning is the new city. Get an early start so you can walk the riverfront promenade before spending several hours in the **Guggenheim Museum** (p. 466). Make sure you've reserved seats on the afternoon train to Barcelona, where you can snooze during the trip. It gets in around 10pm, just as Spaniards are eating dinner.

DAY 6: Barcelona ★★★

Start exploring this capital of Catalan culture by strolling **Les Rambles** (p. 313), which runs from the waterfront uphill to L'Eixample, going from carny to chic along the way. Wander the **Barri Gòtic** (p. 313) and see the **Museu Picasso** (p. 352). Have lunch, catch your breath, and shoot up to Montjuïc to see Gothic Catalan art at **Museu Nacional d'Art de Catalunya** (p. 364) and 20th-century whimsy at the **Fundació Joan Miró** (p. 363).

DAY 7: Barcelona ★★★

Start your day in a state of wonder by visiting Antoni Gaudí's masterpiece basilica **La Sagrada Familia** (p. 355) and his masterpiece apartment house **La Pedrera** (Casa Milà; p. 359). Spend the afternoon on the waterfront visiting the **l'Aquarium de Barcelona** (p. 360) and working on your tan on the beach at **Vila Olímpica** (p. 361). Celebrate the evening in the *xampanyerías* (champagne bars) of L'Eixample.

The Roman Aqueduct of Segovia.

DAY 8: Valencia ★★

Take a morning train to Valencia, and spend the afternoon hitting all the Old Town sights, including the **Catedral** (p. 294) and its cool Gothic tower, **El Miguelete** (p. 294), as well as the **Palacio de Marqués de Dos Aguas** (p. 297) for the best collection of ceramics in Spain. Spend the late afternoon on **Playa Malvarossa,** the best of the in-city beaches; that way you'll be ready to eat Valencia's great paella at one of the beachfront restaurants.

DAY 9: Valencia: City of Arts & Sciences ★★★

Get an early start so you can visit the **Mercado Central** (p. 297) fresh food market first thing in the morning. It is one of the largest in Europe and is a treasure house of locally raised food. Then spend the day at the **City of Arts & Sciences** (p. 294), inhabiting the future. Eat downtown, not too far from the train station, as you'll be taking the midnight hotel train to Granada.

DAY 10: Granada ★★★

You'll arrive early, so after storing your luggage, walk around the central district, visiting the **Catedral** and its adjacent **Capilla Real (Royal Chapel;** p. 223). The chapel contains the impressive sarcophagi of Fernando and Isabel, who completed the Reconquest when they took Granada in 1492. Shop in the souk along **Caldererías Vieja and Nueva** (p. 225), and walk generally uphill through the medieval Moorish quarter, the **Albaicín** (p. 219). End the day at the **Mirador de San Nicolás** (p. 219), where at sunset the Alhambra on the opposite hill glows like an object of desire. Granada's **tapas scene** (p. 226) is one of the best in Spain.

DAY 11: Granada: The Alhambra ★★★

Months ago you reserved a ticket with an entrance time to the **Alhambra** (p. 219) at the beginning of the day. Bring lunch with you so you can linger. The gardens between palaces are a great place for a picnic. The **Palacio de**

Mosaic sculpture in Barcelona's Parc Güell, designed by Gaudí.

Carlos V (p. 222) may lack the beauty of the Nasrid buildings, but it houses the fantastic **Museo de la Alhambra** (p. 222), which contains some of the complex's most beautiful Hispano-Muslim art. You have a choice to make about where you want to sleep. Take the 5pm train to Sevilla to spend the night there, or wait until 8am the next day and lose the morning in Sevilla.

DAY 12: Sevilla ★★★

Whichever time you've chosen to get here, start exploring Sevilla at the palace fortress of the **Alcázar** (p. 242). Its palaces represent the synthesis of Moorish design and Christian will. The adjacent **cathedral** (p. 194) is one of the biggest in Christendom. Explore the warren of streets in the **Barrio de Santa Cruz** (p. 192), making sure that you visit the **Museo del Baile Flamenco** (**Museum of Flamenco Dance;** p. 196). It might inspire you to catch an impromptu performance late at night in **Triana** (p. 200).

DAY 13: Sevilla & Córdoba

Why waste time? Get a bicycle from any SEVICI rack so you can spend the early day exploring beautiful **Parque María Luisa** (p. 196), the museums of **Plaza de América** (p. 197), and the marvelously bizarre architecture of **Plaza d'España** (p. 197). Get back to the station in time to catch a late afternoon train to Córdoba, where you should take the guided night tour of the city offered by **Artencordoba** (p. 202).

DAY 14: Córdoba ★★

Rise early so you can walk back and forth across the **Puente Romano** (p. 206) before the tourist buses arrive. You can also make a free visit in silence at 8:30am to **La Mezquita** (p. 202), seeing the holy place at its most mystical. You'll want to see the **Alcázar,** where Fernando and Isabel based themselves for the conquest of Granada, and wonder over the underground Roman ruins beneath the new version of the **Museo Arqueológico de Córdoba** (p. 209). Depending on the time of your flight the next day, you can spend another night here and take the early train to Madrid, or spend the night back in the capital.

GREEN SPAIN IN 10 DAYS

Except for the Guggenheim Museum in Bilbao, the north of Spain doesn't register with most North Americans, who cannot conceive of a Spain without bullfights, flamenco, and parched plains. Walled off from the rest of Iberia by high mountains, the verdant northern rim is a fascinating region, where ancient Celtic and Basque Spain persists.

DAY 1: Santiago de Compostela ★★★

If you get to the **Catedral de Santiago** (p. 512) early, you can see the highlights, including the Portico and the tomb of St. James, before the cathedral museum opens at 10am. That way you can avoid the rush of pilgrims arriving in the afternoon. The **Museo das Peregrinacións** (p. 513) clues you in on why Santiago is such a big deal. Walking around town and observing the pilgrims is half the fun.

DAY 2: A Coruña ★

Take a morning train from Santiago, stash your luggage, and make a circuit of the waterfront of this peninsula city. Walk out to the Castillo de San Antón to see the Celtic jewelry at the **Museo Arqueológico e Histórico**

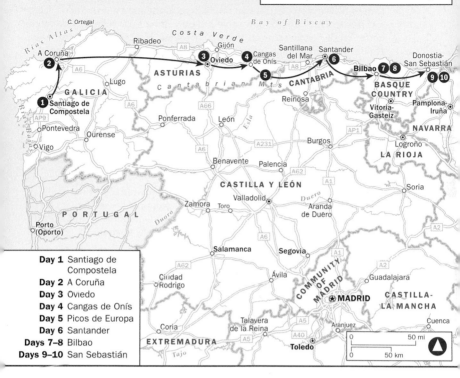

(p. 503). Take Bus 1 to the **Acuarium Finisterrae** (p. 502). Don't miss the oldest lighthouse in Europe, the **Torre de Hércules** (p. 503). Spend your evening socializing at **Praza de María Pita** (p. 503).

DAY 3: Oviedo ★★

Driving to Oviedo takes about 3½ hours and includes some spectacular mountain scenery before you return to the coast. Arrive in time for lunch and visit the **Catedral de San Salvador** (p. 494) after coffee. The two stunning pre-Romanesque churches of **Santa María del Naranco** and **San Miguel de Lillo** (p. 495) re-open for tours at 3:30pm, saving your late afternoon for shopping and evening for dining and strolling.

DAY 4: Cangas de Onís ★★★

The drive east to this outpost of the Picos de Europa takes just more than an hour, giving you plenty of time to visit the **Capilla de Santa Cruz** (p. 486) before heading out of town to the mountain shrine of **Covadonga** (p. 486). Save time for hiking the trails around the ancient battle site and visiting the tomb of Pelayo, high on a cliff behind the waterfall. Spend the night in Cangas listening to hikers' tales.

DAY 5: The Edges of the Picos de Europa ★★★

From Cangas, drive east to **Las Arenas de Cabrales** (p. 487) for a lunch of Cabrales cheese and local cider. Continue east on AS-114 about a half hour to N-621, and go south toward Potes, stopping at the **Centro de Visitantes Sotama** (p. 483) for an orientation to the mountains. Follow signs to **Fuente Dé** (p. 484) for a cable car ride and a ridge hike. In late afternoon, retrace your steps to Potes and follow N-621 to the coast, then E-70/A-8 east to Santander (1½ hours), where you can drop the car.

DAY 6: Santander ★

Enjoy a leisurely day at this elegant beach resort town. Spend a few hours on the beach at **El Sardinero** (p. 472) before visiting the **Museo Maritimo del Cantábrico** (p. 478) to get a handle on the Cantabrian coast and its fishing and mercantile history. If you find time, check out the Roman ruins beneath the lower-level chapel at the **Catedral** (p. 477). Pick up your train tickets so you can catch the 8am (weekdays) FEVE train to Bilbao the next day.

DAYS 7 & 8: Bilbao ★★★

Before you enter the **Guggenheim Bilbao Museum** (p. 466), walk all around it and across the river to see the building in its glorious entirety. Once you've seen the galleries, follow the riverside promenade to **La Parte Vieja** (p. 454). Visit the **Museo Arqueologica de Bizkaia** (p. 467), and immerse yourself in the shops and lively *pintxos* scene.

The next day, see the **Museo de Bellas Artes** (p. 468), focusing on Basque artists. There's still time for a round-trip bus visit to **Gernika** (**Guernica**; p. 459), the Basque village so memorably recalled by Picasso's great canvas.

DAYS 9 & 10: San Sebastián ★★★

From Bilbao, it's a 75-minute bus ride to this resort city. City buses go right to **Playa de la Concha** (p. 453). Over 2 days you'll have time to catch some rays and still hit the sights: the **Museo de Sociedad Vasca y Ciudadanía** (p. 454) for a rundown on the city's history, the docks to see fishermen unloading their catch, and the adjacent **Palacio del Mar** (p. 454), the aquarium. Get a fabulous overview of the city and its long crescent beach by riding the funicular to **Monte Igeldo** (p. 453). **Bar-hopping for *pintxos*** (p. 455) or going out for prolonged dinner are the main activities in San Sebastián. When it's time to go, take a bus direct to the Bilbao airport.

A WEEK IN SPAIN FOR ART LOVERS

This art connoisseur's whirlwind tour ranges from High Gothic to ultra-contemporary. Book 4 nights' hotel in Madrid, because you'll visit two great art towns as day trips.

DAY 1: Madrid's Museo del Prado ★★★ & More

Hold your horses. The Prado is open long hours, but the museum of the **Real Academia de Bellas Artes de San Fernando** (p. 96) is only open until midafternoon. Start here, just outside Puerta del Sol. Goya arranged the permanent collection to show the progression from antiquity to present. Now you can move on to **Museo del Prado** (p. 90), one of the top museums in the world. Almost every good painting by **Velazquez** is here (Galleries 12, 14–16, 18), and most of the famous **Goyas** (Galleries 66–67, 85, 90–94).

DAY 2: Madrid's Reina Sofía ★★ & Thyssen-Bornemisza ★★

The **Museo Nacional Centro de Arte Reina Sofía** (p. 92) picks up chronologically where the Prado left off—the early 20th century. Some of

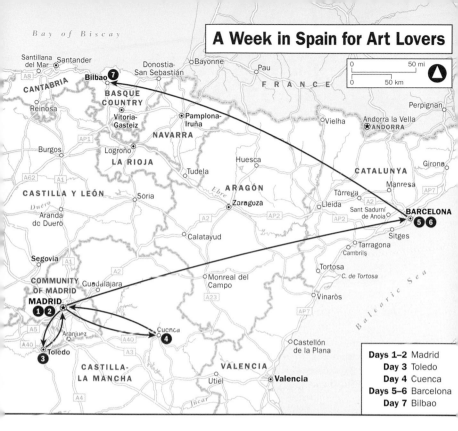

Days 1–2	Madrid
Day 3	Toledo
Day 4	Cuenca
Days 5–6	Barcelona
Day 7	Bilbao

the most fascinating works were made by such famous artists as Joan Miró, Salvador Dalí, and Juan Gris *before* they became famous. Of course, Picasso's *Guernica* is unavoidable (and haunting). Take a long lunch to clear your head before moving on to Madrid's *third* great art museum, the **Museo Thyssen-Bornemisza** (p. 94). Linger in the Gothic galleries assembled by the Baron Thyssen-Bornemisza, or focus on his wife Carmen Cervera's seminal Picassos and American Abstract Expressionists.

DAY 3: El Greco's Toledo ★★★

RENFE whisks you to Toledo in 35 minutes to see the city that inspired El Greco for his whole life. Start with the **Museo del Greco** (p. 130) to set the painter in context. Then see some of his greatest paintings in the **Iglesia de Santo Tomé** (p. 128), the **Catedral** (p. 126), and the **Museo-Hospital de Santa Cruz** (p. 131), where you can get close enough to the works to see every impasto brushstroke.

DAY 4: Ancient Cuenca's Modern Art ★★

Another train will zip you from Madrid to Cuenca in less than an hour—giving you a long day to explore this high-mesa citadel that inspired a movement in modern Spanish art. Begin with the **Museo del Arte Abstracto Español** (p. 140) in one of Cuenca's famous *casa colgadas,* the "hanging houses" cantilevered over the river gorge. The **Fundación Antonio Saura**

Toledo's Plaza Zocodover.

(p. 139) focuses on one of the greatest of the mid-20th-century Grupo El Paso artists. The **Fundación Antonio Pérez** (p. 139) fleshes out Spanish modern art with its overseas influences.

DAY 5: Gaudí ★★★ & Picasso ★★ in Barcelona

Catch an early train from Madrid to Barcelona so you have enough time to tour Antoni Gaudí's masterpiece basilica **La Sagrada Familia** (p. 355) and his masterpiece apartment house **La Pedrera** (Casa Milà; p. 359) before visiting the **Museu Picasso** (p. 352).

DAY 6: Gothic ★★★ to Miró ★★ in Barcelona

Catalan artists might have been Europe's best in the 11th and 12 centuries. The first glimmers of Renaissance perspective and facial modeling appeared centuries ahead of schedule in murals and altarpieces installed in country churches. Fortunately, these treasures are gathered at the **Museu Nacional d'Art de Catalunya** (p. 364) on Montjuïc. Nearby, the **Fundació Joan Miró** (p. 363) concentrates hundreds of paintings and sculptures by that singular Catalan abstract master. Take the late afternoon train to Bilbao.

DAY 7: Frank Gehry's Guggenheim in Bilbao ★★★

You have a full day to enjoy the artistic attractions of Bilbao. Start by having a look at Philippe Starck's design for the **Alhóndiga Bilbao** cultural and sport complex (p. 466), and tour through centuries of mostly Basque art at the **Museo de Bellas Artes** (p. 468). Have lunch on the riverside plaza outside before enjoying the crazy spaces (and sometimes crazier art) inside the **Guggenheim Museum** (p. 466).

EIGHT DAYS IN CATALAN COUNTRY

This itinerary celebrates the Catalan sensibility from its art to its gastronomy as well as its beautiful natural landscapes.

DAY 1: Valencia's City of Arts & Sciences ★★★

To start your tour of Catalan Spain, immerse yourself in visionary Catalan architecture. Valencia's native son, architect, and engineer Santiago Calatrava vaulted Valencia into international prominence with his designs for the **City of Arts & Sciences** (p. 294), a cultural complex. The buildings are

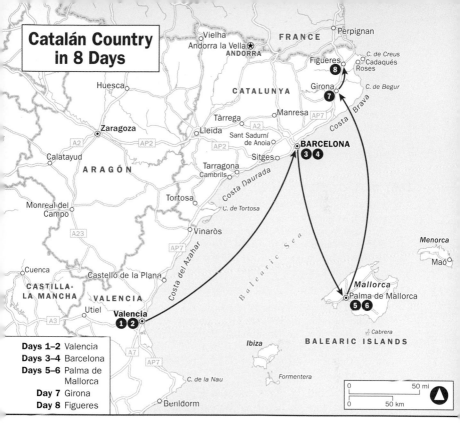

Catalán Country in 8 Days

Days 1–2 Valencia
Days 3–4 Barcelona
Days 5–6 Palma de Mallorca
Day 7 Girona
Day 8 Figueres

amazing in themselves—his planetarium, l'Hemisfèric, actually has a blinking eye—and the reflecting pools only magnify the vision.

DAY 2: Valencia & l'Albufera ★

Rent a bicycle in the morning to pedal south along the coast from Valencia's port to visit the **Parque Natural de l'Albufera** (p. 301). Explore the byways on the coastal side of the road or bike down back roads through the rice paddies. In El Saler, enjoy a lunchtime paella made with rice, vegetables, and fish or meat from the immediate surroundings. In the late afternoon or evening, hop a train to Barcelona (3 hrs.).

DAY 3: Walking Barcelona ★★★

Few streets in the world offer such a passing parade of humanity as **Les Rambles** (p. 313), which runs from the waterfront uphill to L'Eixample. Spend half the day wandering the **Barri Gòtic** (p. 313) and plumbing the Catalan influence on Picasso at the **Museu Picasso** (p. 352), the other half on Montjuïc to see the Gothic art at **Museu Nacional d'Art de Catalunya** (p. 364) and 20th-century whimsy at the **Fundació Joan Miró** (p. 363).

DAY 4: Barcelona Design & Waterfront ★★

You can't leave Barcelona without drinking in the designs of Antoni Gaudí. Arrange a guided tour of his masterpiece basilica **La Sagrada Familia**

(p. 355) to get a look at his upside-down maquette for the church. Spend the afternoon on the waterfront, starting with a great black rice dish at one of the outdoor restaurants. Catch some rays on the beach at **Vila Olímpica** (p. 361), and then head out for a stellar meal (you have many choices).

Tapestry of the Creation, in Girona cathedral.

DAY 5: Majorca: Exploring Palma ★★

Flights from Barcelona into Palma de Majorca take less than an hour, so you'll have plenty of time to visit the **Catedral** (p. 528) and get a visual overview from **Castell de Bellver** (p. 527) before checking out modern Catalan sculpture at **Esbaluard Museu d'Art Modern i Contemporani** (p. 528). Later in the afternoon, hop a city bus to **Playa Nova** (p. 529) to put in some serious beach time.

DAY 6: Majorca: Over the Mountains to Sóller ★★

Spend at least part of your day exploring the erstwhile citrus-growing capital of Sóller by riding the **vintage 1912 narrow-gauge train** (p. 532) over the scenic high Serra de Tramuntana. Reflecting its wealth at the turn of the 19th and 20th centuries, Sóller is filled with superb Modernisme buildings. A 1913 tram takes you from Sóller to its harbor, where beaches are lined with cafes and restaurants.

DAY 7: Exploring Girona ★★★

Catch the early-morning flight from Palma to Girona so you have time to explore the old Jewish quarter, **the Call** (p. 396), and visit the **cathedral and its museum** (p. 397) to see the amazing Romanesque *Tapestry of the Creation.* Be sure to make a walking circuit of the city, strolling the medieval backbone of the hill on which it's built, then the riverfront lined with pastel buildings like a chain of children's blocks.

Vintage narrow-gauge train in Sóller.

DAY 8: Closing with Dalí's Teatro-Museu ★★★

The parched landscapes of painter Salvador Dalí's surrealist period (think limp watches) weren't imagined; **Figueres** (p. 401) looks like that. Take a day trip by train to visit the **Teatre-Museu Dalí** (p. 402). The artist could have been the lost Catalan Marx brother, so don't expect anything about the museum to be serious. It's okay to be convulsed with laughter, whether contemplating his self-portrait in heaven as seen from earth (mostly big feet) or his Warhol-like fascination with pop culture divas. At the end of the day, head to Barcelona for maximum transportation options leaving the area.

ANDALUCÍA IN 10 DAYS

Flamboyant flamenco, matadors in suits of light, casks of sherry, dancing stallions—they all evoke the color and verve of the country-sized region of Andalucía, Spain's passionate south. The Moorish-tinged cities of Córdoba, Sevilla, and Granada would be enough, but Andalucía also boasts historic ports, scenic mountains, and the sherry wine country.

DAY 1: Sevilla ★★★: The Old Town

Andalucía's split personality is cast in stone at the palace fortress of the **Alcázar** (p. 242), where Christian conquerors couldn't resist decorating with Moorish flair. The adjacent **cathedral** (p. 194) is so big because it had to obliterate the Great Mosque that had stood in its spot. Between them, these monuments will take more than half a day. Then wander the **Barrio de Santa Cruz** (p. 192), the quarter that Christian rulers established for their Jewish administrators.

DAY 2: Córdoba's Moorish Yesteryear ★★★

On your second day, take the morning train to **Córdoba** (p. 202). Walk over the **Puente Romano** (p. 206) to visit the **Torre de la Calahorra** (p. 210) for an orientation to the history and cultures of Córdoba. Walk back across to experience the glory of **La Mezquita** (p. 202), one of the great religious sites in Europe. See the elegant gardens of the **Alcázar,** then wander through the medieval warren of the **Judería** (p. 207) until it's time to return to Sevilla for the night.

DAY 3: Gypsy Spirit of Sevilla ★★★

Plunge back into the Barrio de Santa Cruz to spend some time learning the fine points of flamenco styles at the **Museo del Baile Flamenco** (**Museum of Flamenco Dance;** p. 247). Then stroll the banks of the Río Guadalquivír, paying a quick visit to the **Torre del Oro** (p. 198) before exploring the **Barrio de Triana** (p. 193), the traditional quarter of fishermen, sailors, and Gypsies. If you've fallen in love with Andalucían tiles, you can shop in Triana's historic **ceramics factories.**

DAY 4: Exploring Granada ★★★

The train ride from Sevilla eats up most of the morning, but still leaves time to investigate the **Catedral** and its adjacent **Capilla Real** (**Royal Chapel;** p. 223), dominated by the sarcophagi of Fernando and Isabel, who conquered Granada in 1492. Enjoy bargaining with the vendors in the souk along **Caldererías Vieja and Nueva** (p. 225), and walk through the medieval Moorish quarter, the **Albaicín** (p. 219). End the day at the **Mirador**

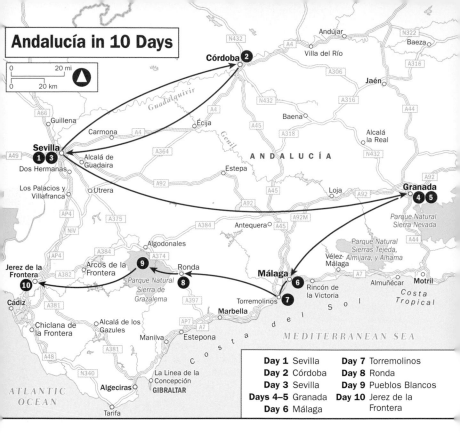

Andújar
Baeza
Villa del Río
Córdoba ②
Jaén
Guadalquivir
A66
Guillena
Carmona
Écija
Baena
Alcalá
la Real
Sevilla ① ③
Alcalá de
Guadaira
A N D A L U C Í A
Dos Hermanas
Estepa
Los Palacios y
Villafranca
Utrera
Loja
Granada ④ ⑤
Parque Natural
Sierra Nevada
Antequera
Parque Natural
Sierras Tejeda,
Almijara, y Alhama
Vélez-
Málaga
Algodonales
Ronda
Arcos de la
Frontera ⑨
Málaga ⑥
Almuñécar
Motril
Jerez de la
Frontera ⑩
⑧
Rincón de
la Victoria
Costa
Tropical
Cádiz
Parque Natural
Sierra de
Grazalema
Torremolinos ⑦
Marbella
Sol
Chiclana de
la Frontera
Alcalá de los
Gazules
Manilva
Estepona
del
MEDITERRANEAN SEA
A48
N340
La Linea de la
Concepción
GIBRALTAR
ATLANTIC
OCEAN
Algeciras
Tarifa

Day 1 Sevilla	**Day 7** Torremolinos
Day 2 Córdoba	**Day 8** Ronda
Day 3 Sevilla	**Day 9** Pueblos Blancos
Days 4–5 Granada	**Day 10** Jerez de la
Day 6 Málaga	Frontera

de San Nicolás (p. 219), where at sunset the Alhambra on the opposite hill glows. Granada's **tapas scene** (p. 226) is one of the best in Spain.

DAY 5: The Alhambra & Generalife ★★★

You were smart enough to purchase a reserved ticket with an entrance time at the beginning of the day, so be prompt for your 15-minute window of entry to the **Alhambra** (p. 219) and bring your lunch with you. Next, the **Palacio de Carlos V** (p. 222) may lack the beauty of the Nasrid buildings, but it houses the fantastic **Museo de la Alhambra** (p. 222), which contains some of the complex's most beautiful Hispano-Muslim art.

DAY 6: Exploring Málaga ★★

The bus from Granada takes less than 2 hours. Once you're settled, let young Picasso show you around. At his birthplace, the **Fundación Picasso** (p. 274), you can get a map of sites important in his childhood and follow the child prodigy around town. To get an idea of the artistic milieu of his father, which influenced young Pablo, visit the **Museo Carmen Thyssen Málaga** (p. 275), which is strong on late 19th- and early 20th-century Spanish painting. Ultimately, you'll want to devote several hours to the **Museo Picasso Málaga** (p. 276).

A pool at the Generalife.

Horses at the Escuela Andaluza del Arte Ecuestre.

DAY 7: A Day at the Beach in Torremolinos

It's a cinch to take the train from Málaga to the beach resort of **Torremolinos** (p. 265), 19 minutes away on the C1 commuter line. Keep walking west on the boardwalk until you reach **Playa La Carihuela.** This former fishing village has the broadest sands and best restaurants for a quintessential beach experience. Return to Málaga to sleep.

DAY 8: Exploring Ronda ★★

Pick up a rental car in the morning and drive the inland route to **Ronda** (p. 229), one of the most dramatic towns in Andalucía. A monster gorge divides old and new towns, and you can get the lowdown on attempts to span it over the centuries at the **Centro de Interpretación del Puente Nuevo** (p. 232). There are many sights in Ronda, but the most evocative are the famous **Plaza de Toros** (p. 233) and its museum, and the **Palacio de Mondragón** (p. 232), which gives you an intimate look at life in Moorish Spain.

DAY 9: Pueblos Blancos

Today's driving tour cuts due west across the Sierra de Grazalema from Ronda through some of the beautiful **Pueblos Blancos** (p. 234)—the white towns clinging to the hillside. Follow signs to **Zahara de la Sierra** (p. 234) for a true mountaintop redoubt, then to **Grazalema** (p. 235), where lunch on the main plaza is a good idea. Continue west to **Arcos de la Frontera** (p. 237), where you should end up at the top of the hill in the tiny square surrounded by a cathedral, a palace, and a parador. Overnight here.

DAY 10: Sherry & Stallions in Jerez de la Frontera ★★

The drive to Jerez from Arcos is just 40 minutes across flat vineyard country. Book a tour at one of the **sherry bodegas** (p. 241). Then be sure to visit the **Escuela Andaluza del Arte Ecuestre** (p. 243). This famed school of equestrian arts puts on weekly shows of dancing horses; you can also visit the rehearsals. It's a 90-minute train ride to Sevilla.

4

MADRID

You'll never forget your first sight of Plaza Mayor. As you emerge from a shady stone portico into a vast sun-struck plaza, you are greeted by a very large and very royal equestrian statue of Felipe III. Surrounded by three-story buildings, Plaza Mayor seems the grandest imaginable stage set, where more than 200 balconies become regal box seats on the scene below. The perimeter is marked with the umbrellas of cafe tables that lure people to while away the afternoon over cold beers or strong coffees. Children race back and forth across the paving stones, flushing pigeons into flight. Travelers with backpacks lean against the plinth of the equestrian monument, eating ice cream. Plaza Mayor may be important—just look at its name, the Major Square—but more than that, it is alive.

It is Madrid in a nutshell. Spain's capital is at once *real* ("ray-AL," as the Spanish say "royal") and real (as English speakers put it). Families row on the lake in Parque del Retiro where kings once staged mock naval battles. When football club Real Madrid wins a cup or league title, the players wrap their team scarves around the elegant Cibeles fountain. People recline in the grass on the green center strips of the paseos, the boulevards built to the king's order. Dog-walkers with packs of canines strut past some of the greatest museums in the world. Tapas-hoppers make the rounds of bars beneath the sculpted visages of Spain's great playwrights. And, yes, Felipe III continues to ignore the backpackers eating ice cream beneath him.

Forever a blend of formal and casual, Madrid wants to be wooed a little before it will give itself to you. Join the Madrileños on the capital's royal stage by getting in step with the urban pace and rhythms—the hurried rush of the subway system, the clip-clop-clip-clop fast walk along Calle Arenal between Sol and Opera, and the languid stroll of the paseos. When you put in the effort, Madrid smiles and tells you its secrets. It is, after all, the sunniest capital in Europe. The weather may be hot in summer and often chilly in winter, but the sky is the very definition of cerulean blue. As Madrileños say, *de Madrid al cielo:* from Madrid to heaven.

ESSENTIALS
Arriving
BY PLANE   Madrid's international airport, **Barajas** (airport code: MAD; www. aena.es), lies 15km (9.3 miles) east of the city center. Its four terminals are connected by a moving sidewalk and light rail. The newest and most comfortable is Terminal 4, which serves Iberia, American, British Airways, Cathay Pacific, El Al, Emirates, Finnair, LAN, Luxair, Qatar, Royal Air Maroc, Vueling, and some small airlines. Terminal 1 serves Air Lingus, Aeroflot, Aerolineas Argentinas, Aeromexico, Air Canada, Air China, most Air Europa flights, Delta, Easyjet, Korean Air,

FACING PAGE: **The cafes of Plaza Mayor.**

The modern terminal at Barajas Airport.

Ryanair, Saudi Arabian Airlines, Transavia, Turkish, and United. Terminal 2's principal airlines include Air France, some Air Europa flights, Alitalia, Brussels Airlines, KLM, Lufthansa, Swiss, and TAP.

Air-conditioned airport **buses** can take you from the ground floor at Terminal 4 or Level 0 at Terminals 1 and 2 to the Atocha train station a few blocks from the Prado. The fare is 5€, and you can buy tickets on the bus but only with cash. Buses leave every 10 to 15 minutes for the 40-minute trip.

By **taxi,** expect to pay 35€ and up, plus surcharges, for the trip to the airport and for baggage handling.

The **subway** is another option, but is cumbersome with luggage and not appreciably cheaper than the airport bus. From the airport, take line 8 to Nuevos Ministerios, exit and re-enter the system, and pay a second fare. The airport supplement is 3€ in addition to the usual 1.50€ to 2€ for travel within metropolitan Madrid.

BY TRAIN   Madrid has two major railway stations: **Atocha** (Glorieta Carlos V; Metro: Atocha RENFE), for trains to and from Lisbon, Toledo, Andalucía, Basque Country, Extremadura, Barcelona, and the French frontier via Catalunya; and **Chamartín** (in the northern suburbs at Augustín de Foxá; Metro: Chamartín), for trains to and from Asturias, Cantabria, Castilla y León, the Basque Country, Aragón, Levante (Valencia), Murcia, and the French frontier via Basque Country. For information about connections from any of these stations, call **RENFE (Spanish Railways)** at ✆ **90-232-03-20** (daily 5am–11:50pm), or visit **www.renfe.com**.

For long-distance tickets, go to RENFE's main office at Alcalá 44 (✆ **90-232-03-20;** www.renfe.com; Metro: Banco de España). The office is open Monday to Friday 9:30am to 11:30pm. Frankly, it is most convenient to purchase tickets on the website and print them out. Phone apps do not permit ticket purchase.

BY BUS   Madrid has at least 14 major bus terminals, including **Estación Sur de Autobuses,** Calle Méndez Álvaro 83 (✆ **91-468-42-00;** www.estacionde autobuses.com; Metro: Méndez Álvaro). Most buses pass through this large station.

BY CAR   All highways within Spain radiate outward from Madrid. The following are the major highways into Madrid, with information on driving distances to the city:

Highways to Madrid

ROUTE	FROM	DISTANCE TO MADRID
N-I	Irún	507km (315 miles)
N-II	Barcelona	626km (389 miles)
N-III	Valencia	349km (217 miles)
N-IV	Cádiz	625km (388 miles)
N-V	Badajoz	409km (254 miles)
N-VI	Galicia	602km (374 miles)

Visitor Information

The most convenient **tourist office** in the heart of tourist attractions is located on Plaza Mayor 27 (Salón de Columnas de la Casa de la Panadería; © **91-454-44-10;** www.esmadrid.com; Metro: Sól or Opera); it's open daily from 9:30am to 8:30pm. In addition to personal advice and information, this center has several terminals to access the esMadrid website. The office also offers free mp3 audioguides. Ask for a street map of the next town on your itinerary, especially if you're driving.

The **Colón Tourist Center** (www.esmadrid.com) is located near the Archaeological Museum on the Paseo de Recoletos in the underground passageway beneath Plaza de Colón. It does not offer telephone service, but is open for visits daily from 9:30am to 8:30pm. Like the Plaza Mayor site, it has terminals for access to esMadrid and offers special counseling for students who have come to Madrid to study Spanish. Similar walk-in information points with the same hours are also available at **Plaza de Cibeles** (opposite the Prado bus stop), **Plaza de Callao** on the corner with calle Preciados, and the **Paseo del Arte** next to the Museo de Reina Sofía.

Madrid's main street, the Gran Via.

City Layout

All roads in Spain ultimately lead to Madrid, which long ago outgrew its original boundaries and continues to sprawl in all directions. But central Madrid can be navigated by its main arteries and squares.

MAIN ARTERIES & SQUARES Every new arrival ultimately stumbles onto the **Gran Vía,** which cuts a diagonal path across the city. It begins at **Plaza de España,** where you'll find the Edificio España, a 25-story, 1920 skyscraper currently vacant while it's being transformed into luxury residences. **Gran Vía** is lined with shops carrying international goods, as well as some of the city's largest cinemas.

South of the Gran Vía lies **Puerta del Sol,** the starting point for all road distances within Spain and the crossroads of Madrid's public transit system.

papa's TOWN

Ernest Hemingway's attachment to Madrid was like an old man's remembrance of the first girl who ever took his breath away. He may have married Paris, but he kept coming back to sleep with Madrid. He was there in the 1920s, looking for a manhood undermined by World War I. He was there in the 1930s, reporting on the fratricidal collapse of a country he loved, and he returned in the 1950s, drawn to the bullring of Las Ventas, where he felt that even in a country in the grip of a dictatorship, some elemental truth could be found in the existential showdown between man and beast.

Madrid is the most Spanish of cities, he once explained to his biographer, A. E. Hotchner. Everyone is from somewhere else. Hotchner took that to mean that everyone in Madrid came from somewhere else in Spain. We think Papa meant that everyone who comes to Madrid from anywhere in the world cannot help but become a Madrileño.

The bustling square is the borderland between Madrid's oldest quarters (La Latina, Lavapiés, Las Letras) and the commercial city center. **Calle de Alcalá** begins at Sol and runs northeast for 4km (2.5 miles) through Plaza de la Independencia and the entrance to Retiro Park. Follow **Carrera de San Jerónimo** east to reach the Paseo del Prado. Follow **Calle Mayor** west to reach Plaza Mayor.

Plaza Mayor lies at the heart of Old Madrid and is an attraction in itself, with its mix of Renaissance and neoclassical architecture. The colonnaded ground level of the plaza is filled with shops and restaurants. Pedestrians pass beneath the arches of the huge square to exit onto the narrow 16th- and 17th-century streets of the district known as La Latina, which are jammed with old-fashioned shops, many bars and taverns.

The area immediately south of Plaza Mayor—known as *barrios bajos*—is a colorful segment of La Latina with cobblestone streets lined with 16th- and 17th-century architecture. Exit Plaza Mayor through the **Arco de Cuchilleros** to Cava Baja, a street packed with markets, restaurants, and taverns. Directly west of Plaza Mayor, where Calle Mayor meets Calle Bailén, stands the **Palacio Royal** (Royal Palace).

Gran Vía ends at Calle de Alcalá, and a few hundred meters east is the grand **Plaza de Cibeles,** with its fountain to Cybele, "the mother of the gods." From Cibeles, the wide **Paseo de Recoletos** begins a short run north to Plaza de Colón. North of Colón, the long serpentine central artery of Madrid begins: **Paseo de la Castellana,** flanked by expensive shops, apartment buildings, luxury hotels, and foreign embassies.

Heading south from Cibeles is **Paseo del Prado,** where you'll find the **Museo del Prado** as well as the striking **Museo Thyssen-Bornemisza** and the **Jardín Botánico** (Botanical Garden). To the east of the garden lies **Parque del Retiro,** a magnificent park once reserved for royalty, with a restaurant, a rose garden, a lake, and two gallery pavilions. (It's best accessed from Plaza de Independencia, north of the Prado.) Paseo del Prado leads south to the Atocha railway station. Just off the roundabout is the third of Madrid's artistic triumvirate, the **Museo Nacional Centro de Arte Reina Sofía.**

STREET MAPS   Arm yourself with a good map before setting out. **Falk** maps are good and are available at most newsstands and kiosks. Free maps given away by tourist offices and hotels are adequate for general orientation, but don't list the maze of small streets in Old Madrid. However, finding your way with a massive folding map is usually impractical and, frankly, makes you more vulnerable to pickpockets. The best bet is to print out a day's itinerary in advance and carry the printouts or use the GPS on your phone.

The Neighborhoods in Brief

Madrid unfolds in three layers. **Old Madrid** lies at the center and contains most of the attractions that travelers come to see. **Modern Madrid,** rebuilt in the last half of the 20th century, envelops Old Madrid on the east and north. It mixes tony residences and shopping with office buildings and some upscale business hotels. **Outer Madrid,** where urban congestion begins to ease into the Castilian countryside, holds less interest for most visitors—unless they have friends or family living there.

ART DISTRICT & PASEOS   Not a real city district, the Paseos form Madrid's north-south axis, and the street name changes along the way. As it approaches Atocha station, the district is suddenly thick with museums and park amenities. The Museo del Prado and some of the city's more expensive hotels are found here. Many restaurants and other hotels are located along its side streets. In summer, the large medians of the Paseos become open-air terraces filled with animated crowds.

PUERTA DEL SOL & LAS LETRAS   Madrid radiated from its eastern gate—Puerta del Sol means "Gate of the Sun"—even before Habsburg kings established their capital in the city. Today Sol is the hub of public transport, connecting ancient and modern Madrid. Sol's central location makes it easy to walk to Plaza Mayor, the Palacio Real, the art museums, Plaza Santa Ana, and the nightlife of bars in La Latina. Metro lines 1, 2, and 3 will take you anyplace else you'll want to go. Although there are some overpriced fleabag hotels in the area (not in this book!), there are also good lodgings at fair prices. Heading south and uphill from Sol is the barrio known as Las Letras because it was home to writers from the 16th through the 20th centuries. Lope de Vega, Cervantes, and Lorca lived and worked here. Plaza Santa Ana, one of the city's best spots for tapas, is central to Las Letras and marks the spot where the districts of Sol, Lavapiés, and La Latina all converge. It can get rowdy at night, but it oozes Old Madrid charm.

PLAZA MAYOR & LA LATINA   Madrid (and its visitors) party in this neighborhood. Sometimes called the "Madrid of the Asturias," it is better known as La Latina. From Plaza Mayor, the Arco de Cuchilleros leads to Cava de San Miguel, Cava Alta, and Cava Baja, all full of taverns and bars. La Latina continues downhill west to the Manzanares River. Also in this area, Muslim Madrid is centered on the Palacio de Oriente and Las Vistillas. What is now Plaza de la Paja was actually the heart of the city and its main marketplace during the medieval period. In 1617, Plaza Mayor became the hub of Madrid, and it remains a center of activity both day and night. The neighborhood around Plaza Mayor is vital and vigorous, which is a good thing when you're out partying at a bar or restaurant and a not-so-good thing when you're trying to sleep. But most lodgings are set up to seal out the racket. The bars start serving coffee on the plaza before the sun comes up, and the neighborhood has many cafes that serve inexpensive breakfasts.

OPERA & PALACIO REAL   Adjacent to Plaza Mayor and La Latina, this section of Madrid revolves around the Teatro Real, the Plaza de Oriente, and the Palacio Real with its parks and gardens. It forms a buffer zone between Puerta del Sol and Plaza Mayor, and the uphill, modern district around Gran Vía. Much of this neighborhood was rebuilt in the 19th century, making it more spacious and less cramped than Sol or La Latina. Several hotels are located in the vicinity of the Opera stop on the Metro. The neighborhood's attractions, both religious and secular, are chiefly related to the monarchy.

GRAN VÍA & PLAZA DE ESPAÑA   Gran Vía was constructed in the early 20th century to be Madrid's main street. It is flanked by cinemas, department stores, and bank and corporate headquarters, although its retail offerings have dimmed in recent years. Gran Vía begins at Plaza de España, with bronze figures of Don Quijote and his faithful squire, Sancho Panza. Hotels with a Gran Vía address seem to believe in *gran precios* (high rates) justified on address rather than amenities. A certain after-dark glamour clings to Gran Vía (along with a number of less-smart creatures of the night), but walk a few steps away from the bright lights and traffic and into the adjoining neighborhoods, and hotels begin to offer more value for price.

CHUECA & MALASAÑA   Chueca is a recently revitalized district north of Gran Vía defined by the the main streets of Hortaleza, Infantas, Barquillo, and San Lucas. It is the center of gay nightlife, with dozens of clubs, good restaurants, and hip shopping. Chueca and adjoining student-heavy Malasaña are gentrifying, often offering basic and old-fashioned *hostales* on the same block with design-conscious (and, thus, more expensive) new hotels. These neighborhoods north of Gran Vía are great for dining and clubbing but are less convenient for seeing the sights. Plan on riding the Metro more if you choose to stay here.

SALAMANCA, RETIRO & CHAMBERÍ   Once Madrid's city walls came down in the 1860s, the district of Salamanca to the northeast of Old Madrid became a fashionable address. Calle de Serrano cuts through this neighborhood and is lined with stores and boutiques. The street is also home to the U.S. Embassy. The adjacent leafy streets near Parque del Retiro and Chamberí (west of the Paseos and due north of Old Madrid) are often lumped with Salamanca because they are also upscale enclaves, though typically more residential.

GETTING AROUND
On Foot

You can walk most places in central Madrid, and it's the best way to experience the city. To save time, it's a good idea to take public transport to a neighborhood and then set off on foot to explore. Madrid was sited on the high ground to command the modest valley of the Manzanares River. The difference in elevation between popular areas of the city is fairly minor, but you will encounter uphill grades between Sol and Las Letras, and between the major art museums and Sol.

Walking, Biking & Blading

Get oriented to Madrid with guided tours from the chief tourist information center (Plaza Mayor, 27; ✆ **90-222-14-24;** www.esmadrid.com/officialguidedtours; Metro: Vodafone Sol or Opera). Tours are given in several languages, including English. **Walking tours** (5.90€) in English primarily focus on Madrid's history, but other options include historic taverns and a ghost tour. A **bicycle tour** (6.90€, without bike rental) covers that same historical ground at a quicker pace. **Rollerblade tours** (6.90€, without skate rental) follow the banks of the Río Manzanares, for example, or explore historic gardens. Tours operate all year, but sizes are limited, so book ahead. Note that rollerblade tours and more specialized bicycle and walking tours are not usually offered in English. Dust off your high school Spanish to expand your choices.

By Public Transit

Madrid has some of the most thorough and least-expensive public transit in Europe. For a full overview, check the website for **Consorcio Transportes Madrid** (www.ctm-madrid.es). This site, available in Spanish and English, has a very useful tool that recommends ways to get from one place to another using any combination of public transit and walking.

By Metro (Subway)

The Metro system (℃ **90-244-44-03;** www.metromadrid.es) is easy to learn and use. The fare is 1.50€ for the first five stations one-way; the price goes up 0.10€ for each additional station up to a 2€ maximum in central Madrid. (Don't expect to game the system—you have to insert your ticket to exit as well as enter the Metro.) A 10-trip **Metrobus** ticket, good on buses and Metro, costs 12€. The Metro operates from 6am to 2am (try to avoid rush hours). Twelve main Metro lines and three additional short lines to connect hub stations cover most of the city. Don't overlook using the **Circular** (which circles around the edges of Old Madrid) as a quick connector among the other lines. Be forewarned that Madrileños are very aggressive when entering and exiting the subway cars. He who hesitates is lost, so push right through. Ever wonder how they manage to stay out late at night and still put in a full day's work? Look for nappers among the lucky few who snag a seat.

By Bus

The **public buses,** marked **emt,** are most useful for moving around the circular roads, or *rondas,* such as getting from Atocha to Puerta de Toledo, or for moving quickly up and down the Paseos. They run 6am to 11pm. Tickets for single bus rides are 1.50€, but few people buy just one. Buy a 10-trip Metrobus ticket (see above), or consider one of the special passes designed for tourists. If your stay is short and you have to move around the city quickly, then it can be worth your while to purchase an **Abono Transportes Turístico** for unlimited rides on Madrid's Metro and buses. The passes, which are available at Metro stations and tourist offices, are sold for 1, 2, 3, 5, and 7 days (for 8.40€, 14€, 18€, 27€, and 35€, respectively). The Abono is valid only for the ticket holder, and you have to show photo ID when you buy it. Unless you'll be a heavy user of the Metro and bus systems, the **Metrobus** ticket is usually a better buy at 12€, especially since two people can share a single ticket.

   Madrid City Tour is the city's hop-on, hop-off double-decker sightseeing bus. Recorded commentary is available through headphones in 14 languages, and separate narration is available for children. The buses' two routes cover most of the city's major attractions. Both start at Calle Felipe IV next to the Museo del Prado. From November to February, buses operate 10am to 6pm, passing each stop about every 14 minutes. From March to October, they operate 9am to 10pm and pass each stop every 8 to 9 minutes. Tickets can be purchased for 1 or 2 days. Adults pay 21€ for 1 day, 25€ for 2 days; ages 7 to 15 and over 65 pay 9€ for 1 day, 12€ for 2 days. Children 6 and under are free. The City Tour has the advantage of letting you get around without having to deal with public transportation. It is, however, more expensive. For more information, call ℃ **90-202-47-58,** or visit www.madridcitytour.es.

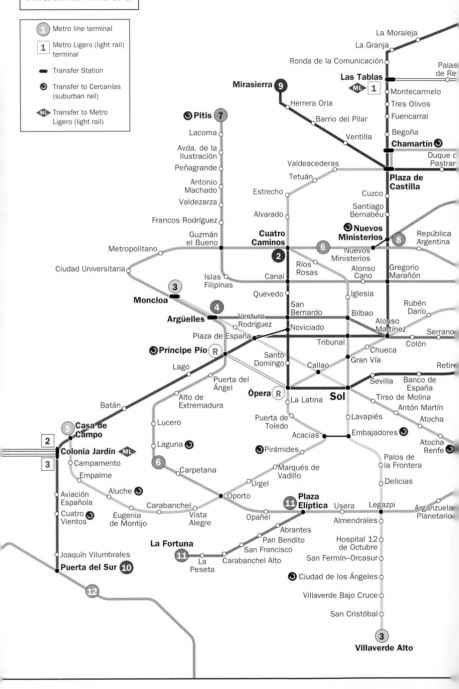

Madrid Metro

Legend:
- Metro line terminal
- Metro Ligero (light rail) terminal
- Transfer Station
- Transfer to Cercanías (suburban rail)
- Transfer to Metro Ligero (light rail)

La Moraleja
La Granja
Ronda de la Comunicación
Palas de Re
Las Tablas
Montecarmelo
Tres Olivos
Fuencarral
Begoña
Chamartín
Duque d
Pastrar
Mirasierra · 9
Herrera Oria
Barrio del Pilar
Ventilla
Pitis · 7
Lacoma
Avda. de la Ilustración
Peñagrande
Valdeacederas
Tetuán
Antonio Machado
Estrecho
Cuzco
Plaza de Castilla
Valdezarza
Alvarado
Santiago Bernabéu
Francos Rodríguez
Cuatro Caminos
Nuevos Ministerios
República Argentina
Guzmán el Bueno
2
6
8
Metropolitano
Nuevos Ministerios
Ríos Rosas
Alonso Cano
Gregorio Marañón
Ciudad Universitaria
Islas Filipinas
Canal
Quevedo
Iglesia
Rubén Darío
Moncloa · 3
San Bernardo
Bilbao
Argüelles · 4
Ventura Rodríguez
Alonso Martínez
Serrano
Plaza de España
Noviciado
Tribunal
Colón
Príncipe Pío · R
Santo Domingo
Chueca
Lago
Callao
Gran Vía
Retir
Puerta del Ángel
Sevilla
Banco de España
Alto de Extremadura
Ópera · R
La Latina
Sol
Tirso de Molina
Antón Martín
Batán
Lucero
Puerta de Toledo
Lavapiés
Atocha
Casa de Campo · 5
Laguna
Acacias
Embajadores
Atocha Renfe
Colonia Jardín
Pirámides
Palos de la Frontera
Campamento
Carpetana
Marqués de Vadillo
Delicias
Empalme
Urgel
Aviación Española
Aluche
Oporto
Plaza Elíptica · 11
Usera
Legazpi
Arganzuela Planetario
Cuatro Vientos
Carabanchel
Vista Alegre
Opañel
Almendrales
Eugenia de Montijo
Abrantes
Hospital 12 de Octubre
Pan Bendito
San Francisco
San Fermín–Orcasur
Joaquín Vilumbrales
La Fortuna · 11
Carabanchel Alto
Ciudad de los Ángeles
Puerta del Sur · 10
La Peseta
Villaverde Bajo Cruce
12
San Cristóbal
3
Villaverde Alto

2
3

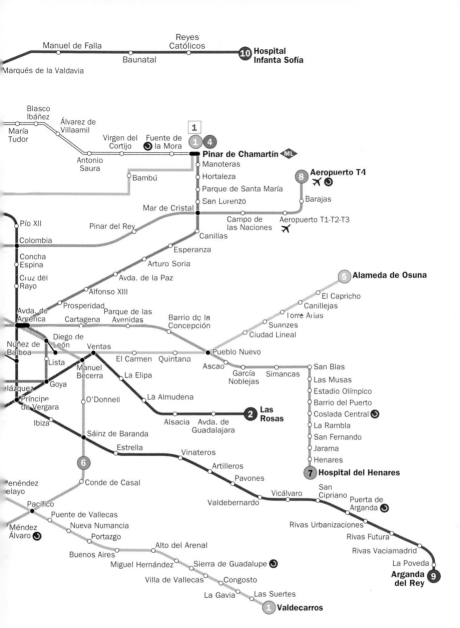

Manuel de Falla

Reyes
Católicos

10 Hospital
Infanta Sofía

Baunatal

Marqués de la Valdavia

Blasco
Ibáñez

Álvarez de
Villaamil

María
Tudor

Virgen del
Cortijo

Fuente de
la Mora

1

1 4

Antonio
Saura

Pinar de Chamartín ML

Manoteras

Bambú

Hortaleza

8 Aeropuerto T4

Parque de Santa María

San Lorenzo

Barajas

Mar de Cristal

Pío XII

Pinar del Rey

Campo de
las Naciones

Aeropuerto T1-T2-T3

Colombia

Canillas

Concha
Espina

Esperanza

Arturo Soria

Cruz del
Rayo

Avda. de la Paz

5 Alameda de Osuna

Alfonso XIII

El Capricho

Avda. de
América

Prosperidad

Parque de las
Avenidas

Canillejas

Torre Arias

Cartagena

Barrio de la
Concepción

Suanzes

Núñez de
Balboa

Diego de
León

Ventas

Ciudad Lineal

Lista

El Carmen

Quintana

Pueblo Nuevo

Velázquez

Manuel
Becerra

La Elipa

Ascao

San Blas

Goya

García
Noblejas

Simancas

Las Musas

Príncipe
de Vergara

O'Donnell

La Almudena

Estadio Olímpico

Barrio del Puerto

Ibiza

Alsacia

Avda. de
Guadalajara

2 Las
Rosas

Coslada Central

La Rambla

Sáinz de Baranda

San Fernando

Estrella

Vinateros

Jarama

6

Conde de Casal

Artilleros

Henares

Pavones

7 Hospital del Henares

Menéndez
Pelayo

Vicálvaro

San
Cipriano

Pacífico

Valdebernardo

Puerta de
Arganda

Puente de Vallecas

Méndez
Álvaro

Nueva Numancia

Rivas Urbanizaciones

Portazgo

Rivas Futura

Buenos Aires

Alto del Arenal

Rivas Vaciamadrid

Miguel Hernández

Sierra de Guadalupe

La Poveda

Villa de Vallecas

Congosto

Arganda
del Rey

9

La Gavia

Las Suertes

1 Valdecarros

61

By Commuter Rail

The **Cercanía** (www.renfe.com/viajeros/cercanias/index.html) train network, designed as suburban commuter rail, is also a convenient way to visit **El Escorial** (from Chamartín station) or **Alcalá de Henares** (from Atocha station). Fares on the *cercanías* run 1.60€ to 8.40€, depending on zone. *Note: Cercanías* are not included in the Abono Transportes Turístico or the Metrobus pass.

By Taxi

Cab fares are pretty reasonable. When you flag down a taxi, the meter should register 2.10€ 6am to 9pm or 2.20€ 9pm to 6am; for every kilometer thereafter, the fare increases between 1€ and 1.20€. A supplement is charged for trips to the railway station, the bullring, or the football stadiums. The ride to Barajas Airport carries a 5.50€ surcharge, and there is a 2.95€ supplement from railway stations and to or from Juan Carlos I Trade Fair. In addition, a 1.20€ supplement is charged on Sundays and holidays. It's customary to tip at least 10% of the fare. Taxis can be hailed on the street or at taxi ranks near attractions and hotels. To call a taxi, call ☏ **91-547-82-00** or 91-405-12-13.

Tip: Be sure that the meter is turned on when you get into a taxi. Drivers prefer to estimate the cost of the ride, which will almost always cost more than the metered fare. You'll also find unmetered taxis that hire out for the day or the afternoon. They are legal, but sometimes charge exorbitant rates. To avoid them, always take a black taxi with horizontal red bands or a white one with diagonal red bands.

If you take a taxi outside the city limits, the driver is entitled to charge you twice the rate shown on the meter.

Driving

Public transit is so good that inside the city you should leave the driving to Madrileños. They're the ones who grew up watching bullfights and understand the balance of aggression and aversion necessary to navigate Madrid's nonsensical intersections.

Renting a car for excursions is another matter, as pickup points are usually at train stations or the airport, where it's easy to reach outlying highways. Citizens of non-E.U. countries should obtain an **International Drivers Permit** before arriving in Spain. Without one, some agencies may refuse to rent you a car. Car rentals at the airport include **Avis** (☏ **91-743-88-67**; www.avis-europe.com), **Hertz** (☏ **91-746-60-04**; www.hertz.es), **Europcar** (☏ **91-743-87-58**; www.europcar.com), and **National Atesa** (☏ **91-746-60-60**; www.atesa.es). Prices vary little among companies, so stick with whichever one dovetails with your frequent-flyer program. Most can also arrange downtown pickup and dropoff.

[Fast FACTS] MADRID

Banks & ATMs You'll find a bank, or at least an ATM, wherever crowds gather in Madrid, especially in shopping districts and around major Metro stations. Most permit cash withdrawals via MasterCard or Visa, and many are linked into networks that will let you access your home bank account. Most offer a choice of language, including English. Major banks include **Banco Santander, Caja**

Madrid, and **BBVA.** Major overseas banks with a presence in Madrid include **Deutsche Bank** and **Citibank.** Most Spanish ATMs only accept 4-digit PINs, so if you have a longer PIN and want to use your card in Spain, change it at least a week before departure.

Business Hours
Opening hours can be complicated in Madrid. Expect small shops and banks to open at 10am, close 2 to 5pm for lunch, and open again from 5 to 8:30pm. Shopping centers and some international shops stay open continuously 10am to 10pm.

Doctors & Dentists
For a list of English-speaking doctors and dentists working in Madrid, visit the website of the U.S. Embassy in Madrid (see below). The PDF of the complete medical services list is available from the website under the tab for "U.S. Citizen Services." For dental services, you can also consult **Unidad Médica Anglo-Americana,** Conde de Arandá 1 (© **91-435-18-23;** www.unidad medica.com). Office hours are Monday to Friday from 9am to 8pm, and Saturday 10am to 1pm.

Embassies
If you lose your passport, fall seriously ill, get into legal trouble, or have some other serious problem, your embassy or consulate can help. These are the Madrid addresses and contact information:

Australia: Torre Espacio, Paseo de la Castellana 259D; © **91-353-66-00;** www.spain.embassy.gov.au;

Canada: Torre Espacio, Paseo de la Castellana 259D; © **91-382-84-00;** www. canadainternational.gc.ca

Ireland: Paseo de la Castellana 46, Ireland House; © **91-436-40-93;** www. irlanda.es

New Zealand: Calle Pinar 7; © **91-523-02-26;** www. nzembassy.com/spain

United Kingdom: Torre Espacio, Paseo de la Castellana 259D; © **91-714-63-00;** www.gov.uk/government/ world/organisations/ british-embassy-madrid

United States: Calle Serrano 75; © **91-587-22-00;** http://madrid.usembassy. gov

Emergencies
Call © **112** for fire, police, and ambulance services.

Hospitals & Clinics
Unidad Médica Anglo-Americana, Conde de Arandá 1 (© **91-435-18-23;** www.unidadmedica.com; Metro: Retiro), is not a hospital but a private outpatient clinic offering specialized services. This is not an emergency clinic, although someone on the staff is always available. It's open Monday to Friday 9am to 8pm, and Saturday 10am to 1pm. In a real medical emergency, call © **112** for an ambulance.

Internet Access
Most lodgings offer free Wi-Fi access, at least in public areas, if you have your own laptop, tablet, phone, or other device. Typically, bandwidth on free hotel Wi-Fi is good enough to surf the Web, use e-mail,

look up maps, and sometimes even make VOIP phone calls. It is not adequate, however, for streaming video or music. Some hotels give away basic Wi-Fi but charge for faster access. Somewhat slower free Wi-Fi is usually available in cafes and some stores. The city government also provides free Wi-Fi at hot spots around the city and on public transit. Buses and some Metro lines also have free Wi-Fi. If you are planning to use a phone or tablet, download the GOWEX Free Wi-Fi app for iOs or Android. With the proliferation of free hotspots, Internet cafes are vanishing.

Mail & Postage
Madrid's central post office is in the Palacio de Comunicaciones at Plaza de Cibeles (© **91-523-06-94**). Hours are Monday to Friday 8:30am to 9:30pm and Saturday 8:30am to 2pm. Sending a postcard or letter to the U.S. starts at 0.90€. To calculate the price, visit http://correos.es. You can also buy stamps at any place that sells tobacco.

Pharmacies
For a late-night pharmacy, look in the daily newspaper under Farmacias de Guardia to learn which drugstores are open after 8pm. Another way to find one is to go to any pharmacy, which, even if closed, always posts a list of nearby pharmacies that are open late. Madrid has hundreds of pharmacies; one of the most central is **Farmacia de la Paloma,**

Calle de Toledo 46 (© **91-365-34-58;** Metro: Puerta del Sol or La Latina.

Police The central police station in Madrid is at Calle Leganitos, 19, next to Plaza de España. It is open daily 9am to midnight. The main phone numbers are © **91-548-85-37** and © **91-549-80-08.** The 24-hour number for reporting a crime is

© **90-210-21-12.** The Madrid City Council and the National Police have instituted a program called the **Foreign Tourist Assistance Service** (acronym in Spanish is SATE) to help tourists in filing a complaint, canceling credit cards or other documents, contacting embassies or consulates, and contacting or locating family members.

Safety As in every big, crowded city around the world, purse snatching and pickpocketing are facts of life in Madrid, especially wherever there are lots of slightly disoriented tourists paying scant attention to their belongings. Don't let down your guard and you're unlikely to be a victim.

WHERE TO STAY

Summer vacationers will be pleased to learn that Madrid hotels consider July and August to be "low" season and price their rooms accordingly. For those who prefer to travel when it is cooler, November rates are also typically low. But the economic crisis has depressed rates overall so that, for now, you can expect good value for your money whenever you travel.

Even in neighborhoods perceived as more upscale—Salamanca and the area around Opera, for example—you can find really good lodgings to suit almost any budget. Admittedly, Chueca and Salamanca hotels put you a little farther from the main attractions, but Madrid is so spread out that no lodging will be within walking distance of everything. Select the neighborhood and lodging that suits your style and price.

If you are staying in Madrid long enough to make an apartment rental worthwhile, **Homes for Travellers** (© **91-444-27-01;** www.homesfortravellers.com) has a carefully curated selection of apartments, mostly in Chueca and Malasaña, as well as near Opera, Gran Vía, Plaza Mayor, and Puerta del Sol. Studio apartments begin around 65€ per night, while one-bedroom units start around 75€ per night. Booking is done online and secured by credit card deposit. Carefully check locations as some residential neighborhoods are inconvenient for sightseeing. Such websites as **VRBO.com, HomeAway.com, AirBnB.com,** and **Flipkey.com** are also primo resources for rentals of full apartments or private rooms within residential aparments.

Arts District & Paseos
EXPENSIVE
The Ritz ★★★ Many hotels claim to be legendary; this one actually is. When Alfonso XIII was married in 1908, he was dismayed that Madrid lacked hotels befitting his guests. He wanted a hotel equal to the Ritz in Paris or London, so he engaged César Ritz to consult on the design and lend his name. Few expenses were spared—the carpets were hand-woven, the tapestries hand-stitched at the Real Fábrica de Tapices, and all the modern amenities of 1910 were installed. The location next to the Museo del Prado on the Plaza de la Lealtad with its Neptuno fountain couldn't be much more prestigious. Time could not diminish its great bones, but some of the brocade and velvet was getting a little worn when Orient Express took over and brought the Ritz back to being, well, The Ritz. Comfort and luxury are givens, and security for celebrity travelers is tight and

professional. The Goya Restaurant here is the successor to the original established with the aid of Auguste Escoffier. You might stay here as a treat, but you can get a hint of the luxury and pampering that guests enjoy by booking afternoon tea or chocolate and churros on the terrace.

Plaza de la Lealtad, 5. ℂ **800/237-1236** in the U.S. and Canada, or 91-701-67-67. www.ritz.es. 167 units. 245€–420€ double; from 425€ junior suite; from 764€ suite. Parking 35€. Metro: Atocha or Banco de España. **Amenities:** Restaurant; bar; concierge; exercise room; room service; sauna; spa; free Wi-Fi.

MODERATE

HUSA Hotel Paseo del Arte ★★   This large modern hotel has a spectacular location across a small plaza from the Reina Sofía, down an alley from the CaixaForum, and a 5-minute walk down Calle Atocha from Casa Patas. Because it hosts many business groups, everything is up for negotiation. Rates skyrocket when it has a conference, and drop through the floor when it doesn't. If you can get HUSA to throw in the buffet breakfast (otherwise a pricey 16€ per person), take the deal. It's a better buffet than the luxury hotels serve. Rooms are modestly sized, so see if you can upgrade to one of the luxurious rooms with a private terrace. Booking through the website gives less room for haggling, but guarantees a room upgrade, if available, and late check-out.

Calle Atocha, 123. ℂ **91-298-48-00.** www.husa.es. 260 units. 75€–140€ double; 142€–224€ terrace executive rooms. Metro: Atocha. **Amenities:** Restaurant; bar; concierge; exercise room; room service; spa; free Wi-Fi.

INEXPENSIVE

Hotel Mediodía ★★   Built back when the Atocha train station was still called Mediodía, this is one of the rare hotels left with true single rooms as well as plenty of doubles, triples, and quadruples. The large rooms are especially handy for families. Like all older hotels, accommodations vary. Some have marble floors, while others have artificial wood parquet; some have older porcelain fixtures in the bathrooms, others have modern tub-showers. Some guests find the variation annoying, but we chalk it up to character, and if we don't like the first room we're shown, we ask nicely to see another. The location is terrific—rooms on the back actually overlook the Reina Sofía (there's a perfect view from the balcony of Room 405), while rooms on the front look across the street to the Atocha train station. The "social lounge" on the ground level is a good place to entertain business associates or new travel friends.

Plaza del Emperador Carlos V, 8. ℂ **91-530-70-08.** www.mediodiahotel.com. 173 units. 61€–70€ double; 72€–83€ triple; 75€–95€ quadruple. Metro: Atocha. **Amenities:** Snack bar; free Wi-Fi.

Puerta del Sol & Las Letras

EXPENSIVE

Hotel Urban ★★   The contemporary take on Art Deco styling makes the Urban perhaps the most sophisticated luxury hotel in the city, while the Puerta del Sol proximity keeps down the price. The soaring central atrium hints of the building's previous life as an office building, but decor wipes away all sense of the workplace. The Derby owners are inveterate art collectors, and they've installed some extremely tall Papua, New Guinea, sculptures in the lobby, while gracing some of the suites with smaller South and Southeast Asian sculptures and art pieces. The large rooms feel rather like a supersized passenger cabin in a Rolls limo—all dark wood and leather, brushed metal, padded upholstery, and glass.

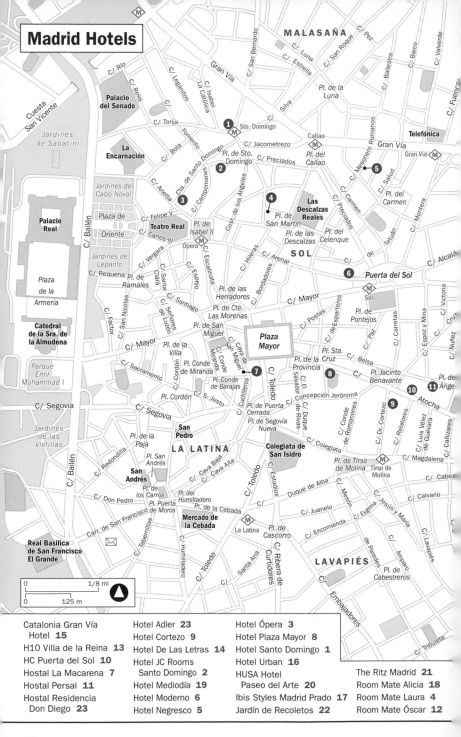

Madrid Hotels

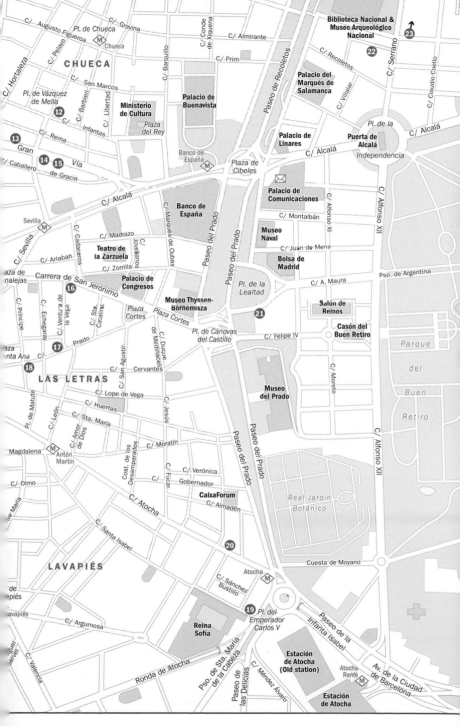

Thorough soundproofing shuts out the outside world. The rooftop terrace has chaise lounges for catching the rays by day (then cooling off in the pool), as well as tables and stools for drinks at night.

Carrera de San Jerónimo. ✆ **91-787-77-70.** www.derbyhotels.com. 96 units. 155€–279€ double; 203€–363€ junior suite; 270€–492€ suite. Parking 30€. Metro: Sevilla. **Amenities:** Restaurant; bar; exercise room; outdoor heated pool; free Wi-Fi.

MODERATE

HC Puerta del Sol ★★   This Catalonia Hoteles property is the Goldilocks of hotels near Plaza Santa Ana—not too big, not too small, just right. It occupies an early-20th-century building (some of the original carved woodwork is maintained in the top-floor suites), but the interior was completely rebuilt in 2011. The cool central courtyard comes as a great surprise in the heart of the city. With a glass roof and air-conditioning, it's so serene that many guests hang out here to read a book and sip a drink from the discreet little bar. The modest-sized rooms have new hardwood floors, marble baths, and low-key brown and gold drapes and bedspreads. Most have large windows opening onto the courtyard or Calle Atocha.

Calle Atocha, 23. ✆ **91-369-71-71.** www.hoteles-catalonia.com. 89€–170€ double. Metro: Vodafone Sol or Tirso de Molina. **Amenities:** Restaurant; bar; cafe; solarium; rooftop terrace; heated outdoor Jacuzzi; free Wi-Fi.

Ibis Styles Madrid Prado ★★   Clever folks, those Ibis designers. This modest modern hotel just outside Plaza Santa Ana lacked all architectural distinction, so Ibis invented a theme to make every room lively and fun. Each of six floors is keyed to a Spanish wine region, while individual rooms are named for a grape grown there. There's a lot of purple and bright green in the accents of the public areas (red and white wine grapes, naturally), while each guest room has a large, scenic mural of vineyards over the bed. This is a budget lodging, so it has no cafe or restaurant (beyond the breakfast buffet), but it has wine dispensers with a nitrogen system to ensure the wines don't fade after opening. During slow season, the hotel invites guests to free tastings in the late afternoon. At other times, you'll pay a small fee per glass.

Calle del Prado, 11. ✆ **91-369-02-34.** www.pradohotel.com. 46 rooms. 85€–129€ double. Metro: Antón Martín. **Amenities:** Wine bar; business corner; free Wi-Fi.

Hotel Moderno ★★   Family-owned and actively managed since it opened in 1939, the Moderno keeps reinventing itself without losing the charm that has always made it one of the nicer lodgings on Puerta del Sol. The building dates from 1857, and some of the internal structure prevents the expansion of the small rooms on the first four floors. Ask for the upper levels for a little more room to spread out. Rooms with an outdoor terrace might be worth an extra 30€ per night during times of year when you might want to sit outside. They have the most space as well as fabulous views of Puerta del Sol. A few triple and family rooms are also available.

Calle Arenal, 2. ✆ **91-531-09-00.** www.hotel-moderno.com. 97 rooms. 68€–132€ double; 92€–159€ triple. Metro: Sol. **Amenities:** Bar, concierge; free Wi-Fi.

INEXPENSIVE

Hostal Persal ★   The era of shared bathrooms has mostly vanished, even in budget hostales like this one, but sometimes architecture doesn't allow a bathroom per bedroom. Persal solved the problem neatly by linking some of the bedrooms into suites sharing a single bath. Rooms within the suite are small—honestly, almost all the doubles are cramped here—but because you get two bedrooms, they're a sensible option for families. Some bathrooms are so tiny that you'll have to turn sideways once inside to close the door. Get claustrophobic? The largest rooms are on the fourth floor. They are also the quietest, which can be an issue on this plaza at night.

Plaza del Angel, 12. ✆ **91-369-46-43.** www.hostalpersal.com. 80 units. 59€–89 double; 69€–109€ triple; 89€–129€ quadruple. Metro: Tirso de Molina. **Amenities:** Restaurant; bar; cafe; concierge; free Wi-Fi.

Hotel Cortezo ★★ New management and a top-to-bottom renovation have given fresh vigor to this bargain hotel adjacent to the Cine Ideal and the Teatro Nuevo Apolo. Decor tends toward the gentleman's club boutique look with white linens, dark wooden headboards, and brushed stainless steel trim. Masterful photography of Madrid architectural details may inspire some of your own shots. The rooftop terrace is small but fitted with a few lounge chairs, teak strip decking, and an outdoor shower to cool off and wash off the tanning lotion. It's very popular with Scandinavian tourists. Guests are encouraged to bring their own wine to the roof for spectacular sunsets over La Latina. Part of what makes Cortezo so welcoming is its ready-to-please staff.

Calle Doctor Cortezo, 3. ✆ **91-369-01-01.** www.hotelcortezo.com. 92 units. 45€–95€ double; 60€–115€ junior suite. Parking 25€. Metro: Vodafone Sol, Tirso de Molina. **Amenities:** Breakfast buffet; bar; room service; free Wi-Fi.

Plaza Mayor & La Latina
INEXPENSIVE
Hostal la Macarena ★ Good looks are this hotel's strong suit, and they shouldn't be underestimated as they can affect the mood of your whole trip. Crisply maintained balconies (with geraniums) are matched inside by simple decor in soothing honey tones. The rooms are also very spacious, especially this close to Plaza Mayor. If they sound too good to be true, there is a catch: no air-conditioning. (It's the only hotel without this amenity that we recommend in Madrid.) The rooms do have very large ceiling fans and excellent insulation, so they don't get any hotter than the outside air. Still, that's pretty warm in the summer. Even the balconies are encased in glass to keep out noise and summer heat. Some larger rooms accommodate three and even four beds. Rates during July and August are about a third lower than the rates given below.

Calle Cava de San Miguel, 8. ✆ **91-365-92-21.** www.silserranos.com. 20 units. 54€–65€ double; 73€–82€ triple; 90€–100€ quadruple. Metro: Vodafone Sol or Opera. **Amenities:** Bar.

Hotel Plaza Mayor ★★ Bright and contemporary, this nicely located budget boutique hotel was carved out of the old Santa Cruz church in 1997, and the mass of that stone building keeps the interior cool in summer and warm in winter. The downside is that some rooms were constructed around architectural barriers and wound up oddly shaped—long and thin in some cases, not quite rectilinear in others. They also vary a lot in size, mostly on the small side. But all have solid, well-made furnishings, shiny wood floors, and wall-mounted flat-screen TVs that don't take up important real estate. There's one penthouse suite, which has to be booked by e-mail or phone. It costs 50% more than the standard doubles, but has an outdoor patio with views across the tiled roofs of La Latina and skylights in the slanted ceiling that flood the room with light. If the penthouse is booked, opt for a "superior" room on the corner to get views of Plaza Santa Cruz, one of our favorites in Madrid's old quarters.

Calle Atocha, 2. ✆ **91-360-06-06.** www.h-plazamayor.com. 34 units. 59€–82€ double; 75€–92€ double superior. Metro: Vodafone Sol or Tirso de Molina. **Amenities:** Cafeteria; free Wi-Fi.

Opera & Palacio Real

MODERATE

Hotel Opera ★   Literally around the corner from the Palacio Real in one direction and the Teatro Real in another, Hotel Opera has a regal but modern feel. The modern-box architecture won't win any awards, but management saved its best touches for the interior. All rooms face the exterior, which means some look out on the palace, and all are flooded with light. The low-key decor uses soft earth tones with large photos and contemporary prints. Terrace rooms on the eighth floor have sweeping views of the city, glass-domed Jacuzzi tubs where you can bathe by starlight, and big skylights that make the rooms themselves bright and airy.

Cuesta de Santo Domingo, 2. ✆ **91-541-28-00.** www.hotelopera.com. 79 units. 82€–140€ double; 175€–219€ terrace rooms. Metro: Opera. **Amenities:** Restaurant; bar; concierge; gym; room service; sauna; free Wi-Fi.

Hotel Santo Domingo ★★   A multi-year renovation project, completed in 2013, transformed one of the most old-fashioned lodgings in central Madrid into the epitome of casual chic. Four of the five different grades of rooms are decorated in the familiar international palette of taupes and tans with dark wood accents and pops of brilliant white in the linens and bathrooms. All have new wooden floors, new bathrooms, and all new furnishings. The least expensive rooms, designated "smart economy," use lollipop color schemes to make them look bigger than they are; queen-size beds eat up most of the space, but the rooms are well designed and a very good deal. They are sold as either singles or doubles. Other doubles are larger, stepping up in size when called standard double and getting downright spacious as superior doubles. There are only a few available, but the corner rooms (premium priced) are as large as a junior suite and feature two glass walls for panoramic city views. Both the bar and hotel restaurant are run by the Arzak family of San Sebastián fame.

Calle San Bernardo 1. ✆ **91-547-98-00.** http://hotelsantodomingo.es. 200 units. 81€–140€ smart economy; 99€–170€ double; 139€–234€ superior double; 153€–227€ corner room. Parking 30€. Metro: Santo Domingo. **Amenities:** Restaurant; bar; room service; free Wi-Fi.

Room Mate Laura ★   Designer Tomás Alía gave this member of the Room Mate chain the personality of a party girl with smarts. Taking a nearly impossible tall triangular space, he hung the rooms off one side behind balconies and left a soaring lobby over the reception area. Low lighting and open railings make Laura a bad choice if you have vision or balance issues, and questionable if you're traveling with children. For everyone else, the rooms are a joy. They have very high ceilings, in some cases so high that the sleeping area is tucked into an overhead loft. Furnishings are spare and contemporary Scandinavian in feel, and the showers are glass display boxes. Several rooms have hideaway cooking facilities for an extra fee. Location is great; almost equidistant from Puerta del Sol, the Teatro Real, and Gran Vía.

Travesia de Trujillos, 3. ✆ **91-701-16-70.** http://laura.room-matehotels.com. 37 units. 62€–109€ double. Metro: Opera or Santo Domingo. **Amenities:** Concierge; free Wi-Fi.

INEXPENSIVE

JC Rooms Santo Domingo ★★   This budget boutique hotel offers brightly decorated rooms aimed at a young clientele. The newest of a small group, it occupies a strategic spot just off Gran Vía. The free minibar is restocked daily, and every room has a computer with Wi-Fi. Rooms are themed to different European countries; some have walls with gigantic photos, others have broad splashes of primary colors. Furnishings are mostly light wood in unadorned Scandinavian style. An A Coruña brewery restaurant is on the premises.

Cuesta de Santo Domingo, 16. ✆ **91-547-60-79.** www.jchoteles-santodomingo.com. 45 units. 59€–90€ double; 75€ 96€ triple; 110€–129€ quadruple. Metro: Santo Domingo. **Amenities:** Restaurant-brewery; free Wi-Fi.

Gran Vía, Chueca & Malasaña
MODERATE

H10 Villa de la Reina ★★   The brown, taupe, and tan color scheme of the decor might seem masculine, but the huge reproduction portraits of Spanish queens in the lobby signal that this really is the "house of the queen." Rooms are feminine, but not in the soft and fluffy sense of the word. The desk has to share the television, but the handsome black-and-white photography of period architectural details (from buildings on Gran Vía) gives the walls and hence the rooms considerable elegance. Marble bathrooms include lighted magnifying mirrors and a small vase with a single calla lily or similar flower.

Gran Vía, 22. ✆ **91-523-91-01.** www.hotelh10villadelareina.com. 74 units. 70€–165€ double; 119€–250€ junior suite. Metro: Gran Vía. **Amenities:** Restaurant; bar; room service; free Wi-Fi.

Hotel Catalonia Gran Vía ★   Location is key for this older hotel. It was one of the first buildings constructed on Gran Vía and was designed by one of Antoni Gaudí's teachers, Emilio Salas y Cortés. Renovated many times since its construction in 1898, it's one of the larger hotels on the street. That footprint allowed owners to install a very nice seasonal rooftop pool with great views of the Cibeles fountain. Rooms are on the small side and feature a milk-chocolate and honey color scheme with hardwood floors. Bathrooms employ a pale honey-colored marble on the floors and walls, but the sink fixture is set in a red-brown marble that looks dated. Some upper-level rooms offer outdoor terraces and junior suites have mini-pools.

Gran Vía, 9. ✆ **91-531-22-22.** www.hoteles-catalonia.es. 185 units. 69€–161€ double; 89€–181€ terrace room; 125€–185€ junior suite. Metro: Gran Vía. **Amenities:** Restaurant; bar; exercise room; Jacuzzi; room service; sauna; free Wi-Fi.

Room Mate Oscar ★★   Perhaps Madrid's first design hotel to openly court a gay clientele (appropriately enough for Chueca), many of Oscar's rooms have walls silkscreened with photos of incredibly fit naked bodies (no frontal nudity) and furniture by Verner Panton and Philippe Starck. The spare and open spaces give the rooms a futuristic air, though if the price is right, spring for a deluxe room (for far more space). Soundproofing is excellent, both inside and out. That's a good thing, because the fictional Oscar is a party animal, and so are many of his guests. You'll see them coming down for breakfast at 11:45am; luckily, the buffet is set until noon.

Plaza Vázquez de Mella, 12. ✆ **91-701-11-73.** http://oscar.room-matehotels.com. 75 units. 71€–125€ double; 125€–160€ junior suite. Metro: Gran Vía. **Amenities:** Concierge; free Wi-Fi.

INEXPENSIVE

Hotel Negresco ★★   This well-run, sweet little hotel is a remarkable deal. The rooms are fresh and beautifully maintained, but they tend to be small. Those with two single beds are actually the smallest, while rooms with a queen-size "cama matrimonial" are marginally larger and definitely more comfortable for reading in bed. (They have padded headboards.) Both configurations have a good work desk, as the hotel caters to economy-minded business travelers. The location on a small street off Gran Vía that ultimately leads into Puerta del Sol is surprisingly quiet. Competing economy hotels on the street are not as nice but have helped drive prices down. There's a flower shop nearby, so if you're staying for a while, brighten the room with a bouquet. At these prices, you can afford the treat. There's a snack-bar room with vending machines and an espresso maker just off reception.

Calle Mesonero Romanos, 12. ✆ **91-523-86-10.** www.hotel-aquaria-negresco-madrid.com. 20 units. 50€–70€ double. Metro: Callao. **Amenities:** Business center; Wi-Fi (free in public areas).

Salamanca, Retiro & Chamberí

EXPENSIVE

Hotel Adler ★★★   This beautiful hotel rescued an architecturally distinct late-19th-century building from an ignominious fate as a parking garage. All that was left of the original was the carved limestone facade, but the boutique hotel constructed inside that shell is perhaps more glamorous than the original structure. All the rooms have soaring ceilings, and many are equipped with decorative marble fireplaces. Plush carpeting underfoot coordinates with upholstered furniture. While decor varies from room to room, many have canopy or four-poster beds—or beds set into alcoves framed by columns. The designer bathrooms are some of the best we have seen in any hotel, and include contemporary marble shower areas as well as deep free-standing soaking tubs. The hotel has no meeting rooms, and hence deals almost entirely with guests on vacation. There's a definite Old World grace about the hotel—front desk staff wear frock coats, for example—yet it is comfortable, low-key, and very warm and inviting.

Calle Velázquez, 33. ✆ **866/376-7831** in the U.S. and Canada, or 91-426-32-20. www.adlerma-drid.com. 44 units. 193€–275€ double; from 375€ junior suite. Parking 30€. Metro: Velázquez. **Amenities:** Restaurant; bar; bikes; concierge; room service; Wi-Fi.

MODERATE

Jardín de Recoletos ★   This contemporary apartment-hotel is just a few blocks north of the Puerta de Alcalá and not far from the Paseo de Recoletos. It is within walking distance of the Parque del Retiro and the boutique shopping of Salamanca. A modern building erected in 1999, it aspires to the grand post-modernism of that period with its vast expanse of marble floor in the lobby and stained glass in the atrium. Less ambitious rooms offer traditional styling, space, and comfort—and a kitchenette adequate for preparing breakfast or a late-night snack. Some suites feature a large outdoor terrace.

Calle Gil de Santivañes, 6. ✆ **91-781-16-40.** www.vphoteles.com. 43 units. 139€–179€ double; 169€–225€ suite. Parking 24€. Metro: Serrano or Recoleto. **Amenities:** Restaurant; room service; free Wi-Fi.

INEXPENSIVE

Hostal Residencia Don Diego ★   Like buying the least expensive house in an exclusive neighborhood, this fifth-floor hostel offers bargain comfort in otherwise pricey Salamanca. The decor is simple and modern with hardwood floors, blond wood bedside tables and desk with brushed stainless pulls, and white walls embellished with lots of mirrors and contemporary art prints. Bathrooms are modern and most units have bidets and full soaking tubs, though the few singles have shower stalls. The reception area, which has a number of comfy leather couches, doubles as a morning breakfast lounge and as a sitting lounge the rest of the day.

Calle de Velázquez, 45. ✆ **91-435-07-60.** www.hostaldondiego.com. 58 units. 54€–81€ double; 81€–102€ triple. Metro: Velázquez or Serrano. **Amenities:** Free Wi-Fi in lounge.

WHERE TO EAT

Madrid has many long-standing gastronomic traditions, the most developed tapas bar scene in the world, and access to everything the country has to offer. If you like regional Spanish food, you'll find good examples here. If you like Spanish seafood, you're in good company. Fresh fish and shellfish are trucked or flown in from the coast daily. Although Madrid does not have the intense foodie culture of Barcelona or San Sebastián, you can get a cutting-edge meal from some of the country's leading chefs. Madrid, however, excels at more casual dining. Once you get past the idea that you must have dinner at a "restaurant," you'll discover you can eat very well indeed at a more casual "bar-restaurante" or a "cafe-bar." Indeed, given the ongoing financial troubles in Spain, casual dining spots are flourishing.

Arts District & Paseos

EXPENSIVE

Gran Café de Gijón ★ SPANISH/CONTINENTAL   A throwback to the era when Madrid's literati flocked here for heated discussions over coffee and brandy, the Gijón attracts older Madrileños who like to remember a quieter time—and a lot of tourists happy for a break from the go-go modern city. This is really three establishments in one: the outdoor terrace where people like to observe the parade up the paseo; the street-level cafe, where the windows swing open to let in the breezes; and the downstairs formal dining room, with expensive Continental food served at beautifully appointed tables. Adjacent to the upstairs cafe is a stand-up bar—the cheapest (non)seat in the house. It's a great spot to pause on a summer day for black coffee with ice cream (a *blanco y negro*) or a mixed drink.

Paseo de Recoletos, 21. ✆ **91-521-54-25.** www.cafegijon.com. Reservations required for restaurant. Main courses 20€–34€; fixed-price menu 29€–60€. Daily 7:30am–2am. Metro: Banco de España.

Horcher ★ CONTINENTAL   You'll pay handsomely to dine at this avatar of old-fashioned grace and haute cuisine, but you'll never forget the experience. The restaurant launched more than a century ago in Berlin and the proprietors relocated to "neutral" Spain in 1943. The restaurant is a period piece; not only are the dishes from another era, so is the impeccable and knowledgeable service. Start with specialties like smoked eel with radish sauce or an individual cheese soufflé before moving on to typical formal dishes like roast pigeon in Perigord truffle sauce, or a simple brochette of red prawns and scallops. Wild boar, duck, and venison abound on the fall menu.

Calle Alfonso XII, 6. ✆ **91-522-07-31.** www.restaurantehorcher.com. Reservations required. Jackets and ties required for men. Main courses 27€–42€. Mon–Fri 1:30–4pm and 8:30pm–midnight; Sat 8:30pm–midnight. Metro: Retiro.

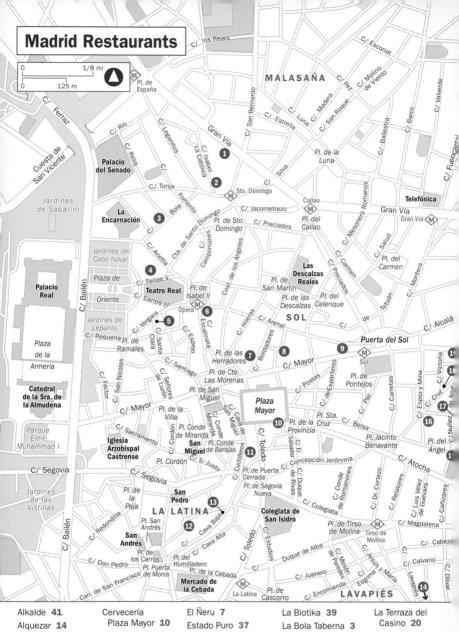

Madrid Restaurants

74

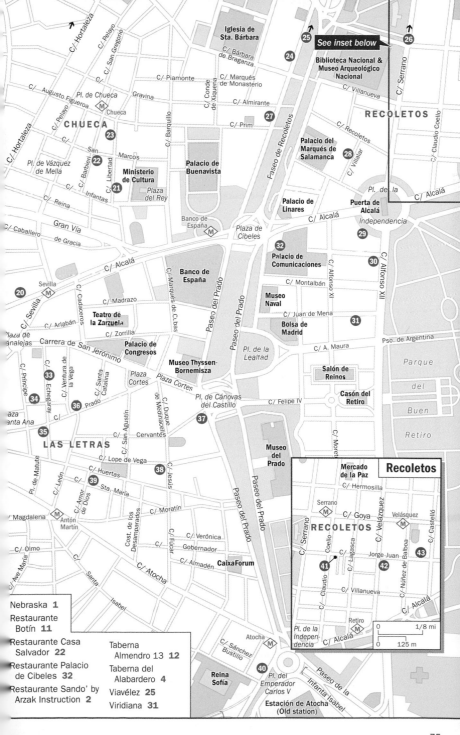

Nebraska **1**

Restaurante Botín **11**

Restaurante Casa Salvador **22**

Restaurante Palacio de Cibeles **32**

Restaurante Sando' by Arzak Instruction **2**

Taberna Almendro 13 **12**

Taberna del Alabardero **4**

Viavélez **25**

Viridiana **31**

Madrid's summer gastronomic festival means great bargains during the last 2 weeks of July. Roughly two dozen restaurants in Salamanca and in the central old city (Sol, Las Letras, La Latina, and near Opera) offer multi-course special menus with beer or water for 25€. At the same time, about 50 bars and taverns participate in the **Ruta de la Tapa.** Each establishment offers a different signature tapa and a beer for 3€. Free shuttle buses take tapas-hoppers between the old city and Salamanca. For more information, see www.esmadrid.com and search for GastroMad.

Restaurante Palacio de Cibeles ★★ SPANISH   Adolfo Muñoz, the inventive chef who brought Toldeo out of the dark ages for dining, opened this gourmet restaurant on the sixth floor of CentroCentro in early 2012. When the weather's good, he also serves a bar menu on the terrace with deals like a burger, fries, and drink for 11€. But gourmets flock to the elegant indoor dining room for Muñoz's creative twists on La Manchan classics, like partridge two ways (stewed with tempranillo red wine sauce and roasted with sherry sauce) or roast leg of lamb with mountain herbs and pisto Manchego—a Spanish version of ratatouille with roasted tomatoes, eggplant, and squash seasoned with sherry vinegar.

Plaza de Cibeles, 1. ✆ **91-523-14-54.** www.adolfo-palaciodecibeles.com. Reservations required. Main courses 25€–33€; terrasse midday menu 16€. Daily 1–4pm; Mon–Sat 10pm–midnight. Metro: Banco de España.

Viridiana ★★ SPANISH   If you like food with wit and panache, you'll love chef Abraham García, who blogs about food in the online edition of *El Mundo*. A film buff, he named the restaurant after the 1961 Luis Buñuel film. (Stills from Buñuel films line the walls.) The look is almost bistro-casual, but the food is creatively prepared, imaginative, and delicious. Ask for fish and you're likely to get a composed plate like grilled butterfish with baby peas, roasted sweet potato, and an almond-garlic sauce. For meat, he might sauté a pork sirloin and serve it with Sicilian dried tomatoes, spring onions, and spiral pasta.

Calle Juan de Mena, 14. ✆ **91-531-10-39.** www.restauranteviridiana.com. Reservations recommended. Main courses 25€–39€. Mon–Sat 1:30–4pm and 8:30pm–midnight. Closed Easter week. Metro: Banco de España.

MODERATE

Café Restaurante El Espejo ★ CONTINENTAL   Opened in 1978, El Espejo looks like an Art Nouveau cafe-restaurant, with its dark wood paneling, glittering chandeliers, and tiles of Rossini-esque maidens with flowers entwined in their hair. For food cooked the way Auguste Escoffier codified it, the set menus offer good bargains. Among the classics are roasted whole bream with a red pepper cream and veal cutlet in mustard sauce. If you crave something more definitively Spanish, oxtail braised in red wine (*rabo de toro*) is dark and unctuous. Desserts are plain; have a sweet sherry instead.

Paseo de Recoletos, 31. ✆ **91-308-23-47.** www.restauranteelespejo.com. Reservations suggested. Main dishes 14€–22€; fixed-price menus 27€–41€. Daily 1–4pm, 9pm–midnight. Metro: Colón.

INEXPENSIVE

El Brillante ★★ SPANISH   Burger King and McDonald's franchises stand near the Reina Sofía, but Spaniards snub them in favor of the equally fast but more varied sandwiches at El Brillante. The finger-sized 4-inch mini-*bocadillos* make a terrific snack, while the 10-inch super *bocatas* are a meal. You can get everything from sliced pork with roasted peppers to an omelet sandwich, but El Brillante is acclaimed for its fried calamari rolls. Tables are few, but there's a certain style to eating while standing at the stainless steel bars, letting your spent napkins float to the floor, just as the Spaniards do. Taking half a city block, El Brillante has a door on the Carlos V roundabout and another on the plaza in front of the Reina Sofía.

Calle Atocha, 122. ℭ **91-468-05-48.** www.barelbrillante.es. Sandwiches 3€–9€. Daily 6:30am– midnight or later. No credit cards. Metro: Atocha.

Estado Puro ★★ SPANISH   Here's the chance for budget diners to sample the food of a top chef. Paco Roncero (see La Terraza del Casino, below) believes that tapas are the purest expression of Spanish gastronomy, so he collaborated with the NH hotel chain to launch this post-modern tapas bar right on the plaza with the Neptune fountain. His most famous tapa is the 21st Century Tortilla, a deconstructed *tortilla Española*. When quaffed from a cordial glass, the layers of liquid egg and liquefied potato taste just like the original. Other dishes depart less from tradition but show a clever mind at work—spiced bread with a slice of foie gras and sweet wine reduction, for example, or tempura-fried asparagus with romesco sauce. It's fun, and there's a nice selection of wines by the glass.

Hotel NH Paseo del Prado, Plaza Cánovas del Castillo, 4. ℭ **91-330-24-00.** http://tapasenesta- dopuro.com. Tapas 2€–11€. Daily noon–midnight. Metro: Banco de España.

Puerta del Sol & Las Letras
EXPENSIVE

Lhardy ★ CONTINENTAL   If you enjoy the Palacio Real (p. 100), you might love dining upstairs in a formal Isabelline dining room at Lhardy. Madrid's elite has been coming here since Lhardy opened in 1839, but most people passing on the street have no idea that the formal rooms exist. That's because Lhardy runs a carriage-trade deli on the first floor along with a bar serving sandwiches, assorted tapas, and ham and cod croquetas. (Think of it as tapas for lawyers and doctors.)

Carrera de San Jerónimo, 8. ℭ **91-521-33-85.** www.lhardy.com. Reservations recommended for dining room. Main dishes 28€–39€. Deli service daily 9:30am–3pm; Mon–Sat 5–9:30pm. Restaurant service Mon 1–3:30pm; Tues–Sat 1–3:30pm and 8:30–11pm. Closed Aug. Metro: Vodafone Sol.

La Terraza del Casino ★★★ SPANISH   Super chef Paco Roncero runs this bastion of contemporary cuisine with Ferran Adrià, the elBulli master of innovation, as an advisor. The restaurant fills the top floor of the Baroque gentleman's club called the Casino, and if that makes you think of waiters in white tuxedo jackets and other luxe touches of a dining room for Madrid's elite, you're on the right track. Yet Roncero's cooking is smart, fresh, seasonal, and devoid of gimmicks. Techniques are au courant—he poaches skate in olive oil, for example, and serves it with a pistou of parsley, garlic, and almonds. It's a variant of a dish the Spanish aristocracy brought back from Italy. He turns the rustic Asturian *fabada* (pork and beans) into an elegant veloute with a bowl of al dente green favas drizzled with Picual olive oil.

Calle Alcalá, 15. ℭ **91-532-12-75.** www.casinodemadrid.es. Main courses 32€–45€. Mon–Fri 1:30–4pm; Mon–Sat 9–11:45pm. Closed Aug. Metro: Sevilla or Vodafone Sol.

Most tapas restaurants outside Spain encourage customers to settle in at a table and order lots and lots of small plates of food. But tapas are ideally eaten standing at a bar and should be a movable feast; enjoy the specialty of the house, and then move on to the next stop. Plaza Santa Ana has one of the best concentrations of tapas bars. They begin serving food between noon and 2pm and remain open until the last customer staggers out in the early morning. Peak tapas hours are usually 6 to 9pm, and a place that was empty at 5pm will have people drinking in the street by 7pm. We find tapas-hopping ideal for an early dinner. It's also a great way to try food you're not sure you'll like (like *callos*, or tripe), or specialties too expensive for a full meal. Many tapas bars don't take credit cards, even if their attached restaurants do. Cash keeps the pace moving. You should do the same.

Las Bravas ★ Fried potatoes smothered in a spicy red paprika-based sauce are a staple in bars all over Spain. This one claims to have invented the dish—known as *patatas bravas*—and even has a patent on the sauce. At Las Bravas, you can also get a pig's ear, fried baby squid, chicken wings, and even a whole 6-inch *tortilla Española* smothered in it. We always grab a ledge on the mirror-covered wall so we can keep track of how much sauce we've dripped on ourselves. Calle Espoz y Mina, 13. ✆ 91-521-35-07. www.lasbravas.com. Tapas 4€ to 9€. Noon to 1am. Cash only. Metro: Sevilla.

Méson Cinco Jotas ★ "Cinco Jotas" (or "5J") refers to the highest possible score in a ham grading system employed in Jabugo in Andalucía. The 5J ham sells at a premium, but once you've tasted it, it's as hard go back to generic *jamón serrano* as to switch from single-malt Scotch to cheap beer. Try it here, where the 5J tapa consists of three paper-thin squares of ham to wrap around five conical crackers. If you like the gamy taste more than the gummy texture, order the *caña de lomo* 5J tapa for a larger helping of sausage made from the same grade of ham. Plaza Santa Ana, 1. ✆ 91-522-63-64. www.mesoncincojotas.com. Tapas 4€ to 18€. Noon to 1am. Metro: Antón Martín.

La Venencia ★ If you're among the fortunate, you'll score standing room at the bar or one of the seats on the elevated platform in the back. If so, you're in for about as Andalucían a drinking

MODERATE

Green & More ★★ SPANISH   Subtitled "La Huerta de Tudela" after the restaurant's farm in the Ebro valley, this venture from Tudela native son Ricardo Gil is a Madrid rarity: a restaurant where vegetables get the respect usually reserved for caviar and prime cuts of meat. Gil has a passion for veggies, and his tasting menu is a nine-course tour de force where meat serves as a seasoning. Typical dishes might be a roll of Swiss chard stuffed with mushrooms and ham served with a little hollandaise, or a potato confit strudel seasoned with ham hock. More than half the menu consists of vegetables, and even fish and meat plates come with roasted vegetables. As Gil writes on the menu, "In our house, the vegetable is the queen." Calle Prado, 15. ✆ **91-420-44-18.** www.greenandmore.es. Main courses 12€–24€; tasting menus 36€–44€. Daily 1:30–4pm; Mon–Sat 8:30–11:30pm. Metro: Antón Martín.

experience as you can find in Madrid. La Venencia serves *fino, oloroso, and amontillado* sherries straight from the cask—or famous marques from the bottle. (Cask sherry is common in Andalucía, but rare in Madrid.) Drinking is primary here, and eating secondary. We like to nibble some pickled sardines or roasted peppers while savoring the taste of Spain's most famous wines. Calle Echegaray, 7. © **91-429-62-61.** Tapas 3€ to 5€. Noon to midnight. Cash only. Metro: Sevilla.

Cervezas La Fábrica ★ On a Sunday afternoon, it seems like everybody here is tossing back draft beer and munching on *montaditos* (tasty bites mounted on a diagonal slice of baguette). The variety is jaw-dropping, especially if you like fish. You'll get the most flavor for your euros with the smoked tuna and the combination of blue cheese with salt-packed anchovies. Calle Jesus, 2. © **91-369-30-67.** www.cervezaslafabrica.com. *Montaditos* 2€ to 3€. Daily 1:30pm to 1am. Metro: Antón Martín.

La Trucha ★ The quintessential fish tapas of Madrid belong to La Trucha, located slightly off the northeast corner of Plaza Santa Ana. You can order a single slice of the house specialty of smoked trout on toast, but it's so good that most people order a whole plate. To save a few euros, try the salad of mixed smoked fish. All that smoke and salt will make you thirsty, but draft beers are some of the cheapest in the neighborhood. Calle Manuel Fernández y González, 3. © **91-429-58-33.** Tapas 2€ to 14€. Daily noon to 1am. Metro: Antón Martín.

La Casa del Abuelo ★ Grandpa really gets around, as "Grandpa's House" is found in three separate locations, all within sight of each other. The main bar is on Calle Victoria, and keeps the longest hours. The others open to accommodate overflow. Choose the original to savor the patina of age—it opened in 1906 and has been serving shrimp specialties ever since. It is good that they accept credit cards, because the bill mounts quickly. We like our *gambas* plainly grilled (*gambas a la plancha*) or grilled with garlic (*gambas al ajillo*), but many customers prefer the smaller plates of breaded shrimp deep-fried in olive oil. The house wine is a steal. Calle Victoria, 12. © **91-521-23-19.** Also Calle Nunez de Arce, 5; Calle Goya, 57. www.lacasadelabuelo.es. Daily 1:30pm to 1am. Metro: Sevilla.

El Ñeru ★ ASTURIAN   You have to push your way through a packed tapas scene in the bar to get to the stairs down to an underground warren of tiled rooms. The cuisine of "The Nest" is Asturian, a regional favorite with Madrileños, and it's reflected in the fish-intensive menu, including the Asturian classic of hake braised in cider. You don't have to be a fish-lover to eat Asturian, though. El Ñeru makes a hearty *fabada Asturiana* of large white beans stewed with ham and sausage, and, for the more adventurous, a stew of tripe and garbanzo beans. A Madrid friend swears that the restaurant also makes the city's best *arroz con leche,* a creamy rice pudding with a caramelized top. Bread service includes a great spread of butter blended with Cabrales blue cheese, and the meal ends with a thimble of a yellow-green digestive liqueur.

Calle Bordadores, 5. © **91-541-11-40.** www.restauranteelneru.com. Main dishes 12€–22€. Tues–Sun 1:30–4:30pm and 8:30–11pm. Metro: Vodafone Sol or Opera.

INEXPENSIVE

La Biotika ★ VEGETARIAN   Vegetarianism is a foreign concept to most Spaniards, whose idea of a vegetable is the garnish that comes with a fried pork steak. But travelers trying to stay meatless are not reduced to living on salad and tortilla Española. Biotika is the longest standing vegetarian and macrobiotic restaurant in Madrid. It's located on the east side of Plaza Santa Ana, and the neo-Sixties Art Nouveau stylings of what's basically a cafeteria can be endearing. Soups and heavy whole-grain breads are made daily on the premises, and the big crisp salads tend to be good and filling. Biotika's signature "meatball without meat" consists of vegetables rolled into a ball and browned. You can also always order sautéed tofu with the vegetable of the moment, with or without brown rice.

Calle Amor de Dios, 3. ✆ **91-429-07-80.** www.labiotika.es. 3-course menus with dessert and beverage 11€–17€. Mon–Sat 10am–11:30pm; Sun 10am–3pm. Metro: Antón Martín.

La Huevería del Ganso ★★ SPANISH   The game at this tongue-in-cheek taberna right outside Plaza Santa Ana is duck-duck-goose—or maybe goose-goose-duck. Big goose eggs figure prominently in the kitchen's reinterpretation of the classics of Spanish bar food. Goose or duck takes the place of the more traditional pork in most cases. The flavors and textures remain remarkably similar—goose "ham" is a lot like pig ham. This being a Spanish kitchen, some ham from Iberian pigs does creep onto the menu. Goose egg *estrellitas* (broken fried egg, usually oozing over fried potatoes), for example, are served over crisp-fried potato straws with slices of air-dried Iberian ham. When the geese stop laying in the summer, the kitchen uses duck eggs.

Calle Echegaray, 26. ✆ **68-599-66-31.** www.lahueveriadelganso.es. Main dishes 3.50€–12€. Daily 1pm–midnight. Metro: Antón Martín.

La Mallorquina ★ PASTRY   This pastry shop at the edge of Puerta del Sol has been a classic hangout for the *merienda* (coffee break) since it opened its doors in 1894. If you can pull yourself away from the downstairs display cases, you'll find a little tearoom upstairs where you can order sandwiches, pastries, or ice cream concoctions. A window seat gives you a great view of the hubbub in Puerta del Sol.

Puerta del Sol, 8. ✆ **91-521-12-01.** www.pastelerialamallorquina.es. Sandwiches 3€–7.50€; pastries 2€–4€. Tearoom 9am–9pm. Metro: Vodafone Sol.

Plaza Mayor & La Latina

MODERATE

Restaurante Botín ★ SPANISH   Ernest Hemingway really ate at Botín, and he set a scene here at the end of *The Sun Also Rises*. The establishment has been trading on that publicity ever since, along with the ruling by the Guinness Book of World Records that it is the world's oldest restaurant still in business (since 1725). It's a charming tourist trap with good-tasting but pricey food. As you enter, peek into the kitchen to see racks of suckling pigs ready to go into the wood-fired oven. If your party is large enough to order a whole pig, it is brought to the table with great ceremony and then—bam!—smashed on top to break it into parts. The daily menu gets you garlic soup as a starter, a serving of roast suckling pig, a drink, and ice cream. But you can enjoy the authentic 18th-century atmosphere and eat as well on roast chicken for much less money. Roast lamb is another house specialty, but most diners opt for the pork.

Calle de Cuchilleros, 17. ✆ **91-366-42-17.** www.botin.es. Reservations recommended. Main courses 15€–32€; fixed-price menu 42€. Daily 1–4pm and 8pm–midnight. Metro: Opera or Vodafone Sol.

Julián de Tolosa ★★ BASQUE   This superb Basque *asador* may be the most elegant restaurant along Cava Baja. Pretty much everything you'll order here will arrive with grill marks, so the house keeps the menu rather simple. Meat eaters can order a sirloin steak or a thick chop, fish eaters get a choice of hake or monkfish. There are two principal side dishes: grilled piquillo peppers, which taste both smoky and sweet, and fat stalks of asparagus. The ambiance is more fine steakhouse than tavern. Large plate glass windows make the street-level dining room a showcase. Many diners prefer the lower dining room with its exposed brick walls and the radiant heat of the wood grill. The wine list is strong on Rioja reds, and even stronger on wines of Navarre.

Calle Cava Baja, 18. ✆ **91-365-82-10.** http://juliandetolosa.com. Main dishes 22€–30€. Daily 1:30–4pm; Mon–Sat 9pm–midnight Metro: La Latina.

INEXPENSIVE

Alquezar ★★ MOROCCAN   If you have ever made couscous from a box of dried semolina, eat at this modest, family-run restaurant with soccer matches on the TV to see what the dish is really like. Try to visit on the weekend when the mother of the clan hand-rolls her own couscous and simmers delicious chicken or lamb tagines to accompany it. On weekdays you'll have to settle for beef or chicken kebab plates accompanied by a pilaf of rice studded with vegetables, raisins, and almonds. By your second visit, the proprietors might hug you like family.

Calle Lavapiés, 53. ✆ **91-527-72-61.** Meals 9€–12€. Daily 1:30–6pm and 8pm–midnight. Cash only. Metro: Lavapiés.

Cervecería Plaza Mayor ★ TAPAS   Basically a beer hall with food rather than a restaurant with drinks, this spot is our first choice for enjoying the atmosphere of Plaza Mayor without breaking the bank. The tapas and *raciones* are traditional and dependable. A few slices of fried chorizo, a slice of *tortilla Española,* maybe a plate of diced potatoes fried with garlic; all you need to make it a meal is a beer. FYI, the draft beer is about half the cost of the bottled suds here, and if you're really frugal, you'll eat inside standing up at the bar to avoid the surcharge for table service and the additional surcharge for the plaza.

Plaza Mayor, 2. ✆ **91-365-06-46.** Plates 4€–12€. Daily 7am–1am. Cash only. Metro: Opera or Vodafone Sol.

Taberna Almendro 13 ★★ ANDALUCÍAN   A Hollywood set designer couldn't imagine a more "typical" Spanish bar, from the dark wood and florid 19th-century tiles to the dim lighting and the barrel of manzanilla sold at a pittance per glass. The perfect complement to that mild sherry is an inexpensive plate of sheep's milk cheese with *membrillo* (quince paste). For a meal, it's hard to beat the ratatouille with fried egg. For authenticity's sake, do your eating and drinking while standing.

Calle Almendro, 13. ✆ **91-365-42-52.** Main dishes 4€–11€. Daily 1:30–4:30pm and 8pm–1am. Cash only. Metro: La Latina.

Opera & Palacio Real

MODERATE

Asador Real ★★ BASQUE   This classic Basque grill is easy to find: Just look for the golden arches. The same building on Plaza Isabel II houses a McDonald's at street level. Asador Real is downstairs and its entry faces Calle Escalinata. Given the proximity to the Teatro Real, the emphasis on substantial cuts of meat, and the formality of the restaurant, Asador Real has surprisingly reasonable prices. If you're so inclined, you can watch the grill masters prepare your food. The best deal is on a quarter lamb or pig, which serves two generously.

Plaza Isabel II, 1. ✆ **91-547-11-11.** www.asadorreal.com. Main dishes 14€–24€. Daily 1:30pm–midnight. Metro: Opera.

La Bola Taberna ★ CASTILIAN   This is possibly the most Madrileño restaurant in the whole city and it is one of the last that makes an old-fashioned *cocido* of long-boiled mixed cuts of meat and sausages. The stew is usually served in three stages—as meat, as vegetables, and as broth. The big pots of *cocido* simmer away over charcoal, and entire families come on Sunday afternoon to make a ceremony of the heavy stew. The menu has changed little since 1870, although (to the dismay of purists) the cooks no longer emphasize organ meats or the more gelatinous cuts in the *cocido*.

Calle Bola, 5. ✆ **91-547-69-30.** www.labola.es. Main dishes 12€–26€. Reservations recommended on weekends. Lunch seatings daily 1:30 and 3:30pm, dinner continuous Mon–Sat 8:30–11pm. Cash only. Metro: Opera.

Restaurante Sandó by Arzak Instruction ★★★ SPANISH   One Spanish gastronome hit the nail on the head when he called Sandó the ready-to-wear version of famed chef Juan Mari Arzak's high-cuisine couture in San Sebastián (p. 451). Of course, the off-the-rack version won't have the hand-stitching or the luxuriant fabric of the runway piece, but it has the style and panache. The dishes at Sandó represent some of the classics that Juan Mari and daughter Elena created in their "laboratory" at Arzak. In classic Arzak style, they marry two seemingly incompatible flavors with great success, like white anchovies and sweet strawberries. One thing is certain: You can eat a tasting menu here for about a quarter the price of Arzak, and it will still include inventive plates like foie gras ravioli with melon and spinach vinaigrette, or roasted monkfish and chorizo with a vegetable sauce sweetened with honey. If you consider yourself a foodie (or even if you don't), Sandó is a treat you should not miss. "Arzak Instruction" (the family company) also runs the bar here at the renovated Hotel Santo Domingo. Try a lunch of two inventive tapas plates and a beer for as little as 10€.

In Hotel Santo Domingo, Calle Isabel la Católica, 2–4. ✆ **91-547-99-11.** http://restaurante-sando.es. Main dishes 21€–28€. Restaurant Tues–Sun 1–4pm; Tues–Thurs 8–11pm; Fri–Sat 8pm–midnight. Bar Mon–Thurs 10:30am–11pm; Fri–Sat 10:30am–midnight. Closed Aug. Metro: Santo Domingo.

Taberna del Alabardero ★★ SPANISH   This handsome restaurant and tapas bar named for the royal guards known as "Beefeaters" opened in 1974 in a historic tavern where nobles and literati rubbed shoulders before the Civil War. There are several small and rather formal dining rooms, including one in the cellars. The dining room menu represents a light approach to contemporary Spanish cooking with dishes like bream roasted in a salt crust and served with a sauce of fresh tomatoes and basil, or oxtail stewed with honey and cinnamon. It's a terrific place to have a civilized Spanish meal. In the bar, on the other hand, you'll probably have to stand and might have to shout to converse, but the food is even lighter (chilled almond soup with prawns and grapes, "meat" balls of fish and shellfish, brochettes of pork with mushrooms and pineapple). The sherry collection behind the bar is excellent.

Calle Felipe V, 6. ✆ **91-547-25-77.** www.grupolezama.es. Reservations required for restaurant. Bar tapas 3€–12€; restaurant main courses 16€–27€; tasting menu 46€. Daily 1–4pm and 9pm–midnight. Metro: Opera.

FOR dipping

At some point, all of Madrid comes into **Chocolatería San Ginés** for a cup of the almost fudgy hot chocolate and the fried dough sticks known as *churros*. When the music stops in the wee hours of the morning, disco queens from Joy Eslava next door pop in for a cup, and later on, before they head to the office, bankers in three-piece suits order breakfast. There's sugar spilled everywhere on the tables, yet the marble counters are an impeccable tableau of cups lined up with the handles all facing at the same angle and a tiny spoon on each saucer. Dipping the sugar-dusted churros into the hot chocolate is de rigeur, and, yes, it's okay to have the snack in the afternoon. Pasadizo San Ginés, 5. ✆ **91-365-65-46.** www.chocolateriasangines.com. Closes briefly early morning for cleaning. Cash only. Metro: Vodafone Sol or Opera.

INEXPENSIVE

Casa Marta ★★ SPANISH   If you always look for the "home cooking" sign when you're on the road, Casa Marta is your kind of place. Although the menu is longer than it would be in most Madrid households, the plain recipes are the sort that home cooks have made since the place was founded in the 1920s as Casa Eladio. We've always held that you can judge a casual restaurant by its croquetas, and these are excellent: lots of flaky tuna, a slight crunch of onion, and a béchamel thick enough to hold its shape and thin enough to explode in your mouth. Other homey plates include calf's liver smothered in onions and roasted peppers stuffed with ground meat.

Calle Santa Clara, 10. ✆ **91-548-28-25.** www.restaurantecasamarta.com. Main courses 8€–14€. Tues–Sun 1:30–4pm; Tues–Sat 9pm–midnight. Metro: Opera.

Gran Vía, Chueca & Malasaña

MODERATE

Restaurante Casa Salvador ★ SPANISH/ANDALUCÍAN   Too bad Hemingway didn't live long enough to eat at Casa Salvador. The place is an instant immersion in Andalucían decor and the cult of the bullfight. The owner is an aficionado of the *corrida* and has photos of bulls, bullfighters, and bullfights everywhere. The food is as simple and unaffected as the atmosphere is overwhelming. House specialties include a delicious soupy casserole of white beans and ham. If the bull photos don't bother you, opt for a grilled veal chop or a gristly but flavorful sirloin steak.

Calle Barbieri, 12. ✆ **91-521-45-24.** Reservations recommended. Main courses 10€–28€. Mon–Sat 1:30–4pm and 9–11:30pm. Closed 2 weeks July–Aug. Metro: Chueca.

INEXPENSIVE

Babel Restaurante B&B ★ SPANISH/AMERICAN   Spaniards have always admired the American grill; fortunately, their imitations of the genre are far more Spanish than American. Some of Babel's burgers, for example, come with caramelized onions, slices of foie gras, or a fried egg. The pizzas include a New Yorker, which for some inexplicable reason has dill pickles and mesclun salad mix on top. It all sounds a little funny until you taste and realize that the dishes please the Spanish palate. One menu standard is the Argentine *parrillada de carne*, which is a non-stop parade of meat and sausage cooked over charcoal on metal skewers and brought to the table until you cry "uncle." We prefer intentionally Spanish dishes, like grilled hake served with clams and a parsley green sauce. Prices are low for such quality and pleasant service.

Calle de la Libertad, 23. ✆ **91-521-61-37.** www.bb-restaurante.com. Main dishes 8€–14€, weekday lunch menu 15€. Tues–Sun 1–4pm; Tues–Sat 8–11pm. Metro: Chueca.

Bocaito ★ SPANISH   This bar-restaurante has separate entries into two barrooms serviced by the same bartenders who stand in the middle surrounded by bar stools. The menu is cheapest if you stand at the bar or even if you score a barroom seat. But it costs little more to dine seated in one of three dining rooms, including the "garden" room that's filled with blue and white Andalucían tiles. The food is traditional working class bar-restaurante fare—a quarter roasted chicken with fried potatoes, pork sweetbreads with green beans, or a grilled pork chop with vegetable of the day—but it's done well and priced fairly. Tapas plates include the usual Andalucían specialties (chicken livers, sardines, anchovies in vinegar) as well as small sandwiches on buns called *bocaitos*.

Calle Libertad, 4–6. ✆ **91-532-12-19.** www.bocaito.com. Main dishes 8€–11€. Mon–Fri 1–4:30pm; Mon–Sat 8:30pm–midnight. Metro: Chueca.

Nebraska ★ SPANISH   The Gran Vía flagship of this small chain of "American" restaurants looks like a cafeteria with its clusters of booths and Formica-topped tables. A pioneer specializing in hamburgers and ice cream sundaes, it is one of the last of the early adopters of American style still standing. The menu emphasizes breakfast egg dishes at all hours, grilled cheese sandwiches, hot dogs baked into a bun ("pigs in a blanket"), and *platos combinados*, which are inexpensive combo plates with meat (pork steak, chicken breast, beef steak tips), starch (fried potatoes or red rice), and the vegetable of the day (best overlooked). The food is freshly and quickly prepared—and they still serve those great ice cream sundaes. It's a sensible compromise when your kids want Mickey D's and you want something Spanish with a cold beer.

Gran Vía, 55. ✆ **91-547-16-35.** www.gruponebraska.com. Main dishes 4€–13€. Daily 8am–1am. Metro: Gran Vía or Santo Domingo.

Salamanca

EXPENSIVE

Alkalde ★★ BASQUE   If you dine on the sidewalk terrace at this tony end of Calle Jorge Juan, you'd never suspect that the main dining rooms downstairs have stone walls and the dark, homey feel of a Basque tavern. This family-run establishment opened nearly a half century ago to bring Basque cuisine to its homesick countrymen. Over time, the cooking has become more modern and sophisticated without deviating from the tried-and-true formula of buying the best available products and being careful not to mess them up. There are some Basque classics that need no updating, including the *sopa de txanguerro* (spider crab soup), *bacalao a pil pil* (cod in an emulsification of olive oil and fish juice), and turbot in garlic sauce.

Calle Jorge Juan, 10. ✆ **91-576-33-59.** www.alkalderestaurante.com. Reservations required. Main courses 17€–40€; *menu del dia* 52€. Daily 1:30–11pm. Metro: Retiro or Serrano.

dASSA bASSA ★★ SPANISH   Anyone who has caught chef Darío Barrio on daytime TV knows that he's a ham. Fortunately, he cooks with as much panache as he emotes. The entrance to his restaurant is on a small street off Puerta de

Alcalá, and the restaurant itself is below grade in a room of whitewashed brick with twinkly LED lights leading the way down the stairs. It's meant to be disorienting—as if you've been spirited away to a dyslexic speakeasy where the staff is determined to feed you dishes you've never tried before. The simple market-based menu features five starters, four meats, and four fish dishes, but what Barrio does with the market provender is complex. He loves to plop salmon eggs or flying fish roe on fish dishes to literally make them pop when you take a bite. Trout eggs find their way into his watermelon gazpacho with scallops. Crepes filled with oxtail stewed in red wine and chocolate are a menu perennial. To enjoy the theater cheaply, opt for the three-course "executive" menu of starter, main dish, pastry of the day, and a glass of wine for only 25€.

Calle Villalar, 7. ✆ **91-576-73-97.** www.dassabassa.com. Reservations required. Fixed-price menus 25€–80€. Tues–Sat 1:30–4pm and 9–11:30pm. Closed Aug 1–21. Metro: Retiro.

La Paloma ★ BASQUE/FRENCH   Chef Segundo Alonso hails from that part of Basque territory where they consider San Sebastián on the Spanish side and Biarritz on the French to be part of the same country. It's certainly part of the same cuisine, and Alonso serves the powerful rustic food of the mountainous countryside, like a tartare of red deer or beef sirloin with a mustard sauce. Perhaps the most celebrated dish is foie-gras-stuffed pigeon roasted in a bed of salt. When the weather calls for it, Alonso can go light as air with cold lobster salad with coriander vinaigrette or poached eggs on puff pastry with smoked salmon. Most dishes are available as full or half portions.

Calle Jorge Juan, 39. ✆ **91-576-86-92.** www.lapalomarestaurante.es. Reservations recommended. Main courses 20€–45€. Mon–Sat 1:30–4pm; Tues–Sat 8pm–11:45. Closed Aug. Metro: Velázquez or Vergara.

MODERATE

Iroco ★★ SPANISH   It's hard to tell which is leafier—the dining room walls covered with botanical prints or the back garden terrace where tables sit among potted trees and shrubs. Either is a good place to enjoy contemporary Spanish cooking that sometimes roams the globe for ingredients. The delicious plate of paella-style rice with cilantro and crisply fried squid is stained black with *huitalacoche* (corn smut) to make a lighter and more original version of a Catalan *arròs negre,* or black rice. Iroco's slow-roasted, boneless kid glazed with honey and served with a turnip purée makes goat a revelation. Garden service carries a 10% surcharge.

Calle Velázquez, 18. ✆ **91-431-73-81.** www.restauranteiroco.es. Reservations required. Main courses 19€–24€. Daily 1:30–4pm and 8:30pm–midnight. Metro: Goya.

Cerveceria José Luís ★★ SPANISH   This is the original in the group of José Luís restaurants, and it has had a shoeshine man in attendance since it opened in 1957. The founder believed that a gentleman should always have clean and shiny shoes, so they can stand at the bar near the door to get their brogues polished. The adjacent dining room is elegant, but many patrons favor the bar where you can perch on a stool and have a complete meal of soup, salad, fish, and dessert. The *cervecería* also has a great selection of *pinchos,* including a signature roll of egg and shrimp salad.

Calle Serrano, 89. ✆ **91-563-09-58.** www.joseluis.es. Main dishes 13€–22€; tapas 3€–5€. Bar daily 9am–1am. Dining room daily noon–4pm and 8pm–midnight. Metro: Gregorio Marañón.

La Terraza ★★ SPANISH   One of Spain's most celebrated chefs, Pedro Larumbe is credited with pioneering a modern, ingredient-driven take on traditional Spanish cooking. His elegant flagship restaurant, Pedro Larumbe, sits on the top floor of the ABC shopping center in Salamanca. La Terraza shares that floor, but is only open from spring to fall because all the tables are on a rooftop terrace. The skyline views are amazing—and so is the food. The lunch menu features light and breezy fare, such as a club sandwich, a chicken breast with lemon and baked potato, or a salad of white asparagus. As the day begins to cool, Larumbe serves a set menu of starter, two mid-sized plates, dessert, bread, water, and coffee. Expect imaginative dishes like duck ravioli with cassis-soaked pears.

Paseo Castellana, 34, 4th floor. ℂ **91-575-11-11.** www.pedrolarumbe.com. Lunch dishes 8€–18€; dinner menu 37€. Tues–Sat 1:30–4pm and 8pm–midnight.

Viavélez ★★★ SPANISH   Asturian Paco Ron walked away from a Michelin star in the little fishing village of Viavélez to make his assault on the big city. This restaurant, named for the town he left behind, may not have attracted the French star-makers, but it has certainly drawn Madrid gourmets who have always been partial to the cold-water fish cuisine of the country's northern Atlantic coast. Ron wisely splits the establishment between a casual *taberna* and a more formal restaurant. The tavern has a short menu of "canapes" (tapas, really) like bonito tuna with sweet red pepper and some simple dishes like steamed mussels, steamed cockles, and pieces of fried cod. The restaurant dishes have a bit more finesse and include treats like squid meatballs, grilled hake with al dente green beans and tomato salad, and, for dessert, dark chocolate cake with dried cherries.

Avenida General Perón, 10. ℂ **91-579-95-39.** www.restauranteviavelez.com. Reservations required. Main courses 18€–27€. Tues–Sun 2–4pm; Tues–Sat 9pm–midnight. Closed 3 weeks in Aug. Metro: Santiago Bernabeu.

INEXPENSIVE

Harina ★ BAKERY CAFE   The watchword here is "healthy." Most dishes are based on the excellent artisanal breads—some not-too-cheesy pizzas, for example, and several kinds of *tostas,* like goat cheese with tomato jam. We love the "anticrisis" menu, which provides six different choices of inexpensive complete meals. The location near the Puerta de Alcalá gate to Parque del Retiro makes Harina a good spot for lunch before or after a park visit. The cakes are better and richer than most in Madrid. There's a bright and cheerful dining room inside the bakery, and a few dozen sidewalk tables where the waiters are a bit overworked.

Plaza de la Independencia, 10. ℂ **91-522-87-85.** www.harinamadrid.com. Main dishes 7€–14€. Mon–Sat 11am–9pm; Sun 11am–4pm. Metro: Retiro.

EXPLORING MADRID

Madrid sprawls, but it has grown organically. Exploring is easy if you think of the neighborhoods as clusters. Plan your day and then take public transit to a central spot and hoof it from there. An excellent and inexpensive Metro system makes it easy.

One of the oldest clusters radiates from Puerta del Sol and its principal Metro stop, known as **Vodafone Sol.** This area includes **Puerta del Sol** and the immediate uphill neighborhood known as **Barrio de las Letras** for its association with the writers of Spain's Golden Age. Here you'll find many of Madrid's historic theaters and top bars.

Plaza Mayor is one of the city's main gathering spots, and the streets behind it flow downhill into the neighborhood known as **La Latina,** as its Metro stop is called. This is another excellent district for tapas bars and nightlife, but is also the site of some of Madrid's oldest structures. The **Museo de Origines**

ARE passes A GOOD DEAL?

Don't jump at either of the Madrid discount cards before you have an idea of what you want to see. The offers all sound good, but you may not reap significant savings.

The most clear-cut is the **Tarjeta Paseo del Arte** (25€), which will save you 25% off the admissions for the Museo Nacional del Prado, Museo Nacional Centro de Arte Reina Sofia, and the Museo Thyssen-Bornemisza, and enable you to skip the lines. You can purchase it at any of the museums. The card is good for a year, but allows just one entry to each museum and is worthwhile only if you're visiting all three.

The big three are among the 50 or so museums and monuments included on the **Madrid Card** (www.madridcard.com; 42€ for 24 hr., 51€ for 48 hr., 61€ for 72 hr., 70€ for 120 hr.). Using the Madrid Card lets you bypass ticket lines, which is

a good thing since you might need to hustle to make the pass worthwhile. Several listed attractions are always free, and the restaurant and shop savings are insignificant. But the card does include free admissions to Bernabéu stadium and the Plaza de Toros de las Ventas. You also get small discounts for the flamenco shows at Cardamomo and Corral de la Morería and on your purchases at El Corte Inglés department store.

You don't need a pass to skip the lines at the Prado, Reina Sofía, and Thyssen-Bornemisza—just buy tickets in advance online. When deciding about discount passes, keep in mind that most Madrid museums have free hours (but are crowded then) and some have no entry fee at all. If you are on a tight budget, it's a better deal to work those free admission hours into your touring plans.

marks the spot where Madrid's patron saint, San Isidro Labrador, and his wife lived in the early 12th century. The city's famous flea market, **El Rastro,** takes over many of the streets on Sunday.

A few blocks away, several attractions cluster around the **Palacio Real.** In addition to the palace, they include royal gardens, the **Teatro Real** (Opera) itself, and the **Convento de las Descalzas Reales,** the beautiful convent founded by the sister of a Spanish king. The main Metro stops are **Opera** and **Santo Domingo.** Nearby but north of the major boulevard **Gran Vía** are the neighborhoods of **Chueca and Malasaña.** Trendy shops, recently renovated museums, and vibrant gay nightlife signal that the neighborhoods' gentrification is well underway. The useful Metro stops here are **Gran Vía, Chueca, Tribunal,** and **Noviciado.**

The **Paseo del Prado** between the **Atocha** and **Banco de España** Metro stops is the mother lode for art lovers with the **Museo del Prado,** the **Museo Thyssen-Bornemisza,** the **Real Jardines Botánicos,** and the **CaixaForum** a few blocks from each other. Practically just around the corner on the Carlos V traffic circle ("glorieta" in Spanish) stands the **Museo Nacional Centro de Arte Reina Sofía.** Most useful Metro stops here are Atocha, Banco de España, and Colón.

The largely 20th-century neighborhood of **Salamanca** is much larger and distances between attractions are greater. Fortunately, good Metro service makes visiting most attractions an easy proposition. This area includes the **Parque del Retiro,** the **Museo Sorolla,** and the **Museo Lázaro Galdiano.** The most useful Metro stops include **Retiro, Serrano, Velázquez,** and **Núñez de Balboa.**

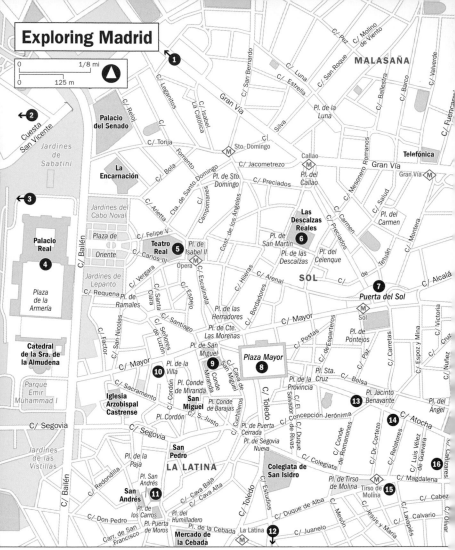

Exploring Madrid

0 — 1/8 mi

0 — 125 m

MALASAÑA

Palacio del Senado

Telefónica

La Encarnación

Las Descalzas Reales **6**

Palacio Real **4**

Teatro Real **5**

SOL

Puerta del Sol **7**

Plaza Mayor **8**

Catedral de la Sra. de la Almudena

Casa de la Villa **10**

Iglesia Arzobispal Castrense

San Miguel **9**

San Pedro

LA LATINA

Colegiata de San Isidro

San Andrés **11**

Mercado de la Cebada **12**

Tirso de Molina **15**

Casa Patas **16**

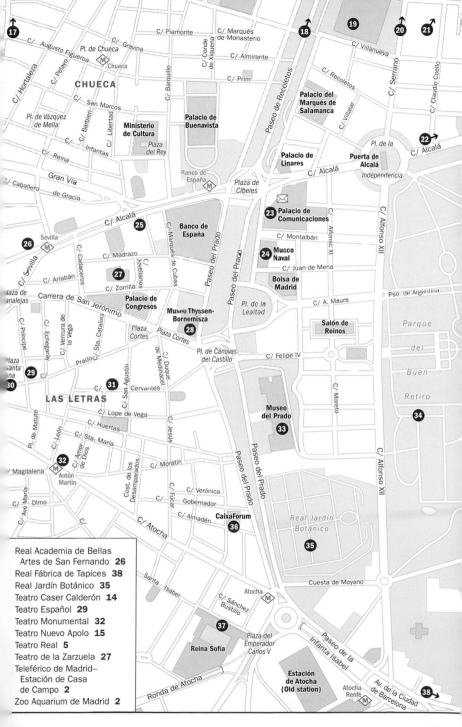

Arts District & Paseos

CaixaForum ★ MUSEUM   It took 5 years to transform the 1901 Mediodia electrical power plant across the Paseo del Prado from the Real Jardín Botánico into a dynamo for contemporary art. Pritzer Prize winners Jacques Herzog and Pierre de Meuron managed to multiply the floor space fivefold while creating a brick structure that seems to levitate (it's actually cantilevered) above its plaza. The building is so strange that you might not immediately notice the 24-meter-high (79-ft.) Jardin Vertical—a wall covered with 250 species of plants that flourish without soil. The interior of the building is equally amazing. The floors are hung on the spine of a winding central staircase that widens as it rises (a trick achieved with rubber molds). Although La Caixa has permanent collections, it is known for its constantly changing exhibitions of contemporary art. Usually three major exhibitions are on display at any given time. Some of the strongest shows are large-format photography, often featuring leading Spanish photographers such as José Manuel Ballester. Many exhibitions are accompanied by lectures, concerts, panel discussions, or other public events.

Paseo del Prado, 36. ✆ **91-330-73-00.** http://obrasocial.lacaixa.es. Building admission free; exhibition halls 4€, free for visitors under 16. Daily 10am–8pm. Metro: Atocha. Bus: 10, 14, 27, 34, 37, or 45.

CentroCentro ★★ MUSEUM   A Baroque Revival palace that once housed the central post office and the city's telecommunications agency, the Palacio de Cibeles became Madrid's City Hall in 2007. Even the city councilors didn't need something quite this huge, so much of the building was recently converted to a series of galleries, a concert hall, and other public spaces called CentroCentro. A reading area has daily papers and free PCs with Internet access. You'll also find lockers, coat check, public restrooms, an excellent store selling Madrid-oriented books and gifts, and a tourist information area. If you're hungry, there's a casual cafeteria and a restaurant for a more leisurely meal (see Restaurante Palacio de Cibeles, p. 76). The Mirador Madrid is perhaps the grandest delight of the whole complex. An elevator whisks you to the seventh floor, where you can walk around on the open-air balcony for one of the best bird's-eye views of the city, especially the Cibeles fountain.

Plaza de Cibeles, 1. ✆ **91-480-00-08.** http://centrocentro.org. Building admission free; admission charged to some exhibitions. Mirador de Madrid 2€, 0.50€ under 12. (Purchase at entry level.) Building Tues–Sun 8am–8pm; Mirador de Madrid Tues–Sun 10am–1pm and 4:30–7:30pm, weather permitting. Metro: Banco de España. Bus: 1, 2, 5, 9, 10, 15, 20, 27, 34, 45, 51, 52, 53, 74, 146, or 150.

Museo Arqueológico Nacional ★★ MUSEUM   Spain's principal archaeological museum spent more than 6 years redesigning its 140-year-old palace and its exhibits. Unlike some parts of the world, Spain recognized the value of its buried culture early on and managed to keep most of the treasures inside the country. They range from wonderful Celto-Iberian statues like La Dama de Elche and La Dama de Baeza to a wealth of Roman sculpture. The Moorish collections are also outstanding. Possibly the most surprising finds are the Visigothic crowns and other royal jewels.

Calle Serrano, 13. ✆ **91-577-79-12.** http://man.mcu.es. Admission and hours to be determined. Metro: Serrano or Colón. Bus: 1, 9, 19, 51, or 74.

Museo del Prado ★★★ MUSEUM   There was a very quiet revolution at the Prado in 2013, when the museum rehung the galleries of paintings by **Diego**

Velázquez (1599–1660), making his psychological masterpiece, *Las Meninas,* the sun at the center of its artistic solar system. They placed it among his royal portraits directly opposite the entry door of Sala 12 on the second level of the Villanueva building. You have probably seen reproductions of this portrait of Felipe IV's royal family (with a shadowy portrait of the painter himself) a thousand times, but the sheer scope and power of the actual canvas will bowl you over. The focus of the painting is on the young infanta Margarita (daughter of Felipe IV) and her diminutive ladies in waiting, including one of the many royal dwarves whom Velázquez never tired of painting. *Las Meninas* is easily the most popular painting in the Prado. (Before you leave, stop by the bookstore in the modern addition by Rafael Moneo to pick up a postcard of the painting. If you visit Barcelona, you'll want a copy to compare to Picasso's homage in the Museu Picasso.) If you want to see *Las Meninas* without crowds, be among the first to enter in the morning—a Madrid Card, Paseo del Arte pass, or printout of an online ticket purchase lets you skip the line.

Even before the rearrangement, there was a logic to gravitating first to Velázquez. Felipe VI ordered the creation of the Prado in 1819 to consolidate the royal art collections (hence all those portraits of Spanish kings and their families), and to prove to the rest of Europe that Spanish art was the equal of any other nation. He was right, and while the Prado has some priceless works by Fra Angelico, Titian, Rembrandt, and Hieronymus Bosch, the Spaniards dominate the collection, and we can't think of a better place to see their work. No matter what else interests you, we suggest focusing first on Velázquez and then turning your attention to Francisco de Goya.

From 1623 until his death in 1660, Velázquez was court painter to Felipe IV, a king only a few years his junior. He painted the king as a vacuous-looking young man, as a thoughtful king in middle age, and as an aging ruler weary from grief and depression—a remarkable psychological progression that the painter witnessed firsthand, and perhaps shared. Goya's early works, hung in **Sala 9A,** show great technique but little reflection. The more palpably human portraits by Francisco de Zurbarán hung in the same room may lack the brush strokes, but carry far more emotion. But Velázquez gets better as the gallery numbers rise. His religious paintings in **Sala 14** derive amazing intensity from the geometric rigor of their compositions. The dead body on the cross in *Cristo Crucificado,* nailed up with four rather than three nails, as 17th-century scholarship suggested, has ceased to be either man or god—he has been transfigured into the devotional icon of Spanish Catholicism.

Most paintings by Velázquez were never seen by anyone but the royal family until they were deposited in the Prado, but **Francisco de Goya** (1746–1828) did get to study them when he began working for the crown in the late 1770s. For the rest of his life, he cited Velázquez as one of his most important influences. Goya's mature work, especially after Carlos IV made him court painter in 1799, shows an understanding of character on a par with Velázquez. *The Family of Carlos IV* in **Sala 32,** painted around 1800, shows a burly king uncomfortable in his finery who would rather hunt than rule. In 1808, Carlos abdicated when the going got tough, and his foolish son invited Napoleon to tidy up Spain.

Goya's cheerful side is on full display in his paintings of countryside idylls that he made as cartoons for tapestries to cover the walls of a royal hunting palace. It was his first royal commission, and he did his level best to be cheerful and witty. Head to **Salas 90 to 94** to experience this youthful joy.

On the darker side, Goya captured the horrors of the French occupation in *Dos de Mayo,* which shows the popular uprising in Puerta del Sol on May 2,

1808, and *El Tres de Mayo,* which depicts the executions of the Spanish partisans by firing squad on Principe Pío hill the following day. These late paintings that made his modern reputation are found in **Salas 64 to 65** on the ground level. The somber Dark Paintings that he made on the walls of his house in the years after 1819 in fits of depression and madness fill adjacent **Salas 66 to 67.** These nightmarish images, such as the heart-breaking *Half Drowned Dog,* didn't reach the Prado until late in the 19th century, where they became inspirations for German Expressionism and for Surrealism.

Goya wasn't the first Spaniard with a fantastical imagination. At the opposite end of the Villanueva building from the Dark Paintings, several Gothic and Romanesque rooms radiate from a central rotunda. Visit **Sala 51C** and wait for your eyes to adjust to the dim illumination. The room re-creates a chapel from the A.D. 1125, Iglesia de la Vera Cruz Maderuelo outside Segovia. Animals high on the wall include the artist's conception of a bear and an elephant—a beast he had heard described but had clearly never seen. The creatures are so abstract they could have been painted by Joan Miró.

Paseo del Prado. © **91-330-28-00.** www.museoprado.es. Admission 14€ adults, 7€ seniors, free for students and children 17 and under, free for all visitors Mon–Sat 6–8pm, Sun 5–8pm. Mon–Sat 10am–8pm; Sun 10am–7pm. Closed Jan 1, Good Friday, May 1, and Dec 25. Metro: Atocha. Bus: 9, 10, 14, 19, 27, 34, 37, or 45.

Museo Nacional Centro de Arte Reina Sofía ★★★ MUSEUM   It's about a 3-block walk—and a much larger aesthetic leap—from the Prado to the Reina Sofia, which holds Spain's most significant collection of 20th- and 21st-century works. In fact, that collection has swelled so extensively in recent years that it now uses the two 19th-century exhibition palaces in the Parque del Retiro (p. 107) as spaces for temporary shows (often installation art) that require large physical spaces. The main museum consists of the neoclassical 18th-century former General Hospital designed by Francisco Sabatini, and the post-modern non-rectilinear addition by Jean Nouvel that opened in 2002.

The Museo Nacional Centro de Arte Reina Sofía.

Every few years the Reina Sofía curators rethink how to present the permanent collection. It is hung in rough chronological order but with various "movements" grouped by room. The movements and their accompanying wall texts change, even when the art remains the same. For the time being, two floors of the Sabatini building contain "permanent" chronological exhibits: "The Irruption of the 20th Century: Utopias and Conflicts (1900–1945)" fills Level 2 (*Guernica* is in Gallery 206); and "Is the War Over? Art in a Divided World (1945–1968)" occupies Level 4. The missing chronological gap is found on Level 1 of the Nouvel building, where "From Revolt to Postmodernity (1962–1982)" covers art as it lost its boundaries with pop culture, and includes a lot of work by American pop artists, just as the 1945 to 1968 galleries have several Abstract Expressionist works, also by Americans.

Current pedagogy declares that in modern art, context is everything because the horrors of the 20th century invalidated old Platonic concepts of art as a reflection of eternal beauty. Abstractions aside, that means that paintings by Picasso, Juan Gris, Joan Miró, and Dalí are surrounded by photographs, posters, advertising art, and short films that provide context for the world in which the art was created. This approach is particularly effective in the galleries that deal with art related to the Spanish Civil War, including *Guernica*. Picasso's response to the unprovoked bombing of a small Basque village remains one of the most powerful antiwar statements ever made.

The sculpture-filled courtyard of the Sabatini building is open during warm weather for light snacks. (Contrary to expectation, the coffee cart, which also sells wine and beer, is not a performance installation.) Admission to blockbuster temporary exhibitions is usually through the Sabatini entrance. Those interested only in the permanent collection enter through the courtyard of the Nouvel building. Pay attention to signage or you could wait an hour or more in the wrong line. Having a Paseo del Arte pass, Madrid Card, or advance online purchase provides priority admission.

Sabatini entrance: Calle Santa Isabel, 52. Nouvel entrance: Ronda de Atocha, s/n. ℂ **91-774-10-00.** www.museoreinasofia.es. Admission 8€ adults; 4€ seniors, students, and visitors 17 and under; 4€ for temporary exhibitions only; free for all Apr–Sept Mon and Wed–Sat 7pm–closing and Sun 3pm–closing. Apr–Sept Wed–Mon 11am–9pm; Oct–Mar Wed–Mon 10am–6pm. Metro: Atocha. Bus: 6, 10, 14, 19, 26, 27, 32, 34, 36, or 37.

Museo Naval ★ MUSEUM We're rarely fans of military museums, but this gem on the ground level of Spanish Navy headquarters is an exception. The museum covers the greatest hits of Spanish naval preeminence, including the discovery and exploration of the Americas, the exploitation of the Pacific trade routes, the Spanish Armada, and the feared Spanish galleons of the 17th and 18th centuries. A scale model of Columbus's flagship, the *Santa Maria,* shows what a fat little tub it was. By contrast, the large cutaway models of a circa-1700 galleon bristling with cannons can be seen as the birth of the modern battleship. The detailed coverage of the Battle of Trafalgar could make you forget that the Spanish lost. We marvel over Juan de la Cosa's handwritten map of 1500, said to be the oldest map of Europe that shows the Americas—including such inhabitants as men with faces in their stomachs. Only 300 visitors at a time are allowed inside; on weekends arrive early to avoid a wait. Security is tight here; you'll need to show your passport to enter.

Paseo del Prado 5. ℂ **91-523-87-89.** www.armada.mde.es/museonaval. Free admission. Tues–Sun 10am–2pm. Metro: Banco de España. Bus: 6, 10, 14, 19, 26, 27, 32, 34, 36, or 37.

Museo Thyssen-Bornemisza ★★★

MUSEUM With the Prado and the Reina Sofía as neighbors, the Thyssen-Bornemisza has to try harder than it might elsewhere. So the museum has made summer even better for art lovers, keeping its temporary exhibitions open until 10pm Tuesday through Saturday and until 9pm Sunday and Monday from mid-June through mid-September. (The permanent collection closes 2 hrs. earlier.) During the same months, the open-air Terrasse bar-restaurant remains open until 2am so you can discuss the art over drinks. That's a good thing, because this museum, dominated by the tastes of two strong personalities, prompts plenty of conversation.

Work by van Gogh at Museo Thyssen-Bornemisza.

The original collection was compiled by the Baron Thyssen-Bornemisza. Covering European art from the 13th through 20th centuries, it was one of the world's great private art collections, which he sold to Spain at a bargain in 1993. Before he sold it, though, he gave some major pieces to his Spanish wife, Carmen, who continued collecting until she donated her collection in 2004. Their collections represent the best art that money could buy in the mid–20th century. Dutch Masters were pretty well picked over by the time they began buying, but a lot of Impressionist art was on the market. The breadth of the collections is astounding, and so is their weight. We advise focusing on the strengths—the Baron amassed great works of Italian and German Gothic art and 20th-century German Expressionism. The Baroness also bought some outstanding German Expressionist works, some beautiful Impressionist paintings, and showed a real affinity for the Spanish Moderns (Picasso, Dalí, and Miró) as well as Abstract Expressionist works by Americans. The museum has also begun to mount blockbuster shows that require borrowing from other collections. These temporary exhibitions have a separate ticket.

Palacio de Villahermosa, Paseo del Prado 8. ✆ **90-276-05-11.** www.museothyssen.org. Admission 9€ adults, 6€ students and seniors, free for children 11 and under; permanent collection free to all Mon noon–4pm. Mon noon–4pm; Tues–Sun 10am–7pm (later hours mid-June–mid-Sept). Metro: Banco de España. Bus: 1, 2, 5, 9, 10, 14, 15, 20, 27, 34, 45, 51, 52, 53, 74, 146, or 150.

Real Fábrica de Tapices ★ FACTORY TOUR

Visiting this working tapestry factory is like opening a time capsule. Founded by Felipe V in 1721, it gave Spain its own version of Paris' Gobelins Manufactory. Almost 3 centuries later, skilled artisans still make rugs and wall tapestries at the original handlooms. Watching their fast-moving fingers will give you a new appreciation for this time-honored craft. Francisco de Goya even designed cartoons for tapestries that still grace the walls of the Palacio Real (p. 100). When you've finished watching the weavers, you can view Goya's original cartoons as well as tapestries from the 18th through 20th centuries. The factory's on the far side of the Atocha train station from the Prado.

Calle Fuenterrabia, 2. ✆ **91-434-05-50.** www.realfabricadetapices.com. Admission 4€ adults; 3€ children. Guided tours every 30 min Mon–Fri 10am–2pm. Closed Aug. Metro: Menéndez Pelayo. Bus: 10, 14, 26, 32, 37, 102, or C.

Real Jardín Botánico ★ GARDEN   The Age of Enlightenment lives on in these formal gardens next to the Museo del Prado and at the southwest corner of the Parque del Retiro. Carlos III, the so-called mayor-king, had Juan de Villanueva (architect of the Prado and the Paseos) design the gardens as a collection of temperate zone plants from around the world. The king himself opened the gardens in 1781. Today the meticulously maintained gardens contain more than 104 species of trees and 3,000 types of plants. Nine self-guided tours focus your interests.

Plaza de Murillo, 2. ℭ **91-420-30-17.** www.rjb.csic.es. Admission 3€ adults, 1.50€ students, free for seniors and children 9 and younger. May–Aug daily 10am–9pm; Mar and Oct daily 10am–7pm; Apr and Sept daily 10am–8pm; Nov–Feb daily 10am–6pm. Closed Dec 25 and Jan 1. Metro: Atocha. Bus: 10, 14, 19, 26, 27, 32, 34, 37, 45, 57, 146, or 150.

Puerta del Sol & Barrio de las Letras

Puerta del Sol is the hub of old Madrid and the principal crossroads of the city's transport systems. It is also the square where Madrileños have always flocked when trouble was afoot—from the uprising against Napoleon in 1808 to the economic protests of May 2011—and when there was a party to be had (the May *feria* or Halloween, for example). The square was originally the eastern gate of the medieval city. Just uphill on the south side are the old streets of the Barrio de las Letras, or "neighborhood of letters," which the city defines as bounded by Calles Atocha and Cruz, the Paseo del Prado, and Carrera de San Jerónimo. Those narrow streets and shady alleys, now paved instead of cobbled, are the same 16th- and 17th-century paths walked by poet and playwright Tirso de Molina (1579–1648), by Miguel de Cervantes (1547–1616), and by the grandest rascal of all, Félix Lope de Vega y Carpio (1562–1635). Now as then, the neighborhood is home to many of Madrid's best theaters and bars. Cervantes' home was razed long ago, although he does have a street named for him with a plaque showing where he lived and died. This neighborhood is served mainly by the Metro stops of **Vodafone Sol, Sevilla,** and **Antón Martín.**

Casa de Lope de Vega ★ HISTORIC HOME   Félix Lope de Vega may have been a more complex and fascinating character than any that he invented in his plays. He purchased this house in 1610 when he was already an established playwright and lived here—close to the theaters of his day—for the last 25 years of his life. Suspend your disbelief and you may be able to get a sense of the daily life of the author, husband, father, and notorious womanizer who became a priest at age 50. The three-story house is an imagined historic restoration, but the furnishings reflect the contents listed in Lope de Vega's will. It's a good chance to see how a well-off figure lived in Habsburg Madrid. Based on his own writings, he was particularly fond of his little walled garden. The most telling details are the low, Moroccan-style furnishings in the women's gathering room and the window in his bedroom that overlooks his in-house chapel. All tours are guided and you're supposed to book in advance, although we've walked in off the street during slow seasons. To guarantee a tour in English, book 2 days ahead.

Calle Cervantes, 11. ℭ **91-429-92-16.** www.madrid.org. Free admission. Tues–Sun 10am–3pm. Metro: Antón Martín. Bus: 6, 9, 10, 14, 26, 27, 32, 34, 37, 45, or 57.

Casa Patas ★★ SHOW   To see authentic flamenco in the company of enthusiasts, head to this Andalucían-style club co-founded by members of the jazz-flamenco band, Pata Negra. You might catch a newly discovered singer-guitarist duo or see members of the Amaya, Montoya, or Habichuela royal families of flamenco. Either way, the performance will be top rate. The bar starts filling up with *flamencos,* as those who live the life of the music are called, about an hour before the nominal start time for a performance. Unshaven men sporting long black ponytails and dressed all in black nurse glasses of sherry amid chic Madrileños in designer jeans tossing back Scotch. Tapas—priced at 4€ to 18€—are available at the bar, and you're welcome to come in for a drink and a tapa anytime after 8pm.

Calle Cañizares, 10. ℭ **91-369-04-96.** www.casapatas.com. Mon–Sat 8pm–2:30am, show times vary. Cover 19€–40€. Metro: Tirso de Molina or Antón Martín. Bus: 6 or 26.

Museo de la Real Academia de Bellas Artes de San Fernando ★★

MUSEUM   The intimate galleries of the Royal Academy Museum are a nice change of pace from Madrid's big art museums. Founded in 1752 as a collection to teach art students, the museum has amassed a fine collection of paintings and sculptures from the Renaissance period to the present. Spanish artists, naturally, are the best represented, but in some cases you can compare their work to that of their Italian and Flemish contemporaries. So good, in fact, is the collection that some pieces have been transferred to the Prado. The Forrest Gump–like Goya became director of the museum in 1795, and the collection features 13 of his paintings, including an equestrian portrait of Fernando VII and an absorbing scene of the Spanish Inquisition. Most revealing are the two self-portraits, one painted when he was not quite 40 and another painted in 1815, several years before he succumbed to the madness that drove his Dark Paintings. The museum also preserves Goya's paint-covered final palette. But it doesn't ignore other Spanish masters, and you will find works by Zurburán, El Greco, Juan Gris, and Picasso, as well as a striking collection of drawings from the 16th through 20th centuries. Second- and third-level galleries show 19th- and 20th-century art, but are sometimes closed due to staff shortages.

Calle Alcalá, 13. ℭ **91-524-08-64.** www.realacademiabellasartessanfernando.com/en. Admission 5€ adults, 2.50€ students, free for children 17 and under; free for all visitors Wed. Tues–Sat 9am–3pm. Metro: Vodafone Sol or Sevilla. Bus: 3, 5, 15, 20, 51, 52, 53, or 150.

Plaza Santa Ana ★★ SQUARE

Sooner or later you'll have a drink or two on Plaza Santa Ana and probably wonder what took you so long to discover the place. The neighborhood has been Madrid's theater district since the Corral des Comedias de Principe, one of Spain's first theaters, began packing in the crowds in 1583. The open-air theaters of that era were famous for producing the plays of Lope de Vega (who lived nearby) and other satirists. When the Teatro Español (see below) was erected here in the mid–19th century, it made Plaza Santa Ana as hip then as it is now. Since the square was firmly established as an entertainment district, dozens of bars and cafes popped up. They (or their successors) are still there and still constitute one of the city's most varied and most civilized tapas scenes.

Metro: Antón Martín.

Puerta del Sol ★★ SQUARE

Some visitors liken Puerta del Sol to New York's Times Square, but we think that's a canard because Puerta del Sol is smaller and friendlier. Alas, the signature neon sign of Puerta del Sol (a colorful rendition of the Tío Pepe sherry bottle) was removed when the old Hotel Paris was sold to developers who replaced Hemingway's favorite hotel with an Apple Store. Moreover, in July 2013, the Sol Metro stop here became officially known as "Vodafone Sol," after the mobile phone service provider. One clerk at the Madrid Tourist Information office commented that, "Soon we will all have to walk around with 'Sony' stamped on our foreheads." Ah, the fallout of the economic crisis. Fortunately, amid all those bankruptcies and loan defaults, Madrid was able to complete its overhaul of the square to make it a central hub for Metro lines and for commuter rail. Auto traffic was further curtailed, the central pedestrian plaza was

ALL THE neighborhood's A STAGE

The earliest record of a theater in Madrid is the Corral de Principe, an open-air venue that began staging plays in 1583. More than 400 years later, the same Plaza Santa Ana neighborhood remains the hub of theatrical activity. Five historic theaters are either on the plaza or in the vicinity. Performances are in Spanish, of course, but you'll find broad comedy and musical theater in its various forms (opera, zarzuela, American-style musicals) really don't depend on a perfect grasp of the language.

Teatro Caser Calderón The largest theater in Madrid seats 2,000. In the past this venue included everything from dramatic theater to flamenco, but in recent years it has taken a more serious turn by presenting mostly opera. Calle Atocha, 18. ✆ **90-200-66-17.** www.teatrocalderon.es. Tickets 5€ to 50€. Metro: Tirso de Molina or Vodafone Sol. Bus: 6, 9, 10, 14, 26, 27, 32, 34, 37, 45, or 57.

Teatro Español This exquisite 19th-century theater continues to anchor the east side of Plaza Santa Ana and presents performances of dance, orchestral and chamber music, and live theater. Medallions on the facade depict the pantheon of Spanish playwrights, from Calderón de la Barca (1600–81) on the right to Federico García Lorca (1898–1936), appropriately enough on the far left. Calle Principe, 25. ✆ **91-360-14-84.** www.teatroespanol.es. Most tickets 15€ to 30€. Metro: Antón Martín or Tirso de Molina. Bus: 6, 26, 32, 57, 65, 15,150, 3, 5, 9, 20, 51, 52, or 53.

Teatro de la Zarzuela If you're curious about Spain's equivalent of

Broadway musicals, this theater is the principal venue for the art form known as zarzuela. It mixes sketch theater, opera, popular song, and spoken narrative—all in Spanish, of course. This theater of potent nostalgia also produces ballet and an occasional opera. Most Wednesday performances are half price. Calle Jovellanos, 4. ✆ **91-524-54-00.** http://teatrodelazarzuela.mcu.es. 5€ to 50€, up to 336€ for boxes. Metro: Banco de España, Sevilla. Bus: 5, 9, 10, 14, 15, 20, 27, 34, 37, 45, 51, 53, or 150.

Teatro Monumental Now that the city's most prestigious symphonic orchestra, Orquestra Sinfónica de Madrid, has moved to the Teatro Real (p. 102), this acoustic gem is home to the Orquesta Sinfónica de Radio Televisión Española, or Spanish Radio and Television Symphonic Orchestra. The RTVE Symphony plays a series of concerts from September through June, and it's worth the price of admission just to see the theater, which was built in 1923 as a lavish movie house. Calle Atocha, 65. ✆ **91-429-81-19.** www.rtve.es/orquesta-coro. Tickets 11€ to 20€. Metro: Antón Martín. Bus: 6, 26, 32, or 57.

Teatro Nuevo Apolo Nuevo Apolo is the permanent home of the renowned Antología de la Zarzuela company. It is on the restored site of the old Teatro Apolo, where these musical variety shows have been performed since the 1930s. Plaza de Tirso de Molina. 1. ✆ **91-369-06-37.** www.teatronuevoapolo.com. Tickets 15€ to 60€. Metro: Tirso de Molina. Bus: 6, 26, 32, 57, or 65.

greatly enlarged, and a new Louvre-like glass entrance was created for the steps down to the trains. The beloved statue of a bear and a *madroña* tree (pictured on the city's coat of arms) was moved out to the middle of the plaza. Embedded in the pavement in front of the old Casa de Correos building is the **Zero Kilometer marker** from which all distances in Spain are calculated. The clock on the former post office displays Spain's official time. When it strikes midnight on New Year's Eve, Spanish revelers eat a dozen grapes—one for each chime.

Plaza Mayor & La Latina

Madrid was born in La Latina. The neighborhood's boundaries conform largely to the walled medina of the 10th-century citadel village known as al-Majrīt, or "place of water" in Arabic. When Alfonso VI of Castilla y León conquered the citadel in 1085, he turned the mosque into a church and left the walls in place. Four centuries would pass before they were fully torn down to let the village grow, and the neighborhood left in the place of the old medina retained its medieval Moorish street pattern. Even today, this original Madrid neighborhood is defined by narrow 10th-century streets punctuated almost randomly by little plazas. The Plaza Mayor was originally the market square on the outskirts, but since the 17th century it has been Madrid's town square.

Casa de la Villa ★ HISTORIC SITE   Of special interest to history buffs, tiny Plaza de la Villa holds some of the city's oldest extant buildings. The plaza has been the site of city government since medieval times, and the Casa de la Villa, the old town hall, is located here. The original medieval structure was rebuilt in Renaissance style in 1645, and modified again when Spanish baroque became the rage. Subsequent modifications, including a stained glass roof over the courtyard, continued to gild the lily. A free tour in both Spanish and English is offered at 5pm on Mondays. The highlight is Goya's painting, *La Alegoria de Madrid,* which personifies the city as a woman standing next to the municipal coat of arms.

Plaza de la Villa, 4–5. ✆ **91-588-10-00.** www.esmadrid.com. Mon 5pm. Free admission. Metro: Opera. Bus: 3 or N16.

Mercado de San Miguel ★★ MARKET   Just outside the walls of Plaza Mayor, the long-dormant Beaux Arts food market has been updated for 21st-century shoppers, with more than three dozen vendors sheltered under the gigantic wood-and-iron roof. The original 1916 Mercado was built to evoke Les Halles in Paris. Today vendors sell everything from fresh pastas and homemade pastries to cooking utensils. Stop by the cafe, tapas bar, or pastry shop for an inexpensive lunch. At night, Madrileños flock here for beer, tapas, wine, and even champagne and oysters.

Plaza de San Miguel. ✆ **91-542-49-39.** www.mercadodesanmiguel.es. Sun–Wed 10am–midnight; Thurs–Sat 10am–2am. Metro: Opera, Vodafone Sol, or Tirso de Molina. Bus: 3 or 148.

Museo de los Orígenes ★ MUSEUM   Renamed from the Museo de San Isidro in 2013, this museum sits on the site where San Isidro Labrador and his wife, Santa Maria de la Cabeza, were said to have lived in the 12th century. The humble farmer was elevated to the patron saint of Madrid (which celebrates him with a festival in May). Legend says their son fell into their well and was miraculously rescued by their prayers—the first public evidence of their holiness. The well remains as one of the museum's chief exhibits. This municipal museum also deals with the secular prehistory and history of Madrid from the arrival of the first humans who hunted along the Río Manzanares some 300,000 years ago through Madrid's apotheosis as Spain's capital. Signage is in Spanish, but the museum makes very good use of portrait reproductions to literally put a face to many of the city's most important movers and shakers.

Plaza de San Andrés, 2. ✆ **91-366-74-15.** www.munimadrid.es/museosanisidro. Free admission. Sept–July Tues–Sun 9:30am–8pm; Aug Tues–Fri 9:30am–1:30pm. Metro: La Latina. Bus: 3, 17, 18, 23, 35, 60, 65, or 148.

Plaza Mayor ★★★ SQUARE   When the sun shines, you'd think Plaza Mayor had been custom-built for outdoor dining and arcade souvenir shopping. But the site was originally a food market just outside the city walls, and the current square

Colorful zodiac murals decorating the Casa de Panadería.

was constructed in 1619 as the mass gathering spot for the city. People came to Plaza Mayor to see bullfights, attend political rallies, celebrate royal weddings, shop for bread and meat, watch hangings, and witness torture-induced confessions during the Spanish Inquisition. With apartments on the square, the royal family had ringside seats. Little remains of that original square, as the buildings surrounding it burned in 1631, 1672, and again in 1790. The plaza was fully enclosed in 1854, creating the great arches that now serve as its gates. Madrileños come to the plaza for the Sunday morning coin and stamp market and for the annual Christmas market. The plaza's acoustics are excellent, and musicians often perform in the center near the equestrian statue of Felipe III. The zodiac murals decorating the Casa de Panadería (originally home to the all-powerful Bakers' Guild) on the north side look appropriately ancient, but they date only from 1992. The most dramatic of the gates is the Arco de Cuchilleros (Arch of the Knife-Sharpeners), on the southwest corner. Beneath Plaza Mayor are the "cave" restaurants that have lured tourists since the days when Washington Irving commented on the spectacle of roast piglet feasts accompanied by copious flagons of wine.

Metro: Vodafone Sol, Opera, or Tirso de Molina. Bus: 3, 17, 18, 23, 31, or 35.

El Rastro ★ MARKET   Foremost among Madrid's street markets, El Rastro (translated as either "flea market" or "thieves' market") sprawls across a roughly triangular district of streets and plazas a few minutes' walk south of Plaza Mayor. Its center is Plaza Cascorro and Ribera de Curtidores. The market comes alive every Sunday morning and will delight anyone attracted to fascinating junk interspersed with antiques, bric-a-brac, paintings, and cheap scarves from India. Bargains can be had, but you'll need to use your haggling skills. Don't expect to find a piece that would light up the eyes of appraisers on TV antiques shows, but you could find something that you want to buy and someone else wants to sell. We often find good buys on flamenco CDs. Take care with your belongings, as pickpockets work the crowds.

Plaza Cascorro and Ribera de Curtidores. www.elrastro.org. Sun 7am–2:30pm. Metro: La Latina. Bus: 3 or 17.

Opera & Palacio Real

As you approach Madrid's regal quarter, the dark and narrow streets of the old city open into sun-splashed plazas. Comparisons to the Paris Opera and the palace of Versailles are inevitable: Everything you see was built under Bourbon kings with French taste. From the Metro stop at Opera, stairs deliver you to Plaza

GET SOAKED (that's a good thing)

Many North Africans have settled in La Latina and adjacent Lavapiés in the last few decades, so it was really only a matter of time before a traditional Arabic bath, a hammam, opened in the neighborhood. **Hammam al Andalus** is modeled on the baths of Moorish Andalucía, and shares the traditional design of arched brick and tile chambers with grill-work windows to let in light. Alternating hot and cold rooms, a warm room where attendants scrub you with soap, a super-hot steam room, and the option of a massage with aromatic oils round out the sensual experience. Calle Atocha, 14. ✆ **90-233-33-34.** http://hammamalanda-lus.com. Rates vary with services 30€ to 73€. Daily 10am to noon, 2 to 4pm, 6 to 8pm and 10pm to midnight. Metro: Tirso de Molina or Vodafone Sol. Bus: 3, 17, 18, 23, 31, or 35.

Isabel II behind Teatro Real. The broad expanse between theater and palace is Plaza de Oriente, constructed in the first half of the 19th century and peopled with statues of Spanish kings and queens. If Plaza Mayor is where people sit at cafes in their shirtsleeves to catch some rays, Plaza de Oriente is where they sit at fancier cafe tables in smart suits to be seen and admired. Main Metro stops are Opera and Santo Domingo.

Monasterio de las Descalzas Reales ★★ MUSEUM   In the 16th century, the daughters of nobility had two choices: to be married off to forge alliances among powerful men or to opt for a life behind the walls of a convent. Many of the wealthiest chose this convent, founded by the powerful and charismatic sister of Felipe II, Juana de Austria. As the widow of the Prince of Portugal, she took over a palace of the royal treasurer in 1557 to establish this Franciscan convent as her own retreat. Each of the noblewomen who took the veil brought a dowry as a bride of Christ, and their treasures still fill the convent. Ironically, by the mid–20th century, all the nuns came from poor families and were literally starving to death amid a priceless art collection that they were forbidden to sell. The state intervened, and Rome granted special dispensation to open the convent as a museum, allowing the public to see the riches. The large hall of the nuns' former dormitory, for example, is hung with 20 tapestries woven in Brussels from cartoons by Rubens. (Take a moment to notice the floor tiles that delineate each nun's tiny sleeping area.) This is still a working convent, home to about 20 nuns. Guided tours are in Spanish, but one glimpse of the massive staircase, with its magnificent murals of saints, angels, and Spanish rulers, immediately explains the conjunction of art, royalty, and faith that defines Spanish history. The guided tour takes at least 1 hour—more if you have to wait for enough people to assemble before the guide will start. Tours are limited to 20 visitors at a time.

Plaza de las Descalzas Reales s/n. ✆ **91-454-88-00.** www.patrimonionacional.es. Admission 7€ adults; 4€ children 5–16 and seniors 65 and older; free for children 4 and under. Tues–Sat 10am–2pm and 4–6:30pm; Sun 10am–3pm. Closed Jan 1, Jan 6, Holy Week, May 1, May 15, Sept 9, Nov 9, Dec 21, and Dec 24–25. Metro: Opera. Bus: 3, 25, 39, or 148. From Plaza del Callao, off Gran Vía, walk down Postigo de San Martín to Plaza de las Descalzas Reales; the convent is on the left.

Palacio Real ★★★ PALACE   Those Bourbons certainly knew how to build a palace! When the old royal palace—a dank, dark, and rather plain *alcázar* captured from the Moors in 1086—burned down in 1734, Felipe V ordered a new palace designed to rival his French cousins' home at Versailles. Having wrested the throne from the Habsburg line in the War of Spanish Succession, it was important for this first king of the Bourbon line to eclipse the previous royal dynasty. He was literally minting money with the gold and silver flowing from the New World colonies, so price was no object and the finished product is one of the grandest, most heavily decorated palaces in Europe. Construction began in 1738, and Felipe's younger son, Carlos III, finally moved into the 2,000-plus-room complex in 1764. Most rooms are reserved for state business, but a significant portion of the palace is open for tours. Although it remains the official residence of the royal family, no monarch has lived here since Alfonso XIII and his wife, Victoria Eugénie, fled Spain in 1931.

Unless you are a VIP, you'll enter on the south side of the palace complex. When you walk into the blinding sunlight of the Plaza de la Armería, everyone else in your line will make a mad dash for the palace. Ignore them and cross the plaza to start at the Armory. You can truly take the measure of the Spanish nobility since the plate and chain armor were individually tailored. Felipe I, the Austrian who married Juana la Loca (daughter of Fernando and Isabel) in 1496, was a medium-slender man nearly 6 feet tall—a giant in his day. Many other royals were almost a foot shorter; generally speaking, the shorter the noble, the larger his metal codpiece by way of compensation.

Once you enter the palace, you're not allowed to backtrack on the rigidly delineated tour. Move quickly through the first few ceremonial rooms until you enter the Throne Room (or Hall of Ambassadors), which marks the start of the Carlos III era. Tiepolo took political flattery to new heights in the vault fresco, The *Apotheosis of the Spanish Monarchy*. It's easy to be overwhelmed by the next sequence of rooms, where decor morphs from baroque into rococo, but you also get a sense how the royals lived in such splendor. You see the drawing room where Carlos III had lunch, the over-the-top Gasparini Room where he dressed, and the bedroom where he died. The Yellow Room, which had been Carlos III's study, is rich with avian and floral tapestries woven at the Real Fabrica de Tapices (p. 94). Finally, you'll reach the grand dining hall, first used by Alfonso XII in November 1879 to celebrate his marriage.

Some of the smaller, more intimate rooms on the tour are not always open, but they show Alfonso XIII as a more domestic king, screening movies with the family on Sunday afternoons. What remains of royal silver and china is also on display (Napoleon's brother Joseph Bonaparte sold the best pieces to finance French military adventures). Unless you have a lot of time, skip the Farmacia Real's numbing collection of apothecary jars in favor of a walk in the **Jardines de Sabatini ★**. Construction of the gardens began in the 1930s on the site of the former royal stables.

The Palacio Real.

WATCH OUT FOR wednesdays

Unless you're a European citizen, you're probably wondering why we are telling you that the **Monasterio de Las Descalzas Reales** and **Palacio Real** are free on Wednesdays for citizens of European Union countries. But free admission swells visitation on those days and can create a real logjam, especially at the monastery, which keeps short hours and limits entry to a few people at a time. Plan accordingly. If you're doing day trips, note that the same deal applies at El Escorial (p. 115).

The formal gardens, dotted with statues of Spanish kings, were opened to the public by King Juan Carlos I in 1978 shortly after he assumed the throne.

The changing-of-the-guard ceremony at noon on the first Wednesday of the month is free to the public.

Plaza de Oriente, Calle de Bailén, 2. ☎ **91-454-88-00.** www.patrimonionacional.es. Admission 10€ adults, 5€ students and children 16 and under, free to all last 2 hr. of each day. Oct–Mar daily 10am–6pm; Apr–Sept daily 10am–8pm. Metro: Opera. Bus: 3, 25, 39, or 148.

Teatro Real ★★ THEATER   One of the world's finest acoustic settings for opera, the up-to-date technical side of this theater is as impressive as its 19th-century over-the-top ornamentation. On November 19, 1850, under the reign of Queen Isabel II, the Royal Opera House opened its doors with Donizetti's "La Favorita." Today the building is the home of the Compañía del Teatro Real, which specializes in opera, as well as the Orquestra Sinfónica de Madrid, which plays classical concerts and accompanies opera and ballet. The best way to appreciate the grand space is to attend a performance, of course, but three different tours are also available. The general tour (limit of 25) shows you the lobby, the Café de Palacio, the formal rooms, the Ballroom restaurant, and the main auditorium (with a peek at the royal box). The "artistic" tour (limit of 15) is a behind-the-curtain look at dressing rooms, rehearsal rooms, the choir, the orchestra pit, and costume workshops. The technical tour (limit of 12) indulges equipment geeks who love ropes and pulleys and other tools of stage magic.

Plaza Isabel II, s/n. ☎ **91-516-06-60.** www.teatro-real.es. Performance tickets 8€–294€. General tour 8€ adults, 6€ for visitors under 26 or over 65; tours daily 10:30am–1pm on the half-hour. Artistic tour 12€ adults, 10€ for visitors under 26 or over 65; tours daily 9:30am and 9:45am. Technical tour 16€ adults, 14€ under 26 or over 65; tours daily 9:30am. Metro: Opera. Bus: 3, 25, 39, or 148.

Gran Vía, Chueca & Malasaña

The slashing diagonal of Gran Vía was built to be Madrid's "modern" street. Alfonso XIII ceremonially inaugurated the demolition work in 1910 with the announced intention of creating a boulevard to rival any in Paris. (Economic collapse in 1929 scaled back the plans.) But Gran Vía was Madrid's first street built for motorcars, and through the first two-thirds of the 20th century, banks, movie theaters, and upscale businesses lined its broad expanse between the Cibeles fountain and Plaza de España. The Circulo de Bellas Artes (Calle Alcalá, 42) was Madrid's first modern cultural center; it's worth visiting to see the effusive blending of Art Deco and classical architecture that embodied the spirit that Gran Vía was meant to symbolize. The street, however, began a long, slow slide in the

1970s and has never quite recaptured its erstwhile glamour, although the opening of some good hotels in recent years has been a step in the right direction. At the same time, the two neighborhoods immediately to its north, Chueca and Malasaña are much further along on their revitalization and have become destinations for shopping, dining, and nightlife.

Museo de Historia de Madrid ★ MUSEUM   This museum re-creates the Madrid of days gone by without wallowing in nostalgia. It was partially closed for several years to restore the marvelous Baroque building and digitize the entire collection. Some of our favorite old-fashioned exhibits were re-installed. There's no substitute for the topographic scale model of the city that was meticulously assembled in 1830. It remains better than any paper or digital map in its overview of the streets of the historic center. Go up on a balcony for an aerial view. Locate the Palacio Real, Plaza Mayor, and Puerta del Sol, and you're good to go. Exhibitions trace the evolution of Madrid since it became the national capital in 1561. It is instructive to see paintings of Plaza Mayor through the ages, for example. The stage set of the plaza barely changes—its inhabitants are simply wearing different costumes.

Calle Fuencarral, 78. ✆ **91-701-18-63.** www.madrid es. Free admission. Sept–June Tues–Sun 9:30am–8pm; July–Aug Tues–Fri 9:30am‑2pm, Sat–Sun 9:30am–8pm. Metro: Bilbao or Tribunal. Bus: 3, 21, 40, 147, or 149.

Museo del Romanticismo ★ MUSEUM   We love it when a "renovation" of a museum takes a fresh look at the collection. This institution set in the 1776 palace of the Marquis and Marchionessa of Matallana used to be the Museo Romántico. It was created by Marquis de Vega-Inclán to house his immense collection of "typical" folk art, porcelain representations of Spanish "types," and visual art from the early 19th century, much of it by the prolific Anonimo. The renovation exorcised the Marquis' ghost by now focusing on upper middle class

The Palacio de Velázquez in Parque del Retiro.

The Museo Lázaro Galdiano in Salamanca.

lifestyle during the reign of Isabel II (1830–68). Spanish Isabelline has a lot in common with British Victorian, despite the very different personalities of the monarchs.

Calle San Mateo, 13. ℂ **91-448-10-45.** http://museoromantico.mcu.es. Admission 3€. May–Oct Tues–Sat 9:30am–8:30pm, Sun 10am–3pm; Nov–Apr Tues–Sat 9:30am–6:30pm, Sun 10am–3pm. Metro: Tribunal or Alonso Martínez. Bus: 3, 37, 40, or 149.

Plaza Dos de Mayo ★ SQUARE   Rebellion echoes through the ages here. The arch in this Malasaña park marks the spot of the Monteleón artillery barracks. When the people of Madrid rose up against Napoleon's troops on May 2, 1808, Spanish troops were ordered to remain confined to barracks. The artillery under command of Luis Daoiz de Torres and Pedro Velarde y Santillán defied the crown and joined the popular uprising. In return, the French reduced the Monteleón barracks to rubble, killed most of the Spanish soldiers, and martyred their leaders. At the end of the Franco era, this park in a largely bohemian neighborhood became a flash point for rebellion against Spanish authoritarianism. In a May 2, 1976, uprising of sorts, a couple undressed on top of the statues to the delight of a crowd—an event often cited as the beginning of the "movida Madrileña." Today the plaza is skateboard turf by day, and a center of cafe life at night.

Metro: Bilbao or Tribunal.

Salamanca

After the narrow streets of Madrid's old city, Salamanca is a welcome change of pace. The Marquis de Salamanca began constructing this quarter in the 1870s and, by the time it was completed around 1920, Salamanca was Madrid's premier address. The neighborhood of broad, tree-lined streets laid out in an orderly grid is lined with elegant buildings, many girded with wrought-iron balconies. Situated east of Paseo de Castellana and north of Parque del Retiro, Salamanca was the first barrio to feature such modern conveniences as electric lights, elevators, and central heating. Today it's a lot like contemporary Spanish fashion: a lively mix of classic formality and radical modernism. The large grid of Salamanca

art ON THE WALLS

In the early 20th century, shopkeepers began the marvelous practice of covering their establishments with beautiful tiled scenes to advertise their products and services. Three great examples still bring life to their surrounding streets.

Farmacia Juanse (Calle San Andres, 5) sits on the corner of Calle San Vicente Ferrer, which gave the ceramic artists plenty of surface to cover with lively scenes of men, women, and children partaking of Juanse's own formulations to cure everything from toothaches to rheumatism. The Malasaña drugstore focuses on more modern medicine, but who would change such a colorful exterior?

Not to be outdone, the proprietors of the **Huevería,** or egg shop, around the corner in Malasaña (Calle San Vicente Ferrer, 32), embellished their establishment with images of sprightly hens. The spot is now a restaurant and tapas bar—and a felicitous spot to enjoy a slice of *tortilla Española.*

Farther afield in La Latina, **La Pelquería Vallejo** (Calle Santa Isabel, 22) was founded in 1908 and, a few years later, added its tiled facade of men and boys being attended to by barbers. Tile signs announce that the services also include hair cuts for women as well as electric and facial massages. The advertising must have worked, as the barbershop is still open and still owned by the same family.

Keep your eye out for colorful tile ornamentation on buildings throughout Madrid. You'll find a number that have been enhanced by the work of Segovia-based master ceramist Daniel Zuloaga, whose family museum is in Segovia (p. 150). For his contribution to advertising art, he created the sign and the beautiful tile clock on the facade of the building that held the printing press of the ABC newspaper. It's now the **ABC Serrano** shopping center (Calle Serrano, 61). But Zuloaga was more artist than ad man. Look for his floral designs and classical motifs on the **Palacio de Cristal** (p. 107) and the **Palacio de Velázquez** (p. 107) in the Parque del Retiro.

You'll find two other wonderful buildings as you tapas-hop around Plaza Santa Ana. The restaurant and flamenco tablao **Villa Rosa** (Plaza de Santa Ana, 15; p. 115) is encrusted with tiled scenes of landmark Spanish buildings and monuments, including Madrid's Cibeles fountain and Granada's La Alhambra. Similar scenes are depicted on **Bar Viva Madrid** (Calle Manuel Fernández y González, 7), though the artists found room to work in reminders that passersby could stop in for "Cervezas, Refrescos Y Cafe." You should do the same, if only to see the original tin counter, dark woodwork, and Andalucían-style patterned tiles of the interior.

is dotted with Metro stations, but the most useful are Retiro, Serrano, Velázquez, Rubén Dario, and Núñez de Balboa.

Carrusel Serrano Madrid ★ CAROUSEL Also known as "Carrusel de Belle Epoque" for its late-19th-century styling, this vintage merry-go-round operates on a plaza in front of Salamanca's branch of El Corte Inglés department store. A step up from conventional street attractions, it has horses with real horsehair tails and such exotic animals as a camel and a tiger. It also features a wonderfully whimsical flying pig.

Calle Serrano, 47 (corner of Calle Marques de Villamagna). No phone. 1.90€ per ride. Mon–Fri 11am–2pm and 5–9pm; Sat–Sun 11am–10pm.

Mercado de la Paz ★★ MARKET   Of Madrid's traditional food markets, Salamanca's is the most beautiful and carries the most expensive luxury items. No market can match it for the presentation of just-misted fresh fish and shell-fish, perfect vegetable specimens, carefully aged meats, perfectly ripe fruit, decadent pastries, and dozens of different varieties of olives. If you consider yourself a foodie, come here to see the provender that the top restaurants use and to buy saffron in bulk to take home.

Calle Ayala, 28; Calle Claudio Coello, 48. ℂ **91-435-07-43.** www.mercadodelapaz.com. Mon–Fri 9am–8:30pm; Sat 9am–2:30pm. Metro: Velázquez.

Museo de Arte Publico ★ MUSEUM   This open-air museum of public sculpture brings whimsy and delight to an otherwise bleak set of steps between Calle Serrano and the busy Paseo de Castellana. The works represent two generations of the Spanish avant-garde including Joan Miró and the Generation of 1950, a defiant group of artists who picked up the mantle of abstraction. Our favorite is the waterfall/fountain of alternating wave forms (it's called "Barandillas en 'S'") created in 1972 by Eusebio Sempere. You can't miss it—the rushing water makes you think that Madrid has suddenly sprung a leak.

Paseo de la Castellana, 41 (beneath Calle Juan Bravo overpass at Calle Eduardo Dato). ℂ **91-467-50-62.** www.munimadrid.es/museoairelibre. Free admission. Open 24 hr. Metro: Serrano.

Museo Lázaro Galdiano ★★ MUSEUM   This highly personalized collection of often extraordinary art ultimately forms a sketch of its collector: José Lázaro Galdiano (1862–1947), a financier, intellectual, collector, and editor. His collections fill the beautiful Palacio Parque Florido. The museum preserves the mural decorations and room layout of the main floor, but during recent renovations the upstairs rooms were modified to better display and preserve the collections. (Each room has a photo showing how the room was decorated and used in Lázaro's day.) As an art aficionado and editor of the journal "Goya," Lazaro held two tenets dear: Painting was the most important of the arts, and every country had a national painting style. He championed the works of Spanish masters, including El Greco, Velázquez, Zurbarán, Ribera, Murillo, and Valdés-Leal. He also collected sculpture and decorative arts that he felt spoke to the Spanish spirit, notably ceramics, silverware, and crystal. But he held special affection for Goya, and managed to acquire an important canvas from the witches' sabbath series Goya painted in 1798 for the Duchess of Osuna. Lazáro did not stop at the Pyrenees, though. He managed to buy several important Dutch and Flemish paintings, including an uncharacteristically meditative image of John the Baptist in the desert painted by Hieronymous Bosch. Several English portrait and landscape paintings by Reynolds, Gainsborough, and Constable were his indulgence of his wife's taste. The museum continues on the upper floors with individual cases of swords and daggers, royal seals, Byzantine jewelry, and even some medieval armor.

Calle de Serrano, 122. ℂ **91-561-60-84.** www.flg.es. Admission 6€ adults, 3€ students and seniors, free for children 12 and under; free for all Mon and Wed–Sat 3:30–4:30pm, Sun 2–3pm. Mon and Wed–Sat 10am–4:30pm; Sun 10am–3pm. Metro: Rubén Darío. Bus: 9, 12, 16, 19, 27, 45, or 51.

Museo Sorolla ★★ MUSEUM   Now offering art workshops for aspiring adult painters, this enchanting house and studio was built between 1910 and 1911 by Joachín Sorolla (1863–1923). The museum is technically on the wrong side of Paseo de la Castellana to be in Salamanca, but the haute bourgeois

Topiaries in Parque del Retiro.

sensibility is a perfect fit. The house offers a window into the comfortable world of the successful painter, who masterfully balanced his work and his domestic life. The home includes three studios with access to the Andalucían-style garden, as well as large living and dining areas on the main floor, maintained as the family used them. There are also four bedrooms on the second floor, now used as galleries. It's easy to imagine Sorolla at work at one of the unfinished paintings on the easels. The galleries display the range of his work from portraits and folkloric paintings to seascapes. But perhaps most telling is the angelic mural of his wife, Clotilde García del Costillo, and children on the dining room ceiling. It was Clotilde who decided to turn the property into a museum as a memorial to her husband. Most visitors fantasize about moving right in.

General Martínez Campos 37. ☎ **91-310-15-84.** http://museosorolla.mcu.es. Admission 3€ adults, 1.50€ students, free for children 17 and under; free for all Sat 2–8pm and all day Sun. Tues–Sat 9:30am–8pm; Sun 10am–3pm. Metro: Iglesia, Gregorio Marañón, or Rubén Darío. Bus: 5, 7, 14, 16, 27, 40, 45, 61, 147, or 150.

Parque del Retiro ★★ PARK   To meet Madrileños at their most relaxed, spend a Sunday among the families in Parque del Retiro. Originally a royal playground for the Spanish monarchs, the park covers 140 hectares (346 acres), but most of the main attractions are located adjacent to the central pathway, best accessed by the gate at the Puerta de Alcalá traffic circle. The park is big enough to be a playground for much of Madrid—whether they want to rent rowboats on the small lake where Felipe IV used to stage mock naval battles, watch puppet shows, practice tai chi, play cards or chess, have their fortunes told, or just lounge on the grass. Even winter chills don't discourage Madrileños with their kids and their dogs. Visitors can also view contemporary art. The Reina Sofia museum mounts large-scale exhibitions in the two grand buildings constructed for the 1887 Philippines Exposition. The **Palacio de Cristal** is literally a glass palace, while the **Palacio de Velázquez** is as opaque as the Cristal is transparent. It was constructed of brick and marble with florid tilework in the Mudéjar Revival style. From May through September, there are free concerts in the park on Saturday and Sunday evenings.

Free admission. Summer daily 7am–midnight; winter daily 7am–10pm. Palacio de Cristal and Palacio de Velázquez Apr–Sept daily 11am–9pm; Oct–Mar daily 10am–6pm. Metro: Retiro.

Outlying Attractions

Casa de Campo ★ PARK   Children love the zoo and the Parque de Atracciones (see "Madrid for Families," p. 109), both in this park formed from former royal hunting grounds south of the Palacio Real across the Río Manzanares. You can see the gate through which the kings rode out of the palace grounds, either on horseback or in carriages, on their way to the tree-lined park. The lake inside Casa de Campo is usually filled with rowers, and you'll find a snack bar here for drinks and light refreshments by the water. A playground by day, the park gets rather dangerous at night.

Daily 8am–9pm. Metro: Lago or Batán.

Ermita de San Antonio de la Florida–Panteón de Goya ★★

CHURCH Goya's tomb reposes in this little hermitage on the banks of the Río Manzanares north of the Palacio Real. The church also contains Goya's elaborately beautiful fresco depicting the miracles of St. Anthony on the dome and cupola. Perhaps because he had to paint on scaffolding, the paintings are sometimes called Goya's Sistine Chapel. He worked in the labor-intensive fresco technique of applying fresh plaster to the surface, incising his design based on a "cartoon" drawing, and then applying pigment with a sponge instead of a brush. Many early viewers were shocked that Goya painted prostitutes, beggars, and hardworking common folk. But the patron, Carlos IV, approved and the work has stood the test of time. The tomb and frescoes are on the right as you enter. Magnifying mirrors on the floor help you see the ceiling without straining your neck.

Glorieta de San Antonio de la Florida, 5. ✆ **91-542-07-22.** www.munimadrid.es/ermita. Free admission. Tues–Sun 9:30am–8pm. Metro: Príncipe Pío. Bus: 76, 46, or 41.

Museo de América ★★ MUSEUM

It is hard to imagine the shock waves that spread through Europe when Christopher Columbus stumbled on a "new" and previously unimagined world in 1492. This earnest museum draws on its significant holdings of objects from scientific research trips and archaeological digs to present a picture of the European interaction with the Americas. Exhibits re-create a "cabinet of curiosities" similar to the one prized by Carlos III, and it's easy to imagine how exciting it would have been to see a beautiful Mayan stone carving or golden funerary figure from Colombia for the first time. But the museum uses its holdings to try to understand and record the rich cultures altered forever by contact with Europeans. It also deals with the exploration of the New World (the progression of knowledge as captured on maps is fascinating) and the life of Spanish colonists there.

Avenida de los Reyes Católicos, 6. ✆ **91-549-26-41.** http://museodeamerica.mcu.es. Admission 3€ adults, 1.50€ seniors and students, free for children 17 and under; free for all Sun. May–Oct Tues–Sat 9:30am–8:30pm, Sun 10am–3pm; Nov–Apr Tues–Sat 9:30am–6:30pm, Sun 10am–3pm. Metro: Moncloa. Bus: 1, 2, 16, 44, 46, 61, 82, 113, 132, or 133.

Museo del Traje ★ MUSEUM

Don't talk to a Spaniard about French or Italian fashion—Spain's been making stylish clothes since the cave dwellers at Altamira introduced the drop-shoulder fur. Shoes don't get quite the attention they could, but this museum does trace the evolution of Spanish dress from the 1800s forward. Spain's modern fashion designers are, in many ways, the culmination of that arc. Look especially for the work of the visionary designer Balenciaga (1895–1972), whose influence is still felt today. While many of the textiles are fragile and must be displayed in low light, the collection also includes jewelry and other accessories.

Avenida Jean de Herrera, 2. ✆ **91-550-47-00.** http://museodeltraje.mcu.es. Admission 3€ adults, free for children 17 and under; free for all Sat 2:30–7pm and all day Sun. Tues–Sat 9:30am–7pm; Sun 10am–3pm. Metro: Moncola. Bus: 46, 82, 83, 132, or 133.

Bullfighting at Plaza de Toros Monumental de Las Ventas.

Plaza de Toros Monumental de Las Ventas ★ BULLRING   This grand Mudéjar-style bullring of red brick, tile, and ornate ironwork is not the largest in the world (that's in Mexico), but it is arguably the most important. It opened in 1931 and seats 24,000 people. The best bullfighters face the best bulls here— and the fans who pack the stands are among the sport's most passionate and knowledgeable. (Many other Spaniards can't stand the sport.) If you would like to try to gain an understanding of the spectacle, it's worth visiting this storied site. Audioguide tours begin at the ceremonial Grand Portal and include the stands, the ring itself, and the patio where matadors pause with their admirers before entering the chapel to pray before they enter the ring.

Calle Alcalá, 237. ℭ **91-356-22-00.** www.las-ventas.com. July–Aug daily 10am–7pm; Sept–June daily 10am–6pm. Mar–Oct tours close 4 hr. before corrida. 10€ adults, 7€ children under 12. Tickets for Sun matches go on sale Fri; box office hours 10am–2pm and 4–7pm, expect to pay 7€–36€ for reasonable seats. Metro: Ventas.

Madrid for Families

Parque del Retiro (p. 107) is the classic family weekend outing, with rowboats to glide over a small lake, puppet shows, street musicians, pony rides, and lots of green grass for running around. The wide, paved paths are one of the few good places in the city for a family bike ride. Rent bikes at nearby **Rent and Roll** (Calle Salustiano Olozaga, 14; ℭ **91-576-35-24;** www.rentandroll.es; from 5€; Metro: Retiro). While you're in the park, pause to see the temporary art exhibitions organized by the Museo Nacional Centro de Arte Reina Sofia in the beautiful 19th-century exhibition halls, the glass house of the **Palacio de Cristal** (p. 107) and the neo-Mudéjar **Palacio de Velázquez** (p. 107). Admission is free.

In fact, you can use the free admission hours at some of Madrid's best museums to work short visits into your day without breaking the bank or taxing your children's attention spans. At the **Museo del Prado** (p. 90), for example, you might want to take your young kids to see the "cartoons" (full-sized colored drawings) that Francisco de Goya created for tapestries. Many of them feature children and animals in bucolic settings. Teenagers, on the other hand, are usually engrossed by Pablo Picasso's *Guernica* in the **Museo Nacional Centro de Arte Reina Sofía** (p. 92). Your children might also enjoy seeing the grand neoclassical fountains of Cibeles and Neptuno as you stroll along the Paseo del Prado. For a grand overview of Cibeles, take them up to the observatory at **CentroCentro** (p. 90) for rooftop views. If your children accompany you on a shopping trip to Salamanca, let them run around and touch the artwork (one of the few places where it is allowed) in the outdoor **Museo de Arte Publico** (p. 106). From there, it's a short walk to the **Carrusel Serrano Madrid** for a ride on the charming merry-go-round.

Madrid's other celebrated gathering place, **Plaza Mayor** (p. 98), is also a fine spot for families. Kids will find plenty of entertainment watching artists at work under the arcade and "living statues" posing for change. Since the plaza is enclosed on all sides, you can keep an eye on your children—and the scene—from a cafe table.

Parque de Atracciones ★ AMUSEMENT PARK   This amusement park opened in 1969 with about 30 rides. It has continued to remodel and add new attractions to keep up with the times. You'll find mini-fire engines for tykes, graceful "flying chairs," water rides, the "cave of tarantulas," and a twisting roller coaster called "Abismo" that climbs to 200m (656 ft.) and reaches a maximum speed of 105kmph (65 mph). If you can keep your eyes open, the city skyline views are amazing.

Casa de Campo. ✆ **90-234-50-01.** www.parquedeatracciones.es. Admission 30€ adults, 23€ children, 16€ seniors; significant discounts available for online advance ticket purchase. July–Aug daily noon–midnight, variable days and hours the rest of the year. Metro: Linea 10. Bus: 33 or 65.

Teleférico de Madrid ★ CABLE CAR   A fun way to reach the Parque de Atracciones (see above), the Teleférico is also an attraction in its own right. It was built in 1969 to connect the fairgrounds of the Casa de Campo (p. 107) with the

Rowboats at Parque del Retiro's lake.

The Teleférico de Madrid.

eastern edge of Parque del Oeste, not far from the Palacio Real. The Disneyland-style cable cars take passengers on an 11-minute ride high above the city with views of parks, buildings, the Río Manzanares, and the Palacio Real. Passengers jump in as the cars slow down, and children under 14 must ride with an adult. Weather junkies will be interested to know that the cable cars operate in rain and snow.

Paseo del Pintor Rosales. ℭ **91-541-74-50.** www.teleferico.com. Fare 4€ one-way, 5.75€ round-trip, free for children under 3. June–Aug daily noon–9pm; variable days and hours the rest of the year.

Zoo Aquarium de Madrid ★ ZOO   When this zoo opened in 1972, it was in the forefront of thinking about how to best let animals and people interact, with animals in simulated natural habitats separated from humans by pits or moats. We like to think that this respectful approach has been a factor in the success of the zoo's breeding programs, which include the first panda born by artificial insemination outside China and the third rhino born by artificial insemination in the world. The zoo is home to about 6,000 animals from 500 different species, and has a tropical marine aquarium.

Casa de Campo. ℭ **90-234-50-14.** www.zoomadrid.com. Admission 23€ adults and children 8 and over, 19€ seniors and children 3–7; significant discounts for online advance ticket purchase. July–Aug daily 10:30am–8:30pm, variable hours and days rest of year. Metro: Linea 10 or Linea 5. Bus: 33.

SHOPPING IN MADRID

There are surprising discoveries to be made throughout Madrid, which is why you should keep your schedule flexible enough that you can stop in the store that catches your eye as you traverse the city. That said, two neighborhoods stand out for shoppers.

Salamanca (p. 156) is the more chic, with the boutiques of Spain's top designers as well as international luxury brands found in similar districts around the world. To keep it local, check out the beautiful tasseled bags, wallets, jackets, and other goods at **Loewe** (Calle Serrano, 26, ℭ **91-577-60-56;** Calle Serrano, 47; ℭ **91-200-44-99;** www.loewe.com; Metro: Serrano), or handle a truly well-made shoe at custom-maker **Gaytan** (Calle Jorge Juan, 15; ℭ **91-435-28-24;** Metro: Serrano or Velázquez). Not surprisingly, Madrid's nicest shopping mall **ABC Serrano** (Calle Serrano, 61; ℭ **91-577-50-31;** www.abcserrano.com;

High-end shopping in Salamanca.

Metro: Serrano) is also in the neighborhood. Even if the goods are too dear for your wallet, you might pick up a few style tips to employ elsewhere. Wherever you shop, keep in mind one of our favorite Spanish words: "rebajas." Translated loosely as "reductions," it signals that a sale is in progress. (Citywide sales generally take place Jan–Feb and July–Aug.)

Shoppers with more limited means will have more luck—and more fun—in the recently trendy neighborhood of **Chueca** (p. 58). It's worth exploring side streets for shops of up-and-coming designers looking for a lower rent. But the main drag of Calle Augusto Figueroa is shoe central, since a number of top-end Spanish shoe manufacturers, including **Barrats** (Calle Augusto Figueroa, 20; ✆ **91-531-65-37**; Metro: Chueca) have outlets here. We have found discounts of 30 to 60%.

Also in the neighborhood, the outlet store of **Salvador Bachiller** (Calle Gravina, 11; ✆ **91-523-30-37**; www.salvadorbachiller.com; Metro: Chueca) is a great source for luggage, purses, and other small leather goods. You can get great buys here (especially on bright colors), but watch for flaws such as broken zippers.

For souvenirs, the store at **CentroCentro** (p. 90) may the best general gift shop in the city. It stocks a good range of Spanish cookbooks in English, jewelry by local designers, and all kinds of clever household goods and novelty items. Our favorite? Mini wind-up *toreadors* and bulls.

In Puerta del Sol, the city's main branch of **El Corte Inglés** (Calle Preciados, 3; ✆ **91-379-80-00**; Metro: Vodafone Sol) department store is another good bet for one-stop souvenir shopping. It carries some fairly predictable merchandise such as embroidered shawls, damascene jewelry, and mass-produced pottery. It's best to think more broadly. Flamenco CDs or specialty food items like saffron (expensive) and smoked paprika (cheap, but packed in charming tins) are easy to pack and make novel gifts. In addition, the city's venerable perfumería Alvarez Gómez closed its retail shop in 2013, but many of the products are available at El Corte Inglés, including a concentrated bath gel that is great for travel.

For more choices, follow some of the streets that radiate out from Puerta del Sol. On Calle Preciados, for example, you'll find an outlet of **Zara** (Calle Preciados, 18; ✆ **91-521-09-58**; www.zara.com; Metro: Vodafone Sol or Callao), the clothing manufacturer that has gained a huge following for its on-trend yet affordable styles. For more timeless fashion, walk uphill to **Capas Seseña** (Calle

Cruz, 23; ✆ **91-531-68-40;** www.sesena.com; Metro: Vodafone Sol), which has been making beautiful capes since 1901. If they suit your style, they are worth the investment.

But there are other, less costly icons of Spanish style, including the constructed Basque cap, Spain's answer to the French beret. **La Favorita** (Plaza Mayor, 25; ✆ **91-366-58-77;** www.lafavoritacb.com; Metro: Vodafone Sol or Opera) has a range of colors and styles for men and women. And right off Plaza Mayor, you can join Spanish women who wait in line to buy hand-sewn espadrilles at local favorite **Casa Hernanz** (Calle Toledo, 18; ✆ **91-366-54-50;** Metro: La Latina).

Before you leave Plaza Mayor, stop at **El Arco de los Cuchilleros Artesania de Hoy** (Plaza Mayor, 9; ✆ **91-365-26-80;** Metro: Vodafone Sol or Opera), which is devoted to contemporary craft items from throughout Spain. If you have a particular interest in Spain's great ceramics traditions, do not miss **Antigua Casa Talavera** (Calle Isabel La Catolica, 2; ✆ **91-547-34-17;** Metro: Santo Domingo), where the beautiful tile facade of the building is only a prelude to the artful ceramics inside. Spanish artisans also excel at guitar-making. The best of the best is **Guitarras Ramirez** (Calle de la Paz, 8; ✆ **91-531-42-29;** www.guitarrasramirez.com; Metro: Sevilla), which was founded in the 1880s and has created instruments for everyone from Andrés Segovia to Eric Clapton. Other good options include **Conde Hermanos** (Calle Arrieta, 4; ✆ **91-541-87-38;** www.condehermanos.com; Metro: Opera), makers of classical and flamenco guitars, and **El Flamenco Vive** (Calle Conde de Lemos, 7; ✆ **91-547-39-17;** www.elflamencovive.com; Metro: Opera), the city's tiny but indispensable flamenco hub with guitars, sheet music, CDs, and more.

Sunday is the day for the famed flea market **El Rastro** (p. 99). We once saw Madrileñas stocking up on armloads of fake pashminas, and you might find other fun fashion pieces among the bric-a-brac. Enjoy the scene, but watch your belongings, as pickpockets work the crowd. If you are a serious antiques collector, it's better to return to the neighborhood on a weekday and check out the

Souvenirs supporting the Real Madrid soccer team.

shops gathered in **Mercado Galerias Piquer** (Calle Ribera de Curtidores, 29; no phone; Metro: Puerto de Toledo).

Madrid's most beautiful food market is **Mercado de la Paz** (p. 106) in Salamanca, where you can peruse the fresh goods and shop for packaged items to take home. On the other hand, Madrid's best market for the beautiful people is **Mercado de San Miguel** (p. 98). This long-shuttered fresh food market has assumed a new identity as a lifestyle emporium with specialty food items to eat on premises or take away.

According to *Forbes,* **Real Madrid** is the most valuable soccer team in the world. You can add to its $3.3 billion net worth by picking up some of the team's training jerseys and shorts, scarves, socks, or hoodies. For the truly obsessed, there are also blankets, sheets, mugs, coasters, electric toothbrushes, and rubber duckies. Official stores include Tienda Carmen (Calle Carmen, 3; ✆ 91-521-79-50; Metro: Vodafone Sol or Callao), Tienda Goya (Calle Goya, 77; ✆ 91-435-79-04; Metro: Goya), and Tienda Gran Vía (Gran Vía, 31; ✆ 91-755-45-38; Metro: Callao or Gran Vía).

ENTERTAINMENT & NIGHTLIFE

If you are only going to hit the town for 1 night, you should see a flamenco show. Madrid is at the forefront of the flamenco revival and much of the credit goes to **Casa Patas** (p. 95), which presents established artists and rising stars. But we also have great respect for some of the showier and more touristic offerings, which help introduce people to the art form. Good choices include **Cardamomo** (Calle Echegaray, 15; ✆ 91-369-07-57; www.cardamomo.es; 39€; Metro: Vodafone Sol), which often features well-known performers, and **Corral de la Morería** (Calle Morería, 17; ✆ 91-365-84-46; www.corraldelamoreria.com; 39€; Metro: Opera), which is located near the Palacio Real and has championed

Madrid's Teatro Real.

flamenco since 1956. Prices above are for the show and one drink. Dinner is available, but you are better off eating elsewhere. For a more casual performance, try **Villa Rosa** (Plaza Santa Ana, 15; ✆ **91-521-36-89**; www.villa-rosa.es; 15€; Metro: Antón Martín), which occupies an historic building on Plaza Santa Ana.

If you prefer cool jazz to hot flamenco, check out **Cafe Central** (Plaza del Angel, 10; ✆ **91-369-41-43**; www.cafecentralmadrid.com; Metro: Antón Martin), which has been presenting touring musicians since the early 1980s. The Malasaña mega-club **Clamores** (Calle Alburquerque, 14; ✆ **91-445-7-38**; www.clamores.es; Metro: Bilbao) often programs live jazz in the early evening, before it turns into a late-night disco. In nearby Chueca, Madrid's premier gay bar **Black & White** (Calle Libertad, 34; ✆ **91-531-11-41**; www.discoblack-white.net; Metro: Chueca) features a basement disco and a street-level bar with drag shows, male strip tease, and other entertainment. For a more centrally located dance club, **Disco-Teatro Joy Eslava** (Arenal 11; ✆ **91-366-37-33**; www.joy-eslava.com; Metro: Vodafone Sol or Opera) occupies a 19th-century theater near Puerta del Sol. For late-night chocolate and churros, Joy Eslava is conveniently located near **Chocolatería San Ginés** (p. 83).

For classical music lovers, **Teatro Real** (p. 102) is known for the fine acoustics that enhance its offerings of opera and classical music. Madrid's largest concentration of theaters is in the vicinity of Plaza Santa Ana (see sidebar on p. 97). For classical music concerts, check **Teatro Monumental** or **Teatro Español,** which schedules dance, orchestral, and chamber music concerts as well as live theater. Both the **Teatro Nuevo Apolo** and the **Teatro de la Zarzuela** specialize in *zarzuela,* the Spanish form of musical entertainment that mixes opera, popular song, and spoken narrative. Performances are in Spanish, of course, but they are so expressive that the language barrier is not necessarily an impediment to enjoying the action.

One of our favorite ways to improve our language skills is to watch American films with Spanish translations. **Cine Ideal** (Doctor Cortezo, 6; ✆ **90-222-09-22**; www.yelmocines.es; Metro: Tirso de Molina) screens current films, including 3D, in their original language, with Spanish subtitles when appropriate.

DAY TRIPS FROM MADRID

The two destinations below offer a switch of attitude and ambiance from central Madrid. Each is key to the Spanish psyche, but they could not be more different. The monastery palace at San Lorenzo de El Escorial, a gigantic mass of heavily decorated stone, might be the weightiest attraction in the country. It is also the embodiment of the religious fervor that seized and motivated some of the

Spanish monarchs. Alcalá de Henares, by contrast, is a pleasantly dusty, flat little town on the plains east of the city where some of the greatest minds of Spanish culture studied and taught.

San Lorenzo de El Escorial ★★

Set in the Guadarrama mountains about 51km (31 miles) northwest of Madrid, El Escorial can be surprisingly cooler than the city. After Toledo (p. 121), a visit to its austere royal palace and monastery is the second most popular day trip from Madrid. The pleasant weather also makes the town a favorite summer getaway for Madrileños. If you don't own a breezy summer home here, plan to spend a half day at the royal site.

ESSENTIALS

GETTING THERE More than two dozen *cercanías* (commuter trains) depart daily from Madrid's Atocha, Nuevos Ministerios, Chamartín, and Recoletos railway stations. During the summer another dozen trains are added. For schedules and information, call ✆ **90-232-03-20,** or visit www.renfe.es. A one-way fare costs 4.50€, round-trip is 6.60€. Trip time is a little more than 1 hour. The railway station is about a mile outside town along Carretera Estación. The Herranz bus company meets all arriving trains to shuttle passengers to and from Plaza Virgen de Gracia, about a block east of the monastery's entrance.

    Empresa Herranz (Calle del Rey, 27, in El Escorial; ✆ **91-890-19-15**) runs some 50 **buses** per day back and forth between Madrid's Moncloa station and El Escorial. On Sunday, service is curtailed to 10 buses. Trip time is an hour, and the one-way fare is 6€. If you're driving, follow the N-VI highway (marked on some maps as A-6) from the northwest perimeter of Madrid toward Lugo, A Coruña, and San Lorenzo de El Escorial. After about a half-hour, fork left onto the C-505 heading toward San Lorenzo de El Escorial. Driving time from Madrid is about an hour.

VISITOR INFORMATION The **tourist information office** (Calle Grimaldi, 4; ✆ **91-890-53-13;** www.sanlorenzoturismo.org) is open Tuesday to Saturday 10am to 2pm and 3 to 6pm, and Sunday 10am to 2pm.

EXPLORING SAN LORENZO DE EL ESCORIAL

Real Monasterio de San Lorenzo de El Escorial ★★★ HISTORIC SITE Felipe II ordered the construction of this stone behemoth in 1563, 2 years after he moved his capital to Madrid. This monument to the Habsburg line was completed in only 21 years. After the death of the original architect, Juan Bautista de Toledo, the structure was completed by Juan de Herrera, often considered the greatest architect of Renaissance Spain. It is an important landmark of Spanish Renaissance style, but the complex does have a rather institutional look, and its sheer size makes it intimidating. The buildings, which include a basilica, a monastery, the royal palace, and a library, are arranged in a quadrangle. Consider the optional guided tour to get an overview and then explore on your own and admire the impressive royal art collection. Felipe II loved Titian, and the artist's *Last Supper* is a highlight. Spain is well-represented with El Greco's *Martyrdom of St. Maurice* and Velázquez's *La Tunica de José.*

    Guides always linger in the basilica, which has 43 ornate altars beneath a dome that emulates St. Peter's in Rome. Habsburg and Bourbon monarchs, including Carlos V, the father of Felipe II, lie in royal vaults beneath the basilica. Much of the mural work in the complex is impressive—from the frescoes of

The Real Monasterio de San Lorenzo de El Escorial.

Habsburg battle victories in the royal palace to the vaulted ceiling in the library painted with allegorical scenes depicting the Liberal Arts and the Sciences. Amid this splendor, the monarch's private quarters are modest, but a window provides a view of the main altar of the basilica.

Calle Juan de Borbón, s/n. © **91-890-59-03.** http://patrimonionacional.es. Admission 10€ adults, 5€ students and children; audio guide 4€; guided tour additional 7€. Apr–Sept Tues–Sun 10am–6pm; Oct–Mar Tues–Sun 10am–5pm.

Alcalá de Henares ★★

The buildings are old and the population is young—as befits the city where the Spanish Renaissance was born when the university was founded here by Cardinal Francisco Jiménez de Cisneros in 1499. While the Inquisition was closing minds, Alcalá was opening them. The progenitor of the modern Spanish language, Miguel de Cervantes, was also born here in 1547. Although the Cervantes family left Alcalá when Miguel was a boy, the central square of the old town is called Plaza de Cervantes and boasts a heroic bronze of the author. The original university moved to Madrid in the 1800s, and the town went into decline. It has established a new identity with residential study programs for several American universities. Commuter rail connections have nearly turned the college town into a suburb, earning the nickname "the bedroom of Madrid."

ESSENTIALS

GETTING THERE   **Trains** travel from Madrid's Chamartín station to Alcalá de Henares four times per day. A one-way fare costs 3€ to 10€, depending on the train. Trip time is 21 to 45 minutes. The train station (© **90-232-03-20;** www.renfe.es) in Alcalá is at Paseo Estación. **Buses** from Madrid depart from Avenida de América 18 (Metro: América) every 15 minutes. A one-way fare is 5€. Bus service is provided by Continental, and the Alcalá bus station is on Avenida Guadalajara, 36 (© **90-242-22-42**), 2 blocks past Calle Libreros. Alcalá lies adjacent to the main national highway (N-II), connecting Madrid with eastern Spain. As you leave central Madrid, follow signs for Barajas Airport and Barcelona.

VISITOR INFORMATION   The **tourist information office,** Callejón de Santa María, 1 (© **91-889-26-94;** www.turismoalcala.com), is open daily 10am to 2pm and 4 to 6:30pm (until 7:30pm July–Sept). It is closed on Monday in July and August.

EXPLORING ALCALÁ DE HENARES

You can easily explore Alcalá in a day, walking everywhere. From February to August, keep an eye out for about 100 pairs of storks that nest on the rooftops and in the bell towers.

The Museo Casa Natal de Cervantes.

Capilla de San Ildefonso ★ CHURCH   Next door to the Colegio (see below) is the Capilla de San Ildefonso, the 15th-century chapel of the old university with an *artesanado* (artisan's) ceiling and intricately stuccoed walls. It houses the Italian marble tomb of Cardinal Cisneros, the founder of the original university.

Plaza San Diego, s/n. ✆ **91-885-41-85.** Admission included in tour of Colegio Mayor de San Ildefonso. Mon–Fri 11am–1pm and 5–7pm; Sat–Sun 11am–2pm and 5–7:30pm.

Colegio Mayor de San Ildefonso ★★ HISTORIC SITE   Adjacent to Plaza de Cervantes (the main square) is this college where Lope de Vega and other famous Spaniards studied. You can see some of their names engraved on plaques in the examination room. The old university's Plateresque **facade** dates from 1543. From here, walk across the Patio of Saint Thomas (from 1662) and the Patio of the Philosophers to reach the Patio of the Three Languages (from 1557), where Greek, Latin, and Hebrew were once taught. The **Paraninfo** (great hall or old examination room) has a Mudéjar carved-panel ceiling and is now used for special events. The Paraninfo is entered through the restaurant Hostería del Estudiante.

Plaza San Diego. ✆ **91-885-41-85.** www.uah.es. Guided tour 4.50€; audio guides 3€. Tours in Spanish or English Tues–Sat noon and 1, 5, 6, and 7pm; Sun noon and 1pm.

Museo Arqueológico Regional ★★ MUSEUM   Clear signage and vivid exhibits make this one of the country's most rewarding archaeological museums. Its coverage includes natural history as well as human occupation. While storks seem to be the most common form of wildlife these days, the beasts were considerably more ferocious some 780,000 years ago, judging by the bones of saber-toothed tigers, ur-wolves, and rhinoceros on display. Don't miss the wonderful murals recovered from Alcalá's Roman era when it was known as Complutum, founded 1 B.C.

Plaza Bernardas, s/n. ✆ **91-879-66-66.** www.madrid.org. Free admission. Tues–Sat 11am–7pm; Sun 11am–3pm.

Museo Casa Natal de Cervantes ★ MUSEUM Miguel de Cervantes, the creator of *Don Quijote,* was born in Alcalá in 1547 and the city remains proud of its association with Spain's literary giant. In the 1940s, research by a Cervantes biographer suggested that this country estate may have been his birthplace, and the city moved quickly to reconstruct the building and establish it as a museum. The handsome brick and stone dwelling has a small courtyard and well. Cervantes' father was a barber-surgeon and the interior of tile floors, white walls, and carved wooden doors conjures the lifestyle of a comfortable family of the time. Displays of Cervantes' manuscripts help to cement the connection to the author. Calle Mayor, 48. ✆ **91-889-96-54.** www.museo-casa-natal-cervantes.org. Free admission. Tues–Sun 10am–6pm.

5

CASTILLA-LA MANCHA

n popular imagination, La Mancha is a vast, arid plain where Don Quijote does battle with windmills. As you travel the region, you will find that every hillock seems to be topped with an old-fashioned windmill or the ruins of a medieval castle. The countryside is a land of olive trees, herds of sheep, and vast tracts of wine grapes, but the cities of Castilla-La Mancha are another story. Crowning high bluffs above the plains' few rivers, the cities are visionary places. Every culture from the Romans onward has made Toledo a citadel on the plain. From its castellated walls, defenders could see attackers coming from days away. But their heights proved as important to art as to war. El Greco looked out from the walls of Toledo and saw the earth far below but the heavens at eye level—a perspective repeated again and again in his paintings of the Ascension. A millennium younger, Cuenca recapitulates the geography of Toledo in easternmost La Mancha, perching at a seemingly impossible height far above its river gorge. In the 20th century, Cuenca became a haven for artists who found in its improbable verticality inspiration for abstract flights of fancy. Cuenca's *casas colgadas*, or "hanging houses," cling to the edges, a perfect balancing act between solid ground and soaring faith.

TOLEDO ★★★

A crossroads of cultures over the millennia, Toledo's strong Arabic, Jewish, and Christian elements have not entirely eclipsed the Roman and Visigothic eras. The hilltop old city is a UNESCO World Heritage Site and surprisingly little of its appearance has changed since El Greco painted his adopted home in the 16th century. Even then it was ancient.

The close medieval streets were deliberately constructed to be barely wide enough for a man and his donkey to pass, but they are strikingly practical—offering cool, welcome shade in the summer and a shield from winter winds. Wrapped on three sides by a bend in the Río Tajo, Toledo overlooks the plains of La Mancha from a high bluff. This outcrop provided a natural fortress in the center of the Iberian Peninsula. The Romans made it the capital of central Iberia, and the Visigoths made it the capital of their kingdom. For roughly a century, it was the capital of a regional Muslim kingdom—an outlier of Córdoba—before it was re-conquered by Alfonso VI in 1085. The kings of Castilla ultimately made Toledo the capital of Spain. Even after the court moved to Madrid in 1561, Toledo remained the national religious center as the seat of the primate of Spain. As the governing city of so many cultures, it retains more layers of history than almost anywhere else in Spain.

FACING PAGE: **A windmill in the La Mancha region of central Spain.**

A view of Toledo from afar.

Although most of Toledo's medieval defensive walls have been taken down, the city still feels like a hilltop fortress. So approach it in that manner, beginning your visit by circumnavigating the roads that once lay just inside the walls, eerily marked by the preserved ceremonial gates (notably the Arabic archway of **Puerta del Sol** on the north side). To better understand how defenders could watch potential enemies as they approached, spend some time surveying the surrounding plain from **Mirador Barrio Nuevo** across the street from the **Museo Sefardí** (see below). Once you begin spiraling into the city interior, two key squares are the centers of life in Toledo. You'll find local children playing street soccer or learning to ride bicycles (as well as travelers visiting the tourist office) at the **Plaza del Ayuntamiento,** southwest of the **cathedral. Plaza de Zocodover,** northeast of the cathedral, is filled with outdoor cafes popular both with visitors and, at night, with young Toledanos. Both squares serve as reference points, as they represent transitions between neighborhoods. Plaza de Zocodover is also the central point where local buses stop in the old city.

Essentials

GETTING THERE   High-speed RENFE Avant **trains** run frequently every day. Those departing Madrid's Atocha railway station for Toledo run daily from 6:50am to 9:50pm; those leaving Toledo for Madrid run daily from 6:50am to 9:30pm. Travel time is approximately 35 minutes. The one-way fare is 13€. For train information in Madrid, call 📞 **90-232-03-20,** or visit www.renfe.com. To reach the old city from Toledo's bus station, take bus 5 to the Plaza de Zocodover (1.40€); a taxi from the station is about 8€).

From Madrid, it's also feasible to take the **bus** instead of the train. The main service is provided by **Alsa** (📞 **90-242-22-42;** www.alsa.es). Buses depart daily from Madrid's Estación de Plaza Elíptica, Avenida Vía Lusitana, between 6:30am and 11pm at 15- to 30-minute intervals. Travel time is 50 minutes to 1¼ hours. A one-way transit costs 5.65€ and can be purchased only at the station. Once you reach Toledo, you'll be deposited at the Estación de Autobuses, which lies beside the river about 1.2km (¾ mile) from the historic center. Although many visitors opt to walk, be ready to climb a hill. Buses 5 and 6 run from the station uphill to Plaza de Zocodover, charging 1.40€ for the brief ride. Pay the driver directly. By **car,** exit Madrid via Cibeles (Paseo del Prado) and take the N-401 south.

VISITOR INFORMATION   The **tourist information office,** Plaza del Consistorio, 1 (*©* **92-525-40-30;** www.toledo-turismo.com), is open daily 10am to 6pm.

Where to Stay

Hostal del Cardenal ★★   You will be immediately charmed when you make your way through an entrance in the thick city walls and find yourself in the tranquil Andalucían-style garden of this former summer home of a very lucky archbishop. The hotel is near the Bisagra Gate on the northern end of the city, roughly 15 minutes on foot from the cathedral. Truthfully, it's a bit difficult to find, but worth the effort for its combination of history and elegance. You will probably find yourself spending a lot of time in the garden or the traditionally furnished sitting areas. The standard double rooms, while bright and cheerful, are somewhat small.

Paseo de Recaredo, 24. *©* **92-522-49-00.** www.elhostaldelcardenal.com. 27 units. 73€–124€ double; 135€–310€ suite. Free street parking about 10-min. walk away. Bus: 5 or 6 from rail station. **Amenities:** Restaurant; bar; free Wi-Fi.

Hotel Santa Isabel ★★   There's an old European tradition that travelers may spend the night unmolested within the shadow of the church. While this delightful B&B inn is not quite as cheap as the cathedral doorway, it's not far from the church and a whole lot more comfortable. It occupies a medieval building across

Toledo

0 100 yds
0 100 m

Roman Circus (Ruins)

Av. de la Reconquista
LOS BLOQUES
C/ Cardenal – Tavera
1
C/ Carrera

Carretera de Carlos III
Glorieta de la Reconquista
Paseo del Circo Romano
i
Puerta de Bisagra
LA ANTEQUERUELA

Avenida de la Cava
2
Puerta de Alfonso VI
C/ Real del Arrabal
C/ Azacanes
C/ Gerardo Lobo

Paseo de Recaredo
SANTIAGO
Subida de la Granja
Puerta del Sol

Paseo de la Cava
3
Plaza de la Merced
Plaza Sta. Clara
C/ Alfileritos
5
C/ La Sillería
6
Palacio Benacazón
Museo de Santa Cruz
7
Plaza de Zocodover

Convento Carmelitas Descalzas
Plaza Sta. Teresa de Jesús
Plaza San Juan de los Reyes
Santo Domingo El Antiguo
4
Pl. de Padilla
Casa de Mesa
Plaza de San Román
Plaza de la Magdalena
Cuesta de Carlos V
Alcázar
8

Palacio de la Cava
SAN MARTIN
Convento de San Pedro Mártir
C/ Bulas
C/ Trinidad
10
11
C/ Hombre de Palo
9
C/ Cadenas

Monasterio de San Juan de los Reyes
17
Museo de Arte Contemporaneo
12
Palacio Arzobispal
Catedral
LA CANDELARIA

C/ Ángel
C/ Reyes Católicos
16
C/ Sto. Tomé
Iglesia Santo Tomé
15
14
Taller del Moro
Plaza Salvador
San Marcos
Plaza del Ayuntamiento
i
Plaza San Justo

JUDERIA
18
19
20
21
Pso. del Tránsito
Jardines del Paseo del Tránsito
EL CALVARIO
C/ Santa Úrsula
13
C/ Pozo Amargo
Plaza Santa Isabela
Conservatorio
Plaza de los Infantes

Madrid
Toledo

C/ Descalzos
Plaza San Ciprano
Plaza Santa Catalina
Plaza Santa Catalina
Seminario
SANTA CATALINA

Carreras de San Sebastián

Río Tajo

HOTELS
Hostal del Cardenal **2**
Hotel Pintor El Greco **21**
Hotel Santa Isabel **9**
Parador de Toledo **3**

RESTAURANTS
Adolfo Colección **12**
Adolfo Restaurante **11**
Alfileritos 24 **5**
El Casón de los López de Toledo **6**
La Campana Gorda **10**

ATTRACTIONS
Convento de Santo Domingo El Antiguo **4**
Hospital de San Juan Batista **1**
Iglesia de Santo Tomé **15**

Mariano Zamorano Fábrica de Espadas **13**
Monasterio de San Juan de los Reyes **17**
Museo del Ejército **8**
Museo del Greco **20**

Museo de Santa Cruz **7**
Museo Sefardi **19**
Museo Victorio Macho **18**
Pasteleria Santo Tomé **14**
Sinagoga de Santa María La Blanca **16**

124

from the Convent of Santa Isabel and near the cathedral. Some guest rooms, in fact, have cathedral views, while the rooftop terrace (reached by a spiral staircase) has panoramic city views. The building became a lodging in 1990, and careful restoration retained the ancient facade while creating a more fresh and airy modern interior. Guest rooms are small but well maintained. Room 215, with a glassed-in balcony, is perhaps the nicest.

Calle Santa Isabel, 24. ✆ **92-525-31-20.** www.hotelsantaisabel.net. 42 units. 54€–108€ double. Underground parking 10€. Bus: 5 or 6. **Amenities:** Free Wi-Fi.

Hotel Pintor El Greco ★★★　One of the city's most romantic lodgings, this hotel is built around the core of a classic 17th-century Toledo house (and former bakery) constructed of brick and stucco both inside and out. Carved wooden furniture upholstered in patterned woven fabrics, wrought-iron banisters and light fixtures, and sunny colors sponged on stucco walls conjure fine living in old Toledo. The new addition, which doubled the size, is as ultra-modern as the original is traditional, with contemporary dark wood and leather furniture, bright splashes of saturated color in pillows and wall decor, white marble floors, and flat-screen TVs. Ironically, many guests prefer the older section for its historical ambiance. The location on the west side of town in the old Jewish Quarter near the Sinagoga del Tránsito and the Convento de San Juan de los Reyes is quiet, but it's only a short walk to the cathedral.

Calle Alamillos del Tránsito, 13. ✆ **92-528-51-91.** www.hotelpintorelgreco.com. 60 units. 60€–188€ double. Parking 14€. Bus: 2. **Amenities:** Free Wi-Fi.

Parador de Toledo ★★★　This *parador* occupies a handsome stone building with tile roof from the 14th century, but travelers choose it less for its historic ambiance and more for its stupendous view. The property sits on a hilly ridge about 4km (2½ miles) from the city center—the perfect vantage point to take in Toledo in all its architectural glory, whether you are sunning by the outdoor pool or enjoying the city lights while eating dinner on the patio. The restaurant serves all the standards of Castilla-La Mancha, including partridge, roast lamb, honey ice cream, and *mazapán*. Guest rooms depart from the usual *parador* approach of antique reproduction furnishings in favor of clean-lined modern pieces that don't detract from the views. The only disadvantage of this location across the Río Tajo is that you will probably want to take taxi rides back and forth to the city center.

Cerro del Emperador. ✆ **92-522-18-50.** www.parador.es. 76 units. 120€–180€ double; 190€–232€ suite. Free parking. **Amenities:** Restaurant; bar; outdoor pool; room service; free Wi-Fi.

Where to Eat

Toledo's cuisine relies heavily on mushrooms foraged from the river gorges, artichokes raised in the dry fields below the city, and wild game. The striking signature dish *perdiz a la Toledana* (partridge cooked with herbs, olive oil, and white wine) is widely imitated all over Spain. The local olive oil is also prized, and you may find some dishes dressed with nothing else.

Adolfo Colleción ★ LA MANCHAN　You don't need to pay haute prices to enjoy star chef Adolfo Muñoz's creative cooking (and some fabulous wines from central Spain) if you head to his bargain-priced wine bar and shop across from the cathedral. It serves tapas and light meals in a hip setting with seating for just 16 people. Game figures prominently, with such treats as venison stuffed with herbs. It's a good spot to try *carcamusas*, a Toledan stewed meat casserole of pork, tomatoes, and green peas, served with fried potatoes. The *menu del día* (2 courses and dessert, but no wine) is always a bargain. More than 300 wines are available, many by the glass.

Calle Nuncio Viejo, 1. ℭ **92-522-42-44.** www.grupoadolfo.com. Most main dishes under 10€. Daily 11am–11:30pm. Bus: 5 or 6.

Adolfo Restaurante ★★ LA MANCHAN   One chef can turn around a city's dining habits. Adolfo Muñoz, the charismatic and talented champion of modernized La Manchan cooking, did that in Toledo. This flagship of his restaurant group, located in a late medieval structure near the cathedral, offers the greatest hits of Toledan cuisine: the dishes served all over Spain but always attributed to Toledo. Game is first and foremost, with a glorious version of *perdiz a la Toledana,* the classic pickled partridge slow-cooked in olive oil. Muñoz serves it with a puddle of reduced cooking juices and a circle of intensely red rice and herbs. Part of what makes Toledan cuisine distinctive is the use of both fresh and dried fruit in many savory dishes. It's part of the Moorish heritage of the city, and Muñoz nods to it by accompanying roast suckling pig with a side of sliced green apples quickly sautéed in pork fat. He also sometimes serves the rack of venison with a sauté of onions, carrots, and dried fruits.

Calle Hombre de Palo, 7. ℭ **92-522-73-21.** www.adolforestaurante.com. Reservations recommended. Main courses 27€–45€; tasting menu 90€–110€. Daily 1–4pm; Mon–Sat 8pm–midnight. Bus: 5 or 6.

Alfileritos 24 Taberna Restaurante ★★ SPANISH   Old Toledo and new Spain come together in this establishment that even has separate rooms for its split personality. It's in a medieval building on a very narrow street almost in the geographic center of Toledo. The tavern side, one of the favorite watering holes for Toledo professionals, can get a bit rowdy on weekends, but it offers one of the best cheap breakfasts in the mornings and a *menu del día* (2 courses, dessert, and choice of drink) for a song (11€). Starters could include a salad of tuna and white asparagus or mixed cheeses and dried fruits with honey vinaigrette. For a main course, choose the deer tacos with mushroom salsa. Prices go up and table settings get more elegant on the restaurant side, where you might find a grilled fish with green pepper sauce or rounds of venison filet mignon with quince and Parmagiano cheese on the 19€ menu. All dishes can also be ordered a la carte.

Calle Alfileritos, 24. ℭ **92-523-96-25.** www.alfileritos24.com. Main dishes 17€–21€. Daily 9am–4pm and 8pm–midnight.

Cervecería Restaurante La Campana Gorda ★ LA MANCHAN   Join Toledo shopkeepers having lunch on such traditional specialties as pickled partridge and vegetables in this dining room near the cathedral. The beer hall in the front room has a long, curving marble bar that is quite beautiful. It serves tapas and *raciónes* such as plates of anchovies in vinegar, wild mushrooms sautéed in butter, or paper-thin slices of air-dried venison. As a general rule, skip the fried food and concentrate on dishes that are either steamed or roasted.

Calle Hombre de Palo, 13. ℭ **92-521-01-46.** Restaurant main dishes 12€–20€, beer hall tapas and *raciónes* 6€–19€. Daily noon–4pm and 8–11pm. Bus: 2.

Exploring Toledo

Catedral de Toledo ★★★ CATHEDRAL   Filled with treasures of religious art and freighted with history as the first cathedral to reclaim central Spain for Christianity, this cathedral remains the ecclesiastical seat of the Roman Catholic church in Spain, long after the political capital moved to Madrid. Set at the center

The Catedral de Toledo.

of the hilltop old city, this structure is one of just three High Gothic cathedrals in Spain and is considered by some critics as the finest example. Construction began in 1226 and was more or less finished in 1463. Keeping with Spanish tradition, the cathedral was built on the site of Toledo's chief mosque, which was in turn built on the foundations of a Visigothic cathedral. The Gothic bones are sometimes hard to see for all the ornate Baroque decoration. The main entrance is off Calle Hombre del Palo (look for the clock tower), and ensures that you pass through the well-stocked cathedral store on your way into church.

From an art historical point of view, the church is rather like a great old-fashioned antique store stuffed with treasures, each remarkable by itself but only tangentially related to its neighbor. Don't expect a harmonious assemblage—concentrate on specific beautiful pieces. The heavily gilded main altar, for example, shows the influence that Moorish damascene decoration would ultimately exert on over-the-top Spanish Baroque. The backs of the lower tier of the seats in the choir, carved by Rodrigo Alemán in 1495, depict the conquest of Granada just a few years earlier. His extraordinary carving of the seat arms in images of knights deep in prayer or thought (some of them hooded like Death himself) may be the most moving statues in a cathedral filled with statuary. VIP tombs—kings Alfonso VII, Sancho II, and Sancho III, as well as Cardinal Mendoza—fill the outer walls.

Fans of Baroque carving are especially enamored of the *transparente*—a wall of marble and alabaster sculpture long overlooked because the cathedral was so poorly lit. The sculptor who created it, Narcisco Tomé, cut a hole in the ceiling so a shaft of light would illuminate the translucent stonework. The window has been restored, throwing highlights on a group of angels, a *Last Supper* rendered in alabaster, and a Virgin ascending into heaven. The side chapels contain some of the cathedral's greatest artistic treasures in rooms small enough to get close to the work and study it.

For an extra fee, you can visit the cathedral museums. The Sacristy contains the modest-sized El Greco portraits of each of the 12 apostles, as well as his recently re-installed 1577–79 masterwork *El Espolio* (The Disrobing of Christ), which starred at the Prado and the Museo de Santa Cruz during the El Greco quadricentennial in 2014.

As the name suggests, the Treasure Room is crammed with precious metals and jewels. The main attraction here is the 500-pound gilded monstrance paraded through the streets on the Feast of Corpus Christi. After years of tourists disobeying the "no flash" rule, the cathedral now bans all photography, filming, and use of cellphones.

Calle Cardenal Cisneros, 1. ✆ **92-522-22-41.** www.catedralprimada.es. Free admission to cathedral; admission to Sacristy and Treasure Room 11€. Mon–Sat 10am–6pm; Sun 2–6pm. Special hours during feast days. Bus: 2.

Hospital de San Juan Bautista ★ ART MUSEUM Cardinal Juan Pardo de Tavera, the 16th-century Toledo archbishop who was a close confident of Emperor Carlos V, was not one to hide his light beneath a bushel. He had this elegant Renaissance palace with beautiful arcaded twin courtyards built in a style far more grandiose than necessary to serve as a hospital for the indigent—but maybe just grandiose enough to serve as a pantheon recalling the greatness of its patron. The building represents the finest mature work of local architect Alonso de Covarrubias, who also designed the Hospital de Santa Cruz, now the Museo de Santa Cruz (below). Cardinal Tavera's mausoleum, designed by Alonso Berruguete, is within the adjacent church, but the hospital now houses the striking Fundación Medinaceli collections of Spanish paintings from the 15th through 18th centuries. Among them are five works by El Greco, including a portrait of Tavera and versions of *The Holy Family* and *The Baptism of Christ.* The building itself is clearly visible in an unfinished state in El Greco's *View and Plan of Toledo* in the Museo del Greco (see below). A portrait of Carlos V by Titian dominates the banquet hall.

Calle Cardenal Tavera, 2. ℂ **92-522-04-51.** www.fundacionmedinaceli.org. Admission 4.50€. Mon–Sat 10am–1:30pm and 3–6:30pm; Sun 10am–2:30pm. Closed Dec 25 and Jan 1. Bus: 2.

Iglesia de Santo Tomé ★ CHURCH This modest little 14th-century chapel, situated on a narrow street in the old Jewish Quarter, holds two treasures: a de Graaf pipe organ that makes it a choice venue for organ concerts, and El Greco's masterpiece *The Burial of the Count of Orgaz* ★★★, created in 1586. The painting is no longer displayed inside the church; it is mounted in a separate entranceway to accommodate both visitors to the painting and the congregants who use the church for worship. Bus groups often descend on the El Greco painting en masse. To avoid big crowds, go when the chapel first opens.

Plaza del Conde, 4. ℂ **92-525-60-98.** www.santotome.org. Admission 2.30€. Daily 10am–6:45pm (closes at 5:45pm in winter). Closed Dec 25 and Jan 1. Bus: 2.

Mariano Zamoraño Fábrica de Espadas y Armas Blancas ★ SHOP Medieval Toledo craftsmen rediscovered the ancient techniques for making weapons of hardened steel, making a sword of "Toledo steel" the gold standard for a crusading knight going to do battle in the Holy Land. The ubiquitous modern souvenir swords are a waste of money, but connoisseurs of fine blades can still find a handful of swordmakers practicing the venerable profession. Mariano Zamoraño's family started making swords in Toledo in the late 19th century, and he continues hammering and honing fine steel just a few blocks from the cathedral. Visit the workshop in the winter, and you can see the artisans heating steel bars red-hot on a bed of charcoal, then stretching and shaping the steel into the final blades. During the rest of the year, the swordmakers attend to less heat-intensive tasks, such as creating foils and tangs, sharpening blades, or painstakingly polishing the high-nickel steel into a mirror finish. (Unlike souvenir swords, Zamaraño's blades are not plated with chrome.) The shop produces everything from fencing rapiers and sabers to cutlasses and ceremonial presentation swords. They also make some kitchen cutlery. Every authentic piece bears the stylized MZ mark.

Calle Ciudad, 19. ℂ **92-522-26-34.** www.marianozamorano.com. Mon–Sat 10am–2pm and 4–6pm.

Monasterio de San Juan de los Reyes ★★ MONASTERY There are no El Grecos in this early Renaissance monastery, but the cloisters work their own kind of magic. Fernando and Isabel had the convent built to mark their 1476

TOLEDO AS el greco SAW IT

While wandering through the heart of Toledo is a delight, it's almost as memorable to view Toledo from afar. In many respects, it still looks as it did when El Greco painted it. For the best perspective, you will need a car. Take the **Carretera de Circunvalación,** the road that runs 3km (1¾ miles) on the far bank of the Río Tajo. This road makes a circular loop of the river from the Alcántara to the San Martín Bridge. Clinging to the hillsides are farmsteads (*cigarrales*) with rustic dwellings and extensive olive groves. The *cigarrales* of the Imperial City were immortalized by Tirso de Molina, the 17th-century dramatist, in his trilogy **Los Cigarrales de Toledo.**

victory over the Portuguese and originally intended to be buried here—until the symbolic importance of being buried in Granada trumped that plan. It is the epitome of a Franciscan retreat· the cloister's jungle-like central garden is filled with birdsong, and the high-vaulted Renaissance arches flood the arcades with reflected light. The convent was not finished until 1504, when it was dedicated to St. John the Evangelist and turned over to the Franciscans. Heavily damaged during Napoleon's invasion, it stood vacant until the late 19th century, when restoration began. In 1954, the state returned the property to the Franciscans and it has been a working friary ever since. Located at the western edge of the old city, midway between the San Martín bridge and the Cambrón gate, it's worth seeking out for the serenity of the courtyard and for the exquisitely graceful stone carvings on the columns of the lower cloister.

Calle Reyes Católicos, 17. © **92-522-38-02.** www.sanjuandelosreyes.org. Admission 2.30€ adults; free for children 10 and under. Daily 10am–6:30pm (closes 5:30pm in winter). Bus: 2.

Museo Convento de Santo Domingo el Antiguo ★★ CHURCH   This monastery church is not the grandest religious site in town, nor does it have the most famed art works. But it does have the distinction of having lured El Greco to Toledo in 1577 with a commission for nine paintings. The rest, as they say, is history. Be sure to see El Greco's *Assumption* over the altar. It's one of the works that made observers sit up and take notice of his talent. The painter and the city proved a good match, and he spent the rest of his life in Toledo, marrying and raising a family. He is buried in the crypt beneath the church. Take the museum tour and you will be able to gaze through the ultimately unsatisfying peephole in the floor at what is purported to be his underground tomb. The museum also contains many other works of art, including some interesting carved wooden statues and painted *retablos*, but El Greco is the main reason to visit.

Plaza Santo Domingo El Antiguo, s/n. © **92-522-29-30.** Museum admission 2€. Mon–Sat 11am–1:30pm; daily 4–7pm.

Museo del Ejército ★★ MUSEUM   As you might imagine for a city that has changed hands many times over the centuries, the Alcázar, or main fortress of Toledo, was rebuilt constantly every time the city fell. The fortress last endured battle in the early months of the Spanish Civil War, when a 70-day siege and bombardment nearly destroyed it. It took more than 70 years of engineering and archaeology to completely reconstruct the historic building and add a modern extension. Given the building's symbolism during the Civil War, it also took some deft political maneuvering to open the Alcázar as Spain's military museum, the Museo del Ejército. The modern portion is devoted to changing exhibits, while the old walls contain some striking collections of Spanish military history, including what is claimed to be the personal sword of El Cid (1043–99). The Spanish armor collection is second only to that at the armory in Madrid's **Palacio Real** (p. 100), and there are some real curiosities, including objects carried by conquistadors Francisco Pizarro and Hernán Cortés, a piece of the cross that Columbus took ashore to claim the New World in the name of Spain, and a tent that sheltered Carlos V in his Tunisian campaign against the Ottoman Empire. Perhaps most stirring, though, are the exhibits on the Siege of the Alcázar, which was ended when Francisco Franco arrived from Morocco with his Army of Africa. It ensured Franco's ascendancy among the Nationalist generals.

Cuesta de Carlos V, 2, near the Plaza de Zocodover. ✆ **92-523-88-00.** www.museo.ejercito.es. Admission 5€ adults; 2.50€ seniors and students; free for children 18 and under. Thurs–Tues 11am–5pm. Closed Jan 1 and 6; May 1, 9, 24, and 25; and Dec 31. Bus: 2.

Museo del Greco ★ ART MUSEUM   This fine little museum adjacent to the old synagogue finally came into its own when Spain celebrated 2014 as the fourth centenary of El Greco's death. A remake of the shabby (and frankly inauthentic) El Greco House, it opened in 2011 with several period gardens, Mudéjar-style cave rooms, and many of El Greco's later works. The museum claims to be the only one in Spain devoted exclusively to El Greco and does an admirable job of tracing the artist's impact on his adopted city—and vice versa. Among the most notable pieces here are a set of portraits of the apostles, the *retablo* of San Bernardino, and one version of the celebrated *View and Plan of Toledo.* But the museum has wisely collected work by other Mannerist and Baroque painters that serve to place El Greco in a broader artistic and historic context.

The exterior of the Museo del Greco.

TOP OF THE pots

Paseo del Tránsito, s/n. ✆ **92-522-36-65.** http://museodelgreco.mcu.es. Admission 3€ adults; 1.50€ students; free for seniors and children 17 and under, free for all Sun and Sat after 4pm. Apr–Sept Tues–Sat 9:30am–8:30pm, Sun 10am–3pm; Oct–Mar Tues–Sat 9:30am–6:30pm, Sun 10am–3pm.

Museo de Santa Cruz ★★★ ART MUSEUM   If you want to get close to masterpieces by El Greco, make this museum your first stop. The museum is the repository for dozens, perhaps hundreds, of 16th- and 17th-century paintings that once decorated Toledo-area churches and convents. About a dozen of them are by El Greco, and the greatest of the lot is *La Asunción de la Virgen* (Assumption of the Virgin), painted 1607–13. If you stand about 18 inches from this late masterpiece, you can see how the paint flows like tiny rivers. You don't have to be religious—or even an art fan—to appreciate the electric excitement in this progenitor of "action painting."

This massive former hospital, an early architectural design by Alonso de Covarrubias, features carved and painted coffered ceilings—some in the Mudéjar style influenced by Muslim decorative arts, some in a pure Renaissance fashion. It was commissioned by Cardinal Mendoza, whom some historians credit (or blame) as the mastermind behind the political machinations of Fernando and Isabel. The museum is divided into three sections, with the ground level devoted to archaeological fragments from Roman, Visigoth, and Muslim periods in Toledo. Another portion of the museum is devoted to popular culture and traditional local crafts including ceramics, glass, and jewelry. The Carranza collection of ceramics of the Iberian peninsula is a thorough but not overwhelming survey of colorful Spanish and Portuguese tile work from the re-conquest of Valencia in 1238 through the 19th century.

The fine art galleries—which include the El Greco works—are the principal reason for visiting. Recent additions to the collection include works by Toledo-born avant-garde sculptor Alberto Sanchez (1895–1962).

Calle Miguel de Cervantes, 3. ✆ **92-522-10-36.** www.toledo-turismo.com/en/santa-cruz_70. Free admission. Mon–Sat 10am–6:30pm; Sun 10am–2pm. Bus: 5 or 6. Pass beneath the granite archway on the eastern edge of Plaza de Zocodover and walk about 1 block.

5

CASTILLA-LA MANCHA

Toledo

Inside the Museum Sefardi.

Museo Sefardí (Sephardic Museum) ★★★ MUSEUM/SYNAGOGUE
It only took 500 years after the expulsion of the Jews from Spain for this museum
to open, in an attempt to explain Judaism and Jewish history to a city where the
Jewish population was essential to the functioning of the court and the country
for centuries. Since 1992, it has blossomed into one of the most visited spots in
Toledo. The most important section is the **Sinagoga del Tránsito,** built in 1355
by Samuel Leví with a special dispensation from Pedro I. Leví had significant
influence with the king, having served Pedro as royal treasurer, among other
roles. It was the only Toledo synagogue untouched in the 1391 attacks on the
city's Jewish ghetto. The building was Christianized after 1492, so only some of
the scrollwork on the walls is original. Restorations in 1910 and 1992 filled in
most of the blanks in the original scripts, which include psalms inscribed along
the tops of the walls and a poetic description of the Temple on the east wall.
Museum display cases chronicle the Jewish communities on the Iberian peninsula from the Roman era to 1492. One gallery deals with slow changes in 19th-
century Spanish law, from the 1802 edict that allowed Jewish religious
observances to the 1869 formal retraction of Fernando and Isabel's expulsion
order. The museum fits nicely with the Museo del Greco next door and San Juan
de los Reyes across the street to make a full morning.

Calle Samuel Leví, s/n. ✆ **92-522-36-65.** http://museosefardi.mcu.es. Admission 3€ adults;
1.50€ students; free for seniors and children 17 and under; free for all after 2pm Sat and all day
Sun. Tues–Sat 9:30am–8:30pm (closes 6:30pm in winter); Sun 10am–3pm. Closed Jan 1, May 1,
June 7, Dec 24–25, and Dec 31. Bus: 2.

Museo Victorio Macho ★ ART MUSEUM   One of Spain's finest modern
sculptors, Macho fled at the outbreak of the Civil War and made his name in
Latin America. When the Franco regime began courting expatriate artists, he
moved back to Toledo in 1953 to build a home and studio on a dramatic rock
outcrop over the Río Tajo, just 150m from the Sinagoga del Tránsito. Following
his death in 1966, the beautiful site was donated to the city as a museum.

Displays include several of Macho's smaller bronzes, some bronze reliefs, and many, many drawings and sketches. The city often uses the site for small art conferences. Visit for the serene gardens and fabulous view of the river below the city walls.

Plaza Victorio Macho, 2. ℭ **92-528-42-25.** Admission 3€. Mon–Sat 10am–7pm; Sun 10am–3pm. Bus: 2.

Santo Tomé Obrador de Mazapán ★ SHOP   The nuns of Toledo began making the sugar and ground-almond confection known elsewhere as marzipan (but called *mazapán* here) in the early 13th century to preserve eggs as emergency rations. The tradition still flourishes, but the nuns face stiff competition from small commercial operations. Some of the best *mazapán* pastries come from this company, founded in 1856. Its principal shop remains in the original location near the Santo Tomé church. Unlike the convents, which sell their pastries in prepackaged boxes, Santo Tomé allows you to assemble your own assortment from the display cases—or just buy one piece for a quick shot of sugar (1.50€– 5€). The Plaza de Zocodover location is known for extravagant *mazapán* sculptures in the main display window.

Calle Santo Tomé, 3; ℭ **92-522-37-63.** Plaza de Zocodover, 7; ℭ **92-522-11-68.** www.mazapan.com.

Sinagoga de Santa María la Blanca ★ SYNAGOGUE   This small synagogue is believed to be the oldest standing European synagogue. It was built in 1203 in the Almohad style with horseshoe arches and intricately carved moldings. The style echoes La Mezquita in Córdoba, the grandest of the Iberian mosques. When it was converted to a Christian church, five naves and much of the decoration were preserved. The Catholic church maintains the building as a museum. Visitors are split on whether the spare decoration makes the synagogue seem barren or more spiritual than the later, far more elaborate Sinagoga del Tránsito a few blocks away.

Calle Reyes Católicos, 4. ℭ **92-522-72-57.** Admission 2.30€. Daily 10am–6:45pm (closes 5:45pm in winter). Bus: 2 or 12.

Marzipan, a local specialty.

Shopping

During the Crusades, the swordsmiths of Toledo were renowned for the quality of their weaponry, and a few still practice the ancient craft. (See **Mariano Zamoraño Fábrica,** above). Kitchen cutlery upholds the same high standard. One good bet for knives that will last a lifetime is **Artesanía Morales** (Plaza de Conde 3; ✆ **92-522-35-86**). Toledo was equally renowned for its *damasquinado,* or damascene work: the Moorish art of inlaying gold, copper, or silver threads against a matte black-steel backdrop. Today Toledo is filled with souvenir shops hawking damascene, much of it inferior machine-made work that can still serve as a cheap souvenir. You can find fine handmade damascene jewelry at **Damasquinados Suárez** (Circo Romano 8 (✆ **92-528-00-27**; www.espaderias-suarez.com).

Marzipan (called *mazapán* locally) is often prepared by nuns and is a local specialty. Many shops in town specialize in this treat made of sweet almond paste, although we think the best is **Santo Tomé** (see above).

The province of Toledo is also renowned for its pottery, which is sold in so many shops at competitive prices that it's not necessary to single any out. Over the years we've found that the large roadside emporiums on the outskirts of town on the main road to Madrid offer better bargains than shops within the city walls.

Entertainment & Nightlife

Come nightfall, the throngs of Toledo tourists seem to vanish, and locals seek out nightlife mainly in the modern city far from the historic attractions. In the old city, you can hear recorded music at **Bar La Abadía,** Plaza San Nicolás 3 (✆ **92-525-11-40**), the restaurant-bar where locals crowd elbow to elbow for pints of beer, glasses of wine, and access to the music of New York, Los Angeles, and London. **O'Brien's Irish Pub,** Armas 12 (✆ **92-521-26-65**), might seem more appropriate for the streets of Dublin than for old Toledo, but like Irish pubs everywhere, it attracts a young and thirsty crowd; there's live music on Thursday nights. A truly hip wine-bar hangout is the gourmet shop owned by super-chef Adolfo Muñoz, **Adolfo Collección** (above). Enjoy wine and tapas, and mingle with Toledo's finest.

CUENCA ★★★

Poised between earth and sky, this small mountaintop city is as improbable as it is beguiling. Moorish soldiers constructed it in 714 on a high limestone spur surrounded by 15-story gorges of the Júcar and Huécar rivers, which converge here. The Moors assumed that their fortification could command every strategic pass between the mountains and the plains of La Mancha. They were right—until Alfonso VIII of Castilla came marching up the hill in 1177. Only a crumbling wall and the Arco de Bezudo remain from the Muslim fortress, but the Christian conquerors shoehorned wonderful Gothic and Renaissance palaces into the medieval street plan. Under Christian rule, Cuenca filled with convents and monasteries. It has always been a place where passion and contemplation walk hand in hand, where the life of the mind meets the unlikely realities of geography.

Although the city hemorrhaged population during and after the Spanish Civil War, it never lost its dramatic appearance as a hilltop fantasy of angular vertical buildings built right to the edges of the gorges. (It is known for its dramatic *casas colgadas,* or "hanging houses," that are cantilevered over the gorges.)

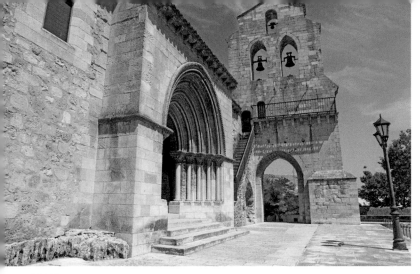

Cuenca.

The Spanish abstract artists of El Grupo Paso (formed in 1957) discovered Cuenca's abstract jumble of angles and peculiar tricks of light, and many relocated here for at least part of the year. Like their art, Cuenca is a city that is more about gesture than image, vector than target, and about finding a place where creativity can take root. The legacy of the art scene has meant more art museums per capita than any other place in central Spain. Simultaneously romantic and artistic, Cuenca became a favorite getaway for middle-class Madrileños even before high-speed rail cut the travel time to less than an hour.

Essentials

GETTING THERE   Ten high-speed RENFE AVE and ALVIA **trains** leave Madrid's Atocha railway station daily and arrive about 50 minutes later at Estación AVE Fernando Zóbel in the modern part of town at Cerro de La Estrella. The one-way high-speed fare begins at 24€. For train information, call ☎ **90-232-03-20,** or visit www.renfe.com. The local bus to the old town from the train station costs 1.20€. There are also about eight intercity **buses** from Madrid every day. Buses arrive at Calle Fermín Caballero 20 (☎ **96-922-70-87** or 96-922-11-84; www.avanzabus.com for information and schedules). A one-way fare costs 12€ to 15€. Cuenca is the junction for several highways and about a dozen lesser roads that connect it to towns within its region. From Madrid, take the N-III to Tarancón, and then take the N-400, which leads directly into Cuenca.

VISITOR INFORMATION   The city **tourist information office,** Calle Alfonso VIII, 2 (http://turismo.cuenca.es; ☎ **96-924-10-51**), is open daily 9am to 8pm. Its city map is a must for exploring.

Where to Stay

Leonor de Aquitania ★   If you are an early riser, ask for a room with a view of the Huécar River gorge so you can open the windows and take in the magnificent sunrise. This hotel occupies an 18th-century building that sits high enough on a hillside to offer views of both the old town and the jaw-dropping gorge. If you want to take it all in, splurge on the "Hebrea Hermosa" (Beautiful Jewish

Cuenca's *casas colgadas,* or hanging houses.

Maiden) suite with a private terrace. In any case, rooms feature handsome red tile floors that are cool underfoot, pale walls, traditional wooden furnishings, and colorful fabrics. They are similar in size to those at the nearby Posada de San José—large enough, but not exactly roomy. While you almost expect a prayer book next to the bed at the Posada, at the Leonor each room is equipped with a copy of *Don Quijote* (in Spanish, of course) on the bedside table.

Calle San Pedro, 60. ✆ **96-923-10-00.** www.hotelleonordeaquitania.com. 49 units. 110€–140€ double; 182€–207€ suite. Weekend lodging/dining specials available. Free parking. **Amenities:** Restaurant; bar; babysitting; room service; free Wi-Fi.

Parador de Cuenca ★★   It's hard to imagine a hotel with a more dramatic location than the Parador de Cuenca. It sits on a high rocky outcrop sandwiched between the deep gorge of the Huécar River and sheer, rocky cliffs. Yet this lodging in a 14th-century convent has an air of permanence and is the best choice in town for quiet luxury. You can even get a sense of monastic life in the church and cloister, and relax in the cafe in a former chapel. The mid-size rooms feature traditional dark wood furniture and some have views of the *casas colgadas,* right across the gorge in Cuenca's old town. The *parador* and the old town are connected by a pedestrian bridge over the gorge, making the *parador* convenient for sightseeing, despite its remove from town. If you are bothered by open heights, this might not be the best lodging choice.

Subida a San Pablo, s/n. ✆ **96-923-23-20.** www.parador.es. 63 units. 110€–194€ double; 290€–336€ suite. Parking 18€. **Amenities:** Restaurant; bar; exercise room; outdoor pool; room service; sauna; outdoor tennis court; free Wi-Fi.

Posada de San José ★★★   Antonio and Jennifer Cortinas have run this lodging in an 18th-century building since 1983, and we like the fact that they have not succumbed to the common practice of decorating the public areas in modern style. Quite the contrary; the public areas of this former boys choir school maintain a rich, ecclesiastical air, with religious frescoes on the walls and statues of saints standing in corners. The rooms are all different shapes and sizes but feature simple, plain wooden furnishings against white walls and paintings by local artists. It's impossible to imagine them any other way. If you're willing to forgo a private bathroom, you can get a double room very inexpensively, and if you're traveling with kids, a couple of these rooms that share one bath may be a good budget option. If you prefer a private bathroom, try to get one of the rooms overlooking the Huécar gorge. They have great views and enjoy cool night breezes. Should you feel the need for a large unit with separate sitting room, TV, and coffee bar, ask for room 12 or 33 (which also has an outdoor terrace). They are among the most expensive but can accommodate an extra bed.

Calle Julián Romero, 4. ✆ **96-921-13-00.** www.posadasanjose.com. 22 units (18 w/private bath). 41€–51€ double without bathroom, 75€–159€ double with bathroom. Bus: 1 or 2. **Amenities:** Restaurant; bar.

Where to Eat

Cuenca's cuisine owes as much to the mountains east of the city as to the plains of La Mancha on the west. Wild game and foraged mushrooms figure prominently, and virtually every eatery offers two Cuenca specialties: *morteruelo* (a pâté of rabbit, partridge, ham, pork liver, pine nuts, clove, and caraway), and *ajoarriero* (a creamy pâté of potato, flaked codfish, oil, and garlic). Both are usually spread on bread or toast as a starter, and one serving makes a fine appetizer for two people. Since this is sheep country, lamb appears on most menus. If you're adventurous, try the *zarajos,* or grilled lamb intestines, sometimes translated on the English menu as "lamb tripe." Chewy and richly flavored, they're usually served coiled like a ball of yarn around a grapevine shoot.

Figón del Huécar ★★ CASTILIAN   Fans of José Luis Perales must get a big kick out of dining in his former home. But even if you are not familiar with the singer-songwriter and composer, you will enjoy your meal in this venerable building where the decor is as smooth as Perales' voice and as elegant as his guitar. For summer dining, try for a table on the outdoor terrace. Inside, the most sought-after tables are those with views of the Huécar gorge, but we also enjoy dining in the book-lined library. Although the kitchen pays homage to tradition (*morteruelo, ajoarriero,* salad with pickled partridge—all available as starters), it brings modern creativity to Cuencan cuisine with dishes like a creamed squash soup with a hint of cheese and parsley-infused oil, or grilled veal sirloin with a Manchego cheese sauce. The restaurant also offers a very reasonable three-course *menu del día.* The wine bar is a good spot to taste the well-made reds now being produced in the D.O. Cuenca region. Take a hint from the staff, who all wear dark suits and ties, and dress for dinner.

Calle Julián Romero, 6. ✆ **96-920-00-62.** www.figondelhuecar.com. Reservations recommended. Main courses 18€–25€; *menu del día* 26€. Tues–Sat 12:30–4pm and 7–11pm. Bus: 1 or 2.

Mesón Casas Colgadas ★★★ CONTEMPORARY SPANISH   Practically next door to the abstract art museum, this longtime Cuenca favorite features a dining room in one of the last surviving medieval "hanging houses." In 2014, Michelin-starred chef Manuel de la Osa took over the property and transformed the traditional Castilian menu into a locavore-centered selection of seasonal dishes. The extraordinarily tender lamb tastes of the wild rosemary that the ewes browse on the hillsides. De la Osa's wine list also features the wines of this corner of Castilla, with an emphasis on powerful Tempranillo-based reds. This is a place to linger over both the food and the views of the river gorge and the surrounding hills. If you're on a budget, you can enjoy a drink and the view in the street-level tavern.

Calle Canónigos, s/n. ✆ **96-922-35-09.** www.mesoncasascolgadas.com. Reservations recommended. Main courses 18€–25€; fixed-price menus 27€–38€; tasting menu 45€. Wed–Mon 1–4pm; Wed–Sun 9–11pm. Bus: 1 or 2.

Mesón El Caserío ★★★ CASTILIAN   As your nose will tell you as you walk up the hill, this casual restaurant just outside the old Moorish gate specializes in wood-grilled meat and vegetables. You can sit indoors at the bar or in the dining room, but you might be alone, as almost everyone gravitates to the casual tables outside. If you have to wait for a table, get a drink at the bar and carry it across the street to the scenic overlook to enjoy great views of the city. None of the savory, smoky meat will put much of a dent in your budget. Beef sirloin steak or a plate of four lamb chops is about as expensive as it gets (less than 17€), and big plates of grilled asparagus that have been drizzled in olive oil are less than half that. *Zarajos* are a popular bar snack here, usually heavily dosed with black pepper and accompanied by a glass of cold beer.

Calle Larga, 25. ℂ **96-923-00-21.** Wed–Mon noon–4:30pm and 8:30pm–2am. Main courses 7€–17€. Bus: 1 or 2.

Posada de San José ★★ CASTILIAN   There's a strong local flavor to the menu at this inn dining room, and many diners start with a small plate of *zarajos* or share a bowl of *morteruelo.* If you've grown tired of organ meats and wild game, order the pork tenderloin braised with apples in cider. The most desirable tables are on the terrace surrounded by rose bushes and an olive tree, but the view of the Huécar gorge is just as impressive from the windows of the semiformal dining room. Like the rest of the property (see above), the restaurant strikes a fine balance between simple, heavy, monastic furniture and outstanding abstract graphic art by contemporary Spanish masters. The restaurant is open to the general public, not just guests of the inn, and tables fill far in advance on the weekends, so reserve early.

Calle Julián Romero, 4. ℂ **96-921-13-00.** www.posadasanjose.com. Reservations required. Tues–Sun 7:30–10:30pm. Main courses 12€–17€. Bus: 1 or 2.

Exploring Cuenca

The new city that puddles at the base of Cuenca is of limited interest to travelers apart from its bus and train stations. Plan to spend your entire time in the old town, a vertical fantasy where medieval foundations have accreted Gothic, Romanesque, and Renaissance upper stories. The sharp angles and exposure to the high-altitude sun give the physical city the look of a cubist puzzle. In fact, spending time in Cuenca feels very much like inhabiting an abstract modern painting.

Plaza Mayor ★★ LANDMARK   This square is the social center of the old city. It is flanked by the *Ayuntamiento* (City Hall) on one side and the cathedral on the other. Only local traffic is permitted in the plaza during most of the day, making it safer for walking around. Cafes spill out into the plaza at mealtimes. **Calle Alfonso VIII** heads downhill from the plaza. Painters and photographers love the faded pastel colors of the houses, many of which have medieval crests above their ancient doors. Be sure to walk (or take the bus for 0.20€) to the top of the hill by the **Arco de Bezudo** for almost unbelievably long vistas. Different but just as dramatic views can be found at the **Mirador de San Miguel,** northwest of Plaza Mayor. It overlooks the Júcar gorge and its green hillsides. Deep gorges give Cuenca an unreal quality, and eight old bridges span two rivers at the bottom to connect the medieval city with the booming new town. Assuming that you're not prone to vertigo, take the leap of faith into thin air and walk across the **Puente de San Pablo ★**, a footbridge between the old city and the *parador* that crosses a 60m (197-ft.) drop. It gives a great perspective on the *casas colgadas ★*, which are illuminated at night. In the summer, the intense heat of the day suddenly dissipates at night and the streets of Cuenca become so cool that you may want a jacket or sweater. At dusk and dawn, thousands of swallows swoop and dart in the high air of the gorges.

Catedral de Cuenca ★★ CATHEDRAL   As soon as Alfonso VIII conquered Cuenca, he commissioned this Anglo-Norman cathedral to please his homesick wife, Eleanor Plantagenet (daughter of England's Henry II and Eleanor of Aquitaine). The masons he brought from Normandy constructed it in the same style as the cathedral at Chartres, which was built at precisely the same time. Major renovations during the Renaissance have obscured the original mystical purity of form, and reconstruction after a partial collapse in the 20th century has required further alterations. But the original soaring alabaster columns are still standing, and there's not another Gothic church like it in Spain. Artistic highlights include the neoclassical altar by Ventura Rodriguez (architect of the Prado), stunning Flemish tapestries, a Gothic statue of Virgen del Sagrario that dates from around the cathedral's founding, and a number of powerful religious paintings (including a pair of El Grecos). Many of the stained-glass windows, which date from the 1990s, were designed by Cuenca's resident abstract artists.

Plaza Mayor de Pío XII. *℃* **96-922-46-26.** Free admission during Mass; other times 2.80€ adults, 2€ students and seniors. Paid admission includes audio guide and admission to museum. July–Sept Mon Fri 10am–2pm and 4–7pm, Sat 10am–7pm, Sun 10am–6:30pm; Oct–Apr daily 10:30am–2pm and 4–7pm; May–June Mon–Sat 10:30am–2pm and 4–7pm, Sun 10:30am–2pm and 5–6:30pm. Bus: 1 or 2.

Fundación Antonio Pérez ★★ ART MUSEUM   Spanish-born Antonio Pérez (b. 1934) has divided much of his life between Cuenca and Paris, but fortunately he chose Cuenca as the site of his foundation. He is usually described as a collector, editor, and artist, and we also suspect that he has a profound sense of humor. His own works fall into the category of found art and often employ common objects to make funny and surprising commentary. For example, he titled three bells without their clappers *Castrati.* Large, airy galleries carved out of a former convent of the Barefoot Carmelites display Peréz's work as well as highlights of his collection of Spanish artists (many of whom are also featured in the Saura foundation and the abstract art museum, both below) and international artists including Andy Warhol. Not surprisingly, Pérez is a big fan of pop art. Two even more extensive collections—one of found objects, the other of graphic art—belong to the Fundación Antonio Pérez but are displayed in a Renaissance palace in the town of San Clemente, 109km (68 miles) south of Cuenca. Objects from each sometimes show up in Cuenca in temporary exhibitions.

Ronda de Julian Romero, 20. *℃* **96-923-06-19.** www.dipucuenca.es/fap/fundacion.asp. 2€ adults, 1€ seniors and students. Wed–Mon 11am–2pm and 5–9pm (winter closes 8pm). Bus: 1 or 2.

Fundación Antonio Saura ★★ ART MUSEUM   Of all the artists inspired by the improbable beauty of Cuenca, Antonio Saura (1930–98) had the most personal connection to the city. He had tuberculosis as a teenager and began coming to Cuenca for his health at age 18. He became fascinated by the view from his sickbed window and it became seminal in his artistic vocabulary. This foundation was established 10 years after the death of this master Abstract Expressionist painter. It displays his work as well as that of his contemporaries, including other members of El Grupo Paso, which Saura helped found. In a late interview, Saura noted that all his life, without realizing it, he had been painting

5

Cuenca

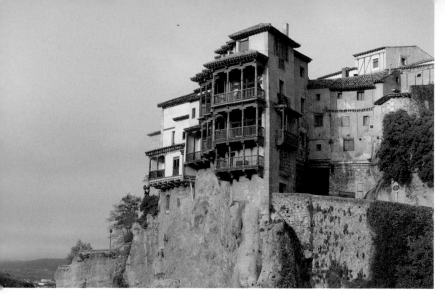

A hanging house, home to the Museo de Arte Abstracto.

"the hypnotic mask between the rocks—the blackberry eyes. The curve of the mountain looks like the mound where the head of Goya's dog emerges."
Plaza de San Nicolas, 4. ✆ **96-923-60-54.** www.fundacionantoniosaura.es. Free admission. Summer Mon and Wed–Sat 11am–2pm and 4–8pm, Sun 11am–2pm; winter daily 11am–2pm and 4–7pm. Bus: 1 or 2.

Museo de Arte Abstracto Español ★★★ ART MUSEUM   You are in for a double treat here. Cuenca's first contemporary art museum, opened in 1966, occupies the largest of the *casas colgadas* and offers a firsthand look inside one of these late Gothic engineering marvels. As if that weren't enough, it also has a vivacious collection of mid-20th-century Spanish abstract art. It's hard to know where to look first—at the details of the building, out the windows to the stomach-lurching gorge, or at the aggressive art on the walls. Studying the art that Cuenca has embraced does, in fact, demonstrate how to look beyond the picturesque to the play of angle and color. Although the museum's art represents an era of pure abstraction, it also echoes the city. Dense, knot-like black snarls on the canvases of Antonio Saura, for example, could be maps of the city's tangled alleyways. The segmented color blocks of José Guerrero resemble the painted walls of the old houses. The thrusting gestures of Fernando Zóbel (founder of the museum) mimic the verticality of the Cuenca streets. The works span a broad period in the output of the artists; while Saura's late work was purely abstract, he went through a much earlier semi-representational surrealist phase represented by a grotesque portrait of Brigitte Bardot that makes the French actress look like an escapee from Picasso's *Guernica*.
Calle los Canónigos, s/n. ✆ **96-921-29-83.** www.march.es. Admission 3€ adults; 1.50€ students and seniors. Tues–Sat 11am–2pm; Sun 11am–2:30pm; Tues–Fri 4–6pm; Sat 4–8pm. Bus: 1 or 2.

Museo de Cuenca ★ MUSEUM   A stark contrast to all the contemporary art museums in the city, this regional history museum takes a broad view, harking back to the Neolithic period with Celtic idols excavated from burials in the region. The Cuenca area was an important mining district for lead and silver, and

Iron Age exhibits show a number of Carthaginian, Greek, and Phoenician arti-facts that found their way to Cuenca through a vigorous trade with the Mediter-ranean coast. The Romans made peace with the local leaders because the mines were so important to the empire, ushering in a long period of Roman life under Ibero-Celtic leadership. Ceramics in the North African style help detail the period of Moorish dominance. Rooms devoted to the medieval period and the 14th through 16th centuries show how Cuenca emerged as a major wine and wool center.

Calle Obispo Valero, 12. ✆ **96-921-30-69.** 1.20€ adults, 0.60€ students, free Sat–Sun. Jun 15–Sept 15 Tues–Sat 10am–2pm and 5–7pm, Sun 11am–2pm; rest of year opens afternoons at 4pm.

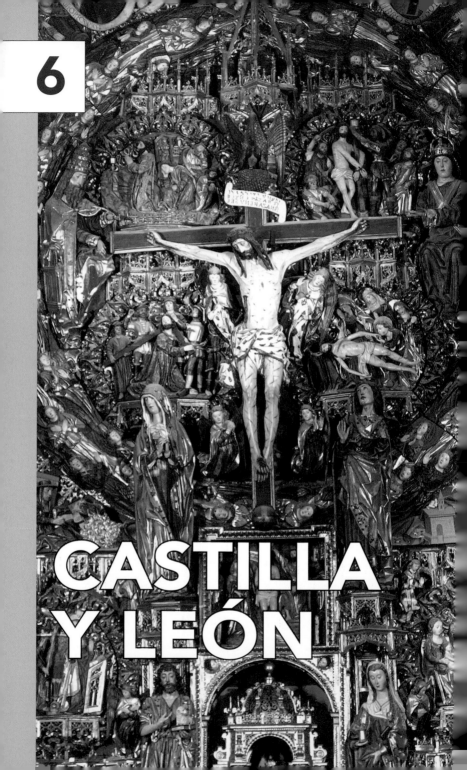

6

CASTILLA
Y LEÓN

N o part of Spain speaks so eloquently of the country's warring past as Castilla y León. Its warrior kings carried the battles of the Reconquista to the Moorish conquerors and won back the Iberian Peninsula league by bloody league. The northern pair of cities in this chapter, León and Burgos, held the grand castles from which the Christian armies marched and the great cathedrals that glorified the faith. Just south of them were the frontier fortresses in the battle between the cross and the crescent. As you approach them, imagine that you are leading an invading army. After a long march, you finally reach the outskirts of Segovia, Avila, or Zamora. You crane your neck to look up at the walled fortress city high on the hill. Its defenders have been watching your arrival for days, and their swords are ready. . . . It is the tale of central Spain written over and over—only the names of the invaders and defenders changed.

SEGOVIA ★★★

Poor Segovia! Because the city's Roman aqueduct appears on every checklist of Spanish monuments, the city often suffers from drive-by tourism. It's easy to park near the aqueduct, take a picture, maybe stop for lunch, and then move on. But Segovia is more than just a pretty face. Outside the perimeter of its old walls lie important religious communities and a mystical shrine of the Knights Templar. In the city proper, Segovia displays a monumental drama from the arches of its Roman aqueduct on one end to the fantasy castle of its Alcázar on the other. The city is built on a large rocky outcrop, resulting in narrow, winding streets that have to be covered on foot to visit the Romanesque churches, early Renaissance palaces, and medieval Judería. This ancient city is located at the heart of the castle-rich part of Castilla. Isabel herself was proclaimed queen of Castilla here in 1474.

Essentials

GETTING THERE   Seventeen **trains** leave Madrid every day. Five take more than 2 hours to reach Segovia (one-way 8.10€; from Chamartín station), but the high-speed trains (13€–24€ one way, from Atocha station) arrive in 26 to 29 minutes. The traditional rail station at Segovia is on Paseo Obispo Quesada s/n (© **90-232-03-20;** www.renfe.com), a 20-minute walk southeast of the town center. The high-speed train arrives at Segovia-Guiomar; it's served every 15 minutes by bus 11 (1€) to the aqueduct.

Buses arrive and depart from **Estacionamiento Municipal de Autobuses,** Paseo de Ezequiel González 10 (© **92-142-77-06**). It's about a 7-minute walk to the aqueduct. There are 20 to 35 buses a day to and from Madrid (which depart from Paseo de la Florida, 11; Metro: Norte), and about four a day traveling between Avila and Segovia. One-way tickets from Madrid cost 8€.

FACING PAGE: **The sculpted altar of Cartuja de Miraflores.**

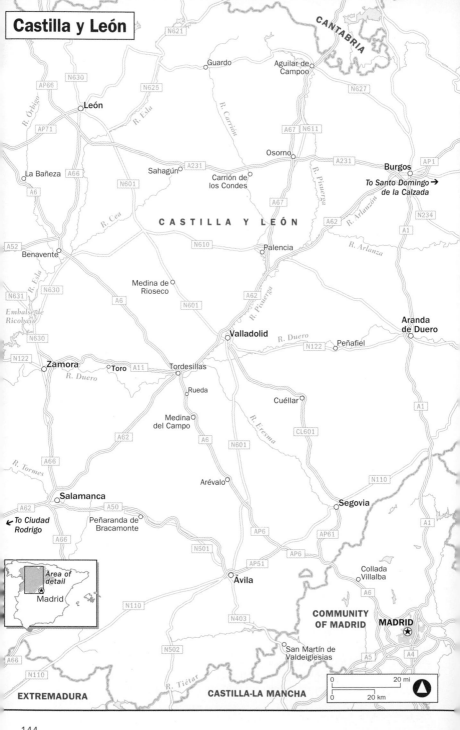

Castilla y León

CANTABRIA

N621

Guardo
Aguilar de
Campoo
N627

N630
AP66

León
N625

A67 N611

R. Orbigo
AP71

Osorno
A231
Burgos AP1

La Bañeza
A66
Sahagún
A231
To Santo Domingo →
de la Calzada

A231
Carrión de
los Condes

A6
N601

N234

A67

A1

CASTILLA Y LEÓN

A62
R. Arlanzón

A52

N610
Palencia

R. Arlanza

Benavente
R. Esla

Medina de
Rioseco
A62

N631
N630

A6
N601
R. Pisuerga

Aranda
de Duero

Embalse de
Ricobayo

Valladolid
R. Duero

N630

N122
Peñafiel

N122
Zamora
Toro
A11
Tordesillas
N122

R. Duero
Rueda

A1

Cuéllar

Medina
del Campo
R. Eresma

CL601

A62

A6
N601

N110

R. Tormes
A66

Arévalo

Salamanca
Segovia

A62
A50

A1

To Ciudad
Rodrigo
Peñaranda de
Bracamonte

AP6
AP61

A66

N501

AP51
AP6

Área of
detail
Collada
Villalba

Madrid

Ávila
A6

N110
COMMUNITY
OF MADRID
MADRID

A66
N403

N110

N502

San Martín de
Valdeiglesias
A5
A4

EXTREMADURA
R. Tiétar
CASTILLA-LA MANCHA

0   20 mi

0   20 km

If you're driving, take the N-VI (on some maps it's known as the A-6) in the direction of A Coruña, northwest from Madrid, toward León and Lugo. At the junction with Rte. 110 (signposted segovia), turn northeast (AP-61 or N-603).

VISITOR INFORMATION   The **Visitor Reception Center,** Plaza del Azoguejo 1 (© **92-146-67-20;** www.segoviaturismo.es), is open daily 10am to 8pm and offers a free city map and sightseeing advice. It's a good place to start if you arrive at the Roman aqueduct. Follow calle Juan Bravo toward Plaza Mayor where you'll find the **Tourist Information of Castilla y León,** Plaza Mayor, 10 (© **92-146-03-34;** www.turismocastillayleon.com), which is open daily from 9am to 3pm and 5 to 7pm. This regional office's city map is easier to use. If you're going to visit Avila, ask for that city's map as well.

Where to Stay

Hostería Ayala Berganza ★★★   Whether you select a room in the 15th-century former noble home or in the modern addition, you will find a feeling of ease and retreat from the modern city. This lodging does lie outside Segovia's ramparts, but is within easy walking distance to the aqueduct and the center of town. Decor varies from room to room, but all share the same approach of incorporating fine fabrics and nice details such as mini-canopies on the beds or handsome carved headboards. Most romantic is the suite in the building's tower; it has its own balcony.

Calle Carretas, 5. © **92-146-04-48.** 1 www.hosteriaayalaberganza.com. 7 units. 52€–175€ double; 165€–255€ suite. Parking 10€. **Amenities:** Restaurant; bar; free Wi-Fi.

Hostería Natura ★★   The owners of this 17th-century palace, just steps from Plaza Mayor, kept the historic exterior intact but took colorful, creative liberties with the interior. The cheerful stylishness almost makes you forget that there's no elevator. Bargain priced rooms 101, 102, and 112 are unusually large quarters furnished with two twin beds, but their airshaft windows don't open. Romantic room 103 has a high, carved-wood four-poster bed, a little private balcony, and walls sponged a deep red. Equally romantic room 114 has a salmon-tinged canopy on the wrought-iron four-poster bed. Room 111 can easily sleep up to five, making it a good bet for families. Parents get a private bath and bedroom suite with a queen-size bed and a balcony overlooking the park next door. It's connected to a narrow interior room with three twin beds lined up along the wall and a separate bath for the kids.

Calle Colón, 5 and 7. © **92-146-67-10.** www.naturadesegovia.com. 17 units. 40€–90€ double; family room 90€–105€. No parking. **Amenities:** Free Wi-Fi.

Hotel Palacio San Facundo ★★★   This hotel in a 16th-century former noble palace exudes character. Sensitive renovations have maintained its Renaissance-era grace while creating 33 unique rooms that surround the central courtyard. They all have tub-showers, glass-slab sinks on stained-wood bases, and flat-screen TVs. Headboards are either wrought iron or padded dark brown leather, with soft leather trim on the decorative pillows. On the second floor, both 202 and 204 have small balconies with a view of the plaza out front. Many third-floor rooms have even more character, with exposed pine beams on the slanting ceilings and skylights with remote-controlled shades. One especially popular room is 306, with a large bed and decor in deep aubergine tones. Sizes vary a bit, of course. Whatever room you choose, you will want to spend time in the glassed-over central courtyard with soaring columns and lots of comfortable seating.

Plaza San Facundo, 4. © **92-146-30-61.** www.hotelpalaciosanfacundo.com. 33 units. 90€–120€ double; 160€–250€ jr. suite. Parking 15€. **Amenities:** Bar; room service; free Wi-Fi.

Hotel Sercotel Infanta Isabel ★ If you like being in the thick of things, this hotel is a good option. It sits on Plaza Mayor right across from the cathedral and some rooms have balconies overlooking the square. The Infanta Isabel (1851–1931), the great-great aunt of King Juan Carlos, used to make a stopover here as she traveled to the summer palace in La Granja. She would probably still recognize the grand staircase of the otherwise updated property and would likely appreciate the combination of luxurious traditional style and modern amenities. Six triple rooms are good for families.

Plaza Mayor. © **92-146-13-00.** http://hotelinfantaisabel.com. 39 units. 55€–135€ double; 92€–177€ triple; 157€–209€ suite. Parking 15€. **Amenities:** Restaurant; bar; babysitting; room service; free Wi-Fi.

Where to Eat

Segovia is justifiably proud—some would say even possessive—of what it considers the city's great contribution to Spanish cuisine: roast suckling pig. There's even a special certification for the dish, *Marca de Garantía "Cochinillo de Segovia,"* indicating that the restaurant only uses milk-fed local pigs less than 21 days old that have been processed and cooked in accordance with a strict set of standards. Restaurants without a special oven will fry the piglet, a dish known as *cochifrito.* As if that were not enough, Segovia is also known for its local lamb, usually offered as *chuletóns de cordero,* or lamb chops, sometimes as *chuletillas de lechal,* or chops from milk-fed lambs. Two common starters on Segovia menus are *sopa castellana*—a soup usually made with a chicken broth base to which chopped ham, bread, sweet paprika, and eggs are added—and *judiones de La Granja,* a dish of white broad beans, chorizo sausage, fresh ham, and onion.

El Bernardino ★ CASTILIAN Just inside the walls of the old city, this traditional *asador* (meat roaster) has been keeping the city fed since 1939. As you look around the dining room (or around at other tables on the terrace), you'll see large wooden platters with roast piglets splayed out on top. You'll also notice that the other diners are having a festive time, scraping off big servings of super-tender pork. The restaurant gives the same wood-fired oven treatment to *cordero lechal* (milk-fed baby lamb), lamb quarters from yearlings, and whole chickens. The rest of the menu is a catalog of Castilian mountain food, from the chicken-garlic soup to the *floron* (a kind of Segovian cake) served on a puddle of crème anglaise.

Calle Cervantes, 2. © **92-146-24-77.** www.elbernardino.com. Reservations recommended. Main courses 12€–18€. Daily 1–4pm and 8–11pm.

La Fogón Sefardí Restaurante ★★ SPANISH/MIDDLE EASTERN The most formal of the dining options at the Casa Mudéjar hotel, "the Sephardic cook" takes the unusual step of incorporating many traditional Spanish Jewish dishes into the otherwise Castilian menu. So while one table might be feasting on the ubiquitous suckling pig, the next will be enjoying a sort of strudel of layers of eggplant with curried lamb and tiny baby vegetables. The kitchen also makes some rather modern dishes, including salmon tacos with a basil-cream sauce. Dessert is the classic *ponche segoviano,* a cake drenched in syrup with the layers separated by a golden custard. The entire dessert is then encased in marzipan.

Hotel Casa Mudéjar, Calle Judería Vieja, 17. © **92-146-62-50.** www.lacasamudejar.com. Main courses 7€–19€; menu del día 23€. Daily 1:30–4:30pm and 8:30–11:30pm.

José María Restaurante ★★★ CASTILIAN Ask any Segoviano where his family goes for *cochinillo,* and you'll get a big smile and a rambling reverie about

bargains **ON SEGOVIAN ROAST SPECIALTIES**

Most restaurants offer roast suckling pig as a huge plate with a lot of accompaniments and roast baby lamb only as a dish for two. But two of our favorite casual dining spots serve these Segovian specialties as *raciones*—entrée-size plates with no side dishes. We like **Restaurante la Churrería de San Lorenzo** ★ because it's in an atmospheric neighborhood outside the old city. Named for its ancient, almost crumbling church, San Lorenzo is about a 10-minute walk from the aqueduct, and La Churrería is the most popular family restaurant on the plaza. The bar looks as if it was built for a tavern scene in *Man of La Mancha*. Plaza San Lorenzo. ✆ **92-143-79-84.** Roast piglet or lamb 20€. Open daily 8am to 4pm and 8pm to midnight.

La Taurina ★, located right on Plaza Mayor, organizes each course of the meal as a stage in a bullfight—no great surprise considering the bullfight-themed tiles on the wall and the profusion of matador memorabilia. Unadorned plates of suckling pig or baby lamb are what most people order, though the full menu that adds some sides, bread, dessert, and wine is only 3€ more. On a nice night, sit outside and enjoy a view of the cathedral with your meal. Plaza Mayor, 8. ✆ **92-146-09-02.** Roast piglet or lamb 18€ to 20€. Daily noon to 5pm and 8pm to midnight.

the crackling skin and succulent meat served at this culinary landmark. Simply put, in pig-roasting circles, chef-proprietor José María Ruiz is the man. As a result, you'll pay a little more for the privilege of eating in the formal white-tablecloth interior dining room, but if you're going to "pig out," it might as well be on the best. Ruiz also excels at roast suckling lamb (*cordero lechal asado*). To the (mock) horror of Spanish dining purists used to overcooked green beans and canned artichokes, he also invents entire dishes to highlight seasonal vegetables.

Calle Cronista Lecea, 11. ✆ **92-146-11-11.** www.rtejosemaria.com. Reservations recommended. Main courses 14€–35€. Daily 1–4pm and 7–11pm.

Exploring Segovia

Segovia is shaped like a wedge of cake plopped on its side. The Roman aqueduct is at the point, while the Alcázar stands atop the thick end above all the frosting. The cathedral and Plaza Mayor are in the middle. You'll find the best shopping in the old city between the aqueduct, the cathedral, and the Alcázar. For local ceramics and souvenirs, cruise **Calle de Juan Bravo, Calle Daoiz,** and **Calle Marqués del Arco.** Thursday is market day.

Alcázar de Segovia ★★ CASTLE   There is a good reason why this fortress looks like a late-19th-century romantic ideal of a medieval castle. Most of it burned in 1862 and was rebuilt to emulate the storybook castles of 16th-century northern Europe rather than the messy fortress-castle of Spain's warrior monarchs of the 1300s. The reconstruction was carried out during shaky political times to burnish the otherwise tarnished the image of the monarchy. In effect, it's a museum of the nobler side of the Reconquista.

As you enter (from the city side), the first thing you'll spy are suits of German plate armor for knights and two for their steeds. Spanish monarchs have cultivated this chivalrous image ever since the Habsburgs came to the throne in the 1500s. The castle was a favorite residence of Castilian monarchs throughout the medieval period, and the sumptuous decoration of tapestries, tiles, and Mudéjar woodwork conjures "days of old when knights were bold."

Isabel took refuge in the original fortress in 1474 when word came that her brother Enrique IV had died. A mural in the Galley Chamber tells the rest of that story: Having mustered the support of the royal army, she marched out of the Alcázar to Segovia's Plaza Mayor to be proclaimed queen of Castilla. She also first met Fernando II of Aragón here, but wisely held onto her rights when they married.

The most dramatic room of the castle is the Hall of Monarchs, with its ceiling-level frieze in a style usually reserved for the depictions of saints. Each king or queen in the Castilian line from Pelayo (Pelagius in Latin) of Asturias, credited with starting the Reconquista in the 720s, to Juana la Loca, Isabel's mad daughter, is shown seated on a golden Gothic throne. This incredible piece of art and history was commissioned by Juana's grandson, Felipe II, to cement his lineage's claim to the Spanish crown.

Walk the battlements of this once-impregnable castle, from which its occupants hurled boiling oil onto the enemy below. Ascend the hazardous stairs of the tower, originally built by Isabel's father as a prison, for a panoramic view of Segovia.

Plaza de la Reina Victoria Eugenia. ✆ **92-146-07-59.** www.alcazardesegovia.com. Admission 5€ adults; 3€ children 6–16; free for children 5 and under; 2€ additional for tower. Apr–Sept daily 10am–7pm; Oct Sun–Thurs 10am–6pm, Fri–Sat 10am–7pm; Nov–Mar daily 10am–6pm. Bus: 3. Take Calle Vallejo, Calle de Velarde, Calle de Daoiz, or Paseo de Ronda.

Cabildo Catedral de Segovia ★ CATHEDRAL   Segovia's original Gothic cathedral was destroyed in 1520 during the short-lived uprising of the Castilian cities against the Habsburg kings. When the smoke cleared and the lords of Segovia were crushed, Carlos V ordered it rebuilt in the same style, making it Spain's last Gothic cathedral. Just to be on the safe side, he also moved it to Plaza Mayor from its old spot next to the Alcázar. Construction began in 1525, and it was finally consecrated in 1768. Even on the brightest days, the interior is gloomy, but it is worth visiting to see the swirling, gold-encrusted altar created by José de Churriguera for the Santisimo Sacramento chapel circa 1700, as well as the stained-glass windows, elaborately carved choir stalls, and 16th- and 17th-century paintings. The serene **cloisters** ★ predate the cathedral.

Plaza Catedral, Marqués del Arco, s/n. ✆ **92-146-22-05.** www.obispadodesegovia.es. Admission to cathedral, cloisters, museum, and chapel room 3€ adults; free for children 13 and under; free admission to cathedral Sun 9am–1:15pm. Daily 9:30am–6:30pm (closes 5:30 in winter).

Casa-Museo Antonio Machado ★ MUSEUM   When the great Spanish poet taught French in Segovia from 1919 to 1932, he lived in this boardinghouse. The modest structure is more a remembrance—almost a shrine—than a true museum. Documents, drawings, and other mementos try to conjure the poet, but they aren't half as evocative as the little courtyard overgrown with flowering cacti and hollyhocks gone to seed.

Calle Desamparados, 5. ✆ **92-146-03-77.** Admission 2.50€; free Wed. Guided tours Wed–Sun 11am, noon, 1pm, 4:30pm, 5:30pm, and 6:30pm. Closed Mon–Tues.

Convento de los Padres Carmelitas Descalzos ★ MONASTERY   The 16th-century mystic and theologian San Juan de la Cruz founded and personally helped build this monastery in 1586. Upon his death in 1591, his body was returned here for burial, where it still rests in the left side chapel of the convent's church. Saint John of the Cross was the confessor of Santa Teresa of Avila (see below) and one of the most significant theologians of the Counter-Reformation.

Cabildo Catedral de Segovia.

His teachings found new audiences among reform-minded Catholics in the late 20th century, and clergy in Segovia speak of him as if he was merely away for the weekend. His central axiom was that a person must empty his or her soul of "self" in order to be filled with God—a mystical tenet akin to Zen Buddhism.

Paseo de Segundo Rincón, 2. ✆ **92-143-19-61.** www.ocdcastilla.org. Admission by donation. Church daily 10am–1:30pm; Tues–Sun 4–8pm.

Iglesia de la Vera Cruz ★ CHURCH   Built in the 12th century by the Knights Templar more as a shrine than a parish church, this Romanesque edifice still resonates with the rough faith of the warrior monks who founded it. The 12-sided shape (copied from Jerusalem's Church of the Holy Sepulchre), the style of the niches, and the fragmentary wall murals all had special significance in the mystic beliefs of the crusader order that built the church to house a piece of the True Cross. Consecrated in 1246 (1208 on the Gregorian calendar), the church's very existence illustrates the strong bond between military and religious life in Segovia. The site was abandoned when the Knights Templar were disbanded by Pope Clement V in the early 14th century, but the structure was partially restored by the Knights of Malta.

Carretera de Zamarramala. ✆ **92-143-14-75.** www.ordendemalta.es. Admission 2€. Tues–Sun 10:30am–1:30pm and 3:30–7pm (closes 6pm in winter). Closed Nov.

Monasterio Santa María del Parral ★ MONASTERY   The restored "Monastery of the Grape" was established for the Jerónimos by Enrique IV, king of Castilla (1425–74) and half-brother to Isabel I. The monastery lies across the Río Eresma about a half-mile north of the city, and it's worth visiting for the exquisite carvings and paintings in the church, which is a medley of Gothic, Renaissance, and Plateresque styles. The facade was never completed, and the monastery itself was abandoned when religious orders were suppressed in 1835. Today, it's been restored and returned to the Jerónimos, Hieronymite priests, and brothers. Inside, a robed novitiate will show you the order's treasures, including a polychrome altarpiece and the alabaster tombs of the Marquis of Villena and his wife—all the work of Juan Rodríguez, also known as Juan de Segovia.

Calle del Marqués de Villena (across the Río Eresma). ✆ **92-143-12-98.** Free admission. Mon–Sat 10am–12:30pm; Sun 10–11:30am; daily 4–6:30pm. Take Ronda de Santa Lucía, cross the Río Eresma, and head down Calle del Marqués de Villena.

Museo de Arte Contemporáneo Esteban Vicente ★ ART MUSEUM
The economic crisis has hit this small museum harder than most, resulting in
hours being truncated on short notice and long gaps between exhibitions. It is
definitely worth a visit, but call ahead to make sure it is open. Spanish-born
Estéban Vicente (1903–2001) found his artistic niche as a member of the pioneering New York School of Abstract Expressionist artists, but chose to donate a
significant body of work to his home country. The collection includes oil paintings, collages, a tapestry, and a number of small sculptures. To house and display
the collection, the mid-15th-century palace of Enrique IV of Castilla y León
(Isabel I's older half-brother) was converted to a white-walled, unadorned, contemporary gallery space. The museum tries to further the spirit of artistic inquiry
that characterized the first generation of Abstract Expressionism through temporary exhibitions, which often focus on video.

Plazuela de las Bellas Artes. ✆ **92-146-20-10.** www.museoestebanvicente.es. Admission 3€
adults, 1.50€ seniors and students, free for children 11 and under; free for all Thurs. Tues–Fri
11am–2pm; Tues–Wed 4–7pm; Thurs–Fri 4–8pm; Sat–Sun 11am–8pm.

Museo Zuloaga ★★ ART MUSEUM   This fascinating little museum occupies the medieval Iglesia San Juan de los Caballeros, where ceramic artist Daniel
Zuloaga based his family pottery studio starting in 1908. The firm made many of
the scenic tiles that decorate the building facades all over Spain, and museum
exhibits elucidate the entire artistic process, with an emphasis on the Zuloaga
family's masterful painting. Other exhibits highlight the history of the church
(parts of it date from the 6th century A.D., making it one of the oldest Christian
sites in Spain).

Plaza de Colmenares. ✆ **92-146-33-48.** Admission 1.20€ adults, free for seniors and students;
free to all Sat–Sun. July–Sept daily 10am–2pm and Tues–Sat 5–8pm; Oct–June daily 10am–2pm
and Tues–Sat 4–7pm.

Segovia's Roman Aqueduct.

Roman Aqueduct (Acueducto Romano) ★★★ ARCHITECTURE
Roughly 2,100 years ago, Roman engineers constructed this architectural marvel—a 15km (9⅓-mile) conduit to bring water from the Guadarrama mountains
to Segovia. The graceful feat of engineering remains as impressive as it was in the
age of the Caesars. While much of the original aqueduct was a ground-level canal,
the concluding segments arch high over the city and then continue underground
all the way to the Alcázar. The entire structure was built of granite blocks without
mortar. Following restorations in the 15th and 16th centuries, it continued to supply the city's water into the late 19th century. The highest of the 166 arches is 28m
(92 ft.), and seems even higher when you stand under it and look up.
Plaza del Azoguejo.

AVILA ★★

A UNESCO World Heritage Site, the ancient city of Avila draws pilgrims for its
physical wonders—most notably the well-preserved 11th-century walls and battlements—and for its spiritual history. It was home base of dynamic mystic
reformer Santa Teresa, co-founder (with San Juan de la Cruz; see p. 148) of the
Carmelitas Descalzos (Barefoot Carmelites). She was born here in 1515, entered
the Carmelites at 19, and began her reform of the order at age 45. Both a prolific
writer and a brilliant organizer, Santa Teresa became the practical and political
mover of the Spanish Counter-Reformation, while her compatriot San Juan de la
Cruz tended to the inner spiritual life of the reform movement. Several sites associated with Santa Teresa remain in Avila, and the pious visit them as a pilgrimage.
If you are coming to Avila to see the walls, make it a day trip. If you want to delve
into the religious history, plan on staying the night.

Essentials

GETTING THERE More than two dozen **trains** leave daily from Madrid for Avila,
about a 1½- to 2-hour trip each way. Trains depart from Madrid's Chamartín station. Tickets cost from about 9€ to 12€. The Avila station is at Avenida José Antonio (📞 **90-232-03-20;** www.renfe.com), 1.6km (1 mile) east of the old city.
You'll find taxis lined up in front of Avila's railway station and at the more central
Plaza Santa Teresa. For taxi information, call 📞 **92-035-35-45.**

    Buses leave Madrid daily from Estación Sur de Autobuses at Calle Méndez
Alvaro. In Avila, the bus terminal (📞 **90-202-00-52;** www.avanzabus.com) is at
the corner of avenidas Madrid and Portugal, northeast of the town center. One-
way tickets from Madrid are 11€.

    To drive here, exit Madrid at its northwest perimeter and head northwest on
Highway N-VI (A-6) toward A Coruña, eventually forking southwest to Avila.
Driving time is around 1¼ hours.

VISITOR INFORMATION The **tourist information office,** Av. Madrid 39
(📞 **92-022-59-69;** www.avilaturismo.com), is open daily 9am to 2pm and 5 to
8pm. July to September it's open Monday to Thursday 9am to 8pm, and Friday
and Saturday 9am to 9pm.

Where to Stay

Avila attracts many religious pilgrims, but the hotels are few. Book ahead, especially for July and August, when Spaniards make their pilgrimages and the searing
heat means you will certainly want air-conditioning.

Avila's well-preserved 11th-century city walls.

Hotel El Rastro ★ The folks who run this hotel seem to have all the lodging (and most of the dining) bases covered in and near Avila. The hotel is a charming but modern adaptation of an old building that's part of the city walls. Exposed walls of brick and stone and floors covered in large tiles in the public areas create an air of antiquity. Bedrooms, however, have been modernized with plastered walls, wooden floors, and small tiled bathrooms with porcelain fixtures. If the hotel is full, the nearby Mesón del Rastro (below) has another 10 very modest rooms over the restaurant. And if *that* isn't adequate, they'll offer you a house in the countryside. Personally, we'd stick with the hotel for price, comfort, and convenience.

Calle Cepedes, s/n. ☎ **92-021-12-18.** www.elrastroavila.com. 19 units. 47€–65€ double. Free parking. **Amenities:** Restaurant; bar; free Wi-Fi.

Hotel Palacio de Los Velada ★★★ With a tiled floor and graceful arched colonnades, the central courtyard of this hotel is one of the most lovely in the city. The 16th-century palace-turned-hotel is located near the cathedral and makes an ideal base for exploring the city. Everything is so close that you can easily return to enjoy one of the comfortable sofas in the courtyard whenever you feel like taking a break. The guest rooms circle the courtyard and mix comfort with a sense of formality that suits the setting. Many rooms feature unique architectural details such as slanting wooden ceilings or big windows framed by stone arches.

Plaza de la Catedral, 10. ☎ **92-025-51-00.** www.veladahoteles.com. 145 units. 60€–112€ double. Parking 17€. **Amenities:** Restaurant; bar; room service; free Wi-Fi.

Parador Raimundo de Borgoña ★★ Located just inside the city walls 2 blocks northwest of Plaza de la Victoria, this hotel can be hard to find. But once you're settled, it makes a good base for exploring the city. Like most properties in rambling historic buildings it features wonderful public spaces, including a lovely central courtyard and a formal garden with some archaeological remnants. Some of the nicest rooms look out on the garden. They all have traditional furnishings that can sometimes seem more dated than evocative of a historic past.

Marqués de Camales de Chozas, 2. ☎ **92-021-13-40.** www.parador.es. 61 units. 140€–264€ double; 315€–340€ suite. Garage 15€; free outside parking. **Amenities:** Restaurant; bar; room service; free Wi-Fi.

Where to Eat

Avila is famous throughout Spain for the quality of its veal ribeye steaks, known as *chuletón de Avila*. The cuisine here is otherwise rather typical Castilian—red meat, dark sauces, wild game, and the potent red wines of the region. Rarely do you need a reservation for dinner—except on Friday and Saturday nights and midday Sunday.

Chocolate ★★ CASTILIAN   You don't need to spend a lot to enjoy a splendid *chuletón de Avila* at this stylish bar-restaurant with foodie aspirations. The steak (about a half-kilo, or 1 lb.) literally hangs over the edge of the plate and comes with roasted red peppers and oven-fried potatoes. Located in a quiet plaza outside the walls, Chocolate seems to have taken its decor from a candy box: dark brown walls, brown banquettes, chocolate brown napkins on the red plastic tables, and Philippe Starck red acrylic chairs. (There are even red "crystal" plastic chandeliers.) Chocolate's other house specialty is a massive hamburger.

Plaza de Nalvillos, 1. ✆ **92-021-16-79.** Main courses 9€–15€. Daily 11am–4pm and 8:30–11:30pm. Cash only.

Las Cancelas ★★ CASTILIAN   The best part of this venerable lodging is the terrific, if slightly expensive restaurant that occupies its central courtyard. The heavy wooden tables are set casually with paper covers for the midday meal, but the restaurant turns romantic at night when candles flicker on linen table settings on the patio surrounded by stone columns. Specialties of the house all issue from the wood-fired oven and include the crusty loaves of hearth breads as well as leg or shoulder of lamb, the inescapable roast suckling pig, or the classic veal chops of Avila (*chuletón de Avila*). It's a popular spot with well-heeled locals, and you'll find the wines of the nearby Castilian countryside to be very good.

Hotel Las Cancelas, Calle Cruz Viejo, 6. ✆ **92-021-22-49.** www.lascancelas.com. Main courses 14€–24€. Daily 1:30–4pm and 8:30–11pm.

Mesón del Rastro ★ CASTILIAN   The inn run by the Hotel El Rastro crew (see above) is a more rustic affair than the hotel, and it's very popular with tourists from other parts of Spain who know good if greasy roast meats when they encounter them. The suckling pig almost goes without mentioning, but the real focus here is on many different roasted preparations of lamb, veal roasts, and—one dish done on top of the stove—pan-fried sweetbreads.

Plaza del Rastro 1. ✆ **92-021-12-18.** www.elrastroavila.com. Main courses 9€–24€; fixed-price menu 26€. Daily 1–4pm and 9–11pm.

El Molino de la Losa ★★ CASTILIAN   Outside the walls and across the river, this 15th-century mill converted to a restaurant has a large dining room that retains its rustic origins—a wooden ceiling, wrought-iron chandeliers—as well as a smaller, modern dining room with a nice view of the Río Adaja and its old bridge. While the kitchen does its part to keep up the image of Avila as carnivore heaven (oven-roasted lamb, baby pig, veal, and duck), the chefs also clearly love vegetables and present them with care and panache. The selection of grilled seasonal vegetables is an excellent option for vegetarians.

Bajada de la Losa, 12. ✆ **92-021-11-01.** www.elmolinodelalosa.com. Main courses 13€–32€. Tues–Sun 1:30–4pm and 9–11pm.

Exploring Avila

A Cubist jumble of Gothic convents and palaces slumping down the top of a hill, entirely surrounded by imposing, castellated stone walls, Avila is the perfect stage set of a Castilian city. It seems a unified whole, making a stronger impression than its individual parts. No visitor can—or should—miss the Murallas, or walls. After that, let your heart and devotion dictate which of the holy spots to visit.

Basílica de San Vicente ★★★ CHURCH   One of Spain's finest Romanesque churches, this faded sandstone basilica with a huge nave and three apses stands outside the medieval ramparts—a defiant Christian structure built to claim the high ground in the name of the cross. Its fiercely moralistic carvings, especially on the cornice of the southern portal, play out the struggle between good and evil. The **western portal ★★**, dating from the 13th century, has the best Romanesque bas-reliefs. Inside is the tomb of San Vincente, martyred here in the 4th century. The tomb's medieval carvings, which depict his torture and martyrdom, are fascinating, if disturbing and revealing of medieval Spanish institutional anti-Semitism. The story casts "a rich Jew" as the villain, and hastens to note that he was saved by repenting, converting to Christianity, and building this church.

Plaza de San Vicente. 🕐 **92-025-52-30.** Admission 1.60€. Daily 10am–1:30pm and 4–6:30pm.

Carmelitas Descalzas de San José (Barefoot Carmelites of St. Joseph) ★ CONVENT   Also known as the Convento de las Madres (Convent of the Mothers), this is the first convent founded by Santa Teresa in 1562 when she began her reform of the Carmelite order. There are two churches: a primitive one, where the first Carmelite nuns took the habit; and one built by Francisco de Mora, architect for Felipe III, after the saint's death. The convent's peculiar little museum, consisting of several rooms behind plate glass, holds personal artifacts of Santa Teresa, including her collarbone and the saddle on which she rode

The Basilica de San Vicente.

around Spain founding convents. One room re-creates her original cell at the convent, including a narrow bed with a log pillow. In the tiny convent church, you might hear the disembodied voices of the cloistered nuns as they sing their prayers.

Calle de las Madres, 4. ✆ **92-022-21-27.** www.sanjosedeavila.es. Admission to museum 1.50€. Apr–Oct daily 10am–1:30pm and 4–7pm; Nov–Mar daily 10am–1:30pm and 3–6pm. From Plaza de Santa Teresa and its nearby Church of San Pedro, follow Calle del Duque de Alba for about 2 blocks.

Catedral del Salvador ★★ CATHEDRAL

Built into the old ramparts of Avila, this cold, austere cathedral and fortress (begun in 1099 under Alfonso VI) bridges the gap between the Romanesque and the Gothic and, as such, enjoys a certain distinction in Spanish architecture. One local writer compared it to a granite mountain. So heavy is the fortified church that a veritable forest of columns in the local mottled red and white stone supports it from within, obscuring many sight lines. Nine hundred years of entombments have filled every nook and cranny of the voluminous cathedral. Dutch artist Cornelius designed the seats of the choir stalls in the Renaissance style. Behind the main chapel is Vasco de Zarza's masterpiece: the beautifully sculpted tomb of Bishop Alonso de Madrigal—nicknamed "El Tostado" ("the toasted one") for his dark complexion. A prominent theologian of his day, he was the powerful bishop of Avila from 1449 to 1455. A side altar, naturally enough, honors local celebrity Santa Teresa. Be sure to stop in the Capilla del Cardenal to marvel at the polychrome wooden statues of saints created by anonymous artists in the 12th and 13th centuries.

Plaza de la Catedral. ✆ **92-021-16-41.** Admission 4€ adults, free for children 9 and under. Apr–Oct Mon–Fri 10am–6pm, Sat 10am–7pm, Sun noon–5pm; Nov–Mar Mon–Fri 10am–5pm, Sat 10am–6pm, Sun noon–5pm.

Murallas de Avila (Walls of Avila) ★★★ ARCHITECTURE

Avila's defensive walls are among the best preserved in Europe. They were begun in 1190 on orders of Alfonso VI as part of the re-conquest of Spain. Since the builders used the foundations of an earlier Roman fortification, they were able to complete the brown-granite construction in 1199, although embellishments continued into the 14th century. Averaging 10m (33 ft.) in height, the walls have 88 semicircular towers and more than 2,300 battlements. Of the nine gateways, the two most famous are the San Vicente and the Alcázar, both on the eastern side. In many respects, the walls are best viewed from the west. You can hire a taxi to drive alongside the walls' entire length of 2km (1¼ miles). Better yet, you can walk the ramparts, looking eye to eye with storks nesting on rooftops and chimneys. Be aware that there are many rough stone steps and some tricky footing, and despite railings, some fully exposed heights. The views are unsurpassed, and it's easy to imagine that the fortifications awed attacking armies.

Carnicerías, Alcázar, or Ronda Vieja gates. ✆ **92-025-50-88.** http://muralladeavila.com. Admission 5€ adults; 3.50€ seniors and students. Daily 10am–8pm (closes 6pm in winter).

Museo Teresiano ★★ MUSEUM

Located below the Convento de Santa Teresa, which was built on the site of her childhood home, this scholarly museum preserves the garden where Teresa recalled her childhood joy at playing with her siblings. Among the museum's more striking artifacts are painted portraits of Teresa by artists who were her contemporaries, as well as letters between Santa Teresa (strong and forceful penmanship!) and San Juan de la Cruz (a more meticulous but rather florid hand). The museum does a good job of placing Teresa in the context of 16th-century Roman Catholicism, and then tracing the influence of her thought down to the present day.

Calle La Dama, s/n. *©* **92-021-10-30** or 92-022-07-08. Admission 2€. Museum Nov–Mar daily 10am–1:30pm and 3:30–5:30pm; Apr–Oct closed Mon.

SALAMANCA ★★★

When the sun is low in the sky, the sandstone cathedrals, convents, and university buildings of Salamanca take on a luminous golden glow. The soft stone lends itself to carving, and virtually every civic structure in the city has been gloriously embellished with flora and fauna, and fables to instruct the illiterate. Only the remnants of a Roman wall suggest historic fortifications—as a university city since 1218, Salamanca has tended to fortify itself with wit and arm itself with wisdom. Instead of archers' battlements or rusted cannons, look for the good-luck frog on the university portal, narrative reliefs of Bible stories on the churches, and sudden surprises of angels or gargoyles overhead.

The University of Salamanca attracts scholars and students from all over the world—including a large contingent of Americans in summer—and their inquiring minds also go out to play, ensuring a lively nightlife. Although greater Salamanca's population exceeds 180,000, the compact old city retains a charming provincial aura. Most attractions are within walking distance of Plaza Mayor, so the best way to explore Salamanca is on foot.

GETTING THERE   Seven **trains** travel directly from Madrid's North station to Salamanca daily (trip time: 2¾ hr.), arriving northeast of the town center on Plaza de la Estación de Ferrocarril (*©* **90-232-03-20;** www.renfe.com). The fare is 24€. More frequent are rail connections between Salamanca and the cities of Avila, Ciudad Rodrigo, and Valladolid (around 6 trains each per day). There is also frequent daily **bus** service from Madrid (trip time: 2½–3 hr.). The fare is 16€ to 23€. Salamanca's bus terminal is at Av. Filiberto Villalobos, 71 (*©* **92-322-60-79**), northwest of the town center. If you're driving from Madrid, take the N-VI northwest, forking off to Salamanca on the N-501.

VISITOR INFORMATION   The **Oficina Municipal de Turismo de Salamanca,** Plaza Mayor, 32 (*©* **92-327-83-42;** www.salamanca.es), is open July to mid-September Monday to Friday 9am to 2pm and 4:30 to 8pm, Saturday 10am to 8pm, and Sunday 10am to 2pm; mid-September to June Monday to Friday 9am to 2pm and 4 to 6:30pm, Saturday 10am to 6:30pm, and Sunday 10am to 2pm. The regional **Oficina de Información Turística de Castilla y León,** Rúa Mayor at Casa de las Conchas (*©* **92-336-85-71;** www.turismocastillayleon), is open mid–September to June daily 9am to 2pm and 5 to 8pm; July to mid-September Sunday to Thursday 9am to 8pm, Friday and Saturday 9am to 7pm.

Where to Stay

You'll want to stay within the old city to avoid a long walk from a hotel on the outskirts. Besides the usual ultra-high seasons of Christmas and Easter, Salamanca hotels also command a premium from late September through October during a succession of festivals and annual conferences.

Abba Fonseca Hotel ★★   Adjoining a classic 17th-century university college, this modern hotel hides inside a massive golden sandstone facade that makes it appear that it's been part of the university campus for centuries. The immediate neighborhood consists of graduate colleges, making on-street parking easy, and the grad-school and scholarly conference clientele guarantee a truly

Salamanca's Plaza Mayor.

usable desk, plenty of outlets to plug in your gear, and Internet that lives up to its high-speed billing. The beds are some of the best we've encountered in Spain, and the hotel is only a short walk to the cathedrals, yet sufficiently removed from the main student areas that it's extremely quiet at night.

Plaza San Blas, 2. ℂ **92-301-10-10.** www. abbahotels.com. 86 units. 65€–110€ double; 110€–200€ suite. **Amenities:** Restaurant; bar; babysitting; fitness center; sauna; room service; free Wi-Fi.

Apartahotel Toboso ★

Bargain-hunters and families rejoice at finding this apartment hotel in the heart of the city near the Plaza Mayor. The furnishings are clean and modern, but hardly stylish. The space, however, is hard to beat. In addition to 23 double rooms, the Toboso has seven apartments—four with two bedrooms that sleep three, and three with three bedrooms that can sleep up to five. The apartments also have kitchens with full-sized stoves and refrigerators, and washing machines. The bathrooms are shiny and new, if a little gaudy with all that red marble. There are two possible drawbacks. Some rooms are over a cabaret/music bar—ask for digs overlooking the quiet interior courtyard instead. Secondly, there is no air-conditioning. The thick stone walls keep it fairly cool even in the summer, but it's not for travelers who can't sleep in a room that isn't chilly.

Calle Clavel, 7. ℂ **92-327-14-62.** www.hoteltoboso.com. 30 units. 45€ double; 70€ 2-bedroom suite, 100€ 3-bedroom suite. **Amenities:** Bar-cafeteria; free Wi-Fi.

Microtel Placentinos ★★

Aptly named—with just nine rooms it really is a micro-hotel—Placentinos is a marvel of design and interior decorating. There are three single rooms and six doubles in this tiny 16th-century building amid the looming blocks of the old university. Most rooms have at least one wall of exposed stone. Comfortable but contemporary furniture may strike a muted palette, but the simple rooms are anything but spartan. Bathrooms in the doubles have whirlpool tubs and some even have a sauna shower. The location is spectacular—steps from the cathedrals.

Calle Placentinos, 9. ℂ **92-328-15-31.** www.microtelplacentinos.com. 57€–100€ single; 73€–122€ double. **Amenities:** Jacuzzi on terrace; high-speed Internet.

Room Mate Vega ★★

All the boutique hotels in the Room Mate group are design-centric, and this one picks up the city's muted sand tones, contrasting them with graphic bed covers and gigantic color photos in the rooms. Vega is located near the city's fresh-food market and about a 90-second walk from Plaza Mayor, making the location extremely convenient for sightseeing. The building is a quirky one, so rooms are all a little different in size and configuration. Most are doubles with two full beds, sometimes pushed together to look like a king. If you opt for an executive room, you get more room to spread out, sometimes with a reading nook, other times with a small balcony. All rooms share the rooftop

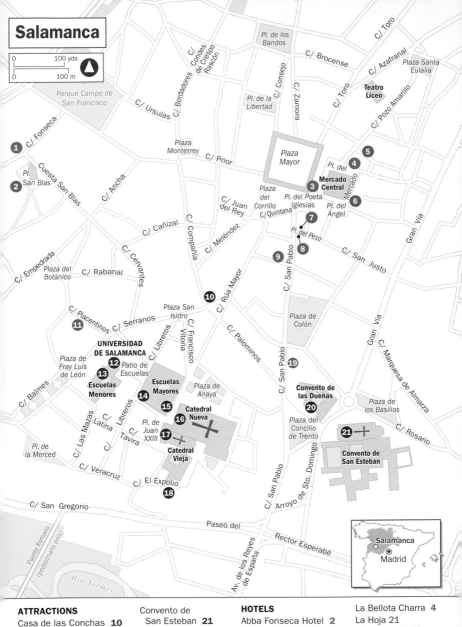

Salamanca

0 — 100 yds
0 — 100 m

Parque Campo de San Francisco

C/ Fonseca
Pl. San Blas
Cuesta San Blas
C/ Empedrada
Plaza del Botánico
C/ Rabanal
C/ Cervantes
C/ Ancha
C/ Ursulas
C/ Bordadores
C/ Condes de Crespo Rascón
Plaza Monterrey
C/ Prior
Pl. de la Libertad
Pl. de los Bandos
C/ Brocense
C/ Consejo
C/ Zamora
C/ Toro
C/ Toro
C/ Azafranal
Plaza Santa Eulalia
Teatro Liceo
C/ Pozo Amarillo
Plaza Mayor
Pl. del Mercado
Mercado Central
Plaza del Corrillo
Pl. del Poeta Iglesias
C/Quintana
Pl. del Ángel
Pl. del Peso
C/ Juan del Rey
C/ Cañizal
C/ Compañía
C/ Meléndez
C/ San Pablo
C/ San Justo
Gran Vía
C/ Placentinos
C/ Serranos
Plaza San Isidro
C/ Libreros
C/ Francisco Vitoria
C/ Rúa Mayor
C/ Palominos
Plaza de Colón
C/ San Pablo
Gran Vía
C/ Marquesa de Almarza
UNIVERSIDAD DE SALAMANCA
Plaza de Fray Luís de León
Patio de Escuelas
Escuelas Menores
Escuelas Mayores
Plaza de Anaya
Catedral Nueva
Pl. de Juan XXIII
Catedral Vieja
C/ Balmes
C/ Las Mazas
C/ Latina
C/ Libreros
C/ Tavira
C/ Veracruz
C/ El Expolio
Pl. de la Merced
C/ San Gregorio
Convento de las Dueñas
Plaza del Concilio de Trento
Plaza de los Basilios
C/ Rosario
Convento de San Esteban
Puente Romano (pedestrians only)
Río Tormes
Paseo del Rector Esperabé
C/ Arroyo de Sto. Domingo
C/ San Pablo
Av. de los Reyes de España

Salamanca
Madrid

ATTRACTIONS

Casa de las Conchas **10**
Casa Museo Unamuno **14**
Catedral Nueva
  de Salamanca **16**
Catedral Vieja **17**
Cielo de Salamanca **13**
Convento de
  las Dueñas **20**
Convento de
  San Esteban **21**
Mercatus **15**
Museo de Art Nouveau
  y Art Déco **18**
Universidad de
  Salamanca **12**

HOTELS

Abba Fonseca Hotel **2**
Aparthotel El Toboso **5**
Microtel Placentinos **11**
Room Mate Vega **6**

RESTAURANTS

Casa Paca **8**
Cepas Viejas **9**
La Bellota Charra **4**
La Hoja 21
  Restaurant **19**
Mesón Cervantes **3**
Restaurante
  Fonseca **1**
Río de la Plata **7**

terrace. There are some tiny singles here, but not Room 003 on the ground level, which has a tiled terrace almost as big as the rest of the room.

Plaza del Mercado, 16. ℂ **92-327-22-50.** www.room-matehotels.com. 38 units. 36€–80€ single; 40€–86€ double; 110€–182€ executive. **Amenities:** Bar; room service; free Wi-Fi; free business center.

Where to Eat

Although Salamancan cuisine is similar to Segovia and Avila, the university city does have a few distinctive specialties: the thinly sliced dry mountain ham from Guijuelo; a spicy, crumbly sausage called *farinato* that is more bread crumbs than meat; and a pastry stuffed with cheese, sausage, and ham, called *hornazo*. Students traditionally feasted on these meat pies during Easter week to celebrate the return of prostitutes to the city after Lent, but the dish is now available year-round and is no longer consumed only by young men with raging hormones. Tourist restaurants along **Rúa Mayor** offer acceptable if uninspired meals at slightly inflated prices, and the restaurants lining **Plaza Mayor** attract tourists and locals alike. To join Salamantinos in a more tranquil setting, walk up to **Paseo Carmelitas** between calle La Fuente and Puerta de Zamora. The leafy green park that lines the street is full of terraces that are popular for afternoon snacks.

La Bellota Charra ★★ CASTILIAN   About as casual and local as restaurants get in Salamanca, this dining room that specializes in sausages is located next door to a sausage maker and across the street from the city fresh market. It's very basic—pale wooden tables and chairs, a tile floor, fluorescent lights—but the food is good and it's cheap. In addition to various sausage plates, you can order a whole meal of meat pâtés and vegetable terrines for a relative song. Beer is always a good choice, but the restaurant stocks some excellent and inexpensive red wines from the nearby Arribes del Duero region, which recently received D.O. (Denominación de Origen) status. Like wines all up and down the river, they are made primarily from the Tempranillo grape.

Plaza del Mercado, 8–10. ℂ **92-321-96-57.** Plates 7€–11€. Daily 1:30–4pm and 8–11:30pm.

Casa Paca ★★ CASTILIAN   The classic choice among Salamantino restaurants, Casa Paca has been serving its meat-heavy menu since 1928. Ancient dishes like *alubias* (white beans stewed with pig's tails and ears) and *cocido* (a meat stew of all the trimmings from several kinds of animals) are on the menu, but diners making a night of it tend to ask for meats *a la brasa volcánica*, or cooked on the wood-fired grill. Favorites include suckling pig, thick beef steaks, and racks of baby goat chops. The atmospheric dining room with alternating wood-paneled and ancient stone walls is a real throwback to old Castilla. Honestly, we find it all a little overwhelming and usually opt to eat and drink on the bar side, where some of the most generous tapas in central Spain are provided "free" with drinks. (Beer and wine go up to 3.50€–5€ at meal times.) There's an array of tapas displayed—slices of *tortilla Española, farinato* sausage with scrambled eggs, pig's ears in tomato sauce (*orillas*), pastry squares filled with goat cheese and quince jam, small casseroles of meatballs, cod-stuffed red peppers, potato salad. Just ask (or point) when you order your drink.

Plaza del Peso, 10. ℂ **92-321-89-93.** www.casapaca.com. Main courses 20€–27€. Daily 2–4:30pm and 9–11:30pm. Bar daily 11am–midnight.

chilling **ON PLAZA MAYOR**

On hot summer nights, you'll find as many people eating ice cream as dining on Plaza Mayor. If you want a cone, join the line outside **Café Novelty** (Plaza Mayor, 2; ✆ **92-321-49-56;** daily 8am–midnight). During colder months, an artsy crowd convenes in the Art Nouveau interior, and you might want to go in just to have a look. Local specialty cold drinks can be just as refreshing, and we like the plaza tables of **Cafetería Las Torres** (Plaza Mayor, 26; ✆ **92-321-44-70;** daily 8am–midnight) for sipping *leche helada* (a smooth concoction with hints of vanilla, cinnamon, and citrus rimmed with whipped cream) or *blanco y negro* (vanilla ice cream melting in a double shot of espresso).

Cepas Viejas ★ CONTEMPORARY SPANISH   Originally a design-centric wine bar with a good and somewhat innovative tapas menu (sliced pickled octopus, small fried sausages, breast of dove, or tuna topped with roasted red pepper), Cepas Viejas has expanded its interior dining room to offer a chef-driven creative cuisine built around oven-roasted meats and fish. The restaurant's motto translates as "when the barrel is empty, the heart has no joy." Not surprisingly, it boasts one of the most extensive wine lists in the city.

Calle Felipe Espino, 6. ✆ **92-326-23-36.** Tapas 2€–3€, main courses 14€–22€. Daily 1–4pm and 8:30pm–midnight.

La Hoja 21 ★★ CONTEMPORARY SPANISH   One of the things we love about the menu at La Hoja 21 is the chef's penchant for cooking with fresh vegetables. Maybe that's because the establishment is just steps from the city's farmer's market. The tasting menu changes only in the seasonal ingredients, but almost always features mushroom risotto with fresh veggies and braised cheeks of the local heritage beef called Morucha. You can also expect crab crepes and little pasta purses filled with cheese, shrimp, and minced vegetables. One of the regional specialties here is roasted leg of mutton with potato cakes.

Calle San Pablo, 21. ✆ **92-326-40-28.** www.lahoja21.com. Reservations recommended. Main courses 15€–20€; tasting menu 33€. Tues–Sun 2–4:30pm; Tues–Sat 9–11:30pm.

Méson Cervantes ★ CASTILIAN   Combination plates are the mainstay of dining on Plaza Mayor, and this venerable restaurant offers some of the best prices as well as some of the best food. For about 10€, you can get a small steak with two fried eggs and fried potatoes, while lamb chops with lettuce, tomato, and fries might set you back a few euros more. It's one of the few spots serving generous vegetarian plates—our favorite includes white asparagus, green beans, peas, lettuce, tomato, marinated artichokes, and steamed squash. The darkly atmospheric upstairs bar (the restaurant has no plaza-level dining room) is jammed at midday with locals drinking beer and eating such plates as rice-filled blood sausage with red peppers or scrambled eggs and *farinato* drizzled with honey.

Plaza Mayor, 15. ✆ **92-321-72-13.** www.mesoncervantes.com. Combination plates 10€–17€; main dishes 15€–22€. Daily 10am–midnight or later.

Restaurante Fonseca ★★★ SPANISH   Every major college town has a restaurant where faculty and staff take guests for inexpensive meals in a fancy setting. In Salamanca, it's this beauty in the formal 16th-century courtyard of the

Colegio Arzobispo. The tables are set in pristine white linens, and you'll be dining with dons and university administrators. The *menu del día* is clearly subsidized, offering a choice of two first plates (typically a salad or a rice dish) and two second plates (sole or chicken, for example), along with wine, bread, and a pastry.

Plaza Fonseca, 4. © **92-326-02-70.** www.restaurantefonseca.com. Main dishes 10€–24€; *menu del día* 11€–13€; menu degustación 33€. Daily 1:30–4pm and 9–11:30pm.

Río de la Plata ★ CASTILIAN   Rafael and Josefa Andrés Lorenzo opened this basement restaurant in 1958, naming it for Josefa's native Argentina. It became a favorite hangout for the bullfight crowd and those ubiquitous Americans, Ernest Hemingway and Orson Welles. It remains a popular dining room for an artsy university crowd as well as curious tourists. Josefa's daughter Paulina oversees the kitchen, making homey dishes like garlic soup, grilled sausages, or local trout with ham. If you hanker for Castilian dishes not available at most restaurants, consider the brains fried in batter or stewed kid with almonds.

Plaza del Peso, 1. © **92-321-90-05.** Reservations recommended. Main courses 10€–27€; *menu del día* 24€. Tues–Sun 1:30–3:30pm and 9pm–12:30am. Closed 2 weeks in July.

Exploring Salamanca

You probably won't want to visit Salamanca in August, when the scorching midday makes even the lizards dash across the plazas in search of a sliver of shade. But at any other time, this is a stroller's city, where new delights catch the eye at every turn. The **Plaza Mayor** ★★★ is the heart of the community, and in true academic fashion, it embodies the conflicting spirits of Spanish intellect. José Benito Churriguera's design of the square is rational, cool, and neoclassical—but the decoration is utterly Baroque. Salamantinos gather here at all hours of the day and night to connect with each other, to talk, and (most of all) to eat and drink. When the sun sets and the stone plaza begins to cool, cafe tables spill out from beneath the arcades and "tunas" (student singers in old-fashioned academic cloaks) wander from table to table singing for tips.

About a quarter of the old city is devoted to buildings of the University of Salamanca, which reached its apex of influence in the 15th and 16th centuries but remains one of Spain's most prestigious centers of scholarship. Courtyards around university buildings are generally open to the public, and the **Patio de Escuelas Menores** is a popular gathering point for tour groups as well as Salamantinos. Standing proudly in the center is a statue of 16th-century poet and scholar **Fray Luis de León,** the city's poster boy for intellectual freedom and defiance of tyranny. Imprisoned for 4 years by the Inquisition for translating the Biblical "Song of Solomon" into Castilian, the scholar began his first lecture after returning to the classroom, *"Decíamos ayer . . . ,"* or "as we were saying yesterday. . . ."

Casa de las Conchas (House of Shells) ★ ARCHITECTURE   It's hard to miss this restored 1483 house on the street between the University and Plaza Mayor because the facade consists of 400 simulated scallop shells, the symbol of Santiago (St. James), the patron saint of the Reconquista. It was created by a medical professor at the university as a tribute to the pilgrimage city of Santiago de Compostela in Galicia. The region of Castilla y León maintains a tourist office here.

Calle de la Compañía, 2. © **92-326-93-17.** Free admission. Courtyard Mon–Fri 9am–9pm; Sat 9am–2pm; Sat–Sun 5–8pm. Bus: 1.

Casa-Museo Unamuno ★★ HISTORIC HOME   The financial crisis has severely limited hours at this delightful little house museum, but make a point of

A twisted FAMILY

Spanish Baroque architecture takes the impulse for distortion to an extreme. The Churriguera family carved out a name for themselves with a family style that owes a great deal to the forms assumed by twisted rope. **José Benito Churriguera** (1665–1725) and his brothers **Joaquin** (1674–1724) and **Alberto** (1676–1750) were stone sculptors who became architects. Their work in Salamanca, especially with altarpieces and the stucco work on building facades, spawned many imitators in Spain as well as in Mexico—hence the term, Churrigueresque.

visiting nonetheless if you want to understand the intellectual, humanistic side of the city. Poet, philosopher, and novelist Miguel de Unamuno lived in this 18th-century home during his first term as university rector. A man of principle, he had to leave the country when dictator Primo de Rivera came to power and demanded that he censor his scholarship. When de Rivera fell, Unamuno returned exultant, but the euphoria was short-lived. Never have we seen a home where the life of the mind was so manifest, from his library of world masterpieces to his own photographs showing him with the top intelligentsia of his era. Unamuno was the symbol of a humanistic era of lofty values and high ideals, crushed in Spain's descent into chaos. Indeed, he died of an apparent broken heart shortly after the Civil War began. Unamuno loved his adopted city deeply, once writing in a poem, "I keep your very soul in my heart. And you, my golden Salamanca, will keep my memory when I die." And so it has.

Calle de Libreros, 25. ✆ **92-329-44-00.** Admission 4€ adults; 2€ students. Tues and Thurs 10am–noon. Bus: 1.

Catedral Nueva (New Cathedral) ★★ CATHEDRAL Salamantinos started constructing their "new" cathedral in 1513 in an old-fashioned style that made it "the last gasp of Gothic style," as architectural historians put it. Located in the south end of the old town, it is the largest and highest building in the city. The soaring spaces inside welcome pious contemplation. All three Churriguera brothers (see box above) served as supervising architects of the late stages of the cathedral's long construction (it wasn't consecrated until 1733), so many of the surface details and twisted-rope columns are truly Churrigueresque. One bas-relief column, for example, resembles a cluster of palm trees. The tradition of inspired stone carving continues. When the lower portion of the Puerta Ramos on the west side was rebuilt in 1992, the stonemason and restorers decided to update the carvings with the image of an astronaut floating in space, a monkey eating an ice cream cone, and a stork carrying a branch in its beak. (Panhandlers hanging out near the entrance will point them out for a tip.)

Plaza Juan XXIII. ✆ **92-321-74-76.** www.catedralsalamanca.org. Free for worship; otherwise 4.75€ adults, 4€ seniors and students. Apr–Sept daily 9am–8pm; Oct and Mar daily 9am–1pm and 4–6pm; Nov–Feb Sun 9am–1pm. Bus: 1.

Catedral Vieja (Old Cathedral) ★★★ CATHEDRAL Functioning more as a museum than a house of worship, the old cathedral is a squat Romanesque structure begun in 1140, and its sight lines to the altar are obscured by the sheer bulk of its interior supports. Nonetheless, it retains some powerful religious art most notably the mid-15th-century altarpiece of 53 compartmentalized scenes painted by Nicholas of Florence to delineate the life of Christ and scenes of th

Virgin Mary. It is not uncommon to see pilgrims entranced by the masterpiece, spending hours on their knees in prayer in the medieval gloom as they contemplate each scene. After viewing the church, stroll through the enclosed cloisters. Two chapels are of particular note: the Capilla de San Martín with frescoes painted in 1242, and the Capilla de Santa Catalina, replete with gargoyles.

Plaza Juan XXIII. ✆ **92-321-74-76.** www.catedralsalamanca.org. Admission 4.75€ adults, 4€ seniors and students. Apr–Sept daily 10am–7:30pm; Oct–Mar daily 10am–12:30pm and 4–5:30pm. Bus: 1.

Cielo de Salamanca ★★ MUSEUM   Sometimes the best attempts at understanding the universe turn out to be bad science but deserve to survive because they are simply beautiful. This fresco of the night sky painted by Francisco Gallego in 1474 is just such an example. It covers part of the ceiling of the old university library and is located just off the plaza that separates the university's graduate school from its undergraduate campus. Working without the benefit of the explorations by Copernicus and Galileo, the artist attempted to merge myth, science, and religion by enjambing astrology and night-sky astronomy. You'll have to wait a few minutes after entering for your eyes to adjust to the low light, but the vision is the very definition of magic.

Patio de Escuelas Menores, s/n. No phone. Free admission. Tues–Sat 10am–2pm and 4–8pm; Sun 10am–2pm.

Convento de las Dueñas ★★★ CONVENT   Unlike the brothers at adjacent San Estéban, the Dominican nuns are cloistered, but the cloister and intensely fragrant rose garden of their convent are open to visitors. Originally a noble palace, it was donated to the order in 1419 and has been subsequently altered and enlarged. The 16th-century cloister designed by Rodrigo Gil de Hontañón is a hidden treasure. The capitals on the arcade pillars represent some of

The Catedral Vieja.

Carved stone pillars at Convento de las Dueñas.

the most inspired stone carving in the entire city, and any fan of gargoyles or modern graphic novels should make the effort to see them. They're a sample book of contorted human bodies, angels, griffons, devils, flying goat heads, winged horses, and other fantastic creatures. The carvings are so vivid that it's hard to believe the poor nuns can sleep at night.

Plaza del Concilio de Trento, s/n. ℂ **92-321-54-42.** Admission 1.50€. Mon–Sat 10:30am–12:45pm; Mon–Fri 4:30–6:45pm. Bus: 1.

Convento de San Estéban ★ MONASTERY   Dominicans from this monastery accompanied Columbus on his voyages. Not only did they proselytize to the natives of the New World, they argued that indigenous people around the world had souls, and human rights. While the dignity of all persons seems common sense in the 21st century, it was a radical concept in the 16th, and the Dominicans of Salamanca suffered for it. Nonetheless, they persevered and continue to agitate for social and economic justice, finally convincing the pope to declare indigenous people as human beings. Their convent is a pleasure to tour, highlighted by the elaborate gilded José Benito Churriguera altar in the church and the stunning Baroque choir with an illustrated hymnal big enough that all 118 monks could read the music from their seats.

Plaza del Concilio de Trento, s/n. ℂ **92-321-50-00.** http://sanesteban.dominicos.es. 3€ adults; 2€ seniors and students. Daily 10am–2pm and 4–7pm. Bus: 1.

Mercatus ★ STORE   The official university store has the usual branded merchandise, but it also sells some terrific souvenirs that won't embarrass you once you get home. If you became enamored of the student singing groups, or "tunas," one night on Plaza Mayor, you can purchase CDs here. Silk scarves that reproduce the Cielo de Salamanca in all its mysterious beauty are worth a splurge, but you can also purchase T-shirts, tote bags, puzzles, and drink coasters emblazoned with the same image. Or go tacky and buy your budding scholar a bright stuffed frog, the good-luck talisman of Salamanca students.

Cardenal Plá y Deniel, s/n. ℂ **92-329-46-92.** http://mercatus.usal.es. Mon–Sat 10am–7pm; Sun 10am–2pm.

Museo de Art Nouveau-Art Déco ★ MUSEUM   Masterful Art Nouveau glass by Emile Gallé and René Lalique are the artistic highlights, but the 1,500-plus piece collection of the Manuel Ramos Andrade Foundation also embraces jewelry, paintings, furniture, and marble and bronze figurines. All the works date from the late 1880s through the 1930s, and while some are mainstream Art Nouveau or Art Deco, others are Spanish outliers of the two styles. Many visitors are surprised to also find a collection of more than 400 porcelain dolls. Manuel Ramos Andrade was a major doll collector, and the pieces represent the top European manufacturers.

Calle El Expolio, 14. ℭ **92-312-14-25.** www.museocasalis.org. Admission 4€ adults; 2€ students; free for children 13 and under. Apr to mid-Oct Tues–Fri 11am–2pm and 5–9pm, Sat–Sun 11am– 9pm; mid-Oct to Mar Tues–Fri 11am–2pm and 4–7pm, Sat–Sun 11am–8pm. Bus: 1.

Museo de Salamanca ★ MUSEUM   Only steps from the grandly carved main entrance of the University, this attractive little museum is packed with religious art confiscated from convents and monasteries in the mid–19th century. Most of the churches from which the 15th- to 17th-century carvings and paintings were taken no longer exist, and in a few cases, the art is exhibited with the altar or niche from its original church. The contrast between rude architecture and polished artistry is striking—a reminder that for rural people, the church was often the most beautiful thing in their lives. One highlight is a golden Churrigueresque altarpiece crafted between 1697 and 1704. In addition to the permanent collections, the museum has begun a very active program of thematic exhibitions combining pieces from its collection with works borrowed from other municipal and regional museums around the region of Castilla y León.

Patio de las Escuelas, 2. ℭ **92-321-22-35.** www.museoscastillayleon.jcyl.es/museodesalamanca. Admission 1.20€ adults, free for seniors and children; free to all Sat–Sun. Oct–June Tues–Sun 10am–2pm, Tues–Sat 4–7pm; July–Sept Tues- Sun 10am–2pm, Tues–Sat 5–8pm.

Universidad de Salamanca ★ HISTORIC SITE   Established in 1213 and granted its full charter in 1254, Salamanca was organized on the model of the University of Bologna—that is, it gave precedence to humanistic scholarship over the study of theology favored by the University of Paris. Its intellectual heyday was in the 15th and 16th centuries, but it remains a major force in Spanish intellectual life and the most popular place in the country for foreigners to study the Spanish language. The original college, the Escuelas Mayores, boasts one of the **best carved portals ★★★** in a city of pretty impressive doorways. Carved in 1534, this "doorway to heaven" was intended to emulate the goldsmith's art. The main medallion in the first register depicts the Catholic monarchs Isabel and Fernando. Crowds gather to scrutinize the fine details, but they are not looking for the Catholic monarchs; they are looking for the carved frog perched on a human skull on the right-hand side of the door. Legend holds that students who can spot it will do well on their exams. Although Salamanca is not known for its business school, Salamantino entrepreneurs have capitalized on the legend by making the *rana* (frog) a whimsical if unofficial symbol of Salamanca. Every imaginable trinket can be purchased emblazoned with its likeness.

Given such a great entrance, it's a little disappointing that the only tour inside the university is restricted to a self-guided walk around the Renaissance arcades of the Escuelas Mayores, the original college of the university. Let your nose lead the way. The chapel has the lingering odor of sanctity (actually, frankincense), while the wonderful old library on the upper level smells of paper and old leather, even through the closed glass doors. You can also visit the lecture hall of Fray Luis de León, fitted with crude wooden benches.

Patio de las Escuelas, 1. ℭ **92-329-44-00.** www.usal.es. Admission 4€. Mon–Sat 9:30am–1pm; Sun 9am–1pm; Mon–Fri 4–7pm; Sat 4–6:30pm. Enter from Patio de las Escuelas, a widening of Calle de Libreros. Bus: 1.

ZAMORA ★

Until the recent installation of high-speed rail, few North Americans beyond architecture buffs ever visited Zamora. Although it does have some modern hotels and terrific restaurants, the city seems little changed since its years of dusty decline in the 17th century, when the majority of its populace emigrated to South America, establishing several Zamoras across that continent. Scholars sometimes refer to Zamora as an open-air museum of Romanesque architecture, and the old churches—most of them well-preserved and still functioning as neighborhood parishes—are powerfully moving. The processions, or *pasos*, during Holy Week (the week before Easter) are some of the largest and most spectacular in Spain. Reserve far ahead to visit then.

It is surprising that Zamora's monuments have survived so many centuries, as the city has been the site of fierce battles. It was here that Leon finally captured the city from the Moors in the 11th century; Zamora was also the scene of fierce battles in the 15th-century war between Isabel I and Juana la Beltraneja, Isabel's illegitimate half-niece—a struggle whose memory is preserved in the old Spanish proverb *No se ganó Zamora en una hora,* or "Zamora wasn't won in an hour."

Essentials

GETTING THERE There are three high-speed **trains** to and from Madrid every day. They take just less than 2 hours and cost 25€ to 31€ each way. The railway station is at Calle Alfonso Peña (© **90-232-03-20;** www.renfe.com), about a 15-minute walk from the edge of the old town. Ten to twenty-three **bus** connections a day from Salamanca are very convenient. The express takes 50 minutes

A procession during Holy Week in Zamora.

(6.30€) while the regular bus (5.25€) takes 1 hour. The town's bus station lies a few paces from the railway station, at Calle Alfonso Peña, 3 (© **98-052-12-81**). Call © **90-202-00-52** for bus schedules and price information. If you're driving from Madrid, take the A-6 superhighway northwest toward Valladolid, cutting west on the N-VI and west again at the turnoff onto 122.

VISITOR INFORMATION The **Oficina Municipal de Turismo,** Plaza de Arias Gonzalo, 6 (© **98-053-36-94;** www.zamora.es/lang), is open daily 10am to 2pm and 4 to 7pm.

Where to Stay

Hotel Horus ★ The former Banco de España building from the 19th century has led many lives. It was transformed into a rich merchant's mansion in the early 20th century and later served as a newspaper headquarters. Just before the financial crisis struck, it was converted into a boutique hotel that retains the Art Nouveau decoration of the original building but upgrades the interiors in a minimalist modern style. Even the smallest rooms are spacious and airy, and the largest rooms are huge. Just a 2-minute walk from the Plaza Mayor, the location is ideal for sightseeing.

Plaza del Mercado, 20. © **98-050-82-82.** www.hotelhorus.com. 45 rooms. 58€–86€ double; 85€–101€ jr. suite. **Amenities:** Bar; restaurant; room service; spa; free Wi-Fi.

NH Palacio del Duero ★★ Barely outside the old city walls of Zamora, the NH Collección hotel (the group's top grade) occupies the 14th- to 15th-century convent of San Juan de Jerusalem as well as the 16th-century Comendadores convent and part of a 20th-century winery. All those properties have been nicely integrated, but the path to some rooms seems a bit like a maze. The rooms themselves are spacious, modern, and serene, and some have private terraces while others open onto a hidden courtyard where some guests like to sunbathe.

Plaza de la Horta, 1. © **98-050-82-62.** www.nh-hotels.com. 49 units. Doubles 54€–85€. **Amenities:** Bar; restaurant; free Wi-Fi.

Parador de Zamora ★ Medieval armor, heavy tapestries, hanging lanterns, and reproduction antique furniture give this *parador* a gravitas that other lodgings in Zamora lack. Built in the mid–15th century on the site of an earlier Roman fortress, the building features a beautiful staircase and a dignified wood and stone interior courtyard with a well in the center. The two levels of guest rooms are arrayed around the central patio and most have big windows with heavy wooden shutters. The decor mixes richly colored fabrics with dark wood furnishings for a modern interpretation of traditional style. The location is within convenient walking distance of attractions.

Plaza de Viriato, 5. © **98-051-44-97.** www.parador.es. 52 units. 115€–165€ double, 170€–230€ superior double. **Amenities:** Restaurant; bar; outdoor pool; room service; free Wi-Fi.

Where to Eat

Zamora sits on the north bank of the Río Duero just downstream from the wine districts of Rueda and Toro (and just upstream from Portugal's port vineyards). To the north, the landscape rises rapidly into mountain woodlands that supply the foraged mushrooms and wild trout often found on Zamoran menus. Historically, the city was an important stop on the Roman "silver road" to Galicia, and the Galician penchant for octopus continues even in this dusty Castilian city.

La Bóveda ★★ CONTEMPORARY SPANISH Located in the old Banco d'España vault at the Hotel Horus, La Bóveda (which translates as The Vault) is a treasure. The chef adapts a number of classic Spanish dishes from different regions—*bacalao al pil-pil* with piquillo peppers from Basque country, for example, or suckling pig with crispy skin from Castilla—and gives them a modern twist. The wine list features the splendid reds from nearby Toro. Although it's perhaps the dressiest restaurant in Zamora, La Bóveda offers exceptional value for the price.

Plaza del Mercado, 20. ✆ **98-050-82-82.** www.hotelhorus.com. Reservations recommended. Main dishes 12€–22€. Daily 1:30pm–3pm; Mon–Sat 9pm–midnight.

El Rincón de Antonio ★★ CASTILIAN The chef at this atmospheric restaurant proves the adage that everything old is new again. He has resurrected some of the classic dishes of this corner of Castilla y León—like garbanzo beans in a garlicky sauce with local *boletus* (porcini or cep mushrooms), or candied artichokes with ham and a mushroom puree. Other Castilian classics like veal tongue and leg of lamb are also featured prominently. Although the menu can be parsed a la carte, almost everyone who dines in the bustling, close-quartered dining rooms, or the greenhouse-like extension, orders one of the tasting menus. There is a vegetarian option as well as five- and six-course menus with meat and fish. The tapas tasting menu of four small plates, wine, dessert, and coffee is one of the best light meals in town (available only in the bar).

Rúa de los Francos, 6. ✆ **98-053-53-70.** www.elrincondeantonio.com. Reservations recommended. Main dishes 14€–28€; fixed-price menus 32€–60€; tapas tasting menu 11€. Daily noon–4pm; Mon–Sat 8pm–midnight.

Serafín ★★ SPANISH Zamora is famous for its rice dish, *arroz al la zamoraña,* and the kitchen at Serafín makes the best version in town. Staff sometimes have trouble explaining the dish to non-Spanish speakers, so you should know that in addition to the minced bits of pig's trotters and pig's ears that characterize the dish, it is redolent with sweet paprika and a combination of sautéed onion and cubed turnip. The restaurant is an unusual hybrid—combining a skillful execution of the roast meat dishes of Castilla y León (accompanied by hearty reds from D.O. Toro) and simple presentations of superb fish and shellfish from the Cantabrian coast on the Bay of Biscay. (With the fish, you drink Rueda whites from about 40 miles east.) Local fish include trout from the mountains north of Zamora, frog legs (an amphibian, but treated as fish on the menu), and sweet river crab.

Plaza Maestro Haedo, 10. ✆ **98-053-14-22.** www.restauranteserafin.com. Main courses 12€–20€; fixed-price menu 17€ and 24€. Fri–Wed 1–4:30pm and 8:30pm–midnight.

Exploring Zamora

Zamora's Romanesque churches are a delight to explore, but you'll have to check the doors for the hours of Mass to get inside most of them. They may be priceless monuments that are 700 to 800 years old, but they are still active parish churches. A handful open for prayers in the mornings at 10am, close before lunch, and open again in the early evening before dinner, 5 to 8pm. It's also a treat to explore the city walls. The **Portillo de la Traición** (Treason Gate) on the northwest corner of the city commemorates the duplicitous assassination of Castilian king Sancho II in 1072 when he and El Cid were laying siege to the city in a battle over succession to the crown of León. The upshot of Sancho's death was that his brother Alfonso united the crowns of Castilla and León.

Catedral San Salvador ★★

CATHEDRAL With its ribbed blue-and-white Byzantine-style dome, there's no mistaking Zamora's cathedral. Built swiftly between 1151 and 1174 (although the transept wasn't finished until 1192), it has a stylistic unity that is unusual in Spain, where cathedrals were generally completed over centuries rather than decades. Set on the high point of Zamora's ridge, the cathedral looks as much like a fortress as a church when viewed from the riverbanks below. Yet it opens into the city with a harmonious plaza that gives viewers the distance to appreciate its full grandeur. Some Gothic towers have been added to the Romanesque temple, of course, and the interior decorations stretch out across the centuries. The choir stalls, carved 1512–16 by Juan de Bruselas, are especially

The Catedral San Salvador.

notable for their lively scenes of country life in addition to the usual images of saints and famous figures from antiquity. The cathedral's museum is located inside the cloister, and it contains the city's greatest artistic treasure, the so-called "Black Tapestries" woven in Flanders in the 15th century. They illustrate scenes from the Trojan War as well as Hannibal's campaign in Italy. They are called "black" because several show people about to be decapitated.

Plaza de la Catedral. ☎ **98-053-06-44.** http://catedraldezamora.wordpress.com. Admission 4€ adults, 2€ seniors and students, 1€ photo permit (no flash). Cathedral admission free during Mass. Mar–Sept daily 10am–2pm and 5–8pm; Oct–Feb daily 10am–2pm and 4:30–6:30pm.

Centro de Interpretación de las Ciudades Medievales ★ MUSEUM

Since so much of Zamora remains medieval, it was a logical spot to open this center for the study of medieval cities. The cutting-edge facility built into the exterior of a city wall has a series of galleries that explore the historical, social, and cultural side of medieval life in central Spain with dioramas, scale models, and multilingual panels. You'll make your way down to the lowest level of the museum, which is known as the Zen overlook, or "Mirador Zen." It overlooks the Rio Duero from a softly lit room filled with faint music.

Cuesta del Pizarro, s/n. ☎ **98-053-62-40.** Free admission. Daily noon–2pm and 5–8pm.

Iglesia de Santa María-Magdalena ★ CHURCH

One of the most beautiful of the many Romanesque churches in Zamora, the Magdalena was begun in 1157 for the Order of San Juan and completed early in the 13th century. The form is a simple parish church of its era—a single narrow rectangular nave with a semicircular apse. What sets this church apart (beyond the extensive restoration carried out in the late 20th century) are the remarkable stone carvings. The capitals of the four pairs of columns supporting the main door are embellished with dragons that have both human and animal heads. The exquisite carvings continue inside the church, with laughing heads on the moldings over the arches.

Two tabernacles are embedded in carved stone, and there is a magnificent tomb of a now-anonymous woman watched over by a pair of carved angels.

Rua de los Francos, s/n. No phone. Free admission. Daily 10am–1pm and 5–8pm.

A Side Trip to Toro ★

Just a 40-minute drive east of Zamora on the A-11, **Toro** is a spectacularly well-preserved medieval city that highlights the third strategy Castilian kings used in the re-conquest of their lands from the Moors. Equal to the sword and the cross was the vine. Building on those first 11th-century plantings, Toro has become the heart of its own D.O. wine district, and ever since scientific winemakers began to tame the powerful *tinto de Toro* grape (a strain of Tempranillo) in the 1980s, the biggest names in Spanish viticulture have flocked to the area to establish vineyards. Some of the best Toro wines are made by **Bodegas Fariña,** and are named for the most beautiful church in town, the **Colegiata.** Toro's single main street is lined with shops offering free tastings and selling the local wines—so many that if you're not careful, you'll be woozy by the time you get to that 13th-century Colegiata, officially **Santa María la Mayor,** located (of course) on Plaza Santa María (no phone; Mon–Fri 10am–2pm and 5–8pm, Sat 10am–2pm). Ironically, you enter the church from the rear so officials can charge a 1€ admission (except during Mass). They do so because the main entrance, the **Pórtico de la Majestad (Portal of Majesty) ★★★**, is one of the most magnificent examples of Gothic stone carving in Spain, and you have to go through the church and back out to view it. The carved figures of the Last Judgment—all still painted in sun-blasted pastels—reveal something of the carver's theology: First to be saved, even before the Virgins and the Martyrs, are the musicians.

Some of the best Toro wines come from Bodegas Fariña.

BURGOS ★★

Burgos has a way of breeding conquerors. El Cid Campeador, the Spanish hero immortalized in the epic "El Cantar de Mío Cid," was born near here and his remains have a king-like prominence in the grand cathedral. Franco made the conservative city his Nationalist army headquarters in the Spanish Civil War. As a result, Burgos remains more intact than most medieval Spanish cities, and it lives up to its roots as the "cradle of Castilla." Employing a distinctive lisp (their hero is "El Theed"), Burgos residents speak textbook Castellano. Of course, they wrote the textbooks. Burgos is a provincial capital on the desert *meseta* (plateau). Ferociously hot in summer, it comes alive at night as students flock to the cafes and dance clubs.

Essentials

GETTING THERE   Burgos is well connected by high-speed **train** from Madrid (trip time: 2–4½ hr.) and Bilbao (trip time: 2½–3 hr.). Fares from Madrid range from 35€ to 43€; from Bilbao, 19€ to 20€. The Burgos-Rosa de Lima railway station is about 7km (4.3 miles) northeast of the old city on Avenida Principes de Asturias, s/n. Call ✆ **90-232-03-20** or visit www.renfe.es.

Some 18 **buses** a day make the 2¾-hour trip from Madrid. A one-way fare costs 19€ to 25€. The bus depot in Burgos is at Calle Miranda 4 (✆ **94-726-20-17;** www.alsa.es), which intersects the large Plaza de Vega, due south of (and across the river from) the cathedral.

Burgos is well connected to its neighbors by a network of highways. From Madrid, follow the N-1 north for about 3 hours. Burgos is a short drive (1½ hr.) from Bilbao.

VISITOR INFORMATION   The **tourist office,** Plaza Alonso Martínez 7 (✆ **94-720-31-25;** www.turismocastillayleon.com), is open July to September daily 9am to 8pm. From October to June it's open Monday to Saturday 9:30am to 2pm and 4 to 7pm, and Sunday 9:30am to 5pm.

Where to Stay

Hotel Rice ★★   It's a bit of a surprise to find a hotel that features classic British-style decor in the heart of Castilian Spain, but this boutique hotel is a good bet for its attention to comfort (including luxury mattresses and excellent marble bathrooms) and convenient location about 0.8km (½ miles) north of the city center. Family rooms can accommodate two adults and two children.

Av. Reyes Católicos 30. ✆ **94-722-23-00.** www.hotelrice.com. 50 rooms. 51€–135€ double; from 67€ suite. Parking 12€. **Amenities:** Restaurant; bar; free Wi-Fi.

Landa Palace ★★★   A small restaurant on the N-1 highway about 2km (1.2 miles) south of Burgos has grown into one of Castilla's most revered hotels. Opened in 1960, it has been in the hands of the Landa family ever since, who have expanded and transformed the old castle into a romantic lodging. Most of the 24 suites, for example, are located in a carefully rebuilt 14th-century defensive tower. Antique furnishings and tile floors give the rooms a historic feel. The property features two restaurants and a bar, but the little details are what set it apart. The indoor swimming pool has a view of a fireplace, for example, and all the bed linen is cared for at the nearby Monasterio de las Huelgas.

Carretera Madrid–Irún Km 235, Burgos. ✆ **94-725-77-77.** www.landahotel.com. 39 units. 170€–200€ double; 200€–290€ suite. MC, V. Free parking. **Amenities:** Restaurant; bar; babysitting; exercise room; 2 heated pools (1 indoor, 1 outdoor); room service. *In room:* A/C, TV, hair dryer, minibar, free Wi-Fi.

Mesón del Cid ★★ CASTILIAN   With its striking views of the adjacent cathedral, it's hard to beat the location of Mesón del Cid. While the decor is rather stodgy, everything about the hotel is welcoming and comfortable, and the old-style Castilian furnishings are actually newly manufactured. Once the city's most elegant address, the hotel has been superseded by several newer chain properties. That competition, combined with the economic slump, means that prices are as old-fashioned as the metal bedframes. The hotel's restaurant is just the place to take your aging aunt for traditional cuisine.

Plaza de Santa María 8. ℂ **94-720-87-15.** www.mesondelcid.es. 56 rooms. 42€–76€ double; from 70€ jr. suite; from 90€ suite. **Amenities:** Restaurant; bar; free Wi-Fi.

Where to Eat

Casa Ojeda ★ BURGALESE   Established in 1912, Casa Ojeda is the Burgos standard-bearer for classical Castilian cuisine. Located in the same building with a modestly priced bar-cafe and a downright inexpensive deli by the same name, Casa Ojeda's spacious dining room features service as classical as the menu and a wood-burning stove to warm up the room in chilly weather. While the spit-roasted meats are excellent (and pricey), the kitchen prides itself on more modest plates like tongue with pickled wild mushrooms, the local blood sausage roasted in the oven with stuffed red peppers, and crab salad with noodles and grated black truffle.

Calle Vitoria 5. ℂ **94-720-90-52.** www.restauranteojeda.com. Reservations required. Main courses 16€–30€. Daily 1:30–4pm; Mon–Sat 9–11:30pm.

Fábula ★★ CONTEMPORARY SPANISH   Perhaps the most consistently inventive restaurant in Burgos, Fábula is a family operation where seasonal market produce stars on the menu. Even the hamburger (made with local grass-fed beef) features ketchup fashioned from Valle de Caderechas tart cherries. Basque fish, especially cod and hake, are featured in a new dish almost every day, and the kitchen makes extensive use of fresh and aged cheeses from Burgos and León. Octopus is popular, both as a tartare starter or deep-fried and smothered with stewed baby onions. For a treat, try the black rice with sautéed lobster.

Calle de la Merced 19. ℂ **94-726-30-92.** www.restaurantefabula.com. Reservations recommended. Main courses 15€–24€. Tues–Sat 2–3:30pm and Tues–Sun 9–11pm.

La Favorita Taberna Urbana ★★ CASTILIAN   Widely acclaimed for the charcoal-grilled beef, pork, and wild game dishes that dominate the dining room menu, La Favorita also has an atmospheric tapas bar where the original exposed brick and stone walls give it a rusticity that belies its urban location. The proprietors are justifiably proud of their regional specialties, many of which are available at the bar as inexpensive tapas. On a chilly day, you can warm up quickly with an order of *estrellitas* (half-cooked eggs over fried potatoes) or a mini-tower of *habitas con foie* (baby broad beans with ham and duck liver).

Calle Avellanos 8 E. ℂ **94-720-59-59.** www.lafavoritaburgos.com. Tapas 2€, *raciones* 6€–12€, main dishes 10€–18€. Daily 11am–11pm.

Exploring Burgos

Casa de Cordón, the historic 15th-century palace on Plaza de Calvo Sotelo, has been restored and is now a bank, but you can still go by and take a look. History records that on April 23, 1497, Columbus met with Isabel and Fernando here after his second voyage to the New World. It was in this building, in 1506, that Felipe Hermoso (the Handsome) suffered a heart attack after a game of jai alai. In her grief, his wife, Juana, dragged his body through the streets of Burgos, earning her the sobriquet Juana la Loca (the Mad).

Cartuja de Miraflores ★ CHURCH Located 4km (2½ miles) east of the center of Burgos, this florid Gothic charterhouse was founded in 1441. King Juan II selected it as the royal tomb for himself and his second wife, Isabel of Portugal. By 1494, the **church ★** was finished, its sober facade belying the treasure-trove of decoration inside. The stunning attraction of the interior is the **sculptured unit ★★★** in the apse, said to have been built with the first gold brought back from the New World. It was the work, in the late 1400s, of Gil de Siloé, who also designed the polychrome wood altarpiece. The remains of the king and queen lie in the white-marble mausoleum, designed like an eight-pointed star. The tomb's decorators gave these parents of Isabel I a fine send-off with exuberant, Gothic decorations such as cherubs, pinnacles, canopies, and scrolls.

Carretera de Burgos a Cardeña Km 3. © **94-725-25-86.** www.cartuja.org. Free admission. Mon–Sat 10:15am–3pm and 4–6pm; Sun 11am–3pm and 4–6pm; Nov–Mar closed Wed.

Catedral de Santa María ★★★ CATHEDRAL Begun in 1221, this cathedral was one of the most celebrated in Europe and certainly one of the best examples of French Gothic on the Iberian Peninsula. Ornamented 15th-century bell towers flank the three main doorways by Juan de Colonia. The 16th-century **Chapel of Condestable,** behind the main altar, embodies Flamboyant Gothic architecture and is richly decorated with heraldic emblems, a sculptured filigree doorway, figures of apostles and saints, balconies, and a stained-glass window of an eight-sided star.

Equally elegant are the two-story 14th-century **cloisters,** filled with haunting Spanish Gothic sculptures. The cathedral's tapestries, including a well-known Gobelin, are rich in detail. In one of the chapels you'll see an old chest linked to the legend of El Cid; it was filled with gravel and used as collateral by the warrior to trick moneylenders. The remains of El Cid himself, together with those of his wife, Doña Ximena, were moved in 1919 to beautifully carved sepulchers in front of the altar and beneath the cathedral's lantern-like dome. At midday, bright colored lights from the stained glass play down on them.

Plaza de Santa María s/n. © **94-720-47-12.** www.catedraldeburgos.es. Admission to chapels, cloisters, and treasury 7€ adults, 6€ seniors, 4.50€ students, 1.50€ children 7–14, and free for children 6 and under. Summer daily 9:30am–7:15pm; spring and fall daily 9:30am–1:15pm and 4–7:15pm; winter daily 10am–1:15pm and 4–6:45pm.

Museo de la Evolución Humana ★★★ MUSEUM Archaeologists have been excited about the finds in the caves in the nearby Sierra Atapuerca since the early 20th century, but only recently did science prove conclusively that some of the human fossil remains date back 800,000 years. That makes Atapuerca the earliest site of human inhabitation in Europe by a long shot—literally hundreds of thousands of years before the emergence of Homo sapiens or even Homo neanderthalis. What is all the more remarkable is that these limestone caves have been in more or less continuous use ever since. This extraordinary museum, which opened in the summer of 2010, chronicles the story of successive waves of hominids in Spain, even explaining what appears to be the oldest use of fire by humans. The subterranean galleries deal with the Atapuerca excavations, while the Evolution gallery dominates the ground floor. The next level up deals with

The Museo de la Evolución Humana.

cultural evolution, and the top floor is a platform for admiring the museum's dramatic and quite beautiful architecture by Juan Navarro Baldeweg.

Paseo Sierra de Atapuerca s/n. ℰ **90-202-42-46.** www.museoevolucionhumana.com. Admission 6€ adults, 4€ seniors and students, free under age 8; free to all Wed. Tue–Fri 10am–2:30pm and 4:30–8pm, Sat 10am–8pm, Sun 10am–3pm.

A Side Trip to Santo Domingo de la Calzada ★

Pilgrims have streamed across northern Spain for nearly 1,000 years to reach Santiago de Compostela (p. 506). If you want to see the pilgrimage route up close, make a day trip to Santo Domingo de la Calzada, 68km (42 miles) east of Burgos. The town was deliberately established by San Domingo in the 12th century as a stopover for pilgrims, and its core has changed little over the centuries. The national landmark 12th-century **cathedral** ★ (ℰ **94-134-00-33**) is mostly Gothic and contains the crypt of its founder. A centuries-old legend is attached to the cathedral: Supposedly a cooked rooster stood up from the dinner table and crowed to protest the innocence of a pilgrim who had been accused of theft and sentenced to hang. To this day, a live cock and hen are kept in a cage up on the church wall, and you can often hear the rooster crowing at Mass. The cathedral is open March to December Monday to Saturday 10am to 1pm and 4 to 6:30pm. Admission is 3.50€ adults, 2.50€ ages 8 to 18, and free for everyone on Sunday for Mass. Motorists can reach Santo Domingo de la Calzada by following either of the traffic arteries paralleling the river, heading west from the Burgos cathedral until signs indicate N-120. If you want to stay the night, you can't do better than the **Parador de Santo Domingo** ★★★, Plaza del Santo 3 (ℰ **94-134-03-00;** www.parador.es; 103€–160€ double). Built next to the cathedral in the 12th century as a hostelry for pilgrims, its modern rich linens, lofty beds, and spacious rooms make it anything but ascetic.

LEÓN ★★

Once the leading city of Christian Spain, León has one of the greatest, most inspiring Gothic cathedrals in Europe. The city was long the capital of a great feudal kingdom that went into eclipse after uniting with Castilla. Today it serves as a gateway between Castilla and the routes to Galicia. The modern city sprawls, but the most important monuments, restaurants, and hotels are concentrated in the center of town. Like Burgos, the region is renowned for its soft-spoken, pristine Castellano Spanish. León is an excellent place to experience the tranquility of the Spanish heartland, as well as an obligatory stop for students of medieval architecture.

Essentials

GETTING THERE León has 10 **trains** daily from Madrid (trip time: 2¾–4½ hr.). The station, Estación del Norte, Av. de Astorga 2 (© **90-232-03-20;** www.renfe. es), is on the western bank of the Bernesga River. Cross the bridge near Plaza de Guzmán el Bueno. A one-way ticket from Madrid ranges from 35€ to 45€.

Most of León's **buses** arrive and depart from the Estación de Autobuses, Paseo Ingeniero Sáenz de Miera (© **98-721-10-00**). Three to five buses per day link León with Zamora and Salamanca, and there are 11 per day from Madrid (trip time: 4¼ hr.). A one-way ticket on a direct regular bus from Madrid is 28€ to 43€ for the *supra* (comfortable) service. For more information on prices, call © **90-242-22-42.**

León lies at the junction of five major highways coming from five different regions of Spain. From Madrid's periphery, head northwest on the N-VI superhighway toward A Coruña. At Benavente, bear right onto the N-630.

VISITOR INFORMATION The **tourist office,** Plaza de la Regla 3 (© **98-723-70-82;** www.turismocastillayleon.com), is open Monday to Saturday 9:30am to 2pm and 4 to 7pm, and Sunday 9:30am to 5pm. From July to mid-September, the office remains open during lunch hours.

Where to Stay

Hotel Alfonso V ★★ We usually expect hotels named after Spanish monarchs to be steeped in history, but this mid-20th-century property in León's commercial center features modern decor. The soaring seven-story lobby is ringed with interior balconies and filled with sculpture. Mid-size guest rooms are not as dramatic. The rooms are decorated in the bright contemporary Spanish style with lots of color pops, simple Scandinavian furniture, and bathrooms awash in marble and nickel-stainless fixtures. Soundproofing is excellent. The top-floor bar is a dramatic place to get a drink at night, with sweeping city views.

Calle Padre Isla 1. © **98-722-09-00.** www.hotelalfonsov.com. 62 units. 60€–163€ double; 180€–259€ suite. Parking 19€. **Amenities:** Restaurant; bar; free Wi-Fi.

Hotel Posada Regia ★ The two buildings renovated to make this hotel neatly bracket León's period of greatest importance as one dates from the 14th century and the other from the 19th. The furnishings evoke the latter, with their Isabelline lines (comparable to Victorian) and the extensive use of silk broadcloth as upholstery. The family that runs the Regia and its tavern took advantage of the different architecture of the buildings to expose beams in some rooms and to strip plaster from brick or stone walls in others. The color palette tends to favor bold, saturated, warm tones. Many of the spacious bathrooms have corner tubs. Top-floor rooms, tucked under the eaves, are the most romantic. The central location makes the Posada Regia very convenient for seeing the sights.

Calle Regidores 11. © **98-721-31-73.** www.regialeon.com. 36 rooms. 59€–130€ double; discounts for Santiago-bound pilgrims with pilgrim card. **Amenities:** Restaurant; bar; free Wi-Fi.

Parador de León/Hostal San Marcos ★★★   One of the most luxurious and desirable hotels in the entire *parador* group, Hostal San Marcos is situated in the 16th-century former monastery built by Fernando (Isabel's husband) for the order of knights who looked after pilgrims on their way to Santiago de Compostela. The building's Plateresque facade is considered one of the country's best examples of Spanish Renaissance architecture. Book early if you have your heart set on spending the night, as the *parador* is one of the most popular in Spain. For a splurge, reserve the Torreon, or tower room, located in one of the turrets. Most rooms are fairly large and sumptuous with traditional furnishings, and you can't beat the sense of history. Also within the complex are an archaeological museum, a church with a scallop-shell facade in homage to St. James, a serene cloister, a library, and a restaurant that brings an elegant touch to local cuisine.

Plaza de San Marcos 7. ℂ **98-723-73-00.** www.parador.es. 203 rooms. 120€–236€ double; 422€ suite. Free parking. Amenities: Restaurant; bar; free Wi-Fi.

Where to Eat

La Formela ★★ CASTILIAN   The Quindós family launched this warm and rather elegant restaurant back in 1989 as an outgrowth of an art gallery run by paterfamilias Jaime. Indeed, one of the small dining rooms, where artists were entertained when their shows opened, retains souvenir napkins and tablecloths that painters spontaneously decorated with ballpoint pens and burnt wine corks. Some of the house specialties include the local version of blood sausage (*morcilla*) sautéed with eggs and served with fried potatoes, as well as a garlicky version of *bacalau a pil pil* (a Basque cod dish). The wine list has kept abreast of developments in Spain, and now offers a number of superb Castilla-León reds as an alternative to the heavier Riojas.

Gran Vía San Marcos 38. ℂ **98-722-45-34.** www.hotelquindos.com. Reservations recommended. Main courses 12€–26€; fixed-price menu 24€. Mon–Sat 1:30–3:30pm and 9–11:30pm. Closed Jan.

Taberna Bar Cuervo ★ TAPAS   The streets and squares just south of the cathedral—Barrio Húmedo—are filled with small restaurants and bars that take advantage of León's cured meats, which are famous throughout Spain. Charcuterie here is often just called *embutidos,* or sausages, and the term goes way beyond ground meats stuffed into casings. Many Spanish gourmets consider the local dried beef, known as *cecina de León,* to be the equal of the best air-dried hams of Andalucía. This tavern has an unusually good selection of charcuterie as well as plates of the local cheeses.

Calle de la Sal 6. ℂ **98-725-40-03.** Raciones 7.50€–15€. Daily 11am–midnight.

Exploring León

Catedral de León (Santa María de Regla) ★★★ CATHEDRAL   This is why almost everyone visits León—to see the sun shine through the most dramatic stained glass windows in Spain. There are 125 in all (plus 57 oculi), dating from the 13th century. They are so heavy that the roof of the cathedral is held up not by the walls, but by flying buttresses. In the church-building frenzy of the Middle Ages, every Gothic cathedral vied to distinguish itself with some superlative trait. Milan Cathedral was the biggest, Chartres had the most inspiring stained-glass windows, Palma de Mallorca had the largest rose window, and so on. Structurally, though, the boldest cathedral was at León. This edifice set a record for the greatest proportion of window space, with stained-glass windows

The Catedral de León.

soaring 34m (112 ft.) to the vaulted ceiling, framed by the slenderest of columns. The windows occupy 1,672 sq. m (nearly 18,000 sq. ft.), or almost all the space where you'd expect the walls to be. Inside, the profusion of light and the illusion of weightlessness astonish even medievalists. The architects (Juan Pérez and Maestro Enrique) who designed the cathedral in the 13th century were, in effect, precursors of architect Mies van der Rohe, 7 centuries before the age of steel girders draped with plate-glass curtain walls. It is the experience of being surrounded by color and light that makes this cathedral so special.

Plaza de Regla. ✆ **98-787-57-70.** www.catedraldeleon.org. Admission to cathedral free; museum 4€; cloisters 1€. Cathedral July–Sept Mon–Sat 9:30am–2pm and 4–7:30pm; Oct–June Mon–Fri 9:30am–1:30pm and 4–7pm, Sat 9:30am–1:30pm. Museum Mon–Fri 9:30am–1:30pm and 4–7pm; Sat 9:30am–1:30pm. Bus: 4.

MUSAC (Museo de Arte Contemporáneo de Castilla y León) ★ ART MUSEUM

We seriously doubt that the city of León will ever rival, say, Berlin for international hipness, but even León deserves a taste of the avant-garde, which this museum supplies in spades. From the exterior, its panels of stained glass evoke a box of Crayola crayons or a rack of paint chips in the "bold" collection. Even on a dreary winter day MUSAC looks cheery and inviting. The collections focus mostly on artists under the age of 40, and the programming has won a number of European awards for daring innovation in presenting conceptual pieces, like a re-created car accident. Marcel Duchamp is no doubt chuckling in his grave.

Av. de los Reyes Leoneses 24. ✆ **98-709-00-00.** www.musac.org.es. Free admission. Tues–Fri 10am–3pm and 5–8pm; Sat–Sun 11am–3pm and 5–9pm. Bus: 7 or 11.

Real Colegiata de San Isidoro ★ CHURCH

The Leónese boast that "León had 24 kings before Castilla even had laws." Eleven of them (along with 14 queens and many other nobles) are entombed here in the 12th-century burial

vault, a marvelously spooky Romanesque room with fanciful ceiling frescoes of biblical scenes and court life. The church is no slouch either. The treasury has some rare finds—10th-century Scandinavian ivory, an 11th-century chalice, and an important collection of 10th- to 12th-century fabrics from Asia. The library museum contains many ancient manuscripts and rare books, including a Book of Job from A.D. 951, a Visigothic Bible, and a Bible from 1162, plus dozens of miniatures.

Plaza San Isidoro 4. ✆ **98-787-61-61.** www.sanisidorodeleon.net. Admission to church free; Pantheon and museum 4€. Church daily 7am–11pm. Pantheon and museum July–Aug Mon–Sat 9am–8pm, Sun 9am–2pm; Sept–June Mon–Sat 10am–1:30pm and 4–6:30pm, Sun 10am–1:30pm. Bus: 4 or 9.

The colorful exterior of the MUSAC.

Entertainment & Nightlife

Few other cities in Spain evoke the mystery of the Middle Ages like León. To best appreciate the old-fashioned eloquence of the city, wander after dark around the Plaza Mayor, the edges of which are peppered with simple cafes and bars. None is particularly distinct from its neighbor, but overall the effect is rich, evocative, and wonderfully conducive to conversation and romance. One of the best places for drinks is **León Antiguo,** Plaza del Cid 16 (no phone), which is open Monday to Wednesday 7pm to midnight and Thursday to Saturday 7pm to 4am. Drinks cost 2€ to 5€.

ANDALUCÍA

7

M uch of what the world imagines as Spain is, in fact, Andalucía. It was the cradle of flamenco, the stomping grounds of the amorous Don Juan, and the tragic setting for *Carmen*. It's the region where bulls are bred and matadors are more famous than rock stars. Nothing in Andalucía is done halfway. The flowers are brighter and the music is both more melancholy and more joyful. Although Andalucía is often a stand-in for Spain in the popular imagination, it was, in fact, the last stronghold of the Moors, who held al-Andalus for over 7 centuries. Consequently, Andalucía shines with all the medieval Muslim glories of Europe: the world-famous Mezquita (mosque) of Córdoba, the Alhambra Palace of Granada, and (in their own way as Christian-Muslim hybrids) Sevilla's imposing Alcázar and looming Gothic cathedral. Its smaller towns can be haunting in their beauty: the whitewashed mountain villages, the Renaissance grace of Ubeda, the drama of gorge-split Ronda, the languor of sherry-besotted Jerez de la Frontera, and the brilliance of gleaming Cádiz. Spend a week or a month, and you'll have only skimmed the surface.

This dry, mountainous region also embraces the Costa del Sol (including Málaga, Marbella, and Torremolinos), developed as the beachside playground of southern Spain and covered in the following chapter. Go to the Costa del Sol for beach resorts, the bar scene, and water sports; visit Andalucía for its architectural wonders, signature cuisine and music, and sheer beauty.

SEVILLA ★★★

Sevilla is Andalucía's largest, most self-assured, and most sophisticated city—the hometown of the passionate Carmen and the lusty Don Juan. Style matters here. Almost every Sevillana owns at least one flamenco dress to wear during the city's famous April *fería*—or to a friend or family member's wedding. It may also be the most ornately decorated city in Spain. No country does baroque like the Spanish, and no city does Spanish baroque like Sevilla, where the style represents the hybrid offspring of Moorish decoration and the Catholic insistence on turning every abstract curlicue of Islam into a Christian angel's wing. Sevilla has been Andalucía's center of power and influence since Fernando III of Castilla tossed out the Almohad rulers in 1248. But Fernando wisely left Barrio Santa Cruz intact, and the tangled ancient streets of the Judería still make the medieval era palpable. As the first major city in the heart of Andalucía to return to Spanish hands, Sevilla has a markedly Christian countenance. The city is studded with churches and former convents funded by the riches that flowed into the city from its 16th to 18th century trade monopoly with the New World.

PREVIOUS PAGE: **Flamenco dancer in Sevilla.**

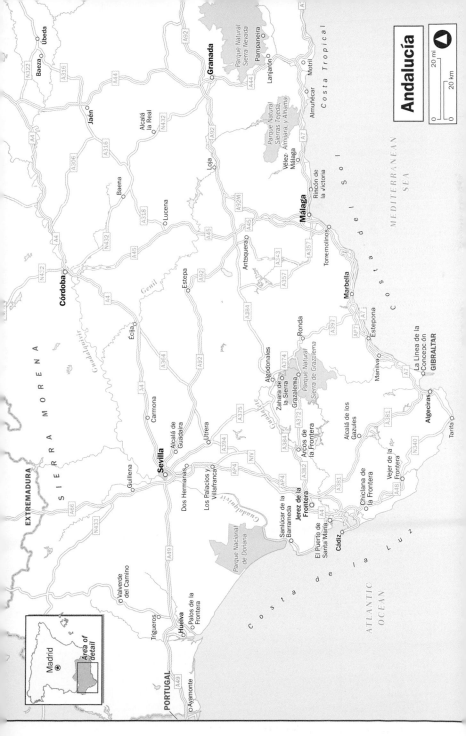

Andalucía

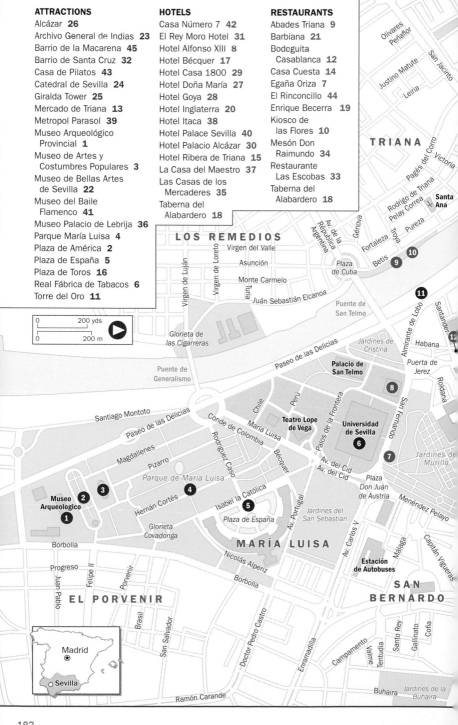

Sevilla

Río Guadalquivir

Descubrimientos

Puente de la Cartuja

Pinzón

Clara de Jesús Montero

Chapina

15

Rafael Salas Gonzalez

Alfarería

Procurador

Castilla

Requena

14

San Jacinto

13

Fabie

Rocio

Belis

Plaza Altozano

Puente de Isabel II

Benidorm

Arjona

Trastmara

Av. Cristo de la Expiración

Puente del Cacherro

Estación de Autobuses

Plaza San Laureano

Antigua Estación de Córdoba

Barca

Rajeles

Darsena

Torneo

Paseo de Cristóbal Colón

Reyes Católicos

Julio Cesar

Marqués de Paradas

Gravina

Canalejas

Museo de Bellas Artes

22

Redes

Goles

Baños

Pascual de Gayangos

Juan Rabadán

Curtidurías

Adriano

Pastor y Landero

Galera

Santas Patronas

San Pablo

San Roque

San Vicente

Miguel Cid

Alphonso XII

Plaza de Toros

16

Castelar

Zaragoza

Morán

Méndez Núñez

Monsalves

San Eloy

Jesus de la Vera Cruz

Martinez Montañes

Cardenal Spinola

Alcoy

Santa Ana

ARENAL

Vartora

General Castaños

Gamazo

Harinas

19

20

Plaza Nueva

Bilbao

21

Tetuán

O'Donnell

Rioja

Velázquez

Campana

CENTRO

Jesus del Gran Poder

San Lorenzo

San Lorenzo

Hospital de la Caridad

Av. de la Constitución

Ayuntamiento

San José

Sierpes

Rivero

Palacio de Lebrija

36

Trajano

Amor de Dios

Martin Villa

Potro

Alameda de Hercules

Archivo de Indias

23

Catedral

Alemanes

33

Álvarez Quintero

Francos

35

Córdoba

Cuna

Ortilla

Larana

Don Pedro Niño

Joaquin Costa

Corredurria

24

25

Argote de Molina

34

Salvador

San Isidoro

Anunciación

Gestoso

Marco Sancho

Pl. del Triunfo

Pl. Virgen de Los Reyes

Palacio Arzobispal

41

39

Plaza de la Encarnación

Virato

Feria

Feria

26

30

29

27

Abades

Pérez Galdós

Santillana

40

Alcázar

Mateos Gago

28

Corral del Rey

Imagen

Sor Ángela de la Cruz

Gonzalez Cuadrado

Pedro Miguel

45

Ila

Agua

Gloria

31

Santa Cruz

Fabiola

San José

Vírgenes

42

Boteros

Apodaca

Gerona

Dueñas

Castellar

Palacio de las Dueñas

Iglesia de San Luis

SANTA CRUZ

32

Santa María la Blanca

Céspedes

Levies

Lirio

Plaza Cristo de Burgos

Alhóndiga

37

44

Bustos Tavera

Sol

Iglesia de San Marcos

San Luis

Menéndez Pelayo

Vidrio

Tintes

Casa de Pilatos

43

San Leandro

Santiago

San Esteban

Azafrán

Jauregui

Plaza Ponce de León

Escuelas Pias

Pinto

Matahacas

Santa Paula

Socorro

Iglesia de San Marcos

Convento de Santa Isabel

Convento de Santa Paula

Demetrio de los Ríos

José María Moreno Galván

La Florida

Juglar

Navarros

Conde Negro

Osario

Valle

Sol

Enladriadas

Iglesia de San Julien

Jiménez Aranda

Blanco White

Av. Luis Montoto

Recaredo

Arroyo

Jardines del Valle

Maria Auxiliadora

Santa Lucia

Ronda de Capuchinos

Trovador

Juan De Vera

Juan Antonio Cabestany

Lope de Vega

Jupiter

Gonzalo Bilbao

Jose Lagullo

Perez Hervas

LA CALZADA

Arroyo

Arroyo

Essentials

GETTING THERE Sevilla's **Aeropuerto San Pablo,** Calle Almirante Lobo (✆ **90-240-47-04;** www.aena-aeropuertos.es), is served by nearly two dozen airlines, including Iberia, Air Europa, Vueling, British Air, EasyJet, and Ryanair. The airport lies 9.6km (6 miles) from the center of the city, along the highway leading to Carmona. A bus run by **Transportes Urbanos de Sevilla** (✆ **90-245-99-54**) meets all incoming flights and transports you into the center of Sevilla for 4€.

Train service into Sevilla is centralized into the **Estación Santa Justa,** Av. Kansas City s/n (✆ **90-242-22-42;** www.renfe.com). Buses C1 and C2 take you from this train station to the bus station at Prado de San Sebastián, and bus EA runs to and from the airport. The high-speed AVE train has reduced travel time from Madrid to Sevilla to 2½ hours. The train makes 18 trips daily, with a stop in Córdoba, and costs 55€ to 86€. About three dozen trains daily connect Sevilla and Córdoba, taking from 45 minutes to 1¼ hours. Ten additional trains run to Málaga (2–2½ hr.) and four trains to Granada (3¼ hr.).

The new bus station at **Plaza de Armas** (✆ **95-490-80-40**) handles most long-distance bus traffic, while most buses within Andalucía use the **Prado de San Sebastián** terminal near Plaza de España, Calle Manuel Vazquez Sagastizabal, s/n. (✆ **95-441-71-11**). For information and ticket prices visit www.alsa.es.

Sevilla is 549km (341 miles) southwest of Madrid and 217km (135 miles) northwest of Málaga. Several major highways converge on Sevilla, connecting it with the rest of Spain and Portugal. Sevilla is easy to drive to, but extremely difficult to drive around in (or to park).

GETTING AROUND Don't even consider driving around Sevilla. If you give up a parking space you will never find another. Fortunately, the city is eminently walkable. If you need to get from one end to another in a hurry, hop an inexpensive bus (1.40€) instead of paying 10€ for a taxi. The city tram and Metro system is good for commuters but of little use to sightseers. The municipal bicycle rental program, **SEVICI,** provides access to bikes for a small subscription charge plus an even smaller hourly fee. The snazzy red bikes are parked in 250 areas all over the city, each with a kiosk where you can subscribe by credit card. A 1-week membership is 12€, and time fees range from 1.05€ to 2.05€ per hour (✆ **90-201-10-32;** www.sevici.es).

VISITOR INFORMATION The tourist office, **Oficina de Información del Turismo,** at Plaza de San Francisco, 15 (Edificio Laredo; ✆ **95-459-52-88;** www.sevilla.org), is open Monday to Friday 9am to 7:30pm, Saturday 9:30am to 7:30pm, and Sunday 9:30am to 3pm.

SPECIAL EVENTS The most popular times to visit Sevilla are during the **April Fair**—the most famous *feria* in Spain—and during **Holy Week (Semana Santa),** when religious floats called *pasos* are carried through the streets by robed penitents. Book lodging far in advance for both.

FAST FACTS There's a **U.S. consulate** at Plaza Nueva, 8 (✆ **95-421-87-51**), open Monday to Friday 11am to 1pm. For **medical emergencies,** go to the Hospital Virgen del Rocío, Av. Manuel Siurot s/n (✆ **95-501-20-00**), about 2km (1¼ miles) from the city center.

If you need a **cab,** call **Tele Taxi** (✆ **95-462-22-22**) or **Radio Taxi** (✆ **95-458-36-05**). Cabs are metered and charge a 2.66€ pickup fee by day, 3.34€ at night. Rates are 0.66€/km by day, 0.81€/km at night.

Where to Stay in Sevilla

If you choose lodging near the cathedral, the bells may jar you awake. Locals who grew up nearby claim they never notice the sound, and it's true that most visitors become accustomed to them quickly. During Semana Santa and *feria*, hotels double or even triple their rates, with increases often announced at the last minute. If you're going to be in Sevilla at these times, arrive with an ironclad reservation and an agreed price before checking in.

EXPENSIVE

Casa Número 7 ★★   You could walk right past this tiny boutique hotel in Barrio Santa Ana and never realize the delights that lie behind its unpresuming facade. This 19th-century mansion features just six tastefully decorated rooms that represent a relaxed version of Spanish hacienda style. The hotel is intended as a place of rest, and it may be in the quietest location in an otherwise noisy city. There is strong Wi-Fi, but there are no televisions. Rooms are named by their dominant decorating color and range from the spacious Yellow Room, which has a balcony opening onto the street, to the snug Blue Room, with just one large bed instead of two. All have sumptuous marble baths.

Calle Vírgenes, 7. ✆ 95-422-15-81. www.casanumero7.com. 6 rooms. 130€–177€ double. Bus: 10, 15, 24, or 32. **Amenities:** Bar; free Wi-Fi.

Hotel Alfonso XIII ★★   Designed to be the model of decadent opulence, this neo-Mudéjar fantasy was built as the most luxurious hotel for the 1929 Exposición Iberoamericana. For generations it was the most exclusive address in Sevilla, and since the complete renovation for the Starwoods Luxury Collection was completed in 2013, the leather upholstery on the chairs is again buttery soft, the gilt-paint highlights and hand-painted tiles gleam, and the rich earth tones of the walls, carpets, and draperies conjure a palace from some land distant. The Alfonso XIII boasts old-fashioned service with 21st-century plumbing and wireless technology.

Calle San Fernando, 2. ✆ 800/325-3589 in the U.S. and Canada, or 95-491-70-00. www.hotel-alfonsoxiii-seville.com. 147 units. 209€–409€ double; from 359€ jr. suite; from 459€ suite. Parking 20€. Bus: 10 or 15. **Amenities:** 2 restaurants; 3 bars; concierge; exercise room; outdoor pool; outdoor tennis court (lit); Wi-Fi for a fee.

Hotel Casa 1800 ★★   This charming boutique hotel steps from the cathedral occupies an 1864 limestone mansion built for the mayor of Sevilla. After 3 years of renovation to preserve its historic details, it opened as a hotel in spring 2011. Many rooms have exposed beams from the original structure and the original plaster-on-stone walls were retained wherever possible. The hotel is filled with original art, giving it the gracious air of a private manse. The decor is luxe—tufted ottomans, overhead chandeliers, beds with artistic and elaborate headboards, and parquet wood floors. The rooftop terrace has stunning views of the Alcázar and the cathedral. Room 302 on the terrace level has a private terrace and is the most requested room in the house. It is one of three deluxe rooms with a terrace and Jacuzzi tub.

Calle Rodrigo Caro, 6. ✆ 95-456-18-00. www.hotelcasa1800.com. 24 rooms. 130€–230€ double. Bus: T1, C5. **Amenities:** Restaurant; 2 bars; concierge; free Wi-Fi.

MODERATE

El Rey Moro Hotel ★★   Created in 2009 from a 16th-century manor house built around a patio with an 8th-century Moorish fountain, the family-run El Rey Moro spans the centuries with colorful contemporary rooms inspired by historic design motifs. Wall colors are warm and intense, and the furnishings tend to be quirky, one-of-a-kind pieces. The rooms are arrayed on two levels around the central courtyard, and many of them retain the old plaster walls and exposed ceiling beams of the original house. This corner of Barrio Santa Cruz is about a 4-minute walk from the cathedral. Guests have free use of house bicycles.

Calle Lope de Rueda, 14. ✆ **95-456-34-68.** www.elreymoro.com. 19 rooms. 79€–189€ double. Bus: T1, C5. **Amenities:** Restaurant; free Wi-Fi.

Hotel Bécquer ★   The palace of the Marquès de Los Torres was converted into this grand hotel in the 1970s, with some antiques saved from the old building. Only two blocks from the Río Guadalquivír, it's close to the Puente Isabel II for walking into Triana, and not far from the bullring, but for other sights you'll likely need to take a taxi. Rooms are small, low-key, and modern with either two twins or one double bed. Guests who book through the hotel website get a laptop, PlayStation, and iPad to use onsite.

Calle Reyes Católicos, 4. ✆ **95-422-89-00.** www.hotelbecquer.com. 141 units. 73€–161€ double. Parking 15€. Bus: C1, C2, or C4. **Amenities:** Restaurant; 2 bars; rooftop pool; spa; free Wi-Fi.

Hotel Doña María ★★   You can never be too close to the centers of power. No doubt that's what Samuel Levi thought when he had his 14th-century in-town palace built here next to the Alcázar so that he could pop in to advise Pedro the Cruel. (Legend holds that there were once underground passageways between the buildings.) By the late 19th century, the structure belonged to the Marquises de Pena, who gave it the current facade for the 1929 Exposición Iberoamerica. In 1965, the Marquise de San Joaquín turned the palace into a hotel, making her Sevilla's first woman hotelier. Alterations over the years have carved out rooms in different shapes and sizes, so ask to move if you're unhappy with what you get. The vast lobby area and hallways are filled with Spanish antiques and old paintings. The rooftop terrace has a small pool, but most guests gravitate to the bar with its in-your-face views of the cathedral and La Giralda. The hotel has a relaxed, old-fashioned feel complemented by the warm and attentive service.

Calle Don Remondo, 19. ✆ **95-422-49-90.** www.hdmaria.com. 64 units. 75€–154€ double. Parking 20€. Bus: C1, C2, or C4. **Amenities:** 2 bars; outdoor pool; free Wi-Fi.

Hotel Inglaterra Sevilla ★   A frankly overdue renovation in 2012 restored this 1857 grande dame to its former glory while reconfiguring the spaces to create fewer, larger rooms. As the name suggests, the hotel emulates *el corte inglés*, the English style that inspired the name of the department store chain. Nowhere is it more evident than in the lounges and bars on the ground level, where the polished wood and the bottles of Scotch make you think that Winston Churchill and his bulldog will come wandering out at any minute. Service here is gracious and old-fashioned. Rooms are fresh and simply decorated with brocaded floral fabrics in subdued gold tones and wooden chairs and headboards; the tile and marble baths all have contemporary fixtures. The Plaza Nueva location could not be more central.

Plaza Nueva, 7. ✆ **94-522-49-70.** www.hotelinglaterra.es. 86 rooms. 79€–184€ double. Bus: T1, C5. **Amenities:** Restaurant; 2 bars; concierge; free Wi-Fi.

Hotel Palace Sevilla ★ Opening onto Plaza de la Encarnación and the monumental "Las Setas" (p. 195, many rooms have views of it), this richly appointed small hotel opened in 2013. The decor references Sevilla's baroque tradition, especially in the swirling forms and heavy ruffles, yet it's all executed with a modern color palette that suggests whimsy rather than slavish imitation. Beds are big and plush and every room is equipped with state-of-the-art hydro-massage showers. Superior doubles even come with a laptop at the desk (though this line of rooms can be snug). The ground-level terrace is a bar, becoming a dinner restaurant in summer.

Plaza de la Encarnación, 17. ℂ **95-531-09-09.** www.hotelsevillapalace.es. 34 rooms. 80€–145€ double. Bus: 27, 32, A2. **Amenities:** Bar; concierge; free Wi-Fi.

Hotel Palacio Alcázar ★ Located on a quiet, orange tree–filled plaza nearly touching the walls of the Alcázar, this breezy and modern boutique guest house occupies the former home and studio of American bullfighter and painter John Fulton. The days when he made it a crash pad for aspiring matadors are long gone, but the tiny property, which became a hotel in 2011, retains his sense of generous hospitality. Bright impressionistic paintings cover the doors of all the units. Some units have small terraces, while the first-floor Room 3 has a small patio and a spiral staircase to a sleeping loft that could be used for children.

Plaza de Allianza, 11. ℂ **95-450-21-90.** www.palacioalcazar.com. 12 rooms. 51€–150€ double. BusL T1. **Amenities:** Free Wi-Fi.

Hotel Ribera de Triana ★ On the Triana side of the Puente Cristo de la Expiración from the Plaza de Armas bus station, this sleekly modern hotel has sweeping views of the Río Guadalquivír from about half the rooms as well as the shared rooftop terrace. The exercise room, also on the roof, has a hot tub with city views. Designed for business travelers, the Ribera de Triana is an excellent buy for leisure travelers as rooms are larger and more modern than at most hotels.

Plaza Chapina, s/n. ℂ **95-426-80-00.** www.hotelriberadetriana.com. 136 units. 74€–161€ double. Parking 16€. Bus: 170, 174, 176. **Amenities:** Restaurant; 2 bars; rooftop pool; spa; free Wi-Fi.

La Casa del Maestro ★ Named for the famed flamenco guitarist "Niño Ricardo" (1904–72) who lived and died in the house, this charming little hotel near Plaza de Encarnación is painted with intense, earthy colors. Lacking a restaurant or even an elevator, it is classified by the city as a one-star hotel, yet rivals many a three-star property for charm. The building is the classic three floors around a central courtyard. The street level includes a large lounge area (with computer corner) where you can get coffee and hang out. Rooms are snug but attractively decorated; most have two twin beds.

Calle Niño Ricardo, 5. ℂ **95-450-00-06.** www.lacasadelmaestro.com. 10 rooms. 60€–160€ double. Bus: 27, 32, A2. **Amenities:** Free Wi-Fi.

Las Casas de los Mercaderes ★ Joining two city palaces around a classic Andalucían patio, this three-story boutique hotel is just far enough away from the cathedral to avoid the crowds yet close to almost everything you might want to see. Public areas are quite grand, with lots of pale marble and handsome antique-styled furniture. Guest rooms are cozier, with heavy draperies and marble floors. This hotel is very popular with Spanish families, who book clusters of small rooms at the end of a hallway. Views from the rooftop terrace include, of course, La Giralda.

Calle Alvarez Quintero 9–13. ℂ **95-422-58-58.** www.casasypalacios.com. 47 units. 78€–123€ double. Parking 22€ per day. Bus: 21, 23, 41, or 42. **Amenities:** 2 bars; free Wi-Fi.

INEXPENSIVE

Hotel Goya ★   With its tiled bathrooms, marble tile floors, and pale wooden furniture, the Hotel Goya may have a lot of hard surfaces, but the staff are warm and welcoming and the rooms, while small, are extremely well designed. It's hard to imagine a better bargain lodging in the city, as everything is kept fresh and functional. The location is also very good for walking to the city sites. The hotel sits in the heart of the oldest part of Barrio de Santa Cruz, no more than a 5-minute stroll from the cathedral. Ask for an interior room off the courtyard in the back to avoid street noise.

Calle Mateus Gago, 31. ℂ **95-421-11-70.** www.hostalgoyasevilla.com. 19 units. 55€–95€ double. Bus: 10, 12, 41, or 42. **Amenities:** Free Wi-Fi.

Hotel Itaca Sevilla ★   Installed in a former private mansion, this handsome hotel opened in 2011 on a quiet street on the south side of Plaza de la Encarnación. Rooms circle a pretty courtyard and all have exterior views through well-soundproofed windows. Modern, dark wood furniture with colorful upholstery, walls painted in warm tones, and crisp white linens give all the rooms a contemporary yet timeless air. Rooms tend to be small, but well designed to make maximum use of the space. You get a lot of style for the price.

Calle Santillana, 5. ℂ **95-422-81-56.** www.itacasevilla. 23 rooms. 55€–95€ double. Bus: 27, 32, A2. **Amenities:** Free Wi-Fi.

Where to Eat in Sevilla

The North African influence on Sevilla cuisine is obvious in the honey-sweetened pastries and the abundant dates, almonds, saffron, and lemons. Gazpacho was made here with almonds and garlic long before tomatoes arrived from the New World, and breads are still baked in ancient ovens.

EXPENSIVE

Egaña Oriza ★★★ BASQUE/SPANISH   Long one of the most elegant haute-cuisine restaurants in Sevilla, Egaña Oriza broadened its appeal in 2010 to include a tapas bar where you can still enjoy the creative cooking of Basque-born chef José Mari Egaña in a casual and less expensive format. (Most tapas are under 4€, and the tapa of the day with a beer or glass of wine is just 3.60€.) The more refined dining room is a model of white linens and crystal glassware, set inside the glassed-over courtyard of a historic mansion next to the Jardins de Murillo. Egaña has simplified his cuisine over the years, adding such dishes as a pappardelle carbonara with caviar (a first course) to Basque classics like hake with fried garlic or his wild boar stew with homemade quince compote.

Calle San Fernando, 41. ℂ **95-422-72-54.** www.restauranteoriza.com. Main courses 14€–28€; daily menu 45€. Mon–Sat 1:30–3:30pm and 8:30–11:30pm. Bus: 21 or 23. Closed Aug.

Taberna del Alabardero ★★ ANDALUCIAN   The upstairs dining rooms of this elegant town house near the Plaza de Toros have earned a reputation as one of the finest upscale restaurants in Sevilla. But it's frankly more fun to eat off the bistro menu in the downstairs tile-encrusted dining room that adjoins the central atrium cafe. The dishes are less precious, and everything is prepared and served by the faculty and students of the hotel and hospitality school, started here many years ago by a priest looking for a way to give street kids some marketable skills. The dishes are rib-stickers: the hearty potato and sausage stew known as Riojanas, cod *a pil pil* served with ratatouille topped with a poached egg, duck in Sevilla orange sauce, and rice pudding with a side of profiteroles. The restored mansion also serves as an inn, with seven spacious and elegant guest rooms.

Calle Zaragoza, 20. © **95-450-27-21.** www.tabernadelalabardero.es. Reservations recommended. Main courses 19€–32€; 3-course bistro menu 13€ weekdays, 18€ weekends. Daily 1:30–4:30pm and 8:30pm–midnight. Inn: 7 rooms. 110€–150€ double; 150€–200€ junior suite. Bus: 21, 25, 30, or 43. Restaurant closed Aug.

MODERATE

Enrique Becerra ★ ANDALUCIAN   The upstairs dining room at this establishment just one street off Plaza Nueva serves excellent grilled meat and fish, but it's frankly too quiet. Everyone prefers to crowd into the bar and adjacent dining room on the ground floor to enjoy creative tapas—soft-cooked foie gras on toast, finger rolls stuffed with spicy steamed mussels, lamb meatballs in mint sauce, or cod in a pasta sack with almond-garlic sauce. The 35 sherries by the glass are very reasonably priced.

Calle Gamazo, 2. © **95-421-30-49.** www.enriquebecerra.com. Tapas 3€–4€; *raciones* 6€–13€; main courses in restaurant 12€–22€. Mon–Sat 1–4:30pm and 8pm–midnight (closed Sat July–Aug). Bus: 21, 25, 30, or 40.

Barbiana ★★ ANDALUCIAN/SEAFOOD   If you've ever tasted the Manzanilla Barbiana from Sanlúcar de Barrameda, you already know what kind of food to expect at this related restaurant planted next to Plaza Nueva. Tangy and yeasty, with a hint of green almonds, it's a perfect complement to fish from the Huelva coast and crustaceans from Sanlúcar itself, and that's exactly what Barbiana serves. The kitchen offers mixed seafood with rice (*not* paella) at midday but not in the evening, when the volume of diners steers the menu toward quicker preparations like *tortillitas de camarones,* a fried batter of chickpea flour with tiny whole shrimp, or grilled rockfish (*sargo*) on garlicky red peppers.

Calle Albareda, 11. © **95-422-44-02.** www.restaurantebarbiana.com. Reservations recommended. Main courses 9€–27€. Mon–Sat noon–5pm and 8pm–midnight. Bus: 21, 25, 30, or 40.

Casa Cuesta ★ ANDALUCIAN   Right across a small plaza from the Mercado de Triana, this historic tapas bar and drinking place of fishermen and bullfighters still boasts the checkerboard marble floors and ornate polished bar of its late 19th-century origins. Known for salty classics such as *jamón serrano,* triangles of Manchego cheese, and potato salad with lots of garlic, Casa Cuesta is also acclaimed for its *flamequines.* They consist of a piece of pork sirloin wrapped in *jamón serrano,* battered, and deep-fried. They make you thirsty for another beer, which is the point.

Calle Castilla 1, Triana. © **95-433-33-35.** www.casacuesta.net. Tapas 3€–5€; larger plates 7€–19€. Daily noon–midnight. Bus: B2 or 43.

Mesón Don Raimundo ★ ANDALUCIAN   You can enjoy the trappings of history when you eat at this formal and classic restaurant in Barrio de Santa Cruz. Originally a Jewish residence, it was converted to a convent in 1362 and served as Sevilla's first post office in the 19th century. The dining rooms are elegant spaces with high-coffered ceilings and moody historic paintings on the walls. The food, we're happy to report, is brighter, more boisterous, and full of flavor. The combination of sweet and savory is typical of Sevillano Mozarabic cooking. Look for it in the venison stew, or the pheasant braised with apples. One of the restaurant's signature seafood dishes is the casserole of squid, grapes, and small fish.

Calle Argote de Molina, 26. © **95-422-33-55.** www.mesondonraimundo.com. Reservations recommended. Main courses 15€–26€. Daily noon–4pm and 7:30pm–midnight. Bus: 21, 23, or 25.

INEXPENSIVE

Bodeguita Casablanca ★★★ ANDALUCIAN   Established in 2005, this little corner bar near the Puerta de Jerez run by Tomás and Antonio Casablanca is justly acclaimed for the kitchen's deft riffs on traditional dishes. The Casablancas convert the humble *tortilla Española* into the noble Tortilla al Whisky, copied by chefs all over Spain. (The sauce is carefully cooked so the alcohol from the Scotch is retained.) In deference to the burger craze, the brothers created a radically Spanish version: two salt cod sliders served on a puddle of melted cheese. Most diners graze on tapas, but Casablanca also offers full plates, including a huge roast leg of lamb.

Calle Adolfo Rodríguez Jurado, 12. ✆ **95-422-41-14.** www.bodeguitacasablanca.com. Tapas 2.50€; plates 12€–20€. Mon–Fri 7am–5pm and 8:15pm–12:30am, Sat 12:30–5:30pm. Bus: T1. Closed Sat-Sun in July, closed August.

El Rinconcillo ★ ANDALUCIAN   El Rinconcillo was established in 1670 on a small street east of Plaza de Encarnación. It was no doubt updated sometime in the last 3-plus centuries, but not recently—which is, of course, its charm. The latest additions to the decor were the Art Nouveau tile murals installed sometime in the late 19th or early 20th century. The lights are dim, and hams and sausage dangle from the heavily beamed ceilings. Good luck scoring one of the marble-topped tables. We usually stand at the bar where the bartender runs our tab in chalk. Some of the most famous tapas are the house *croquetas* and the casserole of chickpeas and spinach.

Calle Gerona, 42. ✆ **95-422-31-83.** www.elrinconcillo.es. Tapas 2.50€–3.50€; plates 9€–18€; set menus 26€–39€. Thurs–Tues 1pm–1:30am. Bus: 12, 27, 32, A2, C5.

Restaurante Las Escobas ★ ANDALUCIAN/CASTILIAN   When Cervantes ate here in the late 16th century, he called Las Escobas a *taberna antigua*, since it had already been around since 1386. That makes it (probably) the oldest eating establishment in Europe. Las Escobas has been in the hands of its current owners for more than 40 years. Of all the restaurants on and just off the cathedral square, we feel this spot gives the best value for the money and does the best job preparing traditional cuisine.

Calle Alvarez Quintero, 62. ✆ **95-456-04-16.** www.lasescobas.com. Tapas 2.80€; main courses 11€–17€; daily menu 16€; tasting menu 44€. Daily noon–midnight. Bus: C5.

Exploring Sevilla

A city of 1.7 million people, Sevilla sprawls in every direction from its historic heart. A Metro system is under construction to speed up getting around, but to date it is of little help in the old city. To see the sights, plan to walk. The cathedral and the Alcázar anchor one end of the city, with the Barrio de Santa Cruz spreading north from them and Parque María Luisa spreading south. Due west of the cathedral, heading toward the river, is Arenal, the former ship-building district now dominated by the bullring and its adjacent concert hall. The old commercial district expands north of Plaza Nueva and Plaza Santiago. Shopping is anchored by Calles Sierpes and Cuna as they reach north to Plaza de Encarnación. The neighborhood north of Encarnación is called Macarena after the basilica, and stretches to the northern limit of the old city at the remains of the Moorish walls.

West of Sevilla's old city and across the river, the Barrio de Triana is the old fishermen's and Gypsy quarter, famed for its bullfighters, flamenco musicians, and ceramics in the North African tradition. The large Isla de Cartuja, north of

RIVERSIDE MEALS WITH A view

Possibly the most scenic overviews of Sevilla are from the Triana side of the Guadalquivír opposite the Torre del Oro. Two dining establishments serve on patios overlooking the river. They're literally next to each other, yet their only similarity is the view. The **Kiosco de las Flores** (Calle Betis, s/n; © **95-427-45-76;** www.kioscodelasflores.com) is a casual fried-fish spot with a large menu that most diners ignore, preferring to order a bottle of wine (10€–20€) and cod, hake, or monkfish battered fish "bites." Main dishes are 8€ to 20€. It's open Tuesday to Saturday noon to 4pm and 8pm to midnight, Sunday noon to 4pm. The hyperelegant **Abades Triana** (Calle Betis, s/n;

© **95-428-64-59;** www.abadestriana. com) is often booked solid for weddings because both the setting and the restaurant are so beautiful. But avoid summer Saturdays, and you can treat yourself to the caviar menu or enjoy contemporary, somewhat lightened preparations of roasted fish and meat, followed by one of the fancy desserts (cheese, strawberries, and caramel, for example). Main dishes are 19€ to 29€. Menus range from 35€ for the business lunch to 80€ for the tasting menu. It's open Tuesday to Saturday noon to 4pm and 8 to 11pm, Sunday noon to 5pm. Both restaurants can be reached by buses C3, 5, 40, and 41.

Triana in the river, was the site of Expo '92 and now holds some museums, performance centers, and an amusement park.

Alcázar ★★★ PALACE   Technically the oldest European royal residence still in use (the king and queen stay here when they're in Sevilla), this complex of palaces and fortifications dates from the Almohad rule of Sevilla. It was, however, almost entirely rebuilt after the 1248 reconquest of Sevilla. The older, more austere building is the **Palacio Gótico ★**, built by Alfonso X ("the Wise") in the 13th century. Carlos V modified the Great Hall and the Sala de Fiestas to celebrate his 1526 wedding to his Habsburg cousin (an unfortunate union that triggered the genetic problems of the dynasty). The far more beautiful and much larger **Palacio Mudéjar ★★★** was built in the 14th century by Pedro I ("the Cruel"), likely employing some of the same artisans who worked on the Alhambra in Granada. It's a tour de force of carved plaster and stone, delicate calligraphic friezes, carved wooden ceilings, and splendid decorative tiles. From the Dolls' Court to the Maidens' Court through the domed Ambassadors' Room, it contains some of the finest work of Sevillano artisans. Fernando and Isabel, who at one time lived in the Alcázar, welcomed Columbus here on his return from America. On the top floor, the Oratory of the Catholic Monarchs has a fine altar in polychrome tiles made by Pisano in 1504. The well-kept **gardens ★** are alone worth the visit. Plan to spend about 1½ hours here.

Plaza del Triunfo s/n. © **95-450-23-23.** www.patronato-alcazarsevilla.es. Admission 9.50€ adults, 2.50€ seniors and students, free under age 17. Oct–Mar daily 9:30am–5pm; Apr–Sept daily 9:30am–7pm. Bus: T1.

Archivo General de Indias ★ LIBRARY   The Spanish crown administered its overseas empire from Sevilla, which also served as the landing port for gold and silver bullion. Such an enterprise generated a lot of paperwork, which was eventually filed away in this building. It is a mother lode of documents, enough of which are shown in rotating exhibitions to make for a fascinating visit. The

WALKING TOURS VIA tour bus

Sightseeing buses face a severe limitation in Sevilla, since many of the city's medieval streets can't accommodate large vehicles. To compensate, **City Sightseeing** (the red bus) offers guided walking tours of Parque María Luisa and the barrios of Santa Cruz, Macarena, and Triana to everyone who buys a bus ticket. The bus makes a circuit on main streets, so it does touch bases with the cathedral, the Alcázar, Torre del Oro, the University of Sevilla, and Isla Mágica on Isla de Cartuja. It can be useful if your time is limited. A free ticket for the Torre de los Perdigones overlook (see below) is one of the discounts included. The buses run every 20 to 30 minutes and cost 17€ for adults and 7€ for children for unlimited use in a 24-hour period. To purchase tickets ahead, visit www.citysightseeing.com.

building was designed by Felipe II's favorite architect, Juan de Herrera, as the Lonja (Stock Exchange). In the 17th century, it was headquarters for the Academy of Sevilla, founded in part by the great Spanish artist Murillo. In 1785, during the reign of Carlos III, the building was turned over for use as a general records office for the Indies. Today's Archivo General de Indias contains some 4 million documents, including letters between patron queen Isabel and explorer Columbus. These very rare documents are locked in air-conditioned storage to keep them from disintegrating. On display in glass cases are fascinating documents in which the dreams of the early explorers come alive.

Av. de la Constitución. © **95-450-05-28.** www.mcu.es. Free admission. Mon–Sat 9:30am–4:45pm; Sun 10am–1:45pm. Bus: T1.

Barrio de La Macarena ★ NEIGHBORHOOD   The district around the **Basilica de La Macarena** ★ (Calle Bécquer, 1; © **95-490-18-00**) is one of the most densely residential parts of the old city. To see the area at its best, spend a Saturday afternoon watching wedding parties come and go at the basilica. Men in traditional suits or tuxedos escort women resplendent in elegant shawls and flamenco-influenced designer dresses. When the happy couple rides off in their limousine, the Sevillanos pack into a bar across the street—and another wedding party floods into the church. You can also visit the church daily 9am to 2pm and 5 to 9pm. The 17th-century image of the **Virgen de Mararena** is one of the most venerated in the Holy Week processions. Church treasures are displayed in a separate **exposition room** ★, open the same hours. Admission with audioguide is 6€ adults, 4€ seniors and ages 16 and under.

Closer to the river than the basilica, the **Torre de los Perdigones** ★ (Calle Resolana, 41; © **95-490-93-53;** www.torredelosperdigones.com) is an 1890 industrial tower that has been converted into a scenic overlook with a camera obscura inside to project images of the city on the wall of a darkened room. It is open Monday to Thursday noon to 7pm, Friday to Sunday 11:30am to midnight. Admission is 4€ adults, 2.50€ ages 5 to 12.

Barrio de Santa Cruz ★★★ NEIGHBORHOOD   What was once a ghetto for Spanish Jews—who were forcibly expelled from Spain in 1492—is today one of Sevilla's most colorful districts. Near the old walls of the Alcázar, winding medieval streets with names like Vida (Life) and Muerte (Death) open onto pocket-size plazas. Part of the quintessential experience of visiting Sevilla is getting lost in the Barrio de Santa Cruz, only to stumble into a plaza where a waiter will offer you a seat and a drink. Flower-filled balconies with draping bougainvillea and potted geraniums jut over this labyrinth, shading you from the ferocious Andalucían sun. In the evening it's common to see Sevillanos sitting in the patios sipping wine under the glow of lanterns. To enter the Barrio de Santa Cruz, turn right after leaving the Patio de Banderas exit of the Alcázar. Turn right again at Plaza de la Alianza, going down Calle Rodrigo Caro to Plaza de Doña Elvira. "Santa Crus" is also loosely applied to the dense streets of the Judería that lie just west of the main portion of Santa Cruz.

Barrio de Triana ★★ NEIGHBORHOOD   Across the Guadalquivir from the city center, Triana is Sevilla with an edge. The working-class neighborhood is the traditional quarter of fishermen and *gitanos,* or Gypsies, and the birthplace of many famous bullfighters memorialized on street corners by commemorative plaques. This is also the neighborhood of *alfarerías,* makers of the traditional decorative tiles for which Sevilla is world famous. The tile companies are concentrated on Calle San Jorge and surrounding streets; most have sales rooms open to the public. Ceramics are very old in Triana—legend says that the neighborhood patrons, 3rd-century martyrs Santa Justa and Santa Rufina, were Triana potters.

The riverfront at the foot of Puente Isabel II is called the Puerto de Triana, and it is filled with small *tabernas* and *marisquerías* (shellfish restaurants) that set up outdoor tables during warm weather. This is the best area to head for early evening tapas as well as casual late-night flamenco (p. 200). Farther east along the river, approaching Puente San Telmo, Triana loses its rough edges and gives way to a number of handsome riverfront restaurants.

The historic public market, the **Mercado de Triana** ★★, is located at the end of Puente Isabel II. Redeveloped in 2012 to 2013, it has become a lively attraction in its own right, with a number of excellent tapas bars that serve food and drink well after the food stalls have closed. There is even a small theater in

The mosaic interior of Sevilla's Alcázar fortress.

Courtyard statue at Casa de Pilatos.

the market, which sometimes has lunchtime flamenco performances. The market sits directly next to the historic Moorish fortress known as the **Castillo de San Jorge ★**. There's no charge to visit San Jorge, which has archaeological exhibits showing its Almohad origins and an exhibition about the Spanish Inquisition, which was based here 1481 to 1785. Don't expect thumbscrews and instruments of torture—the exhibits delve sensitively into the causes (and practical political uses) of intolerance and persecution. San Jorge is open Monday to Friday 9am to 2pm, Saturday and Sunday 10am to 2pm.

Casa de Pilatos ★ HISTORIC HOUSE   This 16th-century Andalucían palace of the dukes of Medinaceli recaptures the splendor of the past, casually combining Gothic, Mudéjar, and Plateresque styles in its courtyards, fountains, and salons. Legend says that the house is a reproduction of Pilate's House in Jerusalem, but the distinctly Sevillano character of the architecture argues otherwise. The house has exhibits, supplemented by an audioguide, on both the ground floor and the first floor, used until recently by the family. The interior includes a collection of paintings by Carreño, Pantoja de la Cruz, Sebastiano del Piombo, Lucas Jordán, Batalloli, Pacheco, and Goya, as well as some atmospheric if not terribly accomplished Greek and Roman statuary. The lush gardens, however, are the highlight and are worth the entrance fee. The cascading magenta bougainvillea at the entrance is an iconic image of great wealth in a desert climate like Sevilla's. The palace is about a 7-minute walk northeast of the cathedral on the northern edge of Barrio de Santa Cruz, in a warren of labyrinthine streets.

Plaza Pilatos 1. ✆ **95-422-52-98.** Entire house 8€; ground floor, patio, and gardens 5€. Apr–Oct daily 9am–7pm; Nov–Mar daily 9am–6pm.

Catedral de Sevilla and La Giralda ★★ CATHEDRAL   The largest Gothic building in the world and the third-largest church in Europe, after St. Peter's in Rome and St. Paul's in London, the Catedral de Sevilla was designed by builders with a stated goal—that "those who come after us will take us for madmen." Construction began in the late 1400s on the site of the Almohad mosque and took centuries to complete. Just inside one portal, the tomb of Columbus is held by four carved pall-bearers.

Works of art abound here, many of them architectural, such as the 15th-century stained-glass windows, the iron screens (*rejas*) closing off the chapels, the elaborate 15th-century choir stalls, and the Gothic reredos above the main altar. On the feasts of Corpus Christi and the Immaculate Conception (and on the 3rd day of Feria), six boys (*Los Seises*) from the choir perform a ceremonial dance on the altar dressed in Renaissance plumed hats and wielding castanets. The treasury has works by Goya, Murillo, and Zurbarán, as well as a display of skulls (*sic transit gloria mundi*). You might spot young women praying before the gigantic Murillo painting of the *Vision de San Antonio.* They're asking St. Anthony, patron of the lovelorn, to send them a husband. After touring the dark interior, you emerge into the sunlight of the Patio de Naranjas (Orange Trees), with its fresh citrus scents and chirping birds.

A detail from the altar at Catedral de Sevilla.

La Giralda, the bell tower of the cathedral, is the city's most emblematic monument. Erected as a minaret in the 12th century, it has seen later additions, such as 16th-century bells. Those who climb to the top ascend on a ramp constructed so that the muezzin could ride up on horseback. Those who make it up get a dazzling view of Sevilla. Entrance is through the cathedral.

Av. de la Constitución s/n. © **95-421-49-71.** www.catedraldesevilla.es. Cathedral and tower 8€ adults, 3€ students 25 and under, free for children 14 and under. Sept–June Mon 11am–3:30pm, Tue–Sat 11am–5pm, Sun 2:30–6pm; July–Aug Mon 9:30am–3:30pm, Tue–Sat 9:30am–4:30pm, Sun 2:30-6:30pm. Bus: T1.

Metropol Parasol ★★ LANDMARK Finally completed in 2011, this sprawling wooden structure overshadows the Plaza de la Encarnación with six parasols in mushroom shapes. Locals simply call it "Las Setas" (Spanish for "mushrooms") and you have to see it to believe it. The plaza had been the site of a public market for more than a century. When excavations began to build a new one, Roman and Moorish ruins were found underground, delaying the process for years. Now the underground portion is the Antiquarium, a well-interpreted archaeological site, and the sculptural Las Setas, designed by German architect Jürgen Mayer-Hermann, towers above a new upscale public market that features tapas bars, delis and food stalls. Upper levels of Las Setas include an observation deck and restaurant.

Plaza de la Encarnación, s/n. © **60-663-52-14.** www.setasdesevilla.com. Viewing level 3€; Antiquarium 2.10€. Market Mon–Sat 8am–3pm. Antiquarium Tues–Sat 10am–8pm, Sun 10am–2pm. Viewing level Sun–Thurs 10:30am–11:45pm, Fri–Sat 10:30am–12:45am. Bus: 27, 32, A2.

Museo de Bellas Artes de Sevilla ★★ MUSEUM The convent building that houses this extensive collection of Spanish art nearly upstages the paintings inside. Built in 1594 for the order of the Merced Calzada de la Asunción, it benefited from Sevilla's golden age of painting and ceramics (the courtyard tiles are enthralling). Inside the galleries are the greatest works of Bartolomé Esteban

ROLLING ON THE river

Spanish galleons may no longer sail up the Río Guadalquivír laden with gold, but the river remains one of the great assets of Sevilla. Sightseeing cruises from **Cruceros Torre del Oro** depart from the embankment just below the Torre del Oro at Paseo Muelle Marqués del Contadero. The cruise gives the best possible perspective on Sevilla's bridges, including the four that were constructed from the city to the Isla de Cartuja for Expo '92. The most dramatic of the group is the counter-balanced cable-stay

Puente Alamillo designed by Santiago Calatrava. The form of the bridge has been variously compared to the prow of a ship or the shape of a harp. Either way, it is a lyrical image on the skyline. April to October, cruises depart every 30 minutes from 10am to 8pm; November to March they depart every half-hour 11am to 7pm. For information, call © **95-456-16-92,** or visit www.crucerostorredeloro. com. The cruise costs 15€ for adults; children under 12 are free.

Murillo, including a gigantic image of the Immaculate Conception originally painted for the Convento de San Francisco. Other highlights include works by Sevilla-born Juan Valdés Leal, and Francisco de Zurbarán.

Plaza del Museo 9. © **95-478-65-00.** www.museosdeandalucia.es. Admission 1.50€, free to E.U. residents and students. Mid-Sept–May Tues–Sat 10am–8:30pm, Sun 10am–5pm; June–mid-Sept Tues–Sat 9am-3:30pm; Sun 10am–5pm. Bus: C5.

Museo del Baile Flamenco ★★ MUSEUM   It has been said that there are no schools to create flamenco dancers, just as there are none to create poets. Cristina Hoyos, the founder of this museum, drew instead on her depth of feeling to become one of the most celebrated flamenco dancers of the late 20th century. The impressionistic museum is relatively short on signage and long on film clips and videos that immerse the viewer in the art of the dance. One of the most engrossing exhibits features short videos that demonstrate the seven representative styles (*palos*) of flamenco from the solea to the tangos. In an opening video, Hoyos advises viewers to follow their emotions. It's not necessary to understand flamenco, she asserts. It must be felt. See for yourself at a nightly show (see below).

Calle Manuel Rojas Marcos, 3. © **95-434-03-11**. www.museoflamenco.com. Admission 10€ adults, 8€ students and seniors, 6€ children. Daily 10am–7pm. Bus: C5.

Museo Palacio de la Condesa de Lebrija ★ HISTORIC HOUSE   Nominally a museum of architecture and interior decoration, this historic house is a portrait of the Countess of Lebrija, who owned the 16th-century palace from 1901 until 1914. She installed a number of ancient mosaics (some Roman, some Moorish) and decorated with a surprisingly harmonious collection of Roman, Greek, and Persian statues as well as Louis XVI furniture to go with her 2nd- and 3rd-century B.C. Roman mosaic floors.

Calle Cuna, 8. © **95-422-78-02**. www.palaciodelebrija.com. Admission 8€ both floors, 5€ ground floor. Sept–June Mon–Fri 1:30am–7:30pm, Sat 10am–2pm and 4–8pm, Sun 10am–2pm; July Mon–Fri 9am–3pm, Sat 10am–2pm; Aug Mon–Fri 10am–3pm, Sat 10am–2pm. Bus: 27, 32, A2.

Parque María Luisa ★ PARK   This park, dedicated to María Luisa, sister of Isabel II, was once the grounds of the **Palacio de San Telmo.** The palace, whose baroque facade is visible behind the deluxe Alfonso XIII Hotel, today houses a seminary. In 1929, Sevilla hosted the Exposición Iberoamericana, and many Latin-American countries erected showcase buildings and pavilions in and around the park. Many pavillions still stand, serving as foreign consulates or university buildings. The park is one of the most tranquil areas in the city and attracts Sevillanos who want to row boats on its ponds, walk along flower-bordered paths, jog, or bicycle. The most romantic (if expensive) way to traverse the park is by horse and carriage.

Plaza de América ★ SQUARE   This landmark square, abloom with flowers, shade trees, and exquisite fountains, represents city planning at its best. It houses a trio of pavilions left over from the 1929 Expo. The center holds government offices; on either side are minor museums worth visiting if you have time to spare.

The **Museo Arqueológico Provincial ★** (© 95-478-64-74) contains many artifacts from prehistoric times and the days of the Romans, Visigoths, and Moors. It's open September to June Tuesday to Saturday 10am to 8:30pm, and Sunday 9am to 2:30pm; in July it's open Monday to Friday 9am to 3pm, Saturday 10am to 2pm; in August it's open Monday to Friday 10am to 3pm and Saturday 10am to 2pm. Admission is 1.50€ for adults and free for E.U. residents and students. Buses 30, 31, and 34 stop there. Nearby is the **Museo de Artes y Costumbres Populares ★** (© 95-471-23-91; www.museosdeandalucia.es). In a Mudéjar pavilion opposite the Museo Arqueológico, this is Sevilla's folklore museum. The ground floor displays artifacts of traditional occupations, including

a forge, a baker's oven, a wine press, and a tanner's shop. The ceramics collection on this floor is first-rate. The upstairs is devoted to fashion and costumes, including court dress of the 19th century and embroideries from the factories of Sevilla. It's open September to June Tuesday to Saturday 9am to 8:30pm, and Sunday 9am to 2:30pm; July to August Tuesday to Saturday 9am to 3:30pm, Sunday 10am to 5pm. Admission is 1.50€ for adults, free to E.U. residents and students.

Plaza de España ★ SQUARE   The major building left over from the Exposición Iberoamericana at the Parque María Luisa is the crescent-shaped Renaissance-style structure set on this landmark square. Architect Aníbal González not only designed but supervised construction of the immense structure. You can rent rowboats for excursions on the canal, or you can walk across bridges spanning it. Set into a curved wall are alcoves focusing on the characteristics of Spain's 50 provinces, as depicted in tile murals.

Torre del Oro.

Torre del Oro ★ MUSEUM   The Almohad rulers of Sevilla erected this tower and another just like it across the river in 1220 as a defensive mechanism. A stout chain linked the two, preventing ships from moving in and out of the port without authorization. The system proved fruitless when a Castillian admiral broke the chain during the 1248 siege. The complementary tower vanished centuries ago, but the Torre del Oro has stood for nearly 9 centuries, serving at various times as administrative offices and a warehouse. Its name derives from the unusual yellow-tinged plaster made of mortar, lime, and straw. These days it serves as the Museo Maritimo and recounts the history of port from its Almohad era to its shipping heyday of the 16th and 17th centuries.

Paseo de Cristóbal Colón, s/n. ✆ **95-422-24-19.** Admission 3€ adults, 1.50€ seniors and students; free Mon. Mon–Fri 9:30am–6:45pm; Sat–Sun 10:30am–6:45pm. Bus: 3, 40, 41, C4, C5. Metro Linea 1: Puerta de Jerez.

Real Plaza de Toros ★ LANDMARK   The Real Maestranza de Caballería de Sevilla began construction of this slightly oval bullring in 1761 to replace earlier wooden rings. It was completed in stages over the following 120 years and is one of the oldest and loveliest rings in the country. Guided tours begin in the stands, which seat 12,000 people. Although visitors cannot step onto the orange earth of the ring, they can survey the five gates that help orchestrate the *corrida*, including the gates where matadors and bulls enter the ring, the gate where dead bulls are carried out by three mules, and the gate where matadors exit in triumph if they receive the highest honors from the officials. The paintings and sculptures in the museum help trace the history of the spectacle from an aristocratic demonstration of bravery to a more populist sport in which talented bullfighters can achieve the fame of nobility. A number of bullfighters' costumes are on display, along with the red capes (*muletas*) that the bullfighter uses to attract the bull. Bulls, by the way, are colorblind; they respond to the motion, not the traditional color.

Paseo Colón, 12. ✆ **95-421-03-15.** www.realmaestranza.com. Admission 7€ adults, 4€ seniors and students. Open Nov–Apr daily 9:30am–7pm, May and Oct daily 9:30am–8pm, June–Sept daily 9:30am–11pm. Bus: 3, 40, 41, C4, C5.

A matador faces down a bull at Real Maestranza de Caballería de Sevilla.

Shopping

Calle Sierpes is the main pedestrian shopping promenade in Sevilla. Shops of note include **Artesanía Textil,** Calle Sierpes, 70 (© **95-456-28-40;** www.artesania-textil.com), which sells investment-quality hand-embroidered silk shawls. The clerks are equally helpful if you're interested in a more modestly priced piece that will still look fabulous back home. **Sombrería Maquedano,** Calle Sierpes, 40 (© **95-456-47-71**), sells beautiful men's felt hats ranging from classic Borsalinos to the flatter, wide-brimmed caballero's hat.

To see the evolution of Sevillana style, stroll Calle Cuna, which runs parallel to Sierpes. The shop windows are a fashion show of flamenco wear and flamenco-inspired contemporary fashion. But it's not all ruffles and dangly earrings. Founded in 1892, **El Caballo,** Calle Adriano, 16 (© **95-421-81-27**), near the bullring, sells traditional saddlery, riding equipment, and fashion accessories, including beautiful leather purses and belts.

It's almost impossible to leave Sevilla without buying a piece of pottery. Near the cathedral, **El Azulejo,** Calle Mateos Gago, 10 (© **95-422-00-85**), has fine ceramic pieces in a wide range of prices as well as handpainted fans. In Santa Cruz, **Las Moradas Artesanía Andalusí,** Calle Rodrigo Caro, 20 (© **95-456-39-17**), has large painted tiles of medieval scenes as well as one of the best selections of gift items (from leatherwork and scarves to hair combs and earrings made of plastic that mimics tortoise shell). It is worth a visit to Triana to see the tile-encrusted facade of **Cerámica Santa Ana,** Calle San Jorge, 31, (© **95-433-39-90**). The factory and showroom, which opened in 1870, has a broad selection of painted tiles, pots, tableware, and decorative items in the *azulejo* tradition. A serving bowl for olives with a separate compartment for pits makes an authentic Spanish souvenir. Right down the street in **Cerámica Rocio-Triana,** Calle Antillano Campos, 8 (© **95-434-06-50**), a husband and wife team create more unusual pieces.

If you want a bullfight poster, skip the tourist shops that offer to print your name on a generic poster and visit the shop at the Plaza de Toros, where artist-designed posters from previous seasons are for sale.

Sevilla for Children

Children delight at feeding cracked corn to the white pigeons in **Plaza de América** (p. 197), and you'll definitely want a photo as the birds flock to their outstretched hands. They'll also get a kick out of climbing the series of ramps to the bell tower of **La Giralda** (p. 194) and taking a cruise on the Río Guadalquivír (p. 196). Across the river at Isla de Cartuja, the site of Expo '92, interactive educational displays at the **Pabellón de la Navegación,** Camino de los Descubrimientos (© **95-404-31-11**), capture the sense of adventure of the early navigators whose discoveries helped make Spain rich and powerful. Many of the accurate ship models on display were made for the Expo. A highlight of the visit is the 50m (164-ft.) Torre Mirador, which offers panoramic views of the city. The Pavilion of Navigation is open from November to April Tuesday to Saturday 10am to 7:30pm; Sunday 10am to 3pm. In May, June, September, and October it is open Tuesday to Saturday 11am to 8:30pm; Sunday 11am to 3pm. In July and August hours are Tuesday to Sunday 10am to 3pm.

Also on the site of Expo '92, the amusement park **Isla Mágica,** Rotonda Isla Mágica (© **90-216-17-16;** www.islamagica.es), captures the fun side of the Expo with rides, entertainment and a waterpark that opened in 2014. Isla Mágica is open daily 11am to 11pm (until midnight on Sat) in July and August with more limited hours April to June and September to early November. Adult admission is 22€ for a full day and 16€ for a half-day. Children and senior citizens are 15€ for a whole day and 10€ for a half-day.

Sevilla Nightlife

FLAMENCO

If you only have one night in Sevilla, you should go to flamenco. The city is a cradle of the art form, and has the busiest performance schedule in the country outside Madrid. There are three formats to choose among.

Two educational centers offer very pure flamenco in a style intended to be as educational as it is entertaining. The **Museo del Baile Flamenco,** Calle Manuel Rojas Marcos, 13 (© **95-434-03-11;** www.museoflamenco.com), offers dance-oriented performances in its courtyard daily at 7pm. Admission is 20€ for adults, 14€ seniors and students, and 12€ children. The **Casa de la Memoria de Al Andalus,** Calle Cuna, 6 (© **95-456-06-70;** www.casadelamemoria.es), has two shows per night in a small courtyard space, usually featuring a small troupe of a musician or two, a singer, and one or two dancers. The emphasis here is on early 20th-century styles that emphasize singing as well as dancing. Shows are at 7:30pm and 9pm. Admission is 16€ adults, 14€ students, and 10€ ages 6 to 11. Arrive early, and you can also tour the flamenco history exhibitions.

The flamenco nightclub spectacle, or *tablao,* of choreographed flamenco performances is an honored tradition in Sevilla. Most *tablaos* give you a drink with basic admission and try to sell you a dinner for an extra 20€ to 40€. The dinner is rarely worth the price, but it is convenient and you may get better seats. **El Patio Sevillano,** Paseo de Cristóbal Colón, 11 (© **95-421-41-20;** www.elpatiosevillano.com), has 90-minute shows twice nightly at 7pm and 9:30pm. Admission is 37€. **El Arenal,** Calle Rodó, 7 (© **95-421-64-92;** www.tablaoelarenal.com), also has two nightly shows at 8pm and 10pm. Admission is 37€. At **Los Gallos,** Plaza de Santa Cruz, 11 (© **95-421-69-81;** www.tablaolosgallos.com), the twice-nightly, 2-hour shows begin at 8pm and 10:30pm. Admission is 35€ adults, 20€ children under 8.

Finally, there is the flamenco bar scene, where you may or may not encounter someone playing and/or dancing, but at least you don't have to sit politely in folding chairs. Three of the best are in Triana: **El Rejoneo,** Calle Betis, 31B; the dance club **Lo Nuestro** next door at Calle Betis, 31A on Tuesdays and Thursdays; and **T de Triana,** Calle Betis, 20. They all open between 11pm and midnight and stay open until dawn.

DRINKS & TAPAS

Most Spaniards consider an evening of snacking and drinking to be the definition of a good time. An excellent tapas scene fills **Calle Joaquín Guichot,** a street parallel with the south side of Plaza Nueva, and spills out westward on **Calle Zaragoza.** Another very popular spot for drinks and tapas is the **Gastrosol,** the bar at Las Setas (Metropol Parasol) in Plaza de Encarnación. As the night advances on Wednesdays through Saturdays, prowl the **Alameda de Hercules** for the best in dance clubs and cocktail bars, which don't open before 10 or 11pm. Most are at least gay-friendly, and those that are overtly gay also welcome a straight crowd. A couple of the best bets are **Bar 1987,** Alameda de Hercules, 93, where shoulder pads, mullets, and Euro disco prove that the Eighties never died. **Bar El Barón Rampante,** Calle Arias Montano, 3, is one of the most popular spots.

PERFORMING ARTS

Though often the setting for operas, Sevilla didn't get its own opera house until the 1990s. The **Teatro de la Maestranza,** Paseo de Colón, 22 (*©* **95-422-33-44;** www.teatromaestranza.com), quickly became one of the world's premier venues for opera. The season focuses on works inspired by the city, including Verdi's *La Forza del Destino* and Mozart's *Marriage of Figaro,* although jazz, classical music, and even Spanish *zarzuelas* (operettas) are also performed here. The opera house may be visited only during performances. Tickets (which vary in price, depending on the event) can be purchased daily from 10am to 2pm and 5:30 to 8:30pm at the box office in front of the theater.

Side Trips from Sevilla

CARMONA ★

An easy hour-long bus trip from the main terminal in Sevilla, Carmona is an ancient city that dates from Neolithic times and contains important Roman ruins. Thirty-four kilometers (21 miles) east of Sevilla, it grew in power and prestige under the Moors, establishing ties with Castilla in 1252.

Surrounded by fortified walls, Carmona has three Moorish fortresses—one a *parador,* and the other two the Alcázar de la Puerta de Córdoba and the Alcázar de la Puerta de Sevilla. The most impressive attraction is **Puerta de Sevilla,** with its double Moorish arch opposite Iglesia de San Pedro. Note, too, **Puerta de Córdoba,** on Calle Santa María de Gracia, which was attached to the ancient Roman walls in the 17th century.

The town itself is a national landmark, filled with narrow streets, whitewashed walls, and Renaissance mansions. The most important square, **Plaza San Fernando,** is lined with elegant 17th century houses. The most important church is dedicated to Santa María and stands on Calle Martín López. You enter a Moorish patio before exploring the interior and its 15th-century white vaulting.

In the area known as Jorge Bonsor (named for the original discoverer of the ruins) is a **Roman amphitheater** as well as a **Roman necropolis** containing the remains of 1,000 families who lived in and around Carmona 2,000 years ago. Of the two important tombs, the Elephant Vault consists of three dining rooms and a kitchen. The other, the Servilia Tomb, is the size of a nobleman's villa. The **Museo de la Ciudad** (*©* **95-423-24-01;** www.museociudad.carmona.org; 3€ adults, free for students and children) displays artifacts discovered at the site. At press time it was closed for renovations (check website for info).

If you're driving to Carmona, exit from Sevilla's eastern periphery onto the N-V superhighway, follow the signs to the airport, and then proceed to Carmona on the road to Madrid. The Carmona turnoff is clearly marked.

To stay overnight, try the elegant **Casa de Carmona ★★**, Plaza de Lasso 1, (*©* **95-419-10-00;** www.casadecarmona.com). This 16th-century private home turned luxury hotel retains the marble columns, imposing masonry, and graceful proportions of the original structure. Each of the 33 units is opulently furnished in a Roman, Moorish, or Renaissance theme. Rates are 68€ to 158€ double, 148€ to 218€ junior suite.

ITÁLICA ★

Lovers of Roman history shouldn't miss Itálica (*©* **95-562-22-66**), the ruins of an ancient city northwest of Sevilla on the major road to Lisbon.

After the battle of Ilipa, Publius Cornelius Scipio Africanus founded Itálica in 206 B.C. Two of the most famous Roman emperors, Trajan and Hadrian, were born here. Indeed, master builder Hadrian was to have a major influence on his hometown. During his reign, the **amphitheater,** the ruins of which can be seen today, was among the largest in the Roman Empire. Lead pipes that carried water from the Río Guadalquivír still remain. A small **museum** displays some of the Roman statuary found here, although the finest pieces have been shipped to Sevilla. Many mosaics, depicting beasts, gods, and birds, are on exhibit, and others are constantly being discovered. The ruins, including a Roman theater, can be explored for 1.50€ (free to E.U. residents). The site is open April to May and the second half of September Tuesday to Saturday 9am to 8pm and Sunday 9am to 3pm. From June to mid-September, it's open Tuesday to Saturday 9am to 3:30pm and Sunday 10am to 5pm. From mid-September to March, it's open Tuesday to Saturday 9am to 6:30pm and Sunday 10am to 4pm.

If you're driving, exit from the northwest periphery of Sevilla, and follow the signs for Highway E-803 in the direction of Zafra and Lisbon. A bus marked M-172 goes to Itália, and departures are from Sevilla's Estación de Autobuses at Plaza de Armas. Buses depart every hour for the 30-minute trip.

CÓRDOBA ★★★

To visit Córdoba is to glimpse what might have been. A millennium ago, Muslims, Christians, and Jews lived and worked together to create western Europe's greatest city—a cosmopolitan center of poetry, art, music, philosophy, cutting-edge science and medicine, and far-ranging scholarship. Until the late 11th century, Córdoba was the capital of western Islam. La Mezquita, the largest medieval mosque in Europe, remains its star attraction. The streets and whitewashed buildings of Andalucía's most intact Moorish city still endure, and visiting Córdoba is ultimately less about monuments and more about getting lost in the maze of cobbled streets that bore witness to an ancient, harmonious world.

You can hit the highlights in a long day, but Córdoba deserves the attention that comes from staying overnight, if only to experience the timeless Judería just after dawn, when you can hear the echoing step of every foot in the narrow streets. There are other advantages to staying the night. Every morning from 8:30 to 9:20am (except Sun), you can visit La Mezquita in silence to get a sense of its truly meditative power (no admission is charged). Moreover, Artencordoba (www. artencordoba.com) offers 2-hour guided night tours of the city.

Essentials

GETTING THERE   Córdoba is a crossroads for high-speed rail between Madrid and Sevilla, Madrid and Málaga, and Málaga and Sevilla, as well as for *media distancia* (MD) trains between Jaen and Sevilla. About 30 **high-speed trains** per day arrive from Madrid, taking about 2 hours and costing 62€ each way. Many use the high-speed link for day trips from Sevilla. The AVE costs 30€, while AVANT trains (20€) and MD trains (13€) take only minutes longer. To visit from the Costa del Sol, take one of the 19 trains per day from Málaga, all take about an hour and cost 41€ for AVE and 27€ for AVANT.

The main train station is north of the old city at Glorieta de las Tres Culturas, off Avenida de América. Bus 3 runs between the rail station and the historic core. Otherwise, it is about a 15-minute walk south on Avenida de Cervantes or Avenida del Gran Capitán. For rail information, call ✆ **90-242-22-42;** for

CÓRDOBA'S gastromarket **IS A HIT**

A short distance northwest of the Judería, a transplanted fair pavilion in the Jardines de Victoria was transformed in May 2013 into the first gastronomic market in Andalucía, **Mercado Victoria,** Paseo de la Victoria, s/n (www.mercadovictoria.com). The 30 food stalls cover all the bases of a conventional fresh-food market—fish, meat, produce, baked goods, and beverages—but most also offer food for immediate consumption on premise. There's also a workshop kitchen for classes and demonstrations. By early evening, the entire glassed-in pavilion is jammed with people eating and drinking, making it one of the most lively tapas scenes in town.

AVE information, call ✆ **90-242-22-42.** The RENFE advance-ticket office in Córdoba is at Ronda de los Tejares 10 (✆ **95-747-58-84;** www.renfe.com).

Alsa (✆ **95-740-40-40;** www.alsa.es) provides **bus** service to Córdoba to the station behind the train depot on Glorieta de las Tres Culturas. The most popular routes are between Córdoba and Sevilla, with seven buses per day. The trip takes 2 hours and costs 12€ one-way. Between Granada and Córdoba eight to nine buses per day make the 3-hour run; the cost is 13€ for a one-way ticket.

VISITOR INFORMATION The **tourist office,** Calle Torrijos, 10 (✆ **95-735-51-79;** www.andalucia.org), is open Monday to Friday 9am to 6:30pm, Saturday and Sunday 9:30am to 3pm.

Where to Stay in Córdoba

At the peak of its summer season, Córdoba has too few hotels to meet the demand, so reserve as far in advance as possible.

EXPENSIVE

Las Casas de la Judería ★★   This romantic hotel sits in the heart of the Judería. Once you step through the heavy wooden door you'll feel as if you're in another world. Created from adjacent 17th- and 18th-century city palaces, the guest rooms feature beds with elaborate headboards and rich bedding. Rooms vary in size and some are quite small. But the public areas are the real joy of the property, and you can experience the Córdoban lifestyle of outdoor living as you enjoy the patios, fountain, and shaded arcades.

Calle Tomás Conde, 10. ✆ **95-720-20-95.** www.casasypalacios.com. 64 rooms. 109€–245€ double; 225€–383€ jr. suites. Parking 19€. Bus: 2, 3, 5, 6. **Amenities:** Restaurant; bar; pool; free Wi-Fi.

MODERATE

NH Amistad Córdoba ★★   The Amistad is literally part of the city—a portion of its back wall is built right into the walls of Córdoba's old city. In the often familiar pattern of historic lodgings, architects combined two 18th-century mansions to make a gracious hotel, and later added another building across the Plaza de Maimónides for suites. In contrast with the historic Mudéjar-style patio at the heart of the property, the generally spacious rooms are decorated in clean-lined modern style of dark woods and richly colored fabrics.

Plaza de Maimónides, 3. ✆ **95-742-03-35.** www.nh-hoteles.com. 108 units. 75€–197€ double; 115€–225€ jr. suite. Parking 20€. Bus: 2, 3, 5, or 6. **Amenities:** Restaurant; bar; pool; free Wi-Fi.

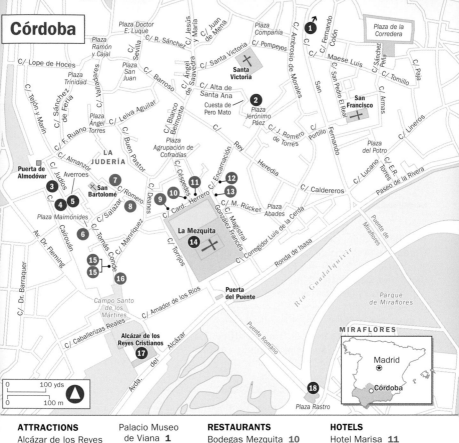

Córdoba

Plaza Doctor E. Luque
Plaza Ramón y Cajal
C/ Lope de Hoces
Plaza Trinidad
C/ Teján y Marín
C/ Sánchez de Feria
C/ Valladares
Plaza San Juan
C/ R. Sánchez
C/ Jesús y María
C/ Juan de Mena
Plaza Compañía
C/ Fernando Colón
Plaza de la Corredera
Maese Luis
C/ Sánchez Peña
C/ Paja
C/ Tomillo
C/ Santa Victoria
C/ Pompeyos
C/ Ambrosio de Morales
San Pedro El Real
C/ Armas
C/ Lineros
C/ Sevilla
C/ Ángel de Saavedra
C/ Barroso
Plaza Ramón y Cajal
C/ Alta de Santa Ana
Santa Victoria
San Francisco
C/ Almanzor
Puerta de Almodóvar
LA JUDERÍA
C/ Averroes
C/ Judíos
San Bartolomé
C/ Romero
C/ Deanes
Plaza Maimónides
C/ Tomás Conde
C/ Manrique
C/ Torrijos
La Mezquita
Puerta del Puente
Plaza Abades
Río Guadalquivir
Parque de Miraflores
MIRAFLORES
Campo Santo de los Mártires
C/ Amador de los Ríos
Alcázar de los Reyes Cristianos
Puente Romano
Madrid
Córdoba
Plaza Rastro
Puente de Miraflores

0 — 100 yds
0 — 100 m

ATTRACTIONS
Alcázar de los Reyes Cristianos **17**
Casa Andalusí **3**
Casa Sefard **5**
La Mezquita **14**
Museo Arqueológico de Córdoba **2**

Palacio Museo de Viana **1**
Sinagoga **4**
Torre de la Calahorra **18**

RESTAURANTS
Bodegas Mezquita **10**
Caravasar de Qurtuba **8**
El Caballo Rojo **9**
El Churrasco **7**
La Almudaina **16**
Los Caballerizas de los Marqueses **15**
Taberna Bar Santos **13**

HOTELS
Hotel Marisa **11**
Las Casas de la Judería **15**
Los Omeyas **12**
NH Amistad Córdoba **6**

INEXPENSIVE

Hotel Marisa ★ Literally across the street from La Mezquita, the Marisa closed for several months at the end of 2013 to paint and refresh all the rooms and improve the heating and air-conditioning. Alas, they could not make the rooms any larger, but what the rooms may lack in dimensions, the hotel makes up for with friendly staff and an excellent location. If you are a light sleeper, ask for a room that looks out on the interior patio. Two rooms at the front of the hotel have views of La Mezquita. All are modestly furnished and well-maintained.

Calle Cardenal Herrero, 6. © **95-747-31-42.** www.hotelmarisa.es. 38 units. 45€–125€ double. Parking 15€. Bus: 3 or 16. **Amenities:** Bar; free Wi-Fi.

Los Omeyas ★ Los Omeyas, in the Juderia, makes a good bargain-priced base for exploring—and for taking a break from the often crowded narrow streets.

The simple front door doesn't really prepare you for the sight of the lovely arched patio at the heart of the building. Rooms are modest with dark wood furniture and light walls and fabrics. For city views, request a room on the top floor.

Calle Encarnación, 17, ✆ **95-749-22-67.** www.hotel-losomeyas.com. 39 units. 40€–80€ double. Parking 15€. Bus: 3 or 16. **Amenities:** Bar; free Wi-Fi.

Where to Eat in Córdoba

Córdoban cuisine probably draws more extensively on Arabic and North African cooking than anywhere else in Spain. Not only does it liberally mix sweet flavors into savory dishes, you'll find a lot of dried fruits and nuts and such spices as cumin, turmeric, and cinnamon. Lamb and kid are usually the meats of choice, although many menus feature beef, a side effect of the local bull-breeding industry. It wouldn't be Spain without a strong complement of pork and shellfish—dishes banned by Jewish and Muslim dietary laws.

MODERATE

Los Caballerizas de los Marqueses ★★ ANDALUCIAN With dining areas in an outdoor patio and a covered dining room inside the hotel Las Casas de la Judería, this exquisite restaurant run by chef Oscar Hidalgo González offers perhaps the most refined dining experience in town. Dishes draw extensively on traditional Córdoban cooking, but they're updated for lighter, more modern tastes. Fish specialties include oven-roasted sea bass with baby green beans and mint. Hidalgo serves roast suckling pig already deboned and topped with an amontillado sauce. The desserts (of which there are many) tend to feature fruit—except the white chocolate mousse with rose-petal ice cream, though it comes garnished with fresh berries.

Calle Tomás Conde, 10. ✆ **95-720-20-95.** www.casasypalacios.com. Main courses 15€–20€. Daily noon–4pm and 8–11pm. Bus: 2, 3, 5, or 6.

La Almudaina ★★ ANDALUCIAN Set into a 16th-century mansion in the old city walls near the Alcázar, Almudaina affects a more international style than most Córdoban restaurants, offering pork sirloin with truffle sauce and finishing swordfish steak in a brandy sauce with wild mushrooms. But the kitchen also prepares some great regional classics. In fact, you can taste six of them plus dessert on the tapas tasting menu that includes *salmorejo* (tomato cream with ham and grated egg), fried meatballs stuffed with mountain ham, stewed oxtail, and fried eggplant with honey.

Plaza Campos de los Santos Mártires 1. ✆ **95-747-43-42.** www.restaurantealmudaina.com. Tapas tasting menu 27€; main courses 12€–25€. Mon–Sat 12:30–4pm and 8:30pm–midnight; Sun 12:30–4pm. Bus: 3 or 16.

El Caballo Rojo ★★ SPANISH Across the street from the Patio de las Naranjas, the Red Horse sits at the end of a whitewashed passageway hung with pots of blooming geraniums, begonias, and impatiens. The restaurant is as lovely as its entrance, spreading 300 seats through two levels of dining rooms. The chef-owner is something of a scholar of Córdoban foodways, which makes for some interesting dishes adapted from Sephardic and Mozarabic traditions. Along with the classics (beef sirloin, roast pork, baked fish), you'll find some dishes here rarely served outside people's homes, such as lamb sweetbreads or partridge stewed with kidney beans. The house version of artichokes steamed in Montilla wine won first prize in a national gastronomic competition. Desserts are a big deal and many are made with egg yolks, almonds, dates, and other flavors of the Moorish tradition. You'll find them hard to resist when the dessert cart rolls by.

Calle Cardinal Herrero, 28. © **95-747-53-75.** www.elcaballorojo.com. Main courses 14€–26€; fixed-price menu 26€. Daily 1–4:30pm and 8pm–midnight. Bus: 2.

El Churrasco ★ ANDALUCIAN   Arabic influences lend interesting flavors to the grilled meats at El Churrasco. Grilled pork sirloin, for example, is served with *salsas arabes,* a gravy seasoned with cumin and cinnamon. But El Churrasco is also a good place to sample the Andalucían standard, *rabo de toro,* or stewed oxtail, especially satisfying for those with hearty appetites. Several fish options are also available, ranging from red tuna tartare with trout eggs to turbot roasted with clams and shrimp.

Calle Romero, 16. © **95-729-08-19.** www.elchurrasco.com. Tapas 2€–11€; main courses 12€–26€; fixed-price menu 32€ (Mon–Fri). Sun–Thurs 1–4:30pm and 8:30–11:30pm; Fri–Sat 1–4pm and 8:30pm–midnight. Bus: 3.

INEXPENSIVE

Bodegas Mezquita ★★ ANDALUCIAN   Originally a deli and wine store, Bodegas Mezquita has expanded to become a full-blown bar and restaurant. The bar opens first; as more customers arrive, the waiters open other rooms until the whole place is packed. The wine list emphasizes bottles from Córdoba province but includes good choices from all over Spain. Most of the dishes are offered in a choice of sizes, making it easy to order tapas and taste several. Crisply fried slices of eggplant are served with honey, and the bodega offers a stew of the day. For a local specialty, try the Córdoban rice pot with stewed Iberian pork and mushrooms, or the Sephardic lamb stew with nuts and raisins and a side of couscous.

Calle Céspedes, 12. © **95-749-00-04.** www.bodegasmezquita.com. Tapas 2.60€–4.50€; main dishes 6.50€–15€; tapas menu 13€; daily menu 15€. Daily noon–midnight. Bus: 2.

Caravasar de Qurtuba ★ ANDALUCIAN   The sign for Lola Hotel still hangs outside (and there is one room available upstairs in this gorgeous central-courtyard building), but Lola Carmona Morales converted the ground level and first floor into a tearoom in 2013, making it a welcome respite from the hubbub of the Judería and the crush of the bars. You can get fruit drinks and coffees here, but the main point is to have a pot of freshly brewed tea and a plate of Arabic pastries.

Calle Romero, 3. © **95-720-03-05.** Arabic pastries and tea 2€–4€. Sun 11–10, Tues–Thurs 11–11, Fri–Sat 11–midnight. Bus: 3, 12.

Taberna Bar Santos ★ ANDALUCIAN   When Francisco Santos opened this tiny bar next to La Mezquita in 1966, he knew he needed something to set his place apart. That something became a massive *tortilla Española,* or potato omelet, that has been called the best in Spain. The creamy slices attract crowds of patrons who spill out into the street. Among the other tapas, we like the tuna topped with roasted red peppers and the bowl of *salmorejo* with slices of bread. This is a cash-only establishment.

Calle Magistral González Frances, 3. © **95-748-89-75.** tabernabarsantos.com. Tapas 2€–7€. Daily 10am–midnight. Bus: 2.

Exploring Córdoba

Among Córdoba's many sights is the **Puente Romano (Roman Bridge)** ★, dating from the time of Caesar Augustus and crossing the Guadalquivir River about a block south of the Mezquita. It's Roman in form only, as all 16 supporting arches have been replaced at one time or another in the last 2,000 years. Sculptor

The Puente Romano, or Roman Bridge, in Córdoba.

Bernabé Gómez del Río erected a statue of archangel San Rafael at the midpoint in 1651; it's a favorite spot for romantic poses.

Chances are, however, that you will spend most of your time in Córdoba within the medieval walled city with its narrow, winding streets. Buildings are so old and have so many layers of whitewash that few of them have a single sharp corner remaining. This area is known as the **Judería ★★★**, although it was, in fact, home to Christians, Jews, and Muslims alike for several hundred years. Most visitors enter the Judería from the streets around La Mezquita, but to get an idea of how the medieval gates looked, enter via the northwest entrance at the **Puerta de Almodóvar ★**.

There's no gate still standing where Calle Manriquez meets Calle Dr. Fleming, as 16th-century houses have taken its place. When construction workers began excavating here under the Plaza Campos de los Santos Mártires, they found the remains of the old Moorish baths associated with the Alcázar, the **Baños del Alcázar Califal de Córdoba ★**. The interpretation is first rate. They are open Tuesday to Friday from 8:30am to 8:45pm, Saturday 8:30am to 4:30pm, and Sunday 8:30am to 2:30pm. Admission is 2.50€ for adults, 1.25€ for students, free under 14 years old, and free to all Tuesday to Friday 8:30 to 9:30am.

Alcázar de los Reyes Cristianos ★★ PALACE   Commissioned in 1328 by Alfonso XI, the Alcázar of the Christian Kings is a fine example of military architecture. Fernando and Isabel governed Spain from this fortress on the river as they prepared to re-conquer Granada, the last Moorish stronghold in Spain. Columbus journeyed here to fill Isabel's ears with his plans for discovery. A statue commemorates Columbus's audience and the rulers' agreement to underwrite his exploratory voyage of 1492.

Two blocks west of La Mezquita, the Alcázar is notable for powerful walls and a trio of towers: the Tower of the Lions, the Tower of Allegiance, and the Tower of the River. While not as inspiring as La Mezquita, the Alcázar was the backdrop to a number of important historical events. The regional branch of the Spanish Inquisition was based here from 1490 until 1821, and Franco later turned the fortress into a prison. But the troubled past is behind it now. Some of the larger halls display 3rd- and 4th-century A.D. Roman mosaics unearthed in Córdoba, while the formal 18th-century gardens hold ever-changing flower beds, long lines of sculpted cypresses, and fragrant orange trees.

There is a sound and light spectacle on Mondays, when the Alcázar is otherwise closed, and on Saturday afternoons from 4:30 to 8pm.

Calle Caballerizas Reales. s/n. ℂ **95-742-01-51.** Admission 4.50€ adults, 2€ students, free ages 1–13, free for all Tues–Fri 8:30–9:30am. Sound and light spectacle 7€ adults, 4.80€ seniors. Tues–Fri 8:30am–8:45pm, Sat 8:30am–4:30pm, Sun 8:30am–2pm. Bus: 3 or 12.

Casa Andalusí ★ MUSEUM   A small fountain strewn with roses welcomes visitors to the ivy-draped main courtyard of this small museum, which tries to re-create daily life in Córdoba during the 12th-century caliphate. Don't spend too much time studying the model of the mill on the Río Guadalquivír, which produced paper for spiritual texts, or reading the often heavy-handed interpretive notes. Instead, take a seat on a low chair, lean against an embroidered cushion, breathe in the scent of the flowers, and listen to the gurgle of the fountain.

Calle Judíos, 12. ℂ **95-729-06-42.** www.lacasaandalusi.com. Admission 2.50€. Daily 10am–7pm. Bus: 3, 12.

Casa Sefarad ★ MUSEUM   This small museum focuses on 11th- and 12th-century daily Jewish life in Córdoba, the de facto capital of Sephardic Jewry. The rooms with the most resonance explicate the traditional craft of making golden thread, highlight Sephardic musical and literary traditions, and celebrate Christian, Jewish, and Islamic women of Córdoba's heyday who were leading poets, philosophers, singers, and scholars.

Corner of calles Judíos and Averroes. ℂ **95-742-14-04.** www.casadesefarad.com. Admission 4€ adults, 3€ students. Mon–Sat 11am–6pm; Sun 11am–2pm. Bus: 3, 12.

Mezquita Catedral de Córdoba ★★★ MOSQUE   From the 8th to 11th centuries, the Mezquita was the crowning architectural achievement of western Islam. It's a fantastic forest of arches painted with alternating red and white stripes—a realization in stone of a billowing desert tent. A Roman Catholic cathedral interrupts the vistas, as it sits awkwardly in the middle of the mosque as an enduring symbol of Christian hubris. The 16th-century cathedral may have

A garden at the Alcázar de los Reyes Cristianos.

INSIDE THE blooming PATIOS

The middle of May is not the time to visit Córdoba for the climate (it's already scorching hot), but it is the season for meeting Córdobans inside their homes. They are so proud of the flowers that they grow in their patios that many of them open to visitors for the **Concurso de los Patios de Córdoba**, or **Córdoba Patio Festival** (www.amigosdelospatios-cordobeses.es). Pick up a map of participants from the tourist office. When you enter people's homes, you will see their ancient patios arranged around a well or fountain with whitewashed walls hung with pots of blazing geraniums, or *gitanillas* ("little Gypsies"). Admission is free, but it's customary to leave a few coins in a tip tray to help with upkeep. If you miss the patio festival, you can still get an idea of the patios so central to Córdoban life by visiting the **Palacio Museo de Viana** ★, Plaza de Don Gome, 2 (© **95-749-67-41;** www.palaciodeviana.com), which is 4 blocks southeast of the Plaza de Colón just outside the Judería. The interior is of most interest to fans of decorative arts, but the 12 patios, representing various eras and architectural styles, are an uplifting sight for all. It's open July to August Tuesday to Sunday 9am to 2pm and 7 to 10pm; September to June Tuesday to Saturday 10am to 7pm, Sunday 10am to 3pm.

been architectural sacrilege, but it does have an intricately carved ceiling and baroque choir stalls. One of the interesting features of the mosque is the **mihrab** ★★, a domed shrine of Byzantine mosaics that once housed the Qu'ran. After exploring the interior, stroll through the Patio de los Naranjos (Courtyard of the Orange Trees), which has a beautiful fountain where worshippers performed their ablutions before prayer and tourists rest their weary feet.

Calles Torrijos and Cardenal Herrero s/n (southeast of the train station, just north of the Roman bridge). © **95-822-52-45.** www.mezquitadecordoba.org. Admission 8€ adults, 4€ children 14 and under. Mon–Sat 10am–6pm; Sun 9–10:30am and 2–6pm. Bus: 3.

Museo Arqueológico de Córdoba ★★ MUSEUM The new museum building for this well-established collection of artifacts opened in 2011 next door to the 1505 palace that had hosted the museum for more than a century. The site was originally a Roman amphitheater, and intact portions of the theater were found and have been revealed in the basement of the new structure. This museum chronicles life in and around Córdoba since the first Neandertals came to the area 300,000 years ago. Those first residents left no artifacts of note, but more recent inhabitants did. Displays of tools and household items begin with Copper and Bronze Age cultures, followed by Phoenician and Greek artifacts, Iberian statuary (circa 500 B.C.), and extensive Roman materials. The Moorish artifacts, of course, are legion. The old home of the museum is closed until further notice, pending an improvement in the economy that will allow restoration.

Plaza Jerónimo Páez, 7. © **95-735-55-17.** www.museosdeandalucia.es. Admission 1.50€. Tues 2:30–8:30pm; Wed–Sat 9am–8:30pm; Sun 9am–2:30pm. Bus: 3.

Sinagoga ★ SYNAGOGUE Córdoba boasts one of Spain's three remaining pre-Inquisition synagogues, built in 1315, two blocks west of the northern wall of La Mezquita (p. 202). The synagogue is noted particularly for its stuccowork, including Mudéjar patterns on the entrance and Hebrew inscriptions from the Psalms inside. The east wall contains a large orifice where the Tabernacle was placed (the scrolls of the Pentateuch were kept inside), and you can still see the balcony where women worshipped. After Spain expelled the Jews in 1492, the synagogue was converted into a hospital, then in 1588, a Catholic chapel.

Calle de los Judíos 20. ℰ **95-720-29-28.** Admission 0.30€. Tues–Sun 9am–2:30pm. Bus: 3.

Torre de la Calahorra ★ MUSEUM   As you cross the Puente Romano (constructed in the reign of Julius Caesar and rebuilt many times since), you'll see herons and egrets wading in the shallows and worshippers crossing themselves and leaving sprigs of rosemary at a small shrine to the archangel San Rafael at the mid-point of the bridge. The display rooms at the Torre are often crowded with school groups, so arrive early. The 1-hour audio tour evokes Córdoba of the 9th to 13th centuries, and is as valuable for vacationers as it is for kids studying history. One room features likenesses of some of Córdoba's great thinkers, including Averroes, Maimonides, and Alfonso X.

Av. de la Confederación, Puente Romano. ℰ **95-729-39-29.** www.torrecalahorra.com. Admission to museum 4.50€ adults, 3€ seniors and students, free ages 8 and under. May–Sept daily 10am–2pm and 4:30–8:30pm; Oct–Apr daily 10am–6pm. Tours daily 11am, noon, 3, and 4pm. Bus: 16.

Shopping

As you walk through the streets of the Judería, you would practically have to wear blinders not to be tempted by the merchandise in the shops, which ranges from tourist trinkets to flamenco-inspired jewelry and shawls to Moorish-inspired textiles, inlaid boxes, and glass tea cups. If you want to concentrate your shopping in one place, check **Arte Zoco,** Calle de Los Judíos, s/n (ℰ **95-729-05-75**), a charming courtyard reached through an arched entry. The site boasts a shop and about a dozen stalls where artists sell jewelry and pottery, along with work in wood, leather, and other materials. Alas, the artists keep irregular hours, but it's worth stopping in for the opportunity to buy a memento of Córdoba from its maker.

The Patio de los Naranjos (Courtyard of the Orange Trees) at Mezquita Catedral de Córdoba.

A CALIPH'S pleasure PALACE

Conjunto Arqueológico Madinat al-Zahra ★, a kind of Moorish Versailles just outside Córdoba, was constructed in the 10th century by the first caliph of al-Andalus, Abd ar-Rahman III. He named it after the favorite of his harem, nicknamed "the brilliant." Thousands of workers and animals slaved to build this mammoth pleasure palace, said to have contained 300 baths and 400 houses. Over the years the site was plundered for building materials; some of its materials may have been used to build the Alcázar in Sevilla. The Royal House, a rendezvous point for the ministers, has been reconstructed. The principal salon remains in fragments, though, so you have to imagine it in its majesty. Just beyond the Royal House are the ruins of a mosque constructed to face Mecca. The Berbers sacked the palace in 1013 when the Umayyad dynasty briefly took control of al-Andalus.

The palace is at Carretera Palma de Río, Km 8 (✆ **95-735-28-74;** www.museosdeandalucia.es). Admission is 1.50€ (free to E.U. residents). From mid-September to March, hours are Tuesday to Saturday 9am to 6:30pm, Sunday 10am to 5pm; in April and May, hours are Tuesday to Saturday 9am to 8pm, Sunday 10am to 5pm; June to mid-September Tuesday to Saturday 10am to 3:30pm, and Sunday 10am to 5pm. Two buses a day leave from Avenida del Alcázar and Paseo de la Victoria (✆ **95-735-51-79**). The roundtrip bus costs 8.50€ adults, 4.25€ ages 5 to 12. Tickets are sold at the tourist office.

GRANADA ★★★

When Boabdil, the last king of Moorish Granada, was exiled to North Africa in 1492, he took the bones of his ancestors with him. But he left behind their fortress-palace, the Alhambra, and a legacy of nearly 8 centuries of Islamic culture. Fernando and Isabel may have won the war and completed the reconquest of al-Andalus, but in Granada they lost the history. Few people come to this beautiful city to see the solemn tombs of Los Reyes Católicos. They come for the joyous ornamentation of the Alhambra, the inextinguishably Arabic face of the Albaícin, and the haunting *zambras* echoing from the Sacromonte hills. As native son Federico García Lorca wrote, "Oh city of gypsies! Who could see you and not remember?"

Essentials

GETTING THERE **Iberia** (✆ **800/772-4642** in the U.S., or 90-240-05-00 toll-free in Spain; www.iberia.com) flies to Granada from Madrid four times daily. **Vueling** (✆ **80-720-01-00** from within Spain; www.vueling.com) has three direct flights a day from Barcelona to Granada. Granada's **Federico García Lorca Airport** (*aeropuerto nacional*) is 16km (10 miles) west of the center of town on Carretera Málaga; call ✆ **90-240-47-04** for information. A bus route links the airport with the center of Granada. The one-way fare is 3€. The bus runs daily 5:30am to 8pm. Trip time is 45 minutes.

The **train** station is **Estación de RENFE de Granada,** Av. Andaluces s/n (✆ **90-232-03-20;** www.renfe.es). Granada is well linked with the most important Spanish cities, especially others in Andalucía. Four trains daily arrive from

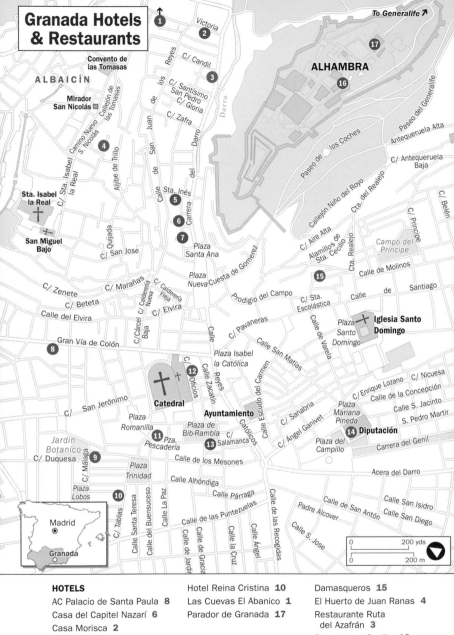

Granada Hotels & Restaurants

ALBAICÍN

Convento de las Tomasas

Mirador San Nicolás

Sta. Isabel la Real

San Miguel Bajo

ALHAMBRA

To Generalife ↗

Madrid
Granada

HOTELS

AC Palacio de Santa Paula **8**
Casa del Capitel Nazarí **6**
Casa Morisca **2**
Hotel América **16**
Hotel Casa 1800 **7**
Hotel Los Tilos **13**
Hotel Palacio de Santa Inés **5**

Hotel Reina Cristina **10**
Las Cuevas El Abanico **1**
Parador de Granada **17**

RESTAURANTS

Botánico **9**
Chikito **14**
Cunini Restaurante & Marisquería **11**

Damasqueros **15**
El Huerto de Juan Ranas **4**
Restaurante Ruta del Azafrán **3**
Restaurante Sevilla **12**

Sevilla, taking 3 to 4 hours, depending on the train, and costing 25€ one-way. From Madrid, two daily trains arrive, taking 4½ hours and costing 68€.

Granada is served by more **buses** than trains. It has links to virtually all the major towns and cities in Andalucía, and even to Madrid. The main bus terminal is **Estación de Autobuses de Granada,** Carretera de Jaén s/n (© **95-818-54-80**). One of the most heavily used bus routes is the one between Sevilla and Granada, with 10 buses run per day, costing 19€ for a one-way ticket. The trip is 3 hours. You can also reach Granada in 3 hours on one of nine daily buses from Córdoba; cost is 14€ for a one-way ticket. If you're on the Costa del Sol, the run is just 2 hours, costing 12€ per one-way ticket. This is a very popular route, with 19 buses going back and forth between Granada and the coast per day. For bus information, contact **Alsa** (© **95-818-54-80;** www.alsa.es).

GETTING AROUND   Just a few buses will take you pretty much anywhere you want to go in Granada. The 30 and 32 city buses (1.50€) run continuously from Plaza Isabel la Catolica to the ticket office of the Alhambra, and the 31 and 32 buses leave from the same spot for Sacromonte. Taxis are relatively inexpensive.

VISITOR INFORMATION   The **Patronato Provincial de Turismo de Granada,** Plaza de Mariana Pineda, 10 (© **95-824-71-46;** www.turgranada. es), is open Monday to Friday 9am to 8pm, Saturday 10am to 7pm, and Sunday 10am to 3pm. For information on both the city and surrounding area, the **Tourist Information Office of Junta de Andalucía,** Calle de Santa Ana. 4 (© **95-857-52-02;** www.andalucia.org), is open Monday to Friday 9am to 7:30pm, Saturday and Sunday 9:30am to 3pm. Two big festivals dominate the agenda—the **International Theater Festival,** which attracts avant-garde theater groups from around the world, and the **Festival Internacional de Música y Danza.**

Where to Stay in Granada
EXPENSIVE
AC Palacio de Santa Paula ★★★   This adaptation of the 16th-century Convento de Santa Paula and a 12th-century Moorish palace bridges the historic structures with an ultra-modern steel and glass shell. The ambiance of the earlier buildings is maintained in some of the public areas, including the beautiful courtyard of the cloister. Rooms are cool and modern, with ample space. Standard rooms have no particular view, while superior rooms overlook the Moorish courtyard and some deluxe rooms look up at the Alhambra. The Palacio de Santa Paula is Granada's most luxurious hotel, rivaled only by the *parador* on the Alhambra grounds (see below).

Gran Vía de Colón, 31. © **95-880-57-40.** www.palaciodesantapaula.com. 75 units. 125€–215€ double; 209€-240€ jr. suite. Parking 18€ per day. Bus: 3, 6, 8, or 11. **Amenities:** Restaurant; bar; exercise room; sauna; free Wi-Fi.

MODERATE
Casa Morisca ★★   Lovingly restored by a Madrid architect, this traditional 16th-century house in the Alabaicín retains its central patio and Moorish fountain, its rough brickwork, its columns with Nasrid capitals, and its narrow view of the Alhambra from the "Mirador" room, which is a suite that costs a lot more than smaller rooms. The Granadino style, so influenced by the decoration of the Alhambra and lingering links with North Africa, carries through in all the decorations. Some parking is available but must be arranged ahead to get a permit to bring the car to the property.

Cuesta de la Victoria, 9. © **95-822-11-00.** www.hotelcasamorisca.com. 14 units. 86€–170€ double; 155€–220€ suite. Free parking. Bus: 31 or 32. **Amenities:** Free Wi-Fi.

STAYING ON THE alhambra GROUNDS

It's not quite the same as staying in one of the rooms of the Alhambra itself, but there are two lodgings—one extremely luxurious, the other more modest—located inside the walls of the palace complex. If you'd like to wander the grounds after the other tourists have gone home, plan to reserve a room far in advance, but keep in mind that both lodgings are inconvenient for visiting the rest of Granada.

The **Parador de Granada ★★★**, Real de Alhambra, s/n (© **95-822-14-40;** www.parador.es) is the harder nut to crack. Its 36 rooms are decorated to reflect the architectural and decorative style of the Alhambra, and it's one of the most luxurious stays in Spain. Try for a room in the atmospheric older section. Double room rates begin at 320€ per night, suites at 618€. For those prices you do get free Wi-Fi.

The **Hotel América ★★**, Real de Alhambra s/n (© **95-822-74-71;** www.hotelamericagranada.com), is a former private home converted in 1936 into an intimate hotel with just 17 small rooms decorated in intense warm colors with sponged walls, hand-painted headboards, and rustic touches like unpainted wood doors and window frames. Some rooms overlook a patio garden with a grape pergola, while others look out on the gardens of the Alhambra Palace. Double room rates range from 110€ to 140€. They also include free Wi-Fi.

Hotel Palacio de Santa Inés ★★ A pioneer in transforming the neighborhood's Mudéjar homes into lodgings for tourists, the Palacio de Santa Inés opened in the mid-1990s. The courtyard architecture and beamed ceilings evoke the building's origins as two private homes. The hotel takes its design cues from the fragmentary 16th-century frescoes in the reception area. Rooms and public areas are decorated throughout with bold hues of Tuscan plaster. Interior balconies with wooden spindles circle the courtyard. Several rooms have partial views of the Alhambra. Reserve well in advance.

Cuesta de Santa Inés, 9. © **95-822-23-62.** www.palaciosantaines.com. 35 units. 60€–145€ double; 145€–225€ suite. Parking 19€. Bus: 30 or 32. **Amenities:** Afternoon tea; free Wi-Fi.

Hotel Reina Cristina ★ Mildly famous as the house where Federico García Lorca was last seen alive when he was abducted by Franco's thugs, this former grand family home has become a charming hotel in the middle of the city. It's only a 5-minute stroll to the cathedral. Guest rooms are modest in size and furnished in a simple, rather old-fashioned style with floral bedspreads and striped curtains.

Calle Tablas, 4. © **95-825-32-11.** www.hotelreinacristina.com. 56 units. 58€–153€ double; 73€–168€ triple. Parking 18€. Bus: 5. **Amenities:** Restaurant; bar; free Wi-Fi.

Casa del Capitel Nazarí ★ Skip the supplement for a room with a view of the Alhambra, since the view is seriously obstructed and the hotel is worth enjoying in its own right. The lodging takes its name from the original Nasrid capital that helps support the 16th-century building. Historic preservation precluded an elevator, but ground-floor rooms are available. Bathrooms are equipped with showers rather than tubs to maximize the living space in the chambers. The rooms have carved wooden ceilings in the Nasrid style, and minibars—a luxury that even the emirs didn't enjoy.

Cuesta Aceituneros, 6. © **95-821-52-60.** www.hotelcasacapitel.com. 18 units. 60€–135€ double. Bus: 5, 11, 31, 32. **Amenities:** Free Wi-Fi.

Hotel Casa 1800 ★★ Sister to the property by the same name in Sevilla (p. 185), this pretty and welcoming hotel is tucked into a small cul-de-sac off Plaza Nueva, making the location both convenient yet surprisingly quiet. The decorative style is a kind of baroque revival, with lots of curlicue flourishes in the decorative painting and a palette of browns, tans, and golds. Standard rooms are quite snug, but feature queen-size beds. Superior and deluxe rooms have either two twins or a king. Several rooms have exposed brick walls and exposed beams on the ceilings.

Calle Benalúa, 11. ✆ **95-821-08-00.** www.hotelcasa1800.com. 25 rooms. 75€–215€ double; 135€–295€ jr. suite. Bus: 5, 11. **Amenities:** Afternoon tea; free Wi-Fi.

INEXPENSIVE

Hotel Los Tilos ★ It helps to enjoy the company of fellow travelers if you opt for Los Tilos: The elevator is tight and guests congregate on the top-floor balcony, where it's fun to spend an evening with a bottle of wine and good company. Rooms are large at this price and are brightly painted in luminous yellows, oranges, and tropical marine blue. Of the hotel's 30 rooms, 22 have views of the lovely plaza filled with good tapas bars and cafes. Location in the heart of city and the availability of triple rooms (good for families) are big pluses. Book three or more nights to get free breakfast.

Plaza Bib-Rambla, 4. ✆ **95-826-67-12.** www.hotellostilos.com. 30 rooms. 40€–70€ double. Bus: 23, 30, 31, 32. **Amenities:** Free Wi-Fi in public areas.

Las Cuevas El Abanico ★ As much an adventure as a lodging, these one- and two-bedroom units in the Gypsy quarter of Sacromonte are fully modernized cave dwellings with whitewashed walls, tiny bathrooms, and a corner equipped for minimal cooking. The kids won't be able to wait to tell their friends they stayed in a Gypsy cave. You, too. Just be aware that the caves are a real uphill schlep from the road and there is a cleaning fee charged when you check out. Most units are rented by the week.

Calle Verea de Enmedio, 89. ✆ **95-822-61-99.** www.el-abanico.com. 5 units. 1-bedroom 68€ per night, 420€ per week; 2-bedroom 110€ per night, 660€ per week. Bus: 35.

Where to Eat in Granada

EXPENSIVE

Damasqueros ★★ ANDALUCIAN Having trained with some of the top names in Spanish cooking (Berasategui and Subijana among them), Lola Marin opened this handsome restaurant in the new part of town in late 2009 and quickly won a dedicated following among Granada gastronomes. Marin cooks from her Andalucían roots, drawing on Jewish and Moorish influences, but she presents the dishes in a carefully edited fashion that could grace the cover of any food magazine. Her barely cooked foie gras, for example, is accompanied by chocolate popcorn and sweet-and-sour quince paste. Her garlic and saffron-infused rice "soup" that's halfway to a risotto is studded with asparagus tips and topped with shaved truffles. She roasts lamb with whole grapes and serves it with fried bread crumbs and melon. It's anyone's guess what she'll be cooking next week, but a peek on the website will tell you what's being served tonight. Damasqueros serves just one menu per day, with or without a wine pairing.

Calle Damasqueros, 3. ✆ **95-821-05-50.** www.damasqueros.com. Tasting menu 40€, with wine pairing 59€. Tues–Sat 1–4:30pm and 8–11:30pm, Sun 1–4:30pm. Closed mid-July to Aug.

El Huerto de Juan Ranas ★ ANDALUCIAN Chef-owner Juan Ranas is a romantic when it comes to dining, and his "garden" at one corner of the Mirador San Nicolás assumes a kind of fairytale elegance once the candles are lit. He serves an excellent tapas menu in the garden terrace upstairs, including his creamy croquettes. The downstairs dining room with linen-clad tables and a profusion of glassware features an updated version of Andalucían classics. The roast lamb shoulder, for example, is cooked slowly at a very low temperature until it falls apart, and the Moorish pastries combine small pieces of fork-tender meat as well as chunks of eggplant.

Calle de Atarazana, 8 (Mirador de San Nicolás). ✆ **95-828-69-25.** www.elhuertodejuanranas. com. Main courses 19€–40€. Fixed-price menus 45€–57€. Daily 8–11:30pm. Bus: 31.

MODERATE

Chikito ★ SPANISH Once upon a time, this spot was the location of the bar-restaurant Alameda, where Federico García Lorca and the rest of the literary circle known as El Rinconcillo used to meet up in the 1920s and trade verses and songs. Should he suddenly materialize, Lorca would probably find the food unchanged from those days. Chef Antonio Torres does an intense version of roast cod with mint and the warm spices of North Africa as well as desserts that feature pastry, nuts, and honey. The plaza is as pleasant as it was in Lorca's day, so that's where most people sit.

Plaza del Campillo 9. ✆ **95-822-33-64.** www.restaurantechikito.com. Main courses 12€–30€. Daily menu 25€. Thurs–Tues 1–4pm and 8–11:30pm. Bus: 1, 2, or 7.

Cunini Restaurante & Marisquería ★★★ SEAFOOD If there is one dining scene in Granada that you should not miss, it is eating seafood tapas at Cunini. Granada restaurants are extraordinarily generous with free tapas, and Cunini is more generous than most. You can sample much of the menu here by standing at the undulating marble bar and ordering drink after drink. (The tapas get better with each drink, and that's not the alcohol talking.) If you want to enjoy the best seafood in Granada, have a seat in the restaurant or on the plaza for the likes of monkfish in white wine or a heaping plate of fried red mullet.

Plaza de Pescadería, 14. ✆ **95-825-07-77.** www.marisqueriacunini.es. Main courses 13€–33€. Mon–Sat noon–2am. Bus: 23, 30, 31, 32.

INEXPENSIVE

Botánico ★ MEDITERRANEAN Located on a small plaza west of the cathedral near the university's law school, Botánico wears many different hats through the day and night. Most of the time it's a bright and cheery cafe-bar where you can get tapas and a beer or a coffee, though it also serves a full, inexpensive dinner menu of Mediterranean and Indian fare. Local artists hang their works on the walls for sale. Around 11pm on weekends, the lights dim, the techno music blasts, and folks start dancing.

Calle Málaga, 3. ✆ **95-827-15-98.** Reservations recommended. Main courses 7.90€–30€; daily menu 15€. Daily 1pm–2am. Bus: 4, 7, or 13.

Restaurante Ruta del Azafrán ★ ANDALUCIAN Contemporary Spanish cooking with a decidedly North African accent is only half the attraction here. There are also great views (looking up) of the Alhambra, and a range of menu choices from inexpensive couscous to veal steaks with foie gras. Most plates are intended to be light and bright, and there are a number of salad entrees at lunch.

The wine list includes some bargains on local white table wines as well as a great selection of bottles from some of Spain's emerging wine regions, such as Jumilla. Paseo del Padre Manjón, 1. ✆ **95-822-68-82.** www.rutadelazafran.com. Main courses 9€–22€. Sun–Thurs 1–4pm, 8–11; Fri–Sat1–4pm, 8pm–midnight. Bus: 31.

Restaurante Sevilla ★ SPANISH   Now run by the Alvarez brothers (Dany the chef and Jorge the maître d'), this old-fashioned favorite sits on a tiny street near the cathedral. So modest is the entrance that you might hear a guitarist playing a Manuel de Falla tune before you find the door. But Restaurante Sevilla has been Granada's see-and-be-seen venue since the 1930s, when de Falla and poet Federico García Lorca used to eat here. The staff pushes the gazpacho, but we suggest the Andalucían lamb with mountain herbs, *cordero a la pastoril*. In season, make reservations.

Calle Oficios, 12. ✆ **95-822-12-23.** www.restaurantesevilla.es. Main courses 12€–26€; tasting menu 36€. Tues–Sat 1–4:30pm and 8–11:30pm. Bus: 32 or 39.

Exploring Granada

One school of thought about visiting Granada says that after seeing the Alhambra you can die happy and need not bestir yourself to see anything else. But Granada is one of the most interesting and sociable cities in Spain, and it would be a pity if you overlooked any of it. After you've visited the Alhambra, spend at least a full day (and evening) to savor the rest.

The **Puerta de Elvira** is the gate through which Fernando and Isabel made their triumphant entry into Granada in 1492 after the last Moorish ruler, Boabdil, fled. It was once a grisly place where the rotting heads of executed criminals hung from its portals. The quarter surrounding the gate was the Muslim section (*morería*) until all Muslims were forced to convert or leave the country about a century after the Reconquest.

One of the more colorful streets is **Calle de Elvira;** west of it, the medieval residential neighborhood of the Albaicín rises on a hill. (Granada's modern mosque is in this quarter.) In the 17th and 18th centuries, many artisans occupied the shops and ateliers along Elvira and its side streets. The **Iglesia de San Andrés,** begun in 1528, and its Mudéjar bell tower are also on Calle de Elvira. Much of the church was destroyed by fire in the early 19th century, but several interesting paintings and sculptures remain. Another old church in this area is the **Iglesia de Santiago,** constructed in 1501 and dedicated to St. James the Apostle, patron saint of Spain. Built on the site of an Arab mosque, it was damaged in an 1884 earthquake. The church contains the tomb of architect Diego de Siloé (1495–1563), who did much to change the face of the city.

Despite its name, the oldest extant square in Granada is **Plaza Nueva,** which, under the Muslims, was the site of the woodcutters' bridge. The Darro has been covered over here, but its waters still flow underneath the square. On the east side of Plaza is the 16th-century Iglesia de Santa Ana, built by Siloé. Inside its five-nave interior you can see Churrigueresque reredos and a coffered ceiling.

The *corrida* has a valiant history in Granada, with the most important bullfights taking place from the 3rd week of May through the 3rd week of June. The final Sunday of September closes out the season with a special card in honor of the Virgen de las Angustias, Granada's patron saint. The 1928 bullring seats 14,500, so there are usually good seats available. The **Plaza de Toros,** the bullring, is on Avenida de Doctor Olóriz, close to the soccer stadium.

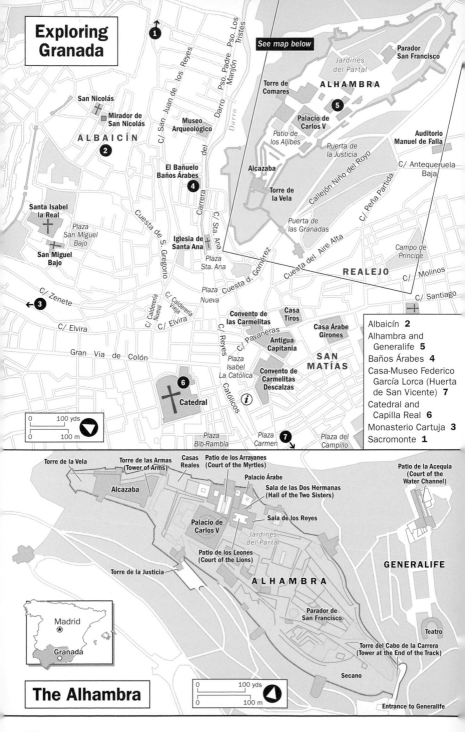

Exploring Granada

See map below

Pso. Los Tristes
Pso. Padre Manjón

San Nicolás

Mirador de San Nicolás

ALBAICÍN 2

C/ San Juan de los Reyes

Darro

Río Darro

Museo Arqueológico

El Bañuelo
Baños Árabes 4

Carrera del Darro

Santa Isabel la Real

Plaza San Miguel Bajo

San Miguel Bajo

Cuesta de S. Gregorio

Iglesia de Santa Ana

C/ Sta. Ana

Plaza Sta. Ana

← 3 *C/ Zenete*

C/ Caldería Nueva
C/ Caldería Vieja

C/ Elvira

C/ Elvira

Plaza Cuesta d. Gomérez

Plaza Nueva

Gran Via de Colón

C/ Reyes Católicos

Convento de las Carmelitas

Casa Tiros

Antigua Capitania

C/ Pavaneras

Casa Árabe Girones

6

Catedral

Plaza Isabel La Católica

Convento de Carmelitas Descalzas

SAN MATÍAS

ℹ️

Torre de Comares

Jardines del Partal

ALHAMBRA

5

Parador San Francisco

Palacio de Carlos V

Patio de los Aljibes

Puerta de la Justicia

Alcazaba

Callejón Niño del Royo

Torre de la Vela

Auditorio Manuel de Falla

C/ Antequeruela Baja

C/ Peña Partida

Puerta de las Granadas

Campo de Principe

Cuesta del Aire Alta

REALEJO

C/ Molinos

C/ Santiago

✝

Plaza Bib-Rambla

Plaza Carmen

7 ↘

Plaza del Campillo

| 0 | 100 yds |
| 0 | 100 m |

Torre de la Vela

Torre de las Armas (Tower of Arms)

Casas Reales

Patio de los Arrayanes (Court of the Myrtles)

Patio de la Acequia (Court of the Water Channel)

Alcazaba

Palacio Árabe

Sala de las Dos Hermanas (Hall of the Two Sisters)

Palacio de Carlos V

Sala de los Reyes

Jardines del Partal

Patio de los Leones (Court of the Lions)

GENERALIFE

Torre de la Justicia

ALHAMBRA

Parador de San Francisco

Teatro

Torre del Cabo de la Carrera (Tower at the End of the Track)

Madrid ✷

Granada

Secano

| 0 | 100 yds |
| 0 | 100 m |

The Alhambra

Entrance to Generalife

Albaicín ★★ NEIGHBORHOOD
This old quarter on one of Granada's two main hills stands apart from the city of 19th-century buildings and wide boulevards. A holdover from the Nasrid empire, it even predates the Renaissance city that sprung up around the cathedral. The Albaicín and Gypsy caves of Sacromonte farther up the hill (see below) were the homes of marginalized Muslims and Gypsies declared beyond the pale by the Christian conquerors. The narrow labyrinth of crooked streets in the Albaicín was too hilly to tear down in the name of progress; ironically, it is now some of the most desirable real estate in Granada.

Houses in Granada's old quarter, the Albaicín.

Its alleyways, cisterns, fountains, plazas, whitewashed houses, villas, and the decaying remnants of the old city gate have all been preserved. Here and there you can catch a glimpse of a private patio filled with fountains and plants, a traditional, elegant way of life that continues. The plaza known as **Mirador San Nicolás** is a delightful spot to enjoy a drink at a cafe. It becomes especially romantic at sunset, when the reflected color makes the Alhambra seem to glow on the opposite hill. During the winter and spring, you may even see snow on the peaks of the Sierra Nevada mountains.
Bus: 31 or 32.

Alhambra and Generalife ★★★ PALACE   One of Europe's greatest attractions, the stunningly beautiful and celebrated **Calat Alhambra (Red Castle)** is perhaps the most celebrated fortress ever constructed. Muslim architecture in Spain reached its apogee at this palace once occupied by Nasrid princes, their families, and their political and personal functionaries. Although the Alhambra was converted into a lavish palace in the 13th and 14th centuries, it was originally constructed for defensive purposes on a rocky hilltop outcropping above the Darro River. The modern city of Granada was built across the river from the Alhambra, about 0.8km (½ mile) from its western foundations.

When you first see the Alhambra, its somewhat somber exterior may surprise you. The true delights of this Moorish palace lie within. If you haven't already purchased your ticket, they are sold in the office at the Entrada del Generalife y de la Alhambra. Enter through the incongruous 14th-century **Puerta de la Justicia (Gateway of Justice)** ★. Most visitors do not need an expensive guide but will be content to stroll through the richly ornamented open-air rooms, with lace-like walls and courtyards with fountains. Many of the Arabic inscriptions translate to "Only Allah is conqueror."

The strictly defined pathway of the tour begins in the **Mexuar** ★★★, also known as Palacio Nazaríes (Palace of the Nasrids), which is the first of three palaces that compose the Alhambra. This was the main council chamber where the chief ministers met. The largest of these chambers was the Hall of the Mexuar, which Spanish rulers converted to a Catholic chapel in the 1600s. From this chapel, there's a panoramic view over the rooftops of the Albaicín.

Pass through another chamber of the sultan's ministers, the Cuarto Dorado (Golden Room), and you'll find yourself in the small but beautiful **Patio del**

Mexuar ★★. Constructed in 1365, this is where the emir sat on giant cushions and listened to the petitions of his subjects, or met privately with his chief ministers. The windows here are surrounded by panels and richly decorated with tiles and stucco.

The Palace of the Nasrids was constructed around two courtyards, the **Patio de los Arrayanes (Court of the Myrtles)** ★★ and the **Patio de los Leones (Court of the Lions)** ★★★. The latter was the royal residence.

The Court of the Myrtles contains a narrow reflecting pool banked by myrtle trees. Note the decorative and rather rare tiles, which are arguably the finest in the Alhambra. Behind it is the **Salón de Embajadores (Hall of the Ambassadors)** ★★, with an elaborately carved throne room that was built between 1334 and 1354. The crowning cedar wood dome of this salon evokes the seven heavens of the Muslim cosmos. Here bay windows open onto **panoramic vistas** of the enveloping countryside.

An opening off the Court of the Myrtles leads to the greatest architectural achievement of the Alhambra, the Patio de los Leones (Court of Lions), constructed by Muhammad V. At its center is Andalucía's finest fountain, which rests on 12 marble lions. The lions represent the hours of the day, the months of the year, and the signs of the zodiac. Legend claims that water flowed from the mouth of a different lion each hour of the day. This courtyard is lined with arcades supported by 124 (count them) slender marble columns. This was the heart of the palace, the private section where the emir and his family retreated.

At the back of the Leones courtyard is the **Sala de los Abencerrajes** ★, named for a noble family whom 16th-century legend says were slaughtered here, either because they were political rivals of the emir, or because one of them was

Detailed mosaic work in the Alhambra.

reserving FOR THE ALHAMBRA

The Alhambra is so popular that the government has limited the number of people who can enter each day and has limited the number of tickets purchased by one individual to 10 per day. The best way to enjoy the Alhambra is to arrive first thing in the morning and proceed to the Nasrid Palaces as soon as possible (you must enter the palaces at the specific time on your ticket). To avoid long ticket lines, buy your tickets in advance. The easiest way is to order online at www.alhambra-tickets.es, or by calling ✆ **95-892-60-31.** Tickets can also be purchased (or picked up) at the Tienda de la Alhambra, Calle Reyes Católicos, 40 in the city center. They may also be picked up at the vending machines at the Alhambra entrance. You will need identification to secure your tickets, but once you have them in hand you can bypass the lines and proceed to the entrance. All advance purchases carry a small (1.3%) surcharge, which is well worth it.

sleeping with the emir's wife. It makes a terrific tale, but there is no historical evidence to support it.

Opening onto the Court of Lions are other salons of intrigue, notably the Hall of the Two Sisters, **Sala de las Dos Hermanas ★★**, which is named for the two identical large white marble slabs in the pavement. Boabdil's stern, unforgiving mother, Ayesha, once inhabited the Hall of the Two Sisters. This salon has a stunning dome of carved plaster and is often cited as one of the finest examples of Spanish Islamic architecture.

The nearby **Sala de los Reyes (Hall of Kings) ★** was the great banquet hall of the Alhambra. Its ceiling paintings are on leather and date from the 1300s. A gallery leads to the **Patio de la Reja (Court of the Window Grille) ★**. This is where Washington Irving lived in furnished rooms, and where he began to write his famous book *Tales of the Alhambra.* The best-known tale is the legend of Zayda, Zorayda, and Zorahayda, the three beautiful princesses who fell in love with three captured Spanish soldiers outside the Torre de las Infantas. Irving credits the French with saving the Alhambra for posterity, but in fact they were responsible for blowing up seven of the towers in 1812, and it was a Spanish soldier who cut the fuse before more damage could be done. When the Duke of Wellington arrived a few years later, he chased out the chickens, the Gypsies, and the transient beggars who were squatting in the Alhambra and set up housekeeping here himself.

Before you proceed to the Emperor Carlos V's palace, look at some other gems around the Court of Lions, including the **Baños Reales (Royal Baths) ★**, with their lavish, multicolored decorations. Light enters through star-shaped apertures. To the immediate east of the baths lies the **Daraxa Garden ★**, and to its immediate south the lovely and resplendent **Mirador de Daraxa ★★**, the sultana's private balcony onto Granada.

To the immediate southeast of these attractions are the **Jardines del Partal ★★** and their perimeter towers. These beautiful gardens occupy a space that once was the kitchen garden, filled with milling servants preparing the sultan's banquets. These gardens are dominated by the **Torre de Las Damas (Ladies' Tower) ★**. This tower and its pavilion, with its five-arched porticoes, are all that are left of the once-famous Palacio del Partal, the oldest palace at the Alhambra. Of less interest are the perimeter towers, including the Mihrab Tower, a former

Nasrid oratory; Torre de las Infantas (Tower of the Princesses); and Torre de la Cautiva (Tower of the Captive). Like the Damas tower, these towers were also once sumptuously decorated inside; today only some decoration remains.

Next you can move to the immediate southwest to visit **Emperor Carlos V's Palace (Palacio de Carlos V)** ★★, where the Holy Roman emperor lived. Carlos might have been horrified when he saw a cathedral placed in the middle of the great mosque at Córdoba, but he's also responsible for some architectural confusion in Granada. He did not consider the Nasrid palace grand enough, so in 1526 he ordered Pedro Machuca, a student of Michelangelo, to design him a fitting royal residence. It's quite beautiful, but terribly out of place in such a setting. Carlos financed the palace by levying a tax on the Muslims. In spite of its incongruous location, the final result is one of the purest examples of classical Renaissance architecture in Spain.

The square exterior opens to reveal a magnificent, circular, two-story courtyard that is open to the sky. Inside the palace is the **Museo de la Alhambra** ★★ (© **95-822-75-27**), a museum of Hispano-Muslim art with its salons opening onto the Myrtle and Mexuar courts. They display artifacts retrieved from the Alcázar, including fragments of sculpture, as well as unusual braziers and even perfume burners used in the harems. The most outstanding object is a **blue amphora** ★ that is 132cm (52 in.) high. It stood for years in the Hall of the Two Sisters. Also look for an ablutions basin dating from the 10th century and adorned with lions chasing stags and an ibex. The museum is open mid-October to mid-March Sunday to Tuesday 8:30am to 2:30pm, Wednesday to Saturday 8:30am to 6pm; from mid-March to mid-October Sunday to Tuesday 8:30am to 2:30pm, Wednesday to Saturday 8:30am to 8pm.

Before leaving the Alhambra precincts, try to see the **Alcazaba** ★, which dates from the 9th century and is the oldest part of the complex. This rugged fortress from the Middle Ages was built for defensive purposes. For a spectacular **view,** climb the **Torre de la Vela (Watchtower)** ★. You look into the lower town onto Plaza Nueva, and you can also see the Sierra Nevada in the distance. From the tower you can also view the Generalife (see below) and the "Gypsy hill" of Sacromonte.

Exit from the Alhambra via the Puerta de la Justicia, and then circumnavigate the Alhambra's southern foundations until you reach the gardens of the summer palace, where Paseo de los Cipreses quickly leads you to the main building of the **Generalife** ★★, built in the 13th century to overlook the Alhambra and set on 30 lush hectares (74 acres). The sultans used to spend their summers in this palace (pronounced Heh-neh-rah-*lee*-feh), safely locked away with their harems. Don't expect an Alhambra in miniature: The Generalife was always meant to be a retreat, even from the splendors of the Alhambra. Lying north of the

A staircase in Emperor Carlos V's Palace.

walking **TO THE ALHAMBRA**

Many visitors opt to take a taxi or the bus to the Alhambra, but some hardy souls enjoy the uphill climb from Plaza Nueva. (Signs indicate the winding roads and the steps that lead to the Alhambra.) If you decide to walk, enter the Alhambra via the Cuesta de Gomérez, which, although steep, is the quickest and shortest pedestrian route. It begins at the Plaza Nueva and goes steeply uphill to the Puerta de las Granadas, the first of two gates to the Alhambra. The second, another 183m (600 ft.) uphill, is the Puerta de la Justicia, which 90% of visitors use. **Caution:** Beware of self-styled guides milling around the parking lot, as they are more interested in separating you and your euros than in providing any real guidance.

Alhambra, this country estate of the Nasrid emirs was begun in the 13th century, but the palace and gardens have been much altered over the years. The palace is mainly noted for its beautiful courtyards, including **Patio de Polo ★**, where the visitors of yore would arrive on horseback.

The highlight of the Generalife is its **gardens ★★★**. Originally, they contained orchards and pastures for domestic animals. Of special note is **Escalera del Agua (the Water Staircase) ★**, with water flowing gently down. An enclosed Oriental garden, **Patio de la Acequía ★**, was constructed around a long pool, with rows of water jets making graceful arches above it. The **Patio de la Sultana ★** (also known as the Patio de los Cipreses) was the secret rendezvous point for Zoraxda, wife of Sultan Abu Hasan, and her lover, the chief of the Abencerrajes.

Palacio de Carlos V. ℂ **90-244-12-21.** www.alhambra-patronato.es. Comprehensive ticket, including Alhambra and Generalife, 14€; Museo de la Alhambra free; garden visits 7€; illuminated visits 14€. Oct 15–Mar 14 daily 8:30am–6pm, floodlit visits Fri–Sat 8–9:30pm; Mar 15–Oct 14 daily 8:30am–8pm, floodlit visits Fri–Sat 10–11:30pm. Bus: 30 or 32.

Baños Arabes ★ LANDMARK   It's remarkable that these 11th-century "baths of the walnut tree," as they were known by the Moors, escaped destruction during the reign of the Reyes Católicos (Fernando and Isabel). Among the oldest buildings still standing in Granada, and among the best-preserved Muslim baths in Spain, they predate the Alhambra. Many of the stones used in their construction show the signs of Visigothic and Roman carving, especially the capitals.

Carrera del Darro 31. ℂ **95-802-78-00.** Free admission. Tues–Sat 9am–2:30pm. Bus: 31 or 32.

Catedral and Capilla Real ★★ CATHEDRAL   This richly ornate Renaissance cathedral with its spectacular altar is one of the country's architectural highlights, acclaimed for its beautiful facade and gold-and-white interior. It was begun in 1521 and completed in 1714. Behind the cathedral (entered separately) is the Flamboyant Gothic **Royal Chapel ★★**, where the remains of Isabel and Fernando lie. It was their wish to be buried in recaptured Granada, not Castilla or Aragón. The coffins are remarkably tiny—a reminder of how short they must have been. Accenting the tombs is a wrought-iron grille, itself a masterpiece. Occupying much larger tombs are the remains of their daughter, Juana la Loca (the Mad), and her husband, Felipe el Hermoso (the Handsome). In the sacristy,

Granada's Baños Arabes.

you can view Isabel's personal **art collection ★★**, including works by Rogier van der Weyden and various Spanish and Italian masters such as Botticelli.

Plaza de la Lonja, Gran Via de Colón, 5. Catedral © **95-822-29-59.** 4€. Mon–Sat 10:45am–1:15pm and 4–7:45pm; closes 6:45pm in winter. Capilla Real © **95-822-78-48.** 4€. Summer Mon–Sat 10:15am–1:30pm and 4–7:30pm, Sun 11am–1:30pm and 4–7:30pm; winter Mon–Sat 10:15am–1:30pm and 3:30–6:30pm, Sun 11am–1:30pm and 3:30–6:30pm. Bus: 6, 9, or 11.

Sacromonte ★ NEIGHBORHOOD   Hundreds of Gypsies once lived on the "Holy Mountain" on the outskirts of Granada above the Albaicín. The mountain was named for the Christians martyred here and for its long-ago role as a pilgrimage site. Many of the caves were heavily damaged by rain in 1962, forcing most occupants to seek shelter elsewhere. Nearly all the Gypsies remaining are in one way or another involved with tourism. (Some don't even live here—they commute from modern apartments in the city.)

You can walk uphill, but you might want to save time by taking a bus or taxi, and you should definitely use a bus or taxi after dark. The best way to see some of the caves and to actually learn something about Gypsy Granada is to visit the **Museo Cuevas del Sacromonte ★**, Barranco de los Negros (© **95-821-51-20;** www.sacromontegranada.com). This interpretation center is a great source of Roma (Gypsy) pride. Several caves are shown as lodgings while others are set up as studios for traditional weaving, pottery, basketry, and metalwork. The museum is open mid-March to mid-October daily 10am to 8pm, mid-October to mid-March daily 10am to 6pm. Admission is 5€, take bus 35 to get here.

In the evenings, many caves become performance venues for the Granada Gypsy flamenco style known as *zambra*. Performances demonstrate varying degrees of authenticity and artistry, but one of the best is presented at **Venta El Gallo, Barranco** Los Negros 5, (© **95-822-84-76;** www.ventaelgallo.com). A *zambra* performance has three stages, corresponding to the three parts of a Gypsy wedding. It is an atmospheric evening that you will not soon forget, but expect a certain amount of ostentatious showmanship for the benefit of tourists and attempts to sell you overpriced drinks. Make your reservation for the show without dinner (unless you feel you have to sit in front), but do pay the extra charge for transportation via minibus because city buses stop running at 11pm, when the musicians and dancers will just be hitting their stride. Admission is 27€, with an additional 6€ for transportation. Dinner and show are 58€.

Monasterio de la Cartuja ★ MONASTERY This 16th-century monastery, off the Albaicín on the outskirts of Granada, is sometimes called the "Christian answer to the Alhambra" because of its ornate stucco and marble and the baroque Churrigueresque fantasy in the sacristy. Its most notable paintings are by Bocanegra, its outstanding sculpture by Mora. The church of this Carthusian monastery was decorated with baroque stucco in the 17th century, and its 18th-century sacristy is an excellent example of latter-day baroque style. Sometimes one of the Carthusian monks will take you on a guided tour.

Paseo de Cartujar s/n. ✆ **95-820-19-32.** Admission 3.50€. Apr–Oct daily 10am–1pm and 4–8pm; Nov–Mar daily 10am–1pm and 3–6pm. Bus: 8 from cathedral.

Shopping

Alcaicería, once the Moorish silk market, is next to the cathedral in the lower city. The narrow streets of this rebuilt village of shops are filled with vendors selling the arts and crafts of Granada province. For the souvenir hunter, the Alcaicería offers a good assortment of tiles, castanets, and wire figures of Don Quijote chasing windmills. Lots of Spanish jewelry can be found here. For the window-shopper in particular, it makes a pleasant stroll. A more interesting shopping experience is found in the souk of the alleyways of **Calderería Vieja** and **Calderería Nueva,** where wall hangings, pillows, silk tassels, and silver teapots abound. The area is a low-key version of what you'd find in North Africa, and a certain amount of bargaining is not only permitted—it's expected.

Handicrafts stores virtually line the main shopping arteries, especially those centered on Puerta Real, including Gran Vía de Colón, Reyes Católicos, and Angel Ganivet. For the best selection of antiques stores, mainly selling furnishings of Andalucía, browse the shops along Cuesta de Elvira.

Inside a Gypsy cave in Sacromonte.

Granada After Dark

Watching the sun set from the **Mirador San Nicolás** (p. 219) is one of the special experiences in this city. But once you have seen the Alhambra glow from the reflected light, the night will still be young.

If you enjoy tapas-hopping, Granada is your city. Its bars usually offer the most generous tapas we have encountered anywhere in Spain. One of the most popular tapas bars is **El Agua Casa de Vinos,** Placeta de Algibe de Trillo, 7 (✆ 95-822-43-46), a lively place with an adjoining restaurant.

Another historic spot with a lovely patio is **Pilar del Toro,** Calle Hospital de Santa Ana, 12 (✆ 95-822-54-70), near the cathedral and Plaza Nueva. After a few stops, you may find that you don't need dinner. In that case, you can consider an evening of flamenco.

For a performance of Gypsy-style flamenco in the Sacromonte caves, see **Venta El Gallo** (p. 224). We also recommend the sporadic performances (usually on Thurs nights Feb–July) at the **Peña de Arte Flamenco la Platería,** Placeta de Toqueros, 7 (✆ 95-821-06-50; www.laplateria.org.es), the oldest flamenco enthusiasts' club in Spain. The setting is a bit like a church hall, but it's a great place to join real fans and see rising stars. Admission is 10€.

One of the most popular discos is **Granada 10,** Calle Carcel Baja, 10 (✆ 95-822-40-01), which opens at midnight daily and doesn't close until at least 6am. Cover charge of 12€ includes the first drink.

Side Trip to Ubeda ★★

Less than 2 hours from Granada by car and a little longer by bus, the Renaissance city of Ubeda could not be more different in demeanor or atmosphere. Granada is the ultimate Moorish city, but Ubeda is filled with Spain's finest Renaissance architecture; it's often called often called the "Florence of Andalucía." The most striking buildings are the work of Andrés de Vandelvira, who created his own vernacular interpretation of the "new" style of Italy. It didn't hurt that his patrons were flush from royal monopolies on the olive oil and wool trade granted by Carlos V (at the cost of a revolt among the nobles of Castilla). The best way to discover the charms of this World Heritage Site is to wander its narrow cobblestone streets and admire the golden-brown Renaissance palaces and tile-roofed whitewashed houses. Definitely allow time for a stroll through Ubeda's shops, which specialize in leather craft goods, esparto grass weaving, and distinctive artisanal olive oils.

The easiest way to visit Ubeda is to take one of the 10 **buses** per day from Granada. They take 2 to 3 hours and cost 13€ each way. For information, call Alsa at ✆ 95-375-21-57, or visit www.alsa.es. The Ubeda bus station is on Calle San José in the new part of the city; signs will point to a downhill walk to the Zona Monumental. To drive here, take the E-902/A-44 north from Granada; at Jaen, follow the A-316 spur northeast. When you arrive, you can pick up a walking map at the **tourist information office,** Calle Baja del Marqués, 4 (✆ 95-377-92-04; www.andalucia.org). It is open Monday to Friday 9am to 7:30pm, Saturday and Sunday 9:30am to 3pm.

WHERE TO STAY & DINE IN UBEDA

Parador de Ubeda ★ ANDALUCIAN   Even if you do not plan to stay overnight in Ubeda, you should take a look at this 16th-century palace. Once you have seen the classic central courtyard, you will almost certainly want to enjoy a meal in the dining room, known as the Restaurante Condestable Dávalos. In *parador*

Sacra Funeraria de El Salvador del Mundo.

style, the menu features classic dishes of the region carefully executed with fresh local ingredients, such as cold soup with almonds, rabbit stew, shoulder of kid, and a savory olive oil ice cream. After you have enjoyed a leisurely meal, you may even want to spend the night. The guest rooms feature high beamed ceilings, traditional furnishings, and tall windows. Many rooms have views of the main plaza.

Plaza Vázquez de Molina, s/n. ℂ **95-375-03-45.** www.parador.es. 36 units. 95€–188 double; 115€–241€ suite. Restaurant main courses 16€–24€; daily menu 34€. Daily 1:30–4pm and 8:30–11pm. **Amenities:** Restaurant; bar; free Wi-Fi.

EXPLORING UBEDA

Centrally located **Plaza Vázquez de Molina** ★★ is flanked by several mansions, including Casa de las Cadenas, now the Town Hall. The mansions suffered from neglect for many years but have all been recently restored, including the *parador* (see above) and El Salvador church (below).

Hospital de Santiago ★ CONCERT HALL   On the western edge of town, off Calle del Obispo Coros, stands the Hospital of Santiago, designed by Andrés de Vandelvira and built between 1562 and 1576. It is still in use as a cultural venue, hosting concerts and containing a minor modern art museum. Over the main entryway is a carving of Santiago Matamoros ("St. James the Moorslayer") in a traditional pose on horseback. Note the monumental staircase leading upstairs from the inner patio. The chapel holds some marvelous woodcarvings.

Av. Cristo Rey. ℂ **95-375-08-42.** Free admission. Mon–Fri 10am–2:30pm and 5–9:30pm; Sat–Sun 10am–2:30pm and 6–9:30pm.

Sacra Funeraria de El Salvador del Mundo ★★ CHURCH   One of the grandest examples of Spanish Renaissance architecture, this church was designed in 1536 by Diego de Siloé as a family chapel and mausoleum for Francisco de los Cobos, secretary to Carlos V. The richly embellished portal is mere window dressing for the wealth of decoration on the **interior** ★ of the church, including a **sacristy** ★★ designed by Andrés de Vandelvira with medallions, caryatids, columns shaped like men (*atlantes*), and coffered decorations and ornamentations. The many sculptures and altarpieces and the spectacular rose windows are also of special interest.

Plaza Vásquez de Molina, s/n. ℂ **60-927-99-05.** www.fundacionmedinaceli.org. Admission 5€ adults, 4.50€ seniors, 2.50€ children. Mon–Sat 9:30am–2pm and 4–6pm; Sun 11:30am–2pm and 4–7pm.

San Pablo ★ CHURCH This Gothic church in the center of old town is almost as fascinating as the El Salvador (see above). The San Pablo church is famous for its 1511 **south portal** ★ in the Isabelline style, and for its **chapels** ★ decorated with exquisite wrought-iron grilles. Vandelvira himself designed the "Heads of the Dead Chapel," the most stunning. Seek out the richly carved Chapel of Las Mercedes, done in florid Isabelline style.

Plaza 1 de Mayo. (© **95-375-06-37.** Free admission. Mon–Sat 7:30–8:39pm; Sun 11:30am–1pm.

Side Trip to the Alpujarra de Granada ★★

No place in Andalucía so retains its Moorish mien as the rustic mountain villages of Granada province on the south flank of the Sierra Nevada. Isolated until the 1950s by poor roads, the architecture echoes Berber houses in northern Morocco. The green valleys and rugged hills terraced with olives and vines are spectacularly scenic. The area is best explored by car; public transit is spotty. The drive is a treat for fans of twisting mountain roads.

LANJARÓN ★

The first town of the Alpujarra that comes up on A-348 is the least typical. Lanjarón is famous all over Spain for water bottled from its springs, and has been a spa town since the Romans. Eight mineral springs bubble up, each with different alleged healing properties. The town revolves around the spa, called the **Balneario de Lanjarón,** Avenida de Madrid, 2. (© **95-877-01-37;** balneariodelanjaron.com; open 9am–2pm and 5–8pm), which was built in 1928. Twice a day, residents and visitors line up in the lobby to fill bottles with water from a flowing spring. The spa makes a relaxing retreat, with services that range from thermal baths to reflexology (11€–56€).

PAMPANEIRA★★

The lowest spot in town is 1,000m (3,281 ft.) above sea level, and every street leads steeply up from there. This village is the tourism and hiking center for the High Alpujarra, and alpine hikers strut up and down the streets with ease. There are a number of small shops selling colorful, shaggy, woven cotton rugs (called *jarapes de Alpujarra*) as well as jewelry and other handicrafts. Two ham producers also sell their wares, and the village even has an artisanal chocolate maker and a gelato outlet.

But the main reason to come here is to hike. Do *not* set out on a trail without first inquiring about trail conditions at the **Punto de Información Parque Natural de Sierra Nevada,** Plaza de la Libertad, s/n. (© **95-876-31-27;** www.nevadensis.com; open Tues–Sat 10am to 2pm and 4 to 6pm, Sun–Mon 10am to 3pm). The center arranges group and privately guided hikes, as well as rock-climbing excursions. Hikers interested in a good afternoon trek are usually encouraged to follow well-marked trails from Pampaneira to the nearby ridgeline villages of Bubión and Capileira. The distance is only about 3km (1.9 mi), with an elevation rise to 1,250m (4,101 ft.) on switchback trails.

If you want to stay overnight in the High Alpujarra, book ahead for the **Hostal Pampaneira,** Avenida de la Alpujarra, 1 (© **95-876-30-02;** www.hostal-pampaneira.com). All 15 cozy and simple rooms have televisions and heat—air-conditioning is never needed. The windows offer million-dollar views, but doubles are only 42€ per night with breakfast. Triples are 50€.

RONDA ★★★

Ronda is an incredible sight. The city is literally split in two by the 150m-deep (492-ft.) Río Guadalevin gorge known as *El Tajo,* and houses hang off both sides of the gorge. In 2,000 years, no one has been able to improve on Pliny the Elder's epithet for the city: "the glorious." But, if you are prone to vertigo, Ronda's high eyrie might feel as if the city were built on a spinning plate on a circus clown's pole. Located at the eastern edge of the mountain ridges that separate the Costa del Sol from the Cádiz plain, Ronda is the gateway to the Serranía de Ronda— the serrated ridges that harbored mountain bandits and political rebels from the age of Caesar through the days of Franco. The city is divided into an older part, which is the Moorish and aristocratic quarter, and the newer section on the south bank of the gorge, built principally after the Reconquest. The old quarter is by far the more fascinating; it contains narrow, rough streets and buildings with a marked Moorish influence. (Look for the minarets.) Walking in the park in the new section, however, provides some truly extraordinary panoramic views as the pathway follows the edge of the cliff.

Essentials

GETTING THERE   Most visitors take a **train** to the main station at Avenida La Victoria (📞 **90-242-22-42;** www.renfe.com). Three trains arrive from Granada per day. The trip takes 2½ to 3 hours and costs 20€ one-way. Three trains also arrive daily from Málaga, taking 2 hours and costing 10€. Three trains daily connect Ronda and Madrid. The trip takes 4 hours and costs 73€ one-way.

The main **bus** station is at Plaza Concepción García Redondo s/n (📞 **90-225-70-25**). There are five buses a day from Sevilla, taking 2½ hours and costing 20€ one-way. There is also service from Málaga, taking 2½ hours and costing 15€ one-way. Also on the Costa del Sol, Marbella runs five buses per day to Ronda, taking 1 hour and costing 14€ one-way.

Major highways circle Ronda, but getting to town requires driving on winding secondary routes. From Sevilla, take N-334 southwest. At El Arahal, continue south along C-339. From Granada, take N-342 west to the junction with N-332, and then take N-332 southwest to the junction with C-339. From Málaga, go northwest on scenic C-344, or from Marbella northwest on C-339.

VISITOR INFORMATION   The **tourist office,** Paseo de Blas Infante s/n (📞 **95-218-71-19;** www.turismoderonda.es), is open daily 10am to 2pm and 3 to 5pm.

Where to Stay in Ronda

EXPENSIVE

Parador de Ronda ★★★   You will not forget your first view of this *parador,* which perches practically on the edge of El Tajo gorge. The city hall used to occupy this site, and its facade, complete with clock, was retained in the design of this thoroughly modern lodging. The large rooms have modern furnishings and color schemes in blue, yellow, green, and red. But as stunning and comfortable as the property may be, the city and its environs take center stage here: rooms look out on the gorge or the old city or toward the bullring. Some rooms have a private terrace, but all guests can enjoy the gardens and the public footpath at the edge of El Tajo.

Plaza de España s/n. 📞 **95-287-75-00.** www.parador.es. 79 units. 120€–223€ double; 180€–292€ suite. Parking 22€. **Amenities:** Restaurant; bar; outdoor pool; free Wi-Fi.

MODERATE

Hotel Catalonia Reina Victoria ★   The Victorian architecture of this hotel, built in 1906 by an Englishman, is a surprising change of pace amid Ronda's more traditional Spanish style. A thorough renovation in 2012 has given the fairly large and airy guest rooms a clean-lined modern feel. But there was no way to improve on the location, amid a lovely garden on the eastern edge of the new town and tucked up close to a 147m (482-ft.) precipice.

Paseo Doctor Fleming, 25. ✆ **95-287-12-40.** www.hoteles-catalonia.com 92 units. 86€–170€ double; 130€–205€ suite. Free parking. **Amenities:** Restaurant; bar; outdoor pool; spa; gym; free Wi-Fi.

INEXPENSIVE

Hotel Ronda ★   You can sense the pride of the family that has turned their home into a small lodging. Located just a block from the upper bridge over the gorge, the typical Andalucían-style home features white walls, tile floors, and lots of ironwork. The five simple but comfortable guest rooms are more colorful, with bright-colored accent walls and bedding. Spacious room 5 was once the stable, while smaller room 3 was where the family kept birds. Hotel Ronda is a good option for a tranquil spot close to the action. Guests often take a bottle of wine to the rooftop terrace to enjoy while admiring the views of Ronda's "new town" and the distant Sierra Nieves mountain range.

Ruedo Doña Elvira, 12. ✆ **95-287-22-32.** www.hotelronda.net. 5 rooms. 72€–98€ double. **Amenities:** Roof terrace, access to health club with pool and tennis courts 6km (4mi) from hotel.

Hotel San Gabriel ★★   This enclave of 21 rooms around several patios on a side street in the old city has a timeless elegance. Built in 1736 as a noble mansion, it was converted to a hotel about 20 years ago and is still run by the family that last occupied it as a private home. The interior is rich in detail, with dark wood, stained glass, artwork, antiques, and traditional furnishings that exude character and comfort. The property also boasts a library, a wine cellar for sipping sherry before dinner, and even a small movie theater with red velvet seats rescued from a local theater. Each room has unique decor, but all are fairly spacious.

Calle Marqués de Moctezuma, 19 (just off Calle Armiñán). ✆ **95-219-03-92.** www.hotelsangabriel. com. 21 rooms. 72€–107€ double; 126€–165€ suite. Closed last two weeks of July, last two weeks of December and first week of January. Parking 10€. **Amenities:** Bar; free Wi-Fi in public areas.

Maestranza ★   This modern hotel faces Ronda's bullring, which must have been handy for legendary matador Pedro Romero, who once lived in a villa on the property. While the hotel is one of the more modern in town, it sits behind a classic facade and features restrained, classic decor with dark wood floors and furnishings, offset with pastel colors.

Calle Virgen de la Paz, 26. ✆ **95-218-70-72.** www.hotelmaestranza.com. 54 units. 66€–85€ double; 110€–150€ suite. Parking 11€. **Amenities:** Restaurant; bar; free Wi-Fi in public areas.

Where to Eat in Ronda

Restaurante Casa Santa Pola ★ ANDALUCIAN   With six dining rooms spread out over five levels built into the side of the hill overlooking El Tajo near the Puente Novo, Casa Santa Pola is very popular for large groups, business meetings, and even flamenco shows. It also makes a nice special-occasion restaurant, as the kitchen tends to produce big, attractive plates laden with meat. The establishment has stopped calling itself an *asador*, since that implies meat roasted over live coals, but many of the dishes are prepared in 19th-century brick ovens. Best bets are roasts and braises that cook a very long time, such as braised lamb shank or the suckling pig, which is cooked sous-vide, then finished in the oven to crisp up the skin.

Cuesta Santo Domingo, 3. ℂ **95-287-92-08.** Main courses 18€–28€; fixed-price menu 38€–60€. Daily 11:30am–5pm and 7:30–11pm.

Restaurante Pedro Romero ★★ ANDALUCIAN   Make a reservation if you expect to eat here on the day of a *corrida.* Bullfight fans mob the place on fight days, as it's Ronda's chief fight-themed restaurant, right down to the color photos of matadors and the stuffed bull's head on the wall. Patriarch Tomás Mayo Fernández opened the restaurant in 1971, and he's still there to greet customers, even as a younger generation has taken over the daily operations. The cuisine is more complex than the decor suggest and includes uncommon mountain dishes like partridge in red sauce with butter beans, or duck liver with a sauce of fresh grapes. There's also a surprisingly good selection of fish.

Virgen de la Paz 18. ℂ **95-287-11-10.** www.rpedroromero.com. Main courses 17€–23€; daily menu 18€. Daily 12:30–4pm and 7:30–11pm. Closed Sun night and Mon June–Aug.

TragaTapas ★★ SPANISH   The gleaming modern decor and minimalist design make this casual spot the ideal place to try contemporary Spanish cuisine in miniature—and we do mean miniature. Each tapa is little more than a bite, but they're all so good you may find yourself simply trying the whole day's selection as outlined on the blackboard. A single spear of grilled asparagus topped with grated cheese and accompanied by a square of quince paste might seem precious, but it's so tasty you'll want another and another. Pork sliders—a very Spanish variant on the hamburger—are big hits, as is the salmon poached in vanilla and lime juice.

Calle Nueva, 4. ℂ **95-287-72-09.** Tapas 2€–6€, *raciones* 10€–14€. Mon–Sat noon–4pm and 8pm–midnight, Sun noon–4pm.

Tragabuches ★★★ ANDALUCIAN   When Tragabuches burst on the scene at the turn of the millennium, it marked the end of the long march of contemporary avant-garde Spanish cuisine from its birth in Basque Country and Catalunya to its conquest of the once-insular gastronomy of Andalucía. Tragabuches continues to innovate and simplify, and eating here lets you bear witness to Spain's culinary revolution. In response to economic hard times, the once astronomically priced tasting menus have been pared back to the level of a special treat. But the same spirit of adventure prevails, with textural contrasts such as yogurt with mint and smoked cod, or foie gras with soft goat cheese and thin slices of tart green apple. The tastes come from Andalucían tradition, but we're pretty sure that no chef's grandmother ever paired shrimp ravioli with an *ajo-blanco* sauce, herring roe, and angel hair pasta.

Calle José Aparicio, 1. ℂ **95-219-02-91.** www.tragabuches.com. Main courses 22€–32€; tasting menus 58€–86€. Tues–Sat 1:30–3:30pm and 8:30–10:30pm, Sun 1:30–3:30pm. Closed Jan.

Exploring Ronda

The still-functional **Baños Arabes ★** are among the best-preserved in Spain. They are on Calle Molino de Alarcón, s/n, and are reached from the turnoff to Puente San Miguel. Dating from the 13th century, the baths have glass-roof windows and hump-shaped cupolas. They're open Monday through Saturday 10am to 6pm (winter) and 10am to 7pm (summer), Sunday 10am to 1pm (winter) and 10am to 3pm (summer). Admission is 3€, free for seniors and students, and free for all on Monday.

Palacio de Mondragón ★, Plaza de Mondragón (ⓒ **95-287-08-18**), was once the 14th-century private home of the Moorish king, Abomelic. But after the Reconquista, it was renovated to receive Fernando and Isabel, who stayed here. The Reyes Católicos had many other more grand dwellings, but few were this charming. Inside you can see a trio of courtyards and a collection of Moorish mosaics. There is also a beautiful carved wooden ceiling. A small museum houses artifacts from regional archaeology. Better than the museum is the restored Mudéjar courtyard where you can take in a panoramic view of El Tajo with the Serranía de Ronda looming in the background. Flanked by two Mudéjar towers, the building now has a baroque facade. It's open Monday through Friday from 10am to 6pm (10am–7pm summer), and Saturday and Sunday 10am to 3pm; admission is 3€, free on Wednesday.

Nearby, the **Casa Palacio del Gigante ★**, Plaza del Gigante, s/n. (ⓒ **67-863-14-45;** www.turismoderonda.es), was named for the Phoenician stone sculpture in the courtyard. Displays in this small in-town Nasrid palace from the 13th to 15th centuries race through Ronda's formation from the geological forces that created the gorge to the Iberian settlement of the city, the Roman occupation, and then the Moorish urban explosion of the 10th and 11th centuries that shaped the city you see today. The palace has been closed for renovation, but pending funding, should re-open in 2015.

One of the great wonders of Ronda is not that the Romans built the first version of Puente San Miguel at the bottom of the gorge, but that the Puente Nuevo spans the gorge at the top. The **Centro de Interpretación del Puente Nuevo ★★**, Plaza de España, s/n (ⓒ **95-287-08-18;** www. turismoderonda.es), tells how it came about. The citizenry successfully petitioned the crown for a new bridge in 1542, but two centuries passed before technology advanced enough to attempt it. The first bridge on this spot opened in 1739—and collapsed in 1741, killing 50 people. The current structure was begun in 1759 and finally inaugurated in 1793. The interpretation center is located inside the bridge's support structure. Exhibits provide an overview of Ronda's geography and the engineering achievements necessary to construct the bridge. The center is open Monday through Friday 10am to 7pm, Saturday and Sunday 10am to 3pm. Admission is 2€ adults, 1€ seniors and students, free for those under 14.

Ronda's Plaza de Toros.

prehistoric CAVE PAINTINGS

Near Benaoján, the **Cueva de la Pileta ★★** (© **95-216-73-43;** www.cuevadela-pileta.org), 25km (16 miles) southwest of Ronda, has been compared to the Caves of Altamira in northern Spain, where prehistoric paintings were discovered toward the end of the 19th century. In a wild area known as the Serranía de Ronda, José Bullón Lobato, grandfather of the present owners, discovered this cave in 1905. More than a mile in length and filled with oddly and beautifully shaped stalagmites and stalactites, the cave also contained five fossilized human skeletons and two animal skeletons.

In the mysterious darkness, **prehistoric paintings** depict animals in yellow, red, black, and ocher, as well as mysterious symbols. One of the highlights of the tour is a trip to the chamber of the fish, which contains a wall painting of a great black seal-like creature about 1m (3¼ ft.) long. This chamber, the innermost heart of the cave, ends in a precipice that drops vertically nearly 75m (246 ft.). Guided visits are limited to 25 people, and the cave is open daily 10am to 1pm and 4 to 6pm. (It closes at 5pm Oct–Mar). Admission, including the hour-long tour, is 8€ adults and 5€ children 5 to 12.

It's easiest to get here by car from Ronda, but you can also take the train to Benaoján. There is no public transportation from the train station, and the walk is 3.5km (just more than 2 miles) uphill. Ronda and the cave are in parallel valleys, separated by a steep range of hills. Driving to the cave requires a rather complicated detour to either the south or the north of Ronda, and then doubling back.

Ronda has the oldest bullring in Spain. Built in 1785, the **Plaza de Toros ★★** is the setting for the yearly **Corrida Goyesca,** in honor of Ronda native son Pedro Romero, one of the greatest bullfighters of all time and the inspiration for Goya's bullfight etchings and paintings. The matadors all dress in the 18th-century style as depicted by Goya's works. The bullring is a work of architectural beauty, built of limestone with double arches and 136 Tuscan-like columns. The town is still talking about the music video Madonna and entourage staged here in 1994. If you want to know more about Ronda bullfighting, head for the **Museo de la Tauromaquia ★★**, Calle Virgen de la Paz (© **95-287-41-32;** www.rmcr. org), reached through the ring. It's open daily (except days of *corrida*) November through February 10am to 6pm; March and October 10am to 7pm; and April to September 10am to 8pm. Admission is 6.50€, or 8€ with audioguide. Exhibits document the exploits of the noted Romero family. Francesco invented the killing sword and the *muleta,* and his grandson Pedro (1754–1839) killed 5,600 bulls during his 30-year career. Pedro was the inspiration for Goya's famous *Tauromaquia* series. There are also exhibits devoted to Cayetano Ordóñez, the matador immortalized by Hemingway in *The Sun Also Rises.*

Because it was so remote, Ronda became a favorite hideout of bandits in 18th and 19th centuries. The **Museo Bandolero ★**, Calle Armiñán, 65 (© **95-287-77-85;** www.museobandolero.com), recounts the history and romantic myths of these colorful characters with historic documents and photos, clothing, and weapons. It's open in summer daily from 11am to 8:30pm and in winter daily from 11am to 7pm. Admission is 3.75€ for adults, 2.80€ for seniors and students.

A DRIVING TOUR OF THE PUEBLOS BLANCOS

The brilliantly whitewashed villages and towns of inland southwestern Andalucía are called Pueblos Blancos (white towns) because they cling to their mountaintops like flocks of white birds roosting together. These archetypal towns and villages dot the steep slopes of the mountains extending north from Gibraltar. They occupy that part of Andalucía that lies between the Atlantic in the west and the Mediterranean extending eastward—the land that flamenco musicians refer to as "Entre Dos Aguas," or "between two waters." One of the most traveled routes through the towns is the road that stretches from Ronda to Arcos de la Frontera on the west.

Many towns have "de la Frontera" as part of their name because they once sat on the frontier between Christian and Muslim towns and villages. Although the Catholic troops eventually triumphed, it is often the Moorish influence that makes these towns architecturally interesting, with their labyrinths of narrow, cobblestone streets, their fortress-like walls, and their little whitewashed houses with the characteristic wrought-iron grilles.

The drive outlined below passes by some of the great scenic landscapes of Spain. It skirts thickly wooded areas that are home to some rare botanical species, including the Spanish fir, *Abies pinsap,* which grows in only four locations, all at more than 1,000m (3,281 ft.). As you drive along you'll approach limestone slopes that rise as high as 6,640m (21,785 ft.). Castle ruins and old church bell towers also form part of the landscape. For those who have been to North Africa, much of the landscape of the Pueblos Blancos will evoke the Berber villages of Morocco's Atlas Mountains. The white towns sprawl across the provinces of Málaga and Cádiz, passing south of Sevilla.

The drive is not difficult, but the roads do twist and turn. At points, they climb very steeply to high mountain passes—some of the highest in southern Europe. In practice, this makes the scenic aspect of the drive better for passengers than for the driver, who should rivet attention on the roadway itself. (There are a few scenic overlooks where you can park and look around.)

The ideal time to drive through the Pueblos Blancos is spring, when the wildflowers in the valleys burst into bloom. Fall is also good. Allow at least a day for Ronda (see p. 229). You can pass through the other villages on this tour to admire the life and the architecture and then move on. The best hotels and restaurants along the entire stretch of the Pueblos Blancos are found in Ronda and Arcos de la Frontera. Elsewhere, lodging options and restaurants are very limited, although we have included some recommendations. The drive from Ronda to Arcos de la Frontera can be done in a day, but outdoor enthusiasts should plan a longer stay for hiking, climbing, and even trout-fishing. Zahara and Grazalema can also be reached by bus from Ronda, but not on the same line. Schedules and lines change often. Inquire at the Ronda tourist office.

Zahara de la Sierra ★

From Ronda, take the A-374 northwest, following the signs to Algodonales, a village best known for **Fly Spain,** Calle Sierra 41 (© **65-173-67-18;** www.fly-spain.co.uk), a first-rate paragliding center. Once you reach Algonadales, head south at the junction with CA-5312 to Zahara de la Sierra, the most perfect of the province's fortified hilltop pueblos. Trip time from Ronda is about 1 hour, and the distance is 51km (32 miles).

Zahara de la Sierra, as seen from afar.

Zahara lies in the heart of the **Natural Park Sierra de Grazalema ★★**, a 50,590-hectare (125,000-acre) park. An important reserve for griffon vultures, the park is studded with pine trees and oak forests. The **Parque Natural Information Office** (℡ **95-612-31-14;** www.zaharadelasierra.cs) lies at Plaza de Zahara, 3 (the eastern end of the main street). Hours are daily from 9am to 2pm and Monday to Saturday from 4 to 7pm. It dispenses information and maps for those who would like to hike in the park. There are five major routes, and for most you'll need to seek permission at the office, which also organizes horseback riding, canoeing, and bike trips.

The white village of Zahara itself zigzags up the foot of a rock topped by a reconstructed Nasrid castle. Houses with red-tile roofs huddle around the base of the fortress hill. Count on a 15- to 20-minute climb to reach what was once a 10th-century Muslim fortress built on Roman foundations 511m (1,677 ft.) above sea level. You can visit the castle, which is always open during daylight hours and offers **panoramic views ★** of the surrounding countryside, including the artificial reservoir at the foot of the mountain.

The cobbled main street of the village below, Calle San Juan, links the two most important churches, **San Juan** and **Santa María de la Mesa.** The latter is an 18th-century baroque church worth a look inside (if it's open). It displays an impressive *retablo* with a 16th-century image of the Madonna. The best time to be here is in June for the Corpus Christi celebration (annual dates vary). Streets and walls seem to disappear under a mass of flowers and greenery.

When you leave town heading south on the Carretera de Grazalema, you'll encounter an olive oil press that, despite modern appearances, has been pressing oil since 1755. **El Vínculo** (℡ **95-612-30-02;** www.molinoelvinculo.com) has displays showing how olive oil is produced from picking to pressing to bottling. In the late fall harvest, you can see the milling; otherwise you can taste and purchase distinctive oils pressed from the Manzanillo and Lechín varieties.

WHERE TO STAY & DINE IN ZAHARA DE LA SIERRA

Arco de la Villa ★ Tugasa, the rural tourism arm of the province of Cádiz, built and maintains this exceptional little stone inn on the west side of the village at the foot of the trail up to the castle. Rooms are spacious if basic. But the beds are comfortable, and the tile bathrooms have modern fixtures and hot water that works. The inn also has a small restaurant, and a cafeteria where you can order simpler (and less expensive) fare. If you want to hike a bit at this great outlook, this is the perfect place to stay.

Camino Nazarí, s/n. ℡ **95-612-32-30.** www.tugasa.com. 17 units. 66€ double. Free parking. **Amenities:** Restaurant; bar; free Wi-Fi in public areas. Cafeteria dishes 4€–9€.

Grazalema ★★

The drive from Zahara to Grazalema is one of the most spectacular in all of Spain, but the roads are narrow and very steep. From Zahara follow the **Carretera de Grazalema,** where the road numbers change often but include CA-9104, CA-5312, and CA-531. You will cross the high point of the mountains at the historic **Puerta de Las Palomas ★★** (Pass of the Doves). This passage stands at an elevation of 1,356m (4,450 ft.), and the switchback road is a sports car driver's dream. When you reach the junction with the main highway A-372, follow the signs east into Grazalema. This 17km (10 miles) drive will take about a half-hour—much more if you stop for photos.

Most towns of the sierra have Roman origins, but Grazalema was founded in the late 8th century A.D. by Berbers from Saddina, a peaceful lot who chose a green valley over an arid peak and never fortified their town. As a result, Christian and Muslim armies alike passed them by. Grazalema lies deep in a pocket between soaring hills, so it comes as a surprise when you round a turn and first spot it settled in the verdant valley of the Río Guadalete. It is the wettest town in Spain, receiving 2,160mm (85 in) of rain annually, making it more a green town than a White Town.

The small **Municipal Tourist Office,** Plaza de España, 11 (✆ **95-613-20-73;** www.turismograzalema.info), is open Monday to Friday 10am to 2pm and 4 to 8pm, Saturday and Sunday 10am to 2pm. It hands out hiking trail maps and serves as a clearinghouse for guide services. Its shop sells scarves, shawls, and blankets woven from local lambs' wool in rich shades of brown and beige.

Towering limestone crags overlook the town. For the best panoramic view, climb to a belvedere near the 18th-century chapel of San José. The town has two beautiful old churches, **Iglesia de la Aurora,** on Plaza de España, and the nearby **Iglesia de la Encarnación.** Both date from the 17th century.

Grazalema is also known for its local crafts, especially hand-woven pure wool blankets and rugs. A 5-minute walk from Plaza de España is **Artesanía Textil de Grazalema,** Carretera de Ronda (✆ **95-613-20-08**). At this small factory, open to the public, you can buy blankets and ponchos that are made from local wool using hand-operated looms and antique machinery. It also sells souvenirs, handicrafts, and traditional gifts. It's open Monday to Friday from 8am to 2pm and 3 to 6:30pm. Closed in August.

The town is also one of the best centers for exploring the **Parque Natural** of the Sierra de Grazalema. For information about walks in the park and horseback riding, see the information office in El Bosque (below).

WHERE TO STAY & EAT IN GRAZALEMA

Villas Turisticas de Grazalema ★★   Built by the provincial tourism agency to encourage family vacations in Grazalema, this little complex of spacious hotel rooms and apartments with one or two bedrooms has split off as a commercial enterprise. The price is still terrific, and the modern apartments even have wood-burning fireplaces with firewood supplied by the hotel. The restaurant at the hotel is known for its local trout dishes. The facility is about a 10-minute walk from the center of Grazalema village but makes a perfect base for a few days of hiking in the natural park.

Carretera Olivar, s/n. ✆ **95-613-22-13.** www.villa-turistica-grazalema.com. 24 rooms, 38 apartments. 42€–72€ doubles; 76€–138€ apartments. **Amenities:** Restaurant; outdoor pool; self-service laundry; free Wi-Fi in common areas.

Cádiz El Chico ★★ ANDALUCIAN   Run by founder Pepe Rojas Gómez and his daughters, this traditional old building on the main square is the best restaurant in town. Rojas was among the first restaurateurs to convince area shepherds to sell him their best lamb and kids instead of shipping the meat to big-city markets. He first made a name for himself among Spanish gastronomes by reviving the region's traditional lamb and kid stews. The restaurant also slow-roasts both animals in a wood-burning brick oven, usually offering the meat with a side of roasted sweet red peppers. This is mountain country cooking at its best.

Plaza de España, 8. © **95-613-20-27.** Main courses 8€–20€. Fixed-price menu 16€. Daily 1–4pm and 8pm–midnight.

El Bosque ★

After the mountain drive from Zahara to Grazalema, the relatively flat westward drive 10km (6.2 miles) through deep forest on A-372 to El Bosque seems like a breeze. Follow signs to **Las Truchas,** which is the combination lodging and restaurant located on Avenida Diputación, s/n (© **95-671-60-61;** www.tugasa. com). The facility was completely renovated in early 2014, and provides double, triple, and quadruple rooms for 66€, and suites for 94€. Rooms are basic but clean and include free Wi-Fi in public areas. Nearby you'll also find the visitor information center for access to the **Natural Park Sierra de Grazalema** (© **95-672-70-29**) from the western side. (The center at Zahara handles eastern access.) The center is at Calle Federico García Lorca, 1, and is open mid-June to mid-September Tuesday to Saturday 8am to 2pm. During cooler spring and fall days, it is open 10am to 2pm and 4 to 6pm. Even if you don't decide to hike in this area, follow the stream across the road from Las Truchas for a 5- to 10-minute stroll. This icy little waterway is the **Río Majaceite,** the southernmost trout stream in Europe. The streamside path is often used by local goatherds, so don't be surprised if you have to step off the path to let a frisky flock pass.

Arcos de la Frontera ★

Along with Ronda, this old Moorish town is a highlight of the Pueblos Blancos and the site of a top lodging. Now a National Historic Monument, Arcos de la Frontera sprawls along the long slope rising to a sheer cliff. The major attraction here is the village itself, with its Renaissance palaces squeezed onto a medieval Muslim street plan. Wander at leisure and don't worry about skipping a particular monument. Nearly all that interests the casual visitor will be found in the elevated **Medina (old town) ★★**, which towers over the flatlands. The old town gathers inside the crenellated castle walls. Unless you are staying at the *parador* and driving a small vehicle, park your car below and walk up until you reach the site built on a crag overlooking a loop in the Guadalete River.

   Plaza del Cabildo ★ is the main square, and the **tourist office,** Calle Cuesta de Belén, 5, (© **95-670-22-64;** www.arcosdelafrontera.es), is open Monday to Saturday 9am to 2pm and 3 to 6pm; Sunday 10am to 2pm. Start your visit at the **Balcón de Arcos** on the Plaza del Cabildo. Don't miss the **view** from this rectangular esplanade overhanging a deep river cleft. You can see the exterior of a Moorish-era castle, but it's privately owned and closed to the public. The main church on this square is **Santa María de la Asunción,** a 13th-century church built atop a mosque that was constructed on the foundations of a 7th-century Latin-Byzantine church. The current facade was last changed in 1732 and bears a blend of Renaissance, Gothic, and baroque styles. The **western**

The hilltop town of Arcos de la Frontera.

facade ★, in the Plateresque style, is its most stunning achievement. The interior is a mix of many styles—Plateresque, Gothic, Mudéjar, and baroque. Look for the beautiful star-vaulting and a late Renaissance altarpiece. The church is open Monday to Friday from 10am to 1pm and 4 to 7pm. Admission is 3€.

Down the main street heading out of Plaza del Cabildo is **Iglesia de San Pedro,** with its baroque bell tower. It is on the other side of the cliff and approached through a charming maze of narrow alleys. You can climb the tower, but it has few guardrails and is ill-suited for those prone to vertigo. Paintings here include *Dolorosa* by Pacheco, the tutor of Velázquez, and works by Zurbarán and Ribera. It's open Monday to Saturday from 10:30am to 2pm. Admission is 2€. Continue down Calle Escribanos to the **Convento de las Mercederías,** where the cloistered nuns sell almond cookies at a revolving window in the wall (a *retorno*) weekdays from 10am to 2pm.

WHERE TO STAY IN ARCOS DE LA FRONTERA

Parador Casa del Corregidor ★★   This *parador* occupies the catbird seat in Arcos, holding down one side of the Plaza del Cabildo. Once the headquarters of the king's magistrate, the 18th-century building was completed renovated to make the wing hanging over the cliff into modern hotel rooms with terraces that overlook the fertile plain of the Río Guadalete—the same river that flows from the mountains around Grazalema all the way to El Puerto de Santa María. The few rooms that overlook the Plaza del Cabildo are larger and more old-fashioned, yet are in least demand.

Plaza del Cabildo, s/n. 🕾 **95-670-05-00.** www.parador.es. 24 units. 90€–145€ double. Limited free parking on plaza. **Amenities:** Restaurant; bar; free Wi-Fi.

WHERE TO EAT IN ARCOS DE LA FRONTERA

Bar Alcaraván ★ ANDALUCIAN   Under new management in 2014, this atmospheric bar sits below the Plaza del Cabildo. In fact, the rooms are actually the vaulted cellars of a palace on the plaza. The menu remains hearty casual food, including regional sausages, fried cuttlefish, baked eggplant stuffed with ham, and stewed octopus. (Arcos has quick road connections to the fishing village of El Puerto de Santa María.) Even on an off night, you're likely to hear a classical guitarist playing. On weekends, there are sometimes flamenco performances.

Calle Nueva 1. 🕾 **95-670-33-97.** Tapas and raciones 4€–12€. Daily 1–5pm and 8pm–midnight.

JEREZ DE LA FRONTERA ★★

Like Kentucky with its thoroughbreds and its bourbon, Jerez is defined by its Andalucían horses and its sherry. Just take a walk down pedestrian Calle Larga, and you'll see what we mean. Fashionable young women wear knee-high black boots with tight pants as a nod to the city's equestrian tradition. And the umbrellas on the cafe tables are emblazoned with the logos of Tío Pepe, Don Patricio, or El Gallo instead of the Cruzcampo beer. The soundtrack, naturally enough, is flamenco's quick-paced *bulería*.

Essentials

GETTING THERE   Several airlines offer **flights** to Jerez from Barcelona, Madrid, Palma, Frankfurt, Dusseldorf, and Munich. For details, call ✆ **90-240-47-04,** or visit www.aena-aeropuertos.es. The airport at Carretera Jerez-Sevilla is about 11km (6¾ miles) northeast of the city center (follow the signs to Sevilla). A *cercanía* train runs from the airport to downtown Jerez.

Most visitors arrive by one of 15 **trains** per day from Sevilla, which take an hour and cost 11€ to 26€ one-way. Eleven trains from Madrid also arrive daily; a ticket costs 71€ to 79€, and the trip takes 4 hours. The beautifully tiled Mudéjar Revival train station is a city landmark on the Plaza de la Estación s/n (✆ **90-242-22-42;** www.renfe.com), at the eastern end of Calle Medina.

Bus connections are also frequent, and the bus terminal is adjacent to the train station on Calle Cartuja at the corner of Calle Madre de Dios, a 12-minute walk east of the Alcázar.

Jerez lies on the highway (E-5) connecting Sevilla with Cádiz.

VISITOR INFORMATION   The **tourist office** is at Plaza del Arenal, s/n. (✆ **95-633-88-74;** www.turismojerez.com). It's open October through May Monday to Friday 8:30am to 3pm and 4 to 6:30pm, Saturday and Sunday 9am to 3pm; June, July, and September, it is open Monday to Friday 9am to 3pm and 5 to 7pm, Saturday and Sunday 9am to 2:30pm; in August it is open Monday to Friday 9am to 3pm and 5 to 7pm, Saturday and Sunday 8am to 4pm. Free walking tours depart from the office Monday through Friday at 10am, noon, and 5pm; Saturday at 10am and noon; and Sunday at noon. Note that the discounts with the **Jerez City Pass,** sold mainly in hotels, are not for the Real Ecuestre (see below) but rather for a stud farm outside the city.

Where to Stay in Jerez de la Frontera

Hotel Bellas Artes ★   Safety is no worry at Bellas Artes, as the regional police headquarters is next door. This refurbished palace is close to the cathedral, and you can study the architecture from the hot tub on the shared rooftop terrace. The high-ceilinged guest rooms with exposed beams and soft pastel decor are downright romantic, but half of them are singles—great for friends traveling together who like their privacy. Two rooms are junior suites, including Room 6 with a small private balcony and stunning cathedral view.

Plaza del Arroyo, 45. ✆ **95-634-84-30.** www.hotelbellasartes.org. 19 rooms. 37€–45€ single; 41€–64€ double; 67€–104€ jr. suite. Amenities: Bar; rooftop terrace with hot tub; free Wi-Fi.

Hotel Casa Grande ★★   The innkeepers at Casa Grande believe in tradition, which is why you'll be given a real metal key to your room instead of a plastic card, and why the small bar is well-stocked with sherry. Many of the 15 rooms circle the central courtyard. They vary in size (some bathrooms are quite small, a few are huge), but all rooms have striking white marble floors, high ceilings, and soothing, low-key traditional furnishings. Room 3, a large superior double, is our favorite. TVs are small, but the Wi-Fi is strong. Guests share a great rooftop terrace.

Plaza de las Angustias, 3. ✆ **95-634-50-70.** www.hotelcasagrande.eu. 15 rooms. 55€–115€ double. Limited free parking. **Amenities:** Bar; free Wi-Fi.

Hotel Villa Jerez ★★ Staying at this boutique hotel north of the old town offers a taste of the the life of the sherry aristocracy. Rooms in the mansion (all except the budget doubles) are spacious and filled with light and look out on terraces, gardens, or the big pool. (The budget rooms are small and in a separate building.) Decor is traditional and elegant with pale walls, classic wooden Spanish furniture, and wrought-iron accents wherever you look. The hotel is plugged into the sherry trade and can easily arrange for private tours of bodegas. The only downside of the Villa Jerez is the 25- to 30-minute walk to Plaza Arenal.

Av. de la Cruz Roja, 7. ✆ **95-615-31-00.** www.villajerez.com. 18 rooms. 65€–115€ double, 113€– 140€ jr. suite. Parking free. **Amenities:** Restaurant; bar; free Wi-Fi.

Where to Eat in Jerez de la Frontera

Bar Juanito ★ SPANISH Jerezanos will tell you that they never visit the extremely popular Bar Juanito because it's too expensive or too touristic, but every time we've visited, everyone is speaking Andalucían Spanish at the outside patio tables, inside bar, and dining room. You might pay a small premium for the quality of the food and the atmosphere, but it's worth a little extra to enjoy fresh tuna loin salad in sherry vinegar, meatballs in oloroso sherry sauce, or the dark and juicy sweetbreads al Jerez.

Calle Pescadería Viejo, 8–10. ✆ **95-633-48-38.** www.bar-juanito.com. Tapas and *raciones* 4.50€–8€. Open Mon–Sat 1–4:30pm and 9–11:30pm, Sun 1–4:30pm.

El Almacén ★ ANDALUCIAN Essentially a long, narrow tapas bar with a few tables for sitting, El Almacén features practically every sherry made in Jerez and most made in Sanlúcar and El Puerto de Santa María. Although the tapas include some excellent standards like *patatas bravas,* many choices are on the lighter side and some—like the tempura-fried eggplant with honey—are suitable for vegetarians.

Calle Latorre, 6. ✆ **69-642-69-53.** Tapas 2.50€–9€. Mon–Thurs noon–4:30pm and 8pm–midnight; Fri–Sat noon–12:45am.

La Carboná Restaurante ★★ ANDALUCIAN This splendid restaurant in what appears to be an old sherry warehouse is really the essence of Jerez. House specialties include big cuts of Cantabrian beef roasted over charcoal and served with a variety of sauces, including a reduction of oloroso sherry. Those same searing flames are used for salmon, hake, and sea bass. Some of the prettiest dishes are presentations of white shrimp from Huelva, *langostinos* (a large prawn) from Sanlúcar, and *carabineros* (scarlet prawns) baked with *oloroso.* Many diners simply opt for the five-course sherry pairing menu, where each course comes with a different glass of sherry.

Calle San Francisco de Paula, 2. ✆ **95-634-74-75.** www.lacarbona.com. Main courses 14€–20€; sherry-pairing menu 32€. Wed–Mon 12:30–4:30pm and 8pm–12:30am.

Reino de León Gastrobar ★ ANDALUCIAN Sleek and rather elegant, this Andalucían gastropub features creative twists on classic tapas. The usual tiny casserole of braised oxtail, or *rabo de toro,* is presented as a pressed cube of braised meat topped with rich beef gravy, carrot cream, and dots of green pea cream. Mini-brochettes of Indian spiced chicken bristle from a Lucite block set on a piece of slate. Expect a more hip crowd than at the usual tapas bar.

Calle Latorre, 8. ✆ **95-632-29-15.** www.reinodeleongastrobar.com. Tapas 3.50€–12€. Daily 8am–1am.

Exploring the Area
TOURING THE BODEGAS ★★

If you want to know Jerez, you must first learn sherry. "I was born in Jerez," a tour guide at **Tío Pepe** once told us. "When we are born in the middle of the grapes, we don't drink milk as a child." We figured she was joking, but there's a grain of truth in the jest.

Jerez is not surrounded by vineyards as you might expect. They lie to the north and west in the "Sherry Triangle" marked by Jerez, Sanlúcar de Barrameda, and El Puerto de Santa María (the latter two towns are on the coast). This is where top quality *albariza* soil is found, the highest quality containing an average of 60% chalk, which is ideal for the cultivation of grapes used in sherry production, principally the white Palomino de Jerez.

In and around Jerez there must be more than 100 bodegas where you can tour and taste. On a typical visit you'll be shown through several buildings in which sherry and brandy are manufactured. In one building, you'll see grapes being pressed and sorted (in the fall); in another, the bottling process; in a third, thousands of large oak casks. Then it's on to an attractive bar where various sherries—amber, dark gold, cream, red, sweet, and velvety—can be sampled. Always start with the lightest and driest sherry, either a *fino* or, on the coast, a *manzanilla*. Keep in mind that sherry is much higher in alcohol than table wine.

You have the most choice of bodegas if you visit Monday to Friday. Many of them close during much of August. Here are a few good choices:

One of the most famous names is **González Byass ★**, the maker of Tío Pepe, Calle Manuel María González, 12 (✆ **95-635-70-00;** www.bodegastiopepe.com). Admission is 13€ (ages 5–18 6.50€). No reservations are required. Tours in English depart Monday to Saturday at noon, 1, 2, and 5pm, and Sunday at noon, 1, and 2pm.

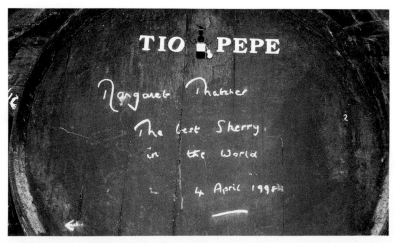

A barrel of Tío Pepe sherry.

Equally famous is **Alvaro Domecq** ★, Calle Madre de Dios, s/n (**©95-633-96-34;** www.alvarodomecq.com). Tours start Monday to Friday at 10 and 11:30am, and 1pm. The cost is 8€; reservations are recommended.

Lovely and romantic, **Bodegas Tradición ★★**, Plaza Cordobeses, 3 (**©95-616-86-28;** www.bodegastradicion.com), focuses exclusively on sherries classified as V.O.S. (aged 20 years or more) and V.O.R.S. (aged more than 30 years). The bodega owner has amassed an impressive collection of Spanish art from the 15th to 19th centuries, including a pair of portraits by Goya. Visitors can see some of it in the bodega gallery—a rare glimpse into the world of sherry privilege. Reservations are required, and the visit and tasting cost 20€.

Alcazár ★ FORTRESS   Jerez was a frontier town that went back and forth between Moors and Christians, and this fortress was built in the 12th century as a rural outpost to hold the line against Christian encroachment. It contains an austerely beautiful mosque, lovely gardens, and some of the best-preserved Moorish baths in Andalucía. Although the mosque was converted to a church in 1264, the mihrab, or prayer niche, was preserved—as was the boiler system of the baths, enabling you to see how they operated. The alcázar also functions as a local history museum, displaying two of the ancient olive mills. (In the 1700s, Jerez had 32 active olive mills.) The fortress also contains the Palacio Villavicencio, a noble palace constructed from the late 1600s to 1927. Its history paintings are mostly remarkable for their immense size. A tower room contains a *camera obscura,* which projects images of the city in a darkened room.

Alameda Vieja, s/n. © **95-632-69-23.** www.turismojerez.com. Alcázar only 5€ adults, 1.80€ students and seniors; with camera obscura 7€ adults, 4.20€ students and seniors. Nov–Feb daily 9:30am–3pm; Mar–June & Sept 16–Oct Mon–Fri 9:30am–8pm & Sat–Sun 9:30am–3pm; July–Sep 15 Mon–Fri 9:30am–10pm, Sat–Sun 9:30am–3pm.

Centro Andaluz de Flamenco ★ CULTURAL INSTITUTION   One of the many cradles of flamenco is Jerez, where Moorish, Gypsy, Jewish, and Andalucían traditions met. This academic center possesses the largest public archive of books, musical scores, and performance videos of flamenco in Spain. Flamenco engravings and paintings line the walls of the central courtyard, and free videos are screened in the auditorium. You'll always hear flamenco in the background—the center features recordings by a different artist every week. Staff are steeped in the local scene; ask about upcoming performances at the city's proliferating *tabanco* sherry bars and commercial nightclub *tablaos.*

Plaza de San Juan, 1. © **95-681-41-32.** www.centroandaluzdeflamenco.es. Free. Mon–Fri 9am–2pm, Wed 4:30–7pm.

DAY TRIP TO SANLÚCAR DE BARRAMEDA ★

This port where the Rio Guadalquivír meets the Bay of Cádiz may have lost its deep harbor of ages past, but its sandbars and silted beaches make it a playground of the south. Well-off Spaniards flock here around Easter to bask in the sun, walk or ride horses on the beach, and eat mounds of fresh seafood in the restaurants. Sanlúcar also produces *manzanilla* sherry, a delicate style that can only be obtained by aging in the salt air by the ocean.

The simplest way to get to Sanlúcar from Jerez is to drive the 25km (15 miles) on the A-480. Alternately, buses run every hour between Jerez and Sanlúcar from 7am to 9pm weekdays, every 2 hours 9am to 9pm on weekends. The **tourist office** is at **Calzada de Ejército** s/n (© **95-636-61-10;** www.sanlucardebarrameda.es). It's open Monday to Friday 10am to 2pm and Saturday and Sunday 10am to 2pm and 6 to 8pm.

ay, **CABALLERO!**

Horses have fascinated Spaniards since Neolithic artists painted images of steeds in the caves outside Ronda 20,000 years ago. The museum at the **Fundación Real Escuela Andaluza del Arte Ecuestre,** Avenida Duque de Abrantes, s/n (© **95-631-80-15;** www.realescuela.org), traces the evolving bond between man and beast, emphasizing horsemanship skills and the breeding of the Pura Raza Española, or "pure Spanish race." The top blood lines of what English-speakers call the Andalucían horse were first established at Carthusian monasteries in the late Middle Ages.

The Real Escuela, founded in 1973, trains horses and riders and operates a breeding farm. Performances of the exquisitely trained, so-called "dancing horses" (always Thurs at noon, but also other days depending on the season; 17€–27€) are a great spectacle. Before the show, you can tour the grounds and visit the saddlery and museums of equestrian art and carriages. On non-performance days, you can also visit the facility (Mon, Wed, and Fri, 10am–2pm; 6.50€–11€) and take in the same sights. But the highlight is the chance to watch a practice session. Even during practice, most horses and riders are a polished team.

The last time we visited, we watched three trainers encourage a nervous horse to perform the signature chorus-line prances. Every few minutes, the trainers stopped to speak softly to the horse, rub his nose and pat his flanks. It was a revealing glimpse at the hard work, patience, and persistence behind the dazzling artistry.

Sanlucár's harbor at the mouth of the Guadalquivir was once so deep that Columbus launched his third voyage to America here. But centuries of silting have made the river shallower, creating lovely in-town beaches and protecting the upstream wetlands of Parque Doñana. The healthy estuarine system is a fisherman's delight. Look for extraordinary shrimp, king prawns, and rock lobster on restaurant menus. Most visitors gravitate to the sandy strand at Bajo de Guia or to restaurant-lined Plaza del Cabildo.

When Magellan sailed from Sanlúcar in 1519 to circumnavigate the globe, he reportedly spent more on *manzanilla* than he did on armaments. To understand why, visit one of the *manzanilla* producers. **Bodegas Barbadillo ★**, Calle Sevilla, 1 (© **95-638-55-21;** www.barbadillo.com) has been crafting and aging sherry since 1821. The bodega offers guided tours in English Tuesday to Saturday at 11am, and Sunday at noon. The price per person is 5€, and reservations are recommended.

The marques emblazoned on cafe umbrellas on **Plaza del Cabildo** ★ signal who owns each bar. Stop at any one to order a plate of shrimp and glass of *manzanilla* to enjoy in the sunshine.

Visiting Parque Doñana

Parque Doñana ★★ NATURE PRESERVE   Sanlúcar is the departure for boat trips to the marshes at the mouth of the Guadalquivír River. More than merely scenic, they sustain the Bay of Cádiz shellfishery, and were finally recognized in the late 20th century as one of the most important estuary systems in Europe. They literally keep millions of birds alive as they migrate each year between Europe and Africa. The marshes are also rich with resident storks, egrets, herons, and songbirds. The interpretive center at the **Fábrica de Hielo (Ice House)** on Bajo de Guia beach explains the marshes, shifting sands, and stabilized sands of the complex ecosystem. The center books 2½-hour riverboat trips into the park, as well as a combined boat and all-terrain vehicle trip to explore different habitats.

Av. Bajo de Guia s/n. ✆ **95-638-16-35.** www.visitasdonana.com. Visitor center free. Daily 9am–8pm. Two riverboat trips daily in morning and afternoon. Prices from 17€ adults, 12€ students & seniors, 8€ children.

Where to Eat in Sanlúcar de Barrameda

Restaurante Mirador de Doñana ★★ ANDALUCIAN   You can get great shrimp and langostinos at almost any bar in Sanlúcar, but if you really want the top of the catch and the best views while enjoying it, the Mirador is the only choice. Many people are perfectly happy eating outside along the beach or in the indoor dining room, but for the best views, head upstairs where the name "scenic overlook of Doñana" is really true. It can be difficult to sort out the different kinds of shrimp and prawns—not to mention the saltwater crayfish and different forms of lobster—but rest assured, they are all good.

Bajo de Guia. ✆ **95-636-42-05.** www.miradordonana.com. Reservations recommended for best views. Main courses 9€–30€. Open daily 1:30-3:30pm and 7:30–11pm, closed Jan–Feb.

CÁDIZ ★

Residents of this seaport city on the Atlantic coast are a forward-thinking lot, yet they still call themselves Gaditanos, a reference to the Phoenician trading post founded here about 1100 B.C. As Western Europe's oldest continuously inhabited city, Cádiz fell under the successive sway of Athens, Carthage, Rome, and finally the Visigoths and Moors. Most traces of that storied past were obliterated in the 1755 earthquake that also leveled Lisbon. The Cádiz of today was conceived as an Enlightenment city with long, straight boulevards and now-abandoned fortifications to protect the galleons of New World trade that Cádiz monopolized when ships became too big to sail upriver to Sevilla. Its stately pastel buildings seem to bleach in the sun along the seaside *paseos*. Reasons to visit include a thriving local culture, great beaches, vibrant music scene, and wonderful seafood restaurants.

Essentials

GETTING THERE   Fifteen daily **trains** arrive from Sevilla (trip time: 2 hr.; 16€–24€ one-way), 12 of them stopping at Jerez de la Frontera and El Puerto de Santa María along the way. The train station is on Avenida del Puerto, Plaza de Sevilla 1 (✆ **90-242-22-42;** www.renfe.com), on the southeast border of the main port.

Four daily **buses** run from Madrid to Cádiz. Trip time is 8¼ hours and a one-way ticket costs 27€. The bus is operated by **Socibus** (✆ **90-222-92-92;**

www.socibus.es), at Avenida José León de Carranza (N-20). The terminal is on the north side of town, a few blocks west of the main port.

Driving from Sevilla, the A-4 (also called E-5), a toll road, or N-IV, a toll-free road running beside it, will bring you into Cádiz.

VISITOR INFORMATION The Cadiz **city tourist office,** Paseo de Canalejas, s/n (© 95-624-10-01; www.cadiz.es), is open in the summer Monday to Friday 9am to 7pm, Saturday to Sunday 9am to 5pm; in the winter Monday to Friday 8:30am to 6:30pm, Saturday to Sunday 9am to 5pm. The office hands out a map detailing four color-coded walking routes to maximize your sightseeing time. The office claims Cádiz is the only city in Spain with such routes painted on the sidewalks.

Where to Stay in Cádiz

Hotel Atlántico, Parador de Cádiz ★★★ A government-run *parador* has held down this beautiful spot between Parque Génoves and Playa La Caleta since the system launched in the 1920s. This latest incarnation, which opened in September 2012, is the third try, and it is the charm. Every room has a terrace overlooking the ocean as well as one or two big beds looking out at the sea through a glass wall, a great writing desk behind the headboards of those beds, and wall-to-wall marble bathrooms. The accompanying spa runs the gamut of beauty and wellness treatments for both men and women, and features a series of splendid rooftop pools, again overlooking the ocean. Staying here is a little like booking a room suspended between sea and sky. La Caleta beach is steps away, while the cathedral is about a 15-minute brisk walk through the city.

Avenida Duque de Nájera, 9. © **95-622-69-05.** www.parador.es. 124 rooms. 150€–220€ double. Bus: 1 or 33. Parking: 16€ per day. **Amenities:** Restaurant; bar; concierge; indoor & outdoor pools; spa; free Wi-Fi.

Hotel de Francia y Paris ★ The name might be French, but the rooms are decorated in modern Spanish taste with a sleek, fresh look. Following the 2013 renovation, rooms feature walnut wood furniture, white walls, new hardwood floors, and floor-to-ceiling draperies that accentuate the high ceilings of this late 19th-century building. All-new bathrooms have spacious shower stalls, sink areas with space to lay out toiletries, and bidets. Most rooms hold two twin beds, a small desk, and one or two chairs. The best have small balconies overlooking the plaza, which is busy in the daytime but relatively quiet by evening. If you visit in the spring, request Room 108, which looks out on blooming bitter orange trees. Leave your windows open, and you'll sleep in the perfume of orange blossoms.

Plaza de San Francisco, 6. © **95-621-23-19.** www.hotelfrancia.com. 58€–79€ double. Bus: 1 or 33. **Amenities:** Free Wi-Fi.

Hotel Patagonia Sur ★★ This limestone-facade hotel fits so seamlessly into the old city that only guests who enjoy the ample hot water in the shower would know that it was newly constructed in 2009 rather than being here since the days of Hercules. Of the 16 rooms, the two penthouse rooms with private terraces are the most desirable and cost only a small premium. The 10 standard doubles are a bit snug, but well designed with ample storage and robust Wi-Fi. Location is just about perfect for walking around Cádiz—steps from the cathedral and the docks, a short walk to the museum and the market, about 15 minutes on foot from La Caleta beach.

Calle Cobos, 11. © **85-617-46-47.** www.hotelpatagoniasur.es. 16 units. 65€–113€ double. Bus: 1, 2, or 7. **Amenities:** Cafeteria; bar; free Wi-Fi.

Where to Eat in Cádiz

El Faro ★★★ SEAFOOD/ANDALUCIAN   The El Faro group got its start in the fishing port of El Puerto de Santa María, but even Porteños profess to prefer the Cádiz branch for staying true to the Bay of Cádiz fish cuisine. Golden walls, painted ceramic plates, and handsome dark woodwork give the dining room an elegance that is only enhanced by crystal glassware and an abundance of fresh flowers. Dishes range from a whole sea bass or gilthead bream cooked in a casing of salt to red tuna with eggplant, caramelized onion, and citrus juices. El Faro is also celebrated for its baked rice dishes, including black rice with squid. Almost all dishes are priced according to the market price on any given day.

Calle San Félix, 15. ✆ **95-621-21-88.** www.elfarodecadiz.com. Reservations recommended. Main courses 17€–25€. Daily 1–4pm and 8:30pm–midnight. Bus: 2 or 7.

Terraza Marisquería Joselito ★ SEAFOOD   One of the more traditional shellfish and seafood spots along the port, Joselito serves both in the bar and on its outside patio just a block from the fishing piers. The menu has three categories: shrimp and clams (including shrimp grilled with olive oil or sautéed with lots of garlic), house "stews" (such as veal meatballs or cuttlefish with small fava beans), and fried and grilled fish. The real treat is grilled fresh tuna landed at Barbete, one of the world's most famous tuna ports a few miles south of Cádiz. All plates come without garnish.

Paseo de Canalejas, s/n. ✆ **95-625-80-86.** Plates 6€–16€. Mon–Fri noon–4pm and 8pm–midnight, Sat–Sun noon–4pm.

Exploring Cádiz

This port city's **seaside promenades ★★** circle the old town and follow the sometimes turbulent Atlantic Ocean. Strolling along them provides a powerful understanding of the city and its relationship to the sea, on which Cádiz has always relied for its life and its commerce. You can only imagine what the port must have looked like when the harbor was filled with Spanish galleons bound for and returning from the New World.

Cádiz's promenade along the sea.

A waterfall in the Parque Genovés.

The southern and western promenades overlook the ocean. Those *paseos* lead to the refreshing public gardens of Cádiz, including **Parque Genovés ★**, with its exotic trees and plants from all over the world. The adjacent leafy **Alameda Marqués de Comillas** also dates from the 19th century, but is less formal, and therefore more welcoming.

The wide oceanfront sidewalks pass the silent remains of the Cádiz fortifications. They were constructed with good reason. In 1587, Sir Francis Drake attacked the harbor and waylaid the Spanish Armada, and in the 1590s, Anglo-Dutch invaders set Cádiz to the torch. The Spanish crown responded by erecting a series of fortifications around the knob of the city. Two remaining forts bracket the cove of La Caleta. At the north end stands **Castillo de Santa Catalina** (✆ 95-622-63-33; daily 11am–7:30pm, until 8:30pm July–Aug; free). Built in 1598, it was the port's main citadel for many decades. It now houses some cultural exhibits, but kids prefer clambering along the ramparts. The **Castillo de San Sebastián** (closed until further notice for renovations) on the south side sits on an island reached across a long causeway favored by surf-casters. The beach at the entrance to the causeway glistens with sea glass cast up by the waves.

The cove between the forts is **Playa La Caleta,** one of two European blue-flag beaches within city limits. The other, more extensive strand, is **Playa La Victoria,** about 32.km (2 miles) farther east on Avenida Fernandez Ladreda. It is best reached by bus 1 (beach route) or bus 7 (central avenue route). Fare is 1.30€. Get off at Plaza Ingenerio La Cierva. This is a good place to join a pickup volleyball game before grabbing a bite at a beachfront snack bar.

Catedral de Cádiz ★ CATHEDRAL   The last great cathedral erected in Spain financed by the riches from the New World, this gold-domed baroque church was begun in 1772. Work halted in 1796 and stalled during the Napoleonic invasion. Finally, the citizens of Cádiz finished the cathedral with volunteer labor in 1838. Like the city, it's a model of openness and light. Even the walls are finished in marble. An excellent audioguide in several languages provides exhaustive detail on each point of interest. Perhaps most remarkable is the monumental carved wooden choir from the Carthusian monastery in Jerez. To get a real sense of devotion, don't miss the 390kg (860-lb) all-silver "paso" that is carried through the streets by 12 men on the feast of Corpus Christi in June. Following renovations, the Torre Poniente was reopened in 2014 and offers panoramic views of the city.

Plaza Catedral. ✆ **95-628-61-54.** www.catedraldecadiz.com. Cathedral admission 5€, 3€ seniors and students; Torre Poniente 5€. Mon–Sat 10am–6pm; Sun 1–6:30pm. Bus: L2.

Centro de Interpretacón del Flamenco ★ CULTURAL CENTER   If you visited the Museo del Baile Flamenco in Sevilla (p. 200), you should come here to get the rest of the story. This small center focuses more on the singing tradition and guitar forms than on dance. A small room set up like a *taberna* has two interactive video screens that let you sample different styles of singing, guitar, dance, and even piano. Spend the extra euro for a glass of wine with admission so that you can relax and linger over this rich source of material. Performances are held in this intimate space at least once a week (see "Cádiz After Dark," below).

Calle Santiago, 12. ⓒ **95-607-36-77.** Admission 4€; 5€ with glass of wine. Mon–Sat 10am–5pm.

Roman hippo statues at the Museo de Cádiz.

Museo de Cádiz ★★ MUSEUM   There's something touching about the two 5th-century B.C. Phoenician sarcophagi in the archaeological collection of this museum. The man's sarcophagus was unearthed in 1887, and when the matching woman's sarcophagus was excavated in 1980, the pair, buried together for eternity, was reunited. In fact, some of the most evocative objects in the archaeological collections are Phoenician—or in the case of the 329 pieces of gold jewelry excavated in 2012, Carthaginian. The ancient jewelry is as advanced in its design and construction as any modern work, and makes an intimate connection to the past. The Roman room is less personal but more monumental, especially the 2.75-m-high (9-ft.) statue of Emperor Trajan excavated near Tarifa in 1980. The fine arts collection on the upper floors is less dramatic.

Plaza de Mina s/n. ⓒ **95-620-33-68.** www.museosdeandalucia.es. Admission 1.50€. Mid-Sept to mid-June Tues–Sat 10am–8:30pm; Sun 10am–5pm; from mid-June to mid-Sept Tues–Sat 9am–5pm, Sun 10am–5pm. Bus: L2, 1, 3, 5.

Torre Tavira ★ LANDMARK   In the late 18th century, when Cádiz handled three-quarters of Spain's commerce with the Americas, the city was dotted with 126 watchtowers to monitor the comings and goings of ships in the harbor. The sole survivor is Torre Tavira, erected on the highest lookout point of the old city. Exhibitions on two levels (a chance to pause in the tiring climb of winding stairs) tell tales of the trading heyday of Cádiz, but the real payoff is the rooftop view of the city, its harbor, and the surrounding seas. When you reach the top, you enter a camera obscura with rotating aperture that casts images of the city on the round walls of a viewing chamber as a guide explains what you are seeing.

Calle Marqués Real Tesoro, 10. ⓒ **95-621-29-10.** www.torretavira.com. Admission 6€; seniors & students 5€. Oct–Apr daily 10am–6pm; May–Sept daily 10am–8pm.

Shopping

The **Mercado Central,** Plaza Libertad, s/n (ⓒ **95-622-08-60;** www.cadiz.es), is the best place to buy stunning Huelva strawberries in season, bananas and oranges from the Canary Islands, and spices to take home. The market is also ringed by a number of tapas bars. On the plaza out front, **El Melli** (ⓒ **95-621-39-33;** elmelli.com) sells an unusually extensive and well-priced selection of flamenco CDs. Two good shopping streets are Calle San Francisco and Calle Compañia. **Spagnolo,** Calle San Francisco, 31 (ⓒ **95-607-90-79;** www.spagnolo.com.es), has been creating preppy clothes with a polo theme since before Ralph Lauren was born. **El Potro,** Calle Companía, 8 (© **95-622-56-73;** www.elpotro.es), the shop of a company based in the leather-working town of Ubrique southeast of Sevilla, has elegant leather goods, and the company's horsehead logo gives many pieces a vaguely Louis Vuitton–like look.

Cádiz After Dark

As in all of Spain, much "nightlife" consists of eating and drinking. For a slightly edgy feel, head to **Taberna Casa Manteca,** Corralón de los Carros, 66 (© **95-621-36-03**), a Barrio La Viña hangout for flamencos, *corrida* aficionados, and lovers of all things pork. The owners are sons of a famous matador, and bull-fight memorabilia decorates the walls like religious paintings in a church. The place opens a little before noon and closes when the last patrons stagger out, usually after 2am.

There are two good options for flamenco. **Peña Flamenco Juanito Villar,** Paseo Fernando Quiñones, s/n, at Playa La Caleta (© **95-622-52-90**), is a small, traditionally tiled *taberna* with a stage at one end for flamenco on Friday nights. There's no admission charge, but you're expected to eat and drink. Call after 1pm to reserve a table. The **Centro de Interpretacón del Flamenco** (p. 247) also hosts flamenco performances on Friday nights. The 20€ price includes a light supper and a drink, but unlike the commercial *tablaos,* this is an intimate show for only about 20 people. Both are great choices, with Juanito Villar being a little more free-wheeling and the center more earnest.

At the other end of the cultural spectrum, the Cádiz city government operates **Gran Téatro Falla,** Plaza Fragela, s/n. (© **95-622-08-34;** institucional. cadiz.es/area/Cultura/35). This imposing 1884 to 1905 neo-Mudéjar brick building presents everything from contemporary and classic theater pieces to star flamenco singers and guitarists, modern dance, opera, and philharmonic orchestras. In May each year, the theater hosts an international music festival of classical music, including the works of Cádiz-born composer Manuel de Falla.

LUNCH TRIP TO EL PUERTO DE SANTA MARÍA ★

The easiest way to get out on the Bay of Cádiz is to take the catamaran ferry, **Muelle Transportes de Maritimo** (© **90-245-05-50;** www.cmtbc.es), to **El Puerto de Santa María ★**. The deepwater port has a long and storied history. Columbus' flagship, the Santa María, hailed from here, and a plaque on the 12th-century castle in the heart of town honors local mariners who took part in the 1492 journey. Today Santa María is primarily a fishing port filled with small shrimpers, deepwater tuna boats, and headquarters of a number of sherry houses. The 30-minute trip only costs 2.65€, which means that you will have plenty of money left for lunch in this foodie town. Even the father of the current king came here to eat lenguado de fideos at **Bar Guadalete Chico ★**, Calle Micaela Aramburu, 3 (© **63-734-12-53**). The deceptively simple soup (media ración, 5.50€) is made with fish stock, a touch of tomato, short noodles, and pieces of flounder. People in the sherry trade favor **Bar Casa Paco Ceballos ★**, Ribera del Mariscos, sn (© **95-654-29-08**), for its tapa of pavía de merluza (2.50€), a long strip of hake breaded and quick-fried in olive oil. Accompany it with a glass of "Bailen," a medium-dry olorosa. Visiting the sherry houses in El Puerto de Santa María requires advance arrangements. One of the most accessible is Osborne, Calle de Moros, s/n (© **95-686-91-00;** www.osborne.es). Tastings and tours range 8€ to 30€, with the top price including tastings of very old, rare sherries.

8

THE COSTA DEL SOL

Some of Spain's nicest beaches—and worst traffic congestion—coexist along the Mediterranean shoreline of the Costa del Sol, the sandy strip along the southern coast of Andalucía. From the quiet sands of **Estepona,** it stretches east to the jet-set resort of **Marbella** and the port city of **Málaga,** then continues east as the Costa Tropical to **Almuñécar.** Along with the strands are sandy coves, whitewashed houses, olive trees, lots of new apartment houses, high-rise hotels, fishing boats, golf courses, souvenir stands, fast-food outlets, theme parks, and widely varied flora and fauna. You'll likely also find bargains on lodging, thanks to overbuilding.

There's good reason why millions of travelers ignore the ugly new architecture and brave the traffic jams. With an average of 325 days of sunshine a year, the Costa del Sol lives up to its name. It's best to know yourself before you go. Do you want to simply bake on the beach? Do you crave nightlife? Do you long to hobnob with the beautiful people? Or do you hanker for the least built-up fishing village? There's an option for everyone.

Golfers won't be disappointed either. If you prefer grassy greens to sandy strands, some of the best resorts are **Los Monteros** (© **95-277-17-00;** www.monteros.com) in Marbella, which has the leading course; **Atalaya Park Golf Hotel & Resort,** in Estepona (© **95-288-90-00;** www.atalaya-park.es); and **Hotel Guadalmina Spa & Golf Resort,** in Marbella (© **95-288-22-11;** www.hotelguadalmina.com). Many golfers like to play a different course every day. Ask your hotel reception desk to arrange tee times at least a day in advance.

Whatever you choose, there's a strategy to enjoying the Costa del Sol. When you leave the highway and enter a thicket of unattractive concrete buildings, keep heading toward the water and look for the old city center, where narrow, twisty streets have defied development. Thanks to highway investments, it's easier to get around. The infamous N-340 highway from Málaga to Estepona has become a fast, safe, six-lane road. For those traveling long distances along the coast, the **Autopista del Sol,** a toll expressway with four lanes, has greatly relieved the traffic congestion.

From June to October, the coast is mobbed, so reserve far in advance. At other times, innkeepers are likely to roll out the red carpet. Northern European pensioners come in droves during the bargain winter season, but many hotels, restaurants, and attractions close or keep limited hours between New Year's Day and Easter, when the weather can be overcast and rainy.

ESTEPONA ★

A town of Roman origin, Estepona is a budding beach resort, less developed than Marbella or Torremolinos and, for that reason, more likable. Estepona contains an interesting 15th-century parish church, with the ruins of an old aqueduct nearby (at Salduba). Its recreational port is an attraction, as are its **beaches:**

FACING PAGE: **A beautiful beach in Marbella.**

The Costa del Sol

Costa Natura, N-340 Km 257, the first legal nude beach of its kind along the Costa del Sol; La Rada, 3km (1¾ miles) long; and El Cristo, only 550m (1,804 ft.) long.

In summer, the cheapest places to eat in Estepona are the *chiringuitos,* little dining areas set up by local fishermen on the beach. They feature seafood, including sole and sardine kebabs grilled over an open fire. Tapas bars are often called *freidurías* (fried-fish bars), and you'll find most of them at the corner of Calle de los Reyes and La Terraza. Tables spill onto the sidewalks in summer. *Gambas a la plancha* (shrimp) are the favorite (but not cheapest) dish to order.

Essentials

GETTING THERE   The nearest rail links are in Fuengirola. However, Estepona is on the **bus** route from Algeciras to Málaga. If you're driving, head east from Algeciras along the E-5/N-340.

VISITOR INFORMATION   The **tourist office,** Av. San Lorenzo, 1 (© **95-280-20-02;** www.estepona.es), is open Monday to Friday 9am to 8pm, Saturday 10am to 1:30pm.

Where to Stay in Estepona

Moderately priced hotels are in the town center, while some of the coast's most expensive and luxurious resorts are out of town along the coast.

Atalaya Park Golf Hotel & Resort ★★   A modern golf and conference complex on the road to Puerto Banús, the low-rise Atalaya Park sprawls along the shore amid 8 hectares (20 acres) of flowering gardens. Public areas are grand, with long vistas along hall-like rooms, while each of the spacious and modern guest rooms has a terrace. With all the on-site amenities and variety of restaurants, many visitors never leave the property until it is time to check out. The two golf courses are among the best on the Costa del Sol, and greens fees are deeply discounted for guests.

Carretera de Cádiz, Km 168.5. ✆ **95-288-90-00.** www.atalaya-park.es. 475 units. 78€–167€ double; 96€–203€ family room, 114€–227€ suite; 215€ –360€ bungalow. Free parking. **Amenities:** 3 restaurants; 3 bars; babysitting; bikes; children's center; exercise room; 2 18-hole golf courses; 6 freshwater pools (2 heated indoor); sauna; 9 outdoor tennis courts (6 lit); watersports equipment/rentals; Wi-Fi (free, in lobby).

Hotel Buenavista ★   We have long loved this modest "hotel *residencia*" in the middle of town just across the road from Estepona's main beach. Rooms on the front have little balconies, and on a clear day you can see the green hills of Africa across the straits. Rooms lack air-conditioning, which is less an issue for comfort as for noise, as traffic on the road and boisterous vacationers can make it loud. But even in the highest season, Buenavista is a bargain for an old-fashioned beach vacation. If you're planning to go in July or August, book far ahead to get a jump on the Spanish families who come here.

Av. de España, 180. ✆ **95-280-01-37.** www.buenavistaestepona.com. 38 units. 50€–90€ double. **Amenities:** Restaurant (separate building); free Wi-Fi.

Hotel TRH Paraíso ★   Panoramic views, dramatic architecture, and all the amenities of a good resort make the TRH Paraíso the leader in the moderate price category along this stretch of the Costa del Sol. It's across the highway from Playa Costalita some 12km (7½ miles) from the center of Estepona. Built in the 1980s, the resort is a little longer in the tooth than some of its competition, which shows in the somewhat smaller bedroom size. But every room has a balcony looking out on the ocean. Guests enjoy discounts at 25 area golf courses, and a special playground and pool are reserved for children.

Carretera de Cádiz, Km 167. ✆ **800-465-9936** in the U.S., or 95-288-30-00. www.hoteltrhparaisocostadelsol.com. 171 units. 50€–129€ double; 165€–212€ suite. Free parking. **Amenities:** 2 restaurants; 4 bars; children's center; Jacuzzi; 2 freshwater pools (1 heated indoor); sauna; free Wi-Fi in common areas.

Kempinski Hotel Bahía Marbella-Estepona ★★★   This sprawling estate hotel between Estepona and Puerto Banús has such broad landscaped lawns that it looks like it should have a golf course. But, no—that landscape is part of the Moroccan style charm of an oasis hotel, though the golf desk can arrange tee times at any of nine nearby courses. All rooms and suites have private balconies or terraces, with garden or sea views. The rooms are spacious, the beds are soft, and the large bathrooms are covered in pale marble. Families favor the Bahia for its excellent children's center and its connections to English-speaking babysitters. Meals are literally a moveable feast, from the indoor breakfast buffet to lunch by the sea to romantic dining in the gardens. The Wi-Fi fee can be waived. Ask.

Carretera de Cádiz, Km 159, Playa el Padrón. ✆ **95-280-95-00.** www.kempinski.com. 145 units. 138€–391€ double; 231€–536€ junior suite; from 600€ suite. Garage parking 15€; outside parking free. **Amenities:** 4 restaurants; 3 bars; children's center; concierge; exercise room; 4 pools (1 heated indoor); spa; outdoor tennis court; watersports equipment rentals; Wi-Fi (20€/day).

beaches: **THE GOOD, THE BAD & THE UGLY**

It was the allure of beaches that originally put the "sol" in the Costa del Sol beginning in the 1950s. But, in truth, not all of the Costa del Sol is a paradise for swimmers.

The roughest beaches—mainly pebbles and slates—are on the east end at Málaga, Nerja, and Almuñécar. Moving westward, you encounter the gritty, grayish sands of Torremolinos. The best beaches here are at El Bajondillo and La Carihuela, which borders an old fishing village. Another good stretch of beach is along the meandering strip between Carvajal, Los Boliches, and Fuengirola. In addition, two good beaches—El Fuerte and La Fontanilla—lie on either side of Marbella. However, all these beaches tend to be overcrowded, especially in July and August. Crowding is worst on Sundays, May through October, when family picnickers join sunbathers on the strands.

All public beaches in Spain are free. Don't expect to find changing facilities—there might be cold showers on the major beaches, but that's it.

Although it's not sanctioned or technically allowed by the government, many women go topless on the beaches. If you do so, you could be subject to arrest by the Guardia Civil. To bare it all, head for the Costa Natura, about 3km (1¾ miles) west of Estepona. This is the only official nudist colony along the Costa del Sol.

Where to Eat in Estepona

La Alcaría de Ramos ★ SPANISH   There's a definite international caste to the nominally Spanish cuisine, betrayed in part by the extensive use of French on the menu. That said, grilled sole with vegetables and potatoes is almost always a pleasant, light dish whatever language it's assumed, and grilled sea bass in a Basque red pepper sauce is a dependable treat. The owners, the Ramos brothers, reserve much of their inventiveness for salads and soups, offering treats like a baby squid salad with Emmenthal cheese and lemon vinaigrette, or a raspberry gazpacho with yogurt and mint sorbet. Opt for dining in the terrace garden if the weather permits.

Carretera de Cádiz, Km 167. ⓒ **95-288-61-78.** www.laalcariaderamos.es. Reservations recommended. Main courses 13€–24€. Mon–Sat 7:30pm–midnight.

PUERTO BANÚS ★

A favorite resort for international celebrities, the coastal village of Puerto Banús was created almost overnight and made to look as if it had been there forever. It's exactly what a set designer would think a Costa del Sol fishing village should look like—except that the harbor is filled with yachts rather than more scruffy fishing boats, and the amplified bells of the mosque built by King Fahd of Saudi Arabia call the faithful to prayer. Expensive bars and restaurants line the waterfront. To reach the town, you can take one of 15 buses that run daily from Marbella, or drive east from Marbella along E-15.

Where to Stay in Puerto Banús

H10 Andalucía Plaza ★   Don't plan on bringing the kids if you stay at this casino hotel. They're not banned, but the atmosphere is clearly adult and the

10-minute walk to the beach is inconvenient, even though an underground walkway scoots beneath the busy highway. This hotel has had many incarnations and had become a frankly seedy tour bus stopover until its last renovation in 2009. Now it's all glitz and glamour, with silver and gold trim on the walls and movie star portraits in the public areas. Rooms vary from tight doubles to larger doubles and suites, but most have balconies or terraces. Admission to the adjacent Marbella Casino is free for guests.

Urbanización Nueva Andalucía, s/n. ℂ **95-281-20-00.** www.hotelh10esteponapalace.com. 400 units. 80€–215€ double; 150€–425€ junior suite. Free parking. **Amenities:** 2 restaurants; 2 bars; bikes; concierge; exercise room; 3 pools (1 indoor); spa; Wi-Fi (free, in lobby).

Park Plaza Suites Hotel ★   Located right next to the yacht harbor, this small hotel often houses yachtsmen in need of a break from the boat. Despite the name, most rooms are doubles (just 6 real suites) but they are spacious and comfortable in a very contemporary style. Floors are wood laminate and bedspreads and draperies are designer Mediterranean chic. Every room has a large balcony or terrace as well as cooking facilities and a washer/dryer. You can walk out the door to restaurants and nightclubs—or enjoy the use of a private stretch of beach. Minimum stays required in July and August.

Paseo Marítimo de Benabola, s/n. ℂ **95-290-90-00.** www.parkplazasuiteshotel.com. 51 units. 90€–304€ double; 105€–790€ suite. Parking 24€. **Amenities:** Restaurant; bar; exercise room; Jacuzzi; room service; Wi-Fi (free, in lobby).

Where to Eat in Puerto Banús

Antonio ★ SEAFOOD/INTERNATIONAL   Old salts and old folks alike recall Antonio from its inception in the early 1970s. It's a testament to the quality of the food and the old-fashioned service by waiters in maroon waistcoats that the place is still thriving. The key to the restaurant's success is that it always gets great fish and the kitchen treats those fish with respect. For the local catch, ask for the mixed fried fish, which will include some tiny squid, red mullet,

The chic harbor at Puerto Banús.

whitebait, and sprats. Roughly every second table orders paella, which is made here with more shellfish than rice. It would make a Valenciano shudder, but Antonio knows what customers like. It's a grand place to watch the action in Puerto Banús—a little like leafing through a gossip magazine without captions to tell you who's who.

Muelle de Ribera 21. ℂ **95-281-35-36.** www.restauranteantoniopuertobanus.com. Reservations suggested. Main courses 16€–32€. Thurs–Tues 1–4pm and 7:30–11pm (until 12:30am Aug–Sept).

El Rodeito ★★ CASTILIAN   Launched in 1988 as a truck-stop restaurant on the road between Málaga and Algeciras (where goods are trans-shipped from Africa), this traditional Castilian grill has made great use of its wood-fired oven. The oven is swept out several times a day, but there is always a fire burning inside—in part because El Rodeito never closes. You can get sit-down meals at normal times, or takeout in the middle of the night. The main focus is on meat— a quarter suckling pig or a chateaubriand, each for two people, or beef tenderloin. All the classic Spanish fish are available roasted in the oven as well, from cod to hake and turbot, but the kitchen really excels with Atlantic lobster (with the big claws) and rock lobster (with the little ones). Portions are immense, so a good strategy is to order entirely from the starters menu or ask for half portions.

Carretera Cádiz, km 173. ℂ **95-281-08-61.** http://elrodeito.com. Main dishes 20€–29€. Daily 1–4pm and 7pm–midnight, takeout 24 hours.

MARBELLA ★★

Although it's nearly as packed with tourists as Torremolinos, Marbella is the nicest resort town along the Costa del Sol. The big difference is money: Some of the region's best upscale resorts coexist here with budget hotels. Marbella also retains traces of its origins as a pleasant seaside town at the foot of the Sierra Blanca. That past persists in the palatial town hall, medieval ruins, and ancient Moorish walls. Marbella's most charming area is the **Old Quarter** of narrow cobblestone streets centered on Plaza de los Naranjos. From the wide promenade along the beach, you simply climb a set of marble stairs past several Salvador Dalí bronze statues and cross the Alameda, a leafy park with tiled benches. Suddenly you're in a tangle of medieval streets and whitewashed houses hung with pots of geraniums. The biggest attractions in Marbella, however, are **El Fuerte** and **La Fontanilla,** the two main beaches. There are other, more secluded beaches, but you need your own transportation to get there. A long-ago visitor to the coast, Queen Isabel II, is said to have exclaimed, *"¡Qué mar tan bello!"* ("What a beautiful sea!"), and the name stuck.

Essentials

GETTING THERE   The main **bus** link is between Málaga and Marbella, with the **Portillo** (ℂ **90-214-31-44;** www.ctsa-portillo.com) running 14 buses a day. The trip takes 1½ to 1¾ hours and costs 6.35€ to 9.55€ one-way. Madrid and Barcelona each have three daily buses to Marbella. The bus station is located on the outskirts of Marbella on Avenida Trapiche, a 5-minute ride from the center of town. If you're driving, Marbella is on the N-340/E-15.

VISITOR INFORMATION   The **tourist office,** Glorieta de la Fontanilla s/n (ℂ **95-277-14-42;** www.marbellaexclusive.com), is open Monday to Friday 9:30am to 9pm, Saturday 10am to 2pm. Another tourist office with the same hours is on the Plaza de los Naranjos (ℂ **95-277-46-93**).

The beachside promenade in Marbella.

Where to Stay in Marbella
EXPENSIVE
Don Carlos Leisure Resort & Spa ★★   This long-time Marbella favorite reinvented itself (yet again) in 2014 with the addition of the "Oasis by Don Carlos" section of the resort. This wing is devoted to fitness and wellness, with an emphasis on slimming and toning already bronzed and pampered bodies. The rest of the resort remains as it has been for years: an oasis of gardens spilling downhill from the stand of pines behind the main hotel to the edge of one of the best beaches on this section of coast. Small business conferences sometimes take over the hotel during the off-season, but Don Carlos is oriented to a leisure clientele.

Carretera de Cádiz Km 192. © **95-276-88-00.** www.hoteldoncarlos.com. 256 units. 175€–571€ double; 517€–2,002€ villa. Free parking. **Amenities:** 3 restaurants; 2 bars; babysitting; exercise room; 2 outdoor freshwater pools; indoor freshwater pool; sauna; spa; 12 outdoor tennis courts (lit); free Wi-Fi.

Gran Meliã Don Pepe ★★   Not far from the center of the Old Town, this grand resort on the beach combines spacious and beautiful rooms (most with terrace or balcony) with tropical gardens on the grounds. It is a chain hotel, but the Meliã group is one of Spain's best, and this particular property has hosted innumerable movie stars and royalty over the years. Live music and other shows are put on every night during the summer—when the resort insists on a 5-night minimum stay.

Calle José Meliá, s/n. © **95-277-03-00.** www.gran-melia-don-pepe.com. 194 rooms. 235€–640€ double; from 578€ suite. Parking 20€. **Amenities:** 4 restaurants; 2 bars; bikes; health club; Jacuzzi; 3 pools (1 heated indoor); sauna; 2 outdoor tennis courts (lit); free Wi-Fi.

Marbella Club ★★★   When the Marbella Club opened in 1954, there was almost nothing else around it. Exclusive and expensive from the outset, it swiftly established Marbella as an alternative to the French and Italian Rivieras for aristocrats, tycoons, and yachtsmen who prefer their weather sunny and their beaches sandy. Six decades later, all those lovely gardens and trees have matured, and the clusters of bungalows and garden pavilions have evolved a homey yet clubby ambience. Rooms vary a lot, but they are without exception spacious and decorated as if a magazine were coming in the next day to shoot a photo spread.

All of them have either private balconies or terraces. Service is discreet and superb.

Bulevar Príncipe Alfonso von Hohenlohe, s/n. 🕿 **800-448-8355** in the U.S., or 95-282-22-11. www.marbellaclub.com. 121 units. 300€–920€ double; from 420€ suite. Free parking. **Amenities:** 2 restaurants; bar; bikes; concierge; golf course; 3 pools (1 heated indoor); spa; free Wi-Fi.

Puente Romano ★★★   Neighbor to the Marbella Club and, for some guests' money, every bit its equal, Puente Romano began as a cluster of vacation apartments but came into its own as a luxurious and beautifully landscaped colony of high-end lodging in the 1970s. The intervening four decades have only seen it mellow further to become an Andalucían seaside village for the well-to-do. Guest rooms are spacious and have private or semi-private balconies or terraces. The grounds are a veritable maze of paths leading past fountains and little waterfalls, beneath arbors enshrouded in vines or flowers, and patches of blooming gardens. Complimentary greens fee and shuttle service to the 18-hole golf course is included with the room.

Bulevar Príncipe Alfonso von Hohenlohe, s/n (Carretera de Cádiz Km 177). 🕿 **95-282-09-00.** www.puenteromano.com. 285 units. 210€–488€ double; 290€–1700€ suite. Limited free parking. **Amenities:** 3 restaurants; 2 bars; babysitting; children's center; concierge; health club; 3 outdoor freshwater pools; sauna; 10 outdoor tennis courts (lit); watersports equipment/rentals; Wi-Fi (19€ per 24 hr.).

MODERATE

The Town House ★★   Looking like a design magazine's idea of a villa on the Mediterranean, this boutique hotel was created from an old house in the center of Marbella's venerable Casco Antiguo, or old quarter. The walls were re-stuccoed and whitewashed and the tile floors re-laid, and it now gleams like a brand new hotel. The architecture helps make the experience, and you'll find yourself spending as much time as possible on the roof terrace at the beginning and end of the day (it's too hot at midday). Views from the terrace stretch over the jumble of Old Town rooftops down to the boardwalk on the beach, a 10-minute walk away.

Plaza Tetuán, Calle Alderete, 7. 🕿/ **95-290-17-91.** www.townhouse.nu. 9 rooms. 125€–160€ double. **Amenities:** Bar; room service; free Wi-Fi.

INEXPENSIVE

Hostal Enriqueta ★★   The most charming of the modest hotels in the old quarter of Marbella, the Enriqueta is a classic example of Andalucían architecture, with its rooms arranged around a flower-filled central courtyard. Rooms 208 and 202 have balconies overlooking that courtyard. All the rooms have air-conditioning, but guests rarely turn it on because the thick-walled old building tends to stay quite cool. Rooms are very plain and very small, but the family that runs the *hostal* is warm and friendly. Stairs are steep and narrow, and there is no elevator. If climbing is a problem, request one of the four rooms on the ground level.

Calle de los Balleros, 18. 🕿 **95-282-75-52.** www.hostalenriqueta.com. 20 rooms. 25€–90€ double. **Amenities:** Free Wi-Fi.

Where to Eat in Marbella

EXPENSIVE

Dani García Restaurante ★★★ CONTEMPORARY SPANISH   New in 2014, this eponymous restaurant at the Puente Romano resort showcases the talents of Marbella's most innovative and star-bedecked chef. García closed the much-beloved Calima at the Don Pepe to launch this elegant new venture with just 50 seats in the main dining room and 20 more in a private dining room. The new venue features some of García's iconic dishes, like the "popcorn" olives (exploded with liquid nitrogen) with lobster salad and suckling pig with pumpkin and orange.

In Puente Romano (p. 258). Bulevar Príncipe Alfonso von Hohenlohe, s/n (Carretera de Cádiz Km 177). ✆ **95-282-09-00.** www.restaurantedanigarcia.es. Reservations required. Fixed-price menu 180€. Tues–Sat 1:30–3:30pm and 8:30–10:30pm.

Marbella Club Grill ★★ INTERNATIONAL   The Marbella Club has reorganized its dining into several discrete venues, all under the talented direction of executive chef Juan Gálvez. Most guests take lunch at the bountiful buffet at the Beach Club. Diners seeking out the avant-garde stylings of contemporary Spanish cuisine gravitate to the MC Café. The old standby, however, remains the Marbella Club Grill, with seating both indoors and outside on the terrace. You dine amid blooming flowers, flickering candles, and strains of live music—perhaps a Spanish classical guitarist, a small chamber orchestra playing 19th-century classics, or a South American vocalist. The contemporary pan-European menu changes with the season. You might begin with a lobster cocktail with diced mango and honey truffle dressing, or perhaps a spicy coconut soup with lemongrass. Specialties include beef entrecôte with a mushroom pepper sauce, and seared tuna with shiitake fried rolls and ginger dressing.

In the Marbella Club (p. 257). Bulevar Príncipe Alfonso von Hohenlohe s/n. ✆ **95-282-22-11.** www.marbellaclub.com. Reservations recommended. Main courses 27€–45€. Summer daily 9pm–12:30am; winter daily 8–11:30pm.

MODERATE

Casa de la Era ★ ANDALUCÍAN   This erstwhile country house retains its rustic charm inside, although the "country" around it has evolved into an industrial park. The restaurant emphasizes coastal Andalucían cuisine with some Moroccan dishes. House specialties include *fideos* (noodles cooked like rice in a paella) with monkfish and clams, fried eggplant drizzled with honey, and braised oxtail in the Córdoban style. One unusual choice is a succession of grilled seasonal vegetables brought to the table on skewers until you say "enough!" The Moroccan couscous is also very good, and you can order a plate of Moroccan honey pastries for dessert.

Carretera de Ojén Km 0.5. ✆ **95-277-06-25.** www.casadelaera.com. Reservations recommended. Main courses 13€–25€. Sept–June Mon–Sat 1–4pm and 8–11pm; July–Aug daily 8–11pm.

Shopping

You will find many international brands in this upscale town, but the **Nueva Andalucía Flea Market,** Avenida Manolete, next to the bullring in Puerto Banús, is of much more local interest. It's one of the largest and most colorful flea markets on the Costa del Sol. More than 120 vendors offer their merchandise on Saturdays from 9am to 2pm. If you'd like to purchase some of Andalucía's regional ceramics, a good bet is **Cerámica San Nicolás,** Plaza de la Iglesia, 1 (✆ **95-277-05-46**). For a serious piece of art, **Galleria d'Arte Van Gestel,** Plaza de los Naranjos, 11 (✆ **95-277-48-19**), in the Old Town is one of the most established galleries in Marbella. It's worth stopping in just to see how harmoniously contemporary art fills the spaces of a historic home.

A MARBELLA *tasca* CRAWL

Marbella boasts more small tapas bars than virtually any other resort town in southern Spain. Even if you set out with a specific place in mind, you'll likely be distracted en route by a newer, older, bigger, smaller, brighter, or just more interesting joint you want to try—which is half the fun.

Prices and hours are remarkably consistent: The coffeehouse that opens at 7am will switch to wine and tapas when the first patron asks for it (sometimes shortly after breakfast), and then continue through the day dispensing wine, sherry, and, more recently, bottles of beer. On average, tapas cost 3€ to 10€, but some foreign visitors configure them into *platos combinados.*

Tapas served along the Costa del Sol are principally Andalucían in origin, with an emphasis on seafood. The most famous plate, *fritura malagueña,* consists of fried fish based on the catch of the day. Sometimes *ajo blanco,* a garlicky local version of gazpacho made with almonds, is served, especially in summer.

Fried squid or octopus is another favorite, as are little Spanish-style herb-flavored meatballs. Other well-known tapas include tuna, grilled shrimp, *piquillos rellenos* (red peppers stuffed with fish), *bacalao* (salt cod), and mushrooms sautéed in olive oil and garlic.

Tapas bars line many of the narrow streets of Marbella's historic core, with rich pickings around Calle del Perral and, to a somewhat lesser extent, Calle Miguel Cana. In August especially, when you want to escape wall-to-wall people and the heat and noise of the Old Town, head for one of the shoreline restaurants and tapas bars called *chiringuitos.* All serve local specialties, and you can order a full meal, a snack, tapas, or a drink. **Restaurante Los Sardinales,** Playa de los Alicates (*©* **95-283-70-12;** www. lossardinales.com), serves some of the best sangria in the area. Another good bet is **Chiringuito La Pesquera,** Playa Marbellamar (*©* **95-277-03-38;** www. lapesquera.com), where you can order a plate of fresh grilled sardines.

Marbella After Dark

You will need to pack more than a bathing suit and flip-flops if you want to join the nightlife scene. There's more international wealth hanging out in the watering holes of Marbella, and a wider choice of glam (or pseudo-glam) discos than virtually anywhere else in Spain. Foremost among them is **Discoteca Olivia Valere** on Carretera Istan, N-340 Km 0.8 (✆ **95-288-88-61;** www.oliviavalere. com), which can hold up to 1,000 people. It's open every night from midnight to 7am and charges a cover of 30€. Fashionable club wear is essential.

If you are in the heart of historic Marbella, you can enjoy a more low-key night in the *bodegas* and taverns. **La Venencia Los Olivos,** Plaza de los Olivos, s/n (✆ **95-285-92-98**), is conveniently located adjacent to one of the town's widest thoroughfares. Its wide choice of sherries, wines, and tapas draws lots of chattering patrons. **Vinacoteca La Cartuja,** Plaza Joaquín Gómez Agüera, 2 (✆ **95-277-52-03;** www.vinoslacartuja.com), is dedicated to carrying as many Spanish wines as possible.

Although hardly authentic, Marbella's best flamenco is offered at **Tablao Flamenco Ana María,** Av. Severo Ochoa 24 (✆ **95-277-56-46**). It's a good start for foreign visitors who speak limited Spanish. The long, often-crowded bar area sells tapas, wine, sherry, and a selection of more international libations. This is late-night entertainment—the doors don't open until 11:30pm, and the crowd really gets going between midnight and 3am. Cover (which includes one drink) is 25€.

Seven kilometers (4⅓ miles) west of Marbella, near Puerto Banús, **Casino Marbella,** Hotel H10 Andalucía Plaza, Urbanización Nueva Andalucía (✆ **95-281-40-00;** www.casinomarbella.com), is a favorite with visitors from northern Europe. Jackets are not required for men, but T-shirts are frowned upon. Casino hours are daily from noon to 4am for slot parlor, daily 8pm to 4am for the main floor. A passport is required for admission (5€). Shorts and athletic shoes are not allowed.

FUENGIROLA & LOS BOLICHES ★

The former fishing towns of Fuengirola and Los Boliches lie halfway between the more famous resorts of Marbella and Torremolinos. Less-developed Los Boliches is just 0.8km (½ mile) from Fuengirola. These towns don't have the facilities or drama of Torremolinos and Marbella, but except for two major luxury hotels, Fuengirola and Los Boliches are cheaper and attract large numbers of budget-conscious northern European tourists. The best beaches—**Santa Amalja, Carvajal,** and **Las Gaviotas**—are broad, clean, and sandy. Everybody goes to the big **flea market** at Fuengirola on Tuesday. Many British retirees who live in the holiday apartments nearby attend this sprawling market, later stopping in at one of the Irish or British pubs for a pint, just like they used to do back home.

Essentials

GETTING THERE Fuengirola is on the C1 commuter rail (*cercanía*) route from Málaga, with trains every half-hour all day. The station is at Avda. Jesús Santos Rein, s/n, 3 blocks from the leisure port and the beach, or a 15-minute stroll down the street from the zoo. The trip takes 45 minutes and costs 3€. If you're driving from Marbella, take the N-340/E-15 east.

The **tourist office,** Paseo Jesús Santos Rein, 6 (✆ **95-246-76-25;** www.fuengirola.org), is open Monday to Friday 9:30am to 2pm and 5 to 7pm, and Saturday 9:30am to 1:30pm.

Where to Stay in Fuengirola & Los Boliches

Hotel Villa de Laredo ★ We always think of the skyline in Fuengirola as "the city by the sea," since so many high-rise hotels shoot straight up into the sky at the edge of the sand. This rather modest hotel with a rooftop swimming pool has a great view of the sandy scene below. It is located smack-dab in the middle of everything, which means that you can easily leave the hotel to dine and shop elsewhere. Some rooms have small terraces opening onto the beachside promenade, but the quarters, even in these, are rather tight. (A mirrored closet door makes the room look a little bigger.) All in all, if you're planning to soak up sun and drink in ambience, a room here offers a pleasant spot to sleep.

Paseo Marítimo Rey de España, 42. ✆ **95-247-76-89.** www.hotelvilladelaredo.es. 74 units. 44€–98€ double. **Amenities:** Restaurant; bar; outdoor pool; free Wi-Fi.

Las Pirámides ★ This pair of 10-story towers joined by a large marble lobby represents the best of the resort's large hotels. The rooms are surprisingly spacious, with wood-paneled walls and carpeted floors. The bathrooms feature shower tubs and marble floors and walls. Best of all, each room has a sea-view balcony with a sliding door and a few chairs for sitting outside and listening to the surf at night. The hotel is a favorite with bus tours and English and Scandinavian holiday packagers, so book ahead.

Calle Miguel Márquez 43. ✆ **95-247-06-00.** www.hotellaspiramides.com. 240 rooms. 60€–85€ double; 80€–151€ triple. Parking 18€. **Amenities:** 2 restaurants; 5 bars; exercise room; Jacuzzi; 2 freshwater pools (1 heated indoor); sauna; watersports equipment/rentals; free Wi-Fi.

Where to Eat Around Fuengirola & Los Boliches

Charolais Bodega Restaurante ★★ SPANISH The Charolais establishment began as a wine bar, and the cellar contains more than 400 choices. You can enjoy a glass of wine with a wide variety of creative tapas in a contemporary bar, or in the more sedate restaurant. The owner is a big fan of Spanish red wines, so the menu tends to emphasize dishes best consumed with *tintos.* House specialties are baby lamb chops and duck breast with mushrooms and port wine sauce. Note that there are separate entrances for the bar and the restaurant.

Calle Larga, 14. ✆ **95-247-54-41.** www.bodegacharolais.com. Reservations recommended on Fri–Sat. Tapas 4€–7€. Main courses 14€–22€. Menus 30€–40€. Mon–Sat 1–4pm and 7–11:30pm. Closed Dec–Feb.

Monopol ★ INTERNATIONAL It takes a little looking to find this rather rustically decorated Fuengirola standby on the small side street several blocks from the waterfront, but it's worth seeking out for the contemporary continental cooking of chef/owner Paul Wartmann. The three-course daily menu is a bargain. Because the staff speak English and German, the restaurant gets a number of repeat visitors who hail from those countries.

Calle Palangreros, 7. ✆ **95-247-44-48.** Reservations recommended. Main courses 10€–14€. Daily menu 20€. Mon–Sat 8–11:30pm.

family-friendly **COSTA DEL SOL**

The Costa del Sol may have one of the hottest nightlife scenes in Spain, but it is also a great destination for families. When you and the kids need a break from the beach, there are plenty of attractions to keep everyone happy. Not surprisingly, many of them concentrate on marine life. **Sea Life Benalmádena** (*(C)* **95-256-01-50;** www.visitsealife.com) at Malapesquera Beach features a tunnel-like aquarium, a rock pool, and habitats for sharks, giant turtles, and rays. It is open daily from 10am to 6pm. Discounted admission, purchased online, is 10€. Treat the kids to a round of minigolf for only 2.50€ more. Also in Benalmádena, **Selwo Marina Delfinarium** (*(C)* **90-219-04-82;** www.selwomarina.es), Parque de la Paloma, s/n, features dolphin and sea lion shows and an exotic bird exhibition. Its Penguinarium has one of the most notable collections of penguins in Europe. The Delfinarium is open mid-February through October daily from at 10am to at least 6pm with later hours in summer. It is open weekends only in November. Adults 19€, seniors and children 15€; significant discounts

for online advance purchases.

In 2010, President Obama and his family visited **Selwo Aventura** (*(C)* **95-257-77-73;** www.selwo.es), highway A7, km 162.5 in Estepona. The wildlife park is home to about 2,000 creatures from five continents, including Asian elephants, cheetahs, lions, giraffes, white rhinoceroses, and hippopotamuses. Daily feeding times for many of the animals are posted. A trampoline area, zipwire, and hanging bridges are great for active kids. The wildlife park is open July and August daily 10am to 8pm with shorter hours the rest of the season. Adults 25€, seniors and children 17€; significant discounts for online advance purchases.

For good old-fashioned fun, **Tivoli World** (*(C)* **95-257-70-16;** www.tivoli.es), Arroyo de la Miel, Benalmadena, has about 40 different amusement rides and a full schedule of entertainment. Open July and August daily 6pm to 2am. More limited days and hours March through June and September and October. Park entrance adults 7.95€, seniors 4.95€; pass for unlimited rides 14€.

Exploring Fuengirola & Los Boliches

Bioparc Fuengirola ★★ ZOO   Now one of Europe's model zoo facilities, this sensitive presentation of animals in three different ecosystems is easily the top attraction on the Costa del Sol. There are no cages, but design keeps animals and humans apart with moats and landscape features. The zoo replicates the tropical rainforests of Madagascar, Equatorial Africa, and Southeast Asia with 1,300 animals representing 140 species. There is a children's play area as well as a couple of restaurants and cafes.

Calle Camilo José Cela, 8–10. *(C)* **95-266-63-01.** www.bioparcfuengirola.es. 18€ adults; 13€ ages 3–9 and seniors. Winter daily 10am–6pm, summer daily 10am–8pm.

Castillo Sohail ★ CASTLE   Fuengirola may have been built up as a discount beach resort town, but it retains this remnant of a Moorish past. The Almohad dynasty built this castle in the 12th century on the hill overlooking the beach where both Romans and Carthaginians settled. To find it, just walk east along Paseo Marítimo toward the elegant cable-stay bridge over the Río Fuengirola. The castle was modified many times after it fell into Christian hands (the armies of Isabel and Fernando) in 1485. Restored by Fuengirola trade school students, it is surrounded by beautiful green lawns.

Paseo Marítimo, s/n. © **95-246-74-57.** 3€ adults, 2€ seniors and children. Spring and fall daily 10am–6:30pm, summer daily 9:30am–9pm, winter daily 10:30am–6pm.

MIJAS ★

Just 8km (5 miles) north of coastal road N-340/E-15, this village is known as "White Mijas" because of its marble-white Andalucían-style houses. Mijas is at the foot of a mountain range near the turnoff to Fuengirola, and from its lofty height—450m (1,476 ft.) above sea level—you get a panoramic view of the Mediterranean.

Celts, Phoenicians, and Moors preceded today's tourist throngs to Mijas. The town itself, rather than a specific monument, is the attraction. The easiest way to get around its cobblestone streets is to walk, but the most colorful is to rent a burro taxi. If you consider Mijas overrun with souvenir shops, head for the park at the top of Cuesta de la Villa, where you'll see the ruins of a **Moorish fortress** dating from A.D. 833. Every Saturday from May into October, busloads of bullfight fans descend on Mijas for the weekly *corridas*.

There's frequent bus service to Mijas from the terminal at Fuengirola, 30 minutes away. To drive from Fuengirola, take the Mijas road north.

Where to Stay & Eat in Mijas

El Padrastro ★ INTERNATIONAL   Mijas has such a small population that isn't involved in tourism that there is no "authentic" village restaurant here. So go with the flow and eat at El Padrastro, reached either by an elevator or by hiking up 77 steps. The food is perhaps fancier than you might expect in a village

A "burro taxi" in Mijas.

that wears rusticity on its sleeve. In addition to roasted sea bass or leg of lamb with mushrooms, you can order lighter dishes like red tuna with a garlic-balsamic vinegar sauce.

Av. del Compás 20–22. © **95-248-50-00.** http://elpadrastro.com. Reservations recommended. Main courses 14€–26€. Daily 12:30–4pm and 7–11:30pm.

Hotel TRH Mijas Beach & Cultural ★   This was one of the pioneer hotels of the Mijas hillside, built in the 1970s before the Mijas-Costa developments got underway. It's not on the beach, but it does have great ocean views from most public areas as well as the guest rooms. You might consider this hotel for the pleasant grounds where you can sit around at tables sipping drinks in the brilliant sun (or beneath an umbrella), leaving it to others to sweat it out on the beach. If you're driving, it can actually be a good spot for touring the region.

Urbanización Tamisa, 2. ✆ **95-248-58-00.** www.trhhoteles.com. 204 units. 50€–115€ double. Parking 12€. **Amenities:** Restaurant; bar; bikes; exercise room; Jacuzzi; outdoor freshwater pool; sauna; outdoor tennis court; free Wi-Fi.

La Cala Resort ★★ Cabell B. Robinson called the terrain here the most challenging of his career when he designed the first two 18-hole courses at this contemporary golf resort (there's now a third). The property is 7km (4⅓ miles) from the beach, so your focus here is likely greens and fairways, and the only sand you'll find is in the bunkers. Rooms are reasonably spacious and are furnished in a low-key contemporary style.

La Cala de Mijas. ✆ **95-266-90-16.** www.lacala.com. 107 units. 117€–144€ double. **Amenities:** 2 restaurants; bar; exercise room; 3 18-hole golf courses; 2 freshwater heated pools (1 indoor); room service; spa; 2 outdoor tennis courts (lit); free Wi-Fi.

TORREMOLINOS ★

This Mediterranean beach resort is the most famous in Spain. It's known as a melting pot for international visitors, mostly Europeans and Americans. Many relax here after a whirlwind tour of Europe—the living is easy, the people are fun, and there are no historical monuments to visit. A sleepy fishing village until the 1950s, Torremolinos has been engulfed in cement-walled resort hotels. Overconstruction makes "Torrie" one of Europe's vacation bargains.

Essentials

GETTING THERE The nearby Málaga airport (p. 269) serves Torremolinos, and frequent **trains** also run from the terminal at Málaga. For train information, call ✆ **90-232-03-20,** or log on to www.renfe.com. **Buses** also run frequently between Málaga and Torremolinos; call ✆ **90-214-31-44** for schedules. If

Beachfront umbrellas in Torremolinos.

you're driving, take the N-340/E-15 west from Málaga or the N-340/E-15 east from Marbella.

VISITOR INFORMATION   The **tourist information office** is at Plaza Comunidades Autónomas (☏ **95-237-19-09**). It's open daily 8am to 3pm (in winter Mon–Fri 9:30am–2:30pm).

Where to Stay in Torremolinos

MODERATE

Hotel Tropicana & Beach Club ★★   Located at the east end of La Carihuela, the Tropicana has an edge on most Torrie hotels because it is a little removed from the human crush of lodgings closer to the city center. It even has its own beach club—i.e., the legal right to claim a piece of the long strand. The Costa del Sol is barely subtropical, yet a "tropical" theme dominates at this hotel, including a preponderance of large palms and hot colors. The somewhat forced conviviality doesn't quite disguise the fact that the Tropicana is yet another salmon-colored concrete hotel bristling with private balconies overlooking the beach. The location puts it close to the many restaurants of La Carihuela.

Calle Trópico, 6. ☏ **95-238-66-00.** www.hoteltropicana.es. 84 units. 55€–220€ double. Free parking. **Amenities:** Restaurant; bar; outdoor freshwater pool; free Wi-Fi.

Meliã Costa del Sol ★   There is no denying the behemoth size of this grand hotel, located right on Playa de Bajondillo. Meliã has remade this veteran of the first generation of Costa del Sol resorts to make the public areas look majestic and elegant, and has fixed up the guest rooms to bring them in line with contemporary expectations. What distinguishes this hotel is the size of the rooms. The smallest are 32 square meters (344 sq. ft.) and suites are nearly twice that size.

Paseo Marítimo, 11. ☏ **95-238-66-77.** www.meliacostadelsol.solmelia.com. 538 units. 69€–225€ double; 133€–299€ junior suite; 298€–530€ suite. Free parking. **Amenities:** 2 restaurants; 2 bars; bikes; concierge; health club and spa; outdoor freshwater pool; free Wi-Fi.

Roc Lago Rojo ★★   The 1970s architecture, drawn from the Habitat apartments built for the 1964 Olympics in Montreal, looks like it was sprung from Woody Allen's *Sleeper,* but complete renovations have kept the studio-style rooms in touch with contemporary decor. Each has a terrace with sea view. Roc Lago Rojo is in the middle of La Carihuela and has a nice seafood restaurant on the premises. In a resort where decorum is often forgotten, Lago Rojo asks that gentlemen wear long pants to dinner (bravo).

Calle Miami, 5. ☏ **95-238-76-66.** www.roc-hotels.com. 144 units. 105€–155€ double. Parking 17€. **Amenities:** Restaurant; bar; babysitting; outdoor freshwater pool; free Wi-Fi.

INEXPENSIVE

Hotel Los Jazmínes ★   We happen to think that Playamar, the stretch of beach in front of Los Jazmines, is one of the best strands in Torremolinos. The location east of the town center means fewer day-trippers bother to walk this far, and the hotel faces a plaza at the foot of the shady Avenida del Lido. Smallish rooms are furnished with queen or double beds and overlook either the hotel garden or the beach. Apartments have two bedrooms, a kitchen, living room, and bath with outdoor terraces.

Av. de Lido, 6. ☏ **95-238-50-33.** www.hotellosjazmines.com. 100 units. 40€–92€ double; 80€–125€ apartment. **Amenities:** Restaurant; bar; outdoor freshwater pool; free Wi-Fi.

Hotel Residencia Miami ★   This white stucco palace was built in 1950 as the summer home of Granada Gypsy queen and flamenco dancer Lola Medina. It became a hotel in 1957, and has matured as a grand complex with an air of mystery. Gardens surround the property and the walls drip with bougainvillea and fuchsia. The rooms are not large, but they feel more compact than small. There's a massive fireplace in the rustic living room.

Calle Aladino. 14. ✆ **95-238-52-55.** www.residencia-miami.com. 26 units. 40€–64€ double. **Amenities:** Bar; outdoor freshwater pool; free Wi-Fi.

Where to Eat

A good spot to try in **Torremolinos** is the food court at La Nogalera, the major gathering place between the coast road and the beach. Head down Calle del Cauce to this compound of modern whitewashed Andalucían buildings. Open to pedestrian traffic only, it's a maze of passageways, courtyards, and patios for eating and drinking. You can find everything from sandwiches and pizza to Belgian waffles and scrambled eggs.

Casa Juan ★ SEAFOOD   We seriously doubt if La Carihuela's shrunken fishing fleet could keep this semiformal, 170-seat restaurant in seafood for more than an hour. It is part of a small empire of seafood restaurants in the immediate neighborhood, but we're suckers for the splendid display of crustaceans and shellfish at the entrance. If you don't order the mixed-shellfish platter (*mariscada de mariscos*), try the cod with saffron sauce or the *zarzuela* (seafood stew) of shellfish.

Calle San Gines, 18–20. ✆ **95-237-35-12.** www.losmellizos.net/casajuan. Reservations recommended. Main courses 12€–45€. Daily 12:30–4:30pm and 7:30–11:30pm. Closed Dec.

El Figón de Montemar ★ ASTURIAN/ANDALUCÍAN   The menu here is a rather unusual combination, matching the bacon and beans (and hard cider) of Asturias with the fried foam of the Andalucían coast. Yet somehow the combination of chilly Cantabrian coast with the sunny Mediterranean works, and the cozy decor with walls covered in wine racks is welcoming. This is one spot where small-time fishermen stream in all day with the whiting, red mullet, and other small fish that they bring up in nets. If one brings a nice fat octopus, then there's suddenly a special on the menu.

Av. Espada 101. ✆ **95-237-26-88.** www.elfigondemontemar.com. Reservations recommended. Main courses 14€–24€. Open daily 1-4pm and 8pm-midnight. Closed Jan 10–Feb 10.

IN BENALMÁDENA-COSTA

Where Torremolinos ends and Benalmádena-Costa to the west begins is hard to say. The two resorts seem to merge (although driving east, there *is* an ancient sign welcoming visitors to Torrie). Benalmádena offers some of the better restaurants in the area.

Ventorrillo de la Perra ★ ANDALUCÍAN/SPANISH   When this 1785 inn turned smugglers' warehouse was rescued from ruin in 1972 to become a restaurant, the owners took great care to restore the original architecture and decorate in an 18th-century style. Some of the crockery and silver dates from the reign of Isabel II, about 50 years later. The menu is equally old-fashioned and, for the most part, Castilian. It features oven-roasted wild game, large portions of meat, and whole fish. But one of the house specialties is also *gazpachuelo malagueño,* a traditional coastal fish stew thickened with new potatoes and spiked with a little sherry and vinegar. It's worth the 15-minute walk from the beach to see one of the rare remnants of coastal life before the concrete high-rises went up.

Av. Constitución 85 Km 13, Arroyo de la Miel. © **95-244-19-66.** Reservations recommended. Main courses 16€–25€. Tues–Sun 1–4pm and 8pm–midnight.

Torremolinos After Dark

Torremolinos has more nightlife than any other spot along the Costa del Sol. The earliest action is always at the bars, which stay lively most of the night, serving drinks and tapas until at least 3am. Note that some bars are open during the day as well.

La Bodega, San Miguel 40 (© **95-238-73-37**), relies on its colorful clientele and the quality of its tapas to draw customers, who seem to rank this place above the dozens of other *tascas* in this popular tourist zone. Many guests come here for lunch or dinner, making a satisfying meal from the plentiful bar food. You'll be lucky if you find space at one of the small tables, but once you begin to order—platters of fried squid, pungent tuna, grilled shrimp, tiny brochettes of sole—you might not be able to stop. Most tapas cost 2€. A beer costs 1.50€, a hard drink at least 3.50€ to 4€. La Bodega is open daily from noon to 5pm and 7:30pm to midnight.

Ready to dance off all those tapas? **Le Room,** Palma de Mallorca, 36 (© **95-238-42-89**), a well-designed nightclub in the town center, is one of the most convivial in Torremolinos. Strobes, spotlights, and a state-of-the-art sound system set the scene. There's even a swimming pool. Expect to pay 3.50€ or more for a drink; cover is 15€, including one drink after 11pm. The club is open from 11pm to 6am in summer months only.

For unabashed tourist flamenco, try **Taberna Flamenca Pepe López,** Plaza de la Gamba Alegre (© **95-238-12-84;** www.tabernaflamencapepelopez. com), in the center of Torremolinos. Many of the artists come from the bars of Sevilla and Granada, and they perform Monday through Saturday at 10pm April to October. The frequency of shows is substantially reduced during the cooler months, and performances are confined mainly to the weekends; call to confirm first. A 27€ cover includes your first drink and the show.

Gay men and women from throughout northern Europe are almost always in residence in Torremolinos. Plaza de la Nogalera and Plaza de los Tientos are centers of gay nightlife.

One of the Costa del Sol's major casinos, **Casino Torrequebrada,** Avenida del Sol, Benalmádena-Costa (© **95-257-73-00;** www.casinotorrequebrada. com), is on the lobby level of the Hotel Torrequebrada. It has tables devoted to blackjack, baccarat, poker, and two kinds of roulette. The gaming hall is open daily from 8pm to 5am. The restaurant is open nightly from 9pm to 2am. There is live music on weekends. Casino admission is 3€. Bring your passport to be admitted.

MÁLAGA ★★

Málaga seems to prove the adage that flamenco styles reflect their birthplace. Andalucía's second-largest city is as deeply nuanced and improvisational as the *malagueña.* Yet travelers often give it short shrift as they rush from the airport or train station to the Costa del Sol resorts, not realizing that Málaga has superb beaches of its own, historic sites, and a strong identity with native son Pablo Picasso. To have it all, base yourself in Málaga, use the train to spend a few hours a day on a Costa del Sol beach, and return to the vibes of a real Spanish city by nightfall. The city of weekday commerce changes into a grand tapas-hopping scene in the evenings and a beach community on the weekends. The redeveloped port district has a striking yacht marina, a romantic walkway by the water, and a new district of shopping, restaurants, and nightlife stretching from the Parque de Málaga to the harbor lighthouse.

Essentials

GETTING THERE Travelers from North America usually transfer for Málaga in London, Paris, Amsterdam, or Madrid. From within Europe, Air Europa, Vueling, and Iberia offer connections from several cities. There's an 8-minute train connection from Terminal 3 to the main rail station on the western edge of the city via a *cercanía* (2.10€); change trains at Estación María Zambrano for a "Centro Ciudad-Alameda" train to get to the town center.

Twelve AVE **trains** per day arrive in Málaga from Madrid (trip time: 2½ hr.). Ten trains a day connect Sevilla and Málaga, usually via Córdoba (trip time: 2–2½ hr.). For ticket prices and rail information in Málaga, contact RENFE (© **90-232-03-20;** www.renfe.com).

Buses from all over Spain arrive at the terminal on the Paseo de los Tilos, behind the RENFE offices. Buses include 8 per day from Madrid (trip time: 7 hr.), 5 per day from Córdoba (trip time: 3 hr.), and 10 per day from Sevilla (trip time: 3 hr.). Call © **90-242-22-42** for bus information.

From coastal resorts, you can drive to Málaga along the N-340/E-15.

VISITOR INFORMATION The tourist office, at Plaza de la Marina, 11 (© **95-192-62-20;** www.malagaturismo.com), is open daily March through September from 9am to 8pm and October to February 9am to 6pm. The website features several themed audiotours in English, and a free downloadable app with extensive detail on 85 sites around the city. For a walking tour with a human guide, 90-minute tours (5€) depart from the office Monday through Saturday at 11:30am.

SPECIAL EVENTS During the second week in August, the city celebrates its Reconquest by Fernando and Isabel in 1487 with parades and bullfights.

Where to Stay in Málaga

EXPENSIVE

AC Málaga Palacio ★★ One of the largest downtown hotels geared to both business and leisure travelers, the Palacio sits across the street from the Parque de Málaga a short distance from the cathedral and at the foot of the pedestrian shopping artery Calle Larios. You'll pay about 20% more for a balcony room with a view of the port and the plaza below. But a basic room here is very pleasant, with a good desk. When booking, negotiate free Wi-Fi, which is often available to members of Marriott Rewards.

Cortina del Muelle, 1. © **95-221-51-85.** www.ac-hotels.com. 214 units. 84€–212€ double; 134€–323€ suite. Parking 25€ nearby. Bus: 4, 18, 19, or 24. **Amenities:** Restaurant; bar; concierge; exercise room; outdoor pool; Wi-Fi (fee).

MODERATE

Hotel MS Maestranza ★ There's a lot to like at the Maestranza, which is named for the adjacent Plaza de Toros. In fact, the bullring is so close that guests in rooms on the Calle Maestranza side can see bullfights from the balconies on floors 9 to 12. The other views are not exactly shabby, either, taking in the beautifully reconstructed yachting port and the lighted Moorish walls rising from the seaside city to the Gibralfaro. Regular rooms are a little tight but well-designed, and the location is perfect for enjoying the nightlife and restaurants of Muelle Uno across the street.

Av. Canóvas del Castillo, 1. ✆ **95-221-36-10.** www.mshoteles.com. 90 units. 72€–180€ double; 90€–210€ jr. suite. **Amenities:** Bar; spa; Jacuzzi; sauna, exercise room; free Wi-Fi.

Hotel Petit Palace Plaza Málaga ★   Tucked into a small street just a few paces off Plaza de la Constitución, this high-tech hotel offers the usual amenities of the chain, including a laptop in every room. Moreover, guests also get 30MB of city Wi-Fi to use in the streets of Málaga. Furnishings are smoothly contemporary and the bathrooms have new porcelain fixtures and high-tech hydromassage showers. Big beds make the small double rooms a little tight, but they are quite functional once you figure out what to do with the luggage. Triple and quad rooms are also available.

Calle Nicasio, 3. ✆ **95-222-21-32.** www.hthoteles.com. 66 units. 80€–110€ double; 105€–129€ triple; 114€–138€ quadruple. **Amenities:** Restaurant; bar; concierge; exercise room; free Wi-Fi.

Room Mate Larios ★★   A striking Art Deco–era building near the head of Calle Larios, this Room Mate is set up with several self-sufficient apartments ranging from studios with a cooking corner to units with a separate bedroom and upstairs loft sleeping area. Expanses of contrasting marble and high-sheen black paint make the public areas look as if they had traveled in time from Paris circa 1930. The rooms continue the deco look with lots of black, gold, and taupe and smoothly streamlined furniture. Standard rooms are tight but well-designed, and apartments are spacious. The Picasso Museum is about a 5-minute walk away, and the city's best shopping is just outside the front door. If Larios is full, Room Mate may suggest its other hotel, Lola, which is a fine hotel in a less convenient neighborhood that will be enduring extensive construction through 2015.

Calle Marqués de Larios, 2. ✆ **95-222-22-00.** www.room-matehotels.com. 41 units. 76€–139€ double; 110€–179€ junior suite; 110€–179€ studio apt.; 154€–204€ duplex apt. **Amenities:** Restaurant; bar; free Wi-Fi.

INEXPENSIVE

Sercotel Los Naranjos ★   Set on the section of Playa Malagueta known as Baños Carmen, about a mile (1.6km) east of central Málaga, Los Naranjos is an ideal setting for spending more time at the beach than sightseeing in the city. Rooms are reasonably spacious and the strand and its accompanying beach bars are literally across the street. It can seem a little desolate in the off-season, but rates are very low then. Several rooms have balconies with a sea view.

Paseo de Sancha, 35. ✆ **95-222-43-16.** www.hotel-losnaranjos.com. 41 units. 50€–146€ double. Parking 13€. Bus: 11. **Amenities:** Restaurant; bar; free Wi-Fi.

Where to Eat in Málaga

EXPENSIVE

José Carlos García Restaurante ★★ SPANISH   Málaga's star chef José Carlos García pioneered fine dining when he opened his waterfront restaurant in 2011. It attracts gastronomes all up and down the Costa del Sol. There are two menus and two dining rooms, with the glass box of a kitchen in between. The a la carte menu features some of the chef's greatest hits (like a sumptuous

WHAT AND HOW TO drink IN MÁLAGA

Malagueños pride themselves on having a slang term for everything, and the place to decipher the language of coffee is **Café Central,** Plaza de la Constitucíon, 11 (**℃ 95-222-49-72;** www.cafecentral-malaga.com), where the tiled lexicon on the wall explains everything from a *solo* (full glass of black coffee) to a *mitad* (half-coffee, half-milk) and a *nube,* or *cloud* (a splash of coffee topped by almost a full glass of milk). Although many people order *churros* with their coffee at Central, the classic spot for thick hot chocolate and *churros* is **Casa**

Aranda, Calle Herrería del Rey (no phone). If it's too warm for hot drinks, **Casa Mira,** Calle Larios, 5 (**℃ 95-221-24-22**), makes excellent crushed-ice drinks called *granizados.* The two traditional flavors are coffee and lemon. But the most traditional drink in the city is the sherry-like Málaga wine, and the most traditional place to drink it is **Antigua Casa de Guardia,** Alameda Principal, 18 (**℃ 95-221-46-80**), founded in 1840. Wines are served from giant oak barrels, and the barman chalks up your tab on the sticky wooden counter.

hand-cut steak tartare) from the former Café de Paris, as well as newer inventions like the white prawns served with frozen white almond-garlic gazpacho. There's also a daily menu of five half portions. The front room is reserved for the tasting menu, a 10- to 14-course extravaganza of incredible bites like sea urchin roe with tapioca pearls or roast suckling pig in pineapple sauce.

Muelle Uno, Plaza de la Capilla. ℃ **95-200-35-88.** www.rcafedeparis.com. Reservations required. Main courses 25€–35€. Daily menu 54€. Tasting menu 90€. Tues–Sat 1:30–3:30pm and 8:30–11pm. Closed July 1–15. Bus: 251.

MODERATE

El Chinitas ★ SPANISH   Heir to the legendary 19th-century cafe-theater by the same name, El Chinitas cultivates a timeless look of straight-backed wooden chairs, wood-paneled walls, and white linen tablecloths. The menu hails from the same era, representing the best of coastal seafood and the meat traditions of central Spain. Fish is mostly fried, while meats are either braised or grilled. In keeping with tradition, other than the obligatory green salad, green beans, artichokes, and asparagus, vegetables are an afterthought. It is a great spot to enjoy *rabo de toro* (braised oxtail), steamed prawns, or scrambled egg dishes. The menu of tapas is a bargain of seven varied tapas and dessert.

Calle Moreno Monroy, 4. ℃ **95-221-09-72.** www.elchinitas.com. Reservations recommended on weekends. Main courses 12€–21€. Daily menu 40€. Tapas menu 17€. Daily noon–midnight.

Godoy Marisquería ★★ SEAFOOD   Like José Carlos García, Godoy was a pioneer on Muelle Uno. This glittering glass jewel box of a restaurant offers a menu primarily of shellfish—augmented by some fin fish, a couple of steaks, and a few ham-based appetizers. The house specialty is a Málagan version of *zarzuela* consisting primarily of large pieces of monkfish with clams and cockles in a tomato-fish broth. For more casual munching, order a good white wine and an assortment of fried anchovies, red mullet, tiny squid, and pieces of flounder.

Muelle Uno, 34–35. ℃ **95-229-03-12.** www.marisqueriagodoy.com. Main courses 12€–25€; shellfish tasting menu 59€. Tues–Sat 1:30–3:30pm and 8:30–11pm. Bus: 251.

A PERFECT MÁLAGA beach EVENING

It takes about an hour to stroll along Playa de la Malagueta from the port to Playa Pedregalejo. You'll pass surfcasters, colonies of feral cats living in the rocks, and on a Saturday afternoon, barefoot brides having their pictures taken on the beach. Fish-house restaurants line the beach at Pedregalejo. One of the value spots is Manuel Cabra's **Restaurante El Cabra ★★**, Paseo Maritimo Pedregal, 17 (✆ **95-225-15-95**). It's open Tuesday to Sunday 2 to 6pm and 8pm to midnight. Main dishes cost 10€ to 21€. His specialties include grilled sardines on a wooden stake and a *fritura Malagueña* of mixed fried fish. Linger as long as you want and then walk 2 blocks up from the beach to Avenida Juan Sebastian Elcano to catch the 11, 33, or 34 bus back to Alameda Principal.

INEXPENSIVE

Gorki ★★ SPANISH   Located just off Calle Larios, this handsome dining room with an equally attractive group of tables in the street can serve you everything from a single oyster with a sip of manzanilla to a full-blown multi-course meal accompanied by a bevy of wines. There are burgers, finger sandwiches of smoked salmon or curried chicken, and big plates of melted goat cheese over fresh tomatoes. For a more substantial meal, order a seared tuna steak or black rice with sautéed cuttlefish and saffron aioli.

Calle Strachan, 6. ✆ **95-222-14-66.** www.gorki.es. Tapas 1.50€–4€; main courses 9€–16€. Daily noon–midnight.

La Bouganvilla ★ SPANISH   Tucked into one corner of Plaza del Siglo, this unprepossessing little eatery resembles an American quiche bar of the 1980s—except that the food is a lot better. The menu consists of about a dozen tapas, ranging from a *pincho de tortilla* to ceviche to a half-dozen shrimp grilled with garlic. Add a few variations on green salad, a range of fresh and aged cheeses, and a couple of variations on small pieces of grilled meat, and you have the full picture. Prices are excellent, service is quick, and the food is some of the best of its kind, making La Bouganvilla a great spot to grab a bite if you're shopping your way across Málaga.

Calle Granada, 22. ✆ **95-100-61-03.** Tapas 2€–7€. Main courses 12€–18€. Daily 10am–11pm.

La Cosmopolita ★ SPANISH   Set a few paces off Plaza del Siglo, this breezy little spot is a midday favorite for Malagueños in the know. Many show up just for the big sandwiches made on baguettes from Las Garrochas bakery. The signature sandwich is the Don José, aka Pepito, with sliced veal, roasted peppers, and grilled octopus. Other highlights include a creamy baby squid risotto, veal steak in mustard sauce, and fried eggs with baby fava beans. On weekdays, La Cosmopolita also serves breakfast.

Calle José Denis Belgrano, 3. ✆ **95-221-58-27.** www.lacosmopolita.es. Tapas 2.50€–3.50€. Main dishes 12€–19€. Mon–Fri 8:30am–midnight, Sat–Sun noon–12:30am.

La Manzanilla ★★ CONTEMPORARY SPANISH   Practically next door to Gorki, Manzanilla is superchef Dani García's homage to the classic tapas bar—with a twist, of course. His reinventions of the classics have an American accent, in part from his experience with his New York outpost of La Manzanilla. Every contemporary chef in Spain does a burger these days, but García is the only one we know offering a *rabo de toro* burger that tastes exactly like braised oxtail. His excellent "pigburguer" is another reimagined classic, made with ground Iberian pork and topped with bacon. One of the most popular tapas is the "tortilla al whisky," which is a classic potato omelet with a whisky sauce—a dish whose origin he duly credits to Bodeguita Casablanca in Sevilla (p. 190). No foodie should miss La Manzanilla, where even the wine is a good buy.

Calle Fresca, 12.. ✆ **95-222-68-51.** www.manzanillamalaga.com. Reservations recommended. Tapas 2.80€–4.50€, other dishes 5.80€–12€. Daily 1–4pm and 8pm–midnight.

Exploring Málaga

Although the train and bus stations are west of the river, almost everything you will want to see is located to the east. The skyline makes it easy to navigate, as the spire of the one-armed cathedral rises in the center of the old city, and the restored Moorish walls stitch their way up the Gibralfaro hillside from the old Alcazaba, or fortress, a short distance from the waterfront. In the main part of town, elegant Calle Larios—paved with marble and lined with top boutiques—links the main Plaza de la Constitución to the waterfront parks. The tree-lined Alameda lies to the west of the port proper. The Parque de Málaga, full of subtropical plants, separates the urban city from the waterfront. The dock areas south of the Parque de Málaga have become the playground of the city, with the former Muelle Dos redeveloped as the delightful walkways of El Palmeral de las Sopresas, and Muelle Uno as a shopping, nightlife, and dining destination.

For an old, congested city, Málaga has convenient and well-marked bicycle paths. For a two-wheel overview of the city, connect with **Bike 2 Málaga,** Calle Vendeja, 6 (✆ **65-067-70-63;** www.biketoursmalaga.com). Of the company's several tours, the general "City Bike Tour" takes 3 hours and costs 22€ adults, 17€ students, and 12€ children.

Alcazaba ★ PALACE   This combination palace and fortress tells the story of the warrior potentates of the Taifa period in Andalucía, when the central Moorish empire had disintegrated into small squabbling kingdoms. It does not occupy

An interior courtyard of Málaga's Alcazaba palace.

the highest ground, but does command an irregular rocky spur that towers over most of the city. Begun shortly after the Arab conquest of 711, the largest sections were built between the 11th and 14th centuries. Just as Catholic churches often reused stones from Moorish buildings, the Alcazaba is filled with fluted Greek-style columns with acanthus capitals from 200 to 300 B.C. and occasional blocks of Roman stones with Latin inscriptions still visible. The well-preserved interior palace retains a palpable air of domesticity and is the most evocative part of the complex. The main entrance to the Alcazaba is up a long series of steps on Plaza de la Aduana, but there is an elevator entrance behind the Ayuntamiento (city hall) at Calle Guillén Sotelo and Calle Francisco Bejarrano Robles.

Plaza de la Aduana, Alcazabilla. ✆ **95-212-20-20.** Admission 2.20€ adults, 0.60€ students and seniors; free Sun 2pm–closing. Combined admission with Castillo de Gibralfaro 3.55€. Apr–Sept 9am–8:15pm (Mon until 8pm); Oct–Mar 8:30am–7:30pm (Mon 9am–6pm). Bus: 4, 18, 19, 24, or 135.

Castillo de Gibralfaro ★ CASTLE   The ruins of this Moorish castle-fortress crown a hill overlooking Málaga and the Mediterranean. The walls are crumbling and the keep is overgrown with weeds, but views are spectacular. Walking to the castle from town is fairly strenuous and muggings have been reported over the years. Still, the walk can be atmospheric if it's not too hot. Otherwise, take the bus from the cathedral.

Castllo del Gibralfaro. Admission 2.20€ adults, 0.60€ students and seniors; free Sun 2pm–closing. Combined admission with Alcazaba 3.55€. Daylight hours. Microbus: 35, hourly from cathedral.

Fundación Picasso ★ MUSEUM   Picasso was born in Málaga in 1881 in a rented apartment at Plaza de la Merced, 15, and moved two doors down in 1883. He lived there until the family moved to A Coruña in 1891. Arguably the greatest painter of the 20th century, Picasso never really worked in Málaga, but the city was a profound influence. The Fundación Picasso preserves his birth home as a small museum, showing artifacts that range from baby Pablo's umbilical band and christening dress to some paintings by his father, painter José Ruiz Blasco. Other exhibits flesh out the family and city influences, and explore Picasso's insistence on his Spanish identity, especially as regards his love of bullfighting and flamenco. When you leave the Casa Natal, look for blue and white tile plaques around the Plaza de la Merced that indicate the second family home, the place where his father used to hang out with other artists, and the Iglesia Santiago where Pablo was baptized.

Plaza de la Merced, 15. ✆ **95-206-02-15.** www.fundacionpicasso.es. Admission with audio-guide 2€; admission to Casa Natal and temporary exhibition hall 3€; free on Sun; free for seniors, students, and under age 17. Daily 9:30am–8pm. Bus: 36, 1, 37.

Málaga Cathedral ★ CATHEDRAL   *La Manquita,* or the "one-armed lady— because its second bell tower was never finished, that's the nickname for the cathedral, which collapses a lot of history into one hulking mass of stone. It sits at the foot of the Alcazaba on the former site of the mosque. The symbolism of obliterating an Islamic house of worship to construct a Catholic one was not lost on the Spanish royalty, who took back Málaga from the Moors in 1487. Construction of the cathedral didn't begin until 1528, and the builders finally threw up their hands in 1782. Skip the guided tour, but step inside briefly to see the 17th-century choir stalls carved of mahogany and cedar. The 40 images of saints are largely the work of Pedro de Mena, one of Spain's most celebrated wood sculptors.

Plaza Obispo. ✆ **95-221-59-17.** Admission 5€, 3€ seniors and students, free under 12. Mon–Fri 10am–6pm; Sat 10am–5pm; Sun 2pm–6pm. Bus: 14, 18, 19, or 24.

Mercado Central ★ MARKET   Also known as the Mercado Atarazanas because it sits on the site of the old Moorish shipyard, this 14th-century building has a front door with a perfectly preserved horseshoe arch from the Nasrid period. The building was substantially changed in the 19th century, when it became the city's food market. Visit for a vivid display of local fish and subtropical fruits and vegetables grown along the coast.

Calle Atarazanas, s/n. No phone. Open Mon–Sat 8am–3pm.

Muelle Uno ★★ LANDMARK   Development of the stretch of waterfront from Plaza de General Torrijos to the 1817 Malagueta lighthouse created Málaga's newest dining, shopping, and nightlife district in 2010 to 2012. Broad walkways line the waterfront, and glass cubes containing boutiques, bars, and restaurants stretch the entire distance. Walking along the waterfront at night provides a romantic vantage back on the lighted Moorish walls that zigzag up the hill from the city below. Right where the waterfront turns onto Muelle Uno, you'll find a number of cruise boats. The 90-minute cruises tour the bay between the two main beaches, one east and one west of the city. Keep your eyes peeled for dolphins.

La Pinta Cruceros, Muelle Uno. ✆ **64-581-59-15.** www.malagaenbarco.com. 10€ adults, 6€ children.

Museo Alborania ★ MUSEUM   If you follow the seashells, starfish, and other marine life forms embedded in the sidewalks around El Palmeral de las Sopresas, you'll end up at this waterfront museum that calls itself a "classroom of the sea." Geared to small children more than to adults, this collection of aquariums showing marine life in reasonable facsimiles of their native habitats is intended to inculcate stewardship of the marine world.

El Palmeral de las Sopresas (Muelle 2), s/n. ✆ **95-160-01-08.** museoalborania.com. 7€ adults, 5€ seniors and students. Ask about family discounts. July to mid-Sept 11am–2pm and 5pm–midnight; mid-Sept to June Tues–Thurs 10:30am–2:30pm and 4:30–9:30pm, Fri–Sun 10:30am–2:30pm and 4:30–11:30pm.

Museo Carmen Thyssen Málaga ★★ MUSEUM   Located just off the Plaza de la Constitución in the Renaissance-era Palacio de Villalón, this museum displays the Spanish paintings circa 1825 to 1925 collected by Carmen Thyssen of the Museo Thyssen-Bornemisza in Madrid. By concentrating on this narrow slice of European art, the baroness was able to acquire the very best work of the era. Moreover, because the museum limits its scope, the interpretation is sharp and succinct. Ground-floor galleries feature the romantic paintings of the early and mid-19th century that would make Spain into one of the most popular artistic clichés of the day. They include colorful landscapes with even more colorful inhabitants: Gypsies, flamenco dancers, bullfighters, and ladies clad in mantillas demurely fluttering their fans. One floor up, galleries showcase a more naturalistic, moody style, as well as the parallel "précieux" style in which every flower petal and costume ruffle is articulated with the detail rivaling damascene work in metal. Alfred Derhondenq's 1851 vision of a Lenten procession in the streets of Sevilla shows the transition from the merely picturesque to a more considered realism. By 1867, Marià Fortuny i Marsal is rendering a bullfight with dramatic intensity and thick palette-knife clusters of paint that show his debt to Cezanne. As the exhibition progresses in time and style, it arrives at possibly one of the greatest paintings in the museum, the 1905 *Salida de un baile de mascaros* (Exit from the Masked Ball). The central figures in this parody of high society are a coachman and a doorman, standing in front of a theater smoking as a man in top

The interior courtyard of Museo Picasso Málaga.

hat and tails and his lady in full ball gown race down the steps. On the right, the red-nosed musicians are taking their leave. On the left, scantily clad and masked ladies are moving in on the society men.

The second floor gallery shows "old masters," a mix of Italian and Spanish sculpture and painting from 13th-century Gothic through the museum's sole Velázquez portrait. The third floor hosts temporary exhibitions.

Plaza Carmen Thyssen, Calle Compañía, 10. © **90-230-31-31.** www.carmenthyssenmalaga.org. Admission 6€, 3.50€ seniors and students, free under age 12. Tues–Sun 10am–8pm.

Museo Picasso Málaga ★★★ MUSEUM   Picasso last visited Málaga at the age of 19, but toward the end of his life expressed the wish that his work be displayed in the city of his birth. That wish became a reality in 2003. Continued gifts by Picasso's daughter-in-law and grandson have brought the collection to 285 works, most of which are unfamiliar since they were kept in the artist's private collection. Because Picasso's greatest hits are elsewhere, this museum focuses on teasing out the artist's multifaceted genius and showing his different styles of working at different times. During the same period that he was making abstract Cubist portraits, for example, he also drew delicate portraits of his son so realistic that they could be photographs.

Calle San Agustín, 8. © **90-244-33-77.** www.museopicassomalaga.org. Permanent collection 6€; temporary exhibitions 4.50€; combination ticket 9€; seniors and students half price; free under age 18. Free to all Sun 6–8pm. Tue–Thurs and Sun 10am–8pm, Fri–Sat 10am–9pm.

Shopping

Calle Larios has most of the city's top boutiques, though many are familiar international brands. For unusual eyewear, stop at the head of the street at **Federoptícos,** Plaza de la Constitucíon, 12 (© **95-221-11-54**), for frames made in Andalucía with intricate inlaid wood designs on the bows. The shop also carries folding reading glasses on a chain from an Andalucían designer. **Calle Nueva,** which runs parallel to Calle Larios, is lined with good, less expensive shops. If you're searching for a fan or beautiful embroidered shawl, check the offerings at charmingly old-fashioned **Ceylon,** Calle Nueva, 2 (℗ **95-222-98-91**). For more hip Spanish fashion, **Piel de Toro,** Calle Nueva, 27 (℗ **95-221-12-20;** www.pieldetoro.com), carries preppy-style clothing for men and women with a playful embroidered bull logo. Sherry drinkers are probably more familiar with the iconic silhouette of the Osborne bull. Near the Museo Carmen Thyssen, the **Toro Store,** Calle Compañia, 2 (℗ **95-125-35-39;** www.tiendastoro.com), has managed to affix the bull to everything from T-shirts and baseball caps to golf balls and espresso cups. The shop is owned by the Osborne family, and you can also buy their sherries and brandy. The clerk will likely offer you a glass while you peruse the merchandise. A rather sweet Málaga tradition is to create porcelain flowers as a way to enjoy their blooming season year round. **Rincón de la Biznaga,** Calle Granada, 53 (℗ **95-222-68-18**), is run by folks who continue this craft. The new **Muelle Uno** is also lined with shops, including **{re}union creadores,** Local 1.B (℗ **62-960-94-04**), which features the work of contemporary craftspeople. Their jewelry and bags are particularly striking. A number of craftspeople set up outdoor booths along the Muelle on Sundays.

Málaga After Dark

Nightlife in Málaga is like nightlife in most big Spanish cities. Spaniards gather at bars and restaurants to drink, snack, and talk. You'll find tapas scenes on the side streets from Calle Larios, along Calle Granada, and along Muelle Uno.

For music and dancing, try the live band venue **ZZ Pub,** Calle Tejón y Rodríguez 6 (℗ **95-244-15-95;** www.zzpub.es), which is big with university students. Performances start around 10:30pm and end 4 to 5am. A more adult crowd frequents the disco **Sala Touch,** Calle José Denis Belgrano, 9 (℗ **64-642-45-63**), which opens Thursday to Saturday 1 to 7am. *Copas* are always 4€.

Shopping along Calle Larios in Málaga.

Two beautifully restored theaters—**Teatro Echegaray,** Calle Echegaray, 6 (✆ **95-222-41-00;** www.teatroechegaray.es), and **Teatro Cervantes de Málaga,** Ramos Marin s/n (✆ **95-222-41-00;** www.teatrocervantes.es), present musical concerts, flamenco, dance, and Spanish-language theater. The Cervantes is also home to the Málaga Symphony Orchestra.

Side Trip from Málaga

EL TORCAL DE ANTEQUERA ★★ Just more than 50km (31 miles) north of Málaga, El Torcal is reached by driving A-45 north to Antequera, A343 south from Antequera, then local road MA-3310 to El Torcal. The drive takes just less than an hour to reach the desert hills that were designated in 1929 as Andalucía's first natural park. A paved road swishes back and forth through the bone-dry landscape, providing constantly changing perspectives on the wind-sculpted limestone hoodoos. Three well-marked trails depart from the visitor center (✆ **95-224-33-24;** www.torcaldeantequera.com; daily Oct–Mar 10am–5pm, Apr–Sept 10am–7pm; free). If you stick to the trails, you run a good chance of spotting several of the 30 species of wild orchids that flourish in this harsh landscape or seeing an eagle swoop down on a lizard. If you deviate from the trails, you run a good chance of becoming utterly lost—to the delight of the griffin vultures gliding overhead. The landscape is so spooky that El Torcal has the dubious distinction of having more UFO sightings than any other place in Spain.

NERJA ★

Nerja is known for its good if pebbly beaches and small coves, its seclusion, its narrow streets and courtyards, and its whitewashed, flat-roofed houses. Nearby is one of Andalucía's top geological attractions, **La Cueva de Nerja** (see below).

At the mouth of the Río Chillar, Nerja gets its name from the Arabic word *narixa,* meaning "bountiful spring." Its most dramatic spot is the **Balcón de Europa ★★,** a palm-shaded promenade that juts out into the Mediterranean. It was built on the site of an earlier fortification, and local lore says that it received its name from King Alfonso XII in 1885 when he visited the area in the wake of an earthquake that had shattered nearby Málaga. He used the phrase during a speech he made in Nerja praising the beauty of the panorama around him. To reach the best beaches, head west from the Balcón and follow the shoreline.

Essentials

GETTING THERE At least 19 buses per day make the 1-hour trip from Málaga to Nerja, costing 5€ one-way. Service is provided by Alsina Graells. If you're driving, head along the N-340/E-15 east from Málaga, or take the N-340/E-15 west from the Motril junction with A-14 coming south from Granada.

VISITOR INFORMATION The tourist office, at Calle Carmen, 1 (✆ **95-252-15-31;** www.nerja.es), is open Monday to Friday 10am to 2pm and 3 to 6:45pm, Saturday and Sunday 10am to 2pm.

Where to Stay in Nerja

EXPENSIVE

Parador de Nerja ★★ The Spanish *parador* system does not let the lack of a suitable historic building stop it from offering a hotel in some of the country's most scenic and popular areas. In Nerja, this modern hotel sits on a cliff above the ocean and compensates for what it might lack in historic atmosphere with

Balcón de Europa in Nerja.

striking views and a lovely garden. In fact, most of the fairly spacious rooms have balconies facing the sea and understated furnishings don't distract from the views. For all the sense of privacy, it's only about a 5-minute walk to town center.

Calle Almuñécar, 8. © **95-252-00-50.** www.parador.es. 98 units. 110€–285€ double. Free parking. **Amenities:** Restaurant; bar; outdoor freshwater pool; outdoor tennis court (lit); free Wi-Fi.

MODERATE

Carabeo ★★ It's hard to find a place with more character than the Carabeo, which occupies a former schoolhouse in Nerja's atmospheric old fisherman's quarters. Owners have done an admirable job of mixing antiques and art to make a comfortable retreat. But however charming the quarters, Nerja is really about the sea, and Carabeo delivers on that front also. The property sits on a cliff overlooking the water and is only about a 5-minute walk to a swimming beach. With so few rooms, the owners could make each unique, but they are all fairly large with rich fabrics and solid wood furniture. Several have a private terrace or balcony.

Hernando de Carabeo, 34. © **95-252-54-44.** www.hotelcarabeo.com. 7 units. 85€–220€ double. Free parking nearby. Closed late Oct to Apr. **Amenities:** Restaurant; bar; exercise room; outdoor pool; sauna; free Wi-Fi.

Hotel Balcón de Europa ★ If you like to be in the heart of the action, this nine-story modern hotel built in the 1970s sits on the right bank of the Balcón de Europa. Most of the rooms have a terrace to enjoy the sea view, and all benefited from a full renovation completed in 2012. Fabrics in rich colors and patterns set a tone of elegance in this beach resort. Views from the pool are stunning, and a small private beach allows guests to escape the crowds.

Paseo Balcón de Europa, 1. © **95-252-08-00.** www.hotelbalconeuropa.com. 110 units. 105€–170€ double; 140€–239€ suite. Parking 12€. **Amenities:** 2 restaurants; bar; outdoor freshwater heated pool; sauna; free Wi-Fi.

INEXPENSIVE

Hostal Ana ★ To save money in this fairly expensive city, book one of the rooms here that has a small kitchen. With a plain white facade and wrought-iron accents, the relatively new building—constructed in 1998—seems right at home in the historic center of the city, yet within easy walking distance of the Balcón de Europa. Liberal use of colorful Andalucían-style tiles adds character. Some of the rooms are small, but all have simple, comfortable furnishings. The innkeepers are friendly and helpful.

Calle La Cruz, 60. © **95-252-30-43.** www.hostalananerja.com. 17 units. 40€–65€ double. **Amenities:** Hot tub; free Wi-Fi.

Hotel Plaza Cavana ★   Small, wrought-iron balconies add an air of grace to this two-story hotel near the Balcón de Europa. Not large enough for lounging, the balconies offer a great vantage point to take in the scene and let fresh sea air into the rooms. The fairly spacious rooms were designed by someone with a good eye for pairing single bright colors with neutrals for a harmonious and tranquil effect. Guests share a garden patio. Innkeepers often offer amenities such as a free buffet breakfast or late checkout for online booking; be sure to ask.

Plaza Cavana, 10. ℂ **95-252-40-00.** www.hotelplazacavana.com. 39 units. 59€–139€ double. Parking 15€. **Amenities:** Restaurant; bar; bikes; exercise room; Jacuzzi; 2 freshwater pools (1 heated indoor); sauna; free Wi-Fi.

Where to Eat in Nerja

Pepe Rico Restaurant ★ INTERNATIONAL   Sometimes it's nice to dress up for dinner, even in a casual beach resort. Pepe Rico, which opened in 1966, is a good bet for a relaxed meal with excellent service in an elegant space. You can choose the dining room with white linens and dark wood furniture or the pretty, tree-shaded patio. The international menu maintains a strong Spanish accent—from Málaga-style white garlic soup to baked cod with scallops and local vegetables. Speaking of vegetables, there is a separate menu for vegetarians, on request.

Calle Almirante Ferrándiz, 28. ℂ **95-252-02-47.** www.peperico.info. Main courses 14€–26€. Mon–Sat 12:30–3pm and 7–11pm. Closed 2 weeks Dec and 1 week in Jan.

Restaurante Rey Alfonso ★ SPANISH/FRENCH   It's easy to miss this restaurant, which is located in a glass case below the Balcón de Europa and reached by small staircases on either side of the promontory. Even if you don't want a meal, stop in for a drink, as you can't really get much closer to the ocean without getting wet, and the views, as well as the sunsets, are quite remarkable. The meals are rather conventional *platos combinados* of meat, starch, and vegetable.

Paseo Balcón de Europa s/n. ℂ **95-252-09-58.** Reservations recommended. Main courses 9€–18€. Mon–Sat noon–3pm and 7–11pm; Sun noon–3pm. Closed 4 weeks Jan–Feb.

Exploring La Cueva de Nerja

The most popular outing from Málaga and Nerja is to the **Cueva de Nerja (Cave of Nerja)** ★★, Carretera de Maro s/n (ℂ **95-252-95-20;** www.cuevadenerja. es). Scientists believe this prehistoric stalactite and stalagmite cave was inhabited from 25,000 to 2000 B.C. It was rediscovered in 1959, when a small group of boys found it by chance. Once fully opened, it revealed a wealth of treasures left from the days of the cave dwellers, including Paleolithic paintings. They depict horses, deer, and other prey, but only a small fraction of the paintings lie in the galleries open to the public. But the striking geology compensates: You can walk through stupendous galleries where ceilings soar to a height of 60m (197 ft.).

The cave is in the hills near Nerja. From here you get panoramic views of the countryside and sea. It's open daily 10am to 1pm and 4 to 6:30pm (until 7:30pm July–Aug). Admission is 9€ adults, 5€ children 6 to 12, and free for children 5 and under. Buses (www.elcapistranonerja.es) to the cave leave from Paseo de los Tilos, s/n in Málaga hourly from 7am to 8:15pm, and from Avenida de Pescia, s/n in Nerja hourly from 8:30am to 9:40pm. Return buses run hourly until 9:45pm. The journey to or from Málaga takes about 1 hour. From Málaga, the roundtrip ticket is 9€, from Nerja it is 2.4€.

The Cueva de Nerja.

ALMUÑÉCAR ★

The Phoenicians founded this seaside town in the 8th century B.C., naming it Sexi, and establishing the first *garum* (fermented fish paste) works just up from the main beach. The Romans took over in 218 B.C. and kept the *garum* business going, as Sexi's fish paste was traded as far away as Greece and Turkey. The town became a more traditional fishing port under the Moors, who also introduced sugar cane farming to the region. Today, most visitors come for the long stony beach dotted with *churrerías,* which open early for breakfast. An extensive complex of parks and ruins in **Barrio San Miguel** near the beach explains Almuñécar's rich history. The most important coastal resort of Granada province, Almuñécar is less crowded than the other beach resorts. Its subtropical climate makes its Rio Verde valley a hothouse for fruits and vegetables. The **Parque Botánico El Majuelo** in the central city next to the ruins of the Roman fish paste factory is filled with tropical and subtropical species that flourish in the warm microclimate.

Essentials

GETTING THERE   At least seven buses per day make the 75-minute trip from Granada to Almuñécar, costing 6.70€ one-way. Service is provided by Alsina Graells (© **95-863-01-40** or 95-888-07-04). From Málaga to Almuñécar, there are 10 buses a day, costing 7.50€ each way. Service is provided by Alsa (www.alsa. es). If you're driving, head along the N-340/E-15 east from Málaga, or take the A-14 south from Granada. Driving time is about 1¼ hours from both cities.

VISITOR INFORMATION   The tourist office at Avenida de Europa s/n (© **95-863-11-325;** www.almunecar.info) is open daily November to March 10am to 2pm and 4:30 to 7pm; April to June and September 16 to October 10am to 2pm and 5 to 8pm; and July to September 15 10am to 2pm and 6 to 9pm. Called the

Palacete de la Najarra and situated among park land, the neo-Mudejar structure is quite possibly Spain's most beautiful tourist office.

Where to Eat & Stay in Almuñécar

Digame Pepe ★ SEAFOOD   This casual restaurant does a bang-up business on English-style breakfasts in the morning, along with *churros* for those who want to sit down, rather than stand at a beachside *churrería* to eat the crisp, hot treats. Digame Pepe is right on the beach, so folks return in the evening to watch the sun set while they eat fried or grilled fish or fish stew.

Paseo de los Flores, s/n. ℭ **95-834-93-15.** Main dishes 8€–20€. Daily 8am–10pm.

Hotel Helios Costa Tropical ★★   Opened in 1989, this large white hotel helped usher in tourism in Almuñécar. It remains our favorite lodging in town. It's located right across the street from the Playa San Cristobal and takes advantage of the setting with sea-view terraces on most of the fairly spacious guest rooms. The Helios has a number of resort features including a pool, game rooms for kids, meeting rooms, and even a hairdresser. But friendly and helpful staff provide the kind of personal attention we usually expect in smaller properties. Two especially nice features are the 10th-floor solarium and the heated pool for winter getaways (Nov–Mar).

Paseo San Cristóbal, 12. ℭ **95-863-44-59.** www.helios-hotels.com/almunecar. 227 units. Doubles 60€–147€. Parking 12€. **Amenities:** Restaurant; bar; exercise room; pool; free Wi-Fi.

Exploring Almuñécar

Castillo San Miguel ★ CASTLE   Archaeologists have found ceramics on the site that date the fortifications back to a Carthaginian compound in the 3rd century B.C., and there is ample evidence that the Romans also fortified the spot. (That *garum* trade was worth protecting, apparently.) The castle that survived, though, was built in the 13th century by the Nasrid dynasty that also constructed the Alhambra. The structure was famous for its prison and the dungeon where

political prisoners were kept. The Spanish monarchs modified the structure but kept its prison operative until 1808, when the castle was severely damaged by English bombardment.

Barrio San Miguel. ℭ **65-002-75-84.** www.almunecar.info. 2.35€ adults, 1.60€ seniors and children (includes Museo Arqueológico). Tue–Sat 10:30am–1:30pm and 5–7:30pm, Sun 10:30am–2pm.

Parque Ornitológico Loro-Sexi ★ ZOO   More than 1,500 birds representing more than 100 species fly in large caged areas in this modern aviary. Scarlet macaws, toucans, and peacocks provide colorful splendor.

Calle Bikini, s/n, Plaza Rahman. ℭ **95-863-11-25.** www.almunecar.info. 4€ adults, 2€ seniors and children. Daily 11am–2pm and 4–6pm.

The beach in Almuñécar.

Museo Arqueológico ★ MUSEUM   The structure itself is perhaps the greatest artifact in this local history museum. It occupies a portion of the Roman ruins (La Cueva de Siete Palacios) set into the city hills. The rather elegant vaulted space contains artifacts from the various cultures that once called Almuñécar home, including the Romans, Moors, and Phoenicians. The most unusual artifact suggests the cosmopolitan nature of the historic city. It's an Egyptian glass with hieroglyphics that date from the 17th century B.C. Carved from solid quartz, the antique curiosity most likely reached Almuñécar aboard a trading vessel.

Calle Cueva de los Siete Palacios, s/n. ✆ **60-786-54-66.** www.almunecar.info. 2.35€ adults, 1.60€ seniors and children. Tue–Sat 10:30am–1:30pm and 5–7:30pm; Sun 10:30am–2pm.

VALENCIA & THE COSTA BLANCA

Spain's third-largest city, Valencia is a lyrical metropolis with world-class architecture, a literal river of museums and parks, excellent beaches, and great food. In fact, it is the gastronomic touchstone for the entire country. The Moors introduced rice to Europe here, and Valencia combined it with the vegetables and legumes of its fertile alluvial plain, the shellfish of its coast, and the rabbits and snails of its gardens to give the world paella.

VALENCIA ★★★

Geography is destiny in Valencia. With the easternmost sheltered harbor on the central Iberian coast, it became a stepping-stone from North Africa to central Spain and back during the Moorish occupation. El Cid prevailed against the Moors here—and they recaptured the strategic port by driving his successors back into the hills. A millennium ago, the city changed hands with staggering frequency. Between container ships shuttling to and from China and petroleum tankers (there are nearly four dozen refineries in or near Valencia), the port is still Valencia's lifeblood. Yet industry is so sequestered and clean that visitors only see it if they bicycle along the coast to L'Albufera (see "Side Trip from Valencia," p. 301).

Floods engulfed Valencia in 1957; to prevent another disaster, the Río Túria, which had encircled the city, was moved underground. This feat of earthworks engineering set Valencia on a path to reimagining itself. The dry riverbed was transformed into a 10km (6¼-mile) linear park, where the City of Arts and Sciences was ultimately erected on the southeastern corner. The futuristic architecture of native son Santiago Calatrava and Spanish-Mexican architect Félix Candela rivals Frank Gehry's Guggenheim Bilbao, and has spurred further renovation and construction throughout Valencia.

Essentials

GETTING THERE Iberia flies to Valencia from Barcelona, Madrid, Málaga, and many other cities. There are also flights between Palma (Mallorca) and Valencia. For flight information, contact the **Iberia Airlines** office, Calle Paz 14 (✆ **90-240-05-00;** www.iberia.com). The airport is 8km (5 miles) southwest of the city center. To reach downtown, take Metro line 3 (1.50€) or bus 150 (1.50€). For more information, call ✆ **90-046-10-46.** A taxi (✆ **96-370-33-33**) from the airport to the town center goes for around 15€.

Trains run to Valencia from all parts of Spain. Estación del Norte (North station), Calle Játiva 2, sits just south of the heart of the city, making it a convenient arrival point. It's also a landmark Modernista building. Its information office on Calle Renfe (✆ **90-232-03-20;** www.renfe.com) is open Monday to Friday 8am to 9pm. From Barcelona, 15 trains—including several TALGOs, which take 3½ hours—arrive daily. At least 14 trains daily connect Madrid with Valencia, with the Alvia high-speed train taking about 2 hours and the AVE only 100 minutes. From Málaga, on the Costa del Sol, the trip takes 4 to 7 hours, depending on connections.

Buses arrive at Valencia's Estació Terminal d'Autobuses, Av. de Menéndez Pidal, 13 (✆ **96-346-62-66**), about a 30-minute walk northwest of the city's

FACING PAGE: **Valencia is known for its rich food culture.**

center. Take bus 8 to reach the Plaza del Ayuntamiento. Thirteen buses a day run from Madrid (trip time: 4 hr.), 10 buses from Barcelona (trip time: 5 hr.), and 5 buses from Málaga (trip time: 8 hr.).

You can take a **ferry** to and from the Balearic Islands (p. 522). Year-round ferries to Palma (Mallorca) take 6 hours. Ferries leave Valencia for Ibiza from March to September; in winter, there is only one ferry per week. Travel agents in Valencia sell tickets, or you can buy them from the Trasmediterránea office at the port, Estació Marítim (☏ **90-245-46-45;** www.trasmediterranea.es), on the day of your departure. To reach the port, take bus 4 or 19 from the Plaza del Ayuntamiento.

From Barcelona, the easiest driving route is the express highway (E-15) south. The Barcelona-Valencia toll is 25€. You can also use a national highway, E-901, from Madrid northwest of Valencia. From Alicante, take the E-15 express highway north. You can drive from Málaga north to Granada and cut across southeastern Spain on the 342, which links with the 340 into Murcia. From there, take the road to Alicante for an easy drive into Valencia.

VISITOR INFORMATION   The chief **tourist information office** is at Calle Paz 48 (☏ **96-398-64-22;** www.visitvalencia.com). It's open Monday to Friday 9am to 8pm, Saturday 10am to 8pm, and Sunday 10am to 2pm.

GETTING AROUND   Most **local buses** leave from Plaza del Ayuntamiento 22. You can buy tickets at any newsstand. The one-way fare is 1.50€; a 10-ride Bonobus Plus card sells for 8€. Bus 8 runs from Plaza del Ayuntamiento to the bus station at Avenida Menéndez Pidal. A bus map is available at the EMT office (Calle Correo Viejo 5; www.emtvalencia.es; Mon–Fri 9am to 2pm and 4:30 to 7:30pm). For bus information, call ☏ **96-315-85-15.** The **Metro** system (☏ **90-046-10-46;** www.metrovalencia.es) is more efficient than the bus, covering the Old Town well and branching out to the outskirts, including the beaches. You can purchase tickets from automatic machines in any station; the cost ranges from 1.50€ for one zone to 1.95€ for two zones. A 10-journey Travelcard is a better deal, selling for 7.20€. If you need a **taxi,** call ☏ **96-370-33-33.**

Valencia is flat and easy to pedal, making it nearly ideal for cycling. One excellent bike rental agency in the heart of the Old Town is **Orange Bikes** (Calle Editor Manuel Aguilar, 1; ☏ **96-391-75-51;** www.orangebikes.net. Mon–Fri 9:30am to 2:30pm and 4:30 to 7:30pm, Sat 10am to 2pm and 7 to 7:30 for bike returns). Rates are 9€ to 12€ per day, 15€ for an electric bike.

[Fast FACTS] VALENCIA

Internet   There are many Internet cafes in Valencia, the most reliable of which is a photocopy and print shop called **Work Center,** open Monday to Friday 7am to 11pm, Saturday and Sunday noon to 9pm; it's at Colón 84 (☏ **96-353-69-19**) in front of the bullring and Estación del Norte.

Language   Don't be surprised if you see signs in a language that's neither Spanish nor Catalan. It is **Valenciano,** closely related to Catalan. Often you'll be handed a "bilingual" menu in Castilian Spanish and in Valenciano. Some older citizens are dubious about this post-Franco cultural resurgence and view the promotion of the language as detrimental to the city's economic goals. Many younger citizens actually speak the language. Most street names appear in Valenciano.

Medical Care   In a medical emergency, call ☏ **112;** or go to the **Hospital Clínico Universitario,** Av. Blasco Ibáñez 17 (☏ **96-386-26-00**).

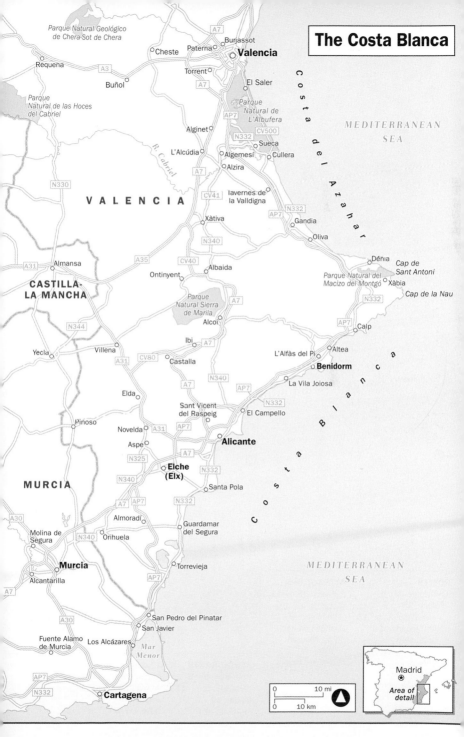

The Costa Blanca

Parque Natural Geológico de Chera-Sot de Chera

Requena

Buñol

Parque Natural de las Hoces del Cabriel

Cheste
Paterna
Burjassot
Valencia
Torrent
El Saler

Parque Natural de L'Albufera

Alginet

L'Alcúdia
Algemesí
Sueca
Cullera
Alzira

V A L E N C I A

Iavernes de la Valldigna

Xàtiva
Gandia
Oliva

Almansa

Ontinyent
Albaida

CASTILLA-
LA MANCHA

Parque Natural Sierra de Marila

Alcoi

Dénia
Cap de Sant Antoni
Parque Natural del Macizo del Montgó
Xàbia
Cap de la Nau

Yecla
Villena
Ibi
Castalla

Calp

L'Alfàs del Pi
Altea
Benidorm

Elda

La Vila Joiosa

Pinoso

Sant Vicent del Raspeig
El Campello

Novelda
Aspe
Alicante

MURCIA

**Elche
(Elx)**
Santa Pola

Almoradí
Guardamar del Segura

Molina de Segura
Orihuela

Murcia
Alcantarilla
Torrevieja

San Pedro del Pinatar
San Javier

Fuente Alamo de Murcia
Los Alcázares
Mar Menor

Cartagena

M E D I T E R R A N E A N   S E A

Costa del Azahar

Costa Blanca

M E D I T E R R A N E A N   S E A

0 — 10 mi
0 — 10 km

Madrid
Area of detail

Valencia

JARDINES DEL TÚRIA

Puente San José
Puente de las Artes

C/ Llano de la Zaidia

0   150 yds
0   150 m

Madrid
Valencia

PONT DE FUSTA Ⓜ

C/ Cronista Rivelles

Real Monasterio de la Trinidad

Museo de Bellas Artes **6**

C/ Guillem de Castro

C/ Salvador Giner

Casa Museo Benlliure

Iglesia del Carmen

C/ Blanquerias

C/ Na Jordana

1 **1**
IVAM

Plaza Carmen

Torres de Serranos

C/ Conde de Trénor

Puente de Serranos

C/ San Pío V

7

8

Centro Cultural la Beneficencia

C/ Alta

C/ Corona

C/ Baja

C/ Portal d. Valldigna

Plaza Fueros

Puente Trinidad

C/ Pintor López

Plaza Cisneros

LA SEU

C/ Dr. Beltrán Bigorra

C/ Serranos

Plaza del Temple

EL CARMEN

C/ Caballeros

C/ Quart

Plaza Tossal **3**

San Nicolás

Basílica de Nuestra Señora de los Desamparados

C/ Trinitarios

Almudín

Museo de la Ciudad

9

Torres de Quart

C/ Murillo

C/ Bolseria

Plaza la Virgen

Catedral **11**

10

LA XEREA

Plaza Tetuán

C/ Pinto Domingo

La Lonja

Santa Catalina

Plaza de la Reina ⓘ

4

C/ del Mar

Santos Tomás y San Felipe Neri

Plaza Don Juan de Vilarrasa

Santos Juanes

Mercado Central

C/ de la Paz

Jardines de la Glorieta

C/ Guillem de Castro

C/ Carniceros

C/ Balmes

C/ Camarón

C/ Bany

EL PILAR

Av. Maria Cristina

Museo de Cerámica **12**

El Patriarca ⓘ

Universidad de Valencia

Plaza Alfonso El Magnánimo

13

14

Iglesia del Pilar

C/ Hospital

Avenida Barón de Cárcer

C/ Músico Peydro

C/ San Vicente Mártir

Plaza R. Botet **15**

16

C/ Pintor Sorella

C/ Poeta Quintana

17

C/ Guillem de Castro

MUVIM

Ayuntamiento

18

Moratín

C/ Barcas ⓘ

19

C/ Don Juan Austria Ⓜ C/ Sorni
COLÓN

San Agustín

Plaza Ayuntamiento

C/ Correos ✉ **20**

C/ Pascual y Genis

C/ Roger de Llúria

C/ Sagasta

EL PLA DEL REMEI

22

C/ Hernán

Av. Marqués de Sotelo

C/ Ribera

Paseo Ruzafa

21

C/ de Colón

C/ Félix

C/ Cirilo Amorós

Cortés

XÀTIVA Ⓜ
ⓘ
Estación del Norte

Xàtiva

Plaza de Toros

C/ Alicante

C/ Ruzafa

23

C/ Pizcueta

C/ Pizarro

Gran Vía del Marqués del Turia

288

Where to Stay

In July and August, when Valencia can be uncomfortably hot and humid, some hoteliers lower prices significantly. It never hurts to ask. In mid-March during Las Fallas (p. 295), expect rates quoted below to double.

EXPENSIVE

Hotel Neptuno Valencia ★★★   A well-established beach hotel right on Playa Malvarrosa, the Neptuno has clean modern lines, and if the standard rooms are a little on the small side, who cares? You're not staying at the beach to spend time in your room. Sea-view rooms command a premium, of course, and the spacious suites command are even pricier. The rooftop solarium has great views along the shore and a tiny pool for cooling off between tanning sessions. The solarium is also a very popular point for watching yacht races in the harbor. The beachfront terrace is serviced by a bar, so you can lie back on a chaise lounge and nurse a cool drink.

Paseo Neptuno, 2. ℂ **96-356-77-77.** www.hotelneptunovalencia.com. 50 units. 133€–160€ double; 324€–360€ suite. Parking 19€. Metro: Marina Reial Joan Carles I or Neptú. **Amenities:** Restaurant; bar; gym; spa; towel rental; free broadband ADSL and Wi-Fi.

Palau de la Mar ★★★   From the classic white exterior of this restored 19th-century *palacio*, guests would never guess at its transformation to a stylish boutique hotel where carved wooden doors, intricate ironwork, and a grand marble staircase artfully mix with such modern elements as steel and glass. Guest rooms feature queen beds and marble bathrooms, but some are small. Families can opt for a room with a queen and twin bed or with three twins. A hidden interior patio with lots of greenery is a nice surprise. The hotel is a little quieter than many because it lies outside the old city—a 10-minute stroll to the cathedral, 15 minutes to the City of Arts & Sciences.

Calle Navarro Reverter, 14–16. ℂ **96-316-28-84.** www.hospes.com. 66 units. 115€–185€ double; 165€–240€ junior suite. Parking 25€. Metro: Colón. **Amenities:** Restaurant; bar; bikes; spa; indoor heated pool; free Wi-Fi.

MODERATE

Ayre Hotel Astoria Palace ★   A location in the heart of the city and within easy walking distance of many attractions makes this modern business hotel an equally good choice for leisure travelers. A recent renovation has given the rooms a fresh, clean style with light walls, wood floors, and dark wood furnishings highlighted by a single bold color in the draperies and bed coverings. Some rooms have views of a charming small plaza, while others overlook an internal courtyard. Rooms and suites on the upper floors are more luxurious and share private lounges, but excellent public spaces extend the living areas for all guests.

Plaza Rodrigo Botet, 5. ℂ **96-398-10-00.** www.ayrehoteles.com. 204 units. 85€–96€ double; 95€–140€ junior suite; 120€–180€ suite. Bus: 9, 10, 27, 70, or 71. **Amenities:** Restaurant; bar; exercise room; Jacuzzi; room service; sauna; free Wi-Fi.

Hotel Ad Hoc Monumental ★★   Exposed brick walls and wooden beams lend a sense of warmth to this small hotel in a restored 1880s building. Well maintained guest rooms are comfortably, if somewhat sparely furnished. Several have outdoor terraces and all have good soundproofing. The hotel's location northeast of but near the cathedral and on the banks of the former riverbed turned green pathway is a real plus. It's convenient for exploring the central city—and for walking or bicycling to the City of Arts and Sciences. Bicycle rental is available.

Calle Boix, 4. ☎ **96-391-91-40.** www.adhochoteles.com. 28 units. 75€–130€ double; 110€–190€ triple. Parking 17€. Bus: 9, 35, 70, 71. Metro: Alameda. **Amenities:** Restaurant; bikes; room service; free Wi-Fi.

HUSA Reina Victoria ★★   The hotel's guest list reads like a "who's who" of Spanish movers and shakers, including everyone from King Alfonso XIII and bullfighter Manolete to Federico García Lorca and Pablo Picasso. The neoclassical-style building dates from 1913, but has been continuously updated to keep up with the needs of contemporary travelers. The decor tends to the traditional and comfortable formula of dark woods, well-padded upholstery, and rich fabrics in subdued colors—with a few neoclassical details for accent. Most rooms are small to mid-size. The central location—roughly equidistant to the Plaza de Toros and the cathedral—is handy for pedestrian sightseeing.

Calle Barcas, 4. ☎ **96-352-04-87.** www.husareinavictoria.com. 96 units. 65€–110€ double. Parking 20€. Bus: 4, 6, 7, 8, 14, or 27. Metro: Colón, Xàtiva. **Amenities:** Restaurant; bar; room service; free Wi-Fi.

Inglés Boutique Hotel ★★   For a treat, try to book a room with a view of the Museo Nacional de Cerámica so that you can wake up to a vision of the stunning baroque facade of the building. The hotel occupies the 18th-century former palace of the Duke of Cardona and maintains a sense of quiet decorum from the graceful main stairway to the tasteful traditional furnishings in the guest rooms. As you might expect of an older building, the rooms tend to vary in size, shape, and amenities. Some have private balconies and others are fairly small; inquire carefully when booking. A central location on an architecturally distinguished street is a plus.

Calle Marqués de Dos Aguas, 6. ☎ **96-351-64-26.** www.hotelinglesboutique.com. 63 units. 65€–132€ double. Parking 25€. Bus: 6, 9, 31, or 32. Metro: Colón. **Amenities:** Restaurant; bar; bikes; room service; Wi-Fi (6.50€/hr.).

Vincci Lys ★★   In many ways, Vincci Lys has the best of two worlds. Although it's close to the train station, it is centrally located for sightseeing, but because it sits on a pedestrian street lined with cafes and restaurants, the hotel has a welcoming, neighborhood feel. Light wood floors, pale walls, and clean-lined furnishings emphasize the generous proportions of many of the rooms, while dark fabrics add a bit of romance. If you are not bothered by street noise, request one of the rooms with a private balcony.

Calle Martínez Cubells, 5. ☎ **96-350-95-50.** www.vinccihoteles.com. 101 units. 65€–110€ double; 135€–200€ junior suite. Parking 27€. Bus: 4, 6, 8, 16, 35, or 36. **Amenities:** Restaurant; bar; concierge; room service; Wi-Fi (12€/day).

INEXPENSIVE

Catalonia Excelsior ★★   This hotel in a 1950s building near the Plaza del Ayuntamiento is a good bet for travelers on a budget. You can opt for a simple, basic double with modest furnishings or upgrade to a larger room, a room with a terrace, or a room with a hydromassage tub to work out the kinks after a day of sightseeing. All guests, however, enjoy the convenient location, good attention to housekeeping, and common terrace.

Calle Barcelonina, 5. ☎ **96-351-46-12.** www.hoteles-catalonia.es. 81 units. 59€–85€ double. Bus: 19, 35, 70, or 71. Metro: Colón. **Amenities:** Restaurant; bar; free Wi-Fi.

Hostal Venecia ★★   Budget travelers are usually pleasantly surprised when they arrive at the Venecia and behold the beautiful building right in the heart of town across the plaza from the town hall (*ayuntamiento*). Because the Venecia shares a staircase with private apartments in the same building, it is considered a *hostal* rather than a hotel, which by law limits the rates it can charge. Travelers reap the benefit, as the Hostal Venecia operates with all the efficiency of a small hotel, and staff tend to be friendly and knowledgeable. Wood paneling and decorative wallpapers lend a touch of style to the clean, simply furnished (and often small) rooms.

Plaza del Ayuntamiento, 3. © **96-352-42-67.** www.hotelvenecia.com. 54 units. 55€–85€ double. Parking nearby 15€. Bus: 19, 35, 70, or 71. Metro: Colón, Xàtiva. **Amenities:** Bikes; free Wi-Fi.

Where to Eat

EXPENSIVE

Eladio ★★ GALICIAN   One glance at the menu signals that chef-owner Eladio Rodríguez has not forgotten his Galician roots, even if he's transplanted them to a warmer and sunnier coast. The tank of live shellfish is just one signal that he's obsessed with freshness, and the menu itself basically advertises the fish of the Galician coast—hake, monkfish, fresh cod, salt cod, and turbot—prepared "Galician style." In general, this means simply roasted in an extremely hot oven with minimal garnish. He does serve cod with the Basque green sauce (*pil pil*), and offers some Valencian treats like red mullet with almond sauce. Meat eaters are in luck at Eladio as well, since Galicia prides itself on extraordinary beef. The kitchen already has a wood charcoal fire going for the fish, so it's no trouble to throw a T-bone on the coals or tuck a chateaubriand (for two) into the grill.

Calle Chiva, 40. © **96-384-22-44.** www.restauranteeladio.es. Reservations recommended. Main courses 20€–28€; tapas 11€–15€; tapas meal menu 30€. Mon 1–4pm; Tues–Sat 1–4pm and 9–11:30pm. Closed Aug. Bus: 3, 70, or 72. Metro: Av. del Cid (line 3 or 5).

La Pepica ★★★ SEAFOOD/VALENCIAN   The Picassos of paella are the cooks in La Pepica's sprawling kitchens. The restaurant faces onto Playa Malvarrosa, but if you approach from the town side, you can walk through those kitchens to the dining room. La Pepica has wowed royalty, movie stars, and—yes, even Ernest Hemingway—with its spectacular seafood and its multiple versions of paella since it was founded in 1898 Order the paella, and don't hesitate to take pictures when the waiter in striped vest and bowtie brings the pan for presentation before taking it to a station for plating. The place is huge, seating more than 400 diners, yet every table gets impeccable service. La Pepica paella is the benchmark for the dish everywhere else in the world.

Paseo Neptuno 6–8, Playa Malvarrosa. © **96-371-03-66.** www.lapepica.com. Reservations recommended. Main courses 20€–35€; tasting menu 27€–40€. Daily 1–4pm; Mon–Sat 8:30–11pm. Closed last 2 weeks of Nov. Bus: 32. Tram: 5. Marina Reial Joan Carles I.

La Sucursal ★★ CONTEMPORARY SPANISH   In a country where cutting-edge food is considered one of the liveliest indigenous art forms, it's only fitting that the contemporary art museum Instituto Valenciano de Arte Moderno (IVAM; p. 297) should boast a delightfully inventive restaurant. Bright and airy, it's easily one of the most glamorous eateries in the city, and the dishes are fascinating reinterpretations of the Spanish culinary canon. The country is obsessed with red meat, so Sucursal offers a tartar—of tomato with pickles and mustard. Scallops are almost always presented grilled or baked on the half shell, but here they're

DRINKING LIKE A LOCAL

To emulate the Valencianos, head to Barrio del Carmen to visit **Sant Jaume,** a cafe at Calle de Cavalleros, 51 (© **96-391-24-01**), and have a drink of *agua de Valencia*. It's a mixture of orange juice, Cointreau, and cava. The drink is said "to cure all that ails you," so it's appropriate that the building itself used to be an apothecary. An easy-to-miss tapas bar, beloved by local foodies, is at the front entrance to the restaurant **Ca'n Bermell,** Calle Santo Tomás, 18 (© **96-391-02-88**). The city's most famous drink, *horchata*, made with ground tiger nuts, is best at **Horchatería El Siglo,** Plaza Plaza Santa Catalina, 11 (© **96-391-84-66**).

featured with edamame in a green soup called "liquid herbs." Instead of paella, there's a soupy *caldoso* of creamy rice with sea lettuce and spinach. Even the venerable roast hake gets a novel treatment with a *pil pil* sauce of soft seaweed.

Calle Guillém de Castro, 118. © **96-374-66-65**. www.restaurantelasucursal.com. Reservations required. Main courses 25€–34€; fixed-price menus 48€–70€. Mon–Fri 1–3:30pm and 8:30–11:30pm; Sat 8:30–11:30pm. Closed 1 week in Aug. Bus: 5. Metro: Túria.

MODERATE

El Poblet ★★★ VALENCIAN/MEDITERANEAN   Chef-owner Quique Dacosta hails from the coastal village of Dénia (famous for its shellfish) and rose to fame as one of Spain's most provocative young chefs. His philosophical writings deconstruct the traditions of seafood cuisine in eastern Iberia and then reconstruct them to match a contemporary avant-garde aesthetic. That all sounds very high-falutin' and has certainly made him the darling of critics, but he can also walk the walk, and his radical cuisine looks beautiful, tastes delicious, and is reasonably priced. The comfortable contemporary dining room in the heart of the city features an a la carte menu grounded in fish and shellfish—dishes like cold red prawns served as a centerpiece of a dinner salad, or grilled fish with grilled snow peas atop a "pasta" of zucchini noodles and bean sprouts. His tasting menus are reasonably priced, and he offers a midday "Grace Kelly" menu (so-called because it is beautiful and elegant) Monday to Friday.

Calle Correos, 8, first floor. © **96-111-11-06**. www.elpobletrestaurante.com. Reservations required. Main courses 18€–20€; Grace Kelly menu 30€; tasting menus 45€–60€. Tues–Sat 1:30–3:30pm and 8:30–10:30pm. Bus: 10, 13, 81, N1 N8. Metro: Colón.

El Timonel ★★ MEDITERRANEAN/SEAFOOD   The decor of this surprisingly good seafood restaurant leans a little too far toward nautical clichés for our taste, but even its looks may be tired, the seafood is fresh and simply presented. El Timonel lists the catch of the day—gilthead bream, cod, flounder, Mediterranean sea bass—and a selection of preparations. They can range from simply grilled or roasted in the oven in a salt crust to steamed in paper or pan-fried with an almond sauce. Meat dishes tend to star the deeply marbled Galician beef from Lugo.

Calle Félix Pizcueta, 13. © **96-352-63-00**. www.eltimonel.com. Reservations recommended. Main courses 17€–29€. Tues–Sun 1:30–4:30pm and 8:15–11:30pm. Metro: Corte Inglés.

La Lola ★ MEDITERRANEAN/INTERNATIONAL   This snazzy little restaurant in Barrio del Carmen has definite attitude, with a contemporary decor that harks back to Op Art and a kitchen inspired by elBulli on a budget—right down to Adrià's rediscovery of simplicity. So it's possible to start with something as straightforward as a single perfect anchovy with toast smeared with tomato, or as complex as braised octopus with creamy potatoes and roasted red peppers. Lola also serves a full range of *caldosas,* rice dishes a little soupier than paellas. Regulars favor the version with duck, wild mushrooms, and crisp bits of ham.

Calle Subida del Toledano, 8. ✆ **96-391-80-45.** www.lalolarestaurante.com. Reservations required. Main courses 17€–25€; fixed-price dinner 25€, lunch 15€ (Mon–Thurs only). Mon–Sat 2–4pm and 9pm–2am; Sun 2–4pm. Bus: 2, 4, 6, or 7.

Palace Fesol ★ VALENCIAN   More than a century old, the "bean palace" earned its name with recherché fava bean dishes, but the restaurant has evolved into a rather elegant dining room specializing in all manner of traditional Valencian cuisine. If you want to know how a local dish is cooked in the classic manner, order it here. There are many variants of paella and *caldosa* on the menu, and even a few fava bean dishes. Chances are, though, the waiter will advise that you try the catch of the day. He'll be right, and you can always get some favas as a side dish. Make reservations.

Calle Hernán Cortés, 7. ✆ **96-352-93-23.** www.palacefesol.com. Main courses 15€–26€. Tues–Sun 1–4pm and 9–11pm. Closed Sat–Sun July–Aug. Bus: 5. Metro: Colón.

INEXPENSIVE

Casa Montaña ★ TAPAS   Hungry Valencianos have bellied up to the bar at this bodega since 1836. The once-rough neighborhood used to be inhabited by fishermen and dock workers, but Casa Montaña led the revival (and some say) gentrification. Dock workers still come in, but they're as likely to be crew off the racing yachts as stevedores. Class truly doesn't matter here, as everyone is welcome. The room is jammed with large wine barrels (most of them full), and the kitchen serves an almost encyclopedic range of tapas, with an emphasis on fish. Don't miss the ancient Saracen *titaina* casserole made with tuna belly, chopped tomatoes and peppers, and graced with toasted pine nuts. The wine cellar is extensive, and if you admire the list, owner Emiliano Garcia might invite you to tour the cellars.

Calle José Benlliure, 69. ✆ **96-367-23-14.** www.emilianobodega.com. Tapas 5€–20€. Mon–Sat noon–3:30pm and 8–11:30pm; Sun 12:30–3:30pm. Metro: Mediterrani. Tram: Grau–Canyamelar.

Exploring Valencia

There are three primary areas of interest in Valencia: the old, formerly walled city centered on the cathedral and Plaza de la Reina, the City of Arts & Sciences southeast of the old city on the dry riverbed, and the port and beach district east of the old city. The 14th-century Gothic Torres de Serranos on the north side of the city formed the main gate to Valencia; the old western gate was formed by the Torres de Quart. The former riverbed is a linear park and often makes pleasant walking. Just west of the old city gate, Torres de Quart, stands the original University of Valencia and the **Jardí Botànic** ★ (Calle Quart, 80; ✆ **96-315-68-00;** www.jardibotanic.org; 2€ adults, 1€ seniors and students, free under age 7; 10am–dusk; Metro: Túria or Angel Guimerà), which makes a pleasant respite from summer heat. Founded by the university in 1567, it was long a garden and orchard of medicinal plants, and botany classes are still offered. Today the botanical garden boasts one of the most important collections of varied tree life and palms in Europe. In all, nearly 45,000 international species are displayed.

Catedral (Seu) ★★ CATHEDRAL   Few buildings in Valencia are as old—or as looming—as its medieval cathedral, built in fortress-like style between 1252 and 1482 on the former site of the Grand Mosque. Naturally enough, the cathedral embodies several design styles, but good old Spanish Gothic predominates. Behind the cathedral proper is a handsome domed basilica. Since the late 15th century, the cathedral's claim to fame is that it possesses the purported **Holy Grail.** The agate and gold chalice figures prominently in such mythic tales as Sir Thomas Malory's *Le Morte d'Arthur,* Tennyson's *Idylls of the King,* and Wagner's *Parsifal.* Depending on which legend you prefer, the vessel was either used by Jesus at the Last Supper or by Joseph of Arimathea to collect Jesus's blood as it dripped from the cross. After touring the cathedral, you can climb the stairway inside the unfinished 47m-high (154-ft.) Gothic tower known as **Miguelete** ★ ("Micalet" in Valenciano). It affords a panoramic view of the city and the fertile orchards and truck gardens beyond. Or visit the **Museo de la Catedral,** which has minor works by Goya and Zurbarán.

Plaza de la Reina. ✆ **96-391-81-27.** www.catedraldevalencia.es. Admission to cathedral free; Miguelete 2€; Museo de la Catedral 4.50€. Cathedral daily 7:30am–1pm and 4:30–8:30pm. Miguelete Mon–Sat 10am–7pm, Sun 10am–1:30pm and 7–9pm. Museo de la Catedral Mon–Fri 10am–1pm and 4–7pm. Bus: 9, 27, 70, or 71.

Ciutat de les Arts i les Ciències (City of Arts and Sciences) ★★★

MUSEUM   Since the Palau de les Arts Reina Sofía opened in 2005 as the final jewel in the cultural crown, the City of Arts and Sciences has become as emblematic of Valencia as Frank O. Gehry's Guggenheim Museum is emblematic of Bilbao. Valencianos' chests swell a little bigger as they inform you that Valencia didn't have to go overseas for a great architect. It already had native son Santiago Calatrava, the engineer-architect previously known for visionary bridge designs. His construction innovations played a large role in creating soaring vistas and

Valencia's Catedral.

THE fires THAT CLEANSE

Valencia goes insane every year March 15 to 19, which is the only way to explain the whirlwind of parades, music, fireworks, controlled explosions outside city hall, and general madcap revelry that continues around the clock. The festival is called **Las Fallas,** and it's not for the faint of heart—or the easily startled.

The origins of Las Fallas are vague but seem to lie in the 18th-century practice of Valencian carpenters celebrating spring by burning their winter lampposts. A century later, the lampposts had morphed into satirical figures that would all be burned in a main plaza on St. Joseph's Day (March 19). New materials like foam core and polyester films have allowed the fallero artists to be ever more outrageous. The figures are erected in 300 or more squares of the city. Some are eight stories high and can cost up to $1 million each. They represent a wide array of political and pop cultural subjects, and the satire can be both biting and bawdy.

Yet solemn piety is also a part of Las Fallas. During the day, parades of characters who seem to have stepped out of a Goya painting bring bouquets of pink, white, and red carnations to the Plaza de la Virgen. The men look like 18th-century dandies, the women like ladies of the court in their full-skirted silk brocade dresses, hair combs, and mantillas. Once they hand over their flowers to be affixed to the skirts of a five-story-high Madonna, they weep and take pictures.

During the 45-minute **Fire Parade,** costumed figures of devils, grim reapers, and jesters whirl down the streets to the pounding rhythms of drum corps. Many swing scythes or carry hoses that spew streams of sparks overhead.

The strangest spectacle of all is the **mascletà,** a pyrotechnic extravaganza whose main purpose must be to sell hearing aids. Thousands of people crowd the streets around City Hall Plaza waiting for the fuses to be lit on approximately 1 million firecrackers and other concussive devices. They begin exploding with an innocuous pop-pop-pop and build to bone-shaking booms.

The grand finale occurs between midnight and 1 am, when all but two "pardoned" figurines are torched in a blazing inferno that feels like a cross between Mardi Gras and the bombing of Baghdad. For Valencianos, it's a way to get rid of the old and welcome in the new. To the uninitiated, it is both unnerving and exhilarating.

The **Museu Faller** (Plaza de Montolivet, 4; © **96-352-54-78, x4625;** www.fallas.com. Tues-Sat 10am-6pm, Sun 10am-3pm;) preserves some historic figures from past festivals along with photos, paintings, and posters of the exuberant excess. Admission is 2€, free on Sunday and holidays.

seemingly weightless structures in the 36-hectare (89-acre) site south of the city on the dry riverbed created by channeling the Río Túria underground. Félix Candela, the Spanish architect who had spent most of his career in exile, contributed one of the structures, and his technical expertise with thin-shell concrete was critical to Calatrava's designs for the other three major buildings. The complex makes a great family outing, and if you plan to visit more than one major structure, check for discounts on combined admissions.

The first building to open (1998) was Calatrava's **L'Hemisfèric ★★**, a structure that resembles a giant eye and eyelid and contains a massive IMAX theater, a planetarium, and a laser show.

The Ciutat de les Arts i les Ciències.

El Museu de les Ciències Príncipe Felipe ★ has a similarly playful construction. The interactive science museum resembles the skeleton of a whale. The exhibits tend to be "gee-whiz" amusements (superheroes, the science of sports, etc.) more than truly educational exhibits, and much of the ground level is now devoted to a basketball court. If your time is limited, this building is perhaps best admired from outside.

Candela's chief design contribution, **L'Oceanogràfic** ★★, is the largest oceanographic aquarium in Europe. He designed it in the shape of a water lily, and used an exaggerated parabola to maximize the ability of the concrete structure to support itself without buttresses. As a result, it is both graceful and otherworldly when viewed from a distance. Within the enveloping structure, the individual displays of marine habitats seem intimate and immediate. The areas are connected by underwater glass walkways.

Panoramic elevators and stairways connect the multiple levels at the airy **Palau de les Arts Reina Sofía** ★★, a 14-story glass-and-metal opera house and performing arts structure. The "palace" contains four massive rooms for performances and is surrounded by walkway plazas and a landscape that contains as much open water as solid ground.

The entire complex is a favorite of skateboarders, who find the angles, ramps, parallel walks, and other features terrifically challenging. It is also popular with fashion photographers, who find the abstraction and grand scale of the architecture a particularly dramatic setting. The "city" also serves as the site of the annual **Festival Eclèctic,** part of the Feria in July. It features four to five free outdoor concerts and several days of free performances by acrobats, martial artists, and street performers.

Av. Autopista del Saler 1, 3, 5, 7. ☏ **90-210-00-31.** www.cac.es. Admission to L'Hemisfèric 8.80€ adults; 6.85€ children 12 and under, students, and seniors. Admission to Museu de les Ciències Príncipe Felipe 8.00€ adults; 6.20€ children 16 and under, students, and seniors. Admission to L'Oceanogràfic 28€ adults; 21€ children 12 and under, students, and seniors. L'Hemisfèric daily 10am–9pm. Museu de les Ciències Príncipe Felipe and L'Oceanogràfic daily 10am–7pm (to midnight July–Sept). Bus: 19, 35, 40, or 95 to Centro Comercio de Saler.

Institut Valencia d'Art Modern (IVAM) ★ ART MUSEUM   IVAM opened in 1989 as Spain's first contemporary art museum. An ultramodern building, it's anchored by the welded-iron sculptures of the abstract/Cubist artist **Julio González** (1876–1942). The museum was bequeathed 394 works by González that range from drawing and paintings to jewelry and his signature welded steel sculpture. The museum also possesses an extensive collection of the works by Valencian painter **Ignacio Pinazo** (1849–1916), whose stylistic experiments were notably abstract and avant-garde in their day. Other strengths of the collections include 20th-century photography and photo-collage, pop art, and new media. Use a separate entrance for the Sala Muralla, so-named because it preserves a portion of the city's medieval walls. The museum is on the western edge of the old city.

Calle Guillém Castro, 118. ✆ **96-386-30-00.** www.ivam.es. Admission 2€ adults, 1€ students, free for seniors. Tues–Sun 10am–7pm. Bus: 8, 28, or 29. Metro: Túria.

Lonja de la Seda ★ LANDMARK   Master mason Pere Compte constructed this fortified hall between 1482 and 1533 as Valencia's silk exchange. Listed as a UNESCO World Heritage Site, it is considered a top example of Gothic civic architecture. A forest of twisted-wheat columns supports the main trading hall, and the tranquil central courtyard features orange trees and a fountain. School children on field trips are usually extremely amused by the gargoyles representing bodily functions usually performed outside of public view.

Plaza Mercado, s/n. ✆ **96-352-54-78.** Free. Tues–Sat 10am–2pm and 4:30–8:30pm, Sun 10am–3pm. Metro: Xàtiva or Colón.

Mercado Central ★★★ MARKET   This Modernista cathedral of food is one of the grandest food markets in Spain, rivaling La Boqueria in Barcelona (p. 342). It's a great place to pick up Valencia oranges (in season) to snack on and to see the exquisite produce grown in the little truck farms (*huertas*) that surround the city. Near the front of the market you will find several stalls where smoked paprika is piled in high cones and tins of saffron can be purchased for a comparative bargain. Even if you're not buying, be sure to visit to see which produce is in season and what fish are truly fresh.

Plaza Mercado, s/n. ✆ **96-382-91-01.** www.mercadocentralvalencia.es. Free. Mon–Sat 7:30am–2:30pm. Metro: Xàtiva or Colón.

Museo de Bellas Artes ★★ ART MUSEUM   In late 2013, the museum inaugurated its **Sala Sorolla,** an exhibition hall hung with 42 major works by the gifted Valencian painter Joaquin Sorolla (1863–1923). It's the most extensive collection of his paintings outside the Museo Sorolla in Madrid (p. 106) and chronicles his career from art student years in Rome to some of his final compositions. The charming museum is also strong in Flemish art and includes a smattering of most of the major Spanish painters from Ribera and Murillo through Goya. Unique is the collection of so-called Valencian "primitives," who continued to work in a Gothic style in the 14th and 15th centuries.

Calle San Pío V, 9. ✆ **96-387-03-00.** www.museobellasartesvalencia.gva.es. Free admission. Tues–Sun 10am–8pm. Bus: 1, 5, 6, 8, 16, 26, 29, 36, 79, or 95. Metro: Alameda, Pont de Fusta.

Palacio de Marqués de Dos Aguas ★ MUSEUM   This late Gothic palace was remade in the 18th century with a rococo exterior dominated by Ignacio Vergara's figures of "Dos Aguas" (Two Waters), the palace's namesake. The building was a landmark long before the private ceramic collections of Manuel González

Martí and his wife Amelia Cuñat were installed here in 1947 to create the **Museo Nacional de Cerámica.** With its long history of fine ceramic art, Valencia was a fitting location. The museum is of most interest to collectors, who will find the nuances of regional styles fascinating.

Calle Poeta Querol, 2. ℰ **96-351-63-92.** http://mnceramica.mcu.es. Admission 3€ adults, 1.50€ students and seniors. Tues–Sun 10am–2pm; Tues–Sat 4–8pm. Metro: Plaza de los Pinazo.

Outdoor Activities

BEACHES
Valencia boasts more than 2.8km (1¾ miles) of beaches (*playas*) with excellent facilities. Just minutes from the city center, **Playa Arenas ★** and **Playa Malvarrosa ★** are certified European blue-flag beaches, an indication of clear, unpolluted waters. Adjoining these beaches is the seafront promenade, **Paseo Marítimo ★.** The beaches to the north and south of the port, Playa de la Punta and Playa de Levante, are too polluted for swimming. However, if you head south, you'll reach **El Saler,** where you'll again see the European blue flag.

BOATING
Real Club Náutico de Valencia, Camí del Canal, 91 (ℰ **96-367-90-11;** www.rcnauticovalencia.com), has a sailing school that rents boats for scuba diving and snorkeling. It maintains a full yacht-service facility.

Shopping
You haven't seen Valencia until you've visited the 1920s **Mercado Central ★★★** (p. 297) to marvel at the beautifully displayed meats, fish, and produce, and to purchase *bomba* rice, smoked paprika, and a paella pan to bring home.

If you are in town on a Sunday morning, head to the open-air market at **Plaza Redonda,** near the cathedral. Vendors offer traditional Valencian handicrafts, including ceramics, ironwork, silver items, and inlaid marquetry. You'll also find equally colorful items from other parts of Spain and even Morocco. If you're more interested in seeing what Valencianos have been storing in their attics, reserve Sunday for the flea market on Avenida de Suecia.

Playa Malvarrosa.

Shop for fresh food at Mercado Central.

Spain's ubiquitous **El Corte Inglés** department store has several locations in Valencia, including Calle Colon, 1 and 27 and Calle Pintor Sorolla, 27 (© **96-315-95-00;** www.clcorteingles.com). We like the fact that these stores stock local handicrafts and other goods along with more general merchandise. They are always a good bet for one-stop shopping.

Serious shoppers will enjoy browsing around the **Plaza del Ayuntamiento** and along the streets of **Don Juan de Austria, Colón, Sorní,** and **Cirilo Amorós.** The **Mercado de Colon** (Calle Jorge Juan, 19; © **96-352-54-78**), a Gaudi-inspired fantasy dating from 1916, is a good stop for a break at one of its cafes. Several streets around the market also attract shoppers, including Calle Conde de Salvatierra, home to **Cacao Sampaka** (Calle Conde de Salvatierra, 19; © **96-353-40-62;** www.cacaosampaka.com), a branch of the original co-founded by Ferran Adrià's brother Albert in Barcelona.

Valencia is known for its embroidered shawls, and **Nela** (Calle San Vicente Mártir, 2; © **96-392-30-23**) has an excellent selection, along with fans, leather goods, and other items. Spain's famous Lladró porcelain figurines are made in a factory just outside the city. For a full range displayed in an elegant setting, seek out **Lladró** (Calle Poeta Querol, 9; © **96-351-16-25;** www.lladro.com). If you wish to visit the **Lladró Museum** in the suburb of Tavernas Blanques, ask the shop staff to assist with reservations.

Entertainment & Nightlife

Where you go at night in Valencia depends on when you visit. The best area in the cooler months is historic **Barrio Carmen,** in the city center. Valencia is famous for its *marcha* (nightlife) and for its bohemian bars. **Calle Alta** is a good street on which to start your bar-crawl, as is the historic core around **Plaza del Ayuntamiento.**

A longtime local favorite is **Cafeteria Barcas 7,** at the same address as the name (© **96-352-12-33**), among banks and office buildings in the heart of town directly north of Estación del Norte. It serves drinks and tapas (including small servings of paella) at the stand-up bar. You could stop here for your first cup of coffee at 7am and for your final nightcap at 1am. There is often live music in the evening. It's open daily from 7am to 1am. Drink prices start at 1.50€, and tapas cost 4€.

In the Barrio Carmen, **Disco City,** Calle Pintor Zariñena 16 (© **96-391-41-51**), is a dance club with black-on-black decor and a wall of mirrors lining the dance floor. It attracts the under-30 crowd, who come here to dance to funk, soul, and R&B. It's definitely for late-nighters: The scene doesn't get rolling until 3am. Cover is usually 15€.

In summer, the emphasis switches to the beach, **Playa Malvarrosa.** Everyone from teens to 40-somethings congregates around open-air bars, which play music, often have dance floors, and are open from late May to September. Drinks usually cost 4€ to 6€. There are also discos in this part of town, one of which is the salsa room at **Akuarela Playa** (© **96-385-93-85;** www.akuarela.es), Calle Eugenia Viñes 152. Cover is 12€ to 17€, and drinks are several euros more than in the open-air bars.

Valencia is Spain's third-largest city and, after Madrid and Barcelona, the country's biggest gay center. Most of the action is in the historic center in the **Barrio Carmen,** particularly along Calle Quart. Valencia is a progressive, liberal city, and visitors need have no fear about being "out" on the street. The best publication for what's happening, and when, is Madrid-based *Shangay,* distributed free in gay establishments and available online at **www.shangay.com.**

The **Palau de la Música ★★**, Paseo de la Alameda, 30 (© **96-357-50-20;** www.palaudevalencia.com; Metro: Alameda), presents an impressive array of 200-plus programs a year. The most prestigious orchestras in the world, as well as directors and soloists, appear here. Between September and October, the Valencia Orchestra is in residence. The hall seats 1,793 and has wonderful acoustics. After a concert here, Plácido Domingo claimed that "Palau is a Stradivarius." An on-site art gallery is open daily from 10:30am to 1:30pm and 5:30 to 9pm. Ticket prices vary, but are generally in the 10€-to-90€ range.

Valencia's Plaza de Toros.

Palau de les Arts Reina Sofía ★★, Autopista del Saler 1 (© **96-197-58-00;** www.lesarts.com), is the grand opera house of Valencia. It's housed in a futuristic, helmet-shaped building that is part of the City of Arts and Sciences (p. 294). Some of the world's most prestigious opera companies perform here. Tickets, costing from 20€ to 175€, are sold at the box office Monday to Friday noon to 8pm.

Neighboring Catalunya may have outlawed bullfights, but *corridas* still figure prominently in Valencian life. The first fight season of the year is during Las Fallas in March. Fights resume from Easter through May, and start up again in early October. Valencia's **Plaza de Toros** is one of the largest rings in Spain; it's adjacent to the rail station at Calle de Xàtiva, 28 (© **96-351-93-15;** www.toros-valencia.com). Tours of the ring and adjacent museum are offered all year Monday to Saturday for 10€ for adults, 8€ ages 7 to 16. Contact TorosValenciaTour at © **65-111-61-39** or www.torosvalenciatour.com.

Side Trip from Valencia

PARQUE NATURAL DE L'ALBUFERA ★★

Only about 13km (8 miles) south of the city center on N-332, this stunning region is also easily visited by bicycle, as much of the roadway is paralleled by a bicycle path. (See "Getting Around," p. 286, for bike-rental details.)

Rice farmers have labored in the flooded fields around **L'Albufera**—an inlet closed off from the sea for so long that the water has become fresh—since the A.D. 700s, but the 21-sq.-km (8-sq.-mile) ecosystem of freshwater lake, lagoons, and barrier beach and dunes was only declared a natural reserve in 1986. Rice fields still cover about two-thirds of the area, and produce the bulk of the tall, hard-to-cultivate Bomba strain that's optimal for paella.

Nowhere is the contrast of built and natural environments as striking as at the beach in the village of **El Saler.** The eastern view zeroes in on cargo ships and tankers in Valencia's industrial port, yet shore birds practically cover the beach of smooth flat stones. El Saler sits between the sea and the freshwater lake. You may see fishermen in small, flat-bottomed boats on the lake, mostly catching mullet or collecting American red crayfish, a crustacean introduced in the 1970s that is prized for paella. The wetlands between fresh water and salt water rank among the Iberian Peninsula's most important breeding grounds for night, squacco, and purple herons (more than 5,000 breeding pairs) and four varieties of terns. For details on birding in the park, see exhibits and bird check-list at the **Racó de l'Olla Centre d'Interpretación** (© **96-162-73-45;** http://parquesnaturales.gva.es), located at the El Palmar turnoff from CV-500. The center is open daily 9am to 2pm, as well as Tuesday and Thursday 4 to 5:30pm from May through October.

ALICANTE ★★

Alicante (Alacant), capital of the Costa Blanca, is popular in both summer and winter, especially with Brits and northern Europeans who have been coming here in droves since the mid–20th century. The compact city combines an atmospheric old quarter, a dramatic and historic bluff-top fortress, a sparkling yacht harbor, and excellent beaches. The waterfront promenade is a swirling delight, and there's even an air of exoticism in the substantial African immigrant population, many of whom wear the native costumes of sub-Saharan Africa.

Playa San Juan ★, the largest beach in Alicante, is 5km (3 miles) east of the old city, and can be quickly reached by tram. It is lined with villas, hotels, and restaurants. The bay of Alicante has two capes, and on the bay is **Playa Postiguet** ★ at the foot of the bluff topped by a castle.

Essentials

GETTING THERE   Alicante's **Internacional El Altet Airport** (✆ **96-691-90-00;** www.aena.es) is 19km (12 miles) from the city. There are up to 11 daily flights from Madrid, about three flights per week each from Sevilla and Barcelona. Fifteen buses daily connect the city to the airport; the fare is 3.50€. The **Iberia Airlines** ticket office (✆ **90-240-05-00;** www.iberia.com) is at the airport.

Ten **trains** a day make the trip from Valencia, taking 1½ to 2 hours. and costing 20€ to 30€. Eight trains a day come from Barcelona (trip time: 5–5½ hr.), and 10 a day from Madrid (trip time: 2¼–4½ hr.). The RENFE office is at **Estación Alicante,** Avenida Salamanca (✆ **90-232-03-20;** www.renfe.es).

Bus lines from various parts of the coast converge at the terminus, Calle Portugal, 17 (✆ **96-513-07-00**). There is almost hourly service from Valencia (trip time: 4 hr.). Buses also run from Madrid, a 5- to 6-hour trip.

To drive here, take the E-15 expressway south along the coast from Valencia. The expressway and N-340 run northeast from Murcia.

VISITOR INFORMATION   The **tourist information office** is at Rambla de Mendez Núñez (✆ **96-520-00-00;** www.alicanteturismo.com). It's open Monday to Friday 9am to 8pm, Saturday 10am to 8pm, and Sunday 10am to 2pm.

FAST FACTS   For medical assistance, go to the **Hospital General,** Calle Maestro Alonso 109 (✆ **96-593-83-00**). In an emergency, dial ✆ **112;** to reach the city police, call ✆ **96-514-95-00.**

Where to Stay

EXPENSIVE

Hotel Spa Porta Maris & Suites del Mar ★★★   Dominating the pier on the cruise port jetty, this pair of sister hotels is our hands-down choice for a luxurious stay in Alicante at a price that doesn't break the bank. We especially enjoy turning off the air-conditioning and sliding open the door to the terrace to go to sleep to the sound of the waves. The Porta Maris section was built first, and the rooms, while spacious by Spanish standards, are smaller than those in the more luxe Suites del Mar. They share an entrance, a reception area (different desks), and a casual restaurant. The Suites del Mar are larger and more comfortable; its guests also have exclusive use of a pool, spa, and lounge, as well as a separate café for breakfast and daytime snacks. Guests at both properties enjoy free admission and drink at Alicante's casino.

Plaza Puerta del Mar, 3. ✆ **96-514-70-21** (Porta Maris) or ✆ **96-514-70-22** (Suites del Mar). www. hotelspaportamaris.com. 132 units in hotel; 47 units in Suites del Mar. 105€–145€ double room; hotel suites 145€–195€; Suites del Mar 150€–260€. Parking 12€. **Amenities:** 2 restaurants; 2 bars; babysitting; children's programs; exercise room; health club; room service; spa; free Wi-Fi.

Meliã Alicante ★★   All 544 rooms at this ocean-liner-sized beach hotel face outward to look at Playa Postiguet on one side or the spiffy Alicante marina on the other, and each has a small balcony to step out and enjoy the sea air. The hotel was built in 1973, and all rooms are identically sized at 26 sq. m (280 sq. ft.), while the junior suites are all 54 sq. m (580 sq. ft.). The current decor plays up the vast expanses of travertine marble and pops of saturated primary colors in the draperies and bed spreads. For a more luxe experience, you can step up to the Meliã chain's "The Level" for rooms with somewhat finer finishes, access to a private lounge with open bar, and an elevation that provides even better views.

Plaza del Puerto, 3. ✆ **800-336-3542** in the U.S., or 96-520-50-00. www.solmelia.com. 544 units. 109€–194€ double; 227€–270€ suite. Parking 23€. **Amenities:** 2 restaurants; 2 bars; babysitting; children's programs; exercise room; health club and spa; 2 freshwater pools (1 heated indoor, 1 outdoor); room service; spa; free ASDL broadband and Wi-Fi.

MODERATE

Abba Centrum Alicante ★   Completely remodeled in 2013, this contemporary business hotel is located in the middle of the commercial district, but really only a 5-minute walk from the waterfront. By stepping away from the sea, you get a lot of room for the price, and it does include Wi-Fi. Room pricing can be erratic, as the hotel is popular with Spanish companies for incentive meetings, and room prices shoot up when the suits are in town. Added perk: The exercise area has a Moroccan-style hammam.

Calle Pinto Lorenzo Casanova, 33. ✆ **96-513-04-40.** www.abbacentrumalicante.com. 148 rooms. 59€–85€ double; 92€–140€ suite. Parking 15€. **Amenities:** Restaurant; bar; concierge; exercise room (w/hamman); room service; sauna; free Wi-Fi.

INEXPENSIVE

Hostal Les Monges Palace ★★   A rather charming hodgepodge of conjoined buildings with exposed brick and stone and extensive tilework, Les Monges has served as a lodging since 1989. The location near the city government offices places you smack in the middle of town, and the decor of the rooms, while modest, is hardly as monkish as the name would suggest. The single suite, in fact, is decorated with Japanese-style furnishings, including a bed so low that you almost have to kneel first to lie down. There's a whimsical charm about it all, and the family that operates the "palace" has a real sense of hospitality. They are genuinely excited to share their beloved Alicante with guests. The shared rooftop patio has charming views of the roofs and chimneys of old Alicante.

Calle San Agustín, 4. ✆ **96-521-50-46.** www.lesmonges.es. 18 rooms. 45€–60€ double; 100€ suite. Parking 12€. Bus: 22. **Amenities:** Bar; free Wi-Fi.

Pensión Portugal ★   Who says you can't do a beach town on the cheap? The tiny but immaculate rooms in this upstairs pension near the bus station are fine places to sleep, and they do have air-conditioning, a must in tight city quarters during most of the year. Some open onto the central courtyard, while the exterior units all have tiny private terraces. Only eight rooms have private bathrooms with showers, but the shared bathrooms in the corridors are actually more spacious. The beach is only a 10-minute walk away, the harbor about 5 minutes.

Calle Portugal, 26. ✆ **96-592-92-44.** www.pensionportugal.es. 20 units, 8 with private bathroom. 36€–40€ double w/shared bathroom; 42€–46€ double w/private bathroom. No credit cards. Bus: 22. **Amenities:** Free Wi-Fi.

Where to Eat

Alicanteros eat rice in almost every imaginable way. The most typical sauce is aioli, a kind of mayonnaise made from oil, egg yolks, and garlic. Dessert selections are the most varied on the Costa Blanca; *turrón de Alicante* (Spanish nougat) is the most popular.

Nou Manolín ★★ TAPAS/VALENCIAN   The fish tapas of Alicante are famous all over Spain—top Michelin-starred chefs often come to town on tapas-eating holidays. One of the places they come is Nou Manolín, where everyone from deckhands to stevedores to upscale tourists mingles at the bar, drinking the local wines and making a meal of little plates of batter-fried anchovies, garlicky grilled shrimp, sizzling casseroles of sausages—more than 50 choices in all. The upstairs dining room is far more elegant, and emphasizes local fish and the beautiful vegetables of the Alicante coast. (In 2012, French chef Joel Robuchon declared it his favorite place to eat in Spain.) The menu features many rice dishes, but the best bet is often the catch of the day baked in a salt crust.

Calle Villegas 3. ℭ **96-520-03-68.** www.noumanolin.com. Reservations recommended. Main courses 17€–32€. Daily 1:15–4pm and 8:15pm–1:15am. Bus: 22.

Restaurante Dársena ★ VALENCIAN   If you're looking for paella in Alicante, look no farther. Dársena offers more than 100 versions of the baked rice dish, including a number using various organ meats. Located on a pier in the harbor, this glamorous dining room is often the first choice of the yachtsmen who put in at Alicante. Generally speaking, all rice dishes are prepared for a minimum of two diners. The menu also offers a half-dozen meat options and another half-dozen fish plates. The fish are usually the best bet, but be sure to ask about the catch of the day. To eat farmed salmon (which is on the menu here) would be a shame, given that the Mediterranean laps at the pilings beneath the restaurant.

Marina Deportiva, Muelle de Levante, 6. ℭ **96-520-75-89.** www.darsena.com. Reservations required at lunch. Main courses 12€–32€; fixed-price menu from 22€. Daily 1:30–4:30pm and Mon–Sat 8:30–11:30pm. Bus: 22.

Restaurante Monastrell ★★★ VALENCIAN   María José San Román is Alicante's only Michelin-starred chef, and she earned it the hard way. Having trained with top Basque chefs Martín Berasategui and Juan Marí Arzak and worked at the El Celler de Can Roca in Girona (p. 395), San Román has developed a sophisticated style all her own that is grounded in the local Levantine gastronomy. The restaurant is named for the indigenous black grape of the area, and the chef probably uses more Alicante saffron in her cooking than any other chef in Spain. In fact, she's celebrated for finding innovative ways to use saffron to enhance flavors without imparting the characteristic aroma. Main dishes draw on hearty cooking of the interior (roast lamb with crisp red peppers and bread crumbs) as well as the coast (tuna neck confit with potato sauce and sea vegetables). The Monastrell Barra on the same premises offers an innovative tapas menu inside a sleek room with walls made of slate.

Calle Rafael Altamira, 7. ℭ **96-520-03-63.** www.monastrell.com. Reservations required. Main courses 17€–25€; daily 5-course menu 38€, personalized 6-course tasting menu 65€. Monastrell Barra tapas 8€, raciones 15€. Tues–Sat 1:15–4pm and 8:15pm–midnight. Bus: 22.

La Taberna del Gourmet ★★ TAPAS/VALENCIAN   This snazzy contemporary tapas restaurant is Alicante's other destination for visiting gourmet chefs. Essentially a gastrobar of what its owners call "auteur cuisine," it is run by María José San Román of Monastrell (above) and her daughter Geni Perramón. Far more than a bar, La Taberna del Gourmet is a deli, a dining room, and a virtual museum of contemporary tapas. The full menu offers more than 100 dishes that range from a few bites of goat cheese with herbs and honey to a bowl of black rice with cuttlefish, prawns, artichokes, and red peppers. Special tasting menus of 9 or 11 tapas are available if at least two people at the table elect the option.

Calle San Fernando, 10. © **96-520-42-33.** www.latabernadelgourmet.com. Tapas 4€–16€, raciones 12€–32€. Daily 11am–12:30am. Bus: 22.

Exploring Alicante

With its wide, palm-lined avenues, this town was made for sauntering. The magnificent **Explanada d'Espanya** ★ wraps around part of the yacht harbor under a parade of palm trees. Its mosaic sidewalks have wave patterns so realistic that they've been known to give inebriated visitors a touch of motion sickness. Off the esplanade are lovely marble-paved squares such as **Plaza Gabriel Miró** and **Portal de Elche.**

High on a hill, the stately if decrepit **Castell de Santa Bárbara** (© **96-526-31-31**) towers over the bay and provincial capital. The Greeks called the fort Akra Leuka (White Peak). Its original defenses, erected by the Carthaginians in 400 b.c. were later used by the Romans and the Arabs. The fortress's grand scale is evident in its moats, drawbridges, tunneled entrances, guardrooms, cisterns, underground storerooms, hospitals, batteries, powder stores, barracks, high breastworks, and deep dungeons, as well as Matanza Tower and the Keep. The castle ramparts offer a panoramic view over land and sea. The castle is accessible two ways. Board the elevator at the Explanada d'Espanya; admission by elevator is 2.50€. In summer the castle is open daily from 10am to midnight; in winter, it closes at 11:30pm. It is also possible to drive to the top. A paved road off Avenida Vásquez de Mella leads directly to a parking lot beside the castle. If you drive, admission is free.

On the slopes of Castillo de Santa Bárbara behind the cathedral is the **Barrio de Santa Cruz** ★. Forming part of the **Villa Vieja (Old Quarter),** it's a colorful section with wrought-iron window grilles, flowers, and a view of the entire harbor.

Alicante isn't all ancient. Facing Iglesia Santa María is the **Museu de Arte del Siglo XX Asegurada** ★, Plaza de Santa María, 3 (© **96-514-07-68;**

Alicante's Explanada d'Espanya.

Castell de Santa Bárbera.

www.maca-alicante.es). Housed in the baroque Casa de la Asegurada, originally constructed in 1685 as a granary, the Museum of Contemporary Art of Alicante features works by Miró, Calder, Cocteau, Dalí, Giacometti, Gris, Picasso, and Tàpies, Chagall, Kandinsky, and Braque. You'll also see a musical score by Manuel de Falla. The museum was formed in 1977 with the donation of a private collection by the painter and sculptor Eusebio Sempere, whose works are on display. It is open Tuesday to Saturday 10am to 2pm and 4 to 8pm, and Sunday 10:30am to 2:30pm. From October to May, the Tuesday-through-Saturday evening hours are 5 to 9pm. Admission is free.

Entertainment & Nightlife

Alicante is a great city for socializing. One of the town's densest concentrations of watering holes lies adjacent to the port. Night owls wander from one bar to the next along the length of **Muelle del Puerto** (a stretch of pavement also known as the Explanada d'Espanya). There are at least 20 spots that rock through the night. Alternatively, barhop on the narrow streets of Alicante's **Villa Vieja.** Some of the most sociable streets are **Calle Laboradores, Calle Cien Fuegos,** and **Plaza Santísima Faz.**

ELCHE

South of Alicante on the road heading toward Murcia, Elche (Elx in Valenciano) is one of the oldest continuously inhabited cities in Spain, and a cradle of Iberian civilization. It is famous for its age-old mystery play, lush groves of date palms, shoe and sandal making, and one of the most accomplished pieces of statuary from Iberian antiquity.

On August 14 and 15 for the last six centuries, the **Misteri d'Elx (Mystery of Elche)** has celebrated the Assumption of the Virgin. It is reputedly the oldest dramatic liturgy in Europe. Songs are performed in an ancient form of Catalan. Admission is free, but it's hard to get a seat unless you book in advance through the tourist office (see "Essentials," below). The play takes place at the Basilica de Santa María, which dates from the 17th century.

Essentials

GETTING THERE   The central train station is Estación Parque, Avenida del Ferrocarril. **Trains** arrive five times a day from Alicante. Call ✆ **90-232-03-20** or visit www.renfe.com for schedules. The bus station (✆ **96-661-50-50**) is at Avenida de la Libertat. **Buses** travel between Alicante and Elche on the hour. If driving, take the N-340 highway from Alicante and proceed southwest.

VISITOR INFORMATION   The **tourist information office** is at Parque Municipal s/n (✆ **96-665-81-95;** www.turismedelx.com). It's open Monday to Saturday 10am to 7pm, Sunday 10am to 2pm.

Where to Stay & Eat

Hotel Huerto del Cura ★★★   If the palm oasis has drawn you to Elche, then you would be nuts to stay anywhere else. This hotel colony of duplex and triplex bungalows sits in the middle of the Huerta del Cura (Priest's Grove), the most beautiful part of the palm forest. Amid the palms are tropical and subtropical fruit trees and flowers, and a winding path of red slates connects the various buildings with patios to sit out and enjoy the beauty and tranquility. Rooms were recently redecorated in a sleek, contemporary styling with a neutral beige, brown, and slate palette. The on-site restaurant, Els Capellans, features contemporary Mediterranean cuisine.

Porta de La Morera, 14. ✆ **96-661-00-11.** www.hotelhuertodelcura.com. 82 units. 68€–115€ double; 112€–132€ suite. Free parking. Restaurant main dishes 14€–28€; tasting menu 50€. **Amenities:** Restaurant; bar; exercise room; outdoor pool; room service; free Wi-Fi.

Elche's Palm Grove.

Restaurante La Finca ★★★ MEDITERRANEAN   A landscaped terrace surrounds this handsome country house on the road to the Elche football stadium. The contemporary cooking is creative and solidly based in local products—including locally farmed caviar. All dishes in each course are priced the same, and the chef encourages diners to assemble their own tasting menus of two snacks, two seasonal appetizers, two starter plates, and two main dishes served in half portions—followed by dessert and coffee. First courses include such surprises as red tuna carpaccio, white asparagus ice cream, and artichokes stuffed with onions and red prawns in aioli. For a main course, consider the grilled pigeon with apples and Calvadós, or lobster with pistachios and baby vegetables. Not surprisingly, La Finca is Elche's only Michelin-starred restaurant.

Partida de Perleta, Poligono 1, 7. ✆ **96-545-60-07.** www.lafinca.es. Reservations recommended. Main courses 25€–29€; fixed-price menus 64€–79€. Tues–Sat 1:30–4pm and 8:30pm–12:30am; Sun 1–4pm. Closed 2 weeks in Jan, 1 week at Easter, and 1 week in Oct.

Exploring Elche

Unless you visit at the time of the mystery play, the town's **Palm Grove ★★** holds the most appeal. The 200,000-tree palm forest is unrivaled in Europe, and there's a 2.5km (1½ miles) walking tour through the grove; ask at the tourist office for a map. It's said that Phoenician (or perhaps Greek) seafarers originally planted the trees. A thousand years ago, the Moors created the irrigation system that still maintains the palms. Even if you don't tour the entire grove, stroll through the **Huerto del Cura (Priest's Grove) ★★**, open daily from 9am to 6pm, to see the palm garden and collection of tropical flowers and cactuses. In the garden, look for the **Palmera del Cura (Priest's Palm)** from the 1840s, with seven branches sprouting from its trunk.

You'll also see a replica of one of the most famous ladies of Spain, *La Dama de Elche*, in the **Museo Arqueológico y de Historia de Elche (MAHE) ★★** at Calle Diagonal del Palau, 7 (© **96-665-82-03**). The museum was installed in 2006 in the old Altamira Palace. The archaeological exhibits, many of which are in underground galleries, explain the significance of Elche as a center of Iberian Celtic culture even before the arrival of Phoenician traders, and cover human habitation here from the late Neolithic to Roman times. It is open Monday to Saturday 10am to 6pm, Sunday 10am to 3pm. Admission is 3€ adults, 1€ students, and 1.50€ seniors and large families.

BARCELONA

10

T he Catalan language has a verb that must have been invented for Barcelona. "Badar" means (more or less) to walk around with your mouth wide open in astonishment. You'll be doing a lot of that in Barcelona. The city's artists have always had a fantastical vision—from the gargoyles along the roofline of the cathedral, to Antoni Gaudí's armored warrior chimneys on La Pedrera, to the surreal amoeboid sculptures of Joan Miró (they're on a roof, too).

Barcelona really is an original, with its own unique history, language, gastronomy, and overall sense of style. When Madrid was still a dusty fortress village on the Río Manzanares, Barcelona was already a force to be reckoned with on the Mediterranean. It has been at the intersection of cultures—Iberian, Roman, Visigothic, Moorish, French, and Aragonese—for 2,000 years. Today it is the capital of the autonomous region of Catalunya, forever chafing to leave the federal fold of Spain but enjoying near-country status within the European Union.

Having won back its identity from Spain, Barcelona is profoundly Catalan, yet generous about conducting business and pleasure alike in Catalan and Castilian—as well as in English. Whatever tongue its visitors speak, Barcelona knows how to impress. Whether you are floating above the city on a cable car, rambling the medieval streets of the Barri Gòtic, devouring peel-and-eat shrimp at a beachside cafe, or sipping fresh strawberry-melon juice at La Boqueria, remember to keep your eyes wide open: You never know what will amaze you next.

ESSENTIALS

Arriving

BY PLANE Barcelona's international airport (BCN) is **El Prat,** located in El Prat de Llobregat (© **90-240-47-04;** www.aena.es), 12km (7½ miles) southwest of the city center. It has two passenger terminals connected by shuttle buses. The newer, flashier terminal is T1, which serves the majority of international carriers, including Air Canada, Air Europa, Air France, Alitalia, American Airlines, British Air, Delta Airlines, El Al, Emirates, Iberia, KLM, Lufthansa, Qatar, Scandinavian Airlines, Swiss International, TAP Portugal, Turkish Airlines, United Airlines, and low-cost carrier Vueling. Most other international carriers—most notably discount airlines Ryanair and easyJet—operate from T2 (formerly terminals A, B, and C).

Most U.S. travelers to Barcelona fly to Madrid and change planes there, although there are seasonal direct flights to Barcelona on various carriers from New York, Washington-Dulles, Philadelphia, and Atlanta. Less expensive routes are sometimes available on Lufthansa, British Air, and Air France with changes elsewhere in Europe. Bargain hunters willing to do the research and put up with some inconvenience can often find the cheapest overall airfare by flying to Ireland or the United Kingdom and taking easyJet, Ryanair, or Vueling from there to Barcelona. **Iberia** (© **800-772-4642;** www.iberia.com) offers daily shuttle

Previous Page: **The ceiling at Palau de la Musica Catalana.**

flights between Barcelona and Madrid—every half-hour at weekday peak hours. Often cheaper than Iberia, **Air Europa** (© **90-240-15-01;** www.air-europa. com) also shuttles between Madrid and Barcelona.

A train runs between the airport and Barcelona's Estació Central de Barcelona-Sants every 15 to 30 minutes daily from 5:40am to 11:10pm (from Sants) or 11:40pm (to Sants). The 20-minute trip costs 4.20€. You can take the Metro from Sants to anywhere in Barcelona. If your hotel is near Plaça d'Espanya or Plaça de Catalunya, it might be worth the slight extra expense to take an **Aerobús** (© **93-415-60-20;** www.aerobusbcn.com). It runs every 5 minutes between 6:10am and 1am from the airport, and until 12:30am from Plaça de Catalunya. The fare is 5.90€ single trip, 10€ round-trip. A taxi from the airport costs about 30€.

BY TRAIN   Barcelona has two major railway stations. Most national and international trains arrive at **Estació Central de Barcelona-Sants,** Plaça de Països Catalanes (Metro: Sants-Estació), including high-speed AVE trains from Madrid and the high-speed Trenhotel from Paris. Some slower trains from northern Spain and just over the French border arrive at **Estació de França,** Avenida Marqués de L'Argentera (Metro: Barceloneta, L3). For general RENFE (Spanish Railways) information, call © **90-232-03-20** or visit www.renfe.com. It's best to purchase tickets, especially on high-speed trains, in advance. There are two train options between Barcelona and Madrid—"express trains" (8½–9½ hr.; 41€–45€) and the high-speed AVE trains (2¾–3¼ hr.; 128€–180€).

BY BUS   Bus travel to Barcelona is possible, but it's pretty slow and less comfortable than the train. Barcelona's Estació del Nord, Carrer d'Alí Bei, 80 (Metro: Arc de Triomf) serves **Alsa** (© **90-242-22-42;** www.alsa.es) buses to and from southern France and Italy. Alsa also operates 27 buses per day to and from Madrid (trip time: 7½– 8½ hr.). A one way ticket from Madrid costs 33€ to 40€. **Linebús** (© 90-233-55-33; www.linebus.com) has six trips a week from Paris. **Eurolines Viagens,** Carrer Viriato (© **93-490-40-00;** www.eurolines.es), operates seven buses a week from Frankfurt and another five per week from Marseille.

BY CAR   From **France** (the usual European road approach to Barcelona), the major access route is at the eastern end of the **Pyrenees.** You can choose the express highway (E-15) or the more scenic coastal road. If you take the coastal road in July and August, you will often face bumper-to-bumper traffic. You can also approach Barcelona via **Toulouse.** Cross the border at **Puigcerdà** (where there are frontier stations), near the Principality of Andorra. From there, take the N-152 to Barcelona.

From **Madrid,** take the N-2 to Zaragoza, and then the A-2 to El Vendrell, followed by the A-7 freeway to Barcelona. From the **Costa Blanca** or **Costa del Sol,** follow the E-15 north from Valencia along the eastern Mediterranean coast.

BY FERRY   **Trasmediterránea,** Muelle de Sant Bertran s/n (© **90-245-46-45;** www.trasmediterranea.es), operates daily trips to and from the Balearic Islands of Mallorca (8 hr.) and Menorca (8 hr.). In summer, it's important to have a reservation as far in advance as possible.

Visitor Information

Barcelona has two types of tourist offices. The Catalunya regional office deals with Spain in general and Catalunya in particular, with basic information about Barcelona. It has two locations at the airport, **El Prat** (Terminal 1: © **93-478-47-04;** Terminal 2: © **93-478-05-65**), both in the Arrivals hall after you pass

Customs. Hours are daily 8:30am to 10pm. These offices are co-managed with **Turisme de Barcelona** (see below). Another large office in the center of Barcelona at the **Palau de Robert,** Passeig de Gràcia, 107 (© **93-238-80-91;** www.gencat.net), is open Monday to Saturday 10am to 8pm, Sunday and holidays 10am to 2:30pm.

The **Oficina de Informació de Turisme de Barcelona,** Plaça de Catalunya 17-S (© **93-285-38-34;** www.barcelonaturisme.com), deals exclusively with the city of Barcelona. The main office is underground on the southeast corner of the plaza. In addition to getting detailed information about the city, you can purchase the **Barcelona Card** (p. 346) here. In the same space is the **FC Barcelona** shop that sells football match tickets along with all the souvenirs imaginable, and the information desk for the **Ruta de Modernisme** (p. 346). The office is open daily 9am to 9pm, although the Modernisme desk is open 10am to 6pm.

City Layout

Barcelona is a port city surrounded by two small mountains (**Montjuïc** on the southwest, **Tibidabo** on the north) that form a natural bowl around the port. Although the city sprawls on its east side, the main sections of interest to travelers are the **waterfront, Ciutat Vell** (old city), **L'Eixample** and **Gràcia** (19th-century extensions inland from the old city), and **Montjuïc.**

The central artery of the Ciutat Vell is **Les Rambles,** a broad avenue with a pedestrian center strip. It begins at the waterfront at Plaça Portal de la Pau, with its 50m-high (174-ft.) monument to Columbus, and stretches north to Plaça de Catalunya, changing names several times along the way. Along this wide promenade you'll find bookshops and newsstands, stalls selling birds and flowers, and benches or cafe tables where you can sit and watch the passing parade. West of Les Rambles is **El Raval,** a sector of the old city that has rebounded in recent years and has evolved a good restaurant and bar scene. Just off Les Rambles to the east is **Plaça Reial,** the most harmoniously proportioned square in Barcelona. The neighborhood immediately east of Les Rambles is the **Barri Gòtic** (or

The Plaça de Catalunya.

Gothic Quarter), and east of the **Barri Gòtic** are the neighborhoods of **El Born** (where the waterfront transitions into the medieval city) and **La Ribera.**

Plaça de Catalunya is intersected by **Gran Via Corts Catalanes,** which is the approximate divider between the old and new cities. Ringed with hotels and restaurants, the plaza is a crossroads of bus and Metro routes. North of Gran Via, the streets of L'Eixample assume an orderly grid. **Passeig de Gràcia** is the most elegant of the north-south boulevards. The exception to the grid is the slash across "new" Barcelona, the **Avinguda Diagonal,** which separates the grid of L'Eixample from the grid of Gràcia.

FINDING AN ADDRESS/MAPS   Barcelona abounds with long boulevards and a complicated maze of narrow, twisting streets. Knowing the street number, if there is one, is essential. The designation s/n (*sin número*) means that the building has no number. It's crucial to learn the cross street if you're seeking a specific address. The rule about street numbers is that there is no rule. Most streets are numbered with odd numbers on one side, even numbers on the other. But because each building counts as a single number and some buildings are much wider than others, consecutive numbers (like 41 and 42, for example) may be a block or more apart.

Arm yourself with a good map before setting out. The free maps given out at the tourist office will do, but they often leave off the names of many of the small streets. The Barcelona Streetwise map from **Falk** is good as well as durable. It is available at most newsstands and kiosks. However, finding your way with a massive folding map is usually impractical and, frankly, makes you more vulnerable to pickpockets. **Google Maps** (http://maps.google.com) are very detailed for Barcelona and largely accurate. If your phone or tablet has local service, you can use them while walking around. Otherwise, download an app that allows you to save the maps for offline reference.

The Neighborhoods in Brief

LES RAMBLES & EL RAVAL   **Les Rambles,** as famous a promenade as Madrid's Paseo del Prado, was originally the drainage canal that ran down the western edge of the city walls erected by Jaume I in the 13th century. Now it's a broad, 1.5km-long (1-mile) avenue that runs between the waterfront and Plaça de Catalunya. The large pedestrian strip down the middle hosts a stream of street entertainers, flower vendors, news dealers, cafe patrons, and strollers.

In the 15th century, convents and monasteries were built on the southwest side of Les Rambles. The last of them was razed in the 19th century, but the succession of names along the promenade—Rambla de Santa Mònica, Rambla dels Caputxins, Rambla de Sant Josep, Rambla dels Estudis, and Rambla de Canaletes—recalls the religious orders. When they left, brothels moved in, and **El Raval,** west of Les Rambles, became Barcelona's red light district. Nonetheless, a few important landmarks of Modernisme were constructed in Raval and by the late 20th century, the city spruced up the quarter. Today it is a resurgent neighborhood where the university campus and contemporary arts scene on the north end encourage both inexpensive restaurants and interesting design shops. The newly developed Rambla del Raval provides a charming neighborhood park complete with Fernando Botero's giant bronze cat, "El Gato del Raval," and a loud flock of wild monk parrots that nest in the trees.

BARRI GÒTIC   East of Les Rambles is Barcelona's main medieval quarter, the **Barri Gòtic.** King Jaume I encircled it with a wall in the 13th century, of which little remains. Built atop the old Roman city of Barcino, it is a tangle of narrow streets that radiate from and connect to slightly larger plazas around the cathedral and a series of other Gothic churches. Buried deep within the Barri Gòtic are the remnants of the **Call,** the medieval Jewish neighborhood. The Barri Gòtic is perhaps the most atmospheric sector of Barcelona, where thoroughly modern shops stand cheek by jowl with museums and historic churches.

LA RIBERA & EL BORN La Ribera—literally, the shore—was constructed in medieval times where the sea encroached just east of the city walls. Part of it was destroyed to build a fortress, now the Parc de la Ciutadella. **El Born** was the name given to the streets west of the fortress that formed the transition between La Ribera and Port Vell. The entire area consists of small, ancient streets, with the straight north-south **Via Laietana** forming its western boundary, and the equally straight **Passeig de Sant Joan** and **Parc de la Ciutadella** forming the eastern boundary. Somewhat more open than the cramped quarters of the Barri Gòtic, this is the area where the **Museu Picasso** stands.

L'EIXAMPLE & GRÀCIA North of Plaça de Catalunya and Gran Via de les Corts Catalanes, **L'Eixample** is the elegant planned "expansion" that unfolded in the late 19th and early 20th centuries. Catalan Modernisme, a colloquial and localized version of Art Nouveau architecture, reached its apex here. Famous landmark buildings include Antoni Gaudí's **Basilica de la Sagrada Familia** and **Casa Milà,** nicknamed La Pedrera (the stone quarry). The main north-south axis is **Passeig de Gràcia.** At its northern end, it is transected by the broad swath of **Avinguda Diagonal.** North of the Diagonal is the working class neighborhood of **Gràcia,** which consists of several formerly rural villages annexed by Barcelona over the years.

LA BARCELONETA & THE WATERFRONT Back when Barcelona was a sailor's town, the waterfront was colorful but a little iffy after dark. The 1992 Olympics changed all that, bringing a complete redevelopment of the Port Vell—now a yacht harbor—and installing **L'Aquarium Barcelona** and the **Maremagnum** shopping center on a newly created island, the Moll d'Espanya. Another quay was transformed into the **Moll de la Fusta,** a popular walking and cycling path. At the east end of Moll de la Fusta, **Passeig de Joan de Borbó** goes to the tip of **La Barceloneta.** Once the neighborhood of fishermen, Barceloneta has become a hip bohemian address and is noted for its seafood restaurants and sandy beaches. Follow the beaches east to **Port Olimpic,** developed for the boating events of the 1992 Olympics.

MONTJUÏC Rather disconnected from the rest of the city, **Montjuïc** is a small mountain that's not so small when you're walking up it in August. It begins at **Plaça d'Espanya,** a traffic rotary where the city's convention center is located, and goes up to the old Palacio Nacional, now the **Museu Nacional d'Art de Catalunya.** The mountain was used for the 1929 Barcelona International Exposition, which created the roadways, many gardens, and the **Poble Espanyol** area of "typical" architecture from around Spain. Many events of the 1992 Olympics were also held here, leaving behind a stadium and a state-of-the-art swimming facility. It is also the home of the **Fundació Joan Miró.**

GETTING AROUND
On Foot

You can walk most places in Barcelona's old city, or through the main districts of interest in L'Eixample. But it's a good idea to use public transport to a starting point and then set off on foot to explore.

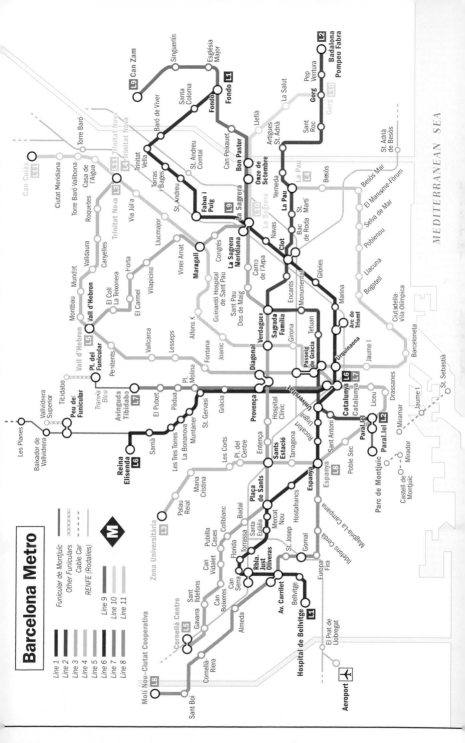

315

READY TO go

By Public Transit

Barcelona's public transit system includes extensive and interlinked networks of buses, subway trains, trams, and "rodalies" (local commuter rail). For a full overview, check the website of **Transports Metropolitans de Barcelona** (www.tmb.cat). This site, available in Catalan, Spanish, and English, has a very useful tool that recommends ways to get from one place to another using any combination of public transit and walking. Individual tickets on subway and buses within the central city cost 2€.

By Subway

Barcelona's Metro system consists of six main lines; it crisscrosses the city more frequently and with greater efficiency than the bus network. Service operates Sunday to Thursday from 5am to midnight, and Friday and Saturday from 5am to 2am. Each Metro station entrance is marked with a red diamond. The major station for all subway lines is **Plaça de Catalunya.**

By Bus

About 190 bus lines traverse the city and, not surprisingly, you don't want to ride them at rush hour. Most buses run daily from 5:30am to 10pm; some night buses go along the principal arteries from 11pm to 4am. You can buy your ticket when boarding. Red buses cut through the city center during the day; yellow ones operate at night.

By Barcelona Bus Turistic

The most established of the sightseeing buses, the double-decker **Barcelona Bus Turistic** makes a circuit on three routes that can deliver you to almost every major tourist attraction in the city. The bus includes running commentary (through headsets) in 10 languages, and a choice of outdoor seating with great views and indoor seating with heat or air-conditioning. It also claims free Wi-Fi on board, but it never worked on any buses where we tried it. The circuits on the red route (old city, Montjuïc, and the waterfront) and the blue route (L'Eixample and Gràcia) each take about 2 hours. The green route, which shuttles along the neighborhoods and beaches east of Port Olimpic, takes 40 minutes. You can get on and off all day, but be forewarned that you can wait as much as a half-hour to get onto a crowded bus during high season. It's useful if you don't want to use regular public transportation, but it's quite a bit less efficient. One day on the bus, however, will get you a booklet of discounts good on many attractions including La Pedrera and La Sagrada Familia. The cost is 26€ for 1 day, 34€ for 2 days (15€ and 19€ for ages 4–12).

By Taxi

Each yellow-and-black taxi bears the letters sp (*Servicio Público*) on its front and rear. A lit green light on the roof and a libre sign in the window indicate the taxi is free to pick up passengers. Make sure that the meter is at zero when you enter. The basic rate begins at 2€. Each additional kilometer costs 1€. Supplements might apply—1€ for a large suitcase placed in the trunk, for instance. Rides to the airport carry a supplement of 3.10€. For a taxi, contact **Ràdio Taxi** (*℡* **93-303-30-33;** www.radiotaxi033.com).

By Funicular & Rail Links

It takes some planning to visit the mountains of Tibidabo or Montjuïc. To visit Tibidabo by public transport, you'll have to take the **Funicular de Tibidabo.** The fare is 7.70€, or 4.10€ if you're also purchasing admission to the Tibidabo amusement park. The funicular operates every 15 to 20 minutes. From mid-April to September service is daily 10am to 8pm. In the off-season it usually operates only Saturday and Sunday 10am to 6pm. To get to the funicular, take Metro Line 7 to Avinguda Tibidabo. Exit onto Plaça Kennedy and take either the 1901 tram called **Tramvía Blau** (Blue Streetcar) or **Bus 196** to the funicular. The bus is the usual 2€ fare. Tickets on the **Tramvia Blau** are 4€.

Getting to Montjuïc by funicular is a simple ride from the Paral.lel Metro station and is considered part of the Metro network, although you need to change and use a new 2€ ticket. Once you're on the mountain, you can ride a cable car to the castle on top. Tickets on **Telefèric de Montjuïc** are 7.30€ one-way, 10€ round-trip (5.50€ or 7.40€ for ages 4–12).

By Car

Driving and trying to park in congested Barcelona is not worth the hassle. Use public transportation and save car rentals for excursions and moving on. Avis and Hertz have offices at the airport and downtown. **Avis,** Carrer Corçega 293–295 (*℡* **90-211-02-75;** www.avis.es), is open Monday to Friday 8am to 9pm, Saturday 8am to 8pm, and Sunday 8am to 1pm. **Hertz,** Carrer de Viriat, 45 (*℡* **93-419-61-56;** www.hertz.es), is located adjacent to the Estació Barcelona-Sants rail station and keeps the same hours. It is usually cheaper and easier to arrange your car rental before leaving home. Given the consolidation in the rental car industry, prices vary little among companies, so stick with whichever one dovetails with your frequent-flyer program.

[Fast FACTS] BARCELONA

Banks & ATMs You can usually find a bank—or at least an ATM—wherever crowds gather in Barcelona, especially in shopping districts and around major Metro stations. Most permit cash withdrawals via MasterCard or Visa, and many are linked to international networks that will let you access your home bank account. Most offer a choice of language, almost always including English. The most prominent banks with large ATM networks in Barcelona are **La Caixa** and **Banco Santander.** Major overseas banks with a presence include **Deutsche Bank** and **Citibank.** Note that most Spanish ATMs only accept 4-digit PINs, so if you have a longer PIN, change it at least a week before departure. Many banks now have "dynamic currency conversion," which means the bank will offer to charge your withdrawal in dollars rather than euros. The exchange rate is even worse than the one your bank at home will give you, so always answer "NO" and ask to be charged in euros. With the proliferation of ATM networks, cash exchanges are uncommon and should be avoided as they usually offer poor exchange rates and/or high service charges.

Business Hours Opening hours are in flux in Barcelona. The lunch break is vanishing faster here than in the rest of Spain, but expect small shops and some old-fashioned places to open at 10am, close 2 to 5pm for lunch, and open again 5 to 8:30pm. Other businesses stay open through the midday.

Consulates National embassies are all located in Madrid, but some consular offices are found in Barcelona. The **U.S. Consulate,** Carrer Reina Elisenda, 23 (✆ **93-280-22-27;** train: Reina Elisenda), is open Monday to Friday 9am to 1pm. The **Canadian Consulate,** Plaça de Catalunya, 9 (✆ **93-412-72-36;** Metro: Plaça de Catalunya), is open Monday to Friday 9am to 12:30pm. The **U.K. Consulate,** Avinguda Diagonal, 477 (✆ **93-366-62-00;** Metro: Hospital Clínic), is open Monday to Friday 8:30am to 1:30pm. **Australia** and **New Zealand** have honorary consuls in Barcelona.

Doctors & Dentists
Barcelona has many hospitals and clinics, including **Clínic Barcelona** (✆ **93-227-54-00;** www.hospitalclinic.org) and **Hospital de la Santa Creu i Sant Pau,** at the intersection of Carrer Cartagena and Carrer Sant Antoni María Claret (✆ **93-291-90-00;** Metro: Hospital de Sant Pau). For dental needs, contact **Clínica Dental Barcelona,** Passeig de Gràcia, 97 (✆ **93-487-83-29;** Metro: Diagonal), open daily 9am to midnight.

Emergencies
Call ✆ **112** for general emergencies. To report a fire, call ✆ **080;** to call an ambulance, ✆ **061;** to call the police, ✆ **088.**

Internet Access
Most lodgings offer free Wi-Fi, at least in public areas. Typically, bandwidth on free hotel Wi-Fi is good enough to surf the Web and check e-mail but not for streaming videos or music. Some hotels give away basic Wi-Fi but charge for faster access. Somewhat slower free Wi-Fi is usually available in cafes and some stores. The city government also provides free Wi-Fi at 109 hotspots in L'Eixample and 61 spots in the old city. You will have to sign up for a free account to use it, however, and it is limited by intention to minimal service to "respect the marketplace." Buses and some Metro lines also have free Wi-Fi. If you are planning to use a phone or tablet, download the GOWEX Free Wi-Fi app

(iOs or Android). With the proliferation of free hotspots, Internet cafes are vanishing. Expect to pay 2€ to 4€ per hour.

Language Catalunya has two official languages: Catalan and Castilian Spanish. Catalan (Catalá in its own language) takes precedence for signage, television and radio, and most publications. As a romance language, it resembles both Spanish, and the two can sound similar. English is widely spoken in the tourism sector, and many websites offer pages in English.

Mail & Postage The main post office is at Plaça d'Antoni López (✆ **93-486-80-50;** www.correos.es; Metro: Jaume I). It's open Monday to Friday 8:30am to 9:30pm and Saturday 8:30am to 2pm for sending letters and telegrams. Sending a postcard or letter to the U.S. starts at 0.90€. To calculate the price, visit http://correos.es. You can also buy stamps at any place that sells tobacco.

Newspapers & Magazines The Paris-based *International New York Times* (formerly the *International Herald Tribune*) is sold at most newsstands in the tourist districts, as are *USA Today* and European editions of *Time* and *Newsweek*. British papers abound on the same newsstands. Barcelona's own leading daily newspapers, which often list cultural events, are *El Periódico* and *La Vanguardia*.

Pharmacies **Farmacia Montserrat,** Les Rambles, 118 (© **93-302-43-45;** Metro: Liceu), is the most centrally located. It's open daily 9am to 8pm. Pharmacies take turns staying open late at night. Those that aren't open post the names and addresses of pharmacies in the area that are.

Safety Barcelona is a big city with many disoriented tourists paying scant attention to their belongings. Pickpockets and purse-snatchers treat the unwary like the weak antelopes straggling at the back of the herd. Don't be one of them. Be careful with cameras, purses, and wallets wherever there are crowds, especially on Les Rambles.

WHERE TO STAY

Hotels in Barcelona are among the most expensive in Spain, but that doesn't mean you can't find good values. Many visitors gravitate to hotels on or near **Les Rambles** for convenience, but better bargains can be found in **El Raval** as well as in the **Barri Gòtic.** Although not quite as convenient to public transit, lodgings in **La Ribera** and **El Born** tend to offer the best combination of price and value. Hotels along the **waterfront** tend to be new and flashy, and priced accordingly. **L'Eixample** hotels, while typically more expensive than in the old city, are also usually more spacious.

Les Rambles & El Raval

EXPENSIVE

Casa Camper ★   The Camper shoe company took its offbeat shoe design aesthetic and used it to convert a 19th-century Raval tenement building near the contemporary art museum into a designer hotel. Rooms have a breezy and playful decor, and each one features a rope hammock as well as a bed. They're designed to appeal to well-heeled hipsters—just spare enough to be modern, not so empty as to look barren, and each is a mini-suite with separate sleeping and sitting areas. There's also one real suite on each floor where the living and sleeping areas are linked through a pocket sliding door. Should you feel overwhelmed by the city, you can catch a nap in a hammock on the roof terrace. The lobby has a snack buffet available around the clock.

Carrer Elisabets, 11. © **93-342-62-80.** www.casacamper.com. 25 units. 238€–282€ double; 256€–293€ suite. Metro: Plaça de Catalunya. **Amenities:** Bar; babysitting; bikes; restaurant; room service; free Wi-Fi.

Hotel Bagues ★★★   This is our choice for a romantic getaway in the old city for both its looks and its high level of hospitality. The staff provides friendly and helpful service without putting on airs. And the hotel's Modernista design is a holdover from the building's heyday as a jewelry store; the modern comforts don't detract one iota from the stunning visuals of the original designs. The walls and wardrobes in the rooms are enhanced with gold leaf accents and panels of Madagascar ebony. The hotel even has a Masriera Museum, showcasing the jewelry of the Art Nouveau master. Most rooms are called "standard," but are larger than most hotel suites.

Les Rambles, 105. © **93-343-50-00.** www.derbyhotels.com. 31 units. 165€–280€ double; suites from 280€. Metro: Plaça de Catalunya. **Amenities:** Bar; restaurant; room service; business center; outdoor swimming pool; solarium; spa; gym; limousine service; free Wi-Fi. Dogs allowed on request.

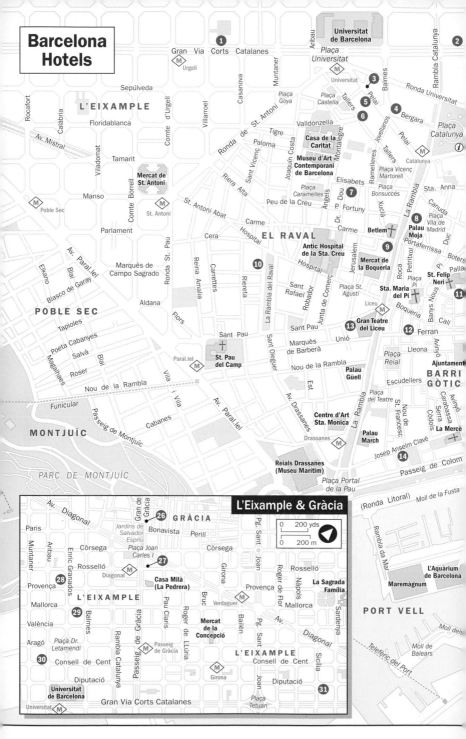

Barcelona Hotels

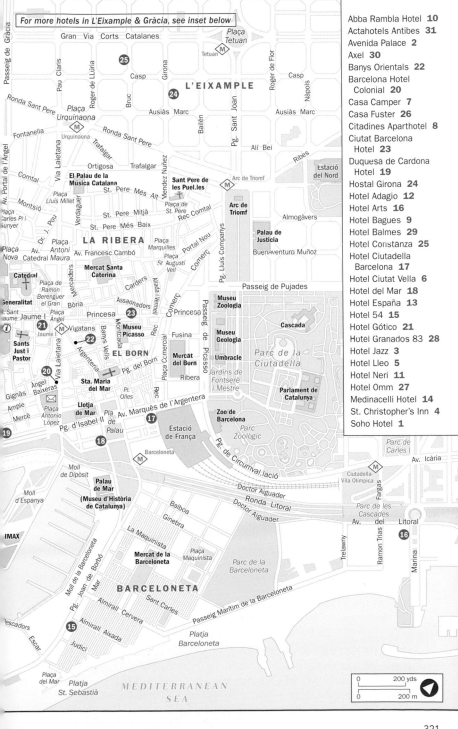

For more hotels in L'Eixample & Gràcia, see inset below

L'EIXAMPLE

LA RIBERA

EL BORN

BARCELONETA

MEDITERRANEAN SEA

Abba Rambla Hotel **10**
Actahotels Antibes **31**
Avenida Palace **2**
Axel **30**
Banys Orientals **22**
Barcelona Hotel
  Colonial **20**
Casa Camper **7**
Casa Fuster **26**
Citadines Aparthotel **8**
Ciutat Barcelona
  Hotel **23**
Duquesa de Cardona
  Hotel **19**
Hostal Girona **24**
Hotel Adagio **12**
Hotel Arts **16**
Hotel Bagues **9**
Hotel Balmes **29**
Hotel Constanza **25**
Hotel Ciutadella
  Barcelona **17**
Hotel Ciutat Vella **6**
Hotel del Mar **18**
Hotel España **13**
Hotel 54 **15**
Hotel Gótico **21**
Hotel Granados 83 **28**
Hotel Jazz **3**
Hotel Lleo **5**
Hotel Neri **11**
Hotel Omm **27**
Medinacelli Hotel **14**
St. Christopher's Inn **4**
Soho Hotel **1**

321

MODERATE

Abba Rambla Hotel ★ Built in 2005, this sleekly modern and friendly hotel was a pioneer of fine lodging in El Raval, an area once known for budget pensions. It fronts the park of La Rambla del Raval, an up-and-coming cafe district. Rooms are compact but well-designed with adequate space and contemporary bathrooms, most with tub-showers. Set just far enough off Les Rambles to avoid the crowds, it's still convenient to walk to the contemporary art museum as well as most attractions in the Barri Gòtic.

Carrer La Rambla del Raval, 4C. ℂ **93-505-54-00.** www.abbahotels.com. 49 units. 60€–140€ double. Parking 22€. Metro: Liceu. **Amenities:** Bar; cafeteria; business center; solarium; free Wi-Fi.

Citadines Aparthotel ★★ At the upper end of Les Rambles near the Plaça de Catalunya, these self-sufficient apartments, constructed in 1994, were renovated and completely refurnished in late 2013. With gray wood floors, muted earth tone bedspreads and draperies, dark wood furniture, large showers in the bathrooms, and fully equipped if compact kitchens, even the smallest of these units is twice the size of most hotel rooms. The kitchen makes it easy (and cheaper) to prepare breakfast and gives you an excuse to shop at La Boqueria. The location, just steps from the Plaça del Pi in the Barri Gòtic, is prime. The Aparthotel has two buildings that share a gym and coin-op laundry. There's no minimum stay, but prices per night decline with longer bookings.

Les Rambles, 122. ℂ **93-270-11-11.** www.citadines.com. 131 units. 110€–245€ studio apt, 200€–490€ 1-bedroom apt. Metro: Plaça de Catalunya. **Amenities:** Gym; free Wi-Fi.

Hotel España ★ Erected as a rooming house in 1859, this handsome structure just steps from Les Rambles was transformed into a Modernista hotel in 1903 by Lluís Domènech i Montaner. Guests get a discount on the guided architectural tour (see "Exploring," below). The hotel was renovated in 2010 to restore its Modernista flair while also installing contemporary technology and plumbing. The styling is serene and simple, with dark wood tones and taupes that coordinate nicely with the Modernista design. The smallest rooms are a little tight (roughly 12×12 ft.), but most are larger.

Carrer Sant Pau, 9–11. ℂ **93-550-00-00.** www.hotelespanya.com. 82 units. 121€–210€ double. Metro: Liceu. **Amenities:** Bar; restaurant; business area; terrace; swimming pool; free Wi-Fi.

Hotel Jazz ★ The Jazz aims to be both clubby and chic. Located off Plaça de Catalunya near the contemporary art museum and the downtown campus of the University of Barcelona, it's true to its name, evoking the Rat Pack era (for some reason, a Spanish fascination) without replicating it. The new renditions of retro design are timeless. This is an unusually family-friendly design hotel, even providing complimentary cradles for infants. In an odd nod to an old-fashioned amenity from the 1950s, the rooms offer piped-in music—a feature that can be easily turned off.

Carrer Pelai, 3. ℂ **93-532-96-96.** www.hoteljazz.com. 108 rooms. 105€–210€ double. Parking 30€. Metro: Plaça de Catalunya. **Amenities:** Bar-cafe; business center; outdoor pool; rooftop terrace; room service; free Wi-Fi.

INEXPENSIVE

Hotel Ciutat Vella ★★ The red-white-and-black color scheme gives this place a lot of visual pop, which is only fitting for a new hostelry around the corner from the contemporary art museum. Rooms have an uncluttered but functional design that has the color and ease of use of a good website. The clientele tends to skew young, but that could be because the art school and university are also nearby. It might be the brightest and airiest lodging in El Raval, and the low-season prices make it one of the best bargains.

Carrer Tallers, 66. ✆ **93-481-37-99.** www.hotelciutatvella.com. 40 units. 70€–140€ double. Metro: Plaça de Catalunya or Universitat. **Amenities:** Free lobby snacks and drinks available 24 hr.; rooftop terrace with Jacuzzi and solarium; free Wi-Fi.

Hotel Lleó ★   Surrounded by designer boutique hotels where all the furnishings are dark wood, all the floors are Pergo, and all the soft goods are shades of brown and taupe, the Lleó is a Spanish throwback of blond wood furniture, tan walls, and hardwood floors. It's like finding a caramel in a box of chocolates—different but just as good in its own way. The hotel is penalized a star in the official ratings for no restaurant, so it's a bargain for the quality. Rooms are adequately sized with decent desks, comfortable beds, and small but well-designed bathrooms. In summer, the rooftop terrace and pool are welcome surprises in this price range.

Carrer Pelai, 22 y 24. ✆ **93-318-12-12.** www.hotel-lleo.com. 92 rooms. 64€–152€ double. **Amenities:** Rooftop terrace and pool; business center; Jacuzzi; billiards room; Wi-Fi.

St. Christopher's Inn ★   One of the newest (2012) in this European chain of deluxe backpacker hostels, the Barcelona version touts the city's late night revelry, the nude beach (there is one, but it's not close), and the youthful vibe of the city. The four private rooms can be as expensive as nearby hotels, but the dorm rooms are a pretty good deal. Male, female, and mixed dormitories are available, and they're clean and bright. All ages are welcome, but most guests are younger than 25.

Carrer Bergara, 3. ✆ **93-667-45-88.** www.bookbeds.com. 11 rooms. 13€–33€ dorm bed; 58€–120€ private double. Metro: Plaça de Catalunya. **Amenities:** Kitchen facilities; bar-restaurant; towel rental; free Wi-Fi.

Barri Gòtic, La Ribera & El Born

For stays of 3 nights or more, a good option is an apartment rental. It has advantages (your own cooking facilities, being embedded in a residential area) and disadvantages (cleaning deposits, no services). One of the better agencies is **apartmentsinbarcelona.net** (Carrer Jaume I, 30; ✆ **93-439-56-64**). You make arrangements online, then check in at the office, where someone will guide you to your apartment. Selections are available citywide and with varying numbers of bedrooms, but most are studios or one-bedroom apartments in the Barri Gòtic and El Born. Rates range from 50€ to 200€ per night depending on location, size, season, and length of stay.

EXPENSIVE

Hotel Neri ★★★   This delightful boutique hotel sits at the edge of the Call in the Barri Gòtic. Most of the hotel lies within a rebuilt medieval noble home, but the restaurant wing is a modern addition that harmonizes nicely with the ancient stone. Reception sits on the Call, while the restaurant terrace opens onto Plaça Sant Felip Neri, one of Barcelona's most storied old squares. The building skillfully combines nine centuries of architecture while keeping the rooms open, airy, and timeless. Abstract Expressionist art hangs throughout the hotel, evoking a modern sensibility in a structure rooted in the very non-abstract materials of stone and exposed wood. The rooftop terrace (complete with hammocks as well as tables and chairs) functions as an auxiliary bar, weather permitting. The Neri's location in the Call makes it a popular choice for travelers on Jewish heritage holidays.

Carrer Sant Severe, 5. ℂ **93-304-06-55.** www.hotelneri.com. 22 units. 225€–335€ double; 290€–470€ suite. Metro: Liceu or Jaume I. **Amenities:** Restaurant; bar-cafe; babysitting; free Wi-Fi.

MODERATE

Banys Orientals ★ Located in El Born at the doorway to the Barri Gòtic, this boutique hotel sits in the most historic part of Barcelona. It offers quality and comfort at an affordable price in a 19th-century private mansion turned modern hotel. The bathrooms gleam with marble, the floors are stained a dark walnut, and the crisp white linens stand out in high contrast. In addition to doubles, there are several suites, some with private patios. If you like the location, consider the upgrade to a suite, as doubles are beautiful but too tight to have more than one suitcase open at a time.

Carrer Argentería, 37. ℂ **93-268-84-60.** www.hotelbanysorientals.com. 43 units. 96€–143€ double; 115€–195€ suite. Metro: Jaume I. **Amenities:** Restaurant; room service; free Wi-Fi.

Hotel Adagio ★ Barcelona hotels with an official two-star rating can be pretty grim, but Adagio is a delightful exception following substantial renovations in early 2013. Located about halfway between Plaça Reial and Plaça de Catalunya, Adagio fronts onto Carrer Ferran, one of the broader east-west streets of the Barri Gòtic. The reception area is tiny, as it was moved back to make room for the excellent tapas restaurant **Adagiotapas** (p. 333) in the front. Rooms are small but very clean. Location is superb, but it's best to keep windows closed and use the air-conditioning as the narrow stone streets can be noisy at night. Exceedingly friendly and eager-to-please staff helps compensate for the lack of luxury.

Carrer Ferran, 21. ℂ **93-318-90-61.** www.adagiohotel.com. 38 units. 104€–144€ double. Metro: Liceu or Jaume I. **Amenities:** Free Wi-Fi.

INEXPENSIVE

Barcelona Hotel Colonial ★★ Set in a handsome 19th-century building that once housed the Banco Hispano, this hotel is convenient for exploring Barcelona's waterfront as well as the old city. It's less than a 5-minute walk from the Moll de la Fusta and just a few hundred yards from the Museu Picasso. Perhaps because it's a former bank building, this lodging has a grander lobby than many old city hotels, especially those in Born. Rooms are rather less spacious than the lobby, though just as sumptuously appointed. Triple rooms with a sleeper couch are available.

Vía Laietana, 3. ℂ **93-315-22-52.** www.hotelcolonialbarcelona.com. 81 rooms. 80€–165€ double; 108€–190€ triple. Metro: Jaume I or Barceloneta. **Amenities:** Cafeteria; free Wi-Fi.

Ciutat Barcelona Hotel ★★ A bargain-priced design hotel for grown-ups, the Ciutat Barcelona has soothing a contemporary look to its rooms, including chairs and light fixtures that could have come straight from the showroom at Design Within Reach. Spaces are compact but well-designed, and the rooftop terrace is like having a private oasis in the middle of the city. There is a side entrance for wheelchair users, and some of the rooms are accessible. The small pool is big enough to make kids happy.

Carrer Princesa, 35. ℂ **93-269-74-75.** www.ciutatbarcelona.com. 78 rooms. 70€–135€ double. Metro: Jaume I. **Amenities:** Internet corner; rooftop pool; free Wi-Fi.

Hotel Gótico ★★ This hotel at the crossroads of Jaume I/Princesa and Via Laietana is our favorite among the cluster of Gargallo family hotels on the same block. The historic building from 1823 was transformed into a hotel in 1999 and completely renovated in 2012. Acres of marble cover the entry foyer (as well as the bathrooms) and golden accents glimmer against wood inlay and exposed brick. Guest rooms are a little snug but are simply decorated with furniture that reinterprets the Modernista aesthetic through the lens of Danish Modern. The location is terrific for walking swiftly to the cathedral in one direction, the Museu Picasso in the other. Friendly and solicitous staff make the experience of staying here all the more pleasant.

Carrer Jaume I, 14. ✆ **93-315-21-13.** www.hotelgotico.com. 81 units. 60€–170€ double. Metro: Jaume I. **Amenities:** Bar-cafe; room service; terrace; free Wi-Fi. Dogs permitted.

L'Eixample
EXPENSIVE

Casa Fuster ★★★   This stunning Modernista building was designed by Lluís Domènech i Montaner for the Fuster family in 1908, and it was reported at the time to be the most expensive home constructed in the city. Modernisme's heyday lives again in this deluxe hotel decked out in a palette of magenta, mauve, and taupe. Private balconies in many rooms open onto leafy Passeig de Gràcia. The hotel's Viennese cafe has become one of Barcelona's best jazz clubs, but soundproofing is so good that you won't hear a single saxophone honk in your room. The location is less convenient than most for exploring the city, but if you have your heart set on sleeping in a full-blown Modernista landmark, Casa Fuster is your place.

Passeig de Gràcia, 132. ✆ **93-255-30-00.** www.hotelcasafuster.com. 96 units. 176€–326€ double; 268€–347€ jr. suite; from 693€ suite. Parking 33€. Metro: Diagonal. **Amenities:** Restaurant; bar; babysitting; concierge; exercise room; Jacuzzi; outdoor heated pool; room service; sauna; free Wi-Fi.

Hotel Omm ★★★   It's almost worth staying at Omm just for the view from the rooftop bar and swimming pool of La Pedrera's fanciful chimneys across the street. Grupo Tragaluz, of Barcelona gourmet restaurant fame, set out to make this boutique property a 21st-century exemplar of style the way Gaudí's Casa Milà (La Pedrera) is the apex of Modernisme. The lobby, restaurant **Roca Moo** (p. 338), and other public areas are all high drama, while the rooms are breezy and relaxing. Guest rooms have parquet wood floors, handwoven rugs, and large windows with views of either the inner courtyard or Passeig de Gràcia.

Carrer Rosselló, 265. ✆ **93-445-40-00.** www.hotelomm.es. 91 units. 199€–355€ double; 499€–650€ suite. Parking 32€. Metro: Diagonal. **Amenities:** Restaurant; bar; babysitting; concierge; rooftop heated pool; room service; spa; free Wi-Fi.

MODERATE

Axel ★   Several gay travel publications give Axel their imprimatur, and it's easy to see why. A huge mural of two men embracing adorns the lobby, there's gay erotic art in most guest rooms, the on-site boutique sells skimpy men's bathing trunks, and there's a strong flirting scene at the rooftop pool, sun deck, and cocktail bar. Still, the hotel advertises itself as being hetero-friendly, and with its larger-than-usual rooms (with true king beds instead of two twins pushed together), rich linens, and a full menu of pillow choices, Axel should appeal to travelers of all orientations.

Carrer Aribau, 33. ✆ **93-323-93-93.** www.axelhotels.com. 105 units. 60€–188€ double; 211€–305€ suites. Parking 25€. Metro: Universitat. **Amenities:** Restaurant; 2 bars; health club and spa; outdoor heated pool; room service; free Wi-Fi.

Hotel Balmes ★★   The bargain-priced member of the Derby group, the Balmes shares the serene modern style of the chain, which we'd call a cross between a small art museum and a well-appointed gentleman's club. (The owner of the hotel group is an indefatigable art collector.) In this case the art consists of an extensive collection of sub-Saharan African masks and small wooden sculptures in both the public areas and the individual guest rooms. Even the standard rooms are spacious, and several superior rooms feature small outdoor terraces. Carrer de Mallorca, 216. ℂ **93-451-19-14.** www.derbyhotels.com. 105 units. 70€–198€ double. Metro: Diagonal. **Amenities:** Bar; restaurant; sauna; free Wi-Fi.

Hotel Granados 83 ★★   The stone and glass facade of this converted 19th-century hospital is accented with oxidized iron trim in an effort to give it what the designer thought was a "New York" Soho look. In truth, it couldn't be anywhere but Barcelona, and the enthusiasms of the architect fortunately do not continue into the hotel itself, which is quietly and confidently posh without being the least bit snooty. Like the Bagues and the Balmes (see above), it is a Derby Hotel, and maintains the company style of dark wood, polished glass, and artwork everywhere. In this case, the art is from South and Southeast Asia. There are also a few Egyptian artifacts, and guests are given a free pass to the Museu Egipci of Barcelona. (The hotel's owner is on the board.) Carrer Enric Granados, 83. ℂ **93-492-96-70.** www.derbyhotels.com. 77 units. 110€–264€ double. Metro: Diagonal. **Amenities:** Restaurant; bar; exercise room; outdoor pool; room service; free Wi-Fi.

Soho Hotel ★★   Barcelona-born designer Alfredo Arribas collaborated with Verner Panton's design company to create the organic minimalist look for this bargain-priced designer hotel. Certain contemporary clichés creep in, like the clear glass cube showers and beds so low that you're nearly on the floor. But those beds are super-comfortable and those showers have great shower heads. Lower-level rooms can be noisy with Gran Via traffic, so ask for a courtyard room. The most expensive rooms are seventh-floor suites that feature wood-decked terraces with terrific city views. Gran Via de les Corts Catalanes, 543. ℂ **93-552-96-10.** www.hotelsohobarcelona.com. 51 units. 58€–165€ double; 108€–256€ terrace suite. Parking 28€. Metro: Plaça de Catalunya. **Amenities:** Bar; outdoor heated pool; free Wi-Fi.

INEXPENSIVE

Actahotels Antibes ★★   Modern and rather pretty with its spare black and white decor with pops of red, this pleasant and functional hotel, just a 7-minute walk from La Sagrada Familia, is a breath of fresh air in a neighborhood where most lodgings have grander pretensions. Rooms are compact, so don't plan on spreading out, but they're tidy and bright, and the staff are cheerful. Lacking a restaurant or even a cafeteria (there is a breakfast room), the hotel only gets two stars from the official rating agency. That's okay—it guarantees a lower price for a quality lodging. Carrer de la Diputació, 394. ℂ **93-232-62-11.** www.hotel-antibesbarcelona.com. 71 units. 46€–87€ double. Parking: 18€. Metro: Tetuan. **Amenities:** Internet corner; free Wi-Fi.

Hostal Girona ★   Early Modernista architect Ildefons Cerada designed this building in the 1860s, and it retains some significant traces of its design heyday. The hostal is located on an upper floor, and only some of the rooms show their history. All units have private bathrooms, though some rooms are quite small.

Four units have balconies, but for the full Modernista effect, ask for one of the two large rooms with terraces.

Carrer Girona, 24 (piso 1, puerta 1). ✆ **93-265-02-59.** www.hostalgirona.com. 19 units. 36€–98€ double. Metro: Girona or Urquinaona. **Amenities:** Free Wi-Fi.

Waterfront

EXPENSIVE

Duquesa de Cardona Hotel ★ This 16th-century former noble home was transformed into a boutique hotel in 2003. The developers' optimism that the strip between the Barri Gòtic and the harbor was going to gentrify was a little premature, as a low-rent backpacker hostel still operates two doors away. But it's hard to fault the fabulous views across the Moll de la Fusta to Port Vell, or the upper-level views back to the Columbus monument and up the coast to Port Olimpic. Rooms on the front (an extra charge for waterfront views) are larger and more romantic than some of the tighter quarters on the back that face into El Born.

Passeig Colom, 12. ✆ **93-268-90-90.** www.hduquesadecardona.com. 40 units. 165€–245€ double; 230€–280€ jr. suite. Parking 30€. Metro: Barceloneta or Jaume I. **Amenities:** Restaurant; babysitting; concierge; room service; free Wi-Fi.

Hotel Arts ★★★ This landmark hotel from the waterfront makeover for the Olympics occupies the lower 33 floors of a 44-story skyscraper and is known for its contemporary art collection. The Ritz-Carlton–managed hotel is about 2.5km (1½ miles) southwest of the old city, next to Port Olimpic. The spacious, well-equipped guest rooms have built-in headboards, bedside tables, generously sized desks, and sumptuous beds. Pink marble dominates the bathrooms, and views from the windows take in the skyline and the Mediterranean. The hotel also has the city's only beachfront pool.

Carrer de la Marina 19–21. ✆ **800/241-3333** in the U.S., or 93-221-10-00. www.ritzcarlton.com. 483 units. 250€–370€ double; 475€–12,000€ suite. Parking 42€. Metro: Ciutadella or Vila Olimpica. **Amenities:** 5 restaurants; 2 bars; children's programs; concierge; exercise room; outdoor heated pool; room service; spa; free Wi-Fi.

MODERATE

Hotel 54 ★ If you can't score a room with a view at this pleasant hostelry in the former fishermen's association building, then console yourself by hanging out on the fifth floor terrace to enjoy a 270-degree view of the harbor and city skyline. The location is terrific: You can cut through residential Barceloneta to walk to Platja San Sebastiá, and Les Rambles is a 15-minute walk up the Moll de la Fusta. A major renovation installed nice decorative touches like colored LED mood lights over the beds and the cast glass sinks in the bathrooms.

Passeig Joan de Borbó, 54. ✆ **93-225-00-54.** www.hotel54barceloneta.com. 28 units. 90€–150€ double. Metro: Barceloneta. **Amenities:** Bar-cafe; room service; rooftop terrace; free Wi-Fi.

Medinacelli Hotel ★★ Built into the old palace of the Dukes of Medinacelli at the waterfront edge of the Barri Gòtic, the hotel expanded into an adjacent building and created 19 new rooms in spring 2013. Rooms are bright with pale modern furnishings and ample windows that are double-glazed to seal out noise. Ceilings in some rooms are surprisingly low for a heritage building, but even the most modest rooms are fairly spacious, averaging around 250 square feet.

Plaça Duc de Medinacelli, 8. ✆ **93-481-77-25.** www.hotelmedinacelli.com. 78 units. 90€–200€ double. Metro: Drassanes. **Amenities:** Free Wi-Fi.

Hotel Ciutadella Barcelona ★★   Set between the Parc de Ciutadella and Barceloneta, this hotel opened in fall 2012 with bargain-priced contemporary design rooms. The location is great for exploring the dining and nightlife of El Born—or spending the day at the beach. Most rooms are compact, but they're so well-designed that they seem more spacious. Views along the avenue are unremarkable, but windows are ample and double-glazed, ensuring that the light gets in and the noise does not. Terrifically friendly and helpful staff make the Ciutadella a very pleasant choice. Avinguda Marquès de L'Argentera, 4. (C) **93-319-19-44.** www.hotelciutadellabarcelona.com. 59 units. 90€–110€. Metro: Barceloneta. **Amenities:** Free Wi-Fi.

WHERE TO EAT

One reason why Barcelona has evolved into one of the world's top gastronomic destinations is La Boqueria. The great market displays *everything* that is available in the city, from the catch of the day to still-warm-from-the-sun berries. With no mystery about ingredients, the chefs and cooks have to work their magic to make a dish that is somehow even better than the pristine ingredients you saw in the market. Sometimes that's as simple as *pá amb tomate*—toasted or grilled bread rubbed with fresh tomato, drizzled with olive oil, and sprinkled with sea salt. In tomato season, it is served instead of a breadbasket.

You can eat fabulously at some of the most old-fashioned and casual spots in the city—places like Cal Pep, Can Ravell, La Gardunya, or even the ultimate comfort food restaurant, Los Caracoles. But Barcelona is one of the world's great eating cities, so it's worth splurging here if you can. It need not break the bank; some of the top chefs have opened tapas restaurants and other bargain venues to showcase their culinary creativity using less expensive materials. Barcelona dining hours are closer to the European standard than in Madrid. Lunch is usually served to -3pm (and can represent a great bargain), and dinner starts around 8pm, although dining before 9pm is unfashionable.

Les Rambles & El Raval
MODERATE

Ca L'Isidre ★★ CATALAN   Isidre Gironés and his wife Montserrat have been serving market cuisine with a seafood emphasis at this El Raval restaurant since 1970. Although the neighborhood was fairly rough until recently, gastronomes have always sought them out for hard-to-find old-fashioned dishes like fried salt cod with white beans. You can also order contemporary preparations like tartare of bream and *cigalas* (the local saltwater crawfish) with parsley oil, or roast kid with baby onions. In summer and early fall, the best available starter is gazpacho with assorted seafood. Carrer Les Flors, 12. (C) **93-441-11-39.** www.calisidre.com. Reservations required. Main courses 18€–40€; weekday lunch menu 40€. Mon–Sat 1:30–4pm and 8:30–11pm. Closed 1st 2 weeks in Aug. Metro: Paral.lel.

Fonda España ★★ BASQUE   The value for price ratio is very high at this superb restaurant in the Hotel España in El Raval. The menu is created by star chef Martín Berasategui (he's based in Basque country but visits often). Because he focuses on traditional fare rather than the more inventive dishes served at his other restaurants, he's charging less (and using fewer organ meats, a blessing for squeamish diners). Look for grilled kid chops (like lamb chops), baked monkfish, or fried mullet. The most Basque of the desserts is a glass of slightly sparkling txacolí wine with strawberries and a scoop of lemon peel ice cream. Management recently restored the main dining room to Lluís Domènech i Montaner's designs; the Art Nouveau mosaics positively gleam.

Hotel España, Carrer Sant Pau, 9. ℂ **93-550-00-10.** www.hotelespanya.com. Reservations suggested. Main courses 9€–26€; weekday lunch menu 26€; dinner tasting menu 55€. Mon–Sat 1–4pm and 8–11pm. Metro: Liceu.

La Gardunya ★★ CATALAN   Tony Magaña Huertas is the boss behind this unexpected little restaurant in the back of Barcelona's covered food market, La Boqueria, and he loves good, simple food. Fancier table settings are available upstairs but most diners opt for the downstairs bar. There are also a few tables by the back door so you can watch the market workers coming and going. The food is "market cuisine" in the most direct sense of the term (it's at the market), but preparations show real imagination. Fresh cod, for example, might be roasted with quince and served with a dab of aioli and wilted spinach. A grilled steak could come with a confit of piquillo peppers. Fixed price menus at lunch and dinner are real bargains.

Carrer Jerusalem, 18. ℂ **93-302-43-23.** Reservations recommended. Main courses 13€–30€; fixed-price lunch 14€, dinner 16€. Bar Mon–Sat 7am–midnight. Restaurant Mon–Sat noon–3pm and 8pm–midnight. Metro: Liceu.

INEXPENSIVE

Dos Palillos Barcelona ★★ ASIAN/SPANISH   Albert Raurich heads this oddball tapas restaurant, and given that he spent 11 years at elBulli (the last 6 as head chef under Ferran Adrià), the restaurant had to have a twist. When he and Adrià ate their way through New York's Chinatown on a visit, Raurich thought up dim sum tapas. Casa Camper thought it was great idea, and the "two sticks" launched in their hotel as homage to the chopsticks of Asian cuisine and the toothpicks of Spanish bar food. Dishes run the gamut from Chinese dumplings filled with Spanish prawns and Iberico pork belly to Japanese-style burgers with ginger, cucumber, and miso. Regulars swear by the combination of tempura vegetables with glasses of sherry.

Carrer Elisabets, 11. ℂ **93-304-05-13.** www.dospalillos.com. Tapas 4€–15€. Thurs–Sat 1:30–3:30pm; Tues–Sat 7:30–11:30pm. Closed 2 weeks in Aug. Metro: Liceu or Catalunya.

Granja M. Viader ★ CATALAN   One of Barcelona's original "milk bars," M. Viader invented the drink you see next to the sodas in every cooler: Cacaolat. It's exactly what you might think from the name—chocolate milk—and Catalans of a certain age gush with nostalgia over it. The founder was instrumental in getting pasteurized milk products out to the public, and this wonderfully old-fashioned cafe, founded in 1870, still serves coffee, pastries, sandwiches, hot chocolate, and (of course!) chocolate milk. In the morning, you can also get hot *churros* to go with the hot chocolate.

Carrer Xucla, 4–6. ℂ **93-318-34-86.** www.granjaviader.cat. Sandwiches 3–5€; pastries 1.80€–4€. Mon–Sat 9am–1:15pm and 5–8:15pm. Metro: Liceu or Catalunya.

Barri Gòtic, La Ribera & Born
EXPENSIVE

Comerç 24 ★★★ CATALAN   Chef-owner Carles Abellan re-invents classic Catalan dishes through the lens of world cuisine. An elBulli alumnus, he experiments with techniques and flavors, an the results are inevitably harmonious. The

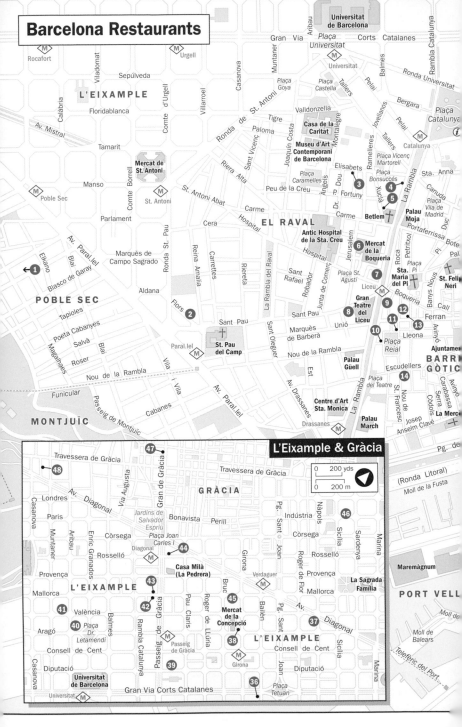

Barcelona Restaurants

L'EIXAMPLE

Rocafort

Urgell

Sepúlveda

Viladomat

Comte d'Urgell

Villarroel

Casanova

Muntaner

Gran Via   Plaça   Corts Catalanes
Universitat

Universitat
de Barcelona

Balmes

Rambla Catalunya

Ronda Universitat

Bergara

Plaça
Catalunya

Floridablanca

Calàbria

Tamarit

Av. Mistral

Manso

Poble Sec

Parlament

Comte Borrell

Ronda de St. Antoni

Mercat de
St. Antoni

St. Antoni

Sant Vicenç

Ronda de

Riera Alta

St. Antoni Abat

Carme

Cera

Reina Amalia

Hospital

Carretes

Riereta

Tigre

Paloma

Valldonzella

Casa de la
Caritat

Museu d'Art
Contemporani
de Barcelona

Plaça
Caramelles

Peu de la Creu

EL RAVAL

Antic Hospital
de la Sta. Creu

Hospital

Plaça
Goya

Plaça
Castella

Tallers

Joaquín Costa

Montalegre

Àngels

Plaça
Vicenç
Martorell

Elisabets

Dou

P. Fortuny

Carme

Jerusalem

Mercat
de la
Boqueria

Ramelleres

Tallers

Jovellanos

Plaça
Bonsuccés

Xuclà

Betlem

Petxina

Sta. Anna

La Rambla

Canuda

Plaça
Vila de
Madrid

Palau
Moja

Portaferrissa

Plaça
del Pi

Sta.
Maria
del Pi

Bote

Pal

St. Feli
Neri

3

4

5

6

7

POBLE SEC

Av. Paral.lel

Blai

Blasco de Garay

Marquès de
Campo Sagrado

Aldana

Flors

Tapioles

Poeta Cabanyes

Salvà

Roser

Nou de la Rambla

Magalhaes

Blai

Vila i Vila

Funicular

Passeig de Montjuïc

Cabanes

MONTJUÏC

Elkano

Ronda St. Pau

Sant Pau

St. Pau
del Camp

Paral.lel

Sant Oleguer

Sant Pau

Sant
Rafael

Robador

Junta de Comerç

La Rambla del Raval

Marquès
de Barberà

Nou de la Rambla

Unió

Plaça St.
Agustí

Gran
Teatre
del
Liceu

Liceu

Palau
Güell

Est

Av. Drassanes

Centre d'Art
Sta. Monica

Drassanes

Palau
March

Plaça
del Teatre

Nou de St. Francesc

Plaça
Reial

Escudellers

Roca

Boqueria

Lleona

BARR
GÒTIC

Josep
Anselm Clavé

La Merc

Ajuntamer

Ferran

Call

Avinyó

Banys Nous

Codols

Serra

Carbassa

Avinyó

Pg. de

1

2

8

9

10

11

12

13

14

L'Eixample & Gràcia

Travessera de Gràcia

Gran de Gràcia

GRÀCIA

Travessera de Gràcia

0   200 yds

0   200 m

(Ronda Litoral)

Moll de la Fusta

Londres

Paris

Còrsega

Rosselló

Provença

Mallorca

València

Aragó

Consell de Cent

Diputació

Casanova

Muntaner

Aribau

Enric Granados

Balmes

Av. Diagonal

Vila Augusta

Jardins de
Salvador
Espriu

Bonavista

Perill

Plaça Joan
Carles I

Diagonal

Casa Milà
(La Pedrera)

Rambla Catalunya

Passeig de Gràcia

Gràcia

Pau Claris

Roger de Llúria

Bruc

Girona

Bailèn

Pg. Sant Joan

Verdaguer

Indústria

Còrsega

Rosselló

Provença

Mallorca

Mercat
de la
Concepció

L'EIXAMPLE

Consell de Cent

Diputació

Plaça
Tetuan

Universitat
de Barcelona

Gran Via Corts Catalanes

Universitat

Nàpols

Sicília

Sardenya

Marina

Roger de Flor

Av. Diagonal

Sicília

Joan

La Sagrada
Família

Maremàgnum

PORT VELL

PORT VEL

Moll d

Moll de
Balears

Telefèric del Port

Plaça
Dr.
Letamendi

47

48

44

43

42

41

40

39

38

45

46

37

36

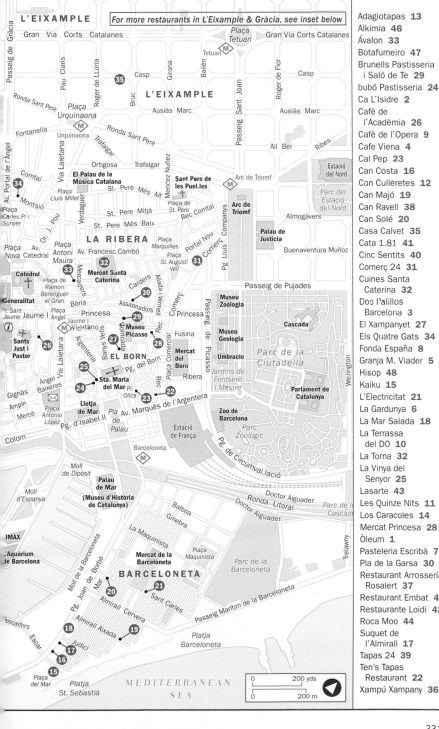

For more restaurants in L'Eixample & Gràcia, see inset below

rabbit paella offers rabbit cooked on a spit. He perfumes fresh salmon with vanilla and serves it with yogurt cheese instead of crème fraîche. His roast suckling pig is done Hanoi-style, gorgeously glazed and scented with astringent herbs. This is vibrant, earthy food—not a speck of foam in sight. Abellan also makes one of the great Catalan classics, *arròç de pato* (duck paella) with dabs of foie gras along with the confit. The dining room is out of the way, up the street from the Museu de Xocolata at the east end of La Ribera. In addition to a la carte service, Abellan offers two tasting menus (7 or 12 courses) with tapas-sized portions.

Carrer Comerç 24. ✆ **93-319-21-02.** www.carlesabellan.es. Reservations required. Main courses 18€–38€; tasting menus 92€ or 116€. Tues–Sat 1:30–3:30pm and 8:30–11:30pm. Closed 10 days in Dec. Metro: Arc de Triomf or Estació de Franca.

Moderate

Cal Pep ★★★ CATALAN   The only bad thing about Cal Pep is that it closes after lunch on Saturday and doesn't reopen until Monday dinner. Folks in Barcelona for the weekend miss out joining the swarm of happy people dining on Pep's small dishes. Plan your time wisely so that you can try what other places call *media raciones,* that is, bigger than a tapa and smaller than a *racion*. There are some Catalan classics among the 70 or so dishes available on a given day, but most are the restaurant's own invention—the "atomic" omelet with crumbled sausage, chewy beans, and potent garlic sauce, for example, or the baked artichokes stuffed with onions and black olives. Pep himself plays host, making sure everyone is having a good time and recommending what they should try next. There's a small dining room inside, but most patrons prefer the counter seats up front.

Plaça des les Olles, 8. ✆ **93-310-79-61.** www.calpep.com. Reservations for groups of 4–20 only. Main courses 14€–28€. Mon–Fri 7:30–11:30pm; Tues–Sat 1–3:45pm. Closed Aug. Metro: Barceloneta or Jaume I.

Cuines Santa Caterina ★★ ASIAN/MEDITERRANEAN   This soaring adjunct to the Mercat Santa Caterina (p. 351) is one of the classiest eating halls in Barcelona. A simple tapas bar stands at the entrance, but the main action is in the dining room of chunky wooden tables surrounded on two sides by open kitchens. That's right, "kitchens" in the plural. Order paella and it comes from the Spanish kitchen; order fried rice and it comes from the Asian kitchen. The restaurant prides itself on total integration with the market, and many of the dishes are suitable for vegetarians, if not always for vegans. Light vegetable tempuras are offered, as are vegetable sushi rolls and excellent sashimi cut to order. Spanish and Catalan market food—roast duck, monkfish, and clams with romesco sauce—is just as plentiful and just as good. You can't make reservations, so show up early or be ready to wait.

Mercat de Santa Caterina, Avinguda Francesc Cambó, 17. ✆ **93-268-99-18.** Main courses 9€–24€. Daily 1–4pm; Sun–Wed 8–11:30pm; Thurs–Sat 8pm–12:30am. Metro: Jaume I.

Els Quatre Gats ★ CATALAN   Founded in 1897 as Barcelona's bohemian hangout, the "four cats" (Catalan slang for "just a few people") hit its mark early on, thanks to backing by artists Santiago Rusiñol and Ramón Casas. The Modernista crowd hung out here, and the owner gave Picasso one of his first paying art jobs by commissioning the illustration still used on the menu cover. In fact, the young Picasso had his first exhibition at El Quatre Gats in 1900. Even the building, designed by Puig i Cadalfach, is a period piece of art. Every tourist comes here at least once; unfortunately, many of them dress poorly and wear flip-flops, which the management bans as in bad taste. (We suspect many of the restaurant's nay-sayers on crowd-sourced websites were bounced for sloppy attire.) The food is hardly revolutionary—cod cooked in ratatouille, roast shoulder of lamb, duck confit with mushrooms—but the midday menu is a good bargain and the memorabilia on the walls can be engrossing.

Carrer Montsió, 3. ✆ **93-302-41-40.** www.4gats.com. Reservations required Sat–Sun. Main courses 12€–28€. Daily 10am–2am. Metro: Plaça de Catalunya.

La Terrassa del DO ★ CATALAN   The casual dining space of the grandly named DO Plaça Reial Boutique Hotel Gastronomic is only marginally more expensive than its less accomplished neighbors on the Plaça Reial. The forte here is drinks with tapas, but even the tapas are a welcome respite from most bar food. Imagine a glass of cava with a salad of escarole, mango, and grilled fresh Atlantic bonito, or a glass of Priorat red with griddled calamari and garlic. The DO kitchen also prepares solid comfort food like charcoal-grilled octopus with mashed potatoes, roasted catch of the day with vegetables of the season, or a burger made with Galician veal (the closest thing to American beef you'll find in Spain). There are many tables inside and (weather permitting) more outdoors, so reservations aren't an issue.

Plaça Reial, 1. ✆ **93-481-36-66.** www.hoteldoreial.com. Tapas 1.50€–10€, main courses 9€–29€. Daily 9–11am, noon–4pm, and 7pm–2am. Metro: Liceu.

INEXPENSIVE

Adagiotapas ★★ CATALAN   Chef/owner Jordi Herrera—a revered former teacher of cuisine at Barcelona's hotel school—is a master of tradition and innovation alike. His capacity for giving old dishes new legs won him a Michelin star at his fine-dining restaurant, but in mid-2013 he also opened this creative tapas operation in a modest hotel in the Barri Gòtic. Some dishes are straightforward, like the briny oyster with ginger mignonette, while others are clever re-inventions of classics, such as the *tortilla* with caramelized onion that's finished in the oven as a small tart cooked in a cupcake paper. Instead of the conventional ham croquettes, he serves delicious rabbit croquettes encrusted with shredded phyllo and accompanied by a few dabs of ratatouille. The wine list is short and inexpensive.

Carrer Ferran, 21. ✆ **93-318-90-61**. www.adagiotapas.com. Tapas 4€–10€. Daily 1–4pm and 7–11pm. Metro: Liceu or Jaume I.

Avalon ★ CATALAN   One salutary effect of Spain's fiscal crisis has been the proliferation of inexpensive restaurants with menus from upmarket chefs. This welcoming, breezy spot in the Grand Hotel Central is the brainchild of rock star chef Ramón Freixa. In contrast to his fine-dining restaurants (where he has four Michelin stars), Avalon feels like a casual American spot with Catalan food. It's bright and unfussy, and offers free Wi-Fi. The dishes are unfussy as well—a dozen little plates ranging from mini-pizzas to green salads and small rice plates, and then nine larger plates: three different burgers topped with fried egg, three different roasted sausage casseroles, three different canneloni. It's playful and very affordable.

Carrer Pare Gallifa, 3. ✆ **93-295-79-05.** www.avalonrestaurant.es. Reservations recommended. Main dishes 12€–17€. Daily 1:30–4pm and 8–11pm. Metro: Jaume I.

Cafè de L'Acadèmia ★★ CATALAN   Set into a 15th-century building opposite the church on the tiny plaza of Sant Just, Cafè de L'Acadèmia is more inventive and less expensive than it looks. Chef-owner Jordí Casteldi prepares Catalan market cuisine, offering a delicious cold carrot soup with a dollop of pesto in warm weather. (It comes paired with a second bowl of gazpacho.) Fish dishes—roasted salt cod gratinée with artichoke mousse, for example—are a little more involved than the usual fare. Like many modern Catalan chefs, he also prepares a number of nominally Italian dishes that can range from lasagna with blood pudding sausage to risotto finished with thin slices of foie gras on top. Caramelized grapes beneath the rice are a foil to the foie. Casteldi owns his own vineyards, so the house wine is truly the wine of the house.

Carrer Lledó, 1. ✆ **93-319-82-53.** Reservations required. Main courses 10€–14€; midday menu 16€. Mon–Fri 1:30–4pm and 8:30pm–1am. Closed last 2 weeks of Aug. Metro: Jaume I.

Can Culleretes ★ CATALAN   Tucked onto a tiny side street near the Plaça Reial, Culleretes has been serving traditional Catalan fare since 1786—dishes like spinach cannoli with salt cod brandade, stewed wild boar, or partridge casserole. The priciest meal (36€ for two) is the assorted fish and shellfish, a three-course spread that starts with garlic shrimp and steamed shellfish, moves on to assorted fried fish (usually monkfish and squid), and concludes with grilled prawns, scampi, and baby calamari.

Carrer Quintana, 5. ✆ **93-317-30-20.** http://culleretes.com. Reservations recommended. Main courses 8€–18€. Tues–Sun 9am–4pm and Tues–Sat 9–11pm. Closed mid-July to mid-Aug.

Los Caracoles ★ SPANISH   It is a rite of passage for tourists to dine at "The Snails," where the Bofarull family has been welcoming hungry travelers since 1835. You may smell the whole chickens roasting over a spit in an open window before you arrive. The snails, for which the restaurant was renamed in the mid–20th century, are good and garlicky, but most diners come for the comfort food: chicken and ham croquettes, roast chicken, roast suckling pig, and the pricey lobster paella. The menu has basically remained unchanged since Los Caracoles was featured in the inaugural edition of *Spain on $5 a Day*. Honest food without subtext never goes out of style.

Carrer Escudellers, 14. ✆ **93-301-20-41.** www.loscaracoles.es. Reservations recommended. Main courses 8€–27€. Daily 1:15pm–midnight. Metro: Liceu or Drassanes.

Pla de la Garsa ★★ CATALAN   Although a new generation is in charge, this venerable family restaurant retains its terrific collection of Modernista graphic art, its 18th-century tiles and wrought iron, and its commitment to the dark and savory side of traditional Catalan cookery. The kitchen makes its own pâtés and terrines—the anchovy-black olive terrine (*garum*) is especially good—and offers a wide array of traditional sausages and cured meats, including the air-dried beef usually only found in mountainous western Catalunya. When it's available, ask for the sturgeon carpaccio with cava vinaigrette as a starter. (Sturgeon cooked in cider is also usually on the menu as a main dish.) Duck is a staple here; one of the restaurant's most popular dishes is duck three ways (gizzards, liver, and thighs). The short and powerful wine list is strong on Priorat, and for dessert you can't go wrong with any of the Catalan cheeses.

Carrer Assaonadors, 13. ✆ **93-315-24-13.** www.pladelagarsa.com. Reservations recommended Fri–Sat. Main courses 9€–14€. Daily 8pm–1am. Metro: Jaume I.

Les Quinze Nits ★ SPANISH   The proprietors of this large restaurant with lots of outdoor tables on Plaça Reial know how to whip up a crowd: Offer the least expensive meals on the scenic plaza. The food is pretty good, especially if you stick to simple preparations like grilled tuna with squash and olives or *arròc negre* (paella-like black rice with squid in its own ink). Be careful with the drink orders, though, as wine, beer, and soft drinks are actually more expensive than at otherwise higher priced restaurants.

Plaça Reial, 6. ℂ **93-317-30-75.** www.lesquinzenits.com. No reservations. Main dishes 7€–13€. Daily 12:30–11:30pm. Metro: Liceu.

Ten's Tapas Restaurant ★★ CATALAN   When culinary magician Jordi Cruz decided to move his two-star Michelin restaurant aBaC out to Tibidabo, he repaid the foodies of El Born by establishing this refreshingly unpretentious tapas restaurant in its space. The tapas menu has a great version of fried potatoes with aioli mousse and spicy *bravas* sauce, but you'll also find more ambitious plates like foie gras with figs, sweet and salted bread crumbs, and Sichuan pepper ice cream. One of the most inspired dishes might be the oysters on the half shell with a dollop of cucumber ice cream, finely minced lemon peel, and a drizzle of arbequina olive oil. Roughly 15 dishes are offered at a time, including one special from the aBaC menu.

Carrer del Rec 79. ℂ **93-319-22-22.** www.tensbarcelona.com. Reservations suggested. Tapas 5€–15€. Sun and Tues–Thurs 1–3:30pm and 8–11:30pm, Fri–Sat 1–3:30pm and 8pm–midnight. Metro: Barceloneta or Jaume I.

La Vinya del Senyor ★ VINOTECA/TAPAS   It doesn't get much better than spending an afternoon on the terrace of La Vinya del Senyor taking in the glorious Gothic facade of the church of Santa María del Mar—especially if there's a wedding taking place. The vinoteca serves glasses of wine with a modest tapas menu. It's not uncommon to find several Priorats, several more Riojas, and a selection of Ruedas and Albariños by the glass. If you're drinking a bottle, you can choose from more than 300 still wines and cavas, sherries, and Moscatels. Tapas include many usual suspects—Manchego cheese, *jamón serrano*—and some Catalan surprises like walnut rolls drizzled with Catalan olive oil. La Vinya also serves the sweet, crisp version of *coca,* a Catalan flatbread scented with anisette and rolled in sugar and pine nuts. Because it absorbs the tannins in your mouth, it's a great complement to a powerful red wine.

Plaça Santa María, 5. ℂ **93-310-33-79.** www.lavinyadelsenyor.com. Tapas 3€–11€. Sun–Thurs noon–1:30am, Fri–Sat noon–2am. Metro: Jaume I or Barceloneta.

El Xampanyet ★   One of the city's best-loved "champagne bars" since 1929, El Xampanyet knows that no bar ever went broke by selling inexpensive drinks. By day it keeps a low profile just across from the Museu Picasso; the corrugated steel door does not roll up until the museum closes. In minutes, Xampanyet is jammed, as drinkers assemble next to wine barrels, marble-topped tables, or the long zinc bar as if someone were about to start shooting a party commercial. Tapas are simple and salty (olives, ham, croquettes), and the house cava (white or pink) is a great deal.

Carrer Montcada, 22. ✆ **93-319-70-03.** Tapas 2€–6€. Mon–Sat 8pm–2am. Metro: Jaume I. Closed in Aug.

L'Eixample

EXPENSIVE

Alkimia ★★ CATALAN   As the name suggests, chef Jordi Vila fashions himself an alchemist, transmuting base materials of Catalan cuisine into a kind of gastronomic gold. Some signature dishes—like a "fried egg" of cauliflower cream—are almost impossibly labor-intensive (and priced accordingly), while others like the roast chicken canneloni, the veal kidneys with coffee crumbs, or the pickled oyster with glazed pork are surprising in their tastes but more straightforward to prepare. Vila can elevate some of the simplest ingredients, poaching red mullet in olive oil and gracing the plate with an apple-cucumber chutney.

Carrer Industria, 79. ✆ **93-207-61-15.** www.alkimia.cat. Reservations required. Main dishes 11€–28€; fixed-price menus 39€–94€. Mon–Fri 1:30–3:30pm and 8:30–10:30pm. Closed 3 weeks in Aug. Metro: Sagrada Família.

Botafumeiro ★★ SEAFOOD   Owner Moncho Neira hails from Galicia and holds the opinion (shared by much of Spain) that Galicians know more about fish than anyone. Neira sources his fish from the auctions on the Catalan and Galician coasts and presents them in a glamorous, old-world fine-dining setting where waiters wear white jackets and diners are expected to dress accordingly. Begin with a selection of clams and oysters from the raw bar, or take Neira's advice and start with his spider crab pie. Because he has access to the Galician catch, he always has live lobsters, "Norway lobster" (scampi), two or three species of crab, clams, mussels, and percebes (goose barnacles) in enormous tanks at the restaurant entrance. Diners who prefer meat can choose from a few steaks, some veal dishes, and traditional Galician stewed pork with turnips. The wine list is as Galician as many of the fish, with several bracing *albariño* whites from the Rias Baixas along with a nice selection of Catalan cavas.

Carrer Gran de Gràcia, 81. ✆ **93-218-42-30.** www.botafumeiro.es. Reservations recommended. Main courses 18€–44€; tasting menu 80€. Daily 1pm–1am. Metro: Fontana.

Casa Calvet ★★ CATALAN   Antoni Gaudí designed this Modernista building in 1899 for a textile manufacturer who lived here with his family and ran the business from the downstairs offices now occupied by the restaurant. Casa Calvet has lovingly preserved the stained glass and wood-trimmed Gaudí design, matching it with a cuisine that is equally ornamented, essentially Catalan, and tempered by French nouvelle. Sherry-roasted lamb chops, for example, are paired with ratatouille-filled ravioli and a beet-garlic sauce, while bonito tuna is seared and served with fresh green melon, spiced yogurt, and green beans. Even vegetarians can find a dedicated dish—a ragout of vegetables with tofu and porcini mushrooms.

Carrer Casp, 48. ✆ **93-412-40-12.** www.casacalvet.es. Reservations recommended. Main courses 18€–28€; tasting menus 44€–68€. Mon–Sat 1–3:30pm and 8:30–11pm. Metro: Passeig de Gràcia.

Hisop ★ CATALAN   Oriol Ivern Bondia and Guillem Pla wowed their fellow chefs when they opened Hisop in 2001 to serve radically reinvented Catalan cuisine at bargain prices. Pla has moved on, but Ivern keeps Hisop percolating in a more streamlined style, constantly reimagining the flavors of the region in pure, unmuddled form. This results in some marvelously stripped-down dishes—whole grilled red mullet with a zucchini flower, or a john dory with cockles steamed in a vanilla broth. There is suckling pig, but it's made all the more unctuous by an accompaniment of roasted plums. The menu changes four times a year, with weekly adjustments. (What chef can resist the tomato harvest or a seasonal fish spawn?) Hisop's desserts are equally brilliant combinations of flavors—peach with ginger and coffee, chocolate with basil and almonds, pistachio with kaffir lime.

Pasatje Marimon, 9. ℂ **93-241-32-33.** www.hisop.com. Reservations required. Main courses 24€–28€; 10-course tasting menu 67€, with wine tasting 90€. Mon–Fri 1:30–3:30pm and 9–11pm; Sat 9–11pm Closed first 3 weeks in Aug. Metro: Hospital Clínic.

Lasarte ★★★ BASQUE   If you consider yourself a foodie and have plans for one big splurge in Barcelona, Lasarte might be your best bet. It's the elegant Barcelona outpost of much-decorated Basque chef Martín Berasategui, and since 2009 has held two Michelin stars of its own. Berasategui is known for his innovations, but also for mentoring young chefs, so chef de cuisine Paolo Casagrande interprets some of the classics of the master and adds some dishes of his own. This is world-class dining, and it doesn't come cheap. Many dishes are no more than four bites, which translates to more than 10€ per bite. But they are dishes that form part of your sensory memory bank—the plates against which you will measure all others. Red prawns, for example, come into the restaurant live from the boat. The kitchen prepares them in a sea urchin flan topped with a sheep's milk "caviar" (thanks to the miracles of spherification) and sends them to the dining room on a wet black slate to evoke the dark ocean where they swam only hours before. Tuna belly might be flash-grilled over charcoal and served with mango and capers in soy sauce and a tiny bowl of raw celery minestrone for an orgy of sweet, salt, and umami. If this is all just too breathtaking (especially the price), consider the more casual sister restaurant across the street, Loidi (see below).

Carrer Mallorca, 259 (in Hotel Condes de Barcelona). ℂ **93-445-00-00.** www.restaurantlasarte. com. Smart dress and reservations required. Main dishes 43€–52€; 7-course luncheon tasting menu 115€, 10-course dinner tasting menu 135€. Tues–Sat 1:30–3:30pm and 8:30–11pm. Closed Aug. Metro: Provença.

Restaurant Arrosseria Rosalert ★ CATALAN/SEAFOOD   Just a few blocks from La Sagrada Familia, Jordi Alert has been serving great grilled seafood and baked rice dishes since the late 1970s. What you order depends on how much of a hurry you're in. The "menu express" offers a choice of shellfish grilled or steamed, a choice of grilled finfish, and a pastry for dessert. The *arròs* menu (minimum two people) is designed for lingering. You get a selection of fish bites and shellfish *para pica,* and then paella or similar *arròs,* and a pastry. Best order a bottle of wine, as you'll be halfway through it before the rice is ready. If you have a voracious appetite, order the *parrillada* of assorted grilled fish and shellfish, and it will just keep coming, plate after plate.

Avinguda Diagonal, 301. ℂ **93-207-10-19.** Reservations recommended. Main courses 22€–50€; express menu 15€; rice menu 27€. Tues–Sat noon–5pm and 8pm–2am; Sun noon–5pm. Closed 10 days in Jan and Aug. Metro: Verdaguer/Sagrada Família.

Restaurante Loidi ★★ BASQUE   Also part of the Hotel Condes de Barcelona, Loidi is Berasategui's gastro bistro. Dishes are less elaborate than at Lasarte, but are available only as set menus, of which the whole table must order the same number of courses. The six-course "Martín Selection" gives you most of the menu for about the cost of a main dish at Lasarte. A three-course version is also available. Dishes might include large veal ravioli candied in carrot juice and served with meat broth, and fish with cauliflower purée and beet couscous. In keeping with the food, Loidi is much more casual, though many diners dress smartly for dinner anyway.

Carrer Mallorca, 248–250. ℂ **93-492-92-92.** www.loidi.com. Martín Selection menu 48€, 64€ with matching wines; 3-course menu 28€. Daily 1–3:30pm, Mon–Sat 8–11pm. Metro: Provença.

Roca Moo ★★★ CATALAN   If you're not planning a gastronomic pilgrimage to Girona to eat at **El Celler de Can Roca** (p. 395), you might want to book a dinner here. Chef de cuisine Felip Llufriu executes Joan Roca's inspired dishes perfectly, and the design-centric decadence of Hotel Omm pumps the otherworldliness up a notch. You might start with *cigalas* (saltwater crayfish) with curry, rose petals, and licorice—a brilliant combination of flavors to give a fairly bland crustacean some real taste. The kitchen also does a *bogavente* (Atlantic lobster) version of the dish with a licorice curry sauce. Kid is slowly braised and finished with a rosemary-honey glaze and served on a "cloud" of goat's milk foam. Jordi Roca designs the desserts, which must be ordered at the start of the meal. His classic "Trip to Havana" features rum sponge cake, lime soup, peppermint granita, and a frozen ice cream cigar with a spice ash. Roca Moo now boasts its own Michelin star (the Roca brothers' establishment in Girona has three) and has become more exclusive, trimming back the size of the dining room to expand the adjacent Roca Bar, where the same kitchen serves innovative tapas.

Carrer Rosselló, 265 (in Hotel Omm). ℂ **93-445-40-00.** www.hotelomm.es. Reservations required. Main courses 22€–30€; 7-course Classics Menu 87€, matching wines 35€; 8-course Joan Roca Menu 110€, matching wines 40€. Mon–Sat 1:30–4pm and 8:30–11pm. Metro: Diagonal.

MODERATE

Can Ravell ★★★ CATALAN   Ignasi Ravell founded this gourmet shop in 1929, and kept it running through the Franco years by having faith that even in the worst of times, some people will be willing to pay for the best of things. Now Ignasi's son Josep runs this monument to the Catalan table. There's always been a small area in the back where Can Ravell served a few plates (pork with snails, *tortilla* with sautéed green peppers) with drinks. But only regular customers know about the full restaurant upstairs. You have to go through the kitchen and climb a very narrow circular stair to reach the airy room filled with solid wooden tables with marble slab tops. The menu is brief, consisting of four starters and four main dishes selected by the chef that day after a visit to the market. In the summer the chef goes wild featuring one vegetable after another—a feast of green beans one week, of tomatoes the next. In the fall, you might find lentils stewed with pig's ear and jowls, a roast quarter lamb (for two or three diners), and the popualr side dish of mashed potatoes with foie gras. The cellar here is very extensive, and includes literally dozens of cava choices in addition to still wines.

Carrer Aragó, 313. ℂ **93-457-51-14.** www.ravell.com. Reservations required. Main courses 13€–32€. Tues–Sat 10am–9pm; Sun 10am–3pm. Metro: Girona.

Cata 1.81 ★★ CATALAN/TAPAS   Calling itself a "wine restaurant," Cata 1.81 serves only tapas, but they're hardly run-of-the-mill small plates. Here you'll find a "bikini" (the ubiquitous grilled ham and cheese sandwich) with black truffle, grilled foie gras with orange marmalade and "caviar" of chocolate grains, and a ground pork burger with curry ketchup and a fried egg. You can order a la carte, or opt for a tasting menu that is cheaper than ordering the dishes separately. The wine list is deep and broad, covering most of Spain and some of France, Italy, and California.

Carrer Valencia, 181. ℂ **93-323-68-18.** www.cata181.com. Reservations required. Tasting menu 30€ for 7 savory dishes and 2 desserts, 45€ with 4 glasses of wine; individual tapas 4.75€–8€. Sun–Fri 1pm–midnight; Sat 8pm–12:30am. Closed 3 weeks in Aug. Metro: Passeig de Gràcia or Hospital Clínic.

Restaurant Embat ★★ CATALAN   Another stalwart of Barcelona's bargain-priced "bistronomic" restaurants, Embat has just 10 tables in a modest little space with white stucco walls. It bustles at lunch, when the menu usually has three main dishes, none more than 12€, and often requires reservations at night, when prices rise and choices expand dramatically. The dishes are not radical—just re-thought. Gazpacho comes with a few shrimp and a small ball of burrata (cream-filled mozzarella) with a flurry of basil. The classic monkfish with spinach and creamy potato is complemented by a thin sheet of crackly almond praline. Desserts are a specialty; one favorite is the hot chocolate pudding with walnut ice cream.

Carrer Mallorca, 304. ℂ **93-458-08-55.** www.restaurantembat.es. Main courses lunch 10€–12€, dinner 18€–22€; dinner 5-course tasting menu 42€. Tue–Fri 1–3:30pm, Sat 2–3:30pm, Thur–Sat 9–10:45pm. Metro: Girona or Diagonal.

INEXPENSIVE

Tapas 24 ★★ TAPAS   Tapas in the morning, tapas in the evening, tapas at suppertime. Carles Abellan of **Comerç 24** (p. 329) set up this basement restaurant in L'Eixample as his personal homage to the tapas lifestyle, and it is, quite simply, a treat. Come for breakfast, and you can order *estrellitas*—fried potatoes with a broken fried egg stirred in on top, with or without extra sausage, ham, or foie gras. (Catalan chefs love foie gras, which is local and inexpensive.) Service is nonstop from morning through evening, but the menu keeps changing as the day progresses. Count on always being able to order a bowl of lentils stewed with chorizo, the "McFoie" burger (a hamburger topped with foie gras), or *cap i pota*, which is a gelatinous stew of calf's head and feet beloved by Catalan bar patrons. (It's said to prevent a hangover.) Abellan is also famous for his "bikini" grilled ham and cheese sandwich with black truffle.

Carrer de la Diputació, 269. ℂ **93-488-09-77.** www.carlesabellan.es. Tapas 4€–15€. Mon–Sat 9am–midnight. Metro: Passeig de Gràcia.

Xampú Xampany ★ CATALAN   One of the last of the city's old-fashioned *xampanyerías*, this spot on the corner of Carrer Bailèn at Plaça de Tetuan functions as a wine store that specializes in cavas, the Catalan sparkling wines that used to be called "champagne" before E.U. rules kicked in. It also functions as a bar that usually has at least a half-dozen cavas in the ice bucket. On top of that, it is also a casual restaurant that serves breakfast food, sandwiches, and small plates of sausages and grilled fish. The omelet sandwich (French omelet—just eggs) makes a very good breakfast for a few euros. This being Spain, many breakfast customers also have a glass of cava. Like most things involving inexpensive sparkling wine, it looks a lot more romantic after dark.

Gran Vía de les Corts Catalanes, 702. ℂ **93-265-04-83.** http://xampuxampany.com. Mon–Sat 8am–1:30am. Metro: Girona or Tetuan

Waterfront & La Barceloneta

EXPENSIVE

La Mar Salada ★ CATALAN/SEAFOOD   One of the more prominent members of Barceloneta Cuina, a restaurant organization that aims to promote the seafood gastronomic traditions of the fishermen's neighborhood, La Mar Salada serves old-fashioned dishes like *bombas* (potato balls with a bit of blood sausage in the middle) or heavily breaded and deep-fried squid. Both dishes are usually bathed in the garlicky Catalan eggless mayonnaise called "allioli." But this inventive restaurant is also known for its lobster fritters and a dynamite version of rape *suquet,* a seafood soup made with monkfish, clams, onions, tomato, saffron, and sweet paprika.

Passeig Juan de Borbo, 58–59. ☎ **93-221-21-27.** www.lamarsalada.cat. Reservations recommended. Main dishes 17€–29€. Mon and Wed–Fri 12:30–4:40pm and 8–11:30pm, Sat–Sun 12:30–11:30pm. Metro: Barceloneta.

Suquet de l'Almirall ★★ CATALAN/SEAFOOD   Quim Marqués worked at some of the leading restaurants in Spain (including elBulli) before taking over this Barceloneta gem from his parents in 1997. He has become a champion of the local, buying all his fish from the auction less than 100 yards away, and supplementing the fish with local milk, cheese, eggs, and organically grown vegetables. He's also the author of two Catalan cookbooks focusing on Barceloneta cuisine, including a new one with his son, Manel Marqués, who works alongside him. All the fish dishes here are terrific, but the *suquet* (a traditional Catalan seafood stew) is a classic. Best of all, this is one place on the street where you can eat the seafood paella and know it's the real thing.

Passeig Joan Borbo, 65. ☎ **93-221-62-33.** www.suquetdelamirall.com. Main dishes 19€–28€. Tues–Sat 1:30–4:30pm and 9–11:30pm, Sun 1:30–4:30pm. Metro: Barceloneta.

MODERATE

Can Costa ★ CATALAN/SEAFOOD   The first seafront fish shack to put up a masonry building, Can Costa has been around since the 1920s when this stretch of Barceloneta was a much saltier locale. With two indoor dining rooms (a warehouse blocks the harbor view anyway), Can Costa seats a lot of diners. This can be a drawback if you mind waiting while your food is cooked, but the seafood is fresh and the kitchen cooks it as simply as possible. The fried baby squid are some of the best in Barceloneta as they're so quickly sautéed that they remain tender. The "fideuà de peix," a dish baked in a shallow paella pan with noodles instead of rice, is a house specialty. Can Costa also makes a black version flavored and colored with squid ink and featuring more calamari than shellfish.

Passeig Don Joan de Borbò, 70. ☎ **93-221-59-03.** www.cancosta.com. Reservations recommended. Main courses 12€–32€. Sun–Tues and Thurs–Sat 12:30–4pm; Mon–Tues and Thurs–Sat 8–11:30pm. Metro: Barceloneta.

Can Majó ★ CATALAN/SEAFOOD   Literally steps from the beach, this family restaurant dates from 1968 and is now run by two generations of the Majó family. The dining room resembles a country tavern, but as long as the weather is good, everyone wants to eat outdoors at the white-linen-clad tables beneath umbrellas. Not all the seafood is local—they fly in amazing oysters from Galicia and France for the raw bar. Many of the shellfish are cooked over a wood-fired grill, which gives them a smoky tang. The restaurant is known, however, for fish soups—both the simple fish and shellfish in a fish broth, and the more elaborate *zarzuela,* a Catalan dish where the mixed fish are more important than the broth. On request, the kitchen will prepare the very similar French dish, bouillabaisse.

Almirall Aixada 23, Barceloneta. ✆ **93-221-54-55.** www.canmajo.es. Reservations recommended. Main courses 12€–32€. Tues–Sat 1–3:30pm and 8–11:30pm; Sun 1–3:30pm. Metro: Barceloneta.

Can Solé ★★ CATALAN/SEAFOOD   Proprietor Josep Maria Garcia adheres to the traditional plates of La Barceloneta. That could mean starting with a briny bowl of tiny sweet clams or cabbage hearts stuffed with tuna. Some vanishing dishes make their last stand here, like the fried cod and onions with sweet currants that hint at its North African roots. And then there's the *zarzuela,* the most expensive dish on the menu because it is an encyclopedia of the Barceloneta catch, jammed with everything including whiting, shrimp, cigalas, bream, mackerel, clams, mussels, and even lobster.

Carrer Sant Carles, 4. ✆ **93-221-50-12.** www.restaurantcansole.com. Reservations suggested. Main courses 12€–28€. Tues–Sat 1:30–4pm and 8:30–11pm; Sun 1:30–4pm. Closed 2 weeks Aug. Metro: Barceloneta.

Kaiku ★★ CATALAN/SEAFOOD   Owner Rafa Alberdi held out as long as he could just serving lunch, but the clamor of customers for dinner at Kaiku finally won out. Diners never really know what's on the menu until they arrive, as Alberdi and his chef are always looking for unusual items at the fish market. There will be some kind of shrimp, some form of finfish, cockles, oysters, sea anemones, smoked rice dishes, and grilled *zaburinyes*—seared scallops with ginger and lime. A few plates are standards, like the sautéed mushrooms with shrimp and egg, and the seared tuna with green apple and mango.

Plaça del Mar, 1. ✆ **93-221-90-82.** www.restaurantkaiku.cat. Main dishes 15€–20€. Tues–Sun 1–3:30pm and Tues–Sat 7–10:30pm. Metro: Barceloneta.

INEXPENSIVE

L'Electricitat ★★ TAPAS   Possibly the favorite neighborhood bar in all of Barceloneta, the atmosphere here at midday matches the name—it's positively electric. It's a great place to have steamed mussels or clams, maybe a bite of fried fish, some anchovies, a finger sandwich with smoked trout, and then perhaps a small crab salad. There's beer on tap and a lot of inexpensive Catalan wines. In cold weather, they also tap the big barrels of house vermouth that are more or less ornamental the rest of the year.

Carrer Sant Carles, 15. ✆ **93-221-50-17.** Tapas and raciones 1.50€–12€. Mon–Sat 8am–3pm and 7–10:30pm, Sun 8–3:45pm. Metro: Barceloneta.

Montjuïc

MODERATE

Òleum ★★ CATALAN   Montjuïc is known for its views of the city, and there's no place more serene to lord it over the metropolis than from the dining room of this restaurant at the Museu Nacional d'Art de Catalunya. Usually there's a reverse correlation between the quality of the food and the quality of the view, but not here. Òleum presents a fairly light menu at midday and evening. All dishes have a little twist, whether it's the nut bread and sliced grilled foie on the venison burger, or the pumpkin with the mushroom and truffle risotto. Prices are reasonable for such an exquisite venue—you may wish you hadn't worn sneakers to the museum.

Palau Nacional, Parc de Montjuïc, s/n. ✆ **93-289-06-79.** www.laierestaurants.es. Main dishes 12€–26€. Tues–Sat 12:30–4pm and 7:30–11pm, Sun 12:30–4pm. Metro: Plaça d'Espanya.

EXPLORING BARCELONA

Barcelona is a compact city easily explored on foot once you take public transit to a starting point. There are four areas of interest: **the medieval old city, the post-1880 new city, the waterfront,** and **Montjuïc.**

The neighborhoods of the old city (Ciutat Vell) combined are smaller in area than the new city, but you'll probably to spend more time exploring the old than the new. We've broken it down into historic neighborhoods for convenience, but as you wander, you'll find that one flows into the next. The central, largely pedestrian, artery of the old city is **Les Rambles.** To the west lies **El Raval;** to the east is the medieval **Barri Gòtic.** Keep going east past the cathedral and you'll enter **La Ribera** and **El Born.** The old city has beautiful Gothic churches (including the cathedral), atmospheric medieval streets, and steady crowds. It also has the **Museu Picasso,** the **Palau de la Música Catalana,** the **Museu d'Art Contemporani de Barcelona,** and the top food markets.

The new city begins north of Plaça de Catalunya and includes **L'Eixample** and **Gràcia,** which are more residential than most of the old city. You'll go here to shop in upscale boutiques and to visit most of the masterpieces of Modernista architecture, including **La Pedrera, Casa Batlló,** and the **Basilica de la Sagrada Familia.** L'Eixample also has several small art museums, including the **Fundació Antoni Tapiès.**

From a practical standpoint, the **waterfront** begins at the base of Les Rambles. It includes the cruise ship port, **Port Vell** (Old Port) yacht basin, the long sandy beach peninsula of **La Barceloneta,** and the more recently developed **Port Olimpic,** east of the older part of the city. The main attractions include boat cruises, **L'Aquàrium de Barcelona,** and the **seafood restaurants and beaches** of Barceloneta.

Last but hardly least is **Montjuïc.** The mountain at the edge of town has been used over the last century for major expositions and events, including the 1929 International Exposition and the 1992 Olympics. It's covered with parkland, and you'll visit for the views, both indoors and out. Several overlooks have great vistas of the city and harbor, but some of the most interesting sights lie within the **Museu Nacional d'Art de Catalunya** and the **Fundació Joan Miró.**

Les Rambles & El Raval

If you're not jazzed walking up and down **Les Rambles ★★★**, check to make sure you still have a pulse. You can spend a day here just exploring the street life, cafes, and shops. But you'll want to take some of that time to turn into El Raval on streets named Nou de la Rambla, Sant Pau, Hospital, Carme, and Elisabets. You'll find both the wonderfully *récherché* world of old Raval, and the modern, hip neighborhood of the arts. Get to Les Rambles by one of three Metro stops: Drassanes at the waterfront, Liceu halfway up, and Plaça de Catalunya at the top.

La Boqueria ★★★ MARKET   Foodies visiting Spain consider the Mercat de Sant Josep de la Boqueria (its official name) a temple deserving reverential pilgrimage. The spot has been a marketplace since medieval days when Raval farmers sold their produce to the inhabitants of the walled city. The current market is the largest of Barcelona's 35 public markets. It has a sidewalk mosaic in front created by Joan Miró in the 1970s, and the metal-roofed structure is an amalgam of building styles erected between 1840 and 1914. From the outside, it resembles a train station. Inside, it is jammed with stalls selling every imaginable type of fresh produce, fish (segregated to one side), and meat (toward the back).

La Boqueria.

There are bakeries and sandwich stalls and juice bars and cafes all tucked into the mix. Even if you're not someone normally intoxicated by food, it's an important spot to visit. By paying attention to what the stalls are selling, you'll quickly learn what's fresh and in season, and can order accordingly at the restaurants.

Les Rambles, 91. No phone. Mon–Sat 8am–8pm. Metro: Liceu.

Gran Teatre del Liceu ★★ THEATER   Despite its plain exterior, this 2,700-seat Belle Epoque opera house is opulent and extravagant inside. One of the world's grand theaters, it was designed in 1861 to replace an earlier o destroyed by fire. Flames gutted the opera house again in 1994, but it was restored to its 19th-century glory. It's also a great place to take in opera, dance, or a concert. The building has a modest cafe on the lower level where you can get an 11€ menu (appetizer, main course, and drink) from 1:30 to 4pm before one of the matinee performances at 3, 5, or 6pm. The Liceu also offers **guided** and **self-guided tours** of the public areas, and a limited number of guided tours of the stage and service areas.

Les Rambles, 51–59. ✆ **93-485-99-13** or 93-485-99-00. www.liceubarcelona.com. 80-min. guided tour of public areas daily at 10am, 11.50€; nonguided tours daily 11:30am–1pm every 30 min., 5.50€; stage and service area tours selected weekdays at 9:15am, 13€. Metro: Liceu.

Hotel España ★ HISTORIC SITE   This mid-19th-century hotel got its most important facelift in 1903 to 1904 under the direction of Modernista architect Lluís Domènech i Montaner. He worked with two of the top artisans of the era to execute the design: sculptor Eusebi Arnau, who created a striking alabaster chimney in one of the dining rooms, and painter Ramon Casas, who did decorative painting and sgraffito work. Domènech i Montaner completed the look with wooden wainscoting and decorative blue and white tiles. The hotel restored some of the Modernista features when it renovated in 2010, and now offers architectural tours.

Carrer Sant Pau, 9–11. ✆ **93-550-00-00.** www.hotelespanya.com. Admission 5€, 2.50€ hotel guests and restaurant diners. Guided tours Mon–Fri 12:15pm and 4:30pm.

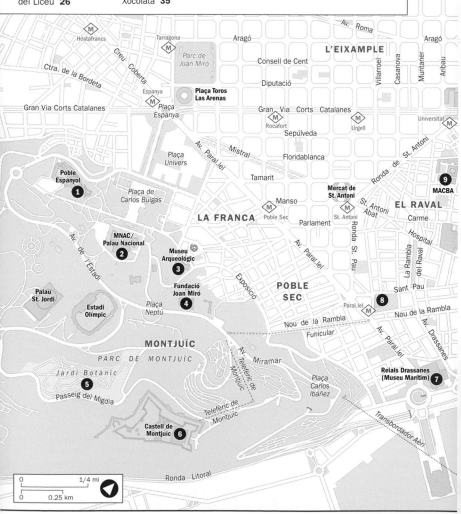

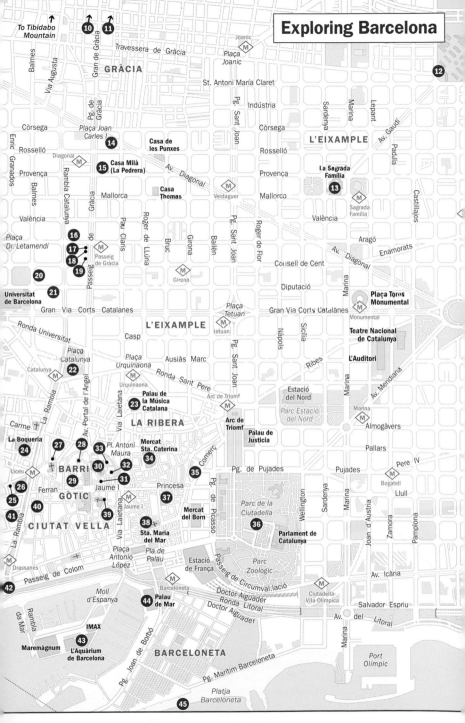

Exploring Barcelona

There are four discount programs that may or may not work for you, depending on what you want to see and how you're planning to get around.

A ticket on the **Barcelona Bus Turistic** (p. 316) gets you a coupon book good for the calendar year. Most discounts are modest, and the Museu Picasso is not included, but if you decide to ride the bus, be sure to use the coupons.

The **Barcelona Card** features several free museum admissions (not Picasso) and allows you to skip the lines. It also provides discounts on other admissions and tours, including 15 to 20% on admissions to major Modernista buildings. Unlimited use of Metro, buses, and commuter rail can be a plus. Available at all Barcelona Turisme offices and El Corte Inglés department stores, it costs 34€ for 2 days, 44€ for 3 days, 52€ for 4 days and 58€ for 5 days. The corresponding prices for children ages 4 to 12 are 14€, 19€, 25€, and 29€.

The **Articket BCN** is geared to the major art museums, providing priority entry to six museums for 30€: Museu Picasso, Museu Nacional d'Art de Catalunya, Fundació Joan Miró, Fundació Antoni Tàpies, the Centre de Cultura Contemporània de Barcelona (CCCB), and the Museu d'Art Contemporani de Barcelona (MACBA). Tickets to the first three alone will cost more than the pass. The pass also allows you to skip the line—a huge timesaver at the Museu Picasso.

Purchasing the **Ruta de Modernisme guide** (12€) at any bookstore or tourist office supplies you with a coupon book with up to 50% off entrance fees to the Modernista buildings. The guide itself and its accompanying map make invaluable, if highly detailed, references to 116 Modernista sites around the city.

When weighing the options, keep in mind that on the first Sunday of each month, **admission is free** at the Museu Picasso, the Museu Nacional d'Art de Catalunya (MNAC), and the Museu d'Història de Catalunya. Museu Picasso is also free every Sunday after 3pm, while MNAC is free every Saturday after 3pm.

Museu d'Art Contemporani de Barcelona ★ MUSEUM   This soaring white structure at the north end of El Raval (just a short distance west of Plaça de Catalunya) has played a key role in the neighborhood's revival. It brings youth and vibrancy to the area—even the ramps around the building are a key gathering spot for Barcelona skateboard athletes. Designed by American architect Richard Meier, the building applies the lessons of Josep Sert's building for the **Fundació Joan Miró** (p. 363) by manipulating angles of exterior walls to allow in natural diffused light. Galleries are often given over to highly conceptual temporary exhibitions, but they do draw on the permanent collection, which is strong in Antoni Tàpies and younger Spanish artists. Guided tours in English are available. The museum is also experimenting with a downloadable app to enable users to access additional audio and video about selected works of art—and to share responses to the work on Facebook and Twitter.

Plaça dels Angels 1. © **93-412-08-10.** www.macba.cat. Admission 10€ adults, 8€ students, free 14 and under and 65 and over. Late June to late Sept Mon and Wed–Fri 11am–8pm; Sat 10am–8pm, Sun 10am–3pm; late Sept to late June Mon and Wed–Fri 11am–7:30pm, Sat 10am–8pm, Sun 10am–3pm. Free guided tours in English Mon 4pm and 6pm, Wed–Sat 4pm. Metro: Plaça de Catalunya.

Museu Maritim ★ MUSEUM   Massive renovations and reconstruction of the historic facility have closed the museum until at least late 2014. In its previous incarnation, the museum's exhibits chronicled Barcelona's maritime history from the time when Rome established the trading port of Barcino up to the 20th century. New exhibits are expected to bring state-of-the-art exhibition technologies to tell that same story. The museum is housed inside medieval royal shipyards, the Drassanes Reiales. So vast were these shipyards, built between 1255 and 1378, that it was possible to construct 30 galleys at a time. As a result, the crown of Aragón became one of the most powerful naval forces in the Mediterranean.

Avinguda de les Drassanes, s/n. ℰ **93-342-99-20.** www.mmb.cat. Hours and admission prices to be announced. Metro: Drassanes.

Palau Güell ★★ HISTORIC SITE   This was Gaudí's second commission and it already looks almost as if it were grown rather than built. Constructed between 1886 and 1890 for aristocrat and industrialist Eusebi Güell, the home shows the architect's budding originality. The family quarters are conventional—"a normal Venetian palace," a guide once sniffed on one of our tours—but the architect's imagination ran wild above and below. The underground forest of brick columns and vaults in 10 musty cellars creates a honeycomb of stables and servants' quarters, and functions as much as the building's root system as its foundation. The rooftop is even more startling. Gaudí wrapped the chimneys with swirling abstract sculptures. Not only are they embedded with mosaics of broken pottery, they also employ artistic symbols from ancient Catalan tradition. After the restraint of the main residence, the rooftop is an exultation of the spirit.

Gaudí's Palau Güell.

Carrer Nou de la Rambla, 3–5. ℰ **93-472-57-75.** www.palauguell.cat. Admission 12€ adults, 8€ students and seniors. Apr–Oct Tues–Sun 10am–7pm, Nov–Mar Tues–Sun 10am–5:30pm. Metro: Liceu.

Plaça de Catalunya ★ PLAZA   Considered the heart of the city, this large circular plaza is where the old city and the 19th-century extension meet. Since its last renovation in 1929, it has also been the crossroads of the Metro system. It is known for its fountains. Legend says that anyone who drinks from the Font de Canaletes will inevitably return to Barcelona.

Metro: Catalunya. Bus: 16, 17, 19, 22, 41, 42, 45, 47, 55, 58, 62, 141, N4, N7, N8, N11, N70–73, N82.

Sant Pau del Camp ★★ RELIGIOUS SITE   The antithesis of Gaudí's La Sagrada Familia, the modest ancient church and monastery of Sant Pau del Camp (St. Paul of the Fields) is one of the most serene and most moving religious spaces in Barcelona. According to his gravestone, which was unearthed in 1596, the monastery was founded between 897 and 911 by Guifré Borrell, then count of Barcelona (and son of Wilfred the Hairy). The church was sacked by Al-Mansur's Moorish troops in 985, but the whole complex was rebuilt during the 13th century—the period of the charming cloister and its stone capitals carved with Biblical tales. Centuries of erosion have not dimmed Eve's sudden embarrassment about her nakedness or the ferocity of the reptilian devil being skewered by archangel Michael. The intimate piety of the church and its small altar are striking. A side chapel holds a beautiful polychrome Gothic statue of María del Deu, as well as the founder's gravestone.

Carrer Sant Pau, 101. ✆ **93-441-00-01.** Admission 3€, Sun morning free. Daily 10am–12:30pm and 4–6:30pm. Masses Sat 8pm in Castilian Spanish, Sun noon in Catalan. Metro: Paral.lel.

Barri Gòtic

Barcelona came into its own as a Mediterranean power in the 12th century when the Aragonese King Jaume I erected a defensive wall around the city. This area— roughly from Les Rambles east to Via Laietana and from the waterfront north to Plaça de Catalunya—is the **Barri Gòtic (Gothic Quarter)** ★★★, which retains much of its medieval street pattern. It's a fascinating neighborhood of narrow streets and pocket squares, most fronting on Gothic churches. Plan on spending at least a half-day exploring, knowing that you will get a little lost, no matter how good your map. The area assumes a special magic on Sunday mornings, when you can emerge from a warren of small streets onto a square where a musician may be playing for change. Metro stops for the Barri Gòtic are Liceu and Jaume I.

Call ★ NEIGHBORHOOD Barcelona had one of the most robust Jewish communities in Iberia from the 12th century until 1391, when the community in the heart of the Barri Gòtic came under siege. Six centuries of absence have wiped away most evidence of Jewish presence, but since the 1990s, a concerted effort by scholars and community activists has helped establish the old limits of the Call and has begun to restore the remains of the principal synagogue. The main street of the Call (a Jewish word meaning "small street" and closely related to the modern Spanish "calle" and Catalan "carrer") was Carrer de Sant Domènc, where the great synagogue, the kosher butcher's shop, and the homes of the leading Jewish citizens were located. An information center and display of artifacts recovered through excavations is operated by the Associació Call de Barcelona in a shop above the remains of the **Sinagoga Mayor.**

Carrer Marlet, 5. Admission 2.50€. Mon–Fri 10:30am–6pm, Sat–Sun 10:30am–3pm. Metro: Jaume I.

The Barri Gòtic.

Inside the Catedral de Barcelona.

Catedral de Barcelona ★★

RELIGIOUS SITE A celebrated example of Catalan Gothic architecture, Barcelona's cathedral was begun at the end of the 13th century and more or less completed by the mid–15th century. One notable exception, the western facade, dates from the 19th century when churchgoers felt that the unadorned Gothic surface was somehow inadequate. If you really want to get a feel for the cathedral, skip the "tourist visit" completely and go to Mass, or at least sit silently and reflect. The high naves, which have been cleaned and lit in recent years, are filled with terrific Gothic architectural details, including the elongated and tapered columns that blossom into arches in their upper reaches. The separate **cloister** has vaulted galleries that surround a garden of magnolias, medlars, and palm trees and the so-called "well of the geese" (13 geese live in the cloister as a symbol of Barcelona co-patron Santa Eulalia). The cloister also contains the cathedral's museum, of which the most notable piece is a 15th-century *pieta* by Bartolomé Bermejo. You can also take an elevator to the roof, which has a number of fanciful gargoyles and terrific views of the rest of the Barri Gòtic. At noon on Sundays (and sometimes on Saturdays), folk dancers gather below the cathedral steps to dance the traditional circular dance, the *sardana*. On the feast of Corpus Christi, the cathedral maintains the Catalan tradition of a dancing egg—a decorated hollow egg that "dances" atop a water jet in one of the fountains.

Plaça de la Seu s/n. 📞 **93-315-15-54.** www.catedralbcn.org. Cathedral free; ticket to museum, choir, rooftop terraces, and towers 6€. Cathedral Mon–Fri 8am–12:45pm and 5:15–7:30pm, Sat–Sun 8am–12:45pm and 5:15–7:30pm; cloister museum daily 10am–12:30pm and 5:15–7pm. Metro: Jaume I.

Museu Frederic Marès ★ MUSEUM

Situated behind the cathedral in part of the old royal palace of the Counts of Barcelona, this striking collection of Iberian sculpture is not for everyone—although its quiet courtyard and hidden plaza are. Marès (1893–1991) was himself a sculptor, but his greatest legacy is the collection that he amassed that covers sculptural styles from the ancient world to the 19th century. The majority of the works are Gothic polychrome statues from around Spain, with emphasis on Castilla and Catalunya. The galleries begin with serene and all-knowing representations of Maria del Deu (Madonna and Child), but Marès seems to have been taken with particularly vivid depictions, especially of gruesome martyrdoms. Crucifixions run the gamut from the sagging flesh of a resigned Christ to more vigorous images of Christ literally writhing on the cross. Small children can find the imagery disturbing. Upper levels of the museum contain some of Marès's peculiar personal collections (locks, especially) that may not appeal to many viewers who nonetheless appreciate the sculptures.

Plaça de San Iu, 5. © **93-256-35-00.** www.museumares.bcn.cat. Admission 4.20€, 2.40€ seniors and students. Mon and Wed–Sat 10am–7pm, Sun 11am–8pm. Metro: Jaume I.

Plaça de Sant Just ★ PLAZA   Most people find this tranquil little plaza because they want to dine at **Cafè de L'Acadèmia** (p. 333), but in Roman times, Jews and Christians came here to trade. The 13th-century church on the plaza, the Basilica dels Sants Just i Pastor, stands on the site of the original 4th-century Christian basilica in Barcino, and the predecessor to this Gothic church functioned as the seat of the archbishop until the city's cathedral was constructed. The plaza's fountain is said to be the oldest water source in the city. Made of Montjuïc stone, it was carved in 1367. Above the three pipes are images of one-handed Sant Just, another of the royal shield, and a third of a shield showing a hawk catching a partridge.

Plaça Sant Just. © **93-301-74-33.** http://basilicasantjust.cat. Free admission. Church open Mon–Sat 11am–2pm and 5–9pm, Sun 10am–1pm. Metro: Jaume I.

Plaça del Pi ★ RELIGIOUS SITE   Three pretty, contiguous plazas surround the 15th-century church of **Santa María del Pi** ★, which is acclaimed for its rose window; at 10m (33 ft.) in diameter, it is considered one of the world's largest. Destroyed at the beginning of the Civil War in 1936, it was slowly restored in the 1950s and is the only window in the basilica to retain its original 14th-century design. It shows the 24 Elders of the Apocalypse with the coats of arms of the church and the Counts of Barcelona. The pews of the church sit on the stones marking graves in the floor. Don't let the skull and crossbones motifs disturb your prayer. During the summer, the church also operates a series of concerts in the basilica's so-called "Secret Garden," with programs that can range from pop music to Vivaldi and include a tour of the church museum. The main square out front is the official Plaça del Pi, but **Plaça de Sant Josep Oriol** adjoins it and flows behind the church to tiny **Placeta del Pi.** The squares are known for the unusual sgraffito decorative technique on the plaster facades of several buildings, an 18th-century style imported from Italy. But the leafy squares are also popular for the weekend artisans' market and open-air cafe-bars.

Santa María del Pi, Carrer del Cardenal Casañas, 16. © **93-318-47-43.** http://basilicadelpi.com. Free. "Secret Garden" concerts 14€. Daily 9am–1pm and 4–9pm.

Plaça del Rei ★ ARCHAEOLOGICAL SITE   Seemingly wedged between the cathedral and the remains of Barcino's Roman walls, this stately square serves as the front porch of the 11th-century Palau Reial Major, palace of the kings of Aragón and Catalunya, and its related complex of buildings, including the **Museu Frederic Marès** (above). The chief attraction here is the guided tour of underground walkways over the excavations of Barcino, the city founded by the Romans in the 1st century B.C. and ruled by the Visigoths until the Moors leveled it in the 8th century A.D. The tour is offered by the **Museu d'Història de la Ciutat.** Although they are partially visible from Plaça del Rei, the last remaining Roman walls and defensive towers of Barcino—a section from the 4th-century A.D. second enclosure—are easier to make out from the opposite side, on **Plaça Ramon Berenguer** on Via Laietana. Embedded within the wall are the royal chapel of Santa Àgata and a 14th-century segment of the Palau Reial.

Plaça del Rei, s/n. © **93-315-11-11.** www.museuhistoria.bcn.es. 7€ adults, 5€ students and seniors, free under age 16. June–Sept Tues–Sat 10am–8pm; Oct–Mar Tues–Sat 10am–2pm and 4–7pm; year-round Sun 10am–3pm. Metro: Jaume I.

Plaça Reial ★ PLAZA   Barcelona's first big urban renewal project in the 19th century, this large and harmonious square occupies the former site of the Santa Madrona Capuchin monastery, which had been demolished at mid-century. Inspired by the renewal projects of Paris, architect Francesc Daniel Molina conceived the Plaça Reial as a residential square formed by buildings with two stories and a partial upper floor. These days it's surrounded largely by cafes, and although it attracts many more tourists than locals, it is still a great place to sit beneath an arcade, drink beer, and observe the scene. The fountain of the three graces in the center is flanked by handsome Art Nouveau lampposts that were Antoni Gaudí's first commission (1878). He decorated them with a caduceus (a messenger's wand with two snakes entwined around it) and winged helmets— attributes of Hermes, patron of shopkeepers.

Metro: Liceu.

Plaça de Sant Felip Neri ★ HISTORIC SITE   This quiet little plaza is one of the few spots in the city to bear witness to Barcelona's suffering during the Civil War. Pockmarks on the facade of the San Felipe Neri church recall the Nationalist bombs that fell here on January 30, 1938. Twenty children and 22 adults who were taking refuge in the church cellars were killed. The fall of Barcelona took place 10 weeks later, when Franco and his forces dropped 44 tons of bombs on the civilian population. Franco saw himself as uniting the country. Many Catalans still see it as genocide.

Metro: Liceu.

Temple d'August ★ ARCHAEOLOGICAL SITE   One of the four columns of this 1st-century A.D. temple is incorporated into the display of the Roman wall on Plaça Ramon Berenguer. The other three remain where they were originally erected, now enclosed by the 19th-century building that houses the Centre Excursionista de Catalunya. The temple once formed part of the Roman Forum dedicated to Emperor Caesar Augustus. The ruins are part of the citywide collection of the Museu d'Història de la Ciutat (see Plaça Reial, above) and can be visited free of charge.

Carrer Paradis, 10. ℭ **93-315-23-11.** www.museuhistoria.bcn.es. Free. June–Sept Tues–Sat 10am–8pm, Sun 10am–2pm; Oct–May Tues–Sat 10am–2pm and 4–8pm, Sun 10am–2pm. Metro: Jaume 1.

La Ribera & El Born

With streets a little wider, buildings a little newer, and street patterns that at least approach a grid, **La Ribera and El Born ★★** push the Barri Gòtic eastward. They are still obviously part of the old city, and can be combined with the Barri Gòtic for a long day or even two of touring. Both La Ribera and El Born combine commercial and residential uses, and both have become gentrified since the 1990s. There's little or no laundry hanging from the balconies in Born these days. In most cases, flower planters have taken its place. Both neighborhoods have sprouted gelaterias and tapas bars every few steps. Metro stops include Jaume I, Arc de Triomf, and Urquinaona.

Mercat Santa Caterina ★★ ARCHAEOLOGICAL SITE/MARKET   La Boqueria's rival in La Ribera, this fresh-food market is a little easier to navigate, if only because it is smaller. It is no less thorough, though prices might be marginally lower. On one side of the market is an archaeological site, another in the collection of the Museu d'Història de la Ciutat (see Plaça Reial, above). The excavations trace Barcelona culture from the Bronze Age to present. Chief among the ruins are the Dominican monastery of Santa Caterina, established here in 1219 and torn down in the anti-clerical fervor in 1835. In 1845, the site was used to erect the city's second enclosed market. The interpretive site, enclosed in glass on one side of the food market, is open Monday through Friday 10am to 2pm and Tuesday and Thursday 4 to 8pm. Admission is free.

Avinguda de Francesc Cambó, 16. ℭ **93-319-57-40.** www.mercatsantacaterina.com. Daily 8am–11:30pm. Metro: Jaume I.

Museu de la Xocolata ★ MUSEUM   Barcelona claims to have been the entry port of chocolate into Europe, based on the arrival of a 1520 shipment of cacao from Mexico. A Cistercian monk in the New World sent it to the Monasterio de Piedra in Aragón complete with a recipe for a chocolate drink. This little museum is full of historical and quasi-historical tidbits, but it's really designed to make you crave chocolate. The first thing you see is a chocolate fountain, and even your ticket is a chocolate bar. Some of the chocolate sculptures are truly amazing—a Komodo dragon, a bullfight, soccer players, the Barcelona Zoo's late and lamented albino gorilla (in white chocolate), and even a tableau of Sancho Panza and Don Quijote.

Carrer Comerç, 36. ℭ **93-368-78-78.** www.museuxocolata.cat. Admission [5€ adults, 4.25€ students and seniors, free under age 7. Mid-Sept to mid-June Mon–Sat 10am–7pm, mid-June to mid-Sept Mon–Sat 10am–8pm.

Museu Picasso ★★★ MUSEUM   This terrific museum celebrated its 50th anniversary in 2013 by rehanging many of the works. So even if you've visited before, a return will likely feel fresh. The first pieces in the collection came mostly from Jaume Sabartés, a childhood friend who became Picasso's personal secretary in 1935. They include a number of works made when Picasso was a student in Barcelona or when he retreated back here to gather himself for another assault on the art world of Paris. As such, they provide a striking portrait of Barcelona at the end of the 19th century as well as an intriguing look at an evolving artistic genius. Picasso also donated generously to the museum, including 2,400 works in memory of his friend Sabartés. His most significant donation was his entire *Las Meninas* series, which he painted as a tribute to and exploration of the art of Velázquez. The large canvas and dozens of smaller studies are the centerpiece of the rehung collection, which fills five adjoining historic townhouses. Allow plenty of time to study *Las Meninas.* It's a rare opportunity to follow Picasso's thought process and artistic instincts at the height of his mature power. It may be true that Picasso's greatest masterpieces are elsewhere, but you will leave this museum wondering how there could possibly be more.

Carrer Montcada, 15–19. ⓒ **93-256-30-00.** www.museupicasso.bcn.cat. Admission 11€ adults (14€ with temporary exhibition), 7€/7.50€ students and ages 16–25; free 15 and under and over 65 ; free Sun 3–8pm and all day first Sun of the month. Tues–Sun 10am–8pm. Metro: Jaume I.

Palau de la Música Catalana ★★★ LANDMARK One of the most extreme and exciting of the Modernista buildings, this structure may be Lluís Domènech i Montaner's masterpiece. Commissioned by the Orfeó Català choral music society, the architect laid the first stone on St. George's Day (May 5, the feast of Catalunya's patron saint) in 1905. It finally opened in 1908—a marvel of stained glass, ceramics, statuary, ornate wrought iron, and carved stone. In keeping with the architect's signature style, the facade features exposed brick combined with colorful ceramic mosaics. The sculptures are symbolic and, frankly, nationalistic. The stone prow, a work by Miquel Blay, is an allegory of popular music with two boys and two old men embracing a nymph while St. George protects them with the Catalan flag. Inside, the vaults of the foyer are lined with Valencian tiles. The concert hall itself is topped with an enormous stained glass skylight representing a circle of female angels surrounding the sun as a choir—quite appropriate for a choral society. If you want a detailed explanation of all the imagery, plan to take a guided tour. We find that the best way to enjoy the hall is to attend a concert. Arrive early and you can study the rich details from your seat.

Carrer Sant Francesc de Paula, 2. ⓒ **93-295-72-00.** www.palaumusica.org. Guided tours 17€. Open daily from 10am–3:30pm. Box office open daily 9:30am–3:30pm. Metro: Urquinaona.

Museu Picasso.

Parc de la Ciutadella.

Parc de la Ciutadella ★ PARK When Barcelona picked the losing side in the War of the Spanish Succession (1701–14), the victorious Felipe V repaid the city by leveling a neighborhood to erect a citadel. The fortification proved of little use against Napoleon, and the fort was torn down in the mid–19th century. Lakes, gardens, and promenades fill most of the park that took its place, and admission to the park itself is free. The large green patch is also the site of the **Zoo de Barcelona ★**, which covers 13 hectares (32 acres) and is home to more than 300 species. Animals run the gamut from lumbering hippos to jumpy Saharan gazelles, from western lowland gorillas to Komodo dragons.

Parc de la Ciutadella. ℂ **90-245-75-45.** www.zoobarcelona.com. Admission 19.90€ adults, 11.95€ ages 3–12, 10.05€ 65 and older. Summer daily 10am–7pm; off-season daily 10am–5:30pm. Metro: Ciutadella.

Santa Maria del Mar ★★ RELIGIOUS SITE Built by the trade guilds rather than the nobility, this church is the city's most harmonious example of the Catalan Gothic style. Construction began in 1329 and was more or less finished in 1383 (the bell towers were added in 1496 and 1902). Three soaring naves are supported by wide-spaced columns that bloom like thick stalks as they reach the ceiling. Stained glass windows throughout fill the church with light during the day. Guided views of the roof and towers are available daily, weather permitting.

Plaça de Santa María. ℂ **93-215-74-11.** www.stamariadelmar.org. Free. Mon–Sat 9am–1:30pm and 4:30–8pm; Sun 9am–2pm and 5–8:30pm. Tours: ℂ 93-343-56-33. www.itineraplus.com. Admission 5€. Tours on the hour Mon–Fri noon–7pm, Sat–Sun 11am–7pm. Metro: Jaume I.

L'Eixample & Gràcia

Where Les Rambles meets Plaça de Catalunya, the tangled streets of the old city turn to the orderly gridiron of **L'Eixample ★★★**, and strolling the wide boulevards can seem like a breath of fresh air. Largely built 1890 to 1910, L'Eixample contains no less than three-dozen Modernista landmarks. You'll want a least a day, perhaps two, to visit the major sites and enjoy some of the shops and cafes. Don't overlook the small details like the Modernista light posts designed by Gaudí, and the hexagonal paving tiles he designed in 1904 that still cover the sidewalks on parts of Passeig de Gràcia. Take a break on the Modernista tile benches on the street corners. Modernisme was one of the first movements that emphasized "design for living," and those designs still bring delight more than a century later. Major Metro stops for the neighborhood include Passeig de Gràcia, Diagonal, Provença, Universitat, Girona, and Sagrada Familia.

Basilica de la Sagrada Familia ★★★ RELIGIOUS SITE   Antoni Gaudí (1852–1926) was a profoundly religious man, and from 1912 forward he made the design of this soaring basilica his life's work. If it is not the grandest church in all of Spain, it is certainly the grandest constructed within living memory. Gaudí originally planned to base the church on all the stories of the Bible, but, as a guide once told us, "he decided that was too long, so he settled on the New Testament." The "church of the Holy Family" is, to say the least, a strange and wonderful building that represents the intersection of the imaginative style of Modernisme with the medieval faith that drove construction of the great Gothic cathedrals. The facades are particularly ornate. Every projection, ledge, window, corner, step, or other surface is encrusted with carvings. Fruits of the seasons surround one set of spires, dragons and gargoyles hang off corners, an entire Noah's ark of preposterous animals (rhinos! elephants!) are carved in stone. One facade tells the stories of the birth and childhood of Jesus, another (completed by modern sculptor Josep Maria Subirachs in 1987) the Passion and crucifixion. And that's just the exterior. Once inside, the light streaming through high stained-glass windows seems to tint the air with colored light. Gaudí conceived the interior as a vast forest, and the columns seem to grow from the floor like powerful trees holding the roof aloft. Construction of the church came to a near halt at the outbreak of the Civil War and languished until the late 1980s. Yet new construction techniques (and more tourist admissions) have sped up the process. The church was consecrated in 2010 by Pope Benedict XVI, and builders hope to

Gaudí's famous Basilica de la Sagrada Familia.

complete construction by the 2026 centenary of Gaudí's death. (He is buried in the Chapel of Carmel, one level down from the main church.) Buy tickets online in advance to avoid the wait of an hour or more during high season.

Entrance from Carrer de Sardenya or Carrer de la Marina. (✆) **93-207-30-31.** www.sagrada-familia.cat. Admission 14.80€ adults, 8.80€ under 18 or retired; elevator for tower tour (about 60m/200 ft.) 4.50€; printed or audio guide additional 4.50€. Online ticket sales at http://ow.ly/lqdwr. Oct–Mar daily 9am–6pm; Apr–Sept daily 9am–8pm. Closed Christmas Day, Dec 26, New Year's Day, and Jan 6. Metro: Sagrada Família.

Modernista light posts, designed by Gaudí.

Casa Amatller ★ LANDMARK

Three of the greatest residential Modernista buildings in Barcelona stand along the single block of Passeig de Gràcia between Carrer del Consell de Cent and Carrer d'Aragó. Architecture critics call it the Mançana de la Discòrdia (Block of Discord), an allusion to the mythical Judgment of Paris over which of three goddesses is the most beautiful. Tourism promoters call the same group the Quadrat d'Or, or "Golden Quarter," which at least points out that they are all wonderful. Casa Amatller is the masterpiece by Josep Puig i Cadalfach. Closed for restoration until late in 2015, this Modernista home designed in 1900 reflects the architect's attachment to northern European Gothic decoration. That makes it a striking contrast to the Gaudí-designed Casa Batlló (see below) next door. Puig i Cadafalch made extensive use of ceramics, wrought iron, and fanciful sculptures. The original Gothic Revival interior is now the headquarters of the Institut Amatller d'Art Hispanic, but the library is normally the only part of the building open to the public.

Passeig de Gràcia, 41. (✆) **93-487-72-17.** www.amatller.org. Free admission. Mon–Sun 10am–8pm. Metro: Passeig de Gràcia.

Casa Batlló ★★ LANDMARK

Next door to Casa Amatller, Casa Batlló was designed by Gaudí in 1905. The facade's sinuous curves in iron and stone give the structure a very lush appeal and the balconies, like those at La Pedrera, seem to be sculpted ocean waves. Floral references in the ornament turn more fauna-like as the building rises. The roof evokes the scaly skin of a dragon. Touring means climbing the spiral staircase around the central light shaft and starting with the Batlló family quarters, where Gaudí's architectural flourishes and his furniture designs vie for your attention. Sr. Batlló's office has a little nook with two benches and a stove for warmth—perfect for a courting couple to sit on one side and their chaperone on the other. Even this smallest of the rooms has a skylight to let in some natural light. The living room overlooks Passeig de Gràcia. All the decor, including the eddies of water in the swirling ceiling, allude to the marine world. The sewing room, which overlooks an interior courtyard, has an ingenious ventilation system of sliding slats that seem inspired by fish gills. The roof terrace has chimneys designed to evoke the backbone of the dragon slain by

Sant Jordi (St. George), patron saint of Catalunya. The outdoor terrace has live music with cocktails from late June through September. An audiotour is included with admission, which has the effect of creating bottlenecks at each spot the tour highlights. Lines for admission can get quite long here; buy your ticket online in advance.

Passeig de Gràcia, 43. © **93-216-03-06.** www.casabatllo.cat. Admission 22€ adults; 19€ ages 7–18, students, and seniors; free for children 7 and under. Music and cocktails mid-June to Sept Tues–Sun from 9pm, 29€. Tours daily 9am–8pm. Metro: Passeig de Gràcia.

Casa Lleó Morera ★ LANDMARK   The third member of the Golden Quarter, Casa Lleó Morera was designed by the remaining member of the Modernista triumvirate, Lluís Domènech i Montaner. The 1905 home was revolutionary in its day for its extensive use of different forms of artisanry on the interior (alas, closed to the public) to realize the architect's distinctly floral design. Because it occupies a corner, the house has two beautiful facades that mirror each other with a tower of sorts dividing them. Domènech i Montaner's signature floral capitals appear in several variants, and he created a gallery of columns on the top floor that evokes the rhythm of a convent cloister. The one part of the ground level that can be visited—the shop of Loewe, purveyor of fine leather goods—does not retain the architect's designs.

Passeig de Gràcia, 35. No phone. Metro: Passeig de Gràcia.

Fundació Antoni Tàpies ★★ MUSEUM   This museum is dedicated to Antoni Tàpies (1923–2012), Catalunya's leading late 20th-century artist. Major holdings consist of gifts from the artist and his wife, and tend to emphasize late works and large-scale pieces. Changing exhibitions show the artist's evolving viewpoints and leave no doubt about his role in bringing unconventional materials (gravel, broken sticks, chunks of cement) into high art. Seeing so many works by Tàpies in one place shows how, like so many Spanish artists, he returned repeatedly to the motif of the cross for works both secular and (in his own abstract way) sacred. Since it's in L'Eixample, it's not really a surprise that the

Casa Batlló.

museum occupies a Modernista landmark. The former home of publishing company Editorial Montaner i Simon was built by Lluís Domènech i Montaner from 1880 to 1882 (the company belonged to his mother's family). The pioneering structure has a jaunty Moorish cast to it.

Carrer Aragó, 255. ✆ **93-487-03-15.** www.fundaciotapies.org. Admission 7€ adults, 5.60€ students and over age 65. Tues–Sun 10am–7pm. Metro: Passeig de Gràcia.

Fundació Francisco Godia ★ MUSEUM   With its gorgeous terrazzo floors, grand marble staircase, high ceilings, and beautifully proportioned rooms, Casa Garriga Nogués runs the risk of overshadowing the art it contains. It was designed by Enric Sagnier and built between 1899 and 1905 and has been impeccably restored. The museum showcases the art collected by entrepreneur and race car driver Francisco Godia Sales (1921–90). He was particularly close to a number of Catalan painters, and collected major canvases by Santiago Rusiñol and Ramon Casas, among others. But his heart belonged to the past. The best works in the museum draw from the seemingly inexhaustible well of Catalan Gothic polychrome sculpture.

Carrer de la Diputació, 250. ✆ **93-272-31-80.** www.fundacionfgodia.org. Admission 5.50€ adults, 3.25€ children 5–16 and students, free for children 4 and under. Mon and Wed–Sat 10am–8pm, Sun 10am–3pm. Metro: Passeig de Gràcia.

Hospital de la Santa Creu i Sant Pau ★★★ LANDMARK   This UNESCO World Heritage complex was designed by Lluis Domènech i Montaner as a hospital village to look after all the lifestyle needs of its patients, providing parks and gardens for the healing powers of pleasant reflection, a freestanding library, and personal services such as a barber shop in the cluster of independent pavilions. The buildings represent the architect at the height of his powers, and his use of graceful sculpture, stained glass, and exquisite mosaic tiles makes the group of buildings perhaps the most beautiful and largest Modernisme/Art Nouveau campus in the world. It covers the equivalent of 9 city blocks, although the architect set it at a 45-degree angle to the grid of the L'Eixample streets to make it an architectural island in the city. The site includes 19 Modernista pavilions, some of which were completed by Domènech i Montaner's son Pere Domènec i Roura after the older architect's death. Declared a UNESCO World Heritage Site in 1997, the hospital complex is only a 10-minute stroll up Avinguda Gaudí from La Sagrada Familia—stop halfway and you can gaze up and down the street for a view of each masterpiece. Renovation and restoration work is ongoing, making much of the site a construction zone. It is really only accessible by guided hard-hat tour.

Carrer Sant Antoni Maria Claret, 167. ✆ **93-317-76-52.** visitsantpau.com. Tour 10€ adults, 5€ students and seniors. English tours daily at 10am, 11am, noon, and 1pm. Metro: Hospital de Sant Pau or Guinardó.

Museu del Modernisme Català ★ MUSEUM   The first museum dedicated exclusively to Catalan Modernisme opened in 2010 on two floors of a Modernist former textile factory designed by Enric Sagnier and built from 1902 to 1904. The ground level is dominated by a mix of graphic art—wonderful posters, in many cases—and furniture designed by Antoni Gaudí, Joan Busquets, and Gaspar Homar. The Gaudí displays include some seminal pieces from his collaborations with Josep Maria Jujol. (They worked together on most of the furniture for Casa Batlló, and Jujol assisted with the ornamentation of Casa Mila.) You can't touch the works, let alone sit in the chairs, but nowhere else can you get so close to pieces and study their design lines and construction techniques. The basement exhibitions include a lot of Modernisme painting and sculpture, including the impassioned marbles of Eusebi Arnau, who did some of the major sculpture for the **Palau de la Música Catalana** (p. 353).

Carrer Balmes, 48. © **93-273-28-96.** www.mmcat.cat. Admission 10€ adults, 5.50€ ages 5–15. Mon–Sat 10am–8pm, Sun 10am–2pm. Metro: Passeig de Gràcia or Universitat.

Palau del Baró de Quadras ★ HISTORIC SITE   Fans of graphic novels and Gothic gargoyles should not miss this extraordinary building. In 1900, Josep Puig i Cadalfach was commissioned by the Baron of Quadras to refurbish this residential block. Over the next 3 years, he completely transformed the structure. The facade is carved in an intricate style that nods to the Plateresque tradition of Castilla, while employing imagery and iconography of French and German medieval stone carving. The long, ornate balcony is covered with busts of eminent medieval and Renaissance figures, floral motifs, and heraldic shields. The carved cornices on columns at the entrance show an archer on one side of the main door firing an arrow at a dragon on the other side. The gargoyles, especially at the lower levels, have unusually expressive faces. The interior has been closed since 2013, but it's worth a detour to see the exterior.

Avinguda Diagonal, 373. Metro: Diagonal.

Parc Güell ★ PARK   Gaudí began this idiosyncratic park in Gràcia as a real-estate venture for his friend and patron, Catalan industrialist Count Eusebi Güell. Although it never came to fruition, Gaudí did complete several public areas, which today look like a surrealist Disneyland, complete with a mosaic-encrusted pagoda and lizard fountain spitting water. (Adults smile and move on, but kids find the fountain fascinating.) The original plans called for a model community of 60 dwellings. Gaudí did construct a grand central plaza with a market below it, and lined the plaza with a long, undulating bench decorated with ceramic fragments. The oddly Doric columns of the would-be market are hollow, part of Gaudí's drainage system. Despite all this effort, only two houses were ever completed. One of them (designed by Ramón Berenguer, not Gaudí) serves as the **Casa-Museu Gaudí** ★. The architect lived here from 1906 to 1925, the period during which he worked on La Pedrera and La Sagrada Familia. The museum contains Gaudí models, furniture, drawings, and other memorabilia.

Calle de Olot for park, Carrer del Carmel, 23 for Casa-Museu Gaudí. © **93-219-38-11.** www.casamuseugaudi.org. Free admission to park. Casa-Museu Gaudí: 5.50€ adults, 4.50€ students and seniors. Park open May–Sept daily 9am–9pm; Oct–Apr daily 9am–7pm; Casa-Museu Gaudí open Apr–Sept 10am–8pm, Oct–Mar 10am–6pm. Metro: Lesseps.

La Pedrera (Casa Milà) ★★★ LANDMARK   It took the neighbors a long time to warm up to Modernisme. When Gaudí's last secular commission, Casa Milà, was finished in 1912, they took one look at the undulating lines of seemingly wind-eroded rock and dubbed the building La Pedrera ("the stone quarry"). The shock of its novelty has faded, but the nickname has stuck as a term of endearment. With a sinuous, rippling facade, it is one of the most beloved of Gaudí's works, and is another spot where purchasing an advance ticket online will save you precious time. The tour includes the patios and the Espai Gaudí (loft and roof). But the best part is visiting the Pedrera Apartment, complete with Gaudí furniture. Substitute a modern music system for the Edison phonograph, and most visitors would be ready to sign a lease on the spot. The Espai Gaudí holds period photographs, drawings, and models that elucidate Gaudí's design

Gaudí's La Pedrera.

techniques. Gaudí may have been a genius, but he was no math whiz. To calculate the loads an arch could bear, he hung weights on knotted cord to get the shapes he wanted, then extrapolated to life size. Gaudí saved his grandest gestures for the rooftop, transforming functional chimneys into a sculpture garden of swirling mosaic forms and ominous hooded warriors. Gaudí intended that the roof be used as an open-air terrace, and during the summer, jazz musicians hold forth several evenings each week. Amid the chimneys Gaudí built a lovely parabolic arch to frame what would become the towering steeples of his masterpiece, La Sagrada Familia. La Pedrera offers special night visits called "The Secret Pedrera" with a very limited number of admissions.

Carrer Provença, 261–265. © **90-220-21-38.** www.lapedrera.com. Admission 16.50€ adults, 14.85€ seniors and students, 8.25€ ages 7–12, free ages 6 and younger; audioguide 4€. Nov–Feb daily 9am–6:30pm; Mar–Oct daily 9am–8pm. Jazz on Rooftop June–Sept Thur–Sat 27€. Secret Pedrera night visits Mar–Oct daily 9:30pm–midnight, Nov–Feb Wed–Sat 8–10:30pm. Metro: Diagonal.

La Barceloneta & the Waterfront

Barcelona has always lived by the water, and fishing boats, trade vessels, and ferries continue to come and go in its harbor. But there's new vitality along the **waterfront ★★**, from the Mirador de Colom east to Port Olimpic along the Passeig de Colom and the pedestrian **Moll de la Fusta ★**. Starting in the late 1980s, Barcelona built new quays and waterfront paths and even constructed new islands to house a world-class aquarium and a shopping and entertainment complex. At the same time, it preserved the barrier-beach sand-spit of **La Barceloneta ★★**, the former fishermen's village that also boasts the city's finest recreational beaches.

Spend some time exploring the back streets of La Barceloneta, where the residents still hang their laundry on the balconies. As you tromp the length of Moll de la Fusta, you'll find two playful pieces of public art: the giant fiberglass lobster that Xavier Mariscal created for the restaurant Gambrinus, and pop artist Roy Lichtenstein's *Barcelona Head* at the foot of Via Laietana. Continue east up the beach to Port Olimpic, and you'll encounter Frank O. Gehry's abstract sculpture called *Peix* (Fish), which has become the de facto symbol of Barcelona's rejuvenated waterfront. This district is the place to enjoy a casual seafood lunch and catch some rays at the beach. Plan on spending a full day, and you'll still have time to take a boat tour and to see some of the sights. Three Metro stops provide access to the sites below. From west to east, they are Drassanes, Barceloneta, and Ciutadella/Vila Olimpica.

L'Aquarium de Barcelona ★★ AQUARIUM   This contemporary aquarium dedicated to Mediterranean species and habitats does its best to make you feel like you're underwater interacting with the fish. The centerpiece of the facility is the giant ocean tank that wraps around an 80m (262-ft.) corridor with a moving walkway on one side. On the other is a strip where you can step off the path to take photos or simply marvel at the flow of creatures swimming by. Another 21 smaller tanks, which ring the ocean tank, focus on different habitats within the Mediterranean. Each is populated with characteristic fish and flora. Some resemble home aquariums full of brightly colored fish, while others are deepwater habitats where bottom-dwelling eels and anglerfish lie in wait for their prey. The dead-eyed sharks are an enduring attraction, and SCUBA-certified visitors with their own gear can arrange to swim with the sharks in the giant tank for a 300€ fee.

Moll d'Espanya, Port Vell. © **93-221-74-74.** www.aquariumbcn.com. Admission 20€ adults, 15€ ages 5–10 and 65 and older, 5€ 0.9m–1.1m tall, free under 0.9m. July–Aug Mon–Fri 9:30am– 9pm, Sat–Sun 9:30am–11pm; June and Sept Mon–Fri 9:30am–9pm, Sat–Sun 9:30am–9:30pm; Oct–May daily 9:30am 9pm. Metro: Drassanes or Barceloneta.

Barcelona Beaches ★★ BEACH   You don't have to leave the city to hit the beach. European blue flags (indicators of the highest water quality) fly on all 10 of Barcelona's beaches. Four of the best lie along the strand from the tip of La Barceloneta east to Port Olimpic. Each has showers, bathrooms, snack bars, umbrella and hammock rentals, and lifeguards. They are all free. Platja de Barceloneta and adjacent Platja del Somorrostro (near Port Olimpic) also have changing rooms and lockers. (Carmen Amaya, perhaps the most famous flamenco dancer of all time, was born in the shanty town that once stood on Platja del Somorrostro.) These two beaches and the more westerly Platja de Sant Sebastià

L'Aquarium de Barcelona.

and Platja de Sant Miquel can be reached from Metro stops Barceloneta or Ciutadella/La Vila Olimpica. A little farther east at Metro stop Poblenou, you'll find the most popular beach with college-age Barcelonans and visitors alike, Platja de Mar Bella. It, too, has all the facilities, including lockers, and is the only beach in Barcelona with a section set off for nude sunbathing and swimming.

Metro: Barceloneta, Ciutadella/Vila Olímpica, or Poblenou. Bus: N6, N8.

Mirador de Colom ★ MONU-MENT   Les Rambles meets the waterfront at this monument to Christopher Columbus that was erected for the Universal Exposition of 1888. Bas-reliefs on the plinth recount the feats of the great navigator, and various symbolic sculptures in florid Victorian style surround the base. At the top of a 50m (174-ft.) column stands a bronze of Columbus pointing to the New World from beneath a white wig of bird droppings that deflate the pomposity of it all. Inside the iron column, a small elevator ascends to the lookout just below Columbus's feet. It provides a panoramic view of Barcelona and the harbor and a chance to play "name that spire," as every church in the city pokes up just above its surrounding buildings. Portal de la Pau. ✆ **93-285-38-32.** Admission 4€ adults, 3€ children 4–12 and seniors, free for children 3 and under. June–Sept daily 9am–1:30pm and 4:30–8:30pm; Oct–May daily 9am–2pm and 3:30–7:30pm. Closed Jan 1, Oct 12, and Dec 25–26. Metro: Drassanes.

Museu d'Història de Catalunya ★★ MUSEUM   This museum uses "the memory of a country" as its tagline, and it's one of the best cultural history museums that we've seen anywhere in the world. The coverage begins in the Lower Paleolithic era and works its way up to the present—quickly. Historic exhibits linger at some of the high points of the Catalan experience, such as the reigns of Jaume I and II when Catalunya was a major power on the Mediterranean, and the 19th-century industrial revolution that made Catalunya in general and Barcelona in particular rich and powerful. The 20th-century coverage is almost giddy with its depictions of a vibrant Barcelona in the first few decades—and almost numbing in its accounting of the horrors of the Civil War and the 4 decades the region spent as Franco's whipping boy. The era since Franco's death seems less well digested, but history museums usually have the advantage of hindsight. It's worth visiting just to appreciate the building, the Palau de Mar, the last survivor among the 19th-century Barcelona warehouses. The fourth-floor restaurant, 1881, has a spectacular terrace with great views of the port and waterfront. It's not necessary to book a meal—most people come just for a drink and the view. Plaça de Pau Vila, 3. ✆ **93-225-47-00.** www.mhcat.cat. Admission 4€ adults, 3€ students and seniors; free first Sun of month. Tues and Thur–Sat 10am–7pm, Wed 10am–8pm, Sun 10am–2:30pm. Metro: Barceloneta.

Montjuïc

Residents of Barcelona used to quarry stone, harvest firewood, and graze livestock on this flat-topped hill southwest of the old city. Montjuïc ★ began to assume its current shape in the early 20th century, when parks were planted and the 1929 International Exposition was held here. Many of the park's structures, including the Palau Nacional, and the Font Màgica date from this period. The 1992 Olympics brought even more structures to Montjuïc, including world-class pools that are still used for international swimming meets. The biggest attractions on the mountain are two stunning art museums, one dedicated exclusively to Joan Miró, the other to the sweep of Catalan art. It takes some effort—and walking—to reach them but it's worth it. The most useful bus lines are Route 55 from Plaça d'Espanya and Route 150 for circling the Montjuïc roads. You can also take the funicular (mostly underground) from the Paral.lel Metro station, which delivers you to the Telefèric de Montjuic station. Many visitors prefer the **Bus Turistic** (p. 316) for visiting Montjuïc, since it makes stops at all the attractions. If you're up for a moderately steep climb, you can also walk from Plaça d'Espanya through the Font Màgica and up the ceremonial staircase of the Palau Nacional, now home of the Museu Nacional d'Art de Catalunya (MNAC), where you can start your explorations.

Castell de Montjuïc ★ HISTORIC SITE   In sharp contrast to its often grim history, this mass of military stone is now surrounded by serene gardens. Barcelonans come here for Sunday picnics. The fort last saw action in the Civil War when it kept changing hands and was used by both sides for political and military executions. In 1940, the Franco government prevailed on Germany to hand over the refugee president of Catalunya and summarily executed him here. The fort then served as a prison for political prisoners until Franco's death. The city assumed control of the property in 2007 and launched a development program to create a memorial to Catalan political martyrs, but the economic crisis halted those plans. Today the fortress is just a place to enjoy the views and the gardens. The best way to get here is on the 8-passenger cable cars of the **Telefèric de Montjuïc.**

Castell: free admission. Telefèric: Avinguda Miramar (opposite Montjuic Municipal Swimming Pool at funicular station). No phone. 11€ round-trip adults, 7.80€ ages 4–12. Mar–May and Oct 10am–7pm, June–Sept 10am–9pm, Jan–Feb and Nov–Dec 10am–6pm. Closed last Mon of Jan to third Fri of Feb. Montjuïc funicular; Bus 55 or 150.

Fundació Joan Miró ★★★ MUSEUM   Revered as the embodiment of the artistic genius of the Catalan people, Joan Miró (1893–1983) was born in Barcelona in the Barri Gòtic and trained locally. This marvelous museum assembles 10,000 of his works, including paintings, graphic art, sculpture, and even tapestries. Like many artists of the early 20th century, Miró gravitated to Paris and ultimately fell in with Andre Breton and the Surrealist movement. But his surrealism was radically different from his slightly younger countryman, Salvador Dalí, and evolved into a personal vocabulary of abstract forms and brilliant colors. His strong sense of line and tendency to lay in patches of color like a cloisonné jeweler (his father was a goldsmith) gave him a style all his own. The original museum building was designed by Miró's close friend, Catalan architect Josep Lluís Sert. A recent extension by Jaume Freixa has made it possible to display a number of pieces donated by Miró and others since the museum opened. The dimly lit **Octagonal Room** contains many of Miró's drawings on paper—the medium where he generally worked out his personal visual language that informed his paintings. Don't miss the amusing sculptures on the rooftop terrace, or the unusually good gift shop.

Plaça de Neptú, Parc de Montjuïc. ✆ **93-443-94-70.** http://fundaciomiro-bcn.org. Admission 11€ adults, 7€ seniors and students, free ages 14 and under. July–Sept Tues–Wed and Fri–Sat 10am–8pm, Thurs 10am–9:30pm, Sun 10am–2:30pm; Oct–June Tues–Wed and Fri–Sat 10am–7pm, Thurs 10am–9:30pm, Sun 10am–2:30pm. Bus: 50 (at Plaça d'Espanya) or 150.

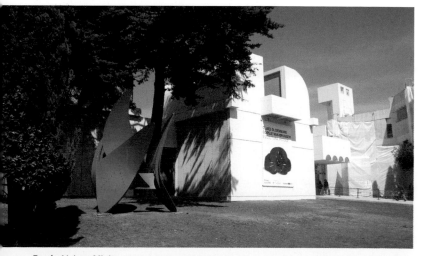

Fundació Joan Miró.

Jardi Botànic ★ GARDEN   The Botanic Gardens of Barcelona, originally established in 1930, were completely overhauled in the 1990s. They are now a beautifully landscaped, green space that showcases Mediterranean-climate plants from all over the globe, including Africa, Australia, California, the Canary Islands, and Chile. The collection continues to evolve. New species are grown in greenhouses every year and planted in the gardens. Those that fail to flourish in Montjuïc's climate and soils are pruned from the collection. The 71 planting zones are connected by walking paths, many of them crossing small bridges and walkways over ponds.

Carrer Dr. Font i Quer, 2, Parc de Montjuïc. ℭ **93-256-41-60.** www.jardibotanic.bcn.es. Admission 3.50€ adults, 1.70€ seniors, free under age 16. Nov–Jan, Apr–May, and Sept daily 10am–5pm; Feb–Mar and Oct daily 10am–6pm; June–Aug daily 10am–8pm.

Museu d'Arqueologia de Catalunya ★   Housed in the former Palace of Graphic Arts built for the 1929 International Exposition, this museum plumbs the history and pre-history of Catalunya with extensive permanent exhibitions of artifacts recovered in archaeological excavations around the region and on the Balearic Islands. The first seven galleries deal with pre-history, but unless you're enamored of the *Clan of the Cave Bear* books, move quickly to the five galleries dealing with the Phoenicians and Greeks ("The Great Blue Sea") where artifacts from early Mediterranean trade show how Catalunya related to the rest of the Mediterranean basin. The Roman era is well-documented. Gallery areas devoted to the native Iberian Celtic culture and the Visigothic period are being substantially re-ordered and should be finished sometime in 2014.

Passeig Santa Madrona, 39–41. ℭ **93-423-21-48.** www.mac.cat. Admission 3€ adults, 2.10€ seniors and students, free under age 16. Tues–Sat 9:30am–7pm, Sun 10am–2:30pm.

Museu Nacional d'Art de Catalunya (MNAC) ★★★ MUSEUM   Some of the greatest Romanesque and early Gothic art in Europe is collected in this stunning museum housed in the Palau Nacional. The collection of Romanesque murals, in particular, is unmatched. Most of them were discovered at the beginning of the 20th century in crumbling ancient churches in the Pyrenees. When one such church was sold to Boston's Museum of Fine Arts, it set off a storm of outrage over losing Catalunya's cultural patrimony. So church after church was purchased by public institutions. Mural paintings were detached from the walls and ultimately moved to this museum. MNAC displays more than 100 pieces from the churches, including wall painting panels and polychrome wood carvings. They date from the 11th to 13th centuries, a fundamental period in Catalan art. The museum chronicles other eras, but the collections are a little thin until they reach Modernisme. As part of the Europeana Partage-Plus project on Art Nouveau, MNAC has been digitizing images of more than 2,000 Modernista objects in its collection, now available at www.partage-plus.eu. The Modernista gallery exhibits have such treasures as the Gaudí-designed furniture from **Casa Lleó Morera** (p. 357), a 1907 fireplace by Lluís Domènech i Montaner, and paintings by second-generation Modernista artist Joaquim Mir and by Catalunya's only noted Impressionist painter, Marià Pidelaserra.

Palau Nacional, Parc de Montjuïc. ℭ **93-622-03-76.** www.mnac.es. Admission 12€ adults, 8.40€ ages 15–20, free under 16 and over 65; free to all Sat after 3pm, first Sun of month. Tues–Sat 10am–7pm; Sun 10am–2:30pm. Metro: Espanya.

Poble Espanyol ★ HISTORIC PARK   This faux Spanish village was designed in 1929 by Josep Puig i Cadalfach for the International Exposition. Each plaza or

BARCELONA | Exploring Barcelona

Museu Nacional d'Art de Catalunya.

street in the village simulates the architecture of some corner of Spain from Galicia to Valencia. Buildings are full-scale, and after more than 8 decades of patina, some portions are authentic enough to make you do a double-take. The main plaza is ringed with restaurants and cafes, and there are many shops selling provincial crafts and souvenirs. To make the site less hokey, management has invited real contemporary craft artists to use the workshops, so you might see someone like jewelry designer and leather worker Diana Cristo at work. Other artists might be printing fabric or blowing glass. The village also houses the Fundació Fran Daurel contemporary Spanish art collection, a small museum that shows about 200 works that range from prints by Eduardo Chillida to ceramics by Pablo Picasso. Note that if you decide to buy tickets for the **Tablao de Carmen flamenco show** (p. 371) you get free admission to Poble Espanyol any time after 4pm, giving you plenty of time to look around and have dinner before the show.

Avinguda Marqués de Comillas, 13, Parc de Montjuïc. © **93-508-63-00.** www.poble-espanyol. com. Admission 11€ adults, 7.40€ seniors and students, 6.25€ ages 4–12, free for children 3 and younger; family rates available. Mon 9am–8pm; Tues–Thurs and Sun 9am–midnight; Fri 9am–3am; Sat 9am–4am. Metro: Espanya. Bus: 55 or 150.

Barcelona for Families

Family-friendly attractions include **L'Aquarium Barcelona** (p. 360), the **Zoo de Barcelona** (p. 354), and, of course, the **beaches** (p. 361). Parents who want to see **La Sagrada Familia** (p. 355) can reward the youngsters with the tower tour, while at **La Pedrera** (p. 359), children are fascinated by Gaudí's mosaic-covered rooftop chimneys that evoke the hooded Darth Vader of *Star Wars.* If the kids accompany you to the Fundació Miró and the Museu d'Art Nacional de Catalunya on Montjuïc, treat them to the Telefèric de Montjuïc cable car ride to the **Castell** (p. 362).

The big family excursion is the trip up **Tibidabo Mountain** to a century-old amusement park. The ride on the **Funicular de Tibidabo** (7.70€, or 4.10€ with amusement park entries) is a treat. To reach the funicular, take Metro Line

The Funicular de Tibidabo.

7 to Avinguda Tibidabo, exit onto Plaça Kennedy, and take either the 1901 **Tramvía Blau** (Blue Streetcar; 4€) or **Bus 196** (2€) to the funicular.

Parc d'Atraccions ★   AMUSEMENT PARK   As fans of Woody Allen's film *Vicky Cristina Barcelona* might recall, this amusement park has some charming retro rides—a carousel, an "airplane" that spins around a pole, whirling teacups—along with modern attractions like a roller coaster, a pirate ship, and a haunted castle. A family visit can be fairly expensive, but you may be able to limit costs by focusing on the Sky Walk section of the park and the adjacent 255m (837-ft.) communications tower, **Torre de Collserola,** with its observation deck.

Plaça Tibidabo 3–4, Cumbre del Tibidabo. ✆ **93-211-79-42.** www.tibidabo.cat. Ticket for all rides: 29€ adults, 10€ ages 60 and over, 10€ children up to 1.2m (4 ft.) in height, free for children under 90cm (3 ft.); Sky Walk: 13€ adults, 7.80€ under 1.2m tall, 6.70€ ages 60 and up; Torre de Collserola: 5.60€ adults, 3.30€ ages 4–12 and 60 and older, free age 3 and younger. Discounts for online purchases. Open Mar–Dec, variable days and times noon–late night.

Organized Tours

Barcelona is best appreciated on foot, and the Barcelona tourist office has developed a number of **Barcelona Walking Tours** that are offered in English and hit the highlights. Tours cover the Barri Gòtic, Picasso's Barcelona (including the Museu Picasso), and Modernisme masterpieces in L'Eixample. A gourmet tour is based in the old city and includes visits to noteworthy shops and food outlets and a few tastings. For full listing of tours, call ✆ **93-285-38-32,** visit bcnshop.barcelonaturisme.cat, or inquire at the tourist office on Plaça Catalunya. Adult tickets start at 16€; some tours free for children, others 7€. Discounts for online purchases.

Free tours of the Barri Gòtic and Gaudí's greatest hits are offered daily by **Runner Bean Tours** (www.runnerbeantours.com). Seasonal ghost tours and a special family itinerary are also available. Guides expect a tip, and most participants give generously. The website gives meeting places and times.

Discover Walks (℗ 93-181-68-10; www.discoverwalks.com) are led by Barcelonans eager to share their enthusiasm for their city. These personal and often quirky walks are held daily from spring through fall (Fri–Mon in winter) and require no advance booking. The Gaudí tour departs from the front of Casa Batlló (p. 356) at 10:30am, the Picasso tour departs from Plaça de l'Angel (Metro: Jaume I) at 5pm, and the Ramblas and Barri Gòtic walk departs from in front of the Teatre del Liceu (p. 343) at 3pm. The walks are free, but tips are expected.

If you are comfortable riding a bicycle in big-city traffic, several firms offer guided bike tours. **Barcelona by Bicycle** (℗ 93-268-21-05; www.bicicletabarcelona.com) offers a daily 3-hour tour in English at 11am, and at 4:30pm Friday to Monday from April to mid-September. The 22€ fee includes bike rental. Tours depart from the Plaça de Sant Jaume (Metro: Jaume I). **Barcelona Ciclo Tour** (℗ 93-317-19-70; www.barcelonaciclotour.com) offers a similar tour at the same price. It departs from the Plaça de Catalunya (Metro: Plaça de Catalunya) daily at 11am and also at 4:30pm from mid-April through October. A "night tour" for the same price is also offered Friday to Sunday June to September and Friday to Saturday in October at 7:30pm.

If you'd rather enjoy the city lights and cooler evening air in a more leisurely fashion, the **Barcelona Bus Turistic** (p. 316) offers a 2½-hour tour starting at 9:30pm June to mid-September. It costs 19€ for adults and 10€ for children, and departs from Plaça de Catalunya (Metro: Plaça de Catalunya).

For a tour that picks you up in your hotel lobby, consider the 4-hour city tour (59€) in 12-passenger vans from **Barcelona Day Tours** (℗ 93-181-52-87; www.barcelonadaytours.com). The same company offers a **half-day tour to Montserrat** (p. 371) for 69€ or full-day options that combine Montserrat with a city tour (99€) or with a **visit to the sparkling wine region** (89€).

SHOPPING IN BARCELONA

If you don't want to spend a lot of time shopping, museum shops are your best bet for unique offerings not available elsewhere. Our favorites are the **Museu Picasso** (p. 352) and the **Fundació Joan Miró** (p. 363). They have broad selections of jewelry, scarves and other accessories, books, posters, and interesting objects for the home at reasonable prices. If, by some chance, you are in the market for an original piece of graphic art by a Spanish master, check out the shop at the **Fundació Antoni Tàpies** (p. 357).

The shops at **La Pedrera** (p. 359) and **Casa Batlló** (p. 356) have merchandise inspired by the Modernisme movement. At Casa Batllo, you can even find nail polish in Gaudí-inspired colors. The shop at **Museu del Modernisme Català** (p. 358) is more limited, but stocks door hardware from an original Gaudí design.

Sports fans should check out the merchandise at **FC Botiga,** the official shops of Barcelona's wildly popular football club. (The most convenient locations are Carrer Jaume 1, 18, ℗ 93-269-15-32, Metro: Jaume I; and Ronda Universitat, 37 at the corner of Plaça de Catalunya, no phone, Metro: Catalunya. For last-minute shopping, there are outlets at terminals T1 and T2 at the airport and at the Sants train station.)

The football club also has shops in two big shopping centers. **Centre Comercial Maremagnum** (Moll d' Espanya s/n; ℗ 93-225-81-00; www.maremagnum.es; Metro: Drassanes or Barceloneta) opened in the early 1990s on the waterfront and is as much a destination for its movie theaters, restaurants, and pubs as it is for its shops. More interesting is **Arenas de Barcelona** (Gran Via, 373–385; ☎ **93-289-02-44;** www.arenasdebarcelona.com; Metro: Plaça d'Espanya), originally Barcelona's bullring, built 1889 to 1900. Six floors of shops and a movie theater are augmented by an excellent food court.

Shoppers and window shoppers alike will probably find neighborhood streets more interesting. To see how the other half lives, check out the boutiques along **Passeig de Gracia,** Barcelona's most prestigious shopping promenade. For our (more limited) money, the streets of the Barri Gòtic and adjacent Born and La Ribera are more interesting to explore and the shops more fun and unpredictable. For an overview of regional handcrafts, check out **Artesania Catalunya** (Carrer dels Banys Nous, 11; ☎ 93-467-46-60; Metro: Liceu or Jaume I). Craft and fashion merge in the humble espadrille. **La Manual Alpargatera** (Carrer Avinyo, 7; ☎ **93-301-01-72;** www.lamanual.net; Metro: Jaume I or Barceloneta) has been making the iconic shoes since the 1940s and claims that Salvador Dalí was an aficionado. Dalí is also an inspiration for jewelry designers at **BCN Art Design** (Carrer Argenteria, 76, Metro: Jaume I; and Carrer Princesa, 24, Metro: Jaume I, ☎ **93-268-13-08;** www.bcnartdesign.es), but you'll find a broader selection of rings, bracelets, necklaces, and earrings inspired by Gaudí and Picasso. **Krappa** (Carrer Freneria, 1; ☎ **93-442-51-00;** www.krappa-bcn.com; Metro: Jaume I) makes engravings based on historic woodcuts. Many maps, cards, bookplates, and larger prints are colored by hand.

Hagglers will enjoy Barcelona's street markets. **El Encants** antiques market is held 9am to 8pm (some dealers leave earlier) on Monday, Wednesday, Friday, and Saturday in Plaça de les Glòries Catalanes (www.encantsbcn.com; Metro: Glòries). A market has operated here since the 14th century, but El Encants moved into a soaring new pavilion in late 2013.

Shopping for antiques at El Encants market.

Mercat Santa Caterina.

One of the best flea markets is held 9am to 8pm on Thursday at **Plaça Nova** at the base of the Cathedral of Barcelona (Metro: Jaume 1). If you miss it, there is a smaller flea market 10am to 5pm Friday to Sunday near the **Mirador de Colom** (Metro: Drassanes). **Plaça Reial** (Metro: Liceu) is the site of a stamp and coin market 10am to 8pm on Sunday. **Plaça del Pi** (Metro: Liceu) hosts an art fair (www.pintorspibarcelona.com) with dozens of artists on Saturday 11am to 8pm and Sunday 11am to 2pm, while contemporary artisans line **Carrer Argentería,** from Santa María del Pi to Via Laietana on weekends 10am to 5pm.

La Boqueria (p. 342) and **Mercat Santa Caterina** (p. 351) are the best fresh food markets. These food extravaganzas are perfect for buying spices and other packaged goods to bring home. For great chocolate, visit **Cacao Sampaka** (Carrer Consell de Cent, 292; ℂ 92-272-08-33; www.cacaosampaka.com; Metro: Passeig de Gràcia), which was co-founded by Albert Adrià, brother of famed chef Ferran. If your taste runs more to nuts or the traditional *torron* (nougat made with honey and almonds), check out the ancient (since 1851) nut roaster **E & A Gispert** (Carrer dels Sombrerers, 23; ℂ **93-319-75-75;** www.casagispert.com; Metro: Jaume I). For gourmet olive oils from around Spain, specialty dried beans, and canned fish and shellfish from Galicia, check the floor-to-ceiling shelves of upscale caterer **Colmado Quilez** (La Rambla de Catalunya, 63; ℂ **93-215-23-56;** www.lafuente.es; Metro: Passeig de Gràcia).

ENTERTAINMENT & NIGHTLIFE

Barcelona is as vibrant by night as it is by day. To get into the rhythm of the city, enjoy an early evening promenade along Les Rambles, and a stop in a tapas bar or two, followed by a late dinner. If you don't want to dine in a nearly deserted restaurant—or among other tourists only—plan to arrive in your chosen restaurant sometime after 9pm. Most nights, that will probably be all the entertainment you need.

But Barcelona also has a rich cultural scene, and the landmark venues of **Palau de la Música Catalana** (p. 353) and **Gran Teatre del Liceu** (p. 343) come alive when performers take the stage. As the name suggests, the Palau de la Musica specializes in musical performances, which present no language barriers. Although the Liceu is known for its opera and theatrical productions, it also schedules an interesting mix of dance and music.

There are also several notable theater venues on Montjuïc, including **Teatre Grec** (Passeig de Santa Madrona, 36; ℂ **93-316-10-00;** www.bcn.cat/grec; Metro: Espanya), an atmospheric open-air amphitheater on the site of a former quarry; and **Mercat de Les Flors** (Carrer Lleida, 59; ✆ **93-426-18-75;** www. mercatflors; Metro: Espanya or Poble Sec), which occupies a building from the 1929 International Exposition and is known for championing innovative drama, dance, and music. These two venues, along with **Teatre Lliure** (Passeig Santa Madrona, 40–46; ✆ **93-289-27-70;** www.teatrelliure.com; Metro: Espanya), host Barcelona's acclaimed Grec Festival in July—an extravaganza of dance, theater, music, and even circus arts.

During the summer, one of the best places to enjoy jazz is on the rooftop of **La Pedrera** (p. 359). Otherwise, check out the schedule of jazz, blues, and world music at **Sala Jamboree** in the Barri Gòtic (Plaça Reial, 17; ✆ **93-319-17-89;** www.masimas.com/jamboree; Metro: Liceu), which features both up-and-coming and established artists. **Santa María del Pi** (p. 350) also has a summer concert series in the church's "Secret Garden."

The concentration of bars at the **Maremagnum shopping complex** (p. 367) is popular with the college crowd and, the somewhat old-fashioned **Poble Espanyol** (p. 364) has a number of popular spots, including the open-air disco **La Terrazza** (✆ **93-272-49-80;** www.laterrazza.com) with its great city views, and **The One** (www.poble-espanyol.com/en/night), a trendy club.

Barcelona is not in the forefront of the flamenco revival, but several venues present colorful and enjoyable performances with dancers, singers, and musicians. **Flamenco Tablao Cordobes** (Les Rambles, 35; ✆ **93-317-57-11;** www.tablaocordobes.com; 42€; Metro: Liceu) occupies a lovely Moorish-style performance space with tilework and arched ceilings. **Flamenco Tablao Patio Andaluz** (Carrer Aribau, 242; ✆ **93-209-35-24;** www.jesuscortes.net; 33€; Metro: Gràcia) features dancer Jesús Cortés, a member of an accomplished

The Palau de la Música Catalana.

The Gran Teatre del Liceu.

family of flamenco artists. At Poble Espanyol, **El Tablao de Carmen** (© **93-325-68-95;** www.tablaodecarmen.com; 39€) is named for the Barcelona born dance legend Carmen Amaya. Note that prices quoted here are for the performance and one drink. Most clubs offer dinner as well, but you are better off eating elsewhere.

Wherever you begin, end your evening with a glass of cava, as Catalunya's sparkling wine is called, at one of the city's classic *xampanyerias,* such as **El Xampanyet** (p. 335) or **Xampú Xampany** (p. 339).

DAY TRIPS FROM BARCELONA

You don't need to pack a suitcase for these day trips into the countryside. And the two destinations could not be more different. The monastery at **Montserrat** is one of the most important religious pilgrimage sites in Spain. **Sant Sadurní d'Anoia** is for oenophiles; more than 40 winemakers in the village open their cellars for tastings of cava, the Catalan sparkling wine.

Montserrat ★★

Thousands flock to this mountainside monastery each year to see and touch the medieval statue of **La Moreneta** (the Black Virgin). Many newly married Catalan couples come here for her blessing on their honeymoon, and many name their daughters "Montserrat" ("Montse" for short). If you want to meet Catalans, visit on Sunday, especially when the weather is nice; for smaller crowds, visit on a weekday. The winds blow cold on the mountain, even during summer, so bring a sweater or jacket.

ESSENTIALS

GETTING THERE   The best way to get to Montserrat is via the Catalunyan railway, **Ferrocarrils de la Generalitat de Catalunya** (FGC; R5-Manresa; © **93-237-71-56;** www.fgc.es), with 12 trains a day leaving from the Plaça d'Espanya in Barcelona. The R5 line connects with an aerial cableway (Aeri de Montserrat), which is included in the fare of 27€ round-trip. An excellent alternative to the Aeri (especially when windy weather grounds the cable car) is the **Cremallera de Montserrat,** a 15-minute funicular ride from the village below the mountain. You get off the train one stop sooner at Olesa de Montserrat, and transfer to the funicular. The fare is also 27€ round-trip. Either combination ticket can be purchased at any FGC train station. Alternatively, a package that includes the train and choice of cable car or funicular, admission to the museum and the new interactive audiovisual gallery, and a self-service lunch is sold online (http://barcelonaturisme.cat) and in the brick-and-mortar stores of **Turisme de Barcelona** (p. 312). Called "Tot Montserrat," it costs 44€.

VISITOR INFORMATION The **tourist office,** Plaça de la Creu (© **93-877-77-01;** www.montserratvisita.com), is open daily from 9am to 5:30pm.

La Moreneta at the Basilica de Montserrat.

EXPLORING MONTSERRAT

You can see Montserrat's jagged peaks from all over eastern Catalunya, and the almost otherworldly serrated ridgeline is a symbol of Catalan identity. As a buffer state between Christian France and often Islamic Spain, medieval Catalunya espoused a fierce and intense Christian faith that reached its apogee in the cult of the **Virgin of Montserrat,** one of the legendary "dark" virgins of Iberian Catholicism. A polychrome carving of the Virgin and Child (a form known in Catalan as Maria del Deu) was discovered in a grotto on the mountainside in the 12th century, and many miracles have been ascribed to the figure.

The **Basilica de Montserrat** and a Benedictine monastery have grown up on the site. But most believers are less interested in the impressive glories of the basilica than they are in getting close to the statue. To view **La Moreneta,** enter the church through a side door to the right. The meter-high carving is mounted in a silver altar in a chapel high above the main altar. You will be in a long line of people who parade past the statue, which is mostly encased in bulletproof acrylic to protect it from vandalism. The casing has a cutout that lets the faithful kiss her extended hand. If you are around at 1pm daily, you can hear the **Escolanía,** a renowned boys' choir established in the 13th century, singing "Salve Regina" and the "Virolai" (hymn of Montserrat). The basilica is open daily from 8 to 10:30am and noon to 6:30pm. Admission is free.

At Plaça de Santa María, you can also visit the **Museu de Montserrat** (© **93-877-77-77;** www.museudemontserrat.com), a repository of art donated by the faithful over the years. While many of the works are religious subjects, some by major artists like Caravaggio and El Greco, others are purely secular pieces, including an early Picasso (*El Viejo Pescador* from 1895) and some lovely Impressionist works by Monet, Sisley, and Degas. The museum is open daily 10am to 5:45pm, charging 7€ adults, 6€ seniors and students, 4€ ages 8 to 16.

BARCELONA | Day Trips from Barcelona

You can also make an excursion to **Santa Cova (Holy Grotto),** the purported site of the discovery of La Moreneta. The natural grotto was reworked in the 17th century, and a small church in the shape of a cross was built here. You go halfway by funicular, but must complete the trip on foot. In 2013, the monastery and the Catalunya government transformed the church into a gallery with a permanent exhibition of religious art. The grotto is open daily from 10am to 1pm and 4 to 7pm. The round-trip fare is 4€.

Sant Sadurní d'Anoia ★

Plenty of terrific wine is made in the countryside around Barcelona, but only Sant Sadurní d'Anoia is easily visited on public transportation—a must if you're planning to taste a number of the sparkling wines (cava) for which the village is famous.

ESSENTIALS

GETTING THERE   The easiest way to get to Sant Sadurní is to take an R4 train from Plaça de Catalunya or Barcelona-Sants station in the direction of Sant Vicenç de Calders. Trains run about every half-hour from 5:30am until 11:15pm, and the journey takes 45 to 50 minutes. The fare is 4.30€ each way.

VISITOR INFORMATION   The tourist office at Carrer del Hosital, 26 (© 93-891-31-88; www.turismesantsadurni.cat), is open Tuesday through Sunday 10am to 2pm.

EXPLORING SANT SADURNÍ D'ANOIA

Thick-walled 19th-century cava cellars fill the town, but you should make your first stop the new **Centre d'Interpretació del Cava ★** (Carrer de l'Hospital, 23; © 93-891-31-88; www.turismesantsadurni.cat). Located inside an old distillery, it mixes old-fashioned and high-tech exhibits to introduce visitors to the history of cava, the grapes used to make it, and the entire production process. You

The interactive Centre d'Interpretació del Cava.

can even hold a (dead) phylloxera louse—just to drive home the history of cava. (When phylloxera struck the vineyards of champagne, the makers there desperately sought new territory, thus giving birth to the Catalan cava industry.) The center charges 6€.

The tourist office inside the center is free and can help you plan your excursion in Sant Sadurní, including making calls to cava operations that require reservations. The cellars that are open for visits and tastes, usually for a token fee or no charge, are listed on the interpretation center's website. Sometimes a paper printout is available, but don't count on it. Some small cellars make a few hundred cases of cava; some are bigger—much bigger. Note that many cellars close on Friday and Saturday afternoons and all day Sunday. Just walking around the village and stopping at some of the tiny operations with open doors by their loading docks can be a lot of fun. Two of the larger producers that put the town on the map offer excellent overviews of the traditional champagne process.

At the edge of town, the massive **Freixenet** ★★ (Carrer Joan Sala, 2; ℂ **93-891-70-96;** www.freixenet.es) pioneered U.S. distribution of cava as a less expensive alternative to champagne. Since the winery gets large groups, much of the tour is via video and includes a heavy dose of marketing, complemented by a quick trip into the deep cellars to see aging bottles and—finally—a tasting. The entire tour takes about 90 minutes and should be reserved in advance. The basic tour costs 7€ for adults, 4.20€ for children 9 to 17, and is free for children 8 and younger. Tours are offered Monday through Saturday 9:30am to 4pm and Sunday 10am to 1pm. Reserve by phone or e-mail at enotourism@ freixenet.es. It's closed the last 2 weeks of December and the first week of January.

The other giant of Sant Sadurní cava production, **Codorníu** ★★ (Avinguda Jaume Codorníu, s/n; ℂ **93-891-33-42;** www.codorniu.es) is worth visiting to see the so-called "Cathedral of Cava," the winemaking and storage facility built 1895 to 1915 and designed by Modernista architect Josep Puig i Cadalfach. If you know Codorníu from its entry-level cava, the tasting will open your eyes (and palate) to some extraordinary high-end selections. Several options are offered, from a standard tour and tasting to extended tastings or even a tapas lunch. The basic tour costs 7€ and is offered Monday through Friday 9am to 5pm and Saturday and Sunday 9am to 1pm. Reserve by phone or e-mail at reserves@ codorniu.es.

COSTA
DAURADA

B efore there was Barcelona, there was Tarragona, which served as the Roman capital of the east end of the Iberian Peninsula for more than 700 years. It still boasts some of the most extensive Roman ruins in the country. They have been respectfully assimilated into the modern city, creating a sense of timelessness that, in its own provincial way, rivals eternal Rome. Closer to Barcelona, Sitges is a beach resort that has grown up into a genuine city that offers art and culture to round out your stay when you've had enough sea, sand, and sun. If you seek more of the shore experience, head south of Tarragona to the long crescents of golden sand—each with a small village—that punctuate the Golden Coast (Costa Daurada) en route to the great fan delta of the Ríu Ebre.

TARRAGONA ★★★

For sheer historic sites, the Roman port city of **Tarragona** is one of the grandest, yet most overlooked cities in Spain. A natural fortress, the city perches on a rocky bluff 82m (269 ft.) above its deep and sheltered harbor. Although the Romans landed farther north at Empúries in 218 B.C. to savage the Carthaginians during the Second Punic War, they made their military and administrative headquarters at Tarraco, now Tarragona. At its Roman apogee, Tarraco boasted a population of nearly 1 million people and launched the legions on the conquest of the peninsula, bringing the western reaches of Europe under Roman control.

The most famous of the Roman roads in Iberia, the Via Augusta, connected Rome to Tarraco, and pieces of it remain in the plazas of the city. In fact, the extensive Roman ruins that survive in Tarragona were declared a UNESCO World Heritage Site in 2000. But not all the architectural elements remain where the Romans placed them. Just as the Catalans absorbed Roman culture, they also appropriated the Roman architecture, mining the monuments for building blocks that show up in the medieval city that clusters around the cathedral.

Essentials

GETTING THERE There are trains from Barcelona-Sants station to Tarragona about every 15 minutes. They take from 31 minutes to 1¼ hours and cost 7.95€ to 32€. AVANT trains have the best combination of speed and value; 35 minutes for 17€. In Tarragona, the RENFE office is in the train station, Plaza Pedrera s/n (© **90-232-03-20;** www.renfe.com). There are also about 10 **buses** per day from Barcelona to Tarragona (trip time: 1½ hr.), but the bus is slower, less convenient, and often more expensive than the train. Call © **97-722-91-26** in Tarragona for more information. To drive, take the A-2 southwest from Barcelona to the A-7, and then take the N-340. It is a fast and costly toll road, with one-way tolls of 18€.

PREVIOUS PAGE: **Sitges' Església de Sant Bartomeu i Santa Tecla, overlooking the harbor.**

The main **tourist office,** at Calle Major, 39 (☎ **97-725-07-95;** www.tarragonaturisme.es), is open July through September Monday through Saturday 10am to 8pm and Sunday 10am to 2pm; October through June Monday through Saturday 10am to 2pm and 4 to 6pm and Sunday 10am to 2pm.

Where to Stay

Ciutat de Tarragona ★★★
Set right on the main city park (a good spot for joggers), this sleekly modern hostelry offers downtown Tarragona's fanciest digs. It's convenient for sightseeing; everything (except the beaches) is within close walking distance. The rooftop deck around the pool is especially popular for families, as are the special family rooms with extra beds and a layout designed to give both parents and kids a little privacy. Triple and quad rooms are also available for adults traveling together. Free parking is provided if booked through the hotel website.

Plaça Imperial Tarraco, 5. ☎ **97-725-09-99.** www.hotelciutatdetarragona.com. 58 units. 75€–141€ double; from 105€ junior suite. **Amenities:** Restaurant; bar; exercise room; outdoor pool; room service; sauna; free Wi-Fi.

HUSA Imperial Tarraco ★★
You can often get a very good deal at business hotels when no conference has been booked. The public rooms here have the usual hallmarks of a HUSA business hotel: lots of polished white marble and furniture upholstered in brown leather. But the Imperial Tarraco was originally built for leisure, and the crescent shape with rooms angling out toward the sea gives most guests a pretty striking view of the water and the Roman ruins from their small balconies.

The Roman Via Augusta in Tarragona.

Passeig Palmeras/Rambla Vella. ☎ **97-723-30-40.** www.hotelhusaimperialtarraco.com. 170 units. 67€–145€ double; 132€–175€ suite. **Amenities:** Restaurant; bar; babysitting; children's center; concierge; outdoor pool; room service; outdoor tennis court; free Wi-Fi.

Hotel Lauria ★
Guests enjoy the large outdoor pool and the close proximity to the Balcony of the Mediterranean promenade. In fact, the hotel is well-situated for sightseeing in general. The rooms range from small to medium and have comfortable, but spare, modern furnishings brightened with bold pops of color. For an ocean view, ask for a room at the back.

Rambla Nova, 20. ☎ **97-723-67-12.** www.hotel-lauria.com. 72 units. 50€–80€ double. Parking 20€ but worth trying to negotiate. **Amenities:** Bar; outdoor freshwater pool; room service; free Wi-Fi.

Hotel Plaça de la Font ★
Photo murals behind the beds bring images of Tarragona's stately architecture and rocky coast into the guest rooms. But if

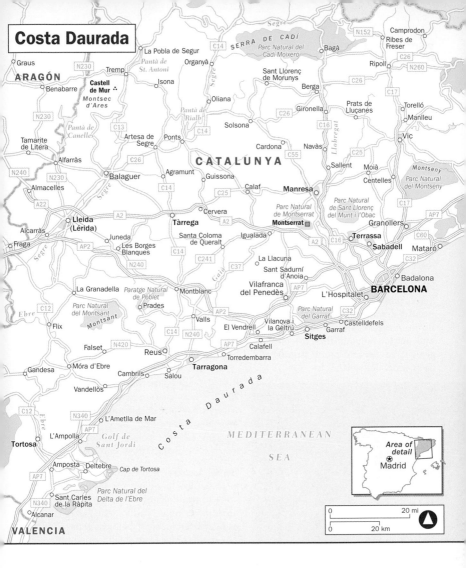

Costa Daurada

you like to turn in early, take note that the hotel sits on a lively old city plaza and you may find that you can't escape the cafe noise at night. Many consider it a minor inconvenience for the charming and convenient location and the good price for simple, modern rooms.

Plaça de la Font, 26. ☎ **97-724-61-34.** www.hotelpdelafont.com. 20 rooms. 55€–72€. **Amenities:** Bar; restaurant; free Wi-Fi.

Where to Eat

Cooking in Tarragona is rather Janus-like, looking out to the sea for all the bounty of the Mediterranean and glancing over its shoulder to the mountainous country that begins a short distance from the coast. As a result, its menus are always brimming with both coastal fish like sea bream and bass, and deepwater predators like yellowfin tuna. At the same time, the local lamb and kid are as good as any in Spain since the herds feed on the rosemary scrub of the nearby hillsides.

Barquet ★★ CATALAN/SEAFOOD   One of Tarragona's most established seafood restaurants (since 1950), Barquet's nautically themed dining rooms may look a bit old-fashioned, but the food is fresh and the kitchen really knows how to cook and present both fish and shellfish. Look for the local specialty of fried fish with toasted noodles called *fideos rossejat*. Local oysters are available on the half-shell as well as roasted, and the garlicky steamed mussels are the equal of any on the coast. One of the best bets is often the grilled catch of the day (usually sea bream or bass), and diners who don't care for fish have a few grilled options of veal and chicken. The house selections of D.O. Terra Alta wines are good, economical complements to most dishes. Once one of Tarragona's more expensive options, Barquet has introduced several less expensive set menus to help diners cope with the ongoing financial crisis.

Carrer Gasometro, 16. ✆ **97-724-00-23.** www.restaurantbarquet.com. Reservations recommended. Main courses 15€–28€; daily menus from 20€, tasting menus 27€–43€. Mon–Sat 1–3:30pm; Tues–Sat 9–10:30pm. Closed Aug 15–Sept 15.

El Llagut Taverna Marinera ★★ CATALAN/SEAFOOD   El Llagut considers itself a Slow Food restaurant, and does indeed use local meat, fish, fruits, and vegetables. But it is blessedly free of foodie pretensions. The rough stone walls and checked tablecloths give diners the message that they can relax and enjoy their meal, and staff take the time to fully explain unfamiliar dishes. Rice dishes with seafood are the sure winners here. Some are a veritable encyclopedia of the local catch, while the *arròs negre* focuses on just one species, gaining its flavor and color from the squid and squid ink.

Carrer Natzaret, 10. ✆ **97-722-89-38.** Main dishes 11€–20€, Slow Food menu 21€–24€. Tue–Sun 1–3:30pm and 9–10:30pm.

The Balcó del Mediterráni.

modernisme **AMID THE ROMANS**

Just as Tarroco was a provincial reflection of the glories of Rome, modern Tarragona can boast some glimmers of the Modernista masterpieces of Barcelona. When you're making your promenade on Rambla Nova in the new city, stop in to see the Modernista interior of the **Teatre Metropol** (Rambla Nova, 46; ℰ **97-724-47-95**), built in 1908 and still used for live theater, dance, and concerts. At the edge of the old city, **L'Església de Sant Francesc** (Rambla Vella, 28) has a striking Modernista chapel well worth the time to visit (Mon–Sat 11am–1pm and 5–8pm; free admission). If you're continuing uphill to the old city through Plaça de la Font, pop into the **Ayuntament** (City Hall) to see the Modernista ship-shaped tomb of Jaume I of Aragón (1208–76), the conqueror who brought together the political fates of Aragón and Catalunya and stands today as a rallying symbol for Catalan autonomy, if not outright independence from Spain. The Ayuntament is open daily 8am to 10pm and admission is free.

La Taula Rodona Brasserie ★★ CATALAN   This casual restaurant offers good value and a warm tavern ambience dominated by the towering chimney. Tarragona may be a city on the sea, but this establishment showcases the excellent veal, pork, lamb, and kid from the nearby mountains. Everything is grilled over an open wood fire, and the place is inevitably packed with local students, courting couples, and even entire large families.

Carrer La Nau, 4. ℰ **97-724-25-92.** Main dishes 9€–17€. Tues–Sun 1–3:30pm; Tues–Sat 9–10:30pm.

Les Coques ★★ CATALAN   If you are looking for a meal with a sense of occasion, Les Coques is a good choice. The restaurant is set within thick stone walls and features arched entrances and wood-beamed ceilings. As befitting the setting, many of the dishes, such as lamb glazed with red wine, can be rather pricey. But you can enjoy the setting and fine service equally well even if you stick with the less expensive and more homey dishes such as whole fish baked in salt or meatballs made with chopped octopus.

Carrer San Llorenç, 15. ℰ **97-722-83-00.** www.les-coques.com. Main dishes 13€–30€. Daily menu 18€. Mon–Sat 1–3pm and 9–11pm.

Les Voltes ★★ CATALAN   Thick plate glass and stainless surfaces harmonize surprisingly well with the ancient stone to create a very upscale look for this modern restaurant in the vaults of the Roman circus. It's a bit of a circus itself, as it seats 250 people and is popular with tour groups as well as individual travelers. Despite an almost all-tourist clientele, Les Voltes has very good prices for expertly grilled and roasted meats, including lamb shoulder and a spicy casserole of pork trotters. The springtime shellfish assortment is a rather spectacular presentation of shrimp, lobster, and Dublin prawns, but it is expensive (40€ and up, depending on market prices) and requires that at least two people at a table order it.

Carrer Trinquet Vell, 12. ℰ **97-723-06-51.** www.restaurantlesvoltes.cat. Main courses 8€–20€. Tues–Sun 1–3:30pm (July–Aug closed Sun at lunch); Tues–Sat 8:30–11:30pm. Closed first half of Jan and last 2 weeks in July.

Exploring Tarragona

Central Tarragona consists of a new city organized around the broad avenues of Les Rambles on fairly flat terrain, and a partially walled old city that huddles around the cathedral on high rocky ground. Traces of Roman Tarroco are found in the both old and new cities, as are a few gems of Modernisme architecture and design. In the new city, the **Balcó del Mediterráni (Balcony of the Mediterranean)** seaside belvedere connects the old and new Rambles. Be sure to stroll the main artery, **Rambla Nova,** a fashionable wide boulevard that is also the site of a flea market Fridays and Saturdays 10am to 4pm. Running parallel with Rambla Nova to the east is the **Rambla Vella,** which marks the beginning of the old town and was once part of the Roman Via Augusta. Just off Rambla Vella, the **Plaça de La Font** functions as the go-between from old to new cities. It has a lively cafe scene as well as the offices of city government.

Catedral ★ RELIGIOUS SITE   Begun in the mid–12th century and finally consecrated in 1331, the cathedral spans the transition from Romanesque to Gothic architecture. It has a fortress-like quality, if for no other reason than it stands at the highest point of the city. The immense rose window of the main facade is balanced by the Gothic upper tier of the octagonal bell tower, where windows flood the interior with light. The most striking work of art in the church is the altarpiece dedicated to Santa Tecla, patron of Tarragona, carved by Père Joan in 1430. Two flamboyant Gothic doors open into the east end of the church, where you'll find the **Museu Diocesà,** with a collection of Catalan religious art.

Plaça de la Seu. ✆ **97-723-86-85.** Cathedral and museum 3.50€. Mar 16–May 31 Mon–Sat 10am–1pm and 4–7pm; June 1–Oct 15 Mon–Sat 10am–7pm; Oct 16–Nov 15 Mon–Sat 10am–5pm; Nov 16–Mar 15 Mon–Sat 10am–2pm. Bus: 1.

Museu d'Art Modern de Tarragona ★ MUSEUM   "Modern" at this museum is more a statement of era than style, as the paintings ignore all the avant-garde movements of the 20th century. It was founded by the donation of several sculptures by Julio Antonio that had been in the possession of his family. Additional bequests have expanded the collection, which includes many more Catalan artists, especially the painter Josep Sancho i Piqué and sculptors Santiago Costa i Vaqué and Salvador Martorell i Ollé. Along the way, curators also acquired an extensive collection of late 20th-century Catalan photography.

Carrer Santa Anna, 8. ✆ **97-723-50-32.** www.altanet.org/MAMT. Free admission. Tues–Fri 10am–8pm; Sat 10am–3pm and 5–8pm; Sun 11am–2pm.

Museu Nacional Arqueològic de Tarragona ★★ MUSEUM   Catalunya's oldest archaeology museum was established in the first half of the 19th century and continued to add to its collection as urban expansion and building projects unearthed more evidence of the city's early history. This is a good place to get an overview of Tarragona's Roman era before you explore the ancient sites that still dot the city. The museum's displays of household objects such as jewelry, cups and plates, cooking utensils, and children's toys bring a human touch to history. They are balanced by works of great artistry, such as a carved head of Medusa, and intricate mosaic murals of peacocks and marine life.

Plaça del Rei 5. ✆ **97-723-62-09.** www.mnat.es. Admission 2.40€. June–Sept Tues–Sat 9:30am–8:30pm; Sun 10am–2pm; Oct–May Tues–Sat 10am–6pm; Sun 10am–2pm. Bus: 8.

The Museu Nacional Arqueològic de Tarragona.

Roman Tarragona

Since the Roman ruins are distributed throughout the city, we have drawn them together here for travelers who want to immerse themselves in the remains of Tarroco. Apart from the sections of the Roman aqueduct still standing on the northern fringe of the city proper, most of the Roman ruins are grouped together under the umbrella of the **Museu d'Història de Tarragona (Tarragona History Museum;** Calle Cavallers, 14; ✆ **97-724-22-20;** www.museutgn.com). The museum itself is distributed among a few historic houses owned by the city (included in the combined admission pass), but visitors will find the Roman sites themselves of greater interest. To see the best Roman artifacts, visit the Museu Nacional Arqueològic de Tarragona (above).

Single site admissions to the Roman monuments are 3.30€ adults, 1.70€ seniors and students, free ages 16 and younger. Combined admission to all the museum's sites (available at any one) is 11€ adults, 5.50€ seniors and students. October to March Tuesday to Saturday 9am to 6:30pm, Sunday and holidays 10am to 3pm; April to September Tuesday to Saturday 9am to 9pm, Sunday and holidays 9am to 3pm. Closed December 25 and 26, January 1, and January 6. All sites can be reached by city bus 2 (1.45€).

Amfiteatre Romà ★★★ HISTORIC SITE This 2nd century A.D. theater was carved from the cliff that rises above the crashing ocean. Contrasted against the vast spread of seaside sky and the abrupt and rugged cliff, the amphitheater must have been one of the most dramatic in the ancient world. Even in ruins, it is not a sight that you will soon forget. In its day, up to 14,000 spectators would gather here for bloody gladiator battles, other games, and executions. The tiered seats that they sat upon are the same ones you'll see today. Lest the beauty of the site entrance you, a monument declares that "Many innocent lives were taken in this amphitheater."

Parc del Milagro. ✆ **97-724-25-79.**

Passeig Arqueològic ★★ HISTORIC SITE   When the Romans decided to enclose their city of Tarraco in the 2nd century A.D., they built their walls on top of huge boulders. Only about a third of the original 3,500m construction still stands, and you can follow a garden-like path for about 0.8km (½ mile) of that length. Historic markers show the way; there are also opportunities to climb up onto the ramparts for views of the sea and country. As a reminder of the progression of history, you'll find cannon placed in battlements by the Spanish in the early 18th century.

El Portal del Roser. ℂ **97-724-57-96.**

Pretorì i Circ Romà ★★ HISTORIC SITE   In the 1st century A.D., the Romans selected a hillside location to build this three-level complex that dedicated a floor each to worship (the top level), government (the middle level), and the circus (the lower level). The well-preserved circus, with a capacity of 30,000 spectators, is the most visited and evocative part of the site. It was used for horse and chariot races, and it's still possible to imagine the winners exiting through the grand, arched Porta Triumphalis.

Plaça del Rei, s/n. ℂ **97-723-01-71.**

Side Trip to Poblet

If you rent a car, you can make a 30- to 45-minute drive through picturesque mountain passes to one of Catalunya's most evocative and atmospheric monasteries. As a side benefit, it's smack-dab in the middle of an up-and-coming winegrowing district. **Real Monestir de Poblet** ★★ (Plaça Corona d'Aragó 11, Poblet; ℂ **97-787-00-89;** www.poblet.cat) is a UNESCO World Heritage Site.

The ancient Amfiteatre Romà.

AT THE shore ON THE COSTA DAURADA

The main segment of the Costa Daurada consists of the sandy beach towns southwest of Tarragona, stretching from Salou, just outside Tarragona, roughly 60km (37 miles) to the old Roman port of L'Ampolla.

Salou is the largest beach town of the Costa Daurada, but the community has managed to hold onto the elegance of its main beach. Local legend has it that the Passeig de les Palmeres, a broad promenade lined with towering palms, was modeled on the promenade in Nice. An impressive sculpture celebrates the departure of Jaume I from Salou in 1229 to recapture Mallorca. Modernista villas lining the promenade attest to Salou's long-standing wealth and good taste. The counterpoint to that graciousness is **Port Aventura** (© 90-220-22-20; www. portaventura.es; adults from 37€, ages 7–17 from 28€, ages 4–11 from 18€, seniors from 28€), located outside of town. Polynesia, Aztec Mexico, China, and Wild West theme areas have their own thrill rides and dance spectacles, and the Costa Caribe Aquatic Park offers dozens of water adventures. Open mid–March through January 6.

Just south of Salou is our choice for a base on Costa Daurada: the salty village of **Cambrils,** where beachgoers and commercial fishermen share the strand, and tourists gather to watch the boats unload their catch around 4pm. Gastronomes will book their fish dinners far ahead at **Joan Gatell Restaurant** (Passeig Miramar, 26; © 97-736-67-82; joangatell@joangatell.com). The tasting menu (75€) includes four grand fish courses.

The easiest (and least expensive way) to get on the water here is to take the **catamaran shuttle service** between Salou and Cambrils (9€ one-way, 12€ round-trip). It is operated by **Creuers Costa Daurada** (Avinguda Diputació, 15; © 97-736-30-90; www.creuerscostadaurada.com; other cruises 15€–41€).

To get up into the hills above Cambrils, hike up the easy **Miró in Montroig del Camp trail** from Pixerota beach for 8km (5 miles) to the hilltop chapel of La Mare de Déu de la Roca. As a young man, Joan Miró spent summers in these hills above Cambrils, and there are 10 benches along the trail marking spots where he painted one of his pictures.

At L'Ampolla, the coast changes character from golden sands to the broad, flat, and stunningly beautiful delta of the Riú Ebre (known elsewhere in Spain as the Río Ebro). Land and water are so interspersed here that it is hard to tell where one ends and the other begins. The delta is a major rice-growing region and an important habitat for water birds. So many thousands of flamingos breed here that they cease to seem like a novelty. Much of the delta lies within the **Parque Natural del Delta de l'Ebre.** Its **Ecomuseu del Parque Natural** (Carrer Doctor Martí Buera, 22; © 97-748-96-79; www.parcsdecatalunya.net; admission by donation; Mon–Sat 10am–2pm and 3–6pm, Sun 10am–2pm Sun) has exhibits explaining both the human and natural features. The information desk can also advise on boat trips, bicycle rentals, and birding guides.

Its most striking feature is the pantheon of the old kings of Aragón—a catacomb of royal tombs. Constructed in the 12th and 13th centuries and still in use, Poblet's immense basilica reflects both Romanesque and Gothic architectural styles. Re-established in 1940 as a Cistercian monastery after remaining vacant since 1835, Poblet is the largest Cistercian community in Europe. The monks pass their days writing, studying, working a printing press, farming, and helping restore the building, which suffered heavy damage during the 1835 revolution.

The monastery is also surrounded by vast stretches of Pinot Noir grapes, originally introduced by Cistercian monks from Burgundy. The monastery's winery has been rebuilt by the Cordoniú group and is open for free tours and sales. It belongs within the D.O. Conca de Barberà wine region, but is one of the few properties making reds from Pinot Noir rather than Garnatxa (Grenache) or Ull de Llebre (a local clone of Tempranillo).

Admission to the monastery costs 7€ adults, 4€ seniors and students. From March 16 to October 12, it's open Monday to Saturday 10am to 12:40pm and 3 to 6pm; October 13 to March 15, it's open daily 10:30am to 12:40pm and 3 to 5:30pm. Except for Monday, when no guide service is available, visits to the monastery usually include tours, mostly in Spanish but with occasional English translations. They depart at 75-minute intervals.

SITGES ★★

Sitges is one of the most popular vacation resorts in southern Europe. Long a beach escape for Barcelonans, it became a resort town in the late 19th century as artists, authors, and industrialists transformed fishermen's houses into summer villas. The Modernisme movement took hold in Sitges by the late 1870s, and the town remained the scene of artistic foment long after the movement waned, attracting such giants as Salvador Dalí and poet Federico García Lorca. The bohemian exuberance and intellectual and artistic ferment came to an abrupt halt with the Spanish Civil War. Although other artists and writers arrived in the decades after World War II, none had the fame or the impact of those who had gone before.

The beach is as dramatic ever, making Sitges the brightest light on Catalunya's Costa Daurada. It becomes especially crowded in the summer with affluent and young northern Europeans, many of them gay, and there's a lively art and gallery scene, mostly featuring bright, loosely representational but expressive painting. A new contemporary art museum has re-introduced a more challenging edginess. Sitges is also famous for its raucous celebration of Carnestoltes, or Carnival, in the days leading up to Lent.

Essentials

GETTING THERE There are commuter rail (*cercanías*) **trains** to Sitges every 15 to 30 minutes between 6am and midnight from Barcelona-Sants station. Travel time is about 30 minutes and the fare is 4.10€. In Barcelona, call © **90-232-03-20** or click the *cercanías* tab at www.renfe.com for details on schedules. Sitges is a 45-minute drive from Barcelona along the C-246, a coastal road. The express highway A-7 is less scenic but faster on weekends when the free coastal road is clogged with traffic.

VISITOR INFORMATION The **tourist office** is at Plaza Eduard Maristany, 2 (© **93-894-42-51**; www.sitgestur.cat). Year-round hours are Monday to Friday 10am to 2pm and 4 to 6:30pm, Saturday 10am to 2pm and 4 to 7pm, and Sunday 10am to 2pm.

Where to Stay

Book far ahead if you're planning a visit in July or August, as every room in Sitges will be full. Between mid-October and Easter, you might find most lodgings closed.

Galeón Hotel ★ Part of a three-hotel group all located a 2-minute walk from the beach near the Plaça d'Espanya, the Galeón offers the best balance between price and comfort. Nicely maintained, it has been updated to place streamlined furniture in the wood-paneled rooms and to provide a pillow menu for the firm and comfortable beds. The public areas are small, but if you're not in your room at Sitges, you're likely at the beach. The hotel provides guests with beach towels and umbrellas—a nice touch.

Carrer Sant Francesc 44. ℂ **93-894-13-79.** www.hotelsitges.com. 74 units. 84€–122€ double. Parking 18€. **Amenities:** Restaurant; bar; outdoor freshwater pool; free Wi-Fi in public areas.

Sitges' beachside promenade.

Hotel Calipolis ★ The graceful curve of this beachfront hotel is echoed in the shape of the outdoor pool. This somewhat conventional resort is under private ownership and management with all the local pride that entails. Mountain-view rooms tend to be a little larger, quieter, and less expensive, but opt for a sea-view room with a balcony if you can afford it. It's a great place to sit outside and enjoy a glass of wine while listening to the surf. The hotel is a 5- to 10-minute stroll from the center of the town and beachside restaurants. It is quiet at night despite the basement nightclub.

Carrer Sofia, 2-6. ℂ **93-894-15-00.** www.hotelcalipolis.com. 170 rooms. 120€–260€. **Amenities:** Bar; restaurant; swimming pool; solarium; nightclub; gym; limited parking.

Hotel El Xalet and Hotel Noucentista ★★ Everyone who sees these adjoining hotels falls in love with them. Set in the city center a good 10-minute walk from the beach, they occupy two adjoining Modernisme landmark buildings constructed by architects Gaietà Buigas i Monravà in 1882 and Gaietà Miret i Raventos in 1881, respectively. The ornate stonework, carved trim, fanciful spires, and stained glass in floral motifs reflect the neo-medieval side of Modernisme design. The lobbies and reception areas are filled with period tile mosaics and marble, while the fairly small guest rooms are more simply furnished and are painted in summery pastels. (Each building also has a few larger suites.) The nicely maintained gardens surround a small pool at El Xalet. Breakfast is served (weather permitting) on the roof terrace, and there is a summer-only restaurant in El Xalet.

Carrer Illa de Cuba, 21 and 35. ℂ **93-811-00-70.** www.elxalet.com. 17 units in Hotel El Xalet, 12 units in Hotel Noucentista. 63€–110€ double; 90€–145€ suite. **Amenities:** Restaurant; outdoor pool; free Wi-Fi.

Hotel Romàntic ★ Created by combining three 19th-century townhouse villas, the Romantic has a kind of casual sprawl that's part of its charm. The hotel makes the most of the art-colony history of Sitges, practically plastering the walls with bright, often whimsical canvases that make up in enthusiasm what they might lack in execution. The paintings continue into the guest rooms, but they certainly beat the generic posters of other hotels striving for an arty, romantic atmosphere. In fact, the name is justified—both gay and straight travelers from all over Europe congregate here and get the day off to a grand start with breakfast in the lovely garden. Note, however, that few of the rooms have en suite bathrooms, and many of the rooms are quite small and furnished with single beds. Companion property, Hotel de la Renaixenca, is used for overflow guests, who have full use of the grounds. The beach and train station are nearby.

Carrer de Sant Isidre, 33. ✆ **93-894-83-75.** www.hotelromantic.com. 60 units (57 w/shared bathroom). 83€–108€ double w/shared bathroom; 99€–126€ double w/private bathroom. **Amenities:** Bar; babysitting.

Where to Eat

Seafood always seems best at the beach, and Sitges restaurants serve a wide variety of Catalan rice plates or stews with fish and shellfish. But hilly pastoral country is literally just a few miles inland on the other side of the coastal mountains, and meat dishes are also popular.

L'Estrella de Xaimar ★ CATALAN   One of the best bargains in Sitges, this tavern has the florid panache of Modernisme decor combined with the casual atmosphere of a *cerveseria* (as the Catalans spell "beer hall"). The menu emphasizes fish and shellfish, often in casserole, as well as lamb, kid, and veal grilled with fresh herbs from the nearby mountainside. Beer is usually the drink of choice. Wine selections are limited but local, featuring reds, whites, and rosés from the nearby Penedès region and cava from Sant Sadurní d'Anoia.

Calle Major, 52. ✆ **93-894-70-54.** Main dishes 11€–26€, menus from 13€. Daily 1:30–4pm and 8:30–11:30pm (in winter, dinner Fri–Sat only).

Fragata ★★ SEAFOOD   Located on the beach at the edge of Plaça Baluarte, Fragata is a contemporary jewel box of a restaurant: all glass, with taupe and nutmeg upholstery and table linens. Even the impressive wine cellar is a frosted glass cube. There's a bit of an international air to parts of the menu—lollypop baby lamb chops, for example—but beautifully presented Catalan seafood carries the day, whether as a *suquet* (the Catalan answer to bouillabaisse), a tossed salad of salt cod and oranges on lettuce, or grilled baby squid in a sauce of their own ink. The mixed grill of fresh fish is always a good bet—except on Sunday, when the fishermen stay ashore.

Passeig de la Ribera, 1. ✆ **93-894-10-86.** www.restaurantefragata.com. Reservations recommended. Main dishes 15€–32€. Daily 1:30–4:30pm and 8:30–11:30pm.

El Velero ★★ SEAFOOD   Florencio Martínez is the big starfish among Sitges chefs, and his venerable El Velero is the city's leading seafood establishment. It sits right on the promenade at the beach; the elegant scene is indoors, but when the weather is balmy, ask for a table on the glassed-in terrace that opens onto the esplanade. The workhorse fish here is daurada (gilthead bream), a member of the bass family, and the size of the catch will determine the preparation. Small bream are often baked in salt or pan-fried like Dover sole, while larger fish are cut into steaks rather than filets and roasted with fresh herbs and a garlicky aioli. If you're in the mood for beef, the chateaubriand for two with a Spanish brandy sauce is both spectacular and a good deal. David Martínez, the chef's son, is the expert sommelier who is happy recommending a brisk Empordà white for the fish or a dignified Poblet red for the meat.

Passeig de la Ribera, 38. ✆ **93-894-20-51.** www.restaurantevelero.com. Reservations required. Main courses 14€–31€; fixed-price menu 45€. Wed–Sun 8:30–11:30pm.

The family-friendly Playa San Sebastián.

Exploring Sitges

Sitges was once a fortified medieval town on the hillside above the beach, and bits and pieces of that fortress persist. The modest former castle, for example, is now the seat of the town government. The oceanfront **Passeig de la Ribera** is much more emblematic of modern Sitges. A favorite spot to promenade in the early evening, it is defined by two landmarks of different eras and sensibilities. A sign on **Chiringuito ★** (Paseo de la Ribera; © 98-894-75-96), a beachside restaurant/bar founded in 1913, identifies it as the probable source of the name now used by all similar casual spots along the Spanish coast.

At the east end of the promenade, booming surf soaks the stone steps leading to Plaça del Baluart, where the 17th-century baroque **Església de Sant Bartomeu i Santa Tecla ★** overlooks the harbor. So does a single cannon, the last of six that drove off English warships in 1797. Behind the landmark church are the Museu Cau Ferrat and the Museu Maricel (see below).

Most people come here to hit the beach, which comes equipped with showers, bathing cabins, and stalls; kiosks rent motorboats and water sports equipment. Beaches on the eastern end and inside the town center, such as **Aiguadoiç** and **Els Balomins,** are the most peaceful. **Playa San Sebastián, Fragata Beach,** and the **"Beach of the Boats"** (below the church and next to the yacht club) are the area's family beaches. A somewhat hipper, more youthful crowd congregates at **Playa de la Ribera** to the west.

All along the coast, women can and certainly do go topless. Farther west are the most solitary beaches, where the attire grows skimpier, especially along the **Playas del Muerto,** where two tiny nude beaches lie between Sitges and Vilanova i la Geltrú. A shuttle bus runs between the cathedral and Golf Terramar. From Golf Terramar, go along the road to the club L'Atlántida, and then walk along the railway. The first beach draws nudists of all sexual orientations, while the second is principally if not exclusively gay.

Fundació Stämpfli-Art Contemporani ★ MUSEUM   This new organization rounds out the artistic reputation of Sitges by bringing it up to date—the oldest works are from the 1960s—and by injecting an international perspective to the seaside art colony. Small but growing, the permanent collection includes more than 80 works by 55 different artists from 22 countries. Changing temporary exhibitions explore aspects of contemporary art from pop art of the 20th century to video art of the 21st.

Plaça de l'Ajuntament, 13. ℂ **93-894-03-64.** www.museusdesitges.com. Admission 3.50€ adults, 2€ seniors and students, free under age 6; combination ticket with Museu Romàntic 6.50€ adults, 4€ students and seniors. Oct–June Fri 3:30–7pm, Sat 10am–2pm and 3:30–7pm, Sun 11am–3pm; July–Sept Thurs–Fri 4–8pm, Sat–Sun 11am–8pm.

Museu Cau Ferrat ★★ MUSEUM   Nearing completion of a several-year restoration project, this museum captures the life, lifestyle, and art of the early years of Sitges as an art colony. In the late 19th century, modern artist Santiago Rusiñol (1861–1931) created his combined studio, home, and art gallery by joining two 16th-century fishermen's cottages. His unique property soon attracted Catalan bohemians whose presence helped spur the transformation of the town into a popular seaside resort. Upon his death in 1931, Rusiñol willed the house and his collection to the city, and visitors can see examples of his work as well as work by his contemporaries. The collection includes a few notable pieces by Picasso and El Greco. But the appeal of the museum lies less in any individual work of art than in the way that it captures the excitement, allure, and tensions of an avant-garde artistic salon in the years before the Spanish Civil War. **Note:** Reopening of the museum has been delayed by the economic crisis, but renovations are expected to be complete in 2014.

The Museu Cau Ferrat.

Carrer Fonollar. ℂ **93-894-03-64.** www. museusdesitges.com. Anticipated admission 3.50€ adults, 2€ seniors and students, free for children 5 and under. Combined ticket with Museu Maricel 6.50€ adults, 4€ seniors and students. June 15–Sept Tues–Sat 9:30am–2pm and 4–7pm, Sun 10am–3pm; Oct–June 14 Tues–Sat 9:30am–2pm and 3:30–6:30pm, Sun 10am–3pm.

Museu Maricel ★ MUSEUM   One of the people attracted to the Sitges art scene was American industrialist Charles Deering (heir to the company that would become International Harvester), who had this charming palace built right after World War I. Today it displays the collection of Dr. Jésus Pérez Rosales, which ranges from Gothic and Renaissance altarpieces to Catalan ceramics. The town's own art collection is of more local interest as it features work created by Sitges artists in the 19th and 20th centuries, including the members of the Sitges "Luminist School," a movement that preceded Catalan Modernisme. Check

SITGES after dark

In true Spanish fashion, nightclubs and bars with live entertainment rarely open before 11pm, and in Sitges, most cater to a gay clientele. The greatest concentration is on **Carrer Sant Bonaventura** in the center of town, a short walk from the beach (near the Museu Romàntic; below). A map detailing gay bars and their style—from leather to black rubber to disco-ball dancing—is available at the bars themselves and online at www. gaysitgesguide.com.

to see if recent renovations are completed before heading over as it may be closed.

Carrer Fonallar. ✆ **93-894-03-64.** www.museusdesitges.com. Anticipated admission 3.50€ adults, 2€ seniors and students, free for children 5 and under. Combined ticket with Museu Cau Ferrat 6.50€ adults, 4€ seniors and students. June 15–Sept Tues–Sat 9:30am–2pm and 4–7pm, Sun 10am–3pm; Oct–June 14 Tues–Sat 9:30am–2pm and 3:30–6:30pm, Sun 10am–3pm.

Museu Romàntic (Can Llopis) ★ MUSEUM   Using furniture and household objects to recreate family rooms in the downstairs section of the building, this museum conjures the daily life of a land-owning Sitges family in the 18th and 19th centuries. The wine cellars are a reminder that the Llopis family, while nominally involved in farming and statecraft, reserved their true passions for making sophisticated wines from the Malvasia grape. The upper level, formerly the servants' quarters, contains a collection of more than 400 dolls donated by writer and illustrator Lola Anglada Barcelona. Made of wood, papier-mâché, and porcelain, they date from the 17th through the 19th centuries. Some feature mechanical or musical movements.

Carrer Sant Gaudenci, 1. ✆ **93-894-29-69.** www.museusdesitges.com. Admission 3.50€ adults, 2€ seniors and students, free for children 5 and under; combination ticket with Fundació Stämpfli 6.50€ adults, 4€ students and seniors. Mon–Sat 10am–1pm and 3–6:30pm; Sun 10am–1pm.

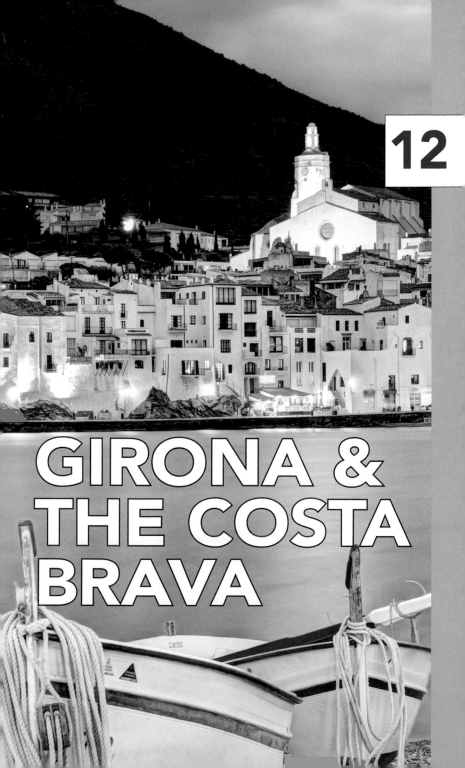

GIRONA & THE COSTA BRAVA

S pain's northeast corner was almost ruined in the 1960s when real estate speculators somehow decided that its medieval fishing coves could be turned into sun-and-sea resorts to rival the already overgrown Costa del Sol in Andalucía. Fortunately, geography conspired against the Costa Brava, or "Wild Coast" (as the region was dubbed), from going too far down the road of overdevelopment. Yes, there are some blights on the landscape, and some of the communities closest to Barcelona sold their character to the holiday package industry. But other communities resisted and have preserved their identities along with their historical buildings, wild natural scenery, and sweeping crescent beaches.

GIRONA ★★★

Girona is Barcelona's country cousin—slower-paced and more compact, yet strikingly sophisticated and cosmopolitan. It is the perfect escape valve when the pressure of the Barcelona crowds begins to get to you. Girona is simply a charming, disarming Catalan city with lots to look at and some delicious things to eat. It was founded by the Romans on a hill crouching above the Ríu Onyar, and the shape of the city remains as Roman as it was 2,000 years ago. As those Romans realized, the river crossing here was so strategically important that Girona has been besieged 25 times over the centuries, beginning with Charlemagne in 785. The most devastating siege was by Napoleon in 1809, when he starved the city into submission.

Fortunately, Napoleon did not destroy Girona, and the elegant and graceful city retains traces of the Roman era along with medieval buildings on the Roman street structure. Gorgeous 19th-century pastel houses line the riverfront. As a citadel city, Girona is blessedly compact and, while steep, walkable. You'll be glad to work up an appetite because, like Barcelona, Girona is a city with a passionate local food culture.

Essentials

GETTING THERE More than 25 **trains** per day run between Girona and Barcelona. Trip time ranges from 37 minutes on AVANT and AVE trains to 1¾ hours on the slow regional. Tickets range from 8.40€ to 29€ one-way, with the best combination of time and price being the AVANT trains at 38 minutes and 15€ to 18€. Trains arrive in Girona at the Plaça Espanya (✆ **90-232-03-20;** www. renfe.com). Barcelona Bus (✆ **97-220-24-32** in Girona; www.barcelonabus. com) operates express buses between Girona and Barcelona at the rate of 6 to 13 runs per day, depending on the season and demand. Fare is 21€. From Barcelona or the French border, drivers connect with the main north-south route (A-7), taking the turnoff to Girona. From Barcelona, take the A-2 north to reach the A-7.

PREVIOUS PAGE: **Off the beaten path in Cadaqués.**

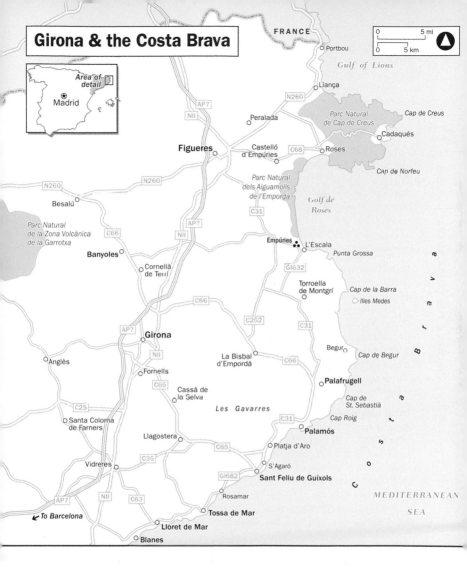

Girona & the Costa Brava

FRANCE

Portbou

Gulf of Lions

Llançà

Madrid

Area of detail

AP7

NII

N260

Peralada

Parc Natural
de Cap de Creus

Cap de Creus

Cadaqués

Figueres

Castelló
d'Empúries

C68

Roses

Cap de Norfeu

N260

N260

Parc Natural
dels Aiguamolls
de l'Empordà

Golf de
Roses

Besalú

C31

Parc Natural
de la Zona Volcànica
de la Garrotxa

C66

NII

AP7

Empúries

L'Escala

Banyoles

Cornellà
de Terri

Punta Grossa

GI632

Torroella
de Montgrí

Cap de la Barra

Illes Medes

C66

C252

C31

AP7

Girona

NII

Begur

Cap de Begur

Anglès

Fornells

La Bisbal
d'Empordà

C66

C65

Palafrugell

C25

Cassà de
la Selva

Les Gavarres

Cap de
St. Sebastià

Santa Coloma
de Farners

C31

Cap Roig

Palamós

Llagostera

C65

Platja d'Aro

Vidreres

C35

S'Agaró

GI682

Sant Feliu de Guíxols

AP7

NII

C63

Rosamar

MEDITERRANEAN
SEA

To Barcelona

Tossa de Mar

Lloret de Mar

Blanes

Costa Brava

0 ——— 5 mi
0 ——— 5 km

VISITOR INFORMATION The **tourist office,** at Rambla de la Llibertat, 1 (✆ **97-201-00-01;** www.girona.cat/turisme), is open Monday through Friday 9am to 8pm, Saturday 9am to 2pm and 4 to 8pm, and Sunday 9am to 2pm. The **Welcome Point,** Carrer Berenguer Carnicer, 3 (✆ **97-221-16-78**), is open July through mid-September Monday through Saturday 9am to 8pm and Sunday 9am to 2pm. The rest of the year it is open Monday through Saturday 9am to 2pm. In addition to providing information on lodging, dining, attractions, and transport, the Welcome Center offers guided tours.

Where to Stay

Bellmirall ★★ At least one rough stone wall in each room reminds visitors that this building in the center of the old Call dates from the 14th century. If you want to immerse yourself in the atmospheric old city, this lodging is a good choice at a good price. The rooms are small to midsize and feature simple furnishings, but you can also take advantage of the small courtyard. You'll find a TV in the common living space, but the bedrooms are TV- and phone-free. There is a garage for bicycles and motorcycles.

Carrer Bellmirall, 3. ✆ **97-220-40-09.** www.bellmirall.eu. 7 units. 65€–85€ double. Closed Jan–Feb.

Ciutat de Girona ★★
This modern hotel is located on the west side of the river between the San Feliu footbridge and Parque de la Devesa, a popular evening gathering spot in the summer. The generously sized bedrooms feature contemporary furnishings and up-to-date technology. Families will be pleased that there's an indoor swimming pool. When you're ready to see the sites, the cathedral is only about a 10-minute walk away.

Carrer Nord, 2. ✆ **97-248-30-38.** www.hotel-ciutatdegirona.com. 44 units. 88€–135€ double. **Amenities:** Restaurant; bar; parking; room service; pool; free Wi-Fi in public areas.

Hotel Historic ★★★
Architecture buffs should not miss this lodging that in a fashion encompasses Girona history. The 9th-century building, now hotel, includes a portion of a Roman wall and a 3rd-century aqueduct. Lodging choices include both guest rooms and apartments that can accommodate three or four people. Most guest rooms have beautiful stone walls, balconies, and stylish modern furniture. The apartments have more rustic, but comfortable, decor and are a good option for families.

Carrer Bellmirall, 4A. ✆ **97-222-35-83.** www.hotelhistoric.com. 15 units. 115€–150€ double; 200€ junior suite. Apartments 90€ up to 3 people, 120€ up to 4. **Amenities:** Restaurant; room service; free Wi-Fi and cable high-speed Internet.

Hotel Llegendes de Girona ★★
Is Girona for lovers? This hotel thinks so. Three "Eros" rooms have two levels and feature romantic decor. The Suite Margarita Bonita goes farther with rather explicit artwork, a bed mounted on a stage, liberal use of mirrors, and a sofa designed for tantric exercise. For those not on honeymoons, the 9th- to 10th-century building adjacent to Sant Feliu also has lovely, unthemed rooms that are comfortable, stylish, and a convenient base for exploring the old city.

Portal de la Barca, 4. ✆ **97-222-09-05.** www.llegendeshotel.com. 15 rooms. 109€–150€ double; 170€–190€ Eros room, 270€ suite. **Amenities:** Restaurant; room service; free Wi-Fi.

Where to Eat

The residents of Girona take Catalan gastronomy very seriously, making it one of the best cities its size for contemporary fine dining. The gourmet emphasis trickles down to more casual and less pricey venues as well, and it's easy to make a meal of tapas. One good area for tapas-hopping is the Plaça de la Independència, just across the Pont Sant Augusti from the Call.

Boira Restaurant ★ CATALAN
Boira has some seating outdoors on Plaça de la Independència, but we prefer a romantic table overlooking the river in the tranquil upstairs dining room. In contrast to the more traditional menus of surrounding restaurants, Boira emphasizes seasonal, local food. Creamy goat cheeses from the Catalan countryside could show up in a small tart, in the spring, local asparagus often graces fish plates, and in the fall, mushrooms abound. Part of Boira's appeal is the daily menu of starter, main dish, dessert, and wine for less than the cost of a main dish in many restaurants. Accordingly, portions are

modest. Some of the most fit people in Girona—professional cyclists who train here—eat regularly at Boira.

Plaça de la Independència, 17. ☏ **97-221-96-05.** Main dishes 12€–14€, daily menu 14€–17€. Daily 1–3:30pm and 8–10:30pm.

Casa Marieta ★★ CATALAN Fans of quirky local foods should try the *trinxat,* a casserole of rice, ham, cabbage, and potatoes. This regional dish is available, appropriately enough, in this, the oldest restaurant in town. Casa Marieta is also a reliable place to enjoy *suquet,* the seafood stew served throughout Catalunya. Art Nouveau–style stained glass and banquette seating enhance the dining experience.

Plaça de la Independència, 5-6. ☏ **97-220-10-16.** www.casamarieta.com. Reservations recommended. Main courses 9€–16€. Tues–Sun 1–3:30pm and 8–10:30pm. Closed Feb.

El Celler de Can Roca ★★★ CATALAN/INTERNATIONAL Named the best restaurant in the world in 2013 by the readers of *Restaurant* magazine in the United Kingdom, El Celler de Can Roca picked up the avant-garde baton when Ferran Adrià closed the famous elBulli. With Roca brothers Joan (head chef), Jordi (head pastry chef), and Josep (sommelier) in charge, the restaurant belies the old trope about too many chefs and spoiled broth. The cuisine is firmly rooted in classic Catalan home cooking but with sometimes surreal twists, as if the ghost of Salvador Dalí were in the kitchen. For example, the simple appetizer of local olives is served as caramelized olives—on a bonsai tree. (Be careful with the branches, as they need the tree for the next customer.) The meal begins with small bites from the El Mundo section of the kitchen (a spicy ball of frozen fish broth coated in cocoa butter, for example), followed by inventive main dishes of the moment. Rarely are they repeated, although the veal tartare with mustard ice cream, spicy ketchup, and fruit compotes is one of the stalwarts. Jordi is famous for inventing desserts that re-create the aromas of classic perfumes. For a once-in-a-lifetime experience, it's worth the splurge and the cost of a cab ride, as the restaurant sits about 2km (1¼ miles) from the center of town. Online reservations open at midnight on the first day of the month; phone reservations can be made farther ahead.

Carrer Can Sunyer, 48. www.cellercanroca.com. ☏ **97-222-21-57.** Reservations essential. Main courses 22€–50€; fixed-price menus 95€–145€. Tues–Sat 1–4pm and 9–11pm.

El Cul de la Lleona ★ MOROCCAN Named for the well-kissed hindquarters of the lion statue in Plaça Sant Feliu, this modest Moroccan restaurant on a quiet street in the Call is a good bet for vegetarians. Whether you opt for the chickpea couscous or a tagine, your dish will be graced with such warm spices as saffron, cumin, and coriander. The spicy roast chicken is topped with a roasted preserved lemon. Simple desserts range from honey pastries to cold mango soup. The inexpensive daily menu includes wine.

Carrer Calderera, 8. ☏ **97-220-31-58.** Main dishes 8€–13€, daily menu 12€ –14€. Mon–Sat 1–3:30pm and 8–10:30pm.

Massana ★★★ CATALAN We love the advice that Pere Massana gives to diners who hesitate to try the sea cucumbers that he offers as a starter. After the description on the menu he adds, "Do not ask. Taste them." That's good advice overall, and diners would be wise to simply trust Massana's sure hand at combining flavors and textures into winning dishes. Even though he is now the proprietor of one of Catalunya's best restaurants and the recipient of a Michelin star, he has not forgotten the great Catalan culinary traditions. One section of the menu is devoted to "The Pure Product, barely touched" and includes such plates as Palamós prawns from the Costa Brava roasted in coarse sea salt.

Bonastruch de Porta 10. ✆ **97-221-38-20.** www.restaurantmassana.com. Reservations recommended. Main courses 25€–40€; tasting menu 85€. Mon–Sat 1:15–3:45pm; Mon and Wed–Sat 8:45–10:45pm.

Mimolet Restaurant ★ CATALAN/FRENCH   French food still has a certain cachet in Catalunya, and Mimolet specializes in French bistro comfort food: cassoulet, duck, roasted daurada with root vegetables, and even steak-frites. Some of the tastiest dishes are found among the starters, including tempura-fried small fish, salmon tartare with basil oil, mussel salad with creamy wasabi dressing, and Iberian ham croquettes with red wine reduction. For a set price, you can choose a starter and a main dish, and the chef will surprise you with dessert (usually some combination of genoise, fresh fruit, cream, and chocolate).

Carrer Pou Rodó, 12. ✆ **97-220-21-24.** www.mimolet.net. Main dishes 13€–22€. Daily menu 22€, 3-course a la carte 30€, tasting menu 40€. Tues–Sat 1–3:30pm and 8–10:30pm, Sun 1–3:30pm.

Exploring Girona

Crossing the **Ríu Onyar** is much easier than it was in Roman times. From the vast city parking lot and train station, simply walk east over the pedestrian footbridge to the 14th-century Romanesque hulk of **Sant Feliu,** one of the oldest churches outside the Roman walls. The **Plaça de Sant Feliu** is a central meeting point for Gironans and visitors alike. Take note of the statue of a lioness mounted on a stone column. Tradition holds that a Gironan returning from a journey must kiss the statue's hindquarters to prove his good citizenship (tourists do it, too).

If you walk around behind the church and uphill, staying outside the walls, you will find the medieval baths (erroneously attributed to the Moors) and the handsome Benedictine monastery of Sant Pere de Galligants (St. Peter of the Cock Crows), which houses the **Museu d'Arqueologia de Catalunya.**

Alternatively, you can pass through the walls at the towering Roman gate on Plaça de Sant Feliu to the plaza in front of the **Catedral de Girona,** centerpiece of the medieval old city. According to another Gironan legend, the witch gargoyle on the cathedral was once a human witch, magically transformed into stone in the midst of curses and rants. Ever since, rainwater has washed blasphemy from her mouth.

Girona's medieval prosperity came in large part from its flourishing Jewish community, which concentrated in the **Call,** or Jewish Quarter, the narrow streets near the cathedral. You can wander for hours through the labyrinthine medieval quarter with its narrow, steep alleyways and lanes, which form a rampart chain along the Onyar. **Carrer de la Força** is the Call's main street, but photographers will want to explore the atmospheric side streets.

The new city is on the west bank of the Ríu Onyar. Its main shopping street is **Carrer Santa Clara.** The new city also has a number of tapas bars, especially on Les Rambles and **Plaça de la Independència,** just across the Pont de Sant Agusti from the Call. One of the most appealing things to do after dark, at least between June and September, is to walk into the new city's **Parque de la Devesa,** an artfully landscaped terrain of stately trees, flowering shrubs, refreshment kiosks, and open-air bars.

A narrow street in the Call, or Jewish Quarter, of Girona.

Els Banys Àrabs ★ HISTORIC SITE Despite their name, these baths were built in 1194, almost two centuries after the Moors were driven from Girona in 1015. They are a terrific example of Romanesque civic architecture. You can visit the **caldarium** (hot bath), with its paved floor, and the **frigidarium** (cold bath), with its central octagonal pool surrounded by pillars that support a prism-like structure in the overhead window.

Carrer Ferran el Católic. ℂ **97-221-32-62.** www.banysarabs.org. Admission 2€ adults, 1€ students and seniors. Apr–Sept Mon–Sat 10am–7pm, Sun 10am–2pm; Oct–Mar Mon–Sat 10am–2pm.

Casa Masó ★ HISTORIC SITE No visitor leaves Girona without a photograph of the picturesque pastel houses along the Riú Onyar. But with a little advance planning, you can also visit one of these iconic homes. Casa Masó, which consists of four houses combined in the late 19th and early 20th centuries, was the birthplace of Catalan architect Rafael Masó (1880–1935). A disciple of Antoni Gaudí, his work was heavily influenced by the British Arts & Crafts movement and the furnishings and decorations in the home show an interesting blend of Catalan Modernisme, British Arts & Crafts, and French Art Nouveau. Admission is by guided tour only and requires an advance reservation.

Carrer Ballesteries, 29. ℂ **97-241-39-89.** www.rafaelmaso.org. Admission 5€ adults, 2.50€ students and seniors; free under 16. Tues–Sat 10am–6pm.

Catedral de Girona ★★★ RELIGIOUS SITE The magnificent cathedral is Girona's leading attraction, but visiting is not for the weak of limb. To enter, you must climb a 17th-century baroque staircase of 89 steep steps. (Fitness enthusiasts race up and down the steps in the early morning.) The cathedral dates from the 14th century, so the basic structure bridges Romanesque and Gothic. What is most evident, though, is the surface decoration that is pure Catalan baroque. As you climb the stairs, you'll be staring at a facade added in the late 17th and early 18th centuries. The bell tower, which rises from a cornice, is crowned by a dome capped with a bronze angel weather vane. Go through the cathedral's main door and enter the nave, which at 23m (75 ft.) is the broadest Gothic nave in the world.

Most of the cathedral's extensive art collection is displayed in its treasury. The prize exhibit is the **Tapestry of the Creation** ★★★, an exquisite piece of 11th- or 12th-century Romanesque embroidery that depicts humans and animals in the Garden of Eden along with portraits of Girona citizens, including members of the city's prominent Jewish population. The other major work is a 10th-century manuscript, the **Códex del Beatus,** which contains an illustrated commentary on the Book of the Apocalypse. From the cathedral's **Chapel of Hope,** a door

The Catedral de Girona.

leads to a **Romanesque cloister** from the 12th and 13th centuries, with an unusual trapezoidal layout. The cloister gallery, with a double colonnade, has a series of friezes that narrate scenes from the New Testament. Guides tout them as the prize jewel of Catalan Romanesque art, but even more fantastic are the carved capitals of the cloister, which vividly narrate moral tales in intricate twists of stone. From the cloister you can view the 12th-century **Torre de Carlemany (Charlemagne's Tower),** the only surviving section of the 12th-century church that the cathedral displaced.

Plaça de la Catedral. ✆ **97-221-58-14.** www.catedraldegirona.org. Admission to cathedral free; cloister and museum with audioguide 7€ adults, 5€ students and seniors; free under 7. (Nave, treasury, and cloister are free Sun, audioguide 1€.) Cathedral daily 9am–1pm and during cloister and museum visiting hours. Cloister and museum Apr–Oct daily 10am–8pm; Nov–Mar daily 10am–7pm.

Església de Sant Feliu ★ RELIGIOUS SITE   Eight Roman and early Christian sepulchers are the main attractions of this Romanesque church with Gothic flourishes. In fact, the two oldest date from the 2nd century A.D. and one shows Pluto carrying Persephone to the underworld. Inside, a chapel contains the remains of city patron Sant Narcís. According to legend, flies escaping from his tomb drove away the French armies during the 1285 siege of Girona. The church itself was built slowly over the 14th to 17th centuries on the spot held by tradition to be the tomb of the 4th-century martyr, Feliu of Africa. The structure is significant in Catalan architectural history because its pillars and arches are Romanesque while the nave is Gothic. Some exceptional works within the church include a 16th-century altarpiece and a 14th-century alabaster statue of a Reclining Christ.

Pujada de San Feliu. ✆ **97-220-14-07.** Free admission. Mon–Sat 7am–12:30pm and 4–6:30pm; Sun and holidays 4–6:30pm.

Museu d'Arqueologia ★ MUSEUM   Everyone from Celtic Iberians, Greeks, and Carthaginians to Romans, Moors, and Visigoths passed through Girona and the surrounding countryside at one point, and the very thorough collections of this regional branch of the **Museu d'Arqueologia de Catalunya** (p. 405) chronicle them all. The museum occupies the Catalan Romanesque building that once housed the Benedictine monastery of Sant Pere de Galligants (St. Peter of the Cock Crows). Most of the artifacts represent the Roman period and the quality overall is very high.

Plaça Santa Llúcia, s/n. ℂ **97-220-26-32.** www.mac.cat. Admission 2.30€ adults, 1.60€ students, free ages 65 and over and under 16. Oct–May Tues–Sat 10am–2pm and 4–6pm, Sun 10am–2pm; June–Sept Tues–Sat 10:30am–1:30pm and 4–7pm, Sun 10am–2pm.

Museu d'Art ★★ MUSEUM   As you have probably already gathered, the people of Girona love a good legend. So it is only fitting that the 10th- to 11th-century altar stone of Sant Pere de Roda is one of the most prized objects in the museum. Made of wood and stone, it depicts both religious stories and Catalan legends. It's just one piece in a collection that brings together Catalan art from the 12th to the 20th centuries. The museum is also the main repository worldwide of 20th-century Noucentisme, a reactionary Catalan art movement that rejected Modernisme in favor of a more ordered and refined classicism. Do not miss the shaded gardens behind the museum, the Jardins de la Francesa. A staircase in the gardens lets you ascend to the ancient city walls, where you can walk for a considerable distance to gain a unique perspective on the medieval city.

Pujada de la Catedral, 12. ℂ **97-220-38-34.** www.museuart.com. Admission 2€ adults; 1.50€ students and seniors. May–Sept Tues–Sat 10am–7pm, Sun 10am–2pm; Oct–Apr Tues–Sat 10am–6pm, Sun 10am–2pm.

Museu del Cinema ★ MUSEUM   Film buff and historian Tomàs Mallol assembled more than 25,000 artifacts from early crude camera obscura devices and Chinese shadow puppets to attempts to animate photography when that technology was still in its infancy. The collection dates from early history (including the original camera of the Lumière brothers) up to about 1970. Cinema aficionados from around the globe come here to study the origins of their art form.

Carrer Sèquia, 1. ℂ **97-241-27-77.** www.girona.cat/cinema. Admission 5€ adults, 2.50€ students, free for children 16 and under. Oct–Apr Tues–Fri 10am–6pm, Sat 10am–8pm, Sun 11am–3pm; May–June and Sept Tues–Sat 10am–8pm, Sun 11am–3pm; July–Aug daily 10am–8pm.

Museu dels Jueus ★★ MUSEUM   The Jewish population of Girona flourished in the 12th century, when scholars, including the great rabbi Nahmanides, established one of Europe's most important philosophical centers of Kabbalistic mysticism. In keeping with European tradition, the Jewish Quarter, or "Call," grew up in the protective shadow of the cathedral—until Isabel and Fernando expelled all the Jews from Spain in 1492. As part of the 1992 nationwide reassessment of Spain's gains and losses from the events of 1492, the Girona government established a nonprofit organization to recover the Jewish history and culture of the city. One part of that effort was to establish this museum. In the decades since it opened, it has grown to an extensive warren of 11 galleries that examine community life, festivals and traditions, synagogues and forms of worship, and even the disapora and the tricky matter of conversions during the Spanish Inquisition. Some of the most striking exhibitions deal with Jewish artistic and cultural traditions specific to Catalunya, while some of the most poignant include carved sepulchers unearthed during excavations at the old Jewish cemetery on Montjuïc.

Carrer Força Vella 8. ℂ **97-221-67-61.** www.ajuntament.gi/call. Admission 4€ adults, 2€ seniors and students. May–Oct Mon–Sat 10am–8pm and Sun 10am–3pm; Nov–Apr Mon–Sat 10am–6pm.

The Museu dels Jueus.

Museu d'Història de la Ciutat ★ MUSEUM   This collection covers the sweep of local history and prehistory from the flint and iron tools of the first Neolithic peoples through the glories of medieval Girona to the dark days of the Spanish Civil War, when the city built an underground shelter to protect its children from the relentless bombardment by Franco's forces. One of the more interesting themed exhibits deals with the traditional sardana circle dance and the cobla band that accompanies the dancers. Although the 18th-century Capuchin Convent de Sant Antoni has been transformed into a modern museum, one room does retain the macabre vision of the 18 niches where dead friars were propped up in a seated position until their bodies became naturally mummified.

Carrer de la Força 27. ✆ **97-222-22-29.** www.ajuntament.gi/museuciutat. Admission 4€ adults, 2€ students, free seniors and 16 and under. Tues–Sat 10am–2pm and 5–7pm; Sun 10am–2pm.

Side Trip from Girona
CASTELL GALA DALÍ DE PÚBOL ★★

Salvador Dalí created a persona that was bigger than life and, in some ways, better known than his actual work. His greatest composite work of the art is the Teatre-Museu in Figueres (below), and it's packed with some of his best works. The **Castell Gala Dalí de Púbol** (Carrer Gala-Salvador Dalí s/n, Púbol; ✆ **97-248-86-55;** www.salvador-dali.org) is less about his art and more about his neuroses and his strangely submissive relationship with his wife, Gala. In 1969, the couple stumbled onto this 11th-century castle, which lay in ruins (no roofs, cracked walls). Dalí promptly bought it for Gala and redecorated the interiors to create a series of comfortable (if often bizarre) rooms without making the exterior look as if the property were repaired. It was Gala's refuge, and he agreed not to visit unless she invited him—something she rarely did. Dalí used the castle as a studio for 2 years after her death, moving out in 1984 when his bedroom caught fire one night. The artistry here is conceptual—it's all in how Dalí treated the architecture and furnished the rooms. Admission is 8€ adults, 6€ students, and free for children 8 and under. It's open mid-March through December 10am to 6pm, with extended evening hours in the summer. Púbol is 21km (13mi) east of Girona on highway C-66.

FIGUERES ★★

The clown prince of modern Spanish art, Salvador Dalí, was born in Figueres, a small city in northern Catalunya where the dry foothills look a lot like the parched landscape of his famous melting clocks. Seeking to capitalize on the artist's fame, the mayor of Figueres invited him to create a museum there in 1961. Dalí chose the ruins of the old municipal theater because his first childhood art show had been hung there. With no disrespect to the community, the chief reason to visit Figueres is to tour the strange and wonderful world of the Teatre-Museu Dalí.

Essentials

GETTING THERE RENFE (*C* **90-232-03-20;** www.renfe.com) has hourly train service between Barcelona-Sants and Figueres. The trip takes around 2 hours, give or take 15 minutes, and costs 12€ to 16€, depending on type of train. Be sure to book for the Figueres station, not Figueres Vilafant, which is the high-speed rail station in a neighboring town. Trains from Girona take 30 to 40 minutes and cost 4.10€ to 5.45€. Figueres can also be reached by car on the AP-7 from Girona.

VISITOR INFORMATION The Figueres **tourist office** is at the Plaça del Sol (*C* **97-250-31-55;** www.figueresciutat.com). The office is open July through September Monday through Saturday 9am to 8pm and Sunday 10am to 3pm; from November to Easter, hours are Monday through Friday 9am to 3pm, and from Easter through June and October, hours are Monday through Friday 9am to 3pm and 4 to 7pm, and Saturday 10am to 2pm and 3:30 to 6:30pm.

Where to Stay & Eat

Duran Hotel & Restaurant ★ CATALAN   We don't know what Salvador Dalí ordered when he ate at this restaurant that occupies an old inn dating from 1855. But you can't go wrong with the sole in orange sauce with shrimp ravioli or a *fideù* (paella with noodles instead of rice) of monkfish and prawns. The Duran also offers a number of game dishes, such as saddle of hare with chestnut puree and raspberry jam. The hotel occupies a newer part of the property and features 65 rooms with crisp, neutral-toned furnishings punctuated by playful headboards of undulating wooden slats. Some rooms can accommodate three or four people, and some have been adapted to be wheelchair accessible.

Carrer Lasauca, 5. *C* **97-250-12-50.** www.hotelduran.com. 65 rooms. 59€–89€ double. Main courses 14€–29€; fixed-price lunch menu 20€. **Amenities:** Restaurant; bar; free Wi-Fi.

Hotel Empordá ★★ CATALAN   This restaurant was founded in 1961 and quickly gained a following for its masterful fish and game dishes. We like the fact that current chef/owner Jaume Subirós has menu offerings for different appetites. On the Market Menu, diners can opt for starter and dessert only, or main course and dessert only. His Tasting Menu is a multi-course extravaganza with appetizer, four main dishes, cheeses, and dessert. Both menus rely on fresh ingredients from the market so you never know what to expect, but Subirós is equally inventive with fish and meat, grilling grouper and serving it with a saffron and quince aioli, for example, or adding sesame to a red wine sauce for venison and accompanying it with sweet potato puree. Like the Duran above, the Empordá is also a hotel. All 42 rooms were recently refurbished in clean-lined modern style. All have terraces and hydromassage tubs in the bathrooms.

Av. Salvador Dalí, 170. *C* **97-250-05-62.** www.hotelemporda.com. 42 rooms. 59€–109€ double. Restaurant main courses 15€–42€; fixed-price menus 20€–60€. Restaurant daily 12:45–3:30pm and 8:30–10:30pm. **Amenities:** Restaurant; bar; free Wi-Fi.

Exploring Figueres

Teatre-Museu Dalí ★★★

MUSEUM This thoroughly bizarre museum is less a monument to Salvador Felipe Jacinto Dalí i Domènech (to use his full name) than a series of snapshots of corners of his psyche all collaged together inside a carnival funhouse. It helps to know a little bit about the artist. He began his career in the 1920s as one of Spain's three *enfants terribles* (the others were Federico García Lorca and Luis Buñuel). For most of his life, Dali was engaged in an obsessive and dependent relationship with Elena Ivanova Diakonova, known as Gala. He remained tenaciously loyal to her until her death in 1982 (although the same can't be said of Gala toward Dalí).

Many of the works in the Teatre-Museu relate to this relationship and Dalí's complicated feelings about sexual intimacy. It took the artist a long time to assemble the museum, since he made all the initial placements of objects. It finally opened in 1974.

The whimsical Teatre-Museu Dalí.

When the artist died in 1989, thousands of artifacts and artworks from throughout his life passed to the Gala-Salvador Dalí Fundació, which maintains the museum, and the exhibits have been moved around—but not so much to jeopardize Dali's claim that it is the largest surreal object in the world. Dalí spent his final 4 years living adjacent to the museum in the Torre Galatea, named for Gala. He was buried beneath the theater's great dome, which he had painted as the eye of a fly as seen through a microscope. Also painted on the ceiling are portraits of himself and Gala as seen from below the ground. (You're looking at them feet first.) Don't miss the artist's first Cadillac in the courtyard, where it rains *inside* the car.

Plaça de Gala-Dalí 5. © **97-267-75-00.** www.salvador-dali.org. Admission 12€ adults, 9€ students and seniors, free ages 9 and under. Mar–June and Oct daily 9:30am–6pm; Nov–Feb daily 10:30am–6pm; July–Sept daily 9am–8pm.

CADAQUES ★★

The last resort on the Costa Brava before the French border, Cadaqués feels truly off the beaten path. Despite the publicity it received when Salvador Dalí lived in the adjacent village of Portlligat, it's still unspoiled and remote. The village wraps around half a dozen small coves, with a narrow street running along the water's edge. Scenically, Cadaqués is a visual feast of blue water, colorful fishing boats, old whitewashed houses, narrow twisting streets, and a 16th-century parish church on a hill.

Essentials

GETTING THERE   Three to four **buses** per day run from Figueres to Cadaqués. Trip time is 1¼ hours. The service is operated by **SARFA** (© **90-230-20-25;** www.sarfa.com). Driving from Barcelona, follow the A-7 northeast until you come to the town of Figueres, where you'll see signs leading east to Cadaqués.

VISITOR INFORMATION   The **tourist office,** Cotxe 2 (© **97-225-83-15;** www. visitcadaques.org), is open Monday to Saturday 9am to 2pm and 3 to 8pm, and Sunday 10:30am to 1pm.

Where to Stay and Eat

Hostal S'Aguarda ★   A good choice if you're planning to visit Dalí's house, this pleasantly old-fashioned casual *hostal* has an elevated view of the village on the high road to Portlligat. Rooms have all the modern conveniences, but none of the slickness of a resort hotel. Bathrooms are unusually large, and many rooms have either a private balcony or access to a shared terrace—both with great panoramic views.

Carretera de Portlligat 30. © **97-225-80-82.** www.hotelsaguarda.com. 28 units. 88€–170€ double; 102€–170€ suite. Free parking. Closed Nov. **Amenities:** Bar; outdoor freshwater pool; room service; free Wi-Fi.

Hotel Rocamar ★   This beachside hotel is elegant enough for a couples getaway, yet has enough activities (indoor and outdoor pools, sauna, mini-golf, and tennis court) to keep a whole family happily entertained. For that romantic getaway, consider one of the rooms with a balcony or terrace and sea views. Many of the other rooms have mountain views, but no balconies. In either case, the rooms feature light walls and yellow and gold fabrics that seem to bring the sun indoors. On-site Sa Concha restaurant features an outdoor terrace dining in good weather.

Dr. Bartomeus, s/n. © **97-225-81-50.** www.rocamar.com. 70 units. 81€–243€ double; 166€–354€ suite. Free parking. Restaurant main dishes 18€–24€. Open daily 1pm–11pm. **Amenities:** Restaurant; bar; children's playground; Jacuzzi; 2 freshwater pools (1 heated indoor, 1 outdoor); room service; sauna; outdoor tennis court; free Wi-Fi.

Exploring Cadaqués

The landmark of Cadaqués is the **Església de Santa María,** Calle Eliseu Meifren, a 16th-century Gothic church with a baroque altar. It dominates the narrow, hilly streets in the old section of town. It's usually open for visits from 9am to 5pm—assuming someone comes to unlock it. Seeing the "sights" in Cadaqués basically means strolling around the narrow streets and enjoying the stony beach. One good stroll from the town center (under an hour along the beach) will take you to the former fishing community of Portlligat and the **Casa-Museo Salvador Dalí** in Portlligat (© **97-225-10-15;** www.salvador-dali.org). Originally a fisherman's hut, Dalí made this his summer home starting in 1930. Over the years he kept adding on and decorated the rooms with collected objects ranging from dried flowers to stuffed animals. He and Gala lived here for many years, and their private quarters are the most interesting rooms. This museum forms part of the "Dalí triangle," which includes the Teatre-Museu Dalí at Figueres (p. 402) and the castle at Púbol (p. 400).

Only two Dalí works remain in the house: a lip-shaped sofa and a pop-art miniature of Granada's Alhambra. Overlooking the beach, the fisherman's house has amusing little white-chimney pots and two egg-shaped towers. Hours are

The Església de Santa Maria.

September to January and February to mid-June daily 10:30am to 6pm, and from mid-June to mid-September daily 9:30am to 9pm. It's closed from January 7 to February 11. Admission is 10€ for adults and 8€ for children, students, and seniors. Reservations are mandatory.

GOLF DE ROSES

This small bay enclosed on the north by the Cap de Norfu and on the south by Punta Gross is lined by a swampy shoreland that forms the **Parc Natural dels Aiguamolls de l'Empordà,** one of the largest wetlands in Catalunya. The marshes are home to more than 300 species of birds, making the park one of the prime birding destinations in Spain. The pink creatures found on the beach, especially in July and August, are the package tourists from northern Europe who flock here to sun on the sands of Roses, the town just north of the natural park. South of the wetlands stand some of the most evocative classical ruins in northeast Spain, **Empúries,** the erstwhile site of Greek Emporion and the landing site of the Romans when they first invaded the Iberian Peninsula to oust the Carthaginians.

Essentials

GETTING THERE Roses can be accessed by bus from Figueres or Cadaqués—**SARFA(© 90-230-20-25;** www.sarfa.com)—but it's easiest to reach driving east from Figueres on C-68. From Roses, the coastal road south leads through the park to the village of L'Escala, where the ruins of Empúries are located.

VISITOR INFORMATION The **Oficina de Turisme de Roses** (© **97-225-73-31;** www.visitroses.cat) is located at Avinguda Rhode, 77–79. It is open Monday to Saturday 10am to 1pm and 4 to 7pm, and Sunday 10am to 2pm.

Exploring the Golf de Roses

Roses is a pretty little town out of season, but resort development has completely obscured the ancient Greek settlement here.

A short distance south of Roses, the wetlands of the **Parc Natural dels Aiguamolls de l'Empordà** ★ begin. The ecological preserve lies at the mouth of Ríu Fluvià and provides an important haven for migratory birds, including pink flamingos. Some birders prefer to explore the waterside paths by bicycle, but there are also well-signed lookout points along the shore road.

The main attraction along the Gulf is **Empúries** ★, where Greek commerce and Roman might are both writ large. The ruins are just north of the village of L'Escala. The archaeological site has been under excavation since 1908. Greeks founded the city in 600 B.C. as a trade port, then built a second city slightly inland in 550 B.C., naming it Emporion, or "trading place." The first settlement lies buried under a fishing village, but the extensive city of Emporion and its cemetery make up the greater part of the ruins. Farther inland, Scipio Africanus founded a military camp in 219 B.C. to stage his first invasion to oust the Carthaginians from the Iberian Peninsula. An amphitheater and villas with mosaics still attest to the flourishing Roman presence. At the site, the **Museu d'Arqueologia de Catalunya** interprets the three towns and chronicles the archaeological excavations. The famous sculpture of Asclepios (god of medicine) was returned to the site from Barcelona in 2008. The museum is on Carrer Puig i Cadafalch s/n (② **97-277-02-08;** www.mac.cat). Admission is 3€ adults, free under 16 and over 60. It is open June to September daily 10am to 8pm, and October to May daily 10am to 6pm.

You can also walk along the seaside path from the ruins to the flourishing village of L'Escala. Salted anchovies from the town are famous all over Spain, and exhibits at the **Museu de l'Anxova i de la Sal** explain the local fishing industry from the 16th century to present. The little museum is at Av. Francesc Macià 1 (② **97-277-68-15;** www.anxova-sal.cat). Admission is 2€. It is open mid-June to September Tuesday to Friday 10am to 1:30pm and 5 to 8pm, Saturday 11am to 1pm and 6 to 8pm, and Sunday 11am to 1pm; from October to mid-June it's closed in the afternoons.

The Empúries ruins.

The Museu d'Arqueologia de Catalunya.

SOMETHING fishy FOR SURE

Founded in 1279 by the king of Aragón, **Palamós** remains the only major fishing port still active on the Costa Brava. Its fleet is legendary for going far to sea for large fin fish such as yellowfin tuna and for harvesting vast quantities of sweet shrimp from coastal waters. Tourism development has been contained south of the village, leaving the medieval architecture and the working docks intact. To understand both the fish and the fishing industry, visit the **Museu de la Pesca** (Moll Pesquer, s/n; $\mathcal{C}$ **97-260-04-24;** www.museudelapesca.org; free; open Tues–Sat 10am–1:30pm and 3–7pm, Sun 10am–2pm and 4–7pm; extended hours in summer). In October, **Palamós Gastronòmic** celebrates the town's foodie heritage with special menus, food demonstrations, cooking classes, and a shrimp-eating contest on the docks.

SANT FELIU DE GUÍXOLS ★★

Sant Feliu de Guíxols is a beautiful harbor and former fishing port framed on one side by a rocky headland holding the luxury residential area of S'Agaro and on the other by a 10th-century Benedictine monastery.

Essentials

GETTING THERE Direct **bus** service from Girona takes about 45 minutes and costs 8.30€ via **SARFA** ($\mathcal{C}$ **90-230-20-25;** www.sarfa.com). If you choose to drive, it takes about 40 minutes on C-45 and C-55.

VISITOR INFORMATION The **Oficina Municipal de Turisme Sant Feliu de Guíxols** ($\mathcal{C}$ **97-282-00-51;** www.guixols.cat) is located on the main beach at Passeig del Mar 8–12. It is open Monday to Saturday 10am to 1pm and 4 to 7pm, and Sunday 10am to 2pm.

Where to Stay & Eat in Sant Feliu de Guíxols

Hostal de la Gavina ★★★ This elegant property is a surprisingly secluded retreat on the often crowded—and not always elegant—Costa Brava. It sits on a small peninsula that juts out into the ocean, with beaches on two quiet bays. The core of the property is a gleaming-white 1932 former private villa with a hint of Moorish style. Expanded over the years, it holds most of the guest rooms, which are confidently luxe in style with rich fabrics, carved and sometimes gilded furniture, and lovely architectural details. Superior double rooms have private balconies. You could easily pass many happy days exploring the manicured grounds and hanging out at the outdoor saltwater pool. There's even a hammam for women in the spa. The Candlelight Restaurant and the adjoining El Patio de Candlelight (in warm weather) epitomize romantic gourmet dining.

Plaça de la Rosaleda, S'Agaro. $\mathcal{C}$ **97-232-11-00.** www.lagavina.com. 74 units. 260€–410€ double; from 565€ suite. Free parking outside; garage 20€. Closed Nov–Apr. **Amenities:** 2 restaurants; 2 bars; bikes; health club; 2 pools (1 heated indoor, 1 saltwater outdoor); room service; spa; 2 outdoor tennis courts; free Wi-Fi.

Hotel Sant Pol ★★ A dozen of this beachside hotel's 22 rooms have direct sea views, and five have hydromassage baths—making the Sant Pol a personalized, small-lodging option to nearby oversized resort hotels. Styling is simple, contemporary, and bright with extensive tile, marble, and nickel-chrome fixtures in the spacious bathrooms. Ideally situated for sunbathing and swimming at the Sant Pol beach (on the north end of the village), the hotel offers free parking if you book online. Note that rates from mid-July through August include half board. The Restaurant Sant Pol is an unpretentious dining room with excellent preparations of local fish and a three-course menu at lunch (17€) and dinner (22€).

Platja de Sant Pol 125. ✆ **97-232-10-70.** www.hotelsantpol.com. 22 units. 87€–236€ double. Parking 10€. Closed Nov. **Amenities:** 2 restaurants; bar; room service; free Wi-Fi.

Exploring Sant Feliu de Guíxols

The chief attraction of Sant Feliu is its natural setting. The Platja Sant Pol is one of the least crowded beaches on the Costa Brava and is well furnished with adjacent bars and restaurants for cold drinks and inexpensive meals. The hills around Sant Feliu are crisscrossed with well-marked hiking paths that offer splendid views of the sea and coast. Ask for a trail map at the tourist office.

The most striking buildings in Sant Feliu are those belonging to the complex of the medieval Benedictine monastery. The monastery is no longer active, and the buildings are undergoing a slow restoration process made even slower by Spain's economic doldrums. But the beautiful Romanesque **Mare de Déu dels Angels** remains an active parish church filled with a millennium of religious art, some of it quite powerful. It's located on the Plaça del Monestir and is open daily 9am to 12:30pm and 7 to 8:30pm at no charge.

The Platja Sant Pol.

Also a part of the monastery complex, the **Museu d'Història** (*C* **97-282-15-75;** www.guixols.cat/museu) explains the local cork industry that made Sant Feliu wealthy in the late 19th century—just in time for cork barons to build the marvelous Modernisme houses along Platja Sant Pol and in S'Agaro. The museum is on the Plaça del Monestir adjacent to the church, and admission is free. It is open Tuesday to Saturday 10am to 1pm and 5 to 8pm, and Sunday 10am to 1pm.

TOSSA DE MAR ★★

The gleaming white town of Tossa de Mar, with its 12th-century walls, labyrinthine old quarter, fishing boats, and good sand beaches, is perhaps the most attractive base for a Costa Brava vacation. Not only does the town have more *joie de vivre* than its competitors, it is shielded from overdevelopment by the towering cliffs that surround its main cove. In the 18th and 19th centuries, Tossa was a significant port for the cork industry. But when the cork business declined in the 20th century, many of its citizens emigrated to America. In the 1950s, thanks in part to the Ava Gardner movie *Pandora and the Flying Dutchman,* tourists began to discover the charms of Tossa, and a new industry was born.

Essentials

GETTING THERE   Direct **bus** service is offered from Blanes and Lloret de Mar. Tossa de Mar is also on the main Barcelona-Palafruggel route. Service from Barcelona is daily from 8am to 8:30pm and takes 1½ hours. For information, call *C* **90-230-20-25.** To drive, head north from Barcelona along the A-19.

VISITOR INFORMATION   The **tourist office** is at Av. El Pelegrí 25 (*C* **97-234-01-08;** www.infotossa.com). In April, May, and October, it's open Monday to Saturday 10am to 2pm and 4 to 8pm; November to March, Monday to Saturday 10am to 1pm and 4 to 7pm; and June to September, Monday to Saturday 9am to 9pm, and Sunday 10am to 2pm and 5 to 8pm.

Where to Stay

EXPENSIVE

Gran Hotel Reymar ★   Built in the 1960s on a rocky outcrop above Mar Menuda beach, this gleaming white hotel has almost become a landmark in its own right. The architectural design allowed for several terraces for sunbathing away from the beach crowds. For more privacy, some rooms have their own balconies with sea and garden views. Modern wood-grained furniture and light walls give a breezy, relaxed feel. The hotel is about a 10-minute walk southeast of the town's historic walls.

Playa Mar Menuda s/n. *C* **97-234-03-12.** www.tossagranhotelreymar.com. 166 units. 127€–274€ double; 184€–387€ suite. Parking 16€. Closed Nov–Apr 17. **Amenities:** Restaurant; 3 bars; bikes; children's center; exercise room; Jacuzzi; outdoor freshwater pool; room service; sauna; outdoor tennis court; Wi-Fi available for fee.

MODERATE

Best Western Mar Menuda ★★   This may not be the fanciest lodging in town, but it has the best terrace with a panoramic view of the sea and the town. Many of the midsize to spacious guest rooms also have sea views, and all are comfortably decorated with clean-lined furniture and bright white linens, and feature good-size bathrooms. If you're interested in watersports (scuba diving, windsurfing, or sailing), staff can offer advice. If you just want to lie by the pool, that's okay, too. Breakfast is included.

Playa Mar Menuda s/n, ☎ **800/528-1234** in the U.S., or 97-234-10-00. www.bestwesternhotel-marmenuda.com. 50 units. 86€–177€ double; 92€–215€ suite. Free parking. Closed Nov–Dec. **Amenities:** Restaurant; bar; babysitting; children's playground; outdoor freshwater pool; room service; free Wi-Fi.

Hotel Diana ★★ This boutique hotel occupies a villa designed by a disciple of Gaudi, who employed decorative paving stones, brightly patterned tiles, and elegant painted ceilings to great effect. Though set back from the esplanade, the hotel has great ocean views, and many rooms have private balconies. Rooms are spacious with traditional furnishings and modern bathrooms, but most guests spend their time on the covered terrace overlooking the beach or on the charming inner patio—a true hidden oasis with vine-covered walls, cafe tables, huge palm trees, and fountains.

Plaça de Espanya, 6. ☎ **97-234-18-86.** www.diana-hotel.com. 21 units. 70€–170€ double; 120€–250€ triple. Parking nearby 10€. Closed Nov–Mar 15. **Amenities:** Restaurant; bar; room service; free Wi-Fi.

INEXPENSIVE

Hotel Cap d'Or ★★ This small hotel has a lot going for it. It's family-run, with good, personal service, and enjoys an enviable location snugged up to the stone walls of the old castle on the south end of town. And it's right on the beach. Small is the operative word, however, and the 11 very tidy and simply decorated rooms tend to be compact. Some have lovely ocean views, but all guests can enjoy the vistas from the outdoor terrace, where the complimentary breakfast and other light fare, prepared by the women in the family, is served. Reserve early.

Passeig de Vila Vella, 1. ☎ **97-234-00-81.** www.hotelcapdor.com. 69€–110€ double; 139€–169€ family room (2 adults and 2 children). Parking nearby 23€. Closed Nov–Mar. **Amenities:** Restaurant; bar; free Wi-Fi.

Hotel Tonet ★ We like the fact that Tossa de Mar is a real little town rather than simply a beach resort. This modest, family-run hotel sits on one of the town plazas and is a good place to hear church bells call people to Mass and to observe daily life from the upper-level terrace/solarium. Yet it is only about a 5-minute walk to the beach. Many of the simply furnished rooms are on the small side and a bit dated, and there is no air-conditioning.

Plaça de l'Església, 1. ☎ **97-234-02-37.** www.hoteltonet.com. 36 units. 51€–65€ double. Nearby parking 10€. **Amenities:** Bar; free lobby Wi-Fi.

Where to Eat

La Cuina de Can Simón ★★ CONTEMPORARY CATALAN This rustic-seeming dining room of rough stone walls dates back to the mid–18th century, when Tossa was a fishing village and fortress town rather than a seaside preserve for the well-to-do. The food here is anything but rustic, representing instead the finesse of contemporary Catalan cooking. Dishes are available a la carte, but most diners opt for the tasting menu, which begins with small bites before moving on to raw oysters (in season), a soup, a fish plate (say, scallops with sea urchin roe), a fish *fideù* (like paella with noodles), a whole baked fish, and then either a small grilled steak or a mound of steak tartare. The dessert platter always features fresh fruit and some form of pudding or ice cream.

The view from Vila Vella.

Carrer Portal, 24. ✆ **97-234-12-69.** www.restaurantcansimon.com. Reservations required. Main courses 18€–28€; fixed-price menu 98€. Wed–Sun 1–3pm and 8–10:30pm. Closed Jan 15–Feb 15 and 2 weeks in Nov.

Restaurant Sa Muralla ★ CATALAN   You needn't get dressed up to eat at "The Wall," a grill restaurant offering simple, straightforward food. Born as a fishermen's bar, it's evolved into one of the best casual restaurants in Tossa. Pescaphobes have a choice of grilled chicken, veal, pork, and lamb, though the grilled catch of the day is what most people order—unless they're enjoying the Tossa classic, *cim-i-tomba,* which consists of layers of fish and potato in a casserole with very garlicky aioli.

Carrer Portal, 16. ✆ **97-234-11-28.** www.samuralla.com. Main dishes 15€–30€. Mid-Mar to Sept daily 1–3pm and 8–10:30pm; Oct to mid-Mar daily 1–3pm.

Exploring Tossa de Mar

To experience the charms of Tossa, walk through the 12th-century walled town, known as **Vila Vella,** built on the site of a Roman villa from the 1st century A.D. Enter through the Torre de les Hores. Tossa was once a getaway for artists and writers—Marc Chagall called it a "blue paradise." Descending from the Old Town, follow signs to Plaça del Pintor J. Villalonga, where you'll find steps that let you walk along the medieval ramparts. In 1914, archaeologists uncovered the ruins of one of the grandest Roman villas on the Costa Brava, **Els Ametllers Roman Villa.** Inhabited from the 1st century B.C. to the 6th century A.D., it was the headquarters of a vast tract of vineyards producing wine for export to Rome. During the summer, beautiful mosaic floors of the rooms are uncovered for viewing. Tossa itself has two main beaches, **Mar Gran** and **La Bauma.** The coast near Tossa, north and south, offers even more possibilities.

ARAGÓN

13

Landlocked Aragón, along with adjacent Navarra, forms the northeastern quadrant of Spain. Most travelers find this ancient land *terra incognita*, which is unfortunate because Aragón is one of the most history-steeped regions of the country. You can visit it as an extension of your trip to Castilla y León to the west, or as a segment of your journey through Catalunya to the east.

Aragón is best known for two former residents: Catalina de Aragón (better known in English as Catherine of Aragón), the unfortunate first wife of Henry VIII of England; and her father, Fernando of Aragón, whose marriage to Isabel, queen of Castilla y León, in the 15th century led to the unification of Spain.

Aragón also prides itself on its exceptional Mudéjar architecture, a synthesis of the architectural forms of Christian Europe with the decorative motifs and construction techniques of the Muslim world.

ZARAGOZA ★★

Zaragoza was the seat of the ancient kingdom of Aragón. Today it is a bustling, prosperous, commercial city of wide boulevards and arcades. Its cathedral is a Mudéjar landmark and its basilica is an important pilgrimage center. According to legend, the Virgin Mary appeared to Santiago (St. James the Apostle), patron saint of Spain, on the banks of the Rio Ebro and ordered him to build a church there.

The city sits at the center of a rich alluvial plain. Founded by Carthaginians, it flourished as the Roman colony of Caesaraugusta, then played a pivotal role in Christian-Muslim political relations as an independent Muslim principality in the 11th century. Today, Zaragoza is a city of more than 750,000 people, slightly less than three-quarters of the entire population of Aragón. The 40,000 students at the Universidad de Zaragoza have livened up this once-staid city. Cafes, theaters, restaurants, music bars, and taverns have boomed in recent years.

Essentials

GETTING THERE Zaragoza's airport (ZAZ) has limited service via Ryanair from London, and by Air Europa from Paris, Brussels, and Milan. It is so well-connected by train that it no longer has commercial domestic flights. A total of 29 **trains** arrive daily from Barcelona (trip time: 1½–5¼ hr.) and 21 from Madrid (1¼–3½ hr.). Trains pull into Estación Zaragoza-Delicias, Calle Rioja, 33 (© **90-232-03-20;** www.renfe.com). All but a few trains per day are high-speed rail. There is one direct **bus** a day between Zaragoza and Barcelona (3½ hr.). By car, Zaragoza is easily reached on the E-90 (A-2) east from Madrid or west from Barcelona.

VISITOR INFORMATION The **tourist office,** Plaza del Pilar s/n. (© **90-214-20-08;** www.turismozaragoza.com), is open daily June to October 9am to 9pm, and November to May 10am to 8pm.

PREVIOUS PAGE: **An example of Mudéjar architecture in Aragón.**

SPECIAL EVENTS One of the city's big festivities is the **Fiesta de la Virgen del Pilar,** held the week of October 12, with top-name bullfighters, religious processions, and general merriment.

Where to Stay in Zaragoza

Hotel Gran Vía ★ Located in the main shopping district, this modern hotel prides itself on being more Spanish than international. That translates into a kind of modesty about the decor and size of the rooms, combined with a fastidious neatness. The beds are cushy and comfortable, and there is soft carpeting underfoot. The main lobby area is larger than you would expect, and that's where many travelers congregate to socialize.

Paseo Gran Vía, 38. © **97-622-92-13.** www.granviahotel.com. 47 units. 45€–65€ double. Parking free. **Amenities:** Bar; room service; exercise room; free Wi-Fi.

ON THE menu IN ARAGÓN

Aragón has a cuisine built on meat, from the famous Teruel ham to mountain lamb. The plains of the Río Ebro produce much of Spain's native wheat and barley. Specialties of the Aragonese table include:

- Lamb or kid roasted on a spit
- Fried slices of Teruel ham with tomato sauce
- Wild trout from mountain streams
- *Cecina* (air-dried beef)
- Wild mushrooms and black truffles
- Artichokes stewed with local ham and almonds

Hotel Reino de Aragón ★★   Our personal favorite in Zaragoza, this up-to-date business hotel is less than a 5-minute walk from the medieval historic center and steps away from the tapas-hopping district on the ladder streets between calles Coso and San Miguel. Service is polite and helpful, and the rooms are comfortable despite the spare, modern decor. This is one high-rise where we opt for an upper floor, as the hotel has enough elevators to avoid long waits. For a slight splurge (about 10€ more), choose one of the superior rooms on the sixth floor to enjoy an outdoor terrace.

Calle Coso, 8. ☎ **97-646-82-00.** www.hoteles-silken.com. 117 rooms. 75€–160€ double. Parking 18€. **Amenities:** Restaurant; bar; free Wi-Fi.

NH Gran Hotel ★   NH Hoteles seems to specialize in finding neglected gems and bringing them back to life. Created by the crown in 1929 as one of a national string of fine hotels, the Gran enjoys wonderful bone structure—that is, a fine Art Deco exterior and well-laid-out public rooms. NH basically gutted the upstairs guest floors to create contemporary rooms with a maximum of marble tiling, contrasting dark wood, and the signature superb NH desk arrangement. The spacious public rooms from the original hotel make it a top venue for weddings and other life-landmark celebrations, while the meeting rooms make it a popular choice with businesses. For sightseers, it's a 10-minute walk to the cathedral or basilica.

Calle Joaquín Costa, 5. ☎ **97-622-19-01.** www.nh-hoteles.com. 134 units. 80€–154€ double; from 117€ junior suite. Parking 16€. **Amenities:** Restaurant; bar; gym; sauna; free Wi-Fi.

Zenit Don Yo ★★   There are budget hotels and then there are bargain-priced hotels. We consider this Zenit affiliate one of the bargains, as the hotel is fresh and contemporary, and while the rooms are modestly furnished, they're pretty large by Spanish standards and their beds are top-notch. The location is best for business but fine for sightseeing—right next to the Plaza de Aragón and Plaza de la Independencia.

Calle Juan Bruil, 4–6. ☎ **97-622-67-41.** www.zenithoteles.com. 147 units. 51€–68€ double; from 75€ junior suite. Parking 13€. **Amenities:** Restaurant; bar; room service; free Wi-Fi.

Where to Eat in Zaragoza

Bal d'Onsera ★★★ CONTEMPORARY SPANISH   Chef Josechu Corella's creative contemporary cooking is a breath of fresh air in this Aragonese capital so often hostage to heavy meats and overcooked vegetables. Every plate is bright and beautifully composed, and could feature saffron-scented scallops with langostinos, poached egg with lobster and white truffle, or pig's trotters with candied squash and black olives. The menu is in constant flux, always depending on what's in the market and what amuses Corella that day. Expect an elegant dinner in a beautifully lit dining room dressed in white linens. Try to reserve as far ahead as possible, as tables have become scarce since the restaurant won a Michelin star in 2013.

Calle Blasón Aragonés 6E. ✆ **97-620-39-36.** www.baldonsera.com. Reservations required. Main courses 20€–32€. Tasting menus 30€ midday, 45€ at night. Tues–Sat 1–4pm and 9pm–midnight.

La Rinconada de Lorenzo ★ ARAGONESE An old-fashioned favorite, "Larry's Little Corner" has acquitted itself of stodginess by introducing a line of creative tapas that have swept the local awards for the last few years. It's in the university area, which means that the bar is always hopping even when the dining room is quiet. The fare is traditional for Aragón, favoring roasted meats, especially the D.O. Ternasco de Aragón, a special variety of lamb. The lamb even shows up stewed, as in the dark and unctuous bowl of trotters. The wine list is short on whites but has multiple reasonably priced red options from the Aragonese delimited wine districts of Calatayud, Somontano, and Cariñena.

Calle La Salle 3. ✆ **97-655-51-08.** www.larinconadadelorenzo.com. Reservations required. Main courses 10€ 22€. Fixed-price menus 15€–44€. Mon–Sat noon–4pm and daily 8–11:30pm (closed Mon July–Aug). Bus: 20, 30, 35, 40, 41, or 45.

Restaurante Riskomar ★★ BASQUE With its self-consciously *vanguardista* design and unabashedly Basque menu, Riskomar offers a full-immersion dining experience of strong flavors, contrasting textures, and a little bit of culinary theater. Many dishes are prepared over an open flame in emulation of Basque master chef Victor Arguinzoniz of Asador Etxebarri, and all thoughts of expense are cast aside when it comes to incorporating glass eels (*angulas*) into dishes around Christmas. (Every Basque grew up eating them as part of the holiday feast.) Several of the best dishes use the cheeks of big hake or cod, so called *cocochas,* which are both the chewiest and most flavorful parts of the fish. Shellfish are impeccable here, and one of the most popular splurges is the *menu mariscada,* which begins with plate after plate of clams, pink and white shrimp, Norway lobster, large prawns, and crayfish before a main course of roasted sea bass.

Calle Francisco de Vitoria, 16–18. ✆ **97-622-50-53.** www.restauranteriskomar.com. Reservations required. Main courses 20€–32€. Tasting menus 35€–45€. Daily 1:30–3:30pm; Mon–Sat 9–11:30pm. Closed 2 weeks at Easter. Bus: 33.

Exploring Zaragoza

Basílica de Nuestra Señora del Pilar ★★ CATHEDRAL This grandiose 16th- and 17th-century basilica on the bank of the Río Ebro has an almost Byzantine aspect with its domes and towers. Thousands of the faithful travel here annually to pay homage to the tiny statue of the *Virgen del Pilar* in the Holy Chapel. The basilica is consider a co-cathedral with La Seo del Salvador, and its name, **El Pilar,** comes from the pillar upon which the Virgin is supposed to have stood when she asked Santiago (St. James) to build the church. (Like "Montserrat," "Pilar" is a common Spanish woman's name, often conferred by devout parents.) During the second week of October, the church is a backdrop for an important festival devoted to Nuestra Señora del Pilar (Our Lady of the Pillar), with parades, bullfights, fireworks, flower offerings, and street dancing. The actual feast day is October 12, and sometimes attracts political terrorists trying to get attention. In the most recent event, in 2013, a homemade bomb went off in the middle of the main chapel, but no one was harmed. The church also contains frescoes painted by Goya, who was born nearby. The baroque cupolas in the Temple of Pilar were decorated by Goya and Francisco Bayeu, another Zaragoza artist and Goya's brother-in-law. You can also visit the **Museo del Pilar,** which houses the jewelry collection used to adorn the Pilar statue as well as sketches by Goya and other local artists.

Plaza de la Nuestra Señora del Pilar. ℂ **97-629-95-64.** Free admission to cathedral; museum 1.50€. Cathedral Tues–Sun 7am–8:30pm; museum daily 9am–2pm and 4–6pm. Bus: 22 or 23.

La Seo del Salvador ★ CATHEDRAL   This Gothic-Mudéjar church, built between 1380 and 1550, is in many ways even more impressive than El Pilar. The rich facade is a fine example of the Aragonese Mudéjar style and the structure is an exemplar of Aragonese Gothic architecture. Among its more important features are the main altar and a fine collection of French and Flemish tapestries from the 15th to the 17th centuries, which are housed in the adjacent museum.

Plaza de la Seo. ℂ **97-629-12-311.** Cathedral free; museum admission 3€. Nov–Apr Tues–Sun 10am–2pm and 4–6pm; May–Oct Tues–Sun 10am–2pm and 4–7pm. Bus: 21, 22, 29, 32, 35, 36, 43, 44, or 45.

Museo de Zaragoza ★ MUSEUM   This museum of local antiquities has a marvelously old-fashioned feel about it, beginning with the flamboyant Beaux-Arts building constructed for the Hispano-French Exposition of 1908 designed to memorialize the centenary of Napoleon's siege of the city. The building survived fierce bombardment during the Spanish Civil War, and the heroic statues

The Gothic-Mudéjar La Seo del Salvador.

that surround it speak of a pre-war era that romanticized antiquity. The three main sculptures represent Painting, Architecture, and Sculpture itself; a pair of Art Nouveau sculptures allude to Archaeology. Most of the ground-floor exhibits are the results of local digs, and represent prehistoric, Carthaginian, Roman, and Muslim eras in Zaragoza. Most notable is a fine bust of Caesar Augustus, for whom the city was named.

Plaza de los Sitios 6. **97-622-21-81.** www.patrimonioculturaldearagon.com. Free admission. Tues and Thurs–Sun 9am–1pm; Wed 9am–1pm and 4–6pm. Bus: 30, 35, or 40.

Museo Ibercaja Camón Aznar ★★ ART MUSEUM   The regional savings bank Ibercaja is one of northern Spain's most active patrons of the arts. This small museum, which augments several Ibercaja exhibition spaces in Zaragoza, fills a marvelous Renaissance home in the middle of the city. The upper-floor galleries are arranged chronologically. The first floor features mostly Spanish paintings from the 15th to 18th centuries, including Pedro Berreguete's *El Salvador*. A few excellent Goya paintings, including a self-portrait, are highlights of the Sala Dorada on the mezzanine, while the low-lit second floor displays five Goya etching series, including *Los Caprichos* and the wrenching *Los Desastres de la Guerra*. The third floor is devoted to 19th- and 20th-century paintings and sculptures.

Calle Espoz y Mina, 23. **97-639-73-28.** http://obrasocial.ibercaja.es. Free. Tue–Sat 10am–2pm and 5–8:30pm, Sun 10am–2pm. Bus: 30, 35, or 40.

Museo Pablo Gargallo ★ ART MUSEUM   Pablo Gargallo (1881–1934) was Aragón's contribution to the artistic avant-garde of the early 20th century. A great friend of Picasso and Juan Gris, he was born in Maella, Aragón, but spent his most productive years in Paris. He introduced Cubism's jarring dimensional changes into sculpture by creating three-dimensional figures from flat metal plates. He was also among the first of the avant-garde to appropriate celebrities as images, creating sculptures modeled on Greta Garbo. The museum holds 100 of his works.

Plaza de San Felipe 3. **97-639-25-24.** www.zaragoza.es. Free admission. Tues–Sat 10am–2pm and 5–9pm; Sun 10am–2pm. Bus: 35 or 36.

Entertainment & Nightlife

Zaragoza is a university town, so things perk up around 11pm. A good place to begin an evening's bar- and pub-crawl is Plaza Santa Cruz.

A popular tapas bar worth a visit is **Casa Luis,** Calle Romea, 8 (**97-629-11-67**). Shellfish tapas include oysters, shrimp, and razor clams in little bundles. The house *cojonudos* (toast topped with quail's eggs, ham, and roasted red pepper) is the best version in town. Casa Luis is open most of the year (closed in June and last 3 weeks of November) Tuesday to Sunday 1 to 4pm and 7 to 11pm. House wine starts at 1.50€, and tapas range from 2€ to 8€.

TARAZONA ★

This handsome city on the border with La Rioja and Navarra is noted for its architectural landmarks in the Mudéjar style that reached its apogee in Aragón, where Christians and Muslims collaborated in the design, decoration, and construction of major buildings. It is laid out in tiers above the quays of the Rio Queiles. The kings of Aragón once lived here, and before them, it was a Roman center.

mudéjar **ARCHITECTURE**

BRICKS: Most Mudéjar buildings in Aragón are constructed of brick, which lends itself well to sophisticated geometric decoration. Walls of Romanesque and Gothic churches tended to be very thick, allowing the craftsmen to configure the surface bricks with protruding corners that create complex decorative patterns.

WOOD: Sophisticated combinations of carved panels and geometrically arrayed beams and boards characterize Mudéjar wooden ceilings. They are usually found in rooms where the ceiling span does not exceed 20 feet, such as private chambers in palaces, small rooms in convents and monasteries, and anterooms in churches. A major exception is the coffered ceiling of the main nave of the Teruel cathedral.

PLASTER: Plaster carving figured prominently in many Islamic architectural styles in Andalucía, and adaptations of those techniques decorate doorways, windows, and even entire walls in Mudéjar buildings constructed in the Christian-dominated north.

TILES: Muslim craftsmen introduced tile artistry to Sevilla in the 8th century, and their abstract geometric tiles still persist as a popular decorative element in Spanish buildings. Mudéjar buildings often feature tiled floors, half-tiled walls, and tile decorations on their exteriors. The tower of San Salvador in Teruel is often cited as one of the most harmonious combinations of Mudéjar tile- and brickwork.

Essentials

GETTING THERE   Six **buses** arrive daily from Zaragoza. Trip time is 1 hour, and a one-way fare costs 8€. For bus information and schedules, contact Therpasa (✆ **97-622-57-23;** www.therpasa.es). If you're driving, head west from Zaragoza along the A-68, connecting with the N-122 to Tarazona.

VISITOR INFORMATION   The **tourist office,** at Plaza San Francisco 1 (✆ **97-664-00-74;** www.tarazona.org), is open daily 9am to 1:30pm and 4:30 to 7pm.

Where to Stay & Eat in Tarazona

Brujas de Bécquer ★   The setting for this well-kept modern hotel couldn't be nicer. Just outside of town on the Zaragoza road, the hotel looks out on the spires of the medieval city on the front, and on a sweeping mountain range in the back. There is a business center and the hotel even has meeting rooms, but the main clientele seems to be tourists. The rooms are modest in size and the bathrooms feature showers but no tubs. The street level has a perfectly pleasant restaurant that serves reasonable fixed-price menus of the meat-intense Aragonese cuisine. Despite the name, you won't find any witches here. The reference is to the title of a book by poet Gustavo Adolfo Béquer that lauds the mountain landscape of Aragón.

Teresa Cajal, 30. ✆ **97-664-04-04.** www.hotelbrujas.com. 56 units. 39€–72€ double. Free parking. **Amenities:** Restaurant; cafeteria; free Wi-Fi.

Condes de Visconti ★★   You definitely feel surrounded by history at this delightful small hotel in a 16th-century in-town palace. Even the Renaissance arcade of the courtyard is lined with Tuscan columns. Because it's right in the heart of the old city, it makes an ideal perch for exploring the medieval streets.

While the bones of the hotel are classic, the decor is a harmonious blend of antiques with contemporary furniture and art. The romantic bedrooms, many with canopy beds, all feature tubs in the bathrooms—whirlpool tubs in most instances.

Calle Visconti, 15. ✆ **97-664-00-74.** www.condesdevisconti.com. 15 rooms. 52€–90€ double. **Amenities:** Bar; free Wi-Fi.

Exploring Tarazona

Tarazona's major attraction is its Gothic **cathedral,** begun in 1152 but essentially reconstructed in the 15th and 16th centuries. The Aragonese Mudéjar style is still much in evidence, especially in the lantern tower and belfry. From June 20 through September, it is open Sunday and Tuesday to Friday 11am to 2pm and 5 to 7pm, Saturday

The 16th-century Ayuntamiento, or Town Hall.

11am to 2pm and 4 to 6pm. From October to late June, it is open Wednesday to Friday noon to 2pm and 4 to 6pm, Saturday 11am to 2pm and 4 to 6pm, Sunday 11am to 2pm. Admission is 4€ adults, 3€ seniors and students, free under age 12.

The handsome 16th-century **Ayuntamiento (Town Hall)** has reliefs across its facade depicting Carlos V entering Bologna in 1529 to be crowned Holy Roman Emperor. The emperor is upstaged, however, by even grander murals depicting heroic deeds of Hercules, which tradition says were performed on a mountain southeast of town. Follow the Ruta Turística, a scenic walk, from city hall up to the church of **Santa Magdalena,** with a Mudéjar tower that forms the chief landmark of the town's skyline; its *mirador* opens onto a panoramic view.

NUÉVALOS/PIEDRA ★

The town of Nuévalos, with its one paved road, isn't much of a lure, but thousands of visitors flock to the **Monasterio de Piedra.**

Getting There

From Madrid, **train** connections reach Alhama de Aragón. Take a taxi from there to the monastery. Driving from Zaragoza, head southwest on the N-II through Calatayud. At the little town of Ateca, take the left turnoff, which is marked for Nuévalos and the Monasterio de Piedra, and continue for 23km (14 miles). If you're driving from Madrid, take the N-II and turn east at the spa town of Alhama de Aragón.

Where to Stay & Eat

Monasterio de Piedra ★★★   You'll feel more like a bishop on retreat than a monk when you stay at this luxurious hotel on the grounds of the monastery. Rooms have views either of the surrounding park or the 12th-century cloister, and the spa is nothing short of sumptuous. The hotel grounds meld into the surrounding park, and guests enjoy free entry to both the monastery and the park. The dining room, which is also open to non-guests, serves traditional Aragonese cuisine.

Calle Afueras, s/n. ℂ **97-684-90-11.** www.monasteriopiedra.com. 61 rooms. 98€–282€ double. Rates include buffet breakfast. Restaurant main dishes 14€–22€. Free parking. **Amenities:** 3 restaurants; 3 bars; outdoor pool; free Wi-Fi.

Touring the Monastery

Nuévalos's major attraction, the **Monasterio de Piedra ★★★** (ℂ **97-684-90-11;** www.monasteriopiedra.com) is a virtual Garden of Eden—it even has a 60m (197-ft.) waterfall. It was here in 1194 that Cistercian monks built a charterhouse on the banks of the Rio Piedra. The monks left in 1835, but their former quarters are now a hotel (above).

Two pathways, marked in blue or red, meander through the grounds, and views are offered from several levels. Tunnels and stairways dating from the 19th century are the work of Juan Federico Mutadas, who created the park. Slippery steps lead down to an iris grotto, just one of many quiet, secluded retreats. It is said the original monks inhabited the site because they wanted a "foretaste of paradise." Actually, they were escaping the political intrigues at the powerful Monestir de Poblet (p. 383) in Catalunya. You can wander through the grounds April to October 10am to 1:15pm and 3 to 7pm. During the rest of the year daily hours are 10am to 1:15pm and 3 to 6pm. Admission is 8€.

TERUEL ★★

Virtually an open-air museum of Mudéjar architecture (see the sidebar on p. 418), Teruel is visually stunning. In 1986, UNESCO designated the cathedral and three other churches in town as the Mudéjar Architecture World Heritage Site. The sheer beauty of the town makes it worth a trip if you're anywhere in the vicinity. That being said, Teruel was once even more architecturally distinguished than you will find it today. It was the site of the bloodiest battle of the Spanish Civil War. As the city changed hands several times between December 1937 and February 1938 in the worst winter cold recorded in Spain up to that time, more than 140,000 soldiers died and many of the city's medieval structures were destroyed in the bombardment.

Essentials

GETTING THERE Four **trains** per day arrive from Zaragoza in the north and Valencia in the south. Travel time is about 2½ hours from either direction and fares range from 15€ to 20€. Trains pull into Estación Teruel, Camino de la Estación (ℂ **90-232-03-20;** www.renfe.com).

VISITOR INFORMATION The **tourist office,** at Plaza de los Amantes, (ℂ **97-862-41-05;** www.dpteruel.es), is open Monday to Friday 10am to 2pm and 4 to 7pm, Saturday 10am to 2pm.

Where to Stay & Eat

Hotel Reina Cristina ★★ Beautifully renovated in 2012 to 2013 by the Gargallo group, one of northeast Spain's leading hoteliers, the Reina Cristina sits just outside the old city walls at the Torre El Salvador. It's an easy, if slightly uphill, walk to see the major sights of town. While the rooms are not especially large, they are carefully thought out to avoid wasting space. Views are either of the city or of the dramatic countryside. Parking is always a problem in Teruel, but the Reina Cristina has its own dedicated lot. The hotel restaurant, which serves traditional Aragonese cuisine, serves an excellent large breakfast buffet (inquire when booking).

Paseo del Óvalo, 1. ✆ **97-860-68-60.** www.hotelreinacristina.com. 83 rooms. 59€–85€ double. Parking 6€.. **Amenities:** Restaurant; bar; free Wi-Fi.

Parador de Teruel ★★   When you drive up to this *parador* on the outskirts of Teruel (about 2km [1.3 miles] from the city center), you might do a double take. The building is a substantial country house built in a modern version of the Mudéjar style, right down to the carved plaster, tile decorations, and the use of repeating ogival arches. The garden landscaping even gives the property a quasi-Moorish feel. Rooms are large and modern, and the bathrooms are filled with marble. The restaurant serves Aragonese cuisine with a special emphasis on roasted, grilled, and stewed lamb.

Carretera Sagunto-Burgos, N-234, km. 122.5. ✆ **97-860-18-00.** www.parador.es. 60 units. 80€–104€ double; 180€–203€ suite. Free parking. **Amenities:** Restaurant; bar; free Wi-Fi.

Exploring Teruel

Most visitors approach the old city from the north, walking up the 1920s neo-Mudéjar **L'Escalinata** stairs to enter town through the arch of the elaborate 14th-century **Torre El Salvador.** The narrow street opens into the city's main

Catedral de Santa María de Mediavilla.

square, **Plaza del Torico,** built around a fountain flowing from the mouth of a bull. The bull has been a civic symbol since Alfonso II captured the city in 1171. Teruel's Mudéjar style helped inspire 19th-century Modernisme architecture, such as the striking **Caja Rural de Teruel,** a lilac-blue confection with white floral designs, on the Plaza del Torico.

Architecture experts consider the **Catedral de Santa María de Mediavilla ★★★** to be the most beautiful surviving example of Mudéjar architecture. Its towers, dome, and roof are all designated as part of UNESCO's World Heritage, but the coffered ceiling of the central nave is also a masterwork. It is located on the Plaza de la Catedral (*©* **97-861-80-16**). Admission is 3€ adults, 2.40€ seniors and students. It is open Monday to Saturday 11am to 2pm and 4 to 8pm.

The 14th-century Mudéjar masterpiece **Iglesia San Pedro ★★** (*©* **97-861-83-98;** www.amantesdeteruel.es) contains a chapel dedicated to Los Amantes, ill-fated medieval lovers whose legend looms larger than the church's towers. The mausoleum, which has high-tech displays about the Romeo-and-Juliet tale, is 4€, while San Pedro alone is only 2€. We recommend the package tour that includes the church, the Mudéjar tower attached to it, and the walkway in between (4€). If you have the time and actually like tales of doomed lovers in antiquity, go for the whole package of mausoleum, church, tower, and walkway for 7€. The complex is open daily 10am to 2pm and 4 to 8pm (10am–8pm in August).

NAVARRA
& LA RIOJA

14

The ancient land of Navarra (Nafarroa in Basque) shares a 130km (82-mile) frontier with France, with nine crossing points making it an important link between Iberia and the rest of the continent. As a border region, Navarra has seen its share of conflict, and to this day the remains of lonely castles and fortified walled towns bear witness to the struggles. But this kingdom, one of the most ancient on the peninsula, has preserved its own government and strong Basque traditions. Euskera and Castilian Spanish are both official languages of the autonomous region.

Romans, Christians, Muslims, and Jews have all left their stamp on Navarra, and its architecture is as diverse as its landscape. It is also a province rich in folklore. Pagan rites were blended with Christian traditions to form a mythology that lives on today in Navarra's many festivals. Dancers and singers wear the famous red berets, the *jota* is the province's most celebrated folk dance, and its best-known sport is *pelota*, sometimes called jai alai in other parts of the world.

Navarra is also rich in natural attractions, but most foreign visitors miss them when they come in July to see the **Fiesta de San Fermín** and the running of the bulls through the streets of Pamplona, Navarra's capital and major city. Even if you do visit for the festival, try to explore the surrounding region.

Adjoining Navarra is **La Rioja,** the smallest autonomous region of mainland Spain. This province has far greater influence than its tiny dimensions would suggest because it's an important wine-growing district. The capital of the province is Logroño, a city of some 200,000 that links the Baja and Alta.

PAMPLONA/IRUÑA ★

Ernest Hemingway's descriptions of the running of the bulls in his 1926 novel, *The Sun Also Rises,* made **Pamplona** famous throughout the world. The romantics who read the book, then rush off to Pamplona to see the *encierro* (running of the bulls) during the Fiesta de San Fermín, generally miss the author's ironic depiction of manliness. Attempts to outlaw this ceremony have failed so far, and it remains a superstar attraction. The riotous festival usually begins on July 6 and lasts to July 14. Fireworks and Basque flute concerts are only some of the spectacles adding color to the fiesta. Those who want to know they'll have a bed after watching the *encierro* should reserve a year in advance at one of the city's hotels, or plan to stay in San Sebastián and "commute" by bus.

But Pamplona is far more than just a city with a popular annual festival. Long the most significant community in Spain's Pyrenean region, it was also a major stopover for those traveling either of two frontier roads: the Roncesvalles Pass or the Velate Pass. Once a fortified city, it became the capital of the ancient Basque kingdom of Navarra in 824.

In its historic core, the Pamplona of legend lives on, but the city has been engulfed by modern real-estate development. The saving grace of new Pamplona

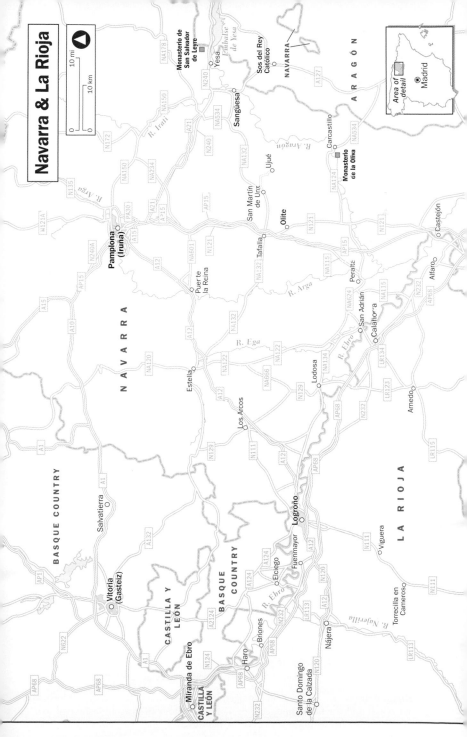

Navarra & La Rioja

is La Taconera, a spacious swath of fountain-filled gardens and parkland west of the old quarter where you will see students from the Universidad de Navarra.

Pamplona's Golden Age came at the beginning of the 15th century during the reign of Carlos III of Navarra (called "the Noble"), who gave the city its cathedral, where he was buried. Over the years, the city has been the scene of many battles, with various factions struggling for control. Those who lived in the old quarter, the Navarrería, wanted to be allied with Castilla y León, whereas those on the outskirts favored a French connection. Castilla y León eventually won out, although some citizens today would prefer Pamplona were part of a new country with a Basque identity.

Essentials

GETTING THERE Few people **fly** to Pamplona since service is limited to a few flights a week from Madrid on Iberia (✆90-240-05-00; www.iberia.com). Arrivals are at **Aeropuerto de Noaín** (✆ 90-240-47-04; www.aena-aeropuertos.es), 6.5km (4 miles) from the city center and accessible only by taxi for about 15€. Ten **trains** a day arrive from Madrid (trip time: 3–5¼ hr.) and five from Barcelona (trip time: 4 hr.). Pamplona also has two daily train connections from San Sebastián to the north (trip time: 1¾ hr.) and four daily from Zaragoza to the south (trip time: 1¾ hr.). Call ✆ **90-232-03-20** or visit www.renfe.com.

Buses connect Pamplona with several major Spanish cities: four per day from Barcelona (trip time: 5½ hr.), eight per day from Zaragoza (trip time: 2 hr.), and seven per day from San Sebastián (trip time: 1 hr.). Instead of calling for information, you'll have to consult the bulletin board's list of destinations at the **Estación de Autobuses** at Calle Conde Olivieto (corner of Calle Yanguas and Miranda). Nearly 20 privately owned bus companies converge here in a mass of confusion.

The A-15 Navarra national highway begins on the outskirts of Pamplona and runs south to join A-68, midway between Zaragoza and Logroño. N-240 connects San Sebastián with Pamplona.

VISITOR INFORMATION The **tourist office,** at Av. de Roncesvalles, 4 (✆ **94-842-04-20**; www.turismo.navarra.es), is open Monday to Saturday 9am to 2pm and 4 to 6pm, and Sunday 10am to 2pm.

Where to Stay in Pamplona

During the Fiesta de San Fermín, prices are three to four times higher than those listed below and some owners charge pretty much what they want. Therefore, agree on the price when making a reservation—that is, if you've been able to get a reservation in the first place.

Gran Hotel La Perla ★★ This dowager lives up to its reputation as Pamplona's grand hotel. When it was built in 1880, it was one of the tallest buildings in Navarra, and its classical facade wears its years with dignity. The most recent renovation in 2013 freshened everything without making radical changes in the low-key modern furnishings. The right address to be in the thick of everything, it sits on the main square and overlooks Calle Estafeta, where the bulls run in the *encierro* of San Fermín.

Plaza del Castillo, 1. ✆ **94-822-30-00.** www.granhotellaperla.com. 44 units. 142€–225€ double; from 530€ suite. Parking 30€. Bus: 3, 4, 9, or 16. **Amenities:** Restaurant; bar; free Wi-Fi.

Hotel Eslava ★ If you're on a budget, the Eslava is the best inexpensive lodging in town. It is clean, fairly quiet, and decorated in a no-nonsense old-fashioned style that doesn't vie to be trendy. It's located a short distance from the Plaza de Recoletas,

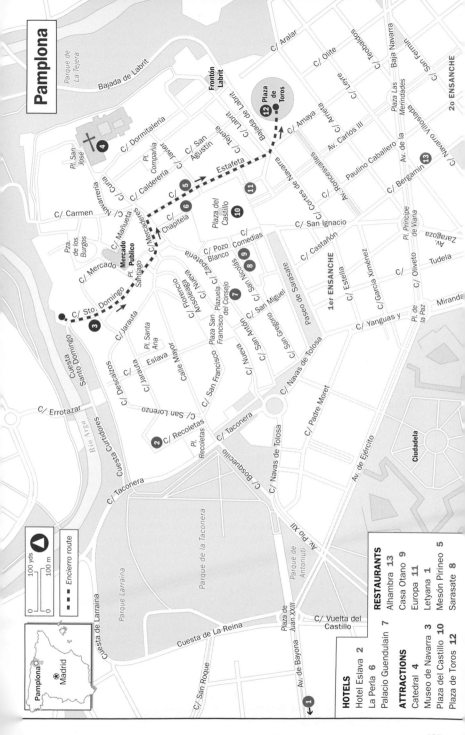

Pamplona

Parque de La Tejera

Bajada de Labrit

Frontón Labrit

Plaza de Toros ⑫

Encierro route

0 100 yds
0 100 m

C/ Aralar
C/ Olite
C/ Teobaldos
Baja Navarra
C/ Leyre
C/ Arrieta
C/ Amaya
C/ San Fermín
Av. Carlos III
Plaza Las Merindades
Paulino Caballero
Av. de la
C/ Navarro Villoslada
2o ENSANCHE
C/ Bergamín ⑬
Av. de la

C/ Dormitalería
Pl. San José ④
Pl. Compañía
C/ Javier
C/ San Agustín
C/ Calderería
C/ Tejería
C/ Labrit
Bajada de Labrit
Estafeta ⑤
C/ Carmen
C/ Curía
C/ Navarrería
C/ Mañueta
C/ Mercaderes
C/ Chapitela ⑥
Plaza del Castillo ⑩
⑪
Av. Roncesvalles
Av. Cortes de Navarra

Pza. de los Burgos
C/ Mercado
Mercado Público
Pl. Santiago
C/ Sto. Domingo ③
C/ Pozo Blanco
C/ Comedias
⑨
Sarasate ⑧
C/ San Ignacio
C/ Castañón
1er ENSANCHE
C/ Estella
C/ García Ximénez
Pl. Príncipe de Viana
Av. Zaragoza
C/ Oliveto
Tudela
Miranda

Río Arga
Cuesta Santo Domingo
C/ Errotazar
C/ Jarauta
Pl. Santa Ana
C/ Florencio Ansoleaga
C/ Nueva
Plaza San Francisco
Plazuela del Consejo
C/ Zapatería
C/ San Nicolás
San Gregorio
C/ San Miguel ⑦
C/ Yanguas y
Pl. de la Paz

C/ Descalzos
C/ Jarauta
Eslava
Calle Mayor
C/ San Francisco
C/ San Antón
C/ Nueva
C/ San Gregorio
Paseo de Sarasate
C/ Navas de Tolosa
C/ Padre Moret
Av. de Ejército
Ciudadela

C/ Taconera
C/ Recoletas ②
Pl. Recoletas
C/ Taconera
C/ Bosquecillo
C/ Navas de Tolosa
Av. Pío XII
Parque de Antoniuti

Cuesta de Larraina
Parque Larraina
Parque de la Taconera
Plaza de Juan XXIII
C/ Vuelta del Castillo

Cuesta de La Reina
C/ San Roque
Av. de Bayona ①

Pamplona
Madrid

HOTELS
Hotel Eslava **2**
La Perla **6**
Palacio Guendulain **7**

ATTRACTIONS
Catedral **4**
Museo de Navarra **3**
Plaza del Castillo **10**
Plaza de Toros **12**

RESTAURANTS
Alhambra **13**
Casa Otano **9**
Europa **11**
Letyana **1**
Mesón Pirineo **5**
Sarasate **8**

and, of course, not far off the Ruta de Santiago. Pilgrims like to stay here because several rooms have big bathtubs where they can soak away the aches of day after day of walking. Staff at the family-run Eslava are extremely hospitable.

Plaza Virgen de la O, 7 (corner with Calle Recoletas 20). ✆ **94-822-22-70.** www.hotel-eslava. com. 28 units. 69€–73€ double. Parking 10€. Bus: 3, 4, 9, or 16. Closed Dec 26–Jan 6. **Amenities:** Bar; free Wi-Fi.

Palacio Guendulain ★★★   You can pretend you were born to nobility when you stay at this plush boutique hotel carved out of the 18th-century family home built by the viceroy of northern South America, Sebastián de Eslava. His descendants still live on the first floor, but the ground level has become the hotel reception area and restaurant, while the second and third floors are given over to sumptuously appointed guest rooms decorated mainly with antique-style furnishings and a smattering of real antiques. The family's collection of fancy carriages is on display, and the polished dark woodwork and gilt-edged furniture can make the hotel sometimes feel like a museum. Nonetheless, it is easy to get used to living in this style, especially since the "classic" rooms are modestly priced. (There are more expensive deluxe rooms and two suites.)

Calle Zapatería, 53. ✆ **94-822-55-32.** www.palacioguendulain.com. 25 units. 121€–179€ double, 256€–377€ suite. Parking 17€. Bus: 3, 4, 9, or 16. **Amenities:** Restaurant; bar; free Wi-Fi.

Where to Eat in Pamplona

Pamplona looks to the Basque country for gastronomic inspiration. Many bars follow the lead of their Bilbao and San Sebastián counterparts by offering creative small plates called *pintxos* here (though they're like tapas).

EXPENSIVE

Alhambra ★★ NAVARRESE/BASQUE   A touchstone of contemporary Navarrese cuisine, Alhambra has been one of Pamplona's top restaurants since it opened in 1985. Chef Javier Diaz knows all the classic dishes, but he is no slave to tradition. Stewed octopus has always been a Navarrese favorite, but Diaz serves it with potato blinis, a pinch of smoked paprika, aioli made with roasted garlic oil, and small side salad of spinach and mint. Slow-roasted pork sirloin is paired with a torchon of foie gras, a bed of crunchy quinoa, and a potato-bacon timbale. Local Araiz pigeon is always on the menu, sometimes stewed with tomatoes, at other times boned and served with a roasted mushroom risotto.

Calle Francisco Bergamín, 7. ✆ **94-824-50-07.** www.restaurantealhambra.es. Reservations recommended. Main courses 19€–24€; fixed-price menus 47€–56€. Mon–Sat 1–3pm and 9–11pm. Bus: 3, 4, or 9.

Europa ★★★ CONTEMPORARY BASQUE   Chef Pilar Idoate likes to play with her food. She'll take the humble *porrusalda,* a Basque potato-leek soup, and substitute green garlic shoots for the leek and accompany the bowl with a mix of shellfish and lightly steamed green asparagus. In a similar fashion, she will substitute sticky rice for the usual paella rice, add a small dice of mixed vegetables, and serve it with grilled squid bodies and quickly fried tentacles (calamari). This sort of inventiveness has won her a Michelin star, but she is equally adept at traditional dishes like slow-cooked milk-fed lamb that comes out golden from the oven and is served with a skewer of lamb sweetbreads. Idoate's three-course menu is an especially good deal as it includes glasses of the excellent Basque country house wines.

Calle Espoz y Mina, 11. ✆ **94-822-18-00.** www.hreuropa.com. Reservations recommended. Main courses 22€–25€; fixed-price menus 41€–62€. Mon–Sat 1–3:30pm and 9–11:30pm. Bus: 3, 4, or 9.

MODERATE

Casa Otano ★★ NAVARRESE/BASQUE   There are two kinds of great eating in Pamplona. The innovative Basque chefs of Alhambra and Europa (above) prepare gorgeous avant-garde food at reasonable prices, making this city one of the better dining cities in Spain. But there's an equally appealing, far more casual style of Navarrese cooking that pops up in old-fashioned taverns like Casa Otano. We like the bar here for its creative *pintxos* in the style of San Sebastián and Bilbao. For the great spit-roasted meats or grilled lamb chops with fried potatoes, you'll have to take a dining room table. Casa Otano has been a local fave since the 1950s.

Calle San Nicolás, 5. ☏ **94-822-70-36**. www.casaotano.com. Reservations recommended Fri–Sat. Main courses 12€–36€. Daily 1–4pm; Mon–Sat 9–11:30pm. Bus: 3, 4, or 9.

INEXPENSIVE

Letyana ★★ BASQUE   Located in a section of town known for its tapas and drinking bars, Letyana is the current king of glorious *pintxos* in Pamplona. One spectacular plate is the medallion of monkfish mounted on a crab shell stuffed with crabmeat on top of scampi cooked in butter and a little squid ink. Another favorite is the loin of venison roasted with prunes and raisins and topped with sauce made with ham, almonds, and cava.

Travesía Bayona, 2. ☏ **94-825-50-45**. *Pintxos* 4€–8€; *raciones* 6€–16€. Daily 1–4pm; Mon–Sat 8–10:30pm. Bus: 3.

Mesón Pirineo ★★ NAVARRESE/BASQUE   Chef Iñaki Rodaballo spends most of his time at his restaurant in Vitoria-Gasteiz, but his spirit is certainly evident in the inventive *pintxos* served at the bar here. The small plates are miniature meals, and several of them have won various tapas contests. One of the most sublime is the beggar's purse, which releases an explosion of chopped shrimp, scallop, and clams in a wine and cream sauce. It may be the best combination seafood stew and small piece of pasta we've ever tried. The restaurant menu is more classic. The wood-fired oven plays a major role here, turning out roasted game and vegetables.

Call Estafeta, 41. ☏ **94-822-20-45**. Tapas 3€–7€; main courses 8€–32€; fixed-price menu (Mon–Fri) 18€. Daily 1–4pm; Mon–Sat 8–10:30pm. Bus: 3, 4, or 9.

Sarasate ★ VEGETARIAN   This lovely, largely midday restaurant is an anomaly in Spain in general and in meat-loving Navarra especially. Except during the San Fermín festival, when they revert to carnivore ways to satisfy the hordes, Sarasate is strictly vegetarian and has been since 1979. The menus are pretty limited, featuring the usual suspects like creamy rice with mushrooms, a strudel of spinach and feta cheese, and roasted green peppers stuffed with tofu and mixed vegetables. Most dishes are gluten-free and several are vegan. All meals are fixed-price, with fruit juices extra.

Calle San Nicolás, 32. ☏ **94-822-57-27**. www.restaurantesarasate.com. Fixed-price menus 11€–15€. Daily 1–4pm; Fri–Sat 8:30–11pm. Bus: 3, 4, or 9.

Exploring Pamplona

The heart of Pamplona is the **Plaza del Castillo,** formerly the bullring, built in 1847. Today it is the seat of the autonomous regional government. This elegant tree-lined plaza becomes something of a communal bedroom during the Fiesta de San Fermín, when visitors without hotel reservations literally sleep in the streets.

The narrow streets of the Old Quarter extend from three sides of the square. The present bullring, the **Plaza de Toros,** is just east and south of this square alongside Paseo Hemingway. Running parallel to the east of the square is **Calle Estafeta,** a narrow street that is the main course of the running of the bulls. With its bars and taverns, it attracts university students and is lively year-round. During the festival it is the most frequented place in town after the Plaza del Castillo. The bulls also run through the barricaded streets of Santo Domingo, Santiago, and Mercaderes.

Catedral de Santa María ★★ CATHEDRAL   This is the most significant historic sight in Pamplona. Dating from the late 14th century, it was built on the site of an earlier Romanesque basilica. The interior is Gothic with lots of fan vaulting. At the center is the alabaster tomb of Carlos III of Navarra and his Castilian wife, Leonor de Trastámara, created in 1416 by Flemish sculptor Janin de Lomme. The alabaster death masks are haunting. (Alas, other early sculptures in the cathedral were vigorously over-cleaned in a misguided restoration that stripped their patina and made them look like modern copies.) The present facade, a mix of neoclassical and baroque, was the work of Ventura Rodríguez, the favorite architect of the other Carlos III, the 18th-century Bourbon king in Madrid. The 14th- and 15th-century Gothic cloisters are a highlight of the cathedral. The Barbazán Chapel, off the east gallery, is noted for its vaulting. The Museo Diocesano, housed in the cathedral's refectory and kitchen, displays religious objects spanning the era from the Middle Ages to the Renaissance.

Calle Curia/Calle Dormitalería, s/n. ✆ **94-821-25-94.** www.catedraldepamplona.com. Free admission to cathedral; museum 5€ adults, 2.50€ children. Mon–Fri 10am–1:30pm and 4–7pm; Sat 10am–1:30pm. Bus: 3, 4, or 9.

A detail from the Catedral de Santa Maria.

A professional jai alai match.

Museo de Navarra ★ MUSEUM   The scope of this museum is impressive. Its earliest piece, the stone carving called the "Mapa de Aboutz," dates from roughly 12,000 years ago, when only spotty areas of Navarra were glacier-free. It is, as the name suggests, a map of the landscape leading from the cave where it was found to the spot where hunters would find a herd of goats. Marvelous stone carvings from the 2nd century A.D. indicate the assimilation of Roman art in the area. One of the most beautiful examples shows Bacchus returning in triumph from India. The hits keep coming over the centuries, with splendid examples of Muslim carving from Córdoba, dignified Gothic religious paintings, and the obligatory Goya—in this case, an excellent portrait of the Marqués de San Adrián painted in 1804.

Cuesta de Santo Domingo, 47. *©* **94-842-64-92.** www.cfnavarra.es/cultura/museo. Admission 2€ adults, 1€ students and seniors, free for children 15 and under, and free for all Sat afternoon and all day Sun. Tues–Sat 9:30am–2pm and 5–7pm; Sun 11am–2pm. Bus: 3, 4, or 9.

ATTENDING A *PELOTA* MATCH

While in Pamplona, you might want to head about 6km (3¾ miles) outside town to **Frontón Euskal–Jai Berri** (*©* **94-833-11-59;** www.fundacionremonte. org), along Avenida de Francia, to check out a professional *pelota* (jai alai) match. Game times are Saturday at 4pm and some Sundays and regional and national holidays. Four matches are usually played on game days, and tickets can be purchased anytime during the sets. Admission to the bleachers is 12€ to 15€.

Shopping

You'll find lots of Navarrese handicrafts in kiosks scattered through the old town. **Bazar Echeve,** Calle Mercaderes, 14 (*©* **94-822-42-15**), sells vests, ceramics, hats, wood carvings, and *botas* (wineskins), which locals use to squirt wine, with great dexterity, into their open mouths. Now in its fourth generation, **Las Tres ZZZ,**

THE RUNNING OF THE bulls

Beginning at noon on July 6 and continuing nonstop to July 14, the Fiesta de San Fermín is one of the most popular events in Europe, drawing thousands of tourists who severely overtax Pamplona's limited facilities.

Get up early (or don't go to bed at all) because to watch you'll need to be in position behind the barricades along Calle Estafeta no later than 6am (the run starts at 8am). Don't even think about running; it may sound like fun but is very dangerous.

Technically, tickets for a good seat in the ring go on sale at 8pm the night before the *corrida* (bullfight), and tickets for standing room go on sale at 4pm the day of the bullfight. Tickets sell out quickly, and because it is impossible to get them through travel agents beforehand, tourists have to use scalpers.

The fiesta draws half a million visitors, many of whom camp in the city parks. Temporary facilities are set up, but there are never enough beds. Hotel reservations should be made a year in advance and confirmed *at least* 6 months beforehand—the tourist office will not make any recommendations during the festival. If you look respectable, some Pamplónicos may rent you a room. Be aware, however, that they may gouge you for the highest price they think you'll pay, and your room might turn out to be a dirty floor shared with others in a slum-like part of the city. Many young visitors sleep on the grounds of the Ciudadela and Plaza Fueros traffic ring, but muggings can occur. Longtime visitors to Pamplona advise that it's better to sleep in a group, on top of your belongings, and during the day. If you can't find a room, check your valuables at the bus station on Calle Conde Olivieto (where there are showers—free, but cold).

As for bars and restaurants, ignore all the times given in the listings beginning on p. 428. Most establishments operate round-the-clock during the festival.

Warning: Some people go to the festival not to watch the bulls but to pick pockets. Also, don't take needless risks, such as leaping from a building in the hope friends below will catch you. Many people do this, and not all are caught.

Calle Comedias, 7 (© 94-822-44-38; www.lastreszzz.com), was founded in 1873 and is one of the best-known makers of wineskins. Goatskin is the traditional material, but the company also produces wineskins from corduroy and synthetics.

Pamplona After Dark

It's not hard to find good nightlife in Pampolan. Three streets in particular—**San Nicolás, Estafeta,** and **Jarauta**—are lined with *tascas,* bars, bodegas, and pubs.

The town's most popular club is **Marengo,** Av. Bayona 2 (© 94-826-55-42; www.discotecamarengo.com), a huge nightspot where a crowd in their 20s and 30s dances the night away. Your dress must pass inspection by a team of hardened doormen before you are allowed inside. Tickets to enter cost 15€, and hours are Thursday and Friday 1:30am to 6am, Saturday 11pm to 6am.

Dating from 1888, the Art Deco **Café Iruña,** Plaza del Castillo 44 (© 94-822-20-64; www.cafeiruna.com), was a Hemingway hangout. Its outdoor terrace is popular in the summer. The winter crowd is likely to congregate around the bar, ordering combination plates and snacks in addition to drinks. During lunch, platters of hot food are served to local office workers and day laborers. The *menú del día* (menu of the day) is 14€. A full lunch, served daily from 1 to 3:30pm, costs 10€ to 12€. The cafe is open Monday to Thursday 8am until midnight, Friday to Sunday 9am to midnight.

Cafetería El Molino, Bayona 13 (© 94-825-10-90), centrally located in the commercial barrio San Juan, doubles as a popular tapas bar. Late in the evening, the action really heats up. The huge assortment of tapas includes fried shrimp, squid, anchovies, fish croquettes, and Russian salad. Most tapas are 3€ to 4€. It's open Thursday to Tuesday 9am to 2am. Closed Wednesday.

OLITE ★

Historic Olite is a castle town that sits in a rich agricultural district with a Mediterranean climate of short winters and long, hot summers. It's also the center of a winemaking industry carried on by cooperative cellars. These wine merchants hold a local festival each year in mid-September, and the town itself holds a Medieval Fair in August.

Essentials

GETTING THERE Four **trains** per day run from Pamplona to Olite, taking 40 minutes one-way. For rail information, call © 90-232-03-20 or visit www.renfe.com. Two **bus** companies, **Alsa** (© 90-242-22-42; www.alsa.es) and **La Tafallesa** (© 94-822-28-86), run from Pamplona to Olite at the rate of 7 to 12 buses per day. The trip takes 35 to 45 minutes. By **car,** take the A-15 expressway south from Pamplona.

VISITOR INFORMATION The **tourist office,** at Plaza Teobaldos (© 94-874-17-03; www.turismo.navarra.es), is open June to September Monday to Saturday 10am to 2pm and 4 to 7pm, and Sunday 10am to 2pm. October to May, hours are weekdays 10am to 5pm and weekends 10am to 2pm.

Where to Eat & Stay

Parador de Olite ★★   Assuming you can afford it, there really is no question that the best place to stay when visiting a castle town is in the castle itself. Part of the national *parador* network, the hotel has just 16 guest rooms in one of the wings

RURAL STAYS IN THE NAVARRA countryside

If you have some time to spend in the area, consider a rental at one of the home stays sponsored by Navarra Tourism. They range from rooms in old farmhouses in the mountains to simple lodgings in homes in the region's small hamlets. Sometimes fully equipped apartments are available. In nearly all cases, these lodgings are extremely reasonable in price and very affordable for families who'd like to experience the great outdoors in this often-overlooked part of Spain. Called *casas rurales,* the lodgings are documented in detail in a helpful guide called "Guía de Alojamientos de Turismo Rural." These guides are distributed free at any of the tourist offices in Navarra, including the one at Pamplona. For more information, call reservation service at ℂ **90-219-64-62,** where some staff members speak English, or visit www.turismorural navarra.com.

of the Palacio Real (see below). It is a late Gothic structure with huge buttresses to support the thick hilltop walls and it fairly bristles with watchtowers. (The kings of Navarra were always at war with someone, usually the French, the Castilians, or the Aragonese.) The other 27 rooms are located in the 1963 addition, which emulates the Gothic style but is clearly modern. The castle evokes the days of Carlos III ("el Noble") and his Castilian queen, Leonor de Trastámara, and two of the most romantic rooms (106 and 107) are named for them.

Plaza de los Teobaldos 2. ℂ **94-874-00-00.** www.parador.es. 43 units. 85€–163€ double. **Amenities:** Restaurant; bar; free Wi-Fi.

Restaurante Túbal ★★★ NAVARRESE　For the full Garden of Eden conceit, try to book an outdoor table during warm weather. The village of Tafalla, just 5.5km (3½ miles) north of Olite, is famous for the bounty of its fields and gardens, and Axten Jiménez and her children, Beatriz and Nicolás, base their cuisine on those fruits and vegetables. The elder Jiménez is famed throughout northern Spain for her research on the traditional gastronomy of Navarra and the Basque region, and the restaurant's interpretation of those traditions combines the hearty flavors with a picture-perfect light, modern presentation. Start with Túdela artichokes grilled with Pio Negro potatoes and garlic shoots, or baked lobster with fresh pasta, bits of Jabugo ham, mushrooms, and a touch of truffle oil. Braised beef cheeks on creamed potatoes or hake with onion sauce makes a good main dish. The restaurant offers an unusually large selection of desserts, ranging from warm chocolate cake with banana ice cream to a classic plate of Spanish cheeses.

Plaza de Navarra 4, Tafalla. ℂ **94-870-08-52.** www.restaurantetubal.com Reservations required. Main courses 16€–27€. Tues–Sun noon–3:30pm and Tues–Sat 8–10:30pm. Closed Aug 21–Sept 4.

Exploring Olite

In the 15th century, this Gothic town was a favorite address of the kings of Navarra. Carlos III put Olite on the map, ordering that the **Palacio Real** (ℂ **94-874-00-35**), Plaza Carlos III el Noble, be built in 1406. It was one of the most luxurious castles of the time. The towers and lookouts make visiting a romantic adventure. April through September, hours are daily 10am to 7pm (to 8pm in July and August); October to March, hours are daily 10am to 6pm. Admission is 3.50€ adults; 2€ children 6 to 16, and seniors. A guided tour is available for 4.90€.

Next to the castle on Plaza Teobaldos stands a Gothic church, **Santa María la Real de Olite** (© 94-874-17-03; www.olite.es), with a splendid 12th-century doorway decorated with flowers—a favorite backdrop for wedding photographs. The church is open for viewing for a half-hour before Mass, which takes place Monday to Saturday at 10am and 7pm and Sunday at 11am and 6:30pm.

Also on the plaza is the fine **Museo de la Viña y el Vino** (© 948-74-12-73; www.museodelvinodenavarra.com), which chronicles winemaking in Navarra since Roman days but concentrates on recent advances in viticulture and technology. Admission is 3.50€ adults, 2€ seniors and students. It is open from Easter to mid-October Monday to Saturday 10am to 2pm and 4 to 7pm, Sunday 10am to 2pm. From mid-October to Easter it is open Monday to Friday 10am to 5pm and Saturday to Sunday 10am to 2pm.

Navarra wines are among the hottest wines in Spain right now, as ancient vineyards have met modern viticulture and an eager domestic market. The local rules permit "French" grapes like Cabernet Sauvignon and Merlot as well as the traditional indigenous varieties like Tempranillo and Graciano. Although the region is just beginning to develop wine tourism, **Bodegas Marco Real** (© 94-871-21-93; www.familiabelasco.com) outside town has tours and tastings that will open your eyes—and taste buds—to Navarra wine. The winery is located at km38 on N-121. A guided tour and tasting costs 7€. Tours run Wednesday and Friday at 9am and 3pm and must be reserved in advance.

Side Trips to a Mountain Fortress, a Historic Monastery & a Town Full of Storks

High up on a mountain of the same name, a short drive east along a secondary road from Olite, **Ujué** seems plucked from the Middle Ages. Built as a defensive town, it has cobbled streets and stone houses clustered around its fortress **Iglesia-Fortaleza de Santa María de Ujué** ★, Calle San Isidro, 8 (© 94-821-15-54),

Olite's Palacio Real.

dating from the 12th to the 14th centuries. The heart of Carlos II ("the Bad") was placed to rest here. The church towers open onto views of the countryside, extending to Olite in the west and the Pyrenees in the east. Recently restored, the main portal is covered with 12th-century stone carvings that show laborers in the vineyards. Admission to the church is free and it is open daily 10am to 6pm.

On the Sunday after St. Mark's Day (April 25), Ujué is an important pilgrimage center for the people of the area, many of whom, barefoot and wearing tunics, carry large crosses. They come to Ujué to worship Santa María, depicted on a Romanesque statue dating from 1190. It was plated in silver during the second half of the 15th century.

You might also consider checking out the **Monasterio de la Oliva ★** (© **94-872-50-06;** www.monasteriodelaoliva.org), 34km (21 miles) south of Olite. It was founded by Navarra king García Ramírez in 1164 and is an excellent example of Cistercian architecture. This monastery, one of the first to be constructed by French monks outside France, once had great influence; today the most notable feature is its 14th-century Gothic cloisters. The late 12th-century church has a distinguished portal and two rose windows. The monastery was built to solidify the Christian hold on what was, in the 12th century, a borderland between Muslim and Christian rule. The Cistercians not only brought their signature architecture and stern Christianity from Burgundy, they also brought wine grapes and the know-how to cultivate them. Today the lands around the monastery produce more good wine than any time in the last 800 years. The monastery is open Monday to Saturday 9am to 12:30pm and 3:30 to 6pm, Sunday 9 to 11:30am and 4 to 8pm. Admission 2€.

It's a modest detour from the monastery across the regional border to the southernmost tip of La Rioja to visit the town of **Alfaro ★**, which has a **tourist office** (© **94-118-01-33;** www.alfaro.es) at Plaza de España 1, open Tuesday to Saturday 10am to 2pm and 5 to 8pm, Sunday 11am to 2pm. The massive 17th-century baroque church on the same plaza is the **Colegiata de San Miguel.** From February to August, more than 400 nests of white storks cover the towers and roofs of the church. Ornithologists say it is the world's largest single concentration of the species, and many studies of stork behavior have been researched in Alfaro. By late August, they begin their migration back to North Africa. The **Mirador de Cigueñas ★** (or "stork overlook") is along one side of the church and provides an ideal vantage for photography.

LOGROÑO ★

The capital of La Rioja, Logroño is also the major distribution center for the area's wines and agricultural products. Because La Rioja is so small, Logroño can serve as your base for touring the autonomous region's major attractions. Although much of Logroño is a typical rural business center, its old quarter is familiar to pilgrims crossing this region to visit the tomb of Santiago at Santiago de Compostela (p. 498). Encased in medieval walls, the old quarter can be explored in about 1½ hours. Its most typical and beautiful streets are **Muro Francisco de la Mata** and **Breton de los Herreros.** But keep in mind that this is a wine town, and the main activity is not sightseeing but rather sipping at a bar, eating a few bites, having a pleasant conversation, and then moving on to another bar to repeat.

Essentials

GETTING THERE There are four daily **trains** (© **90-232-03-20;** www.renfe. com) from Barcelona (trip time: 4–5 hr.) and six per day from Madrid (trip time:

In Spain, architect Frank O. Gehry may be best known as the designer of the Guggenheim Museum Bilbao (p. 466), but he also designed the luxurious **Hotel Marqués de Riscal ★★★**, Calle Torrea, 1 (℮ **94-518-08-80;** www.luxurycollection.com/marquesderiscal), at Elciego, just over the border into the Basque Country. It's 26km (16 miles) northwest of Logroño, and about 129km (80 miles) south of Bilbao, in the heart of La Rioja wine region. The 43-room "new style" hotel, a Starwoods Luxury Collection property, has many of the architectural characteristics of the Guggenheim Museum. The roof, for example, is constructed from curved plates of titanium suspended at different angles and tinted silver, gold, and rose. The design of the exterior of the hotel is meant to evoke a "grapevine just before the fruit is harvested." The elegant rooms are all about windows; there are even window seats that follow the zigzagging contours of the exterior glass. The architect said he

wanted "to make the view part of the room." A stay in this work of art is expensive: 243€ to 437€ for a double, suites 640€ to 835€. A Michelin-starred restaurant is on-site, as is an indoor heated swimming pool, a fitness center, and even a spa offering "wine treatment therapies."

The hotel is part of an entire complex that Gehry designed for venerable La Rioja wine house, the Marques de Riscal. The company modestly calls it **La Ciudad del Vino,** or "City of Wine" (℮ **94-518-08-80;** www.marquesderiscal.com). Gehry incorporated many of the structures of the 19th century winery into his grand gestures of fanciful style. The store and wine bar accept casual visits—you can easily taste and buy. If there's room, you might be able to join a tour, although reservations are technically required. Tour and tasting costs 10€; call to arrange a time. The store and wine bar are open daily 10am to 7pm.

3½–4 hr.). From Bilbao in the north, two trains arrive per day (trip time: 2½ hr.). Five **buses** arrive daily from Pamplona (trip time: 1 hr.) and five from Madrid (trip time: 5 hr.). For information, call ℮ **94-123-58-03.** If you're driving, take N-111 southwest from Pamplona or A-68 northwest from Zaragoza.

VISITOR INFORMATION   The **tourist office,** at Calle Portales, 50 (℮ **94-127-33-53;** www.lariojaturismo.com), is usually open Monday to Saturday 10am to 2pm and 4:30 to 7:30pm, and Sunday 10am to 2pm. From July to September the office is open daily 9am to 2pm and 5 to 8pm. The region has been experimenting with a **Vinobus** to take visitors to several wineries; inquire at the tourist office for details.

Where to Stay in Logroño

Hostal La Numantina ★   You're likely to meet a number of Santiago-bound pilgrims if you stay at this bargain-priced, simple hotel. The rooms are small, the furnishings are basic, and it all feels a little like the guest bedroom in your great-aunt's house. On the plus side, you do get a TV in the room (if you care), a comfortable bed with better-than-average linens, and a compact but scrupulously clean private bathroom.

Calle Sagasta, 4. ℮ **94-125-14-11.** www.hostalnumantina.com. 17 rooms. 59€ double. Closed Dec 22–Jan 7.

Hotel Los Bracos ★   Los Bracos is the classiest address actually in the old city. It is located diagonally across the main plaza from the cathedral and just steps from the narrow streets lined with taverns, restaurants, and bars. Guest rooms are reasonably spacious and modern, with carpeted floors and marble tile in the bathrooms. There are more expensive and even more modern hotels in Logroño, but Los Bracos is the hotel of choice for folks in the wine trade because it blends easy access with atmospheric location and offers true concierge services.

Calle Bretón de los Herreros, 29. ✆ **94-122-66-08.** www.aa-hoteles.com/hotel-los-bracos. 71 rooms. 59€–77€ double; from 118€ suite. Parking 20€. **Amenities:** Restaurant; bar; free Wi-Fi.

Hotel Murrieta ★   The Murrieta probably won't win your heart with its nondescript, boxy international style, but it is regularly renovated (most recently in 2014) to keep the soft goods fresh and the wall paint pristine. The rooms are moderately sized and include a good work desk and a decent Wi-Fi signal. The bathrooms are tiled in marble and the housekeeping is friendly and impeccable. The Camino de Santiago goes right past the front door, as the brass inlays of scallop shells indicate, but the location is in the midst of the modern business center, a block north of the Gran Vía.

Marqués de Murrieta, 1. ✆ **94-122-41-50.** www.pretur.es. 104 units. 55€–85€ double. Parking 15€. **Amenities:** Restaurant; bar; room service; free Wi-Fi.

Where to Eat in Logroño

Asador Emilio ★ RIOJANA   With the exposed wood and stone masonry, you'd think you were still in Castilla, but one look at the menu of roast meat and Bay of Biscay fish and you realize you're within the realm of Basque cuisine as tempered by the vines of La Rioja. Fish dishes range from the predictable hake and cod to bold combinations such as roasted monkfish with grilled octopus and green beans. Meats are spit-roasted over open flames and include suckling pig, milk-fed lamb, and loin of venison. The wine cellar is stocked with both classic and new-style La Rioja wines.

Calle República Argentina, 8. ✆ **94-125-88-44.** www.asadoremilio.com/marcos.htm. Reservations recommended. Main courses 16€–28€; fixed-price menu 25€. Mon–Sat 1:30–4pm and 9–11:30pm. Closed Aug.

La Cocina de Ramón ★★ RIOJANA   Bright and modern, this fresh-market restaurant is one of the most seasonal in Logroño, changing plates as the harvest changes from spring to fall, and relying on root vegetables, meat, and cold-water fish in the winter. The fixed-price menus are often a real steal, as the chef loves to add luxe items (black truffles in particular) to dishes and gets so enthusiastic at the fresh market that he often overbuys highly perishable supplies. Mushroom dishes are sublime, and spring asparagus is as good as it gets in Spain.

Calle Portales, 30E. ✆ **94-128-98-08.** Reservations recommended. Main courses 12€–21€; fixed-price menus 28€–37€. Tues–Sun 1:30–4pm; Tues–Sat 9–11pm. Closed last 2 weeks of both Jan and Aug.

Exploring Logroño

The earliest known guide to the Camino de Santiago, the 12th-century manuscript called the "Codex Calixtinus," makes a point of singling out Logroño as a safe haven for travelers. The pilgrims entered the east end of town on the 11th-century **Puente de Piedra** (stone bridge), which still crosses the Rio Ebro, though it has lost its three fortified guard towers. The street called **Rúa Vieja** is the old pilgrim path, and it leads directly to the ancient **Pilgrim's Fountain,** where pilgrims rest and wash before going to pray in the 16th-century **Iglesia Santiago El Real** at Calle Barriocepo, 6.

Continue on the Camino de Santiago (marked with the scallop shell) a few blocks to the far more ornate **Concatedral de Santa María de la Redonda,** Calle Portales, 14 (✆ **94-125-76-11;** www.laredonda.org). The vaults date from the 1400s, but the baroque facade dates from 1742. Inside, you can visit the 1762 Chapel of Our Lady of the Angels, built in an octagonal shape with rococo adornments. Constructed on top of an earlier Romanesque church, today's cathedral is known for its broad naves and twin towers. Admission is free. It's open Monday to Saturday 8am to 1:30pm and 6:30 to 8:45pm, and Sunday 9am to 2pm and 6:30 to 8:45pm.

From the square on which the cathedral sits, walk up Calle de la Sagasta until you reach the 12th-century **Iglesia de Santa María de Palacio,** on Calle Marqués de San Nicolás, once part of a royal palace. The palace part dates from 1130, when Alfonso VII offered his residence to the Order of the Holy Sepulchre. Most of what he left is long gone, of course, but there remains a pyramid-shaped spire from the 13th century.

Wine shops are ubiquitous in Logroño's old quarter, especially along Calle Portales and the nearby side streets. Continue on the Camino de Santiago to walk through the heart of Logroño, exploring the gardens of the broad **Paseo del Espolón.** In the late afternoon, all the residents turn out for their *paseo,* or stroll.

On the outskirts of town, you can visit **Bodegas Olarra,** Avenida Mendavia, 30 (✆ **90-213-10-44;** www.bodegasolarra.es). It produces wines under the Otonal and Olarra labels. Guided visits and tastings are Monday to Friday 11:30am and 4:30pm, Saturday 11am and 1pm. Admission is 8€ and reservations are required. Bodegas Olarra is closed in August and during the Wine Harvest Festival.

Also on the outskirts, the barrel-aging facility of **Bodegas Ontañón ★**, at Avendia de Aragón, km3 (✆ **94-123-42-00;** www.ontanon.com), receives visitors. You won't see grape-receiving bays or fermentation vessels, but the barrel rooms are highlighted by the Perez family's extensive collection of sculpture, art, and stained glass—almost all with a wine theme. Tours end at the tasting table. The tour and

Stroll along the Paseo del Espolón.

tasting costs 4€ and reservations are required. Tours are offered Tuesday through Saturday at 10:30am, 1:30pm, 4pm, and 6:30pm; Sunday at 10:30am and 1:30pm.

Side Trip to San Millán de la Cogolla

Located about 42km (26 miles) southwest of Logroño, **San Millán de la Cogolla** is often considered the cradle of both the Castilian and Basque languages. The small village was the home of 13th-century poet and author Gonzalo de Berceo, the first major literary figure to write in the Castilian dialect. He was educated here by the monks of **Monasterio de Yuso** (© **94-137-30-49;** www.monasteriodesanmillan.com), a magnificent compound that ranges from an 11th-century walled keep to a striking 16th-century church. The sacristy holds secular as well as religious treasures, including the first written examples of both the Basque and Castilian languages, which were removed from the nearby, vacant Suso monastery for safekeeping. The monastery is open for tours Semana Santa (Holy Week) to September Tuesday to Sunday 10am to 1:30pm and 4 to 6:30pm (also open Mondays in August); from October to Semana Santa Tuesday to Saturday 10am to 1pm and 3:30 to 5:30pm, Sunday 10am to 1pm. The tour costs 6€ adults, 5€ seniors, 2€ ages 7 to 15. A minibus also departs from Yuso to the more ancient **Monasterio de Suso** on the hill above town. Founded in A.D. 550, Suso consists of a Visigothic core with Mozarabic enlargements from the 11th century and a Romanesque section from the 13th. Reservations are required to visit Suso; call © **94-137-30-82.**

The Yuso monastery also makes superb La Rioja wines, which are available on-site at the wing of the compound that was converted in 1995 into a comfortable and serene hotel, **Hospedería del Monasterio de San Millán** (© **94-137-32-77;** www.sanmillan.com). It is also an excellent place to spend the night in any of the 25 large and airy rooms. Double rooms are 99€ to 135€.

HARO

Base for the wine tours of the Rioja Alta district, the region around Haro has been compared to Tuscany. Come here to taste the wine at the bodegas, as international wine merchants do year-round.

Essentials

GETTING THERE Four to five **trains** (© **90-232-03-20;** www.renfe.com) run daily from Logroño (trip time: 45 min.). There are also two to three connections per day from Zaragoza (trip time: 3–3½ hr.). Six to seven **buses** per day run to Haro from Logroño (trip time: 45 min.–1 hr.). For information, call

94-123-59-83. If you're driving, follow the A-68 expressway (south of Logroño) northwest to the turnoff for Haro.

VISITOR INFORMATION The **tourist office,** at Plaza Monseñor Florentino Rodríguez, s/n (**94-130-33-66;** www.lariojaturismo.com), is open October to June Monday to Friday 10am to 2pm, and Saturday 10am to 2pm and 4 to 7pm; July to September Monday to Saturday 10am to 2pm and 4.30 to 7:30pm, and Sunday 10am to 2pm.

SPECIAL EVENTS Every June 29, the **Battle of Wine** erupts. It's an amusing, mock-medieval brawl in which opposing teams splatter each other using wineskins filled with the output from local vineyards.

The entrance to Iglesia de Santo Tomás.

Where to Stay in Haro

Hotel Ciudad De Haro ★ Located outside of town on the highway, this bright, modern hotel is modeled on a Riojan country estate house, right down to the arched entrance from the road to the broad green lawns. Rooms are small but comfortable, and there's plenty of free parking. It's hard to walk into town from here, even though it's less than a half-mile. If it's summer, you might choose to stay here just for the swimming pool.

Carretera N-124, Km 41. **94-131-12-13.** www.ciudadeharo.com. 57 rooms. 54€–77€ double. Free parking. **Amenities:** Restaurant; bar; exercise room; Jacuzzi; outdoor pool; free Wi-Fi.

Hotel Los Agustinos ★★ Haro doesn't get any more historic than this building, an Augustinian monastery founded in 1373. During the 19th and early 20th centuries it served as a military garrison, a school, a hospital, and finally a prison. Renovated by a Basque hotel group, it is now the most elegant and most desirable lodging in Haro. The neighborhood is a pedestrian zone, which keeps the noise level down at night. The large, rather traditionally appointed rooms are distributed on two floors. Most have some exposed stone or overhead beams in addition to white plaster. The floral bedspreads and draperies are not to every taste, but they don't detract from the comfort of the room.

Calle San Agustín, 2. **94-131-13-08.** www.aranzazu-hoteles.com. 62 rooms. 80€–130€ double. Parking 15€. **Amenities:** Restaurant; bar; free Wi-Fi.

Where to Eat in Haro

Beethoven I, II, y III ★ RIOJAN   Chef María Angeles Frenso forages her own wild mushrooms for this trio of adjacent restaurants in the middle of town. They are pretty much interchangeable except for the balance of exposed wood, exposed stone, and contemporary glass. All three serve the same menu, which is organized with musical conceits (melodies, symphonies, etc.). It's a clever way to repackage the usual mix of oven-roasted meats, Basque fish and shellfish, and wild game.

Calle Santo Tomás, 3–5. **94-131-11-81.** www.restaurantebeethoven.com. Reservations required in summer. Main courses 16€–26€. Wed–Mon 1:30–4pm; Wed–Sun 8:30–11:30pm.

Terete ★★ RIOJAN   Alberto Gutiérrez continues in the footsteps of his great-grandfather, Alberto Andrés Alonso, who opened Terete in 1867 to share "the fate God had chosen for him to perfect the art of roasting lamb and serving it with a glass of wine." In other words, eating here is divinely ordained. One starter—Calahorra artichokes sautéed with Swiss chard, peapods, and mushrooms—is almost a meal in itself. Gutiérrez builds his desserts around the succession of local fresh fruits, starting with spring strawberries and ending in the fall with fresh grapes baked into cake.

Calle Lucrecia Arana, 17. ✆ **94-131-00-23.** www.terete.es. Reservations recommended. Main dishes 12€–28€. Tues–Sun 1:15–4pm; Tues–Sat 8:30–11pm. Closed July 1–15 and Oct 15–31.

Exploring Haro & Visiting the Bodegas

The town itself deserves a look before you head for the bodegas. The Old Quarter is filled with mansions, some from the 16th century; the most interesting ones lie along **Calleja del Castillo.** At the center of the Old Quarter is the town's major architectural landmark, **Iglesia de Santo Tomás,** Plaza de la Iglesia. Distinguished by its wedding-cake tower and Plateresque south portal, the 16th-century church has a Gothic interior. The tower's cupola is echoed in the bandstand on the adjacent Plaza de la Paz.

You could spend up to 3 days touring the wineries in town, but chances are that a few visits will satisfy your curiosity. **Bodegas Muga ★**, Av. Vizcaya s/n (✆ **94-130-60-60;** www.bodegasmuga.com), near the rail station, is one of the best wineries for visitors. Tours (8€) are offered in Spanish and English Monday to Saturday by advance reservation. You can also simply pop into the *vinoteca* for a drink. The wine shop is open Monday to Friday 8:30am to 6:30pm and weekends 10am to 2pm. The winery's closed at Easter and August 1 to 15.

You can also visit the atmospheric underground cellars of **Bodegas La Rioja Alta ★**, Av. Vizcaya, 8 (✆ **94-131-03-46**), not far from Muga. Tours, which cost 8€ and must be arranged in advance, are Monday to Friday at 11:30am and Saturday at 12:15pm.

If you want to delve more deeply into the history, science, and aesthetics of La Rioja wines, the very authoritative **Centro de Interpretación del Vino de la Rioja ★★** (✆ **94-130-57-19;** www.vinodelarioja.org) has three floors of exhibits, interactive computer displays, and video clips that cover everything from planting the vines to shipping the bottles. The center is located in the Estación de Enológica de Haro at Calle Bretón de los Herreros, 4. Admission is 3€ adults, 2€ seniors and students. It is open Tuesday to Friday 10am to 2:30pm and 3:30 to 7pm; Saturday 10am to 7pm; and Sunday 10am to 2pm.

Bodegas Muga.

If you arrive in Haro in August or the first 2 weeks in September, when many of the bodegas are closed, settle instead for drinking wine in the *tabernas* that line the streets between Calle Parroquia and Plaza de la Paz. A night spent there will make you forget all about bodega tours. Some of the finest red wines in Spain are sold at these bars, along with tapas—all at bargain prices.

THE
BASQUE
COUNTRY

15

T he Basque Country (El Pais Vasco in Castilian) is seductive. Visitors come in droves to see the Guggenheim Bilbao Museum, only to discover that there is so much more: a dynamic modern city and a nearby coastline of long sandy strands, rocky promontories, and great surfing. They venture a little farther and plumb the depths of Basque identity at Gernika (Guernica in Castilian) and discover the sumptuous pleasures of the Basque table in the Belle Epoque beach resort of San Sebastián. Basque Country is still Spain, but it is Spain with a decidedly piquant accent.

The Basques are the oldest traceable ethnic group in Europe. Their language, Euskera (also spelled Euskara, Uskara, or Eskuara, depending on the dialect), predates any of the commonly spoken Romance languages; its origins, like those of the Basque race itself, are lost in obscurity. One theory holds that the Basques are descended from the original Iberians, who lived in Spain before the arrival of the Celts some 3,500 years ago.

The region calls itself Euskadi, which simply means "collection of Basques". In the strictest sense it refers to three provinces: Guipúzcoa (whose capital, **San Sebastián,** features the Playa de la Concha, one of Spain's best-loved stretches of sand); Bizakaia (whose capital is the exciting, rejuvenated industrial city of **Bilbao**); and inland Álava. Basque nationalists dream of forging a new nation that will one day unite all the Basque lands; in their minds, Euskadi also refers to the northern part of Navarre and three provinces in France.

The Spanish Basque provinces occupy the eastern part of the Cantabrian Mountains between the Pyrenees and the valley of Río Nervión. They maintained a large degree of independence until the 19th century, when they were finally brought to heel by Madrid. The central government continued to recognize the ancient rights and privileges granted by the Romans until 1876, but the region lost its special status when it rebelled over succession to the Spanish throne.

During the Spanish Civil War (1936–39), the Basques were on the losing side, and subsequent oppression under Franco led to deep-seated resentment against Madrid. The Basque separatist movement, ETA (*Euskadi ta Askatasuna,* or Basque Nation and Liberty), and the French organization Enbata (Ocean Wind) engaged unsuccessfully in guerrilla activity in 1968 to secure a united Basque state. Sporadic bombings and kidnappings continued over the next 4 decades. After many false starts, ETA declared a permanent unilateral ceasefire in 2011. Political action continues, but paramilitary activities have halted.

Basques wear a beret of red, blue, or white wool, as a badge of pride and sometimes as a political statement. You may see nationalist graffiti, slogans such as euskadi ta askatasuna (Basque Nation and Liberty). Although the separatist movement simmers on a back burner, economic progress in the Basque region has eroded the appeal of nationalism. The Basques are pragmatists, and compared to the rest of Spain, things are pretty good in Basque Country. You'll find most people friendly and welcoming.

PREVIOUS PAGE: **Louise Bourgeois's spider sculpture, "Maman," outside the Bilbao Guggenheim.**

Bay   of   Biscay

Bermeo
Mundaka
Lekeitio
Hendaye
Fuenterrabía
(Hondarribia)
Irun
FRANCE
BI631
Getxo
Mungia
BI2235
BI2238
Ondárroa
San Sebastián
(Donostia)
A8
BI631
Portugalete
Gernika-Lumo
(Guernica)
Zumaia
Getaria
Zarautz
Hermani
Barakaldo
Deba
A8
Bilbao
BI635
BI633
Andoain
NGJ4
A8
Eibar
A8
Azkoitia
Azpeitia
E5
A15
Llodio
Durango
Elorrio
AP1
Tolosa
N130
NA170
N240
BI623
Zumárraga
E80
Amurrio
BASQUE COUNTRY
Mondragón
Legazpi
Beasain
Idiazábal
A15
AP1
Embalse de
Ulibarri-Ganboa
E5
N622
A1
Altsasu
A10
AP15
AP68
Salvatierra
E5
E80
To Pamplona
Iruña
de Oca
Vitoria
(Gasteiz)
Alegría-
Dulantzi
NAVARRA
R. Ebro
AP68
A1
A132
NA120
CASTILLA
Y LEÓN
Puente
lá Reina
A12
CASTILLA
Y LEÓN
Miranda
de Ebro
Estella
A12
Area of
detail
Haro
Los Arcos
Briones
Madrid
Elciego
LA RIOJA
AP68
N232
Fuenmayor
Logroño
N120
N120
Santo Domingo
de la Calzada
N120
Nájera
N120
AP68
R. Ebro
AP68
0   10 mi
0   10 km

SAN SEBASTIÁN-DONASTIA ★★★

Locals will tell you, "Before God was God and rocks were rocks, the Basques were Basques." San Sebastián (Donastia in Basque) is still a bastion of Basque culture and identity—as well as a resort on par with Nice and Monte Carlo, thanks to flowering gardens, summer festivals, seafront promenades, sandy beaches, green mountains, a scenic, boat-filled Bay of Biscay, and the best restaurants in Spain.

Essentials

GETTING THERE   **Iberia Airlines** (© **90-240-05-00;** www.iberia.com) offers three to six daily flights to San Sebastián from Madrid, plus three daily flights from Barcelona through its regional subsidiaries. The domestic airport is at

The beach in San Sebastián.

nearby Fuenterrabía. From Fuenterrabía, buses run to the center of San Sebastián every 20 minutes Monday to Saturday from 6:45am to 9:05pm, and Sunday every 30 minutes from 7:40am to 9:05pm. Tickets are 5€. Contact **Ekialdebus** (☎ **94-364-13-02;** www.interbus.com.es) for more information.

From Madrid, RENFE runs **trains** to Zaragoza, where passengers change trains to continue on to San Sebastián (5½ hr.). RENFE also provides two trains daily from Barcelona to San Sebastián (5½ hr.). For RENFE information, call ☎ **90-232-03-20** or visit www.renfe.com.

San Sebastián is well linked by a **bus** network to many of Spain's major cities, although it's more convenient to take a train from Madrid. **Continental Auto,** Av. de Sancho el Sabio 31 (☎ **90-242-22-42;** www.alsa.es), runs seven to nine daily buses from Madrid, taking 6 hours and costing 36€. **Vibasa,** Po. De Vizcaya 16 (☎ **94-345-75-00;** www.vibasa.es), operates three buses from Barcelona, a 7-hour trip costing 32€ one-way. Finally, **Transportes PESA,** Av. de Sancho el Sabio 33 (☎ **90-210-12-10;** www.pesa.net), runs buses from Bilbao every 30 minutes during the day, taking 1¼ hours and costing 18€ one-way.

Driving from Madrid, take the N-I toll road north to Burgos, and then follow A-1 to Miranda de Ebro. From here, continue on the A-68 north to Bilbao and then the A-8 east to San Sebastián. From Pamplona, take the A-15 north to the N-I, which leads right into San Sebastián.

VISITOR INFORMATION The **tourist office** is at Boulevard, 8 (☎ **94-348-11-66;** www.sansebastianturismo.com). The office is open year-round Monday to Thursday 9am to 1:30pm and 3:30 to 7pm; Friday to Saturday 10am to 7pm; Sunday 10am to 2pm.

SPECIAL EVENTS In mid-August, San Sebastián stages its annual party, **Aste Nagusia,** a celebration of traditional Basque music and dance, along with fireworks, cooking competitions, and sports events. In mid-September, the **San Sebastián International Film Festival** draws luminaries from America and Europe. In the second half of July, the city hosts the **San Sebastián International Jazz Festival.** The dates of these festivals vary from year to year, so check with the tourist office.

Where to Stay in San Sebastián

Book in advance for the best deals; during high season (May–Sept), many hoteliers will insist you take at least half-board (breakfast plus one meal).

San Sebastián

HOTELS

Adore Plaza **13**
Barceló Costa Vasca **4**
Hostal Bahía **9**
Hotel Astoria 7 **6**
Hotel María Cristina **15**
Hotel Mercure
Monte Igueldo **1**
Londres y de
Inglaterra **10**
Niza **8**

RESTAURANTS

Akelañe **2**
Arzak **16**
Bodegón Alejandro **14**
Casa Vallés **7**
Juanito Kojua **12**
Kokotxa **11**
Martín Berasategui **5**
Rekondo **3**

pil pil: **IT'S ALL IN THE WRIST**

Bacalao al pil pil is perhaps the quintessential Basque fish dish. It is made with salt cod soaked up to 2 days in changes of fresh water to rehydrate the fish and wash away excess salt. The only other ingredients are olive oil, sliced garlic, and a mildly hot guindilla pepper cut into thin rings. The garlic is sautéed in the oil until brown, then removed. The fish is added to the pan and slowly cooked while the chef stirs the oil constantly. Done properly, the fish juices mix with the oil and form an emulsion as thick as mayonnaise. The garlic and peppers go on top.

EXPENSIVE

Hotel María Cristina ★★★   This landmark Belle Epoque hotel underwent a thorough renovation beginning on its centenary in 2012 and finishing in late 2013. Built and named for royalty, it remains the most glamorous address in town. The rooms and suites are decorated in a gray-taupe-white palette that recalls the paint colors of Rolls-Royce automobiles. The María Cristina has very good and very discreet security, providing beautiful public rooms with opulent onyx, marble, and faux painting where celebrities can be photographed during the film and jazz festivals, and secure secondary entrances where they can come and go incognito when they choose. The same glam public areas make the hotel a first choice for many society weddings. Even the least expensive guest rooms are spacious. Bathrooms feature very contemporary fixtures. Beds are deeply luxurious. Each room is equipped with broadband Internet, sometimes included in the price, sometimes ridiculously expensive.

Paseo República Argentina, 4. ✆ **800-325-3589** in the U.S., or 94-343-76-00. www.hotel-maria-cristina.com. 136 rooms and suites. 195€–445€ double; 260€–825 suite. Parking 26€. Bus: 5 or 6. **Amenities:** Restaurant; bar; exercise room; indoor heated pool; spa; Wi-Fi (23€/24 hr.).

Londres y de Inglaterra ★★   When the movie stars and Hollywood directors are in the María Cristina, the supporting actors and the film auteurs from struggling countries try to stay at this dowager property on the northern edge of Playa de la Concha. It's grand in a Belle Epoque style, but has loosened up its corset stays over the years. The semiformal public rooms have large windows that overlook the beach and flood the spaces with light, and comfortable armchairs to sink into to enjoy the comings and goings of the guests. Guest rooms are commodious, with marble bathrooms.

Calle Zubieta, 2. ✆ **94-344-07-70.** www.hlondres.com. 148 rooms and suites. 119€–359€ double; 164€–439€ suites. Bus: 5 or 6. **Amenities:** Restaurant; bar; free Wi-Fi.

MODERATE

Barceló Costa Vasca ★   One of the few northern Spain hotels from this group known for business properties in Latin America and southern Spain, the Costa Vasca is actually a 5-minute walk from the coast—specifically from Ondarreta Beach—and about the same distance from downtown San Sebastián. It does a bustling business during the week with small conferences and other business travel, but offers deals on the weekends. The exterior is red brick set in a wave pattern, while the interior is low-key, tasteful, and contemporary. Rooms all have good work desks. Those with balconies overlook the road, not the beach.

Av. de Pío Baroja, 15. www.barcelo.com. ✆ **94-331-79-50.** 203 units. 64€–205€ double; 200€–450€ suite. Parking outside free; garage 15€. **Amenities:** Restaurant; bar; bikes; outdoor pool; free Wi-Fi.

Hotel Astoria 7 ★★   Which movie star will spend the night with you? That's the come-on at the Astoria 7, a snazzy contemporary hotel in the building that once held San Sebastián's first multiplex cinema. Developers decided to play to that strength, so the entire hotel is themed to classic films. Each room is named for an actor, actress, or director, and there's a small cinema in the basement that screens films every night. The beautiful lobby library is replete with coffee table cinema books, film critiques in a dozen languages, and an extensive collection of DVDs you can check out and watch in your room. The neighborhood seems rather removed from the beach scene, but it's a quick bus ride to the Kursaal complex, where most film festival movies are screened. Rooms are modern and spacious, and even kind of glamorous. The city bus station is a 3-minute walk away.

Calle Sagrada Familia, 1. ✆ **94-344-50-00.** www.astoria7hotel.com. 102 rooms. 77€–178€ double; 105€–215€ suite. Parking garage 16€. **Amenities:** Restaurant; bar; bikes; free Wi-Fi.

Hotel Mercure Monte Igueldo ★   This hotel perches atop Monte Igeldo overlooking the town. It's a 10-minute drive to and from the center, but you should use the bus or funicular since you'll never find parking. Every room in the place, public or private, has a spectacular view. Mind you, guest rooms are not especially large, but they are well-designed, attractively furnished, and spotless. Most have private balconies for enjoying the coastal views.

Paseo del Faro, 134, Monte Igeldo. ✆ **94-321-02-11.** www.mercure.com. 125 rooms. 110€–210€ double; 191€–258€ triple. Free parking. Bus or funicular: Igeldo. **Amenities:** Restaurant; bar; children's center; outdoor pool; free Wi-Fi.

Niza ★★   We have a soft spot for this family-run hotel right on Playa de la Concha because the staff is so genuinely friendly and the hotel oozes character. The rooms are bright and so well ventilated (yes, the windows open!) that you won't need the air-conditioning. Decor is minimal as being outdoors is the main attraction. Eighteen rooms have sea views; those doubles are slightly larger than doubles on the other side, which overlook a landscaped square. The sea-view doubles cost about 50% more, but they can accommodate an extra bed and include a desk. The Niza is easily the best-priced beachfront hotel in town.

Calle Zubieta, 56. ✆ **94-342-66-63.** www.hotelniza.com. 40 units. 70€–178€ double. Bus: 5 or 6. **Amenities:** Restaurant; bar; free Wi-Fi.

INEXPENSIVE

Adore Plaza ★   Lodgings with shared bathrooms aren't quite extinct. This bargain rooming house has nine attractively decorated and comfortable rooms that share five bathrooms located in the halls. Rooms include doubles, triples, quads, and a dormitory room. The building is right on Constitution Plaza in the heart of the old town. The square is busy both day and night, but air-conditioning helps block any noise.

Plaza de la Constitución, 6. ✆ **94-342-22-70.** www.adoreplaza.com. 9 units. 40€–60€ double; 15€–25€ per person sharing dormitory room. Bus: 26 or 28.

Hostal Bahía ★   There's nothing cookie-cutter about this old-fashioned budget hotel located just a block from the beach. Every room seems to have slightly different dimensions, ranging from miniscule to spacious enough for a day bed and an over-stuffed armchair. Usually booked solid from July to September by budget tour companies, the Bahia can be a comfortable bargain at other seasons. During the running of the bulls in Pamplona (p. 432), many travelers stay here and commute by bus.

Calle San Martín, 54B. ✆ **94-346-92-11.** www.hostalbahia.com. 40 rooms. 59€–106€ double. Bus: 5, 6, 7, 8, or 9. **Amenities:** Bar; free Wi-Fi.

pintxo heaven: **AN INTRODUCTION**

Even if it were possible to highlight every great *pintxo* bar in San Sebastián, the resulting list would resemble the phone book. Groups of *pintxos* enthusiasts often spend their evenings on some 20 streets in the old town, each leading toward Monte Urgull, the port, or La Bretxa marketplace. **Alameda del Bulevar** is the most upscale of these streets, and **Calle Fermín Calvetón** is one of the most popular. We like **Calle 31 de Agosto** and the side streets and back alleys that radiate from it.

Here are a few places to get you started. Their hours vacillate with the seasons, but most are open from around noon to mid-afternoon and then again from early evening until midnight. Most *pintxos* run 3€ to 6€. Wine, cider, or beer is typically another 2€ to 3€ per serving.

A Fuego Negro ★★ PINTXOS CREATIVOS   You have to smile when you walk in, for A Fuego Negro is simultaneously witty and a little ridiculous in its self-conscious hipsterdom. The food lives up to the swagger, with funny dishes like "baca-bits" of fried codfish bites that emulate bacon bits and a ketchup-flavored brioche bun that A Fuego Negro uses for its Kobe beef slider. (Calle 31 de Agosto, 31. ℰ **65-013-53-73.** www.afuegonegro. com. Closed Mon.)

Aloña-Berri ★ BASQUE PINTXOS
Run by two smart chefs, José Ramón Elizondo and Conchita Bereciartua, this pretty little bar focuses on "haute cuisine in miniature." That might include a zucchini flower stuffed with mushroom risotto and drizzled with balsamic vinegar, or a beggar's purse of fresh cheese and foie gras with mango. (Calle Berminghan, 24. ℰ **94-329-08-18.** www.alonaberri.com. Closed Sun evening and all day Mon.)

Bar La Cepa ★ BASQUE PINTXOS
Mushrooms, mushrooms, mushrooms! The menu is obvious in this beer bar with heaps of mushrooms on the back counter and hams hanging overhead. (31 de Agosto 7–9. ℰ **94-342-63-94.** www.barlacepa.com. Closed Tues.)

Bar-Restaurante La Viña ★
BASQUE PINTXOS   Once one of the most traditional bars, La Viña got an injection of creativity when chef Santiago

Where to Eat in San Sebastián

We once asked famed Spanish chefs Ferran Adrià and José Andrés where they would go for a gastronomic holiday in Spain. Both answered "¡San Sebastián!" The city's chefs are the most acclaimed in the country. Gourmets devour local specialties such as baby eels in garlic or hake cheeks in green sauce. The local *pintxos* (Basque tapas) are all the rage from London to Los Angeles.

EXPENSIVE

Akelaře ★★★ CONTEMPORARY BASQUE   With his farmstead inspiration, star chef Pedro Subijana prepared the way for the contemporary emphasis on local product. Subijana is not averse to working a little magic in his dishes—the restaurant's name is "Witches' Sabbath" in Basque. Three variations of the tasting menu are offered, and the whole table must take the same menu. The menus are constantly updated, but one choice is always based on Akelaře classics, such as his foamed foie gras with toasted peanut bread, rice with periwinkles and snails, or "Gin and tonic on a plate," a refreshing dessert with a juniper

Rivera took over from his parents in 2013. You can still get great ham and mushroom croquettes, but there are more inventive *pintxos* as well, including a prize-winning "ice cream cone" filled with fresh cheese whipped with white anchovy. (Calle 31 de Agosto 3. © **94-342-74-95**. www.santiagorivera. com. Closed Mon.)

Bergara Bar ★★★ PINTXOS CREATIVOS   Someone should declare this *pintxos* bar a national treasure. The bar is laid out with fabulous spread of up to 60 dishes at a time. Just order by pointing, and the barman will keep your tab running until you're done. These creative bites can be deceptively simple, like the crab salad, grated hard-boiled egg, and swirl of mayo topped with an olive on a plain toast. (Calle General Artetze 8. © **94-327-50-26**. www.pinchosbergara.es. Closed Sun.)

Casa Alcalde ★ BASQUE PINTXOS   Head to the *pintxos* bar at this restaurant for the best variety of ham, cheese, and ham-and-cheese *pintxos* in San Sebastián. The crispy fried calamari aren't bad either. (Calle Mayor 19. © **94-342-62-16**. www.casaalcalde. com. Open daily.)

Ganbara Bar-Asador ★ BASQUE PINTXOS   Local mushroom foragers come here first to sell their finds, and sautéed wild mushrooms are the specialty at the bar. (Calle San Jerónimo 21. © **94-342-25-75**. www.ganbarajatetxea.com. Closed Sun evening and all day Mon.)

La Cuchara de San Telmo ★★ PINTXOS CREATIVOS   The look is traditional, but the kitchen aspires to be avant-garde. Look for squid ink "risotto" made with orzo, foie gras with applesauce, and roasted pig's ears. (Calle 31 de Agosto 28. © **64-778-74-44**. www. lacucharadesantelmo.com. Closed Mon.)

Restaurante Gandarias ★ BASQUE PINTXOS   We only have to close our eyes to recall the grilled sirloin and green pepper on small rounds of bread at this beef-crazy restaurant. Fish lovers adore the crepes filled with salt cod brandade. (Calle 31 de Agosto 23. © **94-342-63-62**. www.restaurantegandarias.com. Open daily.)

berry tang. His roasted wood pigeon is a spectacular little plate of breast pieces glazed with a chocolate mole sauce and dusted in cocoa.

Paseo del Padre Orkolaga, 56. © **94-331-12-09**. www.akelarre.net. Reservations required. Tasting menu 145€. Wed–Sun 1–3:30pm; Wed–Sat 8:30–11pm. Closed Feb and Sept 27–Oct 15, Mon–Tues Jan–June, and Mon July–Dec.

Arzak ★★★ CONTEMPORARY BASQUE   The other progenitor of *la nueva cocina vasca*, Juan Mari Arzak, is based at this modernized family restaurant launched by his grandparents. Arzak grew up in the kitchen, and he has raised co-chef Elena, his daughter, the same way. He and Elena spend at least 1 day a week in their laboratory literally cooking up new dishes and experimenting with novel techniques and presentations. The market dictates the dishes any given day, but apart from chilled raw oysters, don't expect anything to look like any other food you've ever eaten. At our last meal here, we were delighted by a dish where a red liquid was spooned into a tangy clear liquid and spread in fractal patterns. Another dish was enveloped in smoke once the sauce was added. A main dish called "low tide" featured a monkfish fillet in the shape of a monkfish (a bottom-dweller) along with other fish cast as scallop and clam shells, little blue starfish of agar-agar, and "caviar" of spherified pureed red pepper. In other words, you get a lot of gastronomic theater with the meal.

Av. Alcade Elosegui, 273. © **94-328-55-93.** www.arzak.info. Reservations required. Main courses 48€–72€; tasting menu 190€, excluding drinks. Tues–Sat 1:30–3pm and 8:30–11pm. Closed June 13–30 and Nov 5–Dec 1.

Martín Berasategui ★★★ CONTEMPORARY BASQUE   A generation younger than Subijana and Arzak, Martín Berasategui has grown a culinary empire from this eponymous restaurant, earning a total of six Michelin stars (including three for this place, which opened in 1993). Berasategui began working in the family restaurant at age 14 before being sent to France to train as a pastry chef at age 17. At age 20 he took over the family operation. What distinguishes Berasategui from his fellow three-star chefs in San Sebastián is a kind of simplicity. Ultimately, the success of the plates comes down to perfect product— tuna belly fresh from the boat that he grills over wood charcoal; little peels of raw fennel served with risotto; or pig's trotters stuffed with quince, cabbage, and Manchego cheese. Of course, he's equally adept at spectacular presentations, like the roasted red mullet presented with edible "scales" of crystalized fish juices. Few dishes are more than two or three bites, but each bite is packed with more flavor than entire meals elsewhere. He does offer a la carte selections, but almost everyone opts for the tasting menu.

Calle Loidi, 4, Lasarte. © **94-336-64-71.** www.martinberasategui.com. Reservations required. Main courses 49€–62€; tasting menu 195€. Wed–Sat 1–3:30pm and 8:30–11pm; Sun 1–3:30pm. Closed Dec 15–Jan 17.

MODERATE

Bodegón Alejandro ★★ BASQUE   This was the casual family restaurant where Martín Berasategui won his first Michelin star at the age of 25, and it's still a destination for gourmets in the know. Now run by chef Inaxio Valverde, Alejandro remains an exemplar of classic Basque cooking and hospitality. While he always offers a version of cod *pil pil,* Valverde is not a slave to tradition. He's likely to present the cod as a confit in olive oil with steamed spider crab, for example. His appetizer of sautéed octopus comes with smoked tuna juices and paprika potatoes. And he does a brilliant riff on apple pie, making it with tart green apples sided by cheese ice cream.

Calle Fermín Calbetón, 4. www.bodegonalejandro.com. © **94-342-71-58.** Reservations recommended Fri–Sat. Main courses 15€–22€; fixed-price lunch 16€–25€ and dinner 39€. Wed–Sun 1–3:30pm; Wed–Sat 8:30–10:30pm. Closed Dec 23–Jan 15.

Juanito Kojua ★ BASQUE/SEAFOOD   A destination for traditional Basque seafood dishes since 1947, this modest spot began as a meeting place for fishermen's eating clubs and has persisted over the years because its chefs always seem to manage to get the top of the catch. There are four dining rooms of various traditional decor, but you don't go here so much for ambience as for the food. Fish and shellfish are prepared simply: grilled, baked, sometimes steamed. The classic hake cheeks in *pil pil* is probably the most ordered dish on the menu, but to branch out you could try char-grilled line-caught red sea bream (a member of the bass family), tangy with salt. Meat dishes are limited, but the chef is proud of his filet mignon served with a torchon of foie gras, grilled red piquillo peppers, and sautéed mushrooms.

Calle Puerto, 14. © **94-342-01-80.** www.juanitokojua.com. Reservations recommended. Main courses 16€–25€. Tues–Sun 1–3:30pm; Wed–Sun 8–11pm. Closed 3 weeks in Feb and 2 weeks in June.

Rekondo ★ BASQUE You will likely smell the wood smoke from Rekondo even before you reach the old stone house that holds this terrific Basque *asador*. The Basques have made a specialty of roasting meat over open flame, adeptly grilling chops and steaks or spit-roasting haunches of beef or whole kid or lamb. Rekondo branches out to all manner of seafood, grilling garlic-marinated squid and roasting whole spider crab directly over the coals before breaking it down to finish in a casserole tucked into a corner of the grill. The sommelier favors red wines as bold as the food—old-style Riojas and premier cru Bordeaux. In 2014, "Wine Spectator" cited Rekondo for one of the five best restaurant wine cellars in the world.

Paseo Igeldo, 57. ✆ **94-321-29-07.** www.rekondo.com. Reservations recommended. Main courses 24€–55€. Thurs–Tues 1–3:30pm; Thurs–Mon 8:30–11pm. Closed 2 weeks in June and 3 weeks in Nov.

Kokotxo ★★ BASQUE Daniel López creates an updated version of traditional Basque flavors, served on minimalist plates in a pure white dining room flooded with light. Bright pops of color, intense flavors, and irresistible aromas prevent the experience from seeming too clinical. Portions are predictably small, and most diners opt for one of the menus to ensure variety (and volume). These dishes are treats you're unlikely to encounter anywhere but on the Basque coast—plates like sea robin (a gumard, a fish with huge fins that tastes like sweeter, firmer flounder) served with goose barnacles and little spheres of grassy olive oil. Even the sole comes with a gazpacho-like sauce and bright gnocchi made with beets rather than potato. For dessert, don't miss the "bread and tomato," which is gingerbread with a dollop of tomato-raspberry jam and a scoop of tarragon-olive oil ice cream.

Calle Campanario, 11 E. ✆ **94-342-19-04.** www.restaurantekokotxa.com. Main courses 27€–31€; daily menu 27€; market menu 50€; tasting menu 78€. Jan–June Wed–Sat 1:30–3:30pm and 8:45–11pm; July–Dec Tues-Sun 1:30–3:30 and Tues–Sat 8:45–11pm. Closed last 3 weeks of Feb, first week of June, last 2 weeks of Oct.

INEXPENSIVE

Casa Vallés ★ SPANISH/BASQUE We think of Casa Vallés as a time capsule, since little about it seems to have changed since it opened in 1942. The ground-level tapas bar has ignored the *pintxos creativos* craze that's swept the rest of the city. This is where you come for a bite of *tortilla Española* (potato omelet), a casserole of pork-veal meatballs, or a plate of canned anchovies laid out solemnly on a plate. The restaurant upstairs is spare and features old-fashioned wood paneling on the walls. The kitchen keeps it simple: grilled fish, veal, pork, chicken. The oven-roasted spider crab is exceptional, and many locals stream here for the Madrid-style tripe.

Calle Reyes Católicos, 10. ✆ **94-345-22-10.** www.barvalles.com. Main courses 7€–21€. Fixed-price menu 18€ weekdays, 25€ weekends. Restaurant Thurs–Tues 1–3pm; Thurs–Mon 8:30–11pm. Bar daily 8:30am–11pm. Closed 2 weeks in late May.

Exploring San Sebastián

Both locals and scantily clad international visitors can be found on shell-shaped **Playa de la Concha ★★**, opening onto the half-moon **Bay of Biscay.** Popular since the mid–19th century, it's one of the finest urban beaches in Atlantic Europe. When you tire of the sands, take the funicular to the top of **Monte Igeldo** for panoramic views. You can also hike Igeldo and **Monte Urgull,** which bracket the city, and wander the narrow streets of **La Parte Vieja** (old town). Cap your day with an early evening *paseo* (stroll) along Playa de la Concha.

The monuments, such as they are, can easily be viewed before lunch, though the main museum and aquarium might hold your attention longer.

Museo de Sociedad Vasca y Ciudadanía ★, Plaza Zuloaga 1 (℃ **94-348-15-80;** www.santelmomuseoa.com), completed a multi-year reconstruction in 2012 that resulted in an aluminum facade around the ancient walls of the San Telmo monastery. Expanding beyond the original walls, the new museum has several galleries with state-of-the-art exhibitions as well as a theater, library, and cafe. The collections include an impressive array of Basque artifacts from prehistoric times as well as works by Zuloaga, Golden Age artists such as El Greco and Ribera, and a large number of Basque painters. Located in the Old Town at the base of Monte Urgull, the museum is open Tuesday to Sunday 10am to 8pm. Admission is 5€ adults, 3€ students and seniors.

The wide promenade **Paseo Nuevo** almost encircles Monte Urgull, one of the two mountains between which San Sebastián is nestled. (Monte Igeldo is the other one.) The *paseo* comes to an end at **Palacio del Mar ★**, Plaza Carlos, Blasco de Imaz s/n (℃ **94-344-00-99;** www.aquariumss.com), an oceanographic museum/aquarium with a mesmerizing collection of huge tanks containing myriad marine species. A transparent underwater walkway allows a 360-degree view of sharks, rays, and other fish that seem to surround you. A maritime museum upstairs presents a fascinating synopsis of humankind's precarious relationship with the sea through the ages. Here you can also see the skeleton of the next-to-last whale caught in the Bay of Biscay, in 1878. The museum is open October to March Monday to Friday 10am to 7pm, Saturday to Sunday 10am to 8pm; April to June and September Monday to Friday 10am to 8pm, Saturday to Sunday 10am to 9pm; and Semana Santa (Holy Week) and July to August 10am to 10pm. Admission is 13€ adults, 9€ students and seniors, 6.50€ ages 4 to 12.

The **Palacio de Miramar** (℃ **94-321-90-22**) stands on its own hill on the point dividing Playa de la Concha from Playa de Ondarreta. It was a summer palace favored by Queen María Cristina (namesake of the grandest hotel in town). She

The underwater walkway at Palacio del Mar.

San Sebastián-Donastia

THE BASQUE COUNTRY

SPEAKING basque IN STEEL & STONE

Eduardo Chillida Juantegui (1924–2002) was the greatest Basque sculptor of the 20th century, known mainly for his monumental abstract works in steel and stone. Born in San Sebastián, he returned to the city in 1959 and worked at his beautifully sited studio in the hills outside town in the village of Hernani. Visitors don't have to go far to see one of Chillida's signature works, the "Comb of the Wind." It rises from the rocks at the base of Monte Igeldo, where it meets the sea at the west end of Playa de la Concha. Like his best works, it combines an abstract beauty of form with an analytical precision that makes the viewer contemplate both the object and the space it inhabits.

Viewed from one direction, the "Comb of the Wind" resembles giant calipers, a tool associated with Basque mariners and their legendary charts.

---

opened the palace in 1893 but once the monarchy fled Spain, the building fell into disrepair. The city council took it over in 1971. You can visit daily from 8am to 9pm for a look at the lawns and gardens, but the palace is closed to visitors.

For the best view of the city, ride the funicular to the top of **Monte Igeldo ★** (✆ **94-321-02-11;** www.monteigeldo.es), where you can take in a panoramic view of the bay and the Cantabrian coastline. From July to October, the funicular runs Monday to Friday 10am to 9pm, Saturday and Sunday 10am to 10pm. From April to June, it runs Monday to Friday 10am to 8pm, Saturday and Sunday 10am to 9pm. Round-trip fare is 3.10€ adults, 2.30€ children 7 and under. It's also possible to drive up or even to walk, if you don't mind a fairly steep climb without sidewalks. A small amusement park with a variety of rides, **Parque de Atraciones,** is located on top of Monte Igeldo. Open roughly the same hours as the funicular, it charges 1€ for most games, 1.80€ to 2.50€ for rides.

Shopping

One of the best outlets for Basque handicrafts and accessories is **Txapela,** Calle Puerto, 3 (✆ **94-342-02-43**), which sells the rough cotton shirts for which the Basques are famous. If you're looking for a beret or any other form of headgear, visit **Casa Ponsol Sombrería,** Calle Narrica, 4 or Calle Sarriegui, 3 (✆ **94-342-08-76**), San Sebastián's oldest hat manufacturer. For virtually anything else, try the most congested shopping district, **La Parte Vieja,** where merchants hawk everything from T-shirts to cameras.

San Sebastián After Dark

The best evening entertainment is to go *pintxos* tasting in the old quarter. In San Sebastián it's called an *ir-de-pintxos-y-poteo,* which translates roughly as "going out for snacks and drinks."

San Sebastián's only venue for gambling is the **Casino Kursaal,** Mayor 1 (✆ **94-342-92-14;** www.casinokursaal.com). Entrance costs 5€ per person after 10:30pm and requires an ID card with photo or a passport. Jackets and ties for men are not required. The casino is open daily from 5pm to 5am.

The big cultural center is **Centro Kursaal,** Av. de Zurriola, 1 (© **94-300-30-00;** www.kursaal.org), an avant-garde building designed by Rafael Moneo and positioned on the Baie de la Concha. A cultural, sporting, and leisure center, it is the venue for almost any major event.

The Kursaal, along with the Guggenheim museum in Bilbao, has helped put the Basque Country on the cultural map. Some tradition-minded locals find the modern architecture to be at odds with the city's essential Belle Epoque look, but it is really only the late 20th-century equivalent of the city's late 19th-century style. All of San Sebastián's major festivals are staged here. There is a 1,800-seat theater for plays, music, dance, and *zarzuela* performances. You can also take a guided tour for 2€ (Fri–Sun at 1:30pm).

THE BASQUE COAST ★★

The coastline between San Sebastián and Bilbao is a land of mythic proportions. The mountains of the Cordillera Cantábrico come down to the sea, where their fractured faces form the rocky cliffs and headlands that surround astonishing sandy beaches. Tides are long and currents strong in the river outlets, making for some of Europe's most spectacular waves. About half the coastal villages are beach resorts; the other half remain fishing villages in the tradition of those intrepid Basque whalers and cod fishermen who plied the coast of North America a century or more before Columbus set sail. They knew the way to the New World, but exhibiting the Basque head for business, they didn't see the point in sharing their secret.

The coast is best explored by automobile. Begin by driving west from San Sebastian on the AP-1/AP-8 for 20km (13 miles) to **Zarautz ★** (Zarauz in Castilian). Originally a whale-hunting village, it is now the largest Basque resort outside of San Sebastián. Waves crash along the 3km (1¾-mile) main beach with surf that nearly rivals Mundaka (see below). The seaside promenade is lined with contemporary avant-garde sculpture, giving Zarautz a hip, edgy look. The **Photomuseum ★**, Calle San Inazio, 11 (© **94-313-09-06;** www.photomuseum.es), has extensive exhibits detailing the evolution of the medium from wet-plate view cameras to digital imaging. Changing exhibitions usually feature Basque photographers. The museum is open Tuesday to Sunday 10am to 1pm and 5 to 8pm. Admission is 6€ adults, 3€ seniors and students.

Continue west for 7km (4 miles) on the scenic coastal road, N-634, to **Getaria ★**, a fishing village that gave the world Juan Sebastián Elcano (Magellen's navigator) and fashion genius Cristóbal Balenciaga. Still primarily a fishing port, Getaria also has two long, sandy beaches. The hillsides above the coastal plain are renowned for the quality of their *txakolí* grapes. You'll find the bracing white wine served from the barrel in the portside *tascas.*

Just another 7km (4 miles) west on N-634, **Zumaia ★** is a fortified town with two great beaches flanking cliffs studded with fossils. The shore light is quite special here, seeming to come from all directions. Painter Ignacio Zuloaga (1870–1945) lived and worked here, and the **Espacio Cultural Ignacio Zuloaga ★** (© **94-386-22-41;** www.espaciozuloaga.com), Calle Santiago Etxea, s/n, fills a former hermitage that the painter bought to store his canvases. It is open from mid-April to mid-September Friday to Sunday 4 to 8pm.

It's a bit longer drive west along the coast via N-634 (24km/15 miles) and GI-638 (8km/5 miles) to reach **Ondarroa ★**. As you come into town, you'll see signs for **Playa Saturrarán,** a white-sand beach between two rocky headlands that is the Basque Country's best-known nudist beach. Ondarroa is the leading Basque fishing port, and its atmospheric medieval center surrounds a harbor packed with lively bars. The two principal landmarks in town are the 15th-century **Torre Likon** watchtower and the fortress-like Gothic church of **Santa María,** which seems to have grown out of the rock on which it stands.

Twisted roads follow seaside cliffs west to **Lekeitio ★**, 15km (9⅓ miles) from Ondarroa. The landscape changes once you arrive: The mouth of the Río Lea defines the harbor. The river is lined by two shallow swimming beaches. The town itself is mixed between fishing (tuna, mainly) and tourism. Overlooking the harbor, the **Basilica de Santa María de la Asunción,** Calle Abaroa, s/n (*C* **94-684-09-54;** www.basilicadelekeitio.com), has dramatic flying buttresses. The gold-plated Flemish altarpiece depicts scenes from the life of the Virgin and the Passion of Christ. It's open for (free) visits Monday to Saturday 8am to noon and 5 to 7:30pm.

Getting to the next coastal village calls for a long detour upriver to Gernika (see below). Go 22km (14 miles) west on BI-2238, then 11km (6¾ miles) north on BI-2235 to **Mundaka ★**, the surfing capital of Spain's north coast. Long rollers and huge left-curling pipelines speed up the narrowing mouth of the river here, creating some of Spain's top surfing conditions in what is otherwise a gentle little fishing town with great swimming beaches. During the first quarter of the year (always announced at the last minute), you might encounter the Billabong Pro Challenge that pits some of the world's top pro surfers against the best of the Basque coast. The **Mundaka Surf Shop,** Paseo Txorrokopunta, 8 (*C* **94-687-67-21;** www.mundakasurfshop.com), rents gear and offers lessons, and sells a variety of cool Mundaka tees and sweatshirts. If you want to pick the brains of local surfers about the best breaks, try buying them a beer at **Bar Los Txopos** at Calle Txopuetak, 1 (*C* **94-687-64-82**).

This tour of the Basque coast concludes with the medieval fishing village of **Bermeo ★**, just 5km (3 miles) north on BI-2235. Pleasure boats have largely replaced fishing vessels in the pocket harbor, but big diesel-powered trawlers lie at anchor in deeper water just offshore. Renovation of the stone wharves in 2013 to 2014 put a crimp in tourism, as the replica whaling schooner *Aita Guria Baleontzia ★*, Calle Lamera, s/n (*C* **94-617-91-21;** www.aitaguria.bermeo.org), was forced to curtail its tours. The ship is, nonetheless, a reminder that Bermeo's whalers hunted along the Cantabrian coast until the late 15th century, but soon began to venture to Greenland, Canada, and Maine. Normally, it is open April through October Tuesday to Saturday 10am to 2pm and 4 to 7pm, Sunday 11am to 2pm. Cost is 5€ adults, 3€ ages 4 to 14. The last fortified tower of the town, the 15th century Torre Ercilla, is home of the **Museo del Pescador ★** (*C* **94-688-11-71;** www.bermeokoudala.net). Like the wharves below it, the tower is undergoing restoration and is likely to re-open in 2015. Exhibits cast back to Bermeo's involvement with Magellan's voyage, but focus more on the modern in-shore fishery, especially for anchovies. Stirring displays explain how the fishermen created their brotherhood in the 19th century to manage the fishery, extract a fair price, and help families of men lost at sea. Hours and entry fees were not yet posted as we went to press.

Where to Stay on the Basque Coast

Atalaya Hotel ★ Built in 1911 to emulate a British seaside lodging, the Atalaya is skillfully maintained and utterly charming. It sits next to a shady waterfront park. Walk past the trees and down a set of stairs, and you're on the point where you can catch a pipeline and ride it all the way upriver to the sandy beach. It is convenient for surfers, and charges low-season rates during the winter when the big waves roll in. Be sure to wipe your feet before entering—you don't want to track in sand to scratch the polished wood floors.

Calle Itxaropen, 1, Mundaka. © **94-617-70-00.** www.atalayahotel.es. 13 units. Doubles 79€– 110€. **Amenities:** Cafe; sauna; free parking; free Wi-Fi.

Emperatriz Zita ★★   Sandwiched between the mountains and the sea, this modern spa hotel is built atop the ruins of the palace where empress Zita, last monarch of the Austro-Hungarian Empire, lived out her days in exile. She couldn't have chosen a prettier spot. The balcony looks out on the Cantabrian Sea, with the Isla San Nicolás just offshore, and the fishing village of Lekeitio off to one side. Lushly landscaped grounds make it a popular wedding and honeymoon venue; in the off season, many of the guests come for the thermal waters and thalassotherapy.

Calle Santa Elena, s/n, Lekeitio. © **94-684-26-55.** www.aisiahoteles.com. 42 units. 75€–116€ double, 108€ –132€ suite. **Amenities:** Restaurant; sauna; spa; free parking; free Wi-Fi.

Where to Eat on the Basque Coast

Gure Txokoa ★★ BASQUE   Joxe Mari Mitxelena and Elena Aizpurua took over this Basque classic restaurant in 2003 and built it into a dining destination in Zarautz. The menu on any given day depends on what's in the market, and the couple emphasizes seasonal dishes that employ garden vegetables. Even basics like oven-roasted crab, for example, are served with a salad of frisée wrapped in paper-thin slices of zucchini and carrot. The fish are purchased daily at the docks of several villages along the coast, and the couple buys their nicely marbled beef by entire sides. Like so many coastal cooks, Mitxelena works with charcoal and open wood fires to cook most meat and fish. The wine cellar has an excellent selection of the bright, slightly tart local Txacolina wines made in the nearby hills.

Calle de Gipuzkoa, 22, Zarautz. © **94-383-59-59.** www.restauranteguretxokoa.es. Main dishes 18€–24€, tasting menu 60€. Thurs–Tues 1–3:30pm, Fri–Sat 8–10:30pm.

Restaurante Elkano ★★★ BASQUE SEAFOOD   This legendary seafood grill, created by Pedro Arregui, was a pioneer in cooking all manner of fish outdoors over a wood fire. He recalls the exact date in 1968 when he grilled the first whole monkfish and immediately proceeded to try lobster, Norway lobster, and other fish, eventually perfecting a series of techniques for almost every type of seafood. Pedro's son Aitor joined his father in 2002 and shares the cooking duties. Almost everything here is grilled, including whole clams cooked in a basket and glass eels (in season) cooked in a perforated pan. Steaks and chops are also available, but the fish are Elkano's signature plates. Don't be surprised if your waiter suggests that you really don't need the silverware because it "tastes better" eaten with your hands.

Calle Herrerieta, 2, Getaria. © **94-314-00-24.** www.restauranteelkano.com. Main dishes 16€– 40€. Tues–Sun 1–3:30pm, Tues–Sat 8–10:30pm. Closed first half of Apr.

Restaurante Jokin ★ BASQUE SEAFOOD   The stone wharves of the harbor at Bermeo look so much like a Hollywood idea of a fishing village that it should make you hungry. If it does, Jokin can sate that desire. Start with the big *gambas* (prawns) wrapped around balls of rice and minced shrimp, or a cup of *marmitako,* the great spicy Basque fish chowder made with bonito or skipjack. The restaurant perches on one of those stone embankments overlooking the fishing fleet, so you can see exactly where your dinner came from.

Calle Eupeme Deuna, 13, Bermeo. © **94-688-40-89.** www.restaurantejokin.com. Main dishes 12€–26€; daily menu 20€. Daily 1–3:30pm, Mon–Sat 8–10pm.

GERNIKA-LUMO

The subject of Picasso's most famous painting (now displayed at the Reina Sofía Museum in Madrid, p. 92), Gernika-Lumo was the spiritual home of the Basques and the seat of Basque nationalism. The town was destroyed in a Nazi air raid on April 26, 1937, during the Spanish Civil War, and may have been targeted because it was the site of a revered oak tree under whose branches Basques had elected their officials since medieval times. No one knows how many died during the attack—estimates range from 200 to 2,000. The bombers reduced the town to rubble, but a powerful symbol of independence was born. Although activists around the world attempted to rally support for the embattled Spanish Republicans, governments everywhere, including that of the United States, left the Spaniards to fend for themselves, refusing to supply them with arms.

Picasso knew the town by its Castilian name—hence the title of the painting—but "Guernica" is not used here. A symbol of Basque resilience, it goes by Gernika-Lumo. The town has been attractively rebuilt close to its former style. A church bell chimes softly, and laughing children play in the street. In the midst of this peace, however, you suddenly come upon a sign: SOUVENIRS . . . REMEMBER.

Essentials

GETTING THERE **Bizkaibus,** at Calle Iparraguirre, 4, runs buses throughout the Basque country. For information, call ✆ **90-222-22-65,** or visit www.bizkaia.net. Several buses per day run to and from Bilbao, costing only 2.30€ in each direction.

If you're driving from Bilbao, head east along the A-8 superhighway; cut north on the 6315 and follow the signs for Gernika. From San Sebastián, drive west along A-8, and cut north on the 6315. A more scenic but slightly longer route involves driving west from San Sebastián on A-8, branching off on the coastal road to Ondarroa and continuing on as the road turns south, following the signs to Gernika.

VISITOR INFORMATION The **tourist office** is at Calle Artekalea, 8 (✆ **94-625-58-92;** www.gernika-lumo.net). In summer, hours are Monday to Saturday 10am to 7pm, Sunday 10am to 2pm; off season, it is open Monday to Saturday 10am to 2pm and 4 to 7pm, Sunday 10am to 2pm.

Where to Eat & Stay in Gernika

Hotel Gernika ★ For many years the only places to stay overnight in Gernika were little pensions and home-stays. One sign of the town's recovery was the construction of this small brick-and-stone hotel in 1987. Rooms are plain but feature well-maintained dark wood furniture (including a desk in each room) as well as marble-tiled baths with gleaming white porcelain fixtures. The bar/cafeteria serves breakfast but no other meals. It makes a comfortable base for touring the town's few attractions, especially if you're trying to avoid overnighting in a more expensive city hotel.

Carlos Gangoiti, 17. ✆ **94-625-03-50.** www.hotel-gernika.com. 40 rooms. 77€–92€ double. Free parking. **Amenities:** Bar; babysitting; free Wi-Fi.

Restaurante Zallo Barri ★★ BASQUE This family restaurant was launched in 1975 as a casual tavern serving traditional Basque food. But in 2001, Iñigo Ordorika, son of the owners, took over the kitchen and brought the cuisine up to date. At the same time, the restaurant was redone in a modern, minimalist style to reflect the food. Ordorika keeps the dishes rather simple—mussels

steamed with a saffron fish broth, oven-roasted scorpionfish with roasted vegetables and shrimp vinaigrette, or a salad of tuna belly with a cold ratatouille.
Calle Juan Calzada, 79. ✆ **94-625-18-00.** www.zallobarri.com. Reservations recommended. Main courses 15€–22€; fixed-price menus 26€–50€. Sun–Thurs 1–5pm, Fri–Sat 1–11pm.

Exploring Gernika-Lumo

The former Basque parliament, **Casa de Juntas,** Juntetxea (✆ **94-625-11-38**), is the principal attraction in town. It contains a historical display of Gernika and is open June to September daily 10am to 2pm and 4 to 7pm, October to May daily 10am to 2pm and 4 to 6pm. Admission is free. Outside are the remains of the ancient communal oak tree, which wasn't uprooted by Hitler's bombs. From the train station, head up Calle Urioste.

    Fundación Museo de la Paz de Gernika, Foru Plaza 1 (✆ **94-627-02-13;** www.museodelapaz.org), contains a permanent exhibition of the bombing as depicted in photographs and artifacts, including bomb fragments bearing Luft-

waffe markings. The bombing on a market day (greater casualties that way) began at 4pm and lasted for 1 to 3 hours, as Nazi bombers unloaded thousand-pound bombs and incendiary projectiles on the helpless Basque populace. On one wall of the museum is a framed letter from President Roman Herzog of Germany, dated March 27, 1997, acknowledging German responsibility for the indefensible act and calling for reconciliation and peace. Copies of Picasso's working drawings for *Guernica* are also displayed.

    During July and August, the museum is open Tuesday to Saturday from 10am to 7pm, and Sunday 10am to 3pm; September to June, it's open Tuesday to Saturday from 10am to 2pm and 4 to 7pm, Sunday from 10am to 2pm. Admission is 5€ for adults, 3€ for students and seniors, and free for kids under 12.

Stained glass windows at Casa de Juntas.

BILBAO ★★★

The 21st-century edition of Bilbao (Bilbo in Basque) is a case study in the transformative power of art, or at least of architecture. As recently as the 1980s, Bilbao was a smoky steel-making and ship-building city on the banks of a severely polluted river. Today it is a graceful small metropolis with a global appeal. Instead of seeing smoke and grime, visitors behold broad avenues, lovely river vistas, and a cornucopia of cutting-edge architecture.

    The audacity of the government to court the Guggenheim Museum in New York and to engage controversial architect Frank O. Gehry to design the Guggenheim Bilbao has paid off. The opening of the Guggenheim in 1997 began the

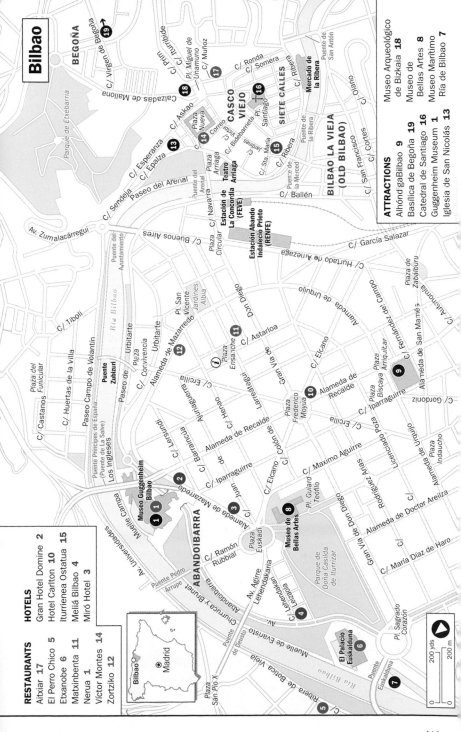

Bilbao

BEGOÑA

CASCO VIEJO

SIETE CALLES

BILBAO LA VIEJA (OLD BILBAO)

ABANDOIBARRA

RESTAURANTS
Aitxiar **17**
El Perro Chico **5**
Etxanobe **6**
Matxinbenta **11**
Nerua **1**
Víctor Montes **14**
Zortziko **12**

HOTELS
Gran Hotel Domine **2**
Hotel Carlton **10**
Iturrienea Ostatua **15**
Meliá Bilbao **4**
Miró Hotel **3**

ATTRACTIONS
Alhóndiga Bilbao **9**
Basílica de Begoña **19**
Catedral de Santiago **16**
Guggenheim Museum **1**
Iglesia de San Nicolás **13**
Museo Arqueológico de Bizkaia **18**
Museo de Bellas Artes **8**
Museo Marítimo Ría de Bilbao **7**

Museo Guggenheim Bilbao

Museo de Bellas Artes

El Palacio Euskalduna

Estación de La Concordia (FEVE)

Estación Abando Indalecio Prieto (RENFE)

Mercado de la Ribera

Teatro Arriaga

Madrid

Bilbao

0   200 yds
0   200 m

transformation of the riverfront and turned a provincial city of 355,000 into what Gehry has called a laboratory for contemporary architecture. Among architects, you're nobody until you have a building in Bilbao.

Bilbao continues to flourish as a banking and services center, long after most of the manufacturing has fled. At the same time, the city government has upgraded the transportation infrastructure, installing a new airport by Calatrava and an efficient and attractive Metro system. Its entrances are a futuristic version of the Paris Metro entrances; locals call the glass hoods *fosteritos* in deference to their designer, Sir Norman Foster.

Essentials

GETTING THERE **Bilbao Airport** (*℃* **90-240-47-04;** www.aena-aeropuertos. es) is 8km (5 miles) north of the city, near the town of Erandio. Flights arrive from Madrid, Barcelona, Alicante, Arrecife, Fuenteventura, Las Palmas, Málaga, Menorca, Palma, Santiago de Compostela, Sevilla, Tenerife, Valencia, Vigo, Brussels, Frankfurt, Lisbon, London, Manchester, Milan, and Paris. **Iberia**'s main booking office in Bilbao is at the airport (*℃* **90-240-05-00;** www.iberia. com). From the airport into town, take bus A3247 for 3.50€.

The **train** station, Estación de Abando (*℃* **90-232-03-20;** www.renfe. com), is on Plaza Circular 2, just off Plaza de España. From here, you can catch short-distance trains within the metropolitan area of Bilbao (Euskotren), medium-distance trains along the north coast (FEVE), and long-distance trains (RENFE) to most parts of Spain. Four trains per day run to and from Madrid on weekdays, two on weekends (5–6¼ hr.). Two trains per day run to and from Barcelona (trip time: 6¼ hr.), and one train per day goes to and from Galicia (trip time: 10½ hr.).

PESA, at the Estación de Buses de Garillano (*℃* **90-210-12-10;** www.pesa. net), operates more than a dozen **buses** per day to and from San Sebastián (trip time: 1¼ hr.). **Continental Auto,** Calle Gurtubay 1 (*℃* **90-242-22-42;** www.alsa. es), has nine buses per day from Madrid (trip time: 5 hr.). If you'd like to explore either Lekeitio (p. 457) or Gernika (p. 460) by bus, use the services of **Bizkaibus** (*℃* **90-222-22-65;** www.bizkaia.net). Fifteen buses per day go to Lekeitio Monday to Saturday and two on Sunday. Trip time is 45 minutes. Ten buses run each weekday to Gernika (trip time: 45 min.). On weekends, only five buses per day go to Gernika. For general bus information, call *℃* **94-439-50-77.**

Bilbao is on the A-8, which links the cities of Spain's northern Atlantic seacoast to western France. It is connected by superhighway to both Barcelona and Madrid.

VISITOR INFORMATION The **tourist office,** at Plaza Ensanche 11 (*℃* **94-479-57-60;** www.bilbaoturismo.net), is open Monday to Friday 9am to 2pm and 4 to 7:30pm. Depending on funding, it is also open weekends in the summer. **Satellite tourist offices** are located at the **Guggenheim Bilbao Museum** (no phone) and in the **old quarter at the Arriaga Theater** on Plaza Arriaga (no phone). They are both open daily.

SPECIAL EVENTS The biggest and most widely publicized festival is **La Semana Grande,** dedicated to the Virgin of Begoña and lasting from mid-August to early September. During the celebration, the Río Nervión is the site of many flotillas and regattas. July 25 brings the festival of Bilbao's patron saint, **Santiago (St. James);** July 31 is the holiday devoted to the region's patron saint, **St. Ignatius.**

Where to Stay in Bilbao

MODERATE

Gran Hotel Domine ★★ If you're going to Bilbao mainly to visit the Guggenheim, it's almost impossible to beat this whimsical, charming hotel located right next door. Iñaki Aurreroextea was tasked with a nearly impossible job: Make a hotel that looks good next to Gehry's museum without copying the form or style. He came up with a skin of polished stone and cantilevered black glass windows. Their odd angles echo the Guggenheim in a fractured plane of small reflections. Inside, each floor has a distinct color scheme in jewel and chocolatebox tones. We generally stay in less expensive interior rooms, which overlook the central atrium. The price is right and we enjoy the view of the Guggenheim from the rooftop terrace every morning at breakfast.

Alameda de Mazarredo 61. ℂ **94-425-33-00.** www.granhoteldominebilbao.com. 135 units. 110€–160€ double; 230€–570€ suite. Parking 20€. Metro: Moyúa. Bus: 38 or 48. **Amenities:** Restaurant; bar; exercise room; free Wi-Fi.

Hotel Carlton ★ Built in 1926 in a grand imperial style that recalled the previous century, this grande dame still features an over-the-top (literally) stained glass dome in the lobby. With 142 rooms on six floors and an array of meeting and ballrooms, it has long been the chosen venue for weddings and political functions. (The hotel actually housed the Basque government during the Civil War.) Owners managed to get the building declared a "historic, artistic, and cultural monument," and the sense of superiority unfortunately carries over to some of the staff.

Plaza de Federico Moyúa, 2. ℂ **94-416-22-00.** www.aranzazu-hoteles.com. 143 units. 87€–135€ double; 210€–275€ junior suite. Parking 24€. Metro: Moyúa. Bus: 38 or 48. **Amenities:** Restaurant; bar; exercise room; sauna; free Wi-Fi.

Meliã Bilbao ★ This giant pink skyscraper of a hotel stands on the Rio Nervión opposite the Euskalduna Palace. The work of Basque architect Ricardo Legorreta, the hotel was inspired by the site-specific sculptures of Eduardo Chillida (p. 455). The soaring lobby (40m/131 ft. high) is filled with large-scale contemporary art, as are many of the public rooms. All the bathrooms feature marble tubs, and guest rooms are oversized and well-equipped for both business and leisure travelers with power sockets on every wall. The hotel stands at one of the high points of the city, and most guest rooms have dramatic views.

Calle Lehendakari Leizaola, 29. ℂ **94-428-00-00.** www.melia-bilbao.com. 211 units. 126€–230€ double; from 295€ suite. Parking 23€. Metro: Moyúa. Bus: 13. **Amenities:** Restaurant; bar; exercise room; outdoor heated pool; sauna; Wi-Fi.

Miró Hotel ★ Almost as close to the Guggenheim as the Hotel Domine, the Miró is the signature hotel decorated by Spanish fashion designer Antonio Miró, who is to Spanish menswear what Calvin Klein is to American. The hotel exterior is a neo-Bauhaus checkerboard of gray steel and tinted glass, and the reserved style keeps the building from competing with the architecture of the Guggenheim. Inside, it's 21st-century minimalism all the way with black carpets on the floors and so much black marble in the bathroom that you'll want to turn on all the lights to see. Some rooms are a little tight on size, but suites have plenty of room to stretch out. Exterior rooms with a view of the Guggenheim fetch a premium price.

Alameda Mazarredo, 77. ℂ **94-661-18-80.** www.mirohotelbilbao.com. 50 units. 88€–137€ double; 155€–175€ suite. Parking 20€. Metro: Moyúa. **Amenities:** Bar; exercise room; room service; spa; free Wi-Fi.

INEXPENSIVE

Iturrienea Ostatua ★ There's no air-conditioning at this old-fashioned townhouse hotel in the old quarter, but thick walls with exposed oak beams and 19th-century solid stone floors keep the rooms from getting very hot, even in the middle of August. There is, however, heat available for the dank months of the year. Paintings and etchings of historic life in Bilbao cover the walls, and the furnishings and lighting were chosen by a pair of Basque sculptors. Rooms on the front can be noisy at night, since you'll likely want to leave the windows open for ventilation. The breakfast (always included) features natural foods.

Calle Santa María, 14. ✆ **94-416-15-00.** www.iturrieneaostatua.com. 21 units. 50€–70€ double. Metro: Casco Viejo. **Amenities:** Bar; free Wi-Fi.

Where to Eat in Bilbao

EXPENSIVE

Etxanobe ★★★ CONTEMPORARY BASQUE   Fernando Canales is a rock star among Bilbao chefs. Turn on any local food show and he's likely to pop up with his chiseled good looks to show viewers precisely how to make some avantgarde creation with three ingredients and a little magic. Yet somehow he finds time to run the kitchen in this sumptuous, post-modern glass dining room in the Palacio Euskalduna. Part of the secret to the terrific dishes is that Canales goes the extra mile to get the very best product. He counts as a personal friend the president of a Basque fishing brotherhood who can acquire ingredients that no one else has, like local goose barnacles (percebes). When other chefs lament the end of summer, Canales celebrates with a glorious menu he calls "the treasures of winter," starting with cauliflower and trout eggs on toast, then moving on to dishes employing different kinds of truffles, artichoke with saffron cream, baked rice and rabbit, a fish stew of winter species, braised partridge. . . . He's convinced there is always something good to eat, and he's ready to prove it.

Av. de Abandoibarra 4. ✆ **94-442-10-71.** www.etxanobe.com. Reservations required. Main courses 22€–38€; tasting menus 69€–85€. Mon–Sat 1:30–3:30pm and 8:30–11:30pm (Fri–Sat until midnight). Closed Aug 1–15.

Nerua ★★★ CONTEMPORARY BASQUE   It only took the prodigy chef Josean Alija a few months to win his first Michelin star at this elegant fine-dining venue in the Guggenheim Bilbao. Alija won accolades early in his career for creating prize-winning dishes like whipped milk-protein ice cream with candied violets, or roasted foie gras with candied carrots. Like many of the artists shown at the Guggenheim, Alija loves to confound expectation. Instead of serving roast pork with a leek sauce, he serves roast leek with an Iberian pork sauce and rice germ. To play off his famed foie gras, he makes a vegetarian version. His "simple" consommé turns out to contain little roasted cubes of foie gras, diced carrot, and anise, borage, and clams in a Parmesan infusion—dressed with truffle "tears" and croutons. To eat here is to enjoy dining as performance art. **Note:** The restaurant has a separate exterior entrance, but it can also be accessed from inside the museum next to the "The Matter of Time" constructions by Richard Serra.

Abandoibarra Etorbidea, 2. ✆ **94-400-04-30.** www.nerua.com. Reservations required. Main courses 22€–35€; tasting menu 70€. Tues–Sun 1:30–3:15pm; Wed–Sat 9–10:30pm. Closed 2 weeks at Christmas. Metro: Moyúa. Bus: 1, 10, 13, or 18.

Zortziko ★★★ CONTEMPORARY BASQUE   Chef Daniel Garcia elevates traditional Basque foodstuffs to a level of refinement not seen since the heyday of Escoffier. The main dining room of this beautiful and formal restaurant glitters in French Empire style, but Garcia's conceptual dishes and their execution are very much 21st century. Not content to simply roast wood pigeon, he presents a plate in five forms: roasted, confit, grilled, fried, and emulsified and frozen into an ice cream. He reimagines the Basque staple monkfish by roasting it, then serving it in a taco with a couscous of roasted cauliflower and dried fruit. For dessert, he proposes a gin and tonic juniper cream, blood orange jelly, and lemon granita.

Alameda de Mazarredo, 17. © **94-423-97-43.** www.zortziko.es. Reservations recommended. Main courses 25€–39€; fixed-price menus 50€–88€. Tues–Sat 1–3:30pm and 9–11:30pm. Metro: Abando.

MODERATE

El Perro Chico ★ BASQUE   One wonders when the "Little Dog" will repaint the blue walls said to have inspired Frank O. Gehry, as half the travelers who stop in come only to see the color. They'd be smarter to stick around and eat. If you choose to sit, by all means opt for a Basque classic like the oven roasted spider crab or the roasted hake *a pil pil.* If you're willing to stand, the choices are actually more imaginative, as El Perro Chico prides itself on *pintxos creativos*—bite-sized compositions that wow the eyes as well as the taste buds. The faux *angulas* (eels) are garlicky and delicious. Like many good places, you can simply point to order, perhaps asking *Que es?* (what is it?) before popping it into your mouth.

Calle Aretxaga, 2. © **94-415-05-19.** Reservations required for restaurant. *Pintxos* 4€–6€; main courses 14€–30€. Tues–Sat 1:30–3:30pm and 9:15–11:30pm.

Matxinbenta ★ BASQUE   Proudly serving excellent Basque fare for more than a half century, Matxinbenta remains particularly popular for the business lunch. The three dining rooms share a fresh, modern look with perhaps an excess of potted plants and last-generation modern furniture. Among the house specialties, the fresh bonito in tomato sauce has a zesty tang that stands out from the somewhat milder fish options like the flounder with fresh dill. Apart from the usual steaks and roast chicken, look for unusual meat choices like the goose drumstick roasted with herbs, or oxtail and sweetbreads stewed with mushrooms.

Calle Ledesma, 26. © **94-424-84-95.** http://matxinbenta.restaurantesok.com. Reservations required Fri–Sat. Main courses 15€–28€; daily menu 30€. Mon–Sat 1–4pm and 8–11pm; Sun 1–4pm. Metro: Moyúa.

INEXPENSIVE

Aitxiar ★ BASQUE   This Casco Viejo standby serves solid traditional Basque fare at bargain prices in an old-fashioned room with stone walls and exposed beams. In addition to standards like steak Wellington with foie gras, cod *a pil pil,* and oxtail braised in red wine, Aitxiar plays little tricks with some of the classics, like the grilled calamari with "crispy beards" served with potato and onion puree flavored with aioli. The roasted duck breast is browned on top and served with a port wine-chocolate sauce over yucca. The potato soup with cubes of fresh tuna is always good, as is the grilled foie gras over eggplant, zucchini, and grilled mushrooms.

Calle María Muñoz 8. © **94-415-09-17.** www.restauranteaitxiar.com. Main courses 11€–17€; fixed-price lunch 9€–25€. Tues–Sun 1–3:30pm and 8:30–11:30pm. Closed: 3 weeks in Aug. Metro: Plaza Unamuno.

Víctor Montes ★ BASQUE   Once you stumble into Plaza Nueva, it's hard to miss Victor Montes, which dominates the plaza with tables in good weather and has plenty of indoor seating in three packed dining rooms in back. And those are just for the sit-down diners, who swarm in for home-cooking favorites like fish and meat stews, and the myriad Basque preparations of different flaky white fish. Salads are copious and every plate comes with fresh vegetables. The bar has a grand selection of *pintxos* or *raciones*, ranging from simple tastes like Idiazabel cheese with walnut and honey to stewed meatballs to small plates of fried squid or cod nuggets.

Plaza Nueva, 8. *©* **94-415-70-67.** www.victormontesbilbao.com. Reservations recommended for full meals; not necessary for tapas bar. *Pintxos* from 1.50€, *raciones* from 4€′ main courses 10€–24€′ fixed-price menus 36€–50€. Daily 11am–11pm. Metro: Casco Viejo.

Exploring Bilbao

Even with all the cranes erecting new stadiums and skyscrapers along the riverbanks, Bilbao still feels very open, extending more than 8km (5 miles) along the valley of the Río Nervión. The shipyards and factories of the waterfront have been replaced with channeled banks, and a ribbon-like park stretches from the old quarter, **Bilbao La Vieja,** east of the modern commercial center around Gran Vía, all the way to the **Abandoibarra** barrio, which includes the Guggenheim. Under a master plan by architect Cesar Pelli, the waterfront was reshaped as a green, human-scale place. The elegant footbridge over the river near the Guggenheim, the **Pasarela Zubizuri,** summarizes the spirit of the new Bilbao. Designed by Santiago Calatrava, it is sinuous and monumental, yet it is for walkers, not vehicles.

Alhóndiga Bilbao ★ CULTURAL CENTER   French furniture and product designer Philippe Starck made his public debut as an architect by remaking this one-time Modernisme white elephant as Bilbao's cultural and sporting center. Opened in 1909 as a wine storage facility, the building was devastated by fire 10 years later. The shell of brick, iron, and concrete waited decades for this reincarnation before finally opening in 2010. The subterranean levels contain an exhibition gallery and a concert hall. Starck kept the ground level intentionally dark to encourage romantic trysts, and it is a forest of columns decorated in different whimsical motifs. They support brick and glass cubes containing a multimedia public library, a state-of-the-art gym, and a rooftop swimming pool. The Alhóndiga also has its own cafes, restaurants, and bars.

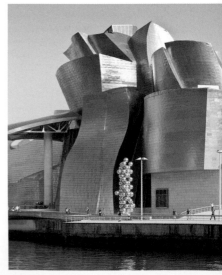

Plaza Arriquibar 4. *©* **94-401-40-14.** www. alhondigabilbao.com. Mon–Thurs 7am–11pm, Fri 7am–midnight, Sat 8:30am–midnight, Sun 8:30am–11pm. Free. 7€ per day to use gym or pool. Metro: Indautxu or Moyua.

Guggenheim Museum ★★★ ART MUSEUM   Skeptics said Bilbao would get a temporary bump in tourism from the curiosity factor as people came to see what Frank O. Gehry hath wrought on the once-industrial waterfront. Nearly 2 decades later, more than 1 million people each year visit

Frank O. Gehry's Guggenheim Museum.

THEY CALL IT puppy LOVE

Critics love to debate the merits of Frank O. Gehry's Guggenheim Bilbao Museum, but considering the museum in isolation misses the point. Bilbainos have embraced the surrounding plazas and made the pavements their own. Skateboard kids love the ramps and smooth-rolling runs, while soccer tykes kick balls against the walls. The greatest irony might be that Jeff Koons' goofy 43-foot-tall flower-sprouting puppy has almost upstaged the limestone and titanium building. Installed as a temporary exhibit for the 1997 opening, it was saved from demolition through a letter-writing campaign by local schoolchildren. The send-up of kitsch is now more or less permanent.

the museum, and the flow shows no sign of abating. The strange building seemingly assembled of gargantuan parts from a titanium-clad fish no longer seems so alien. In fact, it has become as iconic as Eiffel's tower in Paris. Admittedly, there's something appealingly primitive about the squat beast, best viewed from across the river so you can take it all in.

The interior is radical and often disorienting (the lack of right angles will do that), but the building is essentially a soaring 50m-high (164-ft.) atrium with exhibition floors cantilevered off a central support. Unless you've visited often, take the free audioguide when you enter, as it will explain how to navigate.

The Guggenheim Foundation has traditionally focused on major post-1950 artists, including Picasso, Robert Motherwell, Robert Rauschenberg, and Antoni Tàpies. The Bilbao branch has increasingly gone its own way, collecting and showing contemporary Basque art and favoring sculptors, painters, performance artists, and video artists who are still living and working. The Bilbao branch has also instituted a vigorous temporary exhibition schedule, often featuring avant-garde work from China, Korea, and Japan. Signage is trilingual—in Basque, Castilian, and English.

Calle Abandoibarra, 2. © **94-435-90-80.** www.guggenheim-bilbao.es. Admission prices vary by season. From July–Aug they are 13€ adults, 7.50€ seniors and students, free for children 11 and under; Sept–June 8€ adults, 5€ seniors and students. Bono Artean (joint admission to Museo de Bellas Artes and Guggenheim Bilbao) 14€. Sept–June Tues–Sun 10am–8pm; July–Aug daily 10am–8pm. Closed Jan 1 and Dec 25. Bus: 1, 10, 13, or 18. Metro: Moyúa, Tranvia: Guggenheim. If driving, park in the underground **Pio Baroja** garage accessed from Av. Abandoibarra.

Museo Arqueologica de Bizkaia ★★ MUSEUM When academics points out that the Basque language is unlike any other in Europe, Basque archaeologists counter that the Basques were living in northern Spain long before the Neolithic people who spoke proto-Indo-European ever set foot in Europe. This striking facility uses state-of-the-art museum display techniques to make the most of a handful of artifacts elucidating early Basque history. The exhibits vividly chronicle human habitation of the shores of the Bay of Biscay over the last 100,000 years, beginning with the carbon date for the earliest Neandertal fossils in the region. The artifacts and timelines carry through the arrival of Homo Sapiens and cave dwellers during the last Ice Age. They continue all the way up to around A.D. 900 and the first Basque kingdom.

Calzadas de Mallona, 2. © **94-404-09-90.** bizkaikoa.bizkaia.net. Tues–Sat 10am–2pm and 4–7:30pm, Sun 10:30am–2pm. 3€ adults, 1.50€ students and seniors, free under 12, free last Fri of month. Metro: Casco Viejo, Tranvia: Unamuno.

Museo de Bellas Artes ★★ ART MUSEUM   It's tempting to feel sorry for this fine arts museum, since the Guggenheim gets all the attention. But it's worth visiting for two reasons: First, its tidy linear organization by art historical category seems a reassuring return to order after the disorienting galleries of the Guggenheim. Second, it has a few outstanding pieces of art you'd be sorry to miss. Some big names of Spanish painting are represented by mostly minor works, including Velázquez, Zurbarán, El Greco, and Goya. But be sure to catch the Spanish Gothic painting and sculpture, with its images of suffering Christs, sad-eyed Madonnas, and otherworldly angels. Regional paintings from the early 20th century show both folkloric subjects and a striking sense of moral outrage, particularly about the mistreatment of miners and factory workers.

Plaza del Museo, 2. ✆ **94-439-60-60.** www.museobilbao.com. Admission 7€ adults, 5€ seniors and students, free for children 11 and under; free for all on Wed. Bono Artean (joint admission to Museo de Bellas Artes and Guggenheim Bilbao 14€. Wed–Mon 10am–8pm. Metro: Moyúa.

Museo Marítimo Ría de Bilbao ★ MUSEUM   You know that an industry is really finished when the city builds a museum about it. Bilbao was a great shipbuilding center on Spain's north coast since the beginning of the Industrial Revolution. Now it is a city about information and information technology, so this excellent maritime museum, built on the site of the last active shipyard, is a requiem for Bilbao's seagoing era. Outdoor exhibits display several restored historic vessels, and visitors can board them and let their imaginations run wild. Other exhibitions focus on the transformation of the riverfront into an amenity to be enjoyed by all.

Muelle Ramón de la Sota, 1. ✆ **94-608-55-00.** www.museomaritimobilbao.org. Admission 6€ adults, 3.50€ students and seniors, free under age 6. Oct–June Tues–Sat 10am–6pm and Sun 10am–8pm; July–Sept daily 10am–8pm. Metro: San Mamés (exit Sabino Arana). Tranvía: Euskalduna.

The Museo de Bellas Artes.

Bilbao's Old Quarter.

EXPLORING BILBAO LA VIEJA (OLD QUARTER) ★

Even though Bilbao was established around 1300, it has curiously few medieval monuments. It does have an intriguing, bar and restaurant filled Old Quarter on the east side of the Río Nervión.

The Old Quarter of Bilbao is connected to the much larger modern section on the opposite bank by four bridges. A few paces north of the Old Quarter's center are graceful arches, 64 in all, enclosing **Plaza Nueva,** also called the Plaza de los Mártires, completed in 1826. (Only in a city dating from 1300 could a square built in 1826 be called "new.")

The entire barrio has been declared a national landmark. Its most important church is **Iglesia de San Nicolás** (© 94-416-34-24), Plaza de San Nicolás, built in 1756 with a notable baroque facade. Behind the church you'll find an **elevator** on Calle Esperanza Ascao, which rises to the upper town. It is usually open daily from 10:30am to 12:30pm and 3:30 to 8pm. You can also climb 64 steps from the Plaza Unamuno. From here it's a short walk to the **Basilica de Begoña,** Calle Virgen de Begoña, 8 (© 94-412-70-91), built largely in the early 1500s. Inside the dimly lit church is a brightly illuminated depiction of the Virgen de Begoña dressed in long, flowing robes. The Virgin is the patron saint of Bizkaia and many boats are named for her. A long-standing custom calls for sailors to sing the "Salve Regina" when they spot the church tower as they return to port. Hours are daily 10:30am to 2pm and 5:30 to 8:30pm. While in the Old Quarter, you might visit the **Catedral de Santiago,** Plaza Santiago (© 94-432-01-25), which was built in the 15th century and dedicated to Bilbao's patron saint. The church is an important pilgrimage site and its neo-Gothic tower is said to demonstrate the "good taste of the cultured population of Bilbao." It is open daily 11am to 1pm and 4 to 6:30pm. On Sunday, a **flea market** starts at 8am on the streets of the Old Quarter.

To reach the Old Quarter on foot, the only way to explore it, take the Puente del Arenal from the Gran Vía, Bilbao's main street. From the Guggenheim Bilbao, hop the Tranvía to Pio Baroja or the Metro to Casco Viejo—or enjoy the walk down the riverfront promenade.

Shopping

Many visitors can't resist buying a beret in Basque Country. The best selection is found at **Sombrería Gorostiaga,** Calle Victor, 9 (© **94-416-12-76**), a family-owned business since 1854. If you'd like to purchase Basque artisanal products, one good option is **Basandere, Calle Iparraguirre,** 4 (© **94-423-63-86**) near the Guggenheim Museum. The shop also stages exhibitions by local artists and sells gourmet Basque food items.

Even if you are not a foodie, be sure to check out **Mercado de la Ribera,** Calle Ribera, s/n (© **94-602-37-91;** www.mercadodelaribera.net). The 1929 Art Deco–style building sits on the site of markets dating back to the 14th century, and is a marvel of decorative tile, brick, and glass. With more than 186 shops on three levels, it claims to be one of the largest markets in Europe. It is open Monday to Friday 8am to 2pm and 4:30 to 7pm, Saturday 8:30am to 2:30pm. From mid-June to mid-September, it is closed afternoons Monday to Thursday and Saturday.

Bilbao After Dark

Going out for drinks and *pintxos* is one of the chief forms of evening entertainment here. There is a good concentration of tapas bars on **Calle Licenciado Poza,** between Alameda del Doctor Areilza and Calle Iparraguirre, in the Ensanche neighborhood. **Plaza Nueva** in the Old Quarter is another good choice for bar-hopping. **Café Bar Bilbao,** Plaza Nueva, 6 (© **94-415-16-71;** www.bilbao-cafebar.com), has a classic look and serves two very traditional *pintxos* that are perfectly executed: fresh anchovies wrapped around green olives, and *bacalao al pil-pil.*

If you'd rather dance and mingle than eat, one of the most popular spots is **Cotton Club,** Calle Gregorio de la Revilla, 25 (© **94-410-49-51;** www.cotton clubbilbao.es), which bears little resemblance to its Harlem namesake. A DJ spins the latest tunes for a crowd in their 20s and 30s. The club is at its most frenzied on Friday and Saturday when it is open from 6:30pm to 6:30am. There is no cover; beer begins at 3€, whiskey at 6€.

The major cultural venue in Bilbao is the **Teatro Arriaga Antzoika,** Plaza Arriaga, 1 (© **94-479-20-36;** www.teatroarriaga.com), on the banks of the Río Nervión. This is the setting for world-class opera, classical music concerts, ballet, and even *zarzuelas* (comic operas). Announcements of cultural events are available at the tourist office. The **Gran Casino Bilbao,** Alameda Urquijo, 13, (© **94-424-00-07;** www.casinobilbao.es), combines slot machine parlors and table games (roulette, poker, black jack) with dining. The slot machine parlors are open Sunday to Wednesday 10am to 5am, Thursday to Saturday 10am to 6pm. The gaming room is open Sunday to Wednesday from 4pm to 5am, Thursday to Saturday from 4pm to 6am.

16

CANTABRIA
& ASTURIAS

C linging to the northern coast of Spain as a succession of coastal fishing villages, verdant lowlands, and high rolling hills and mountains, the autonomous regions of Cantabria and Asturias are united by geography and history. They are the core of "green Spain," flanked on the west by Galicia and the east by Basque Country. The high peaks and ridges of the Cordillero Cantábrico capture the moisture rolling off the Atlantic, dumping it on the green fields and mountain forests of Cantabria and Asturias.

Some of the earliest evidence of human habitation in Europe (as long ago as 140,000 years) has been found in the limestone caves of this region. When the Romans arrived they found thriving Celtic communities on the coast, and when the Moors came riding in, they were fiercely resisted by local Visigothic warlords.

Protected by the mountains, many Christians found refuge along this northern strip during the centuries of Moorish domination of lands farther south. By tradition, the Christian Reconquista began with the A.D. 722 Battle of Covadonga, led by the warrior Pelayo, later crowned king of Asturias. A great deal of religious architecture remains in the region, including a handful of country churches in a style between Gothic and Romanesque.

This chapter begins in Cantabria and works westward toward Asturias. It is a portion of Spain best seen by car, since connections between the coastal communities are not always convenient, and public transport is inadequate or nonexistent in the interior. **Santander,** a rail terminus and the regional capital, makes the best center for touring Cantabria; it also has the most tourist facilities. From Santander, you can get nearly anywhere in Cantabria within a 3-hour drive. To explore Asturias, the best base is its capital, **Oviedo.**

The most attractive portion of the Cordillera is the scenic and topographic summit known as the **Picos de Europa,** located mostly in Asturias but creeping over the border into Cantabria. In 1918 the region was made Spain's first national natural park.

SANTANDER ★

Santander, capital city of Cantabria, has always been a rival of San Sebastián in the east, but has never attained the premier status of that Basque resort. It did become a royal residence from 1913 to 1930, after city officials presented the English-style Magdalena Palace to Alfonso XIII. Don't expect much in the way of medieval ambience here, but there's plenty of more modern charm. After Santander was ravaged by a 1941 fire that destroyed the old quarter, it was rebuilt in a grand resort style with wide boulevards, a waterfront promenade, sidewalk cafes, restaurants, and hotels.

Many visitors to Santander head for **El Sardinero ★★**, a resort less than 2.5km (1½ miles) from the city center. Buses and trolleys make the short run

El Sardinero.

between downtown and the resort both day and night. Besides hotels and restaurants, the area has three main **beaches:** Playa de Castaneda, Playa del Sardinero, and Playa de la Concha. If they become too crowded, take a 15-minute boat ride to **El Puntal,** a beautiful beach that is rarely crowded, even in August. If you don't like crowds or beaches, go up to the lighthouse, a little more than 2km (1¼ miles) from El Sardinero, where the views are wide-ranging. A restaurant serves snacks both indoors and outdoors. Here, you can hike along the green cliffs or loll in the grass.

Essentials

GETTING THERE   Five to 10 daily **flights** from Madrid and Barcelona land at **Aeropuerto de Santander** (© **90-240-47-04;** www.aena-aeropuertos.es), a little more than 6.5km (4 miles) from the town center. It's accessible by taxi and costs 20€. Much cheaper is the regular bus service that runs between the airport and the train station (3€ one-way). The local office of **Iberia** is at the airport (© **90-240-05-00;** www.iberia.com).

There are four **trains** daily from Madrid (trip time: 4½–6 hr.); a one-way fare costs 50€. For national rail information, call © **90-232-03-20,** or visit www.renfe.com.

Buses are the best way to get to Santander from Bilbao or Oviedo, as the narrow-gauge FEVE trains have been curtailed. Buses arrive at Calle Navas de Tolosa (© **90-242-22-42;** www.alsa.es). There are 22 connections a day to and from Bilbao (trip time: 1½ hr.); a one-way ticket costs 14€.

VISITOR INFORMATION   The **tourist information office** is at Paseo Pereda (© **94-220-30-00;** www.ayto-santander.es). It's open September to June Monday to Friday 9am to 7pm, Saturday 10am to 7pm; Sunday 10am to 2pm; and July to August daily 9am to 9pm.

SPECIAL EVENTS   The **Festival Internacional de Santander** in August is one of the most important music and dance events in Spain. Occasionally, this festival coincides with religious celebrations honoring Santiago (St. James), the patron saint of Spain. For information, visit www.festivalsantander.com.

Where to Stay in Santander
IN TOWN
Abba Santander Hotel ★   All the rooms in this long-standing hotel have outside windows with good insulation so that guests can enjoy maximum light with minimum disturbance from street noise. The location near the bus and rail

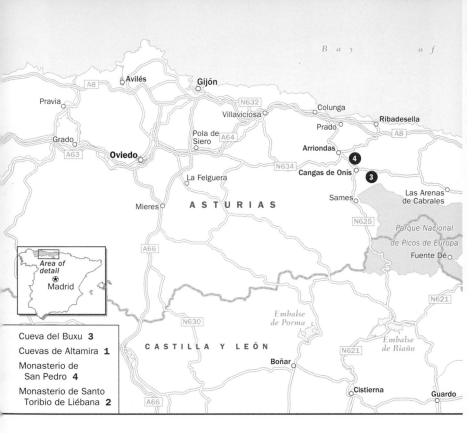

Bay of

Avilés
Gijón
Pravia
N632
Colunga
Villaviciosa
Prado
Ribadesella
A8
A8
Pola de
Siero
A64
Grado
Arriondas
A63
Oviedo
4
N634
Cangas de Onís
3
La Felguera
Las Arenas
de Cabrales
A S T U R I A S
Sames
Mieres
N625
Parque Nacional
de Picos de Europa
Fuente Dé
A66
N621

Area of
detail
Madrid

Embalse
de Porma
N630
Embalse
de Riaño
C A S T I L L A Y L E Ó N
N621
Boñar

Cueva del Buxu **3**
Cuevas de Altamira **1**
Monasterio de
San Pedro **4**
Monasterio de Santo
Toribio de Liébana **2**

A66
Cistierna
Guardo

---

stations is rather congested, but is a bonus for those without a car. Furnishings in the mid-size rooms are rather spare, but marble bathrooms add a touch of style. More importantly, the rooms are fresh and clean. Friendly staff is a big plus. They even arrange "room service" from a couple of local fast food restaurants for those who need a quiet evening.

Calle Calderón de la Barca, 3. ✆ **94-221-24-50.** www.abbasantanderhotel.com. 37 units. 59€–171€ double. Parking 6€. **Amenities:** Free Wi-Fi.

Hotel Bahía ★★   This long-time city social center received a makeover and reopened in 1999 to offer guests a more contemporary and relaxed sense of style. Liberal use of marble in the lobby sets the tone for the modern color schemes and traditional furnishings in the guest rooms, many of which have views of the ocean or of the cathedral. It's not right on the beach, but Bahia is convenient for exploring the waterfront and the old town and sits at the head of the Jardines de Pereda, a charming city park.

Av. Alfonso XIII, 6. ✆ **90-257-06-27.** www.hotelbahiasantander.com. 188 units. 77€–160€ double. Parking 16€. **Amenities:** Restaurant; bar; exercise room; spa; free Wi-Fi.

Hotel Central ★   It's hard to miss this bright blue hotel in the heart of the historic city center. The Beaux Arts building, a neighborhood landmark, has been modernized without losing its charm. Guest rooms feature simple, comfortable furnishings and several of them can be connected for families or a group of

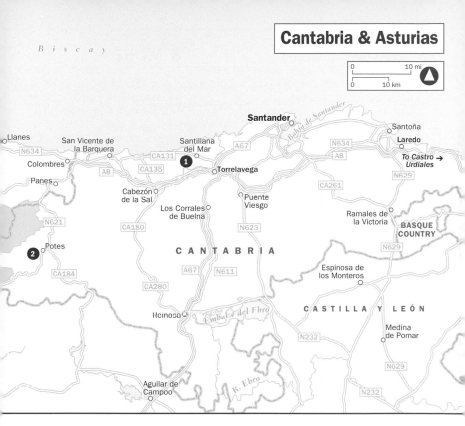

Biscay

Santander

Santoña

Llanes

San Vicente de
la Barquera

Santillana
del Mar

A67

N634

Laredo

Colombres

N634

CA131

To Castro →
Urdiales

Panes

A8

CA135

Torrelavega

A8

N629

Cabezón
de la Sal

Puente
Viesgo

CA261

Los Corrales
de Buelna

Ramales de
la Victoria

BASQUE
COUNTRY

N621

CA180

N623

CANTABRIA

N629

Potes

Espinosa de
los Monteros

CA184

A67

N611

CA280

CASTILLA Y LEÓN

Reinosa

Embalse del Ebro

Medina
de Pomar

N232

Aguilar de
Campoo

R. Ebro

N629

N232

---

friends. Some rooms have sea views, but all guests can enjoy the sun and the views from a lounge chair on the 6th-floor terrace.

Calle General Mola, 5. © **94-222-24-00.** www.elcentral.com. 41 units. 50€–160€ double; 80€–180€ suite. **Amenities:** Restaurant; bar; free Wi-Fi.

AT EL SARDINERO

Eurostars Hotel Real ★★★ Being part of a royal entourage can have its advantages. This gracious white hotel, located on beautifully landscaped grounds above Playa de los Peligros, opened in 1917 to accommodate the guests of King Alfonso XIII and his family on their annual summer vacations in Santander. Today's vacationers may not have the ear of the king, but they enjoy equally glamorous surroundings and impeccable service. All the spacious rooms have exterior views and sumptuous traditional furnishings that harmonize with modern technology and contemporary art. For even more relaxation, the old garages on the property have been renovated and converted into a thalassotherapy spa center. This is *the* address in Santander and one of the top properties in northern Spain.

Paseo Pérez Galdós, 28. © **94-227-25-50.** www.hotelreal.es. 123 units. 95€–250€ double; from 450€ suite. Free parking. Bus: 1, 2, or 7. **Amenities:** Restaurant; bar; exercise room; spa; free Wi-Fi.

Las Brisas ★ This 19th-century palace turned boutique hotel is a good option for travelers seeking an intimate property with lots of character. The white building with red tile roof makes a great first impression, and once inside you won't be

GAUDI'S summer palace **& MORE**

The town of Comillas lies 49km (30 miles) to the west of Santander and only a short drive to the west of Santillana del Mar. Its major attraction is **El Capricho de Gaudí,** Barrio de Sobrellano (© **94-272-03-65;** www.elcaprichodegaudi.com). The fabled Catalan architect, Antoni Gaudí, designed his summer palace in the Mudéjar Revival style. The tile-covered villa was built in 1883. The exterior is a marvel, but it's worth checking to see if it's open for tours at the time of your visit. The town also has the Modernisme **Palacio de Sobrellano** (© **94-272-03-39**) and **La Capilla Panteón,** designed by Catalan architects Joan Martorell and Josep Llimona y Agapit Vallmitjana, respectively, in the late 1870s. The exteriors are updated Gothic buildings—the magical modern details are all inside. Admission each to the palace and chapel is 3€. They are usually open for guided tours Tuesday to Sunday, but check first at the tourist office at Calle Joaquín del

Piélago, 1 (© **94-277-25-91;** www.comillas.es). The **town cemetery gates** (above the main beach) are a Modernisme masterpiece created in 1893 by Lluís Doménech i Montaner.

disappointed. Public areas and guest rooms feature a mix of antiques and traditional furnishings liberally enhanced with rich fabrics, art work, plants, and flowers. Each room is different, but each received a sleek new bathroom in 2011.

Calle la Braña, 14. © **94-227-01-11.** www.hotellasbrisas.net. 13 units. 39€–119€ double; 75€–150€ triple. Amenities: free Wi-Fi.

Sercotel Palacio del Mar ★ About two-thirds of the rooms in this modern mid-1990s hotel are junior suites that feature a separate sitting area and can accommodate up to five people. All rooms are fairly large and have clean-lined modern furnishings and a terrace or balcony. Guests have access to a nearby health club with pool, though the hotel does have its own lovely terrace for catching the sun.

Av. de Cantabria, 5. © **94-239-24-00.** www.hotel-palaciodelmar.com. 67 units. 60€–198€ double; 77€–215€ jr. suite. Free parking. **Amenities:** Restaurant; bar; access to nearby health club with pool; free Wi-Fi.

Where to Eat in Santander

Bodega del Riojano ★★ SPANISH The decor of this restaurant in an ancient wine cellar could not be more fitting. The walls are covered with the ends of wine barrels that have been signed and decorated by contemporary Spanish artists. In 2009, new ownership injected fresh energy into this well-established and respected restaurant. The wines may be, as the name suggests, mostly from La Rioja, but the cuisine is Cantabrian through and through. You can count on some highly regional dishes, like mackerel dumplings and plates of meatballs surrounded by steamed clams and prawns. The kitchen goes the extra mile to make dishes special, even marinating fresh strawberries in Armagnac to serve with puff pastry for a simple seasonal dessert.

Calle Río de la Pila, 5. ℂ **94-221-67-50.** www.bodegadelriojano.com. Main courses 14€–22€; set menus 29€–46€, minimum 4 people. Mon–Sat 1:30–4pm and 7:30pm–midnight, Sun 1:30–4pm. Closed Mon Sept–June.

El Serbal ★★★ CANTABRIAN   This elegant, contemporary restaurant is a top spot to enjoy fine food paired with fine wines. The wine cellar features about 500 bottles from 15 different countries and the menu is short and sweet. Cod *a pil pil* is found all along the coast, but El Serbal is the only place we know where artichokes, clams, and octopus find their way into the dish. The contrast of colors and textures makes it look almost too pretty to eat. The classic roast suckling pig gets an entirely novel treatment. It is roasted with oranges, then flambéed with peach liqueur, and served with a mound of chia seeds.

Calle Andrés del Río, 7. ℂ **94-222-25-15.** www.restaurantesdesantander.es. Reservations requi red. Main courses 23€–25€; 4-course menu 38€; 7-course menu 58€. Tues–Sat 1:30–4pm and 8:30–11:30pm. Closed Sun night, Mon and Feb 1–2. Bus: 7.

Zacarías ★ CANTABRIAN   Chef Zacarías Puente Herboso may have studied geology, business, and tourism, but food is his real passion and he relishes nothing more than seeking out the freshest fish and the finest artisanal cheeses to help highlight the cuisine of the Cantabrian coast and countryside. Most of the menu consists of lists of available fish and meat with prices given by the kilo. How it will be prepared is something you need to negotiate with your waiter. There are some "creations" on the menu, like scrambled eggs with Jabugo ham and roasted red peppers, or tagalog (a fish) roe with lobster, but dining here is really a celebration of great foodstuffs. Puente Herboso has written several books on Cantabrian cuisine (including one in English) that are available in the restaurant.

Calle Hernán Cortés, 38. ℂ **94-221-23-33.** www.restaurantezacarias.com. Main courses 15€–30€. Daily 1–4pm and 8pm–12:30am.

Exploring Santander

Biblioteca de Menéndez Pelayo ★ LIBRARY   Located in the same building as the art museum, this 50,000-volume library was amassed by historian/writer Marcelino Menéndez y Pelayo (1856–1912), Santander's most illustrious man of letters, and left to Santander upon his death in 1912. Guided tours are available. Nearby is the Casa Museo, which displays this great man's study and shows how modestly he lived.

Calle Rubio, 6. ℂ **94-223-45-34.** www.bibliotecademenendezpelayo.org. Free admission. Mon–Sat 9am–1:30pm and 4:30–9pm.

Catedral de Santa María de la Asunción ★ CATHEDRAL   Greatly damaged in the 1941 fire, this restored, fortress-like 13th-century cathedral holds the tomb of Menéndez y Pelayo (see above). The 12th-century **Capilla del Cristo** sits beneath the main church and consists of a trio of low-slung aisles that can be entered through the south portico. The Gothic cloister was restored after the fire. Roman ruins were discovered beneath the north aisle in 1983 and are visible through a glass floor.

Plaza José Equino Trecu, Somorrostro s/n. ℂ **94-222-60-24.** Free admission. Mon–Fri 10am–1pm and 4–7pm, Sat 10am–1pm and 4:30–8pm, Sun 10am–1:30pm and 7–9pm. Closed during Mass. Free guided visits July–Aug.

Museo de Arte Moderno y Contemporáneo de Santander y Cantabria ★ MUSEUM The former Museo de Bellas Artes has taken on a new identity and a new mission to stage exhibitions and installations of contemporary art of national and international interest, often featuring Cantabrian artists. The museum still displays its permanent collection, which does have works by some of the top names in Spanish art, including Goya and Zurburán. But, when visiting a regional museum it's always best to seek out more unique and local work. In this case, it's northern Spanish landscape paintings, many from the 19th and 20th centuries, that give a real feel for the Cantabrian coast and countryside.

Calle Rubio, 6. ℂ **94-220-31-20.** www.museosdesantander.com. Free admission. Tues–Sat 10am–1:30pm and 6–9pm, Sun 11am–1:30pm.

Museo Maritimo del Cantábrico ★★ MUSEUM When you're ready for a break from the beach, this engaging modern museum does a good job of tracing the importance of the sea to the history and economy of the region. Children will probably be most interested in the aquariums and interactive exhibits. That will give parents time to study the photographs, artifacts, and displays that trace Cantabria's 3,000 years as a shipping port.

Calle Muelle de San Martín, s/n ℂ **94-227-49-62.** www.museosdecantabria.com. 6€ adults, 4€ ages 4–12. May–Sept Tues–Sun 10am–7:30pm; Oct–Apr Tues–Sun 10am–6pm. Bus 1–4, 7, 13.

Santander After Dark

The most exciting thing to do in the evening is head for the gaming tables of the **Gran Casino Sardinero,** Plaza de Italia (ℂ **94-227-60-54;** www.grancasino-sardinero.es), which has a cover charge of 3€. The gaming room is open daily from 8pm to 4am; the slot machine parlor is open daily 2pm to 4am. Be sure to bring your passport for entry.

SANTILLANA DEL MAR & ALTAMIRA CAVES ★★
The Village of Santillana

Among the most perfectly preserved medieval villages in Europe, the Cantabrian town of **Santillana del Mar** is now a famous Spanish national landmark. A monastery houses the relics of Santa Juliana, an Asia Minor martyr who refused to surrender her virginity to her husband. The name Santillana is a contraction of "Santa Juliana." The "del Mar" is misleading, as Santillana is not on the water but inland. Jean-Paul Sartre called Santillana "the prettiest village in Spain," and we wouldn't want to dispute his esteemed judgment. Despite all the tour buses, Santillana retains its medieval atmosphere and is very much a village of dairy farmers to this day.

Santillana del Mar was the traditional base for visiting the **caves of Altamira** (see below), which contain some of the most famous Stone Age paintings in the world. The caves have been closed to protect them, but you can visit an amazingly faithful facsimile.

ESSENTIALS

GETTING THERE Autobuses La Cantábrica (ℂ **94-272-08-22**) operates four to seven **buses** a day from Santander but cuts back to four between September and June. Trip time is 45 minutes, and a one-way fare costs 9€. To drive, take the N-611 from Santander to the C-6316 cutoff to Santillana.

VISITOR INFORMATION The **tourist information office** is at Av. Escultor Jesús Otero 20 (℃ **94-281-88-12;** www.santillana-del-mar.com). It's open daily 9:30am to 1:30pm and 4 to 7pm.

WHERE TO STAY IN SANTILLANA

Moderate

Casa del Marqués ★★ For such a tiny place, Santillana del Mar has a lot of classy lodging, and this old manor house converted to a hotel is a terrific alternative to the two *paradors.* The foundations of the manor date from the 11th century, when this was a convent town, but the decor goes for generic antique. The exposed stone walls emphasize the antiquity of the structure. Exposed ceiling beams and broad wooden floors add to the effect. The staircase was carved in one piece from a 700-year-old oak tree when this version of the house was built in the 1440s. Guest rooms are comfortably furnished with rustic-looking furniture. The house is surrounded by lush gardens.

Calle Cantón, 26. ℃ **94-281-88-88.** www.hotelcasadelmarques.com. 15 units. 69€–144€ double; 159€–189€ suite. Parking 14€. Closed Jan–Mar. **Amenities:** Bar; free Wi-Fi.

Parador de Santillana Gil Blas/Parador de Santillana del Mar ★★★ If you want to stay in a 400-year-old noble house with all the attendant noble decor (including suits of armor), then book the Gil Blas. If you just want to stay in Santillana in comfort, choose the Parador Santillana del Mar, which was created for overflow from the historic building but looks like it has been on the same square for centuries. The price is a little lower in the newly built hotel, and we especially like the rooms with big windows opening onto the square. Rooms in the Parador Gil Blas are exceptionally large, but all the plumbing, heating, and wiring systems are quite old.

Plaza de Ramón Pelayo 11. ℃ **94-202-80-28** for Parador de Santillana Gil Blas; ℃ **94-281-80-00** for Parador de Santillana del Mar. www.parador.es. 56 units. Santillana del Mar: 90€–164€ double. Santillana Gil Blas: 100€–188€ double. Free parking. **Amenities:** Restaurant; bar; sauna; free Wi-Fi.

The medieval Santillana del Mar.

Inexpensive

Casa del Organista ★   Make your own romantic music at this 18th-century stone manse originally built for the organist at the Colegiata de Santillana. Lovingly restored by artisan stonemasons and carpenters who specialize in heritage buildings, the three-story structure still has wooden balconies hanging off the exterior and exposed wooden ceiling beams inside. The guest rooms are surprisingly ample for a building its age, and are furnished in a simple but warm style.

Calle Los Hornos, 4. ☏ **94-284-03-52.** www.casadelorganista.com. 14 units. 60€–93€ double. Free parking. **Amenities:** Bar; free Wi-Fi.

Hotel Altamira ★   With its exposed stone walls, broad wooden floors, and exposed beam ceilings, the Altamira can hold its own for historic ambience with any old hotel in town, *paradors* included. This was not a noble residence, but judging by the spacious stairways and large rooms, it was constructed for someone of considerable means. It also boasts a pretty good restaurant specializing in local dishes (see below).

Calle Cantón, 1. ☏ **94-281-80-25.** www.hotelaltamira.com. 32 units. 55€–100€ double. **Amenities:** Restaurant; bar; free Wi-Fi.

WHERE TO EAT IN SANTILLANA

Restaurante Altamira ★ CANTABRIAN   Noted for its Cantabrian specialties, this hotel-restaurant is the best place in town to eat a full meal. The menu emphasizes the inland dishes of the region, notably "meat of the pasture"—as in lamb, mutton, veal, and beef. The grasses are thick and nutritious around Santillana, and the local meat is outstanding. The different stews, known as *cocido,* are always a good bet. Unlike the Madrid version, they emphasize either a lot of fresh vegetables or a lot of legumes. The *cocido montañes* is a little richer and meatier, containing bacon, sausage, pork ribs, lots of shredded white cabbage, and the local white beans.

In the Hotel Altamira, Calle Cantón, 1. ☏ **94-281-80-25.** www.hotelaltamira.com. Main courses 12€–22€. Fixed-price menus 14€–17€. Daily 1:15–4pm and 8–11pm.

EXPLORING SANTILLANA

Wander on foot throughout the village, taking in its principal sites, including **Plaza de Ramón Pelayo** (sometimes called Plaza Mayor), which is dominated by the twin *paradors.*

A 15th-century tower, facing Calle de Juan Infante, is known for its pointed arched doorway. A walk along Calle de las Lindas (Street of Beautiful Women) will take you past many of the oldest buildings in Santillana and two towers dating from the 14th and 15th centuries. Calle del Río gets its name from a stream running through town to a central fountain.

Visit the 800-year-old church, **Colegiata de Santa Juliana** ★, Calle Santo Domingo (☏ **94-281-80-04**), which shelters the tomb of the village's patron saint, Juliana, and walk through its ivy-covered cloister. Among the treasures displayed are 1,000-year-old documents and a 17th-century Mexican silver altarpiece. It's open Tuesday to Sunday 10am to 1:30pm and 4 to 7:30pm. In winter, it closes at 6:30pm. The 3€ admission (1.50€ students and seniors) includes the Convent of Las Clarisas.

At the other end of the main street, the 400-year-old Convento de Regina Coelí, also called the **Convento de las Clarisas** (**Convent of the Poor Clares;** Museo Diocesano; ☏ **94-281-80-04**), houses a rich art collection inspired by a Madrid art professor who encouraged the nuns to collect and

Altamira isn't the only ancient cave in the region. At Puente Viesgo you can visit **El Castillo ★★★**, found at Carretera N623 Km 28, 27km (17 miles) from Santander (**© 94-259-84-25**). Lying in a medieval hamlet in the Pas Valley, this cave was excavated under the 350m (1,150-ft.) peak of the mountain, Monte del Castillo. Decorated by artists 15,000 years ago, the cave has several different sections. Admittedly, the art is not as advanced or concentrated as the works found at Altamira, but seeing the handprints, the clan marks, and the graceful images of deer, bison, and horses that must have seemed to dance in the flicker of firelight could make the hair stand up on the back of your neck. Small groups enter with a guide and must stay close, even in some of the palace-sized chambers. The caves are open April to October Tuesday to Sunday 9am to noon and 3 to 6:30pm; November to March, hours are Wednesday to Sunday 9am to 2pm. Admission is 3€ for adults, 1.50€ for children 4 to 12. Since numbers of visitors are strictly limited, you can save yourself some heartache by reserving admission at a particular date and time at http://cuevas.culturadecantabria.com.

restore religious paintings and statues damaged or abandoned during the Spanish Civil War. The collection is constantly expanding. The convent is open Tuesday to Sunday 10am to 1:30pm and 4 to 8pm (until 6:30pm in winter). If you didn't visit the Colegiata, admission is 3€, 1.50€ students and seniors.

The Altamira Caves

About 2.5km (1½ miles) from Santillana del Mar are the **Cuevas de Altamira,** famous for prehistoric paintings dating from the end of the Ice Age. The cave paintings at Altamira are ranked among the finest prehistoric paintings ever discovered, and, as a result, they are often called the "Sistine Chapel of prehistoric art." These ancient depictions of bison and horses, painted vividly in reds and blacks on the caves' ceilings, were not discovered until the late 19th century. Once their authenticity was established, scholars and laypersons alike flocked to see these works of art, which provide a fragile link to our remote ancestors. Bacteria from visitors caused severe damage, so the Research Center and Museum of Altamira is no longer open to the public.

The **Museo de Altamira ★★** (**© 94-281-80-05;** museodealtamira.mcu. es) is located not far from the original caves. (Authorities are vague to discourage vandals.) Altamira's main cave chambers are painstakingly recreated with computerized digital-transfer technology. The result is that the faux cave has every crack, bump, and hollow of the original. The paintings of 21 bison in iron oxide pigment are perhaps the highlight. The modern museum exhibits go into considerable detail about the lives of the people who made this art. The museum is superb, but it does fall short of the magic of seeing one of these ancient caves — like El Castillo (below)—in person.

If you don't have a car, you have to walk from Santillana del Mar, as there is no bus service. From spring to fall, however, it's a pretty stroll past long green pastures filled with grazing milk cows. From May to October, hours are Tuesday to Saturday 9:30am to 8pm, and Sunday 9:30am to 3pm. November to April, hours are Tuesday to Saturday 9:30am to 6pm, and Sunday 9:30am to 3pm.

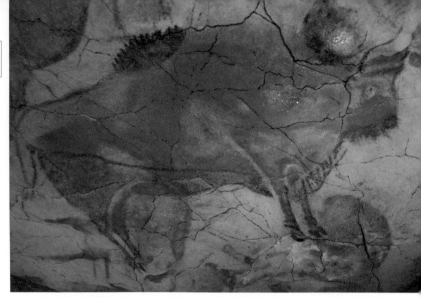

A prehistoric painting at the Cuevas de Altamira.

Admission is 3€ for adults, 1.50€ for students, and free for those 18 and under and seniors. Admission is free to all on Saturday and Sunday after 2:30pm. The center is closed January 1 and 6, May 1, and December 24, 25, and 31.

LOS PICOS DE EUROPA ★★★

These mountains are technically part of the Cordillera Cantábrica, which runs parallel to the northern coastline of Spain. The narrow green band known as Los Picos de Europa is clearly the most dramatic segment. They are the most famous and most legend-riddled mountains in Spain. Rising more than 2,590m (8,500 ft.), they are not high by alpine standards, but their proximity to the sea and sheer vertical drop makes their height all the more impressive. Romans constructed a north-south road whose stones are still visible in some places, but during the Middle Ages, the mountains were passable only with great difficulty. The abundance of wildlife (including some endangered species), dramatic rocky heights, and the medieval battles that took place in the hills all contribute to the legends and myths of the principality of Asturias.

As you tour the Picos de Europa, be on the lookout for some rare **wildlife.** On the beech-covered slopes of these mountains and in gorges laden with jasmine, you might spot the increasingly rare Asturcón, a shaggy, rather chubby wild horse so small it first looks like a toy pony. Another endangered species is the Iberian brown bear. The park is also home to the sure-footed chamois goat, rare butterflies, peregrine falcons, buzzards, and golden eagles. All wildlife is strictly protected by the government.

If you **hike** in this region, be prepared. Many slopes are covered with loosely compacted shale, making good hiking boots essential. Inexperienced hikers should stick to well-established paths. In summer, the weather can get hot and humid, and sudden downpours sweeping in from the coastline are common in any season. Hiking is not recommended between October and May.

The best way to see this region is **by car.** Most drivers arrive in the region on the N-621 highway, heading southwest from Santander, or on the same highway northeast from the cities of north-central Spain (especially León and Valladolid). This highway connects many of the region's best vistas in a straight line. It also defines the region's eastern boundary. If you're driving east from Oviedo, you'll take the N-632, coming first to Cangas de Onís.

Bus travel is much less convenient but possible if you have lots of time. The region's tourist hubs are the towns of Panes and Potes; both have bus service (two buses per day in summer, one per day in winter) from Santander and León (one bus per day in summer). The same buses come to Panes and Potes from the coastal town of Unquera. From Oviedo, there are two buses daily to the district's easternmost town of Cangas de Onís; they continue a short distance farther southeast to Covadonga. Within the region, a small local bus runs once a day, according to an erratic schedule, along the northern rim of the Picos, connecting Cangas de Onís with Las Arenas.

Exploring the Region

If you have a car, the number and variety of tours in this region are almost endless, but for this guide, we have devised three driving tours that form a loop. Any of them, with their side excursions, can fill an entire day; if you're rushed and omit some of the side excursions, you can spend a half-day.

DRIVING TOUR 1: **PANES TO POTES** ★★

DISTANCE: **29km (18 miles); 45 minutes**

Except for one optional detour, this drive extends entirely along one of the region's best roads, N-621, which links León and Valladolid to Santander. The drive is most noteworthy for its views of the ravine containing the Deva River, a ravine so steep that direct sunlight rarely penetrates it.

About two-thirds of the way to Potes, signs point you on a detour to the village of:

1 Liébana

This village is .8km (½ mile) off the main road. Here you'll find the church of Nuestra Señora de Liébana, built in the 10th century in the Mozarabic style. Some people consider it the best example of Arabicized Christian architecture in Europe, with Islamic-inspired geometric motifs. If it isn't open, knock at the door of the first house you see as you enter the village; it's the home of the guardian, who will unlock the church if she's around. For this, she will expect a tip. If she's not around, content yourself with admiring the church from the outside.

Return to N-621 and continue another 5.6km (3.5 miles) to Tama. Watch for turnoff to Centro de Visitantes de Sotama.

2 Centro de Visitantes Sotama

This state-of-the-art **visitors center** (✆ 94-273-05-55; www.mma.es) is filled with life-size photos and striking sound effects that bring the mountains of the Picos de Europa alive. You will feel like you are hiking the trails and encountering the wildlife. An excellent section on cave life makes the Ice Age seem like yesterday. The center is open daily 9am to 6pm (July–August until 8pm). Admission is free.

Fuente Dé.

Continue another 3.4km (2 miles) to reach the village of:

3 Potes

This is a charming place with well-kept alpine houses against a backdrop of jagged mountains.

Three kilometers (1¾ miles) southwest of Potes, near Turiano, stands the:

4 Monasterio de Santo Toribio de Liébana

The monastery dates from the 17th century. Restored to the transitional Romanesque style it enjoyed at the peak of its vast power, it contains what is reputed to be a splinter from the True Cross, brought from Jerusalem in the 8th century by the bishop of Astorga. The monastery is also famous as the former home of Beatus de Liébana, the 8th-century author of *Commentary on the Apocalypse,* one of Spain's most famous ecclesiastical documents. Ring the bell during daylight hours, and one of the brothers will let you enter if you are dressed respectfully.

Drive the 19km (12-mile) winding and beautiful road west from Potes, following the path of the Río Deva to the:

5 Parador de Fuente Dé

You can spend the night here (p. 489) or just stop for lunch.

6 Fuente Dé

Only a few hundred meters beyond the *parador,* a **teleférico,** the third-largest cable-car system in the world (© **94-273-66-10;** www.cantur.com), carries you 800m (2,625 ft.) up to an observation platform above a wind-scoured rock face. The cable car operates July to August daily 9am to 8pm, September to June daily 10am to 6pm. A one-way fare costs 10€; round-trip is 16€. At the top you can walk 5km (3 miles) along a footpath to the rustic **Refugio de Aliva** (© 94-273-09-99), open between June and September 15. Double rooms cost 80€. If you opt for just a meal or a snack at the hostel's simple restaurant, remember to allow enough time to return to the *teleférico* before its last trip down.

DRIVING TOUR 2: **POTES TO CANGAS DE ONÍS** ★

DISTANCE: **85km (53 miles); 2 hours**

This tour includes not only the Quiviesa Valley and some of the region's most vertiginous mountain passes, but also some of its most verdant fields and most elevated pastures. You might stop at an occasional village, but most of the time you will be going through deserted countryside. Your route will take you through several tunnels and high above mountain streams set deep into gorges. The occasional belvederes along the way always deliver on their promise of panoramic views.

The village of Potes (see "Driving Tour 1," above) is your starting point. Take N-621 southwest to Riaño. At Riaño, turn north for a brief ride on N-625. Then take a winding route through the heart of the region by driving northwest on N-637. Although it's beautiful all along the way, the first really important place you'll reach is:

1 Cangas de Onís

This is the westernmost town in the region, where you can get a hotel room and a solid meal after a trek through the mountains. It serves as base camp for many hiking and climbing expeditions into the mountains and has a wealth of guides and outfitters along its main street. The biggest attraction in Cangas de Onís proper is an ivy-covered **Roman bridge,** lying west of

The Roman Bridge in Cangas de Onis.

the center, spanning the Sella River. Also of interest is the **Capilla de Santa Cruz,** immediately west of the center. One of the earliest remaining Christian sites in Spain, it was originally constructed in the 8th century over a Celtic dolmen and rebuilt in the 15th century.

About 1.5km (1 mile) northwest of Cangas de Onís, beside the road leading to Arriondas, stands the:

2 Monasterio de San Pedro

This is a Benedictine monastery in the village of **Villanueva.** The church that you see was originally built in the 17th century, when it enclosed the ruins of a much older Romanesque church. It has some unusual carved capitals showing the unhappy end of the medieval King Favila, supposedly devoured by a Cantabrian bear.

DRIVING TOUR 3: CANGAS DE ONÍS TO PANES ★★

DISTANCE: **56km (35 miles); 1 hour**

This tour travels along the relatively straight C-6312 from the western to the eastern entrance to the Picos de Europa region. A number of unusual excursions can easily stretch this into an all-day outing.

From Cangas de Onís (see "Driving Tour 2," above), head west about 1.6km (1 mile). You'll reach the turnoff to:

1 Cueva del Buxu

Inside the cave are a limited number of prehistoric rock engravings and charcoal drawings, somewhat disappointingly small. Only 25 people per day are allowed inside (respiration erodes the drawings). It's open Wednesday to Sunday at 10:30am, 11:30am, 12:30pm, 3:15pm, and 4:15pm. Advance reservation is essential and must be made by telephone (© **60-817-54-67**) Wednesday to Sunday between 3 and 5pm. Admission is 3€ adults, 1.50€ ages 7 to 12 and over 65.

Some 6.5km (4 miles) east, signs point south in the direction of:

2 Covadonga

Revered as the birthplace of Christian Spain, Covadonga is about 9.5km (6 miles) off the main highway. A battle here in A.D. 722 pitted a ragged band of Christian Visigoths against a small band of Muslim soldiers. The resulting victory established the first niche of Christian Europe in Moorish Iberia, and the leader of the Goths, Pelayo, was crowned

The basilica in Covadonga.

La Santa Cueva.

The blue-veined cheese of Cabrales.

king. The town's most important monuments are **La Santa Cueva ★★**, a cave containing the sarcophagus of Pelayo (d. 737), king of the Visigothic Christians, in a slot tomb; and an enormous neo-Romanesque basilica, built between 1886 and 1901, commemorating the Christianization of Spain. At the end of the long boulevard that funnels into the base of the church stands a statue of Pelayo.

Return to the highway and continue east. You'll come to the village of Las Estazadas; then after another 11km (6¾ miles) you'll reach:

3 Las Arenas de Cabrales

Note that some maps refer to this town simply as Arenas. This is the headquarters of a cheese-producing region whose Cabrales, a blue-veined cheese made from ewes' milk, is avidly consumed throughout Spain. Stop at any of the bars here to sample some Cabrales with the local hard cider. You can also see how it is made in the exhibition center at the **Cueva del Queso ★** (*✆* **98-584-51-23;** www.fundacioncabrales.com), Barrio Pares s/n. The Cueva is open May through August 10am to 2pm and 4 to 8pm, September to April on weekends only. Tours begin quarter after the hour and cost 4.50€ adults, 2€ children.

Drive 5km (3 miles) south from Arenas, following signs to the village of:

4 Puente de Poncebos

This is shown on some maps simply as Poncebos. This village is several miles downstream from the source of Spain's most famous salmon-fishing river, the Río Cares, which flows through deep ravines from its source near the more southerly village of Caín.

Beginning at Poncebos, a footpath has been cut into the ravine on either side of the Río Cares. It is one of the engineering marvels of Spain, known for centuries as the **Divine Gorge.** It crosses the ravine many times over footbridges and sometimes through tunnels chiseled into the rock face beside the water, making a hike along the banks of this river a memorable outing. You can climb up the riverbed from Poncebos, overland to the village of Caín, a total distance of 11km (6¾ miles). Allow between 3 and 4 hours. At Caín, you can take a taxi back to where you left your car in Poncebos if you don't want to retrace your steps.

After your trek up the riverbed, continue your drive to the village of:

5 Panes

This village lies at a distance of 23km (14 miles) to the eastern extremity of the Picos de Europa.

Where to Eat & Stay in the Region

Once you leave Cangas de Onís, lodging options are very limited in these mountain towns. If you're planning an overnight stop, make sure you have a reservation. Directly north of Cangas de Onís, the unprepossessing little village of Arriondas has not one but two Michelin-starred restaurants. Nowhere in the Picos de Europa area can you dine so well as you can here.

IN ARRIONDAS

Casa Marcial ★★★ CREATIVE ASTURIAN   Londoners might know chef Nacho Mendez for his pair of Ibérico restaurants in the British capital, but to find such a culinary genius in this remote mountain town is a delightful surprise. The restaurant occupies the old farmhouse in the hilly country north of town where Mendez was born and grew up. His parents used to operate a small traditional Asturian restaurant on premise. Since their son took over, it's become a mountain pilgrimage site for Spanish gourmands. Yes, he still serves a remarkably traditional *fabada*—Asturian pork and beans—but in a small portion with the beans still toothy and topped with a drizzle of very green olive oil. Lighter fare is where he shines, whether it's the cold cucumber soup poured over green pepper sorbet, local salmon sauced with melon gazpacho, or roast woodcock with oysters and mountain eels. Most diners opt for one of the three menus: a 7-course menu of traditional Asturian dishes, a 7-course classic *dégustación* menu, or the 10-course gastronomic menu where Mendez pulls out all the stops and serves his latest inventions.

Carretera AS-342, La Salgar, 10, 4.5km (2¾ miles) north of Arriondas. ✆ **98-584-09-91.** www.casamarcial.com. Reservations required. Main courses 32€–39€. Fixed-price menus 49€–105€. Tues–Sat 1–4pm and 9–11:30pm; Sun 1–4pm. Closed 5 weeks in Jan–Feb (dates vary).

El Corral del Indianu ★★★ CREATIVE ASTURIAN   Gastronomic pilgrims also beat a path to the door of Chef José Antonio Campoviejo, who is something of a self-styled madman with wild hair and a penchant for reimagining traditional Asturian flavors in new ways. He glazes the local organically raised veal with whiskey, herbs, and mushrooms, and he turns paella rice into Asian-style sticky rice with sautéed vegetables, meats, and local kelp. Asturian cooking has never been considered anything but hearty. It is a cuisine of fatty meats, strongly flavored fish, and lots and lots of beans. But in Campoviejo's hands, it becomes light and even delicate, with dishes like a *salmorejo* of wild strawberries and local heavy cream, or a shot glass–sized serving of *fabada* with perfect white beans enrobed with liquefied bacon and puréed cabbage and topped with a thin slice of raw onion and tiny cubes of blood sausage. The restaurant has a rustic yet modern dining room, as well as a glass-enclosed room that enjoys views of the patio gardens. The a la carte menu is brief, but most diners come for the 10-course tasting menu, which changes with Campoviejo's whims.

Av. de Europa, 14. ✆ **98-584-10-72.** www.elcorraldelindianu.com. Reservations required. Main courses 27€–31€. Tasting menu 77€. Fri–Wed 1:30–4pm; Fri–Sat and Mon–Tues 9–11pm.

Unlike the rest of Spain, Asturias does not make wine. But it does have wonderful apple orchards and excels at making hard cider, or **sidra.** It is the perfect accompaniment to most Asturian cuisine, especially the tangy blue Cabrales cheese. Cider is fermented exceptionally dry from rather tart apples. It should be poured with the bottle raised a meter (3 ft.) above the glass to oxygenate the brew. When you order *sidra*, you get a theatrical show with the drink.

IN CANGAS DE ONIS

Hotel Aultre Naray ★   Steps away from the Roman bridge, this country house built in 1873 is a great example of the stone masonry of the area. Inside, it's a display case of contemporary Madrileño interior design. Rooms are spacious enough and each has a tiled bathroom. Because Cangas de Onís is strategically located at the foothills of the Sierra Escapa, this hotel is favored by sportsmen who flock to the area for fly-fishing, canoeing, and hiking in the mountains.

Calle Peruyes, s/n. ✆ **98-584-08-08.** www.aultrenaray.com. 10 units. 70€–100€ double; 113€–163€ family room for 4. Free parking. **Amenities:** Restaurant; bar; free Wi-Fi.

La Palmera ★ ASTURIAN   Located by the river on the road heading east from Cangas de Onís to Covadonga, La Palmera serves rib-sticking Asturian cuisine at prices far lower than the mountain lakes area just a few miles up the road. The cooking is all about the bounty of the Asturian mountains, so look for excellent grilled beef steak, slow-roasted leg of lamb, and several versions of the local Atlantic salmon and trout. The owners support local farmers by carrying their farmstead cheeses—far less pungent than Cabrales, but delicious nonetheless.

Soto de Cangas s/n, La Rotunda. ✆ **98-594-00-96.** Main courses 12€–22€. Wed–Mon 10am–11pm. Closed Aug.

IN COSGAYA

Hotel del Oso ★   You're really in the countryside by the time you reach Cosgaya, so it's a treat to encounter the Hotel of the Bear next to the Río Deva in the Liébana valley. The rooms are small and feature just a bed or two and a chair and table, but they all have modern private baths. Two-thirds of the rooms are in the main building, the remainder in a small annex. The main building also has the restaurant, Mesón del Oso, which serves big portions of local cooking. In season, the best dishes on the menu feature trout from the river outside the door. Grilled steak with Cabrales cheese sauce is also a specialty. Desserts are all homemade; you can't go wrong with any of the tarts made with local fruits.

Carretera Potes–Fuente Dé, Km 14. ✆ **94-273-30-18.** www.hoteldeloso.com. 50 units. 71€–86€ double. Free parking. **Amenities:** Restaurant; bar; outdoor pool; outdoor tennis court; free Wi-Fi. Restaurant main courses 10€–24€. Daily 1–3:45pm and 9–10:45pm. Closed Jan 7–Feb 15. From Potes, take the road signposted to Espinama 15km (9⅓ miles) south.

IN FUENTE DÉ

Parador de Fuente Dé ★★   This modern mountain lodge attracts a clientele more interested in the mountains than in being pampered at a *parador*. It sits literally at the end of the road to Fuente Dé; to continue on into the mountains, you have to take the cable car (p. 484) to the ridgeline. There are two wings, with somewhat smaller rooms in the older wing, but even those are spacious enough to spread out a bit. In the summer, rooms are often filled with people who have come to hike in the mountains, or those who have come to climb and bring all their technical gear. In the fall, the *parador* is very popular with hunters, as the hills are full of wild game.

At Km 3.5 de Espinama. ✆ **94-273-66-51.** www.parador.es. 77 rooms. 65€–85€ double. Free parking. Closed Dec–Feb. Drive 26km (16 miles) west of Potes. **Amenities:** Restaurant; bar; free Wi-Fi.

GIJÓN

The major port of Asturias and its largest city is a summer resort and an industrial center rolled into one. As a port, Gijón (pronounced Hee-*hohn*) is said to predate the Romans. The Visigoths ruled here, and in the 8th century the Moors wandered through but never took possession of the area.

Essentials

GETTING THERE Gijón doesn't have an airport, but **Iberia** flies to the airport at Santiago del Monte, Ranón (✆ **90-240-05-00;** www.iberia.com), 42km (26 miles) away, a facility it shares with Oviedo-bound passengers.

Gijón has good rail links and makes a good gateway into Asturias. High-speed **RENFE Alvia trains** (✆ **90-232-03-20;** www.renfe.com) arrive from Madrid in 5½ to 6 hours; the one-way trip costs 51€ to 54€. There is also twice-daily service from Oviedo. The trip takes 35 minutes from Oviedo to Gijón; a one-way ticket costs 3.60€.

There is frequent **bus service** (✆ **90-242-22-42** for information). Fifteen buses per day arrive from Madrid, taking 5½ hours and costing 53€ one-way. There is also service from Bilbao at the rate of 10 buses per day; the one-way trip takes 5 hours and costs 31€. Service is every hour from Oviedo; the one-way trip takes only an hour and costs 3€.

Driving from Santander in the east, head west along the N-634. At Ribadesella, you can take the turnoff to the N-632, the scenic coastal road to Gijón. To save time, continue on N-634 until you reach the outskirts of Oviedo, and then cut north on A-66, the express highway to Gijón.

VISITOR INFORMATION The **tourist information office** is at Calle Rodríguez San Pedro (✆ **98-534-17-71;** www.gijon.info). It's open in summer daily 10am to 10pm, off-season daily 10am to 2:30pm and 4:30 to 7:30pm. Visit the website for the excellent downloadable app for iOs and Android that covers more than 100 points of interest.

Where to Stay in Gijón

MODERATE

Hotel Hernán Cortés ★ Gijón's leading downtown hotel is just about midway between the harbor and Playa San Lorenzo, making it fairly convenient. It was renovated in 2009, and some rooms and suites have been given rather luxurious makeovers since. These rooms are a bargain, since they tend to have space for extra beds if you're traveling with children, and some of the suites have large lounges with an extra sofa bed. The hotel does not have its own restaurant, but there is a breakfast room. Moreover, the Casino de Asturias and its Restaurante-Cafetería As de Picas share the imposing neoclassical building, so you can get a bite to eat any time before midnight.

Calle Fernández Vallín, 5. ✆ **98-534-60-00.** www.hotelhernancortes.es. 60 units. 42€–180€ double; 74€–210€ suite. Bus: 4 or 11. **Amenities:** Bar; free Wi-Fi.

Parador de Gijón (Parador Molino Viejo) ★★ Local color abounds at this charmingly old-fashioned hotel with an 18th-century cider mill at its core. It sits right in the middle of the Parque Isabel la Católica, a 10-minute stroll from the town center. Gardens wrap around the hotel, and a colony of swans makes its home in the stream running through the landscape. The rooms are quite modest but atmospheric with heavy wooden furniture, shutters on the deep windows, and broad wooden floors.

Parque Isabel la Católica, s/n. ℂ **800/223-1356** in the U.S., or 98-537-05-11. www.parador.es. 40 units. 75€–125€ double. Free parking. Bus: 4 or 11. **Amenities:** Restaurant; bar; children's center; free Wi-Fi.

INEXPENSIVE

La Casona de Jovellanos ★ This 18th-century building once housed the Asturian Royal Institute of Marine Life and Mineralogy, established here in 1794 by the author Jovellanos. It is a boxy structure, often renovated over the centuries, but hardly grand. When it was built, it stood on the site where Gijón still had fortifications against pirates. Rooms are small but attractive, and the hotel is within easy walking distance of the yacht harbor and the beach.

Plaza de Jovellanos, 1. ℂ **98-534-12-64.** www.lacasonadejovellanos.com. 13 units. 54€–81€ double. Bus: 4 or 11. **Amenities:** Restaurant; bar; free Wi-Fi.

Where to Eat in Gijón

Casa Tino ★ ASTURIAN The Tino for whom the restaurant is named started in the trade as a waiter in 1940 and founded this restaurant in 1965 on a nearby street. (It moved here in 1969.) Pictures of Tino and his co-workers and friends are all over the walls, signaling before you even look at the menu that this is a friendly, family operation where they prize their customers. The menu is filled with Asturian and general Spanish home-cooking dishes like braised pig's feet with roasted potatoes, big meatballs simmered in gravy, and fish chowders with large pieces of hake, turbot, or cod.

Calle Alfredo Truan, 9 ℂ **98-513-84-97.** www.restaurantecasatino.com. Main courses 6€–18€. Daily menu 15€. Mon–Sat 1:15–3:30pm and 8:45–11:30pm. Bus: 4 or 11.

Auga ★★ ASTURIAN This spectacular contemporary restaurant is perfectly situated to get the top of the catch. It literally sits at the end of a pier in the middle of the harbor. The indoor dining room has wood floors and ceilings, but whenever the weather permits, most diners prefer to sit out on the terrace to eat and watch the boats. Chef Gonzalo Pañeda began his career as a pastry chef (his desserts are still fabulous). He was converted to the savory side of the kitchen after eating at Akelaŕe (p. 450) in San Sebastián and left a resort job to found his own place. He has since won a Michelin star of his own for his imaginative market dishes. He has an uncanny ability to combine flavors not usually associated with each other. For example, he serves seared scallops with shavings of black truffle, green apple, and cauliflower. He roasts sea bass with lime zest on a bed of mushrooms and onions. All the plates are beautifully presented.

Calle Claudio Alvargonzález, s/n. ℂ **98-516-81-86.** www.restauranteauga.com. Main courses 25€–29€; tasting menu 65€. Mon and Wed–Sat 1–3:30pm; Mon–Sat 8:30–11pm. Closed mid-Dec to mid-Jan. Bus: 10.

Exploring Gijón

The most interesting quarter of Gijón is the barrio of **Cimadevilla,** with its maze of alleys and leaning houses. This fishermen's village, on a peninsula jutting into

Jurassic park **IN ASTURIAS**

Dinosaur buffs from around the world flock to one of the most extensive dinosaur museums in the world, **Museo del Jurásico de Asturias ★★**, San Juan de Duz at Colunga (© **90-230-66-00;** www.museojurasicoasturias.com), 32km (20 miles) east of Gijón and 40km (25 miles) northeast of Oviedo. The 209km (130-mile) stretch of sandy beaches and towering cliffs along this coast have produced so many dinosaur bones that the area is dubbed "the Dinosaur Coast." In all, 800 fossils, representing dinosaurs that inhabited the earth 65 million to 280 million years ago, are displayed in a trio of large exhibition spaces. The bones are presented in life-size versions, and the museum itself is built in the shape of a big hoof print. Admission is 7.10€ adults, 4.60€ children 4 to 11 and seniors 66 and up; free on Wednesdays. From June to August, hours are daily 10:30am to 8pm. Off-season visits are possible Wednesday to Friday 10:30am to 2:30pm and 3:30 to 6pm, Saturday and Sunday 10:30am to 2:30 pm and 4 to 7pm. First 2 weeks of September it is open weekends only.

the ocean to the north of the new town, spills over an elevated piece of land known as Santa Catalina. It forms a headland at the west end of the **Playa San Lorenzo,** the city's best beach. It stretches for about 2.5km (1½ miles) and has good facilities.

After time at the beach, you can stroll through **Parque Isabel la Católica,** at its eastern end. You can also visit the **Termas Romanas,** or Roman Baths, at Campos Valdés (© **98-534-51-47;** museos.gijon.es), which are underground at the end of the old town, opening onto Playa de San Lorenzo. Discovered in 1903, these baths are now fully excavated, and the town has opened a museum here. Near the baths are reconstructed parts of the old Roman wall. The baths are open July to August Tuesday to Saturday 11am to 1:30pm and 5 to 9pm, Sunday 11am to 2pm and 5 to 8pm. From September to June they are open Tuesday to Saturday 10am to 1pm and 5 to 8pm, Sunday 11am to 2pm and 5 to 7pm. Admission is 2.50€, 1.40€ seniors and students, and free to all on Sundays.

Gijón is short on major monuments. The city was the birthplace of Gaspar Melchor de Jovellanos (1744–1811), one of Spain's most prominent men of letters, as well as an agrarian reformer and liberal economist. Manuel de Godoy, the notorious minister, ordered that Jovellanos be held prisoner for 7 years in Bellver Castle on Mallorca. In Gijón, his birthplace has been restored and turned into the **Museo-Casa Natal de Jovellanos,** Plaza de Jovellanos (© **98-518-51-52;** www.jovellanos.net), open July to August Tuesday to Saturday from 11am to 1:30pm and 5 to 9pm, and Sunday 11am to 2pm. September to June, hours are Tuesday to Saturday 10am to 1pm and 5 to 8pm, and Sunday 11am to 2pm. Admission is free.

OVIEDO ★★

Oviedo is the capital of Asturias. Only 26km (16 miles) from the coast, the city is very pleasant in summer, when much of Spain is unbearably hot. Despite its high concentration of industry and mining, the area has unspoiled scenery. Razed in the 8th century during the Reconquest, Oviedo was rebuilt in an architectural style known as Asturian pre-Romanesque, which predated many of the greatest achievements under the Moors. Remarkably this architectural movement was in flower when the rest of Europe lay under the black cloud of the Dark Ages. As late as the 1930s, Oviedo was suffering violent upheavals. An insurrection in the mining areas on October 5, 1934, led to a seizure of the town by miners, who set up a revolutionary government. The subsequent repression by General Francisco Franco and his Moroccan troops led to a bloodbath and the destruction of many historical monuments. The cathedral was also damaged, and the university was set on fire. Even more destruction came during the Spanish Civil War, when Falangist forces held an uprising in the city and withstood a 3-month siege by Republicans. For all its brutal past, Oviedo today is a lyrical and upbeat little city, with an impressive old quarter and a new section that is filled with parks and fine boulevards with restaurants and boutiques.

Essentials

GETTING THERE Oviedo doesn't have an airport. The nearest one is at Santiago del Monte, Ranón, 52km (32 miles) away, which it shares with Gijón-bound passengers. Call ✆ 98-512-75-00 for information.

RENFE (✆ 90-232-03-20; www.renfe.com) offers three **trains** per day from Madrid; the one-way trip takes 4½ hours and costs 50€. **ALSA** (✆ 90-242-22-42; www.alsa.es) operates **buses** from Madrid; the trip one-way takes 5½ to 6 hours and costs 32€ to 43€. Driving from the east or west, take N-634 across the coast of northern Spain. From the south, take N-630 or A-66 from León.

VISITOR INFORMATION The **tourist information office** is at Plaza de La Constitución 4 (✆ 90-230-02-02; www.turismoviedo.es). Regular hours are daily from 10am to 2pm and 4:30 to 7pm, but from July to September hours are daily 9:30am to 7:30pm.

Where to Stay in Oviedo

Hotel El Magistral ★ This 1997 hotel is within easy walking distance of Oviedo's old town, but provides an interesting counterpoint with its sleek chrome staircase in the lobby and cafeteria/bar constructed with glass bricks. The guest rooms cut back on the high style for an emphasis on comfort with parquet floors, simple bed coverings, and good lighting.

Calle Jovellanos, 3. ✆ 98-520-42-42. www.elmagistral.com. 52 rooms. 43€–121€ double. Parking 10€. Bus: 1 or 2. **Amenities:** Cafeteria; business corner; free Wi-Fi.

Meliã Hotel de la Reconquista ★★★ It's hard to imagine that this elegant 18th-century building started life as an orphanage and children's hospital. It was renovated and opened as a hotel in 1974 and quickly became a social center for the city. You might recognize the beautiful arcaded lobby from Woody Allen's film *Vicky Cristina Barcelona*. Spacious guest rooms all face outward and feature traditional furnishings in soothing neutral tones. In nice weather, guests enjoy two outdoor patios; in cooler weather, they relax in the huge lobby, with comfortable tables and chairs resting on a beautifully woven 250-sq-m (2,690-sq.-ft.) carpet. You get a lot of history and style for the relatively reasonable price.

Calle Gil de Jaz, 16. ✆ 98-524-11-00. www.melia.com. 142 units. 120€–162€ double; 283€–470€ suite. Parking 24€. Bus: 1, 2, or 3. **Amenities:** 2 restaurants; bar; sauna; free Wi-Fi.

Room Mate Marcos ★★ The Room Mate hotel chain excels at converting older buildings to unique hotels. One of their trademarks is to use bright colors and patterns on the guest room walls to make even small spaces seem lively and welcoming. Marcos is no exception and makes liberal use of black and white in the decor to give the property a sophisticated Art Deco feel. Some rooms have an additional sofa bed and others have a small sitting area. The excellent buffet breakfast is served until noon.

Calle Caveda, 23. ☏ **98-522-72-72.** www.room-matehotels.com. 47 units. 44€–80€ double. Bus: 1, 2, or 3. **Amenities:** Bar; free Wi-Fi.

Where to Eat in Oviedo

Casa Conrado ★ ASTURIAN   Diners are mixed on whether they consider the decor of Casa Conrado to be classic or old fashioned. Suffice it to say that Conrado is a fixture on the dining scene in Oviedo and is known for its preparations of classic dishes such as beans with partridge, creamed prawns on croutons, or baked rice with clams, hake, and artichokes. If you're not in the mood for a full meal, stop in the lovely bar with polished wood and stained glass for tapas such as octopus with apple aioli and onion, or a small toast with ham and fresh duck liver.

Calle Argüelles, 1. ☏ **98-522-39-19.** www.casaconrado.com. Reservations recommended. Main courses 13€–22€; fixed-price menu 21€. Mon–Sat 1–4pm and 9pm–midnight. Closed Aug. Bus: 1.

Casa Fermín ★★ ASTURIAN   The plates are so lovely that you'll want your camera at the ready when the waiter delivers your food to the table. And the food is as good—if not even better—than it looks. Using the best culinary techniques and local products, the chefs have transformed simple Asturian home cooking into elegant cuisine. Many of the novel dishes—roast loin of venison with fruit chutney, for example, or steak tartare with mustard ice cream and jalapeño peppers—go together so well that it's amazing no one has offered them before.

Calle San Francisco, 8. ☏ **98-521-64-52.** www.casafermin.com. Reservations recommended. Main courses 24€–30€; tasting menu 62€. Mon–Sat 1:30–4pm and 9pm–midnight. Bus: 1 or 2.

El Fontán ★★ ASTURIAN   If you work up an appetite looking at the fresh meats, fish, produce, cheeses, and more in El Mercado Fontán, there's a simple solution. Climb the stairs to market restaurant, El Fontán, for hearty home cooking in a lively room overlooking the main floor of the 1885 market hall. There's a daily menu that is a super-bargain as it includes a half-bottle of wine. Market workers swear by the restaurant's *pote Asturiana,* a stew of white beans (of course), potatoes, assorted sausage, and shredded kale with a hambone tossed in for seasoning.

Calle Fierro, 2. ☏ **98-522-23-60.** Main dishes 11€–23€; daily menu 10€. Mon–Sat 9am–8pm.

Exploring Oviedo

Oviedo has been rebuilt into a modern city around Campo de San Francisco, a large green park, but the historical and artistic monuments still cluster along the stone streets and plazas of the Old Quarter. The **Catedral de San Salvador** ★ , on the Plaza de Alfonso II el Casto (☏ **98-520-31-17**), is the most important landmark. The original church—now little more than the foundation—dates to the 8th century, but the Gothic cathedral was begun at the end of the 13th century and completed in the late 16th century (except for the spire, which dates from 1556). Inside is an altarpiece in the florid Gothic style, dating from the 14th and 15th centuries. The cathedral's 9th-century **Cámara Santa (Holy Chamber)** is famous for the Cross of Don Pelayo, the Cross of the Victory, and the Cross of the Angels, the finest specimens of Asturian art in the world. The pieces show the continuing evolution of the already highly sophisticated goldsmithing of

Santa Maria del Naranco in Oviedo.

the Visigoths. Admission to the cathedral is free, but entrance to the Holy Chamber is 2€ for adults, 1€ for children ages 10 to 15, and free for children 9 and under. You can buy a package ticket (3.50€ adults, 2€ children) to also visit the cathedral museum and the Gothic cloister. The cathedral is open for tours Monday through Saturday 10am to 2pm and 4 to 6pm. Take bus no. 1.

Right near the cathedral, the **Museo de Bellas Artes de Asturias ★★**, Calle Santa Ana, 1 (© **98-521-30-61;** www.museobbaa.com), exemplifies a civic tendency in parts of Spain to dump all the art that used to be in churches and private collections into one big museum. This museum, where the majority of the work represents Spanish painting and sculpture from the 14th through the 19th centuries, does an admirable job. The representations of other European schools are only of passing interest, but there are some extraordinary works here, including one of only three sets of portraits of the apostles painted by El Greco and a marvelous multi-panel representation of the martyrdom and life of Santa Marina. In one panel, she is miraculously resurrected from the split belly of a dragon. Admission is free. The museum is open September to June Tuesday through Friday 10:30am to 2pm and 4:30 to 8:30pm, Saturday 11:30am to 2pm and 5 to 8pm, Sunday 11:30am to 2:30pm. In July and August, it is open Tuesday through Saturday 10:30am to 2pm and 4 to 8pm, Sunday 10:30am to 2pm.

From the cathedral plaza, walk down Calle Rúa, which becomes Calle Cimadevilla. It leads into the boxed-in square called **Plaza Constitución,** where the Ayuntamiento (town hall) makes the square the secular counterpart to the cathedral plaza. Calle de Fierro leads past the fresh market to **Plaza del Fontán** and adjacent **Plaza Daoíz y Vélarde.** Bagpipe and folk troupes often perform here during tourist season (May–Sept), and on Thursdays a vigorous street market takes over the squares. A flea market of antiques and collectibles sets up shop on Sundays.

Standing above Oviedo, on Monte Naranco, are two of the most famous examples of Asturian pre-Romanesque architecture. **Santa María del Naranco ★★** (© **98-529-56-85;** www.santamariadelnaranco.blogspot.com), originally a 9th-century palace and hunting lodge of Ramiro I, offers views of Oviedo and the snowcapped Picos de Europa. Once containing baths and private apartments, it was converted into a church in the 12th century. Intricate stonework depicts

Vicky, Cristina Oviedo

Writer-director Woody Allen and Oviedo (the romantic getaway city in his 2008 film *Vicky Cristina Barcelona*) seem to have a mutual admiration society. In 2002, the Principality of Asturias, where Oviedo is the capital, awarded Woody the Premio Principe de Asturias de Las Artes (the Prince's Prize for the Arts). In accepting the award, Woody called Oviedo "delicious, exotic, pretty, clean, and agreeable." The Asturians liked that so much that they ordered a life-size bronze statue of the actor/director/author/comedian striding down Calle Uria in his characteristic slump. It's one of more than 100 sculptures that enliven the streets and plazas of the city.

hunting scenes, and barrel vaulting rests on a network of blind arches. The open porticoes at both ends were architecturally 200 years ahead of their time. From April to September, the church is open Sunday and Monday 9:30am to 1pm, and Tuesday to Saturday 9:30am to 1pm and 3:30 to 7pm. Off-season hours are Sunday and Monday 10am to 12:30pm, Tuesday to Saturday 10am to 2:30pm. Admission is 3€ and includes admission to San Miguel de Lillo. Entrance is free on Monday.

About 90m (295 ft.) away is **San Miguel de Lillo** ★ (© **98-529-56-85;** www.santamariadelnaranco.blogspot.com). It, too, was built by Ramiro I as a royal chapel and was no doubt a magnificent specimen of Asturian pre-Romanesque architecture until 15th-century architects marred its grace. The stone carvings that remain, however, are exemplary. Most of the sculptures have been transferred to the archaeological museum in town. The church is open the same hours as Santa María del Naranco (see above). Ask the tourist office for its walking tour map from Oviedo center to the churches or take bus 10 from Calle Uría.

Shopping

Serious shoppers know that Oviedo offers some of Spain's best outlets for handbags and shoes. For a number of the finest boutiques, head for the intersection of **Uria** and **Gil de Jaz.** In this district, and on adjoining side streets, you'll find some of the country's best-known designer boutiques selling the same merchandise that often fetches higher prices in Madrid and Barcelona. You'll also come across good sales on Asturian ceramic ware. The Sunday flea market on **Plaza Daoíz y Vélarde** tends to focus on small items—everything from vintage jewelry to mid-20th-century cameras. The market operates 10am to 2:30pm.

GALICIA

Extending above Portugal in the northwest corner of Spain, Galicia is a rain-swept land of grass and granite, much of its coastline gouged by fjord-like inlets called *rías*. It is a land steeped in Celtic tradition. In many areas its citizens, called Galegos, speak their own language, closely akin to Portuguese. Although much of the region is mountainous interior, Galicia is famous across Europe for its fisheries, including the extremely expensive *percebes* (goose barnacles) and its swordfish catch.

The Romans made quite an impression on the region. The Tower of Hercules at **A Coruña** is part of that legacy. The Moors came, too, and did a lot of damage along the way. But finding the natives none too friendly and other battlefields more promising, they moved on.

Nothing did more to put Galicia on the tourist map than **Camino de Santiago,** the route of religious pilgrims. It is the oldest, most traveled, and most famous route in continental Europe. To guarantee a place in heaven, pilgrims journeyed to the supposed tomb of Santiago (St. James the Apostle), patron saint of Spain. They trekked across the Pyrenees by the thousands, risking their lives in transit. The Camino de Santiago contributed to the development and spread of Romanesque art and architecture across Spain and provided a rallying point for Christian armies to expel Muslim conquerors. More than 140,000 people make the trek each year.

A CORUÑA ★

Whichever direction you face in this financial and industrial capital of Galicia, the smell of the sea is always with you. The city perches on a fist of land jutting into the Atlantic and pointing toward Ireland. Another Spanish city legendarily founded by Hercules, A Coruña was overrun in succession by Phoenicians, Celts, and Romans. Its defining historical moment, however, came in 1588, when it launched Felipe II's "Invincible Armada" on its ill-fated attack on England. Only half the ships made it back to Spain. The following year, Sir Francis Drake paid a visit, burning and looting A Coruña in reprisal.

Today it is a big-shouldered, rugged city that draws its living from the sea, as so many Galicians have since time immemorial. One side of its isthmus is lined with sandy beaches, while headlands protect a deepwater port on the other. The port splits between container ships and the *lonja,* the fish market that feeds all of Spain. Glassed-in balconies along the high buildings at the edge of the port gave A Coruña its 19th-century nickname, "City of Crystal."

Essentials

GETTING THERE Seven flights a week wing their way from Madrid to A Coruña. **Aeropuerto de Alvedro** (✆ **90-240-47-04;** www.aena-aeropuertos.es) lies 10km (6¼ miles) from the heart of the city and is serviced by **Iberia** (✆ **800-772-4642;** www.iberia.com;), **Air Nostrum** (✆ **96-196-03-19;** www.airnostrum.es;),

PREVIOUS PAGE: **A fishing boat in O Grove.**

The seaside promenade in A Coruña.

TAP Portugal (© 351-707-205-700; www.flytap.com), and **Vueling Airlines** (© 34-807-20-01-00; www.vueling.com).

   Trains arrive at Estación San Cristóbal, Praza San Cristóbal (© 90-232-03-20; www.renfe.com). Depending on the train, the one-way ride from Madrid lasts 6 to 9 hours and costs 54€ to 57€. **Monbus** (© 90-229-29-00; www.monbus.es) runs **buses** between A Coruña and Santiago de Compostela every hour. The trip takes between 50 minutes and 1½ hours one-way, and costs 13€.

   By **car**, A Coruña is reached from Madrid by the N-VI. You can also follow the coastal highway, N-634, which runs all the way across the northern rim of Spain from San Sebastián to the east.

GETTING AROUND A Coruña is remarkably compact, since the ancient port city sits on a thumb-like peninsula. It is easy to walk from one point of interest to another. The port side of town (the east) has the working port, the seaside gardens, and the old fort. The port area opens into Praza (Plaza) de María Pita, which divides the Old Town from the newer city. It is an easy 10-minute walk across the peninsula to Riazor and Orzan beaches on the west side of the peninsula. The Beach Promenade is a paved walkway along the waterfront that covers 13km (8 miles) of the periphery of A Coruña's peninsula. More far-flung attractions can be reached on Bus 3, which makes a circuit of the peninsula. Fare is 1.20€ adults, 0.30€ seniors and students.

VISITOR INFORMATION The **tourist office** at Praza María Pita, 6 (© 98-192-30-93; www.turismocoruna.com) is open to January to October Monday to Friday 9am to 8:30pm, Saturday 10am to 2pm and 4 to 8pm, Sunday 10am to 3pm; in off-season, it closes 1 hour earlier in evening.

Where to Stay in A Coruña
MODERATE
Hesperia Finisterre ★   This high-rise hotel at water's edge is often booked by business travelers, but it must be hard to concentrate on work when the nearest beach is less than a half-mile away (it's also an easy walk into the old town). Recently refurbished guest rooms are of average size, with tasteful contemporary furnishings and bathrooms with hydromassage tubs. All rooms have sea views. Advance booking often garners discounts.

Paseo del Parrote, 2–4. © **98-120-54-00**. www.nh-hotels.com. 92 units. 80€–139€ double; from 128€ suite. Parking 15€. Bus: 1, 2, 3, or 5. **Amenities:** Restaurant; bar; bikes; concierge; health club; Jacuzzi; outdoor heated pool; sauna; 2 outdoor tennis courts; free Wi-Fi.

Meliã Maria Pita ★★   The walls of this high-rise modern hotel appear to be made of glass; all the better for guests to enjoy the views from this property

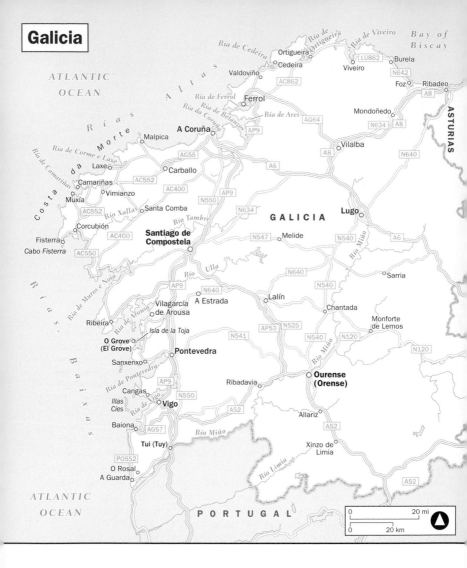

located on the point of the waterfront across from both Orzán and Riazor beaches. Rooms are fairly large, and the decorators weren't afraid to add strong colors and patterned fabrics into the mix of tasteful traditional furnishings and wood floors. *Tip:* Free Wi-Fi can often be negotiated.

Av. Pedro Barrié de la Maza, 1. © **98-120-50-00.** www.melia.com. 183 units. 63€–130€ double; from 139€ suite. Parking 15€. Bus: 2 or 3. **Amenities:** Restaurant; bar; Wi-Fi (12€/24 hr.).

INEXPENSIVE

Hotel Riazor ★ This hotel near the convention center overlooks the beach and boasts incredible views of the bay. It's only about a 20-minute walk into the center of town. The low-key modern decor takes its cues from the colors of sand and water. Some bathrooms have showers only, so if you prefer a tub, be sure to ask. Well-laid out room configurations include triples and quadruples, well-suited for families.

Av. Pedro Barrié de la Maza, 29. ℂ **98-125-34-00.** www.riazorhotel.com. 174 units. 50€–85€ double, 70€–97€ triple, 72€–113€ quadruple. Parking 14€. Bus: 2 or 3. **Amenities:** Restaurant; bar; free Wi-Fi.

NH Atlántico ★ This boxy modern hotel won't win any awards for architecture, but it sits in a prime location equally convenient to explore city sights or head to the beach. You might also run into a few high rollers here, since it also houses the Casino Atlántico. Guest rooms are of ample size and feature well-chosen contemporary furnishings. All rooms have exterior views, which can range from the beach or gardens to city buildings.

Jardines de Méndez Núñez, s/n. ℂ **91-122-65-00.** www.nh-hotels.com. 199 units. 64€–130€ double. Parking 17€. Bus: 1, 2, or 3. **Amenities:** Restaurant; bar; sauna; free Wi-Fi.

Where to Eat in A Coruña

It's customary to go window-shopping here for dinner. The restaurants along two of the principal streets—Calle de la Estrella and Calle de los Olmos—all have display counters up front.

Adega O Bebedeiro ★ GALICIAN Stone and wood—that's the theme of Bebedeiro, where stone walls, a stone fireplace, hardwood floors, and rustic pine tables and stools for the diners set the tone. Now in the second generation of the same family, the restaurant specializes in local fish and shellfish, mostly cooked in a wood-burning oven. Some unusual plates include turnip greens with fried cracklings served with a San Simon cheese puff pastry, and a beautiful plate of asparagus spears draped with *langostinos* and served with a pair of garlic mousselines. Puff pastry is popular in this kitchen (the heat of the fire makes it very dramatic); a great seasonal fish dish pairs roasted sea bass with puff pastry filled with scallops.

Calle Ángel Rebollo 34. ℂ **98-121-06-09.** www.adegaobebedeiro.com. Reservations recommended Fri–Sat. Main courses 13€–25€. Tues–Sun 1–4pm; Tues–Sat 8pm–midnight. Closed 2 weeks in both June and Dec. Bus: 2 or 3.

Casa Pardo ★★ GALICIAN Easily the city's most elegant dining room, Pardo arrays black tables clad in white linen beneath very contemporary sculptural chandeliers. In the 3 decades since Ana Gago and Eduardo Pardo founded the restaurant, it's become known across northern Spain for elegant presentations of innovative seafood dishes. These might include such delights as sea bass braised in crab cream, pan-fried monkfish medallions, or the famous house *caldeirada* (seafood stew) based on monkfish and earthy Galician potatoes. Galician beef is famous throughout the country, and Pardo does a primo sirloin steak with foie gras.

Calle Novoa Santos, 15. ℂ **98-128-00-21.** www.casapardo-domus.com. Reservations recommended. Main courses 12€–30€; fixed-price menus 43€–60€. Mon–Sat 1:30–4pm; Tues–Sat 9pm–midnight. Bus: Any city bus.

El Coral ★ GALICIAN/SEAFOOD The front window of this family-run eatery may have a better and more varied array of sea life than any aquarium. The sole here is the real Dover sole, most of which is caught just outside the port. Icy waters guarantee that the local oysters from the Rias Altas and lobster and crab from all along the coast are sweet and briny. The selection of Galician wines is excellent.

Av. de la Marina Callejón de la Estacada, 9. ℂ **98-120-05-69.** www.restaurantemarisqueria coral.com. Main courses 16€–26€. Mon–Sat 1–4pm and 9pm–midnight. Bus: 1, 2, 5, or 17.

Pablo Gallego Restaurante ★★ SEAFOOD We ate here on the advice of a fishmonger the first time we visited A Coruña and will probably never eat *pulpo Galego*—octopus stewed with potatoes and paprika—anywhere else again. In fact, this charmingly casual spot just off Praza María Pita is where fishmongers and fishermen alike go to eat. The menu runs the gamut from simple anchovies to monkfish medallions and giant prawns roasted on skewers. The restaurant has a clay tandoor oven, which it uses to good effect with chicken dishes and fatty fish—like red tuna belly.

Calle Capitan Troncoso, 4 bajo. ✆ **98-120-88-88.** www.pablogallego.com. Main courses 12€–28€. Mon–Sat 1:30–4pm and 8pm–midnight. Closed second half of Jan. Bus: Any city bus.

Exploring A Coruña

Acuarium Finisterrae ★★ AQUARIUM Few subjects are so dear to the hearts of Galegos as the ocean and its creatures, and one of the exhibits here is literally the ocean on the other side of a glass wall from the aquarium. Fish swim by and crabs scuttle across the ocean floor. The underwater experience is amplified in an exhibit room that simulates the experience inside Captain Nemo's *Nautilus* in the Jules Verne adventure tale, *20,000 Leagues Under the Sea.* Other tanks replicate marine environments around the world. Atlantic harbor seals cavort in their own pool. Changing exhibits highlight subjects as diverse as the effects of global warming on coral reefs or the promises and problems of aquaculture.

Paseo Alcalde Francisco Vázquez, 34. ✆ **98-118-98-42.** www.mc2coruna.org.es. Admission 10€ adults, 4€ seniors and students. May–June and Sept–Dec Mon–Fri 10am–7pm, Sat–Sun 11am–8pm; Jul–Aug daily 10am–9pm; Jan–Apr Mon–Fri 10am–6pm, Sat–Sun 11am–8pm. Bus: 3.

Elevador Panorámico Monte San Pedro ★ NATURAL ATTRACTION This glass elevator climbs 100m (328 ft.) to the top of a small mountain at the western edge of town—a great spot for sunsets or for looking down on the Torre de Hércules.

Parque San Pedro at the Millennium Obelisk. ✆ **98-110-08-23.** www.miradordesanpedro.es. 2€ each way. Operates every half-hour Oct–May Sun–Fri 11:30am–7:30pm and Sat 11:30am–9:30pm; June–Sept Tue–Sun 11:30am–9pm.

Convento da Santa Bárbara ★ CONVENT The cobbled Prazuela de Santa Bárbara is a tiny, tree-shaded plaza flanked by old houses and the high walls of the Santa Bárbara convent. The Clarisas nuns (Poor Clares) are cloistered, but you might hear them singing their prayers at midday services, and you can purchase pastries from their *torno,* a small revolving window built into the convent's vestibule.

Prazuela de Santa Bárbara. The *torno* operates Mon–Fri 10:30am–12:30pm and 4:30–5:45pm, Sat 10:30am–noon.

Domus ★ MUSEUM The so-called "House of Man" is intended to provoke curiosity—starting with its unusual curved building designed by Japanese architect Arata Isozaki. The museum bills itself as the "first interactive museum in the world devoted to the human being." It explores such concrete subjects as the brain, the heart, and the senses, and also probes more intriguing and philosophical ideas such as identity.

Calle Ángel Rebollo, 91. ✆ **98-118-98-40.** www.mc2coruna.org.es. Admission 4€ adults, 2€ seniors and students. July–Aug daily 10am–8pm; Sept–Dec Mon–Fri 10am–7pm, Sat–Sun 11am–7pm; Jan–Apr Mon–Fri 10am–6pm, Sat–Sun 11am–7pm; May–June Mon–Fri 10am–7pm, Sat–Sun 11am–7pm.

Jardín de San Carlos ★ PARK/GARDEN These gardens near the Casa de la Cultura date from 1843 and cover the site of an old fortress that once guarded the harbor. Their views make the gardens a terrific picnic spot. Within the gardens is the tomb of Gen. John Moore, a British commander who fought unsuccessfully against Napoleon's troops. He retreated with his British forces to A Coruña, where he was shot in a final battle.

Paseo del Parrote.

Jardines de Méndez Núñez ★ PARK/GARDEN These gardens in the center of town make a restful interlude while sightseeing. The scent of roses is almost overpowering during May and June.

Between the harbor and Los Cantones (Cantón Grande and Cantón Pequeño).

Museo Arqueológico e Histórico Castillo de Santo Antón ★ MUSEUM The sturdy stone *castillo* was built in the 16th century to fortify the harbor after Drake's raid and later served to hold prisoners and sailors who arrived in port with infectious diseases. It became a museum in 1968. Some artifacts date back to the mysterious megalithic culture of the late Paleolithic era, while others were discovered in medieval burial sites. There's also Roman metalwork and pottery, but visitors are most amazed at the level of artistry in the Celtic gold jewelry created 2500 to 500 B.C.

Paseo Marítimo Alcalde Francisco Vázquez, 2. ✆ **98-118-98-50.** turismocoruna.com. July–Aug Tues–Sat 10am–9pm, Sun 10am–3pm; Sept–June Tues–Sat 10am–7:30pm, Sun 10am–2:30pm. Admission 2€ adults, 1€ for seniors and children. Bus: 3 or 3A.

Praza (Plaza) de María Pita ★ SQUARE This plaza divides the Old Town from the newer city and honors the memory of the woman who helped save many of A Coruña's citizens from slaughter by the English. According to legend, she spotted the approach of Drake's troops, and, risking her own life, fired a cannon to alert the citizens to an imminent invasion. Today the Praza is the social and political center of the city. It is hard to say where more business gets done: in City Hall or in the cafes and bars on the square.

Bus: 1, 1A, 2, 2A, 3A, 17, 23A.

Santa María del Campo ★ CHURCH This 13th-century church can only be viewed from the exterior, but it offers extraordinarily beautiful architectural details. The west door is elaborately carved in the traditional Romanesque-Gothic style. Beneath its rose window you'll see a Gothic portal from the 13th or 14th century. The tympanum is carved with a scene depicting the Adoration of the Magi.

Calle de Santa María.

Torre de Hércules ★ LANDMARK Europe's oldest working lighthouse, this structure was first erected by the Romans in the 2nd century, although continued modernization has obscured its origins. A climb to the top provides great views of A Coruña's bay and port.

Av. de Navarra, s/n. ✆ **98-122-37-30.** 3€ adults, 1.50€ seniors and students. June–Sept daily 10am–9pm, Oct–May 10am–6pm.

A Coruña After Dark

Some of the most appealing bars in A Coruña are atmospheric holes in the wall with a local clientele and decor that has remained virtually unchanged since the mid–20th century. Start your evening at **Mesón A Roda,** Capitán Troncoso, 8 (✆ **98-122-86-71;** daily 1–4pm and 8pm–midnight), which is known for its tapas. For a late night, the town's most appealing and most popular disco is **Playa Club,** Andén de Riazor (© **98-125-00-63;** www.playaclub.net). Set on an oceanfront terrace, a few feet from the waves of Playa Riazor, it does not open until 3am Thursday through Saturday.

Side Trips from A Coruña
THE COAST OF DEATH & THE END OF THE WORLD ★★

For the ancients, **Cabo Fisterra ★** was the end of the world as they knew it. The 145km (90 miles) route takes you along **A Costa da Morte** (the **Coast of Death;** in Castilian, La Costa de la Muerte), so called because of the numerous shipwrecks that have occurred here. It is some of the most majestic and rugged coastline in Spain.

Leaving A Coruña, take the coastal road west (Hwy. 552), heading first to the road junction of **Carballo,** a distance of 36km (22 miles). From this little town, many of the small coastal harbors are within an easy drive. **Malpica ★**, to the northwest, is the most interesting, with its own beach and offshore seabird sanctuary. From Malpica, continue to the sheltered fishing village of **Corme ★** at Punta Roncudo. It has lovely beaches backed by sand dunes.

From Corme, continue along the winding roads to the whitewashed village of **Camariñas ★★**, which stands on the *ría* of the same name. Camariñas is known as a village of expert lace makers, and you'll see their work for sale in many shops. You can also see historic lacework at the **Museo do Encaixe ★** (Praza Insuela s/n, © **98-173-63-40;** www.camarina.net; 2€). From Camariñas, a road leads all the way to the lighthouse at Cabo Vilán.

The road leads first to **Muxia ★** (shown on some maps as Mugia), below which stands the lighthouse at Cabo Touriñán. Continue driving south along clearly marked coastal roads that are sometimes perched precariously on cliff tops overlooking the sea. They will lead you to **Corcubión,** a village with a Romanesque church. From here, follow signs that lead you along a lonely south-bound secondary road to the end of the line, **Cabo Fisterra ★★★**, for a panoramic view. This rocky promontory topped by a lighthouse is one of the westernmost points in continental Europe The sunsets from here are among the

Cabo Fisterra.

Rock formations on the Galician Coast outside of Vicedo.

most spectacular in the world. The bronze hiking boot mounted near the lighthouse commemorates the fact that diehard Santiago pilgrims continue walking from the cathedral to this distant westward point.

SCENIC RÍAS ALTAS ★

In Norway, they're called fjords; in Brittany, abers; in Scotland, lochs; and in Galicia, *rías*. These tidal inlets have been cut into the rocky Galician coastline by the turbulent Atlantic Ocean pounding against its shores. Rías Altas is a relatively modern name applied to all the estuaries on the northern Galician coast. The sinuous and panoramic cornice roads hug the coastline. With their narrow pavements and steep drop-offs, they are not for all drivers. If your nerve fails, default to the adjacent coastal highway.

From A Coruña, head east on the AP-6 to pick up N-651 to **Puentedeume** (also spelled Pontedeume), on the Rías Ares. Historically, it was the center of the counts of Andrade. The remains of their 14th-century palace can be seen, along with the ruins of a 13th-century castle, rising to the east.

Continue north on C-642 to **O Ferrol** (**El Ferrol** in Castilian), which used to be called El Caudillo in honor of the late dictator Francisco Franco, who was born here. O Ferrol is one of the major shipbuilding centers of Spain, and since the 18th century has been a center of the Spanish navy. It's a gritty town, but it lies on one of the region's most beautiful *rías*. Few tourists linger at O Ferrol.

Stay on C-642 to **Ortigueira,** a major fishing village at the head of the *ría* (estuary) from which it takes its name. Driving on, you'll notice the coastline becoming more saw-toothed as you approach **Vicedo.**

Next, you will enter the historic village of **Viveiro.** Part of its medieval walls and an old gate, Puerta de Carlos V, have been preserved. The town has many old churches of interest, including the Gothic-style Iglesia San Francisco. Viveiro is a summer resort, attracting vacationers to its beach, Playa Covas. A great place to stop for seafood here is **Restaurante Nito,** in the Hotel Ego, Playa de Area, 1 (© **98-256-09-87;** www.hotelego.es).

The coastal highway (C-642) will take you through **Burela,** another fishing village. From here you can take the high cornice road east (N-634), where you will see the **Iglesia de San Martín de Mondoñeda,** part of a monastery that dates from 1112. It stands in splendid isolation atop a hill. The road continues down into the little town of **Foz,** a fishing village and summer resort with beaches separated by a cliff. Pick up E-70 west here for the 1½-hour inland drive back to A Coruña.

SANTIAGO DE COMPOSTELA ★★★

All roads in Spain once led to the northwestern pilgrimage city of Santiago de Compostela. A journey to the tomb of the beheaded apostle, St. James, was a high point for the medieval faithful—peasant and prince alike—who converged here from across Europe. They still do, at the rate of more than 140,000 per year.

Santiago de Compostela's link with legend began in A.D. 813, when an urn was discovered containing what were believed to be the remains of St. James, an apostle of Jesus who was beheaded in Jerusalem. A temple was erected over the spot, but in the 16th century, church fathers hid the remains of the saint, fearing they might be destroyed in raids along the coast by Sir Francis Drake. Somewhat amazingly, the alleged remains—subject of millions of pilgrimages from across Europe—lay relatively forgotten.

For decades no one was certain where they were. Then, in 1879, a workman making repairs on the church discovered what were supposed to be the remains, hidden since the 1500s. To prove it was the actual corpse of St. James, church officials brought back a sliver of the skull of St. James from Italy. They claimed that it fit perfectly, like a puzzle piece, into the recently discovered skeleton.

In addition to being the third-most-holy city of the Christian world (after Rome and Jerusalem), Santiago de Compostela is a university town and a marketplace for Galician farmers. With its flagstone streets, churches, and shrines, it is one of the most romantic and historic of Spain's great cities. Santiago also has the dubious distinction of being the rainiest city in Spain, but the showers tend to arrive and end suddenly.

Essentials

GETTING THERE From Madrid, Iberia has five daily **flights** to Santiago, and there is one daily flight from Barcelona. The only international airport in Galicia is east of Santiago de Compostela at Lavacolla (© **90-240-47-04** for flight information), 11km (6¾ miles) from the center on the road to Lugo.

From A Coruña, 21 **trains** make the 1-hour trip daily at a cost of 6€ to 20€. Two high-speed and two slower trains arrive daily from Madrid; the 5- to 8½-hour trip costs 51€ to 54€. For information, call © **90-232-03-20,** or visit www. renfe.com.

Buses leave on the hour, connecting A Coruña with Santiago (trip time: 1 hr.), and cost 13€ one-way. For information, contact **Monbus** (© **98-229-29-00;** www.monbus.es). Eight buses a day arrive in Santiago from Madrid, taking 8 hours and costing 74€ one-way. For information, call **Alsa** at © **90-242-22-42,** or visit www.alsa.es.

If you're driving, take the express highway (A-9/E-50) south from A Coruña to reach Santiago. From Madrid, N-VI runs to Galicia. From Lugo, head south along N-640.

VISITOR INFORMATION The **tourist office,** at Rúa del Vilar 43 (© **98-158-40-81;** www.santiagoturismo.com or www.turgalicia.es), is open Monday to Friday 10am to 8pm, Saturday 11am to 2pm and 5 to 7pm, and Sunday 11am to 2pm.

Where to Stay in Santiago

EXPENSIVE

Hostal de los Reyes Católicos ★★★ It's hard to imagine that the first visitors to this magnificent property slept on straw mattresses that were changed every 6 months. The traditional heavy wooden furniture, soft mattresses, and luxurious

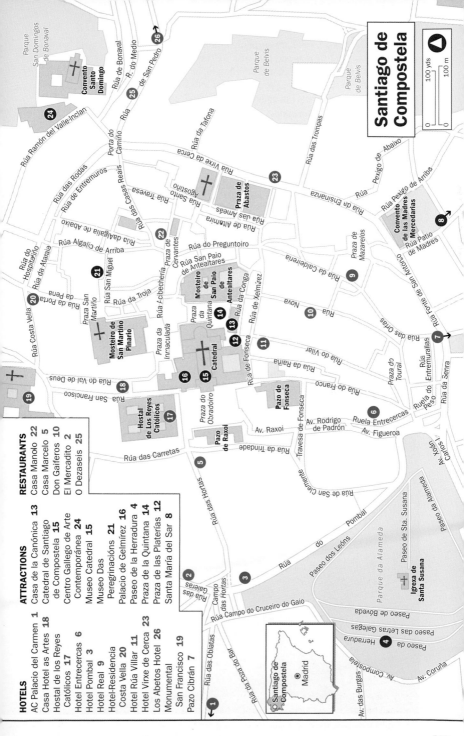

Santiago de Compostela

0   100 yds
0   100 m

HOTELS

AC Palacio del Carmen **1**
Casa Hotel as Artes **18**
Hostal de los Reyes
  Católicos **17**
Hotel Entrecercas **6**
Hotel Pombal **3**
Hotel Real **9**
Hotel-Residencia
  Costa Vella **20**
Hotel Rúa Villar **11**
Hotel Virxe de Cerca **23**
Los Abetos Hotel **26**
Monumental
  San Francisco **19**
Pazo Cibrán **7**

ATTRACTIONS

Casa de la Canónica **13**
Catedral de Santiago
  de Compostela **15**
Centro Gallego de Arte
  Contemporánea **24**
Museo Catedral **15**
Museo Das **21**
Peregrinacións **21**
Palacio de Gelmírez **16**
Paseo de la Herradura **4**
Praza de la Quintana **14**
Praza de las Platerías **12**
Santa María del Sar **8**

RESTAURANTS

Casa Manolo **22**
Casa Marcelo **5**
Don Gaiferos **10**
El Mercadito **2**
O Dezaseis **25**

507

bedding in the guest rooms are certainly much more comfortable. It's well worth a splurge to stay here so that you can soak up the centuries of history as you explore the hallways, visit the cloisters, and simply sink into a chair in the stunning lobby. If you can't swing a stay, inquire about a guided tour, or enjoy a drink at the bar.

Praza do Obradoiro, 1. ℂ **98-158-22-00.** www.parador.es. 128 units. 155€–230€ double; from 218€ jr. suite. Parking 18€. **Amenities:** 2 restaurants; bar; free Wi-Fi.

MODERATE

AC Palacio del Carmen ★
If you'd prefer to get away from the crowds in Praza do Obradoiro, this property in a former convent is a good bet. It's very close to the plaza, but just far enough away so that you can enjoy the peaceful environment, lovely patio, and park-like grounds. Rooms are small to mid-size with traditional furnishings, wooden beamed ceilings, and tiled bathrooms.

Calle Oblatas, s/n. ℂ **98-155-24-44.** www.ac-hotels.com. 74 units. 90€–120€ double; 149€–275€ suite. Parking 15€. **Amenities:** Restaurant; bar; concierge; exercise room; Wi-Fi (free in public areas).

Hotel Rúa Villar ★
This 18th-century manor house with a graceful arched arcade sits practically next to the cathedral in the historic center of Santiago. The owners also collect art, and their sure sense of taste is evident in the harmonious mix of modern furnishings with the stone and wood of the old building. If you visit during winter, request a room with a gas fireplace. Two rooms have lovely if small, glassed-in sitting areas with views.

Rúa do Vilar, 8–10. ℂ **98-151-98-58.** www.hotelruavillar.com. 14 units. 70€–210€ double. No parking. **Amenities:** Restaurant; bar; free Wi-Fi.

San Francisco Hotel Monumento ★★
From the hotel's indoor pool, big windows in the rough stone walls look out on gardens and a distant mountain. Yet

The Catedral de Santiago de Compostela at sunset.

SLEEPING IN historic places

A marvelous new way of staying in Galicia is a web of historic inns and manor houses that have been restored with an eye to comfort and quality. Now welcoming visitors, they are organized through **Pazos de Galicia** (www.pazosdegalicia.com).

You can obtain a map on the Web showing historic homes around the cities you plan to visit in Galicia, with A Coruña, Santiago de Compostela, and Pontevedra being the most preferred

choices. Of course, you'll need a car to reach these places, which lie outside cities or towns of historic interest. They include Pazo La Buzaca, Lugar de San Lorenzo, 36, Morana (© **98-655-36-84;** www.pazolabuzaca.com), a 13-room, 17th-century structure (part of the complex was a former hunting lodge), and Pazo do Souto, Calle Torre, 1, Carballo (© **98-175-60-65;** www.pazodosouto.com), a restored rustic manor house with a pool.

this hotel in an 18th-century former convent building sits near the cathedral in the heart of the narrow streets of the Old Quarter. The public areas are rich in architectural details, while the rooms feature hardwood floors, wooden beamed ceilings, and traditional furnishings.

Campillo San Francisco, 3. © **98-158-16-34.** www.sanfranciscohm.com. 82 units. 121€–165€ double; 200€–220€ suite. Free parking. **Amenities:** Restaurant; bar; indoor pool; free Wi-Fi.

INEXPENSIVE

Casa Hotel as Artes ★ This small hotel represents a real change of pace for history-soaked Santiago. Many of the rooms do feature lovely old exposed stone walls. But rather than playing off the architecture, the innkeepers have named each room for an artist and have used that artist as inspiration for the colorful and somewhat whimsical decor. The small size of the property makes it a nice choice for a romantic getaway.

Travesía de Dos Puertas, 2 (off Rúa San Francisco). © **98-155-52-54.** www.asartes.com. 7 units. 52€–110€ double. Free parking. **Amenities:** Free Wi-Fi.

Hotel Pombal ★ Pilgrims who have completed their journey to Santiago often choose this small hotel that is about a 10-minute walk from the cathedral. Some of the rooms and public areas have views of the cathedral, which is particularly stunning when it is illuminated at night. Rooms feature traditional wooden furnishings. Soft rugs underfoot are a nice touch for the pilgrims.

Rúa do Pombal, 12. © **98-156-93-50.** www.pousadasdecompostela.com. 15 units. 64€–105€ double. **Amenities:** Free Wi-Fi.

Hotel Real ★ Rooms here are on the small side, but each has a balcony which somehow makes the rooms seem more expansive. Simple furnishings in neutral colors are restful and let the views take center stage. Bathrooms are equally small but well maintained.

Calle Calderería, 49. © **98-156-92-90.** www.hotelreal.com. 13 units. 60€–70€ double. **Amenities:** Free Wi-Fi.

Los Abetos Hotel ★★ This modern property about a 5-minute drive from the center of Santiago calls itself a hotel, but has many of the amenities of a resort, including an outdoor pool, tennis courts, and beautiful grounds with stone walkways. High-quality furnishings are in tasteful, classic style. Family rooms, with two queen beds, can accommodate four guests.

Calle San Lázaro, s/n. ℂ **98-155-70-26.** www.hotellosabetos.com. 148 units. 50€–70€ double; 60€–80€ family room. Free parking. **Amenities:** Restaurant; bar; exercise room; outdoor pool; sauna; outdoor tennis court; free Wi-Fi.

Where to Eat in Santiago

MODERATE

Don Gaiferos ★ GALICIAN   Old-fashioned and proud of it, this traditional restaurant next to the Church of Santa María Salomé emphasizes seafood, which arrives by truck from the *lonja* at A Coruña. Good starters include a plate of raw cockles or anchovies with giant capers. The fare is straightforward and simple—roasted hake with potatoes, peas, and, this being Santiago, a few scallops (symbol of Santiago). The beef and veal dishes are also quite good. Among the desserts, the almond tart is the best.

Rúa Nova 23. ℂ **98-158-38-94.** www.dongaiferos.com. Reservations required. Main courses 16€–24€; fixed-price menu 35€. Daily 1:15–3:45pm; Tues–Sat 8:15–11:30pm.

El Mercadito ★★ CREATIVE GALICIAN   The young chef here, Gonzalo Rei, is one to watch, as he counts himself a disciple of Joan Roca of El Cellar de Can Roca (p. 395). You can look out the windows in the suave contemporary restaurant and see the towers of the cathedral in the distance, but as long as you're eating here, you might as well be a world away from hearty pilgrim food. Rei serves modernized Galician food with a creative flair and an emphasis on fresh, local products. For example, he uses mackerel from A Coruña in a couscous with cream peas, crunchy bits of Iberian ham, and wilted spinach. Roasted capon is paired with truffle and served on a bed of quinoa laced with sautéed green peppers.

Rúa Galeras, 18. ℂ **98-157-42-39.** www.elmercadito.es. Reservations required. Main courses 18€–27€; daily menu 37€; tasting menu 53€. Tues-Sun 1:30–4pm; Tues–Sat 8:30pm–midnight.

O Dezaseis ★ TAPAS/GALICIAN   This subterranean haunt specializes in tapas and empanadas with the aim of communicating to non-Spaniards that it really is okay to make a meal of small plates. The dishes are not the creative concoctions you'd find at Casa Marcelo, but rather the small plates that sustain Spaniards all over the country. So expect *tortilla Española* (potato omelet), little casseroles of meatballs, sliced ham and cheese, sizzling plates of grilled chorizo or blood sausage, and the ubiquitous pieces of roast chicken. Or try slices of Galician empanada, which is akin to a pot pie with less runny filling. The traditional one is filled with chunks of fresh tuna, potato, onion, and carrot in a light béchamel sauce. "Sixteen" (as the restaurant's name translates) also grills whole fish.

Rúa San Pedro 16. ℂ **98-156-48-80.** www.dezaseis.com. Tapas 3.50€–14€; *raciones* 11€–13€; fixed-price menus 12€–20€. Mon–Sat 2–4pm and 8:30pm–midnight.

INEXPENSIVE

Casa Manolo ★ GALICIAN   As you might expect of a dining room only 100 paces from the cathedral, Casa Manolo feeds a lot of hungry pilgrims. In fact, there's just one choice of meal each day, called the Pilgrim's Menu, and it reflects the kind of pasta- and rice-heavy fare that sustains the walkers on the road. So don't be surprised if the meal of the day is breaded veal cutlet on spaghetti with red sauce, or an approximation of paella. It's not fancy, but the price is right and the company terrific.

Praza Cervantes, s/n. ℂ **98-158-29-50.** www.casamanolo.es. Fixed-price menu 10€. Daily 1–4pm; Mon–Sat 8:30–11:30pm. Closed in Jan.

Casa Marcelo ★★ CREATIVE GALICIAN   Created as a cutting-edge restaurant, Marcelo has evolved in these impecunious times into a gastropub with an exposed kitchen that still features exciting dishes. They're just smaller and hence less expensive, and the house counts on making up the profit with the margin on the wines by the glass. There's still a distinct Japanese influence, especially in the beautiful presentation and use of bright colors to make the plate pop.

Rúa Hortas, 1. ℂ **98-155-85-80.** www.casamarcelo.net. Tapas 5€; *raciones* 12€; fixed-price menu 60€ –75€. Tues–Sun 1:30–3:30pm and Tues–Sat 9–11:30pm. Closed Feb.

Exploring Santiago

Santiago de Compostela's highlight is undoubtedly its storied cathedral, and you should take at least 2 hours to see it. Most of the other impressive buildings are on Praza do Obradoiro, also called Praza de España. After visiting them, take a stroll through this enchanting town, which has a number of other worthwhile monuments as well as many stately mansions along Rúa del Vilar and Rúa Nueva. One of the most important squares in the Old Town is **Praza de la Quintana,** to the left of the cathedral's Puerta de Orfebrería (Goldsmith's Doorway). It's dominated by **Casa de la Canónica,** the former residence of the canon. South of the square is the Renaissance-style **Plaza de las Platerías (Silversmiths' Square),** which has an elaborate fountain. Cap off a day of sightseeing with a walk along **Paseo de la Herradura,** the gardens southwest of the Old Town, from where you have an all-encompassing view of the cathedral and the Old City.

Plaza de las Platerías.

Catedral de Santiago de Compostela ★★★ CATHEDRAL

Begun in the 11th century, this cathedral is the crowning achievement of Spanish Romanesque architecture, even though it actually reflects a number of styles. Maestro Mateo's **Pórtico de la Gloria ★★★**, carved in 1188, ranks among the finest produced in Europe at that time. The three arches of the portico are adorned with figures from the Last Judgment. In the center, Christ is flanked by apostles and the 24 Elders of the Apocalypse. Below the Christ figure is a depiction of St. James himself. He crowns a carved column that includes a self-portrait statue of Mateo at the bottom. If you observe this column, you will see that five deep indentations have been worn into it by pilgrims. Even today, they line up here to lean forward, place their hands on the pillar, and touch foreheads with Mateo. Mothers bring their infants

Pórtico de la Gloria at Catedral de Santiago de Compostela.

here to do the same thing: bump foreheads with one of Europe's greatest artistic masters in hopes some of the genius will rub off.

The cathedral has three naves in cruciform shape and several chapels and cloisters. The altar, with its blend of Gothic simplicity and baroque decor, is extraordinary. In the crypt, a silver urn contains what the faithful accept as the remains of the apostle St. James. A cathedral museum, **Museo de Catedral ★★**, displays tapestries, archaeological fragments, and the ruins of a circa-1200 A.D. masterpiece, a stone choir carved by Maestro Mateo. Next door, **Palacio de Gelmírez** (☎ 98-157-23-00), an archbishop's palace built during the 12th century, is an outstanding example of Romanesque architecture.

A number of guided tours are available, but the real thrill of visiting here is seeing the relief and joy of pilgrims as they reach their destination.

Praza do Obradoiro, s/n. ☎ **98-156-05-27.** www.catedraldesantiago.es. Admission to the cathedral and to the Palacio de Gelmírez is free. Hours for the cathedral are daily 7am–8:30pm. The museum is open Apr–Oct daily 9am–8pm, Nov–March 10am–8pm. Admission 6€, guided tours 10€–15€; reserve a time slot in advance.

Centro Galego de Arte Contemporánea ★ ART MUSEUM

Portuguese architect Álvaro Siza Vieira took the traditional building material of granite and used it to create a sleek modern building that somehow manages not to look out of place in the historic center. Opened in the early 1990s, the center hosts changing exhibitions of contemporary art and is slowly building a permanent collection of work from Spanish, Portuguese, and Latin American artists. The terrace offers stunning views.

Rúa Valle-Inclán s/n. ☎ **98-154-66-19.** www.cgac.org. Free. Winter Tues–Sun 11am–8pm, summer Tues–Sun noon–9pm.

Colexiata de Santa María do Sar ★ CHURCH   Although a little removed from the center of town, this church is one of the architectural gems of the Romanesque style in Galicia. Its walls and columns are on a 15-degree slant thought to be attributable to either a fragile foundation or an architect's fancy. Visit the charming cloister with its slender columns.

Castrón d'Ouro, .8km (½ mile) down Calle de Sar, which begins at the Rúa do Patio de Madres. ℭ **98-156-28-91.** Admission 1€. Mon–Sat 10am–1pm and 4–7pm.

Museo das Peregrinacións ★ MUSEUM   If you'd like to know more about the life of St. James and the growth of Santiago de Compostela as a pilgrimage site, it's worth spending some time here. Maps and displays outline the major pilgrimage routes; exhibits elucidate what motivates people to embark on this challenging journey.

Rua San Miguel, 4. ℭ **98-158-15-58.** www.mdperegrinacions.com. Admission 2.40€ adults, 1.20€ students, free for seniors. Tues–Fri 10am–8pm, Sat 10:30am–1:30pm and 5:30–8pm, Sun 10:30am–1:30pm.

Shopping

The artful blue-and-white porcelain that is the town's trademark is available for sale at **Sargadelos,** Rúa Nueva 16 (ℭ **98-158-19-05;** www.sargadelos.com/sargadelos), **Amboa Maeloc,** Rúa Nueva, 44 (ℭ **98 158-33-59;** www.amboamaeloc.com), stocks similar ceramics, plus a wide range of other regional handicrafts.

A favorite of most tourists is *tarta Santiago,* a tart sold at virtually every pastry shop in the city. Also very popular is *queso de tetilla,* a mild local cheese shaped like a woman's breast.

Many of the local wines, including assorted bottles of Ribeiro, Condado, and, most famous of all, Albariño, are sold without fanfare in grocery stores throughout Galicia. But for a specialist in the subtleties of these tipples, head for **Charcuterías Seco,** San Pedro Mezonzo, 3 (ℭ **98-159-12-67;** www.charcuteriaseco.com).

Santiago After Dark

In the religious center of Galicia, there's a lot more to do after dark than pray. An estimated 200 bars and *cafeterías* are found on the Rúa do Franco and its neighbor, Rúa da Raíña. The pavement along those streets on weekend evenings at around 11pm is mobbed. Particularly convivial is **Bar/Cafetería Dakar,** at Rúa do Franco 13 (ℭ **98-157-81-92**).

Obeiro, Rúa da Raíña 3 (ℭ **98-158-13-70;** www.obeiro.com), is one of the town's better wine bars, with a good selection of bottles from throughout the country, especially wines from Galicia itself.

One of the town's hot spots is **Pub Modus Vivendi,** Praza Feixoó 1 (ℭ **98-157-61-09;** www.pubmodusvivendi.net), where rock music blasts the night away in a cozy but too crowded interior. It's very psychedelic in decor and attracts local students and young visiting foreigners Sunday to Thursday 6:30pm to 3am, Friday and Saturday 6:30pm to 4:30am. Techno, house, pop, and rock music are played at the garishly decorated **Retablo Café-Concerto,** Rúa Nova 13 (ℭ **98-156-48-51;** www.retablocafeconcerto.com). It's open daily noon to 5am.

PONTEVEDRA ★

An aristocratic old Spanish town on the Lérez River and the capital of Pontevedra province, the city of Pontevedra still has vestiges of an ancient wall that once encircled the town. In medieval days, the town was called Pontis Veteris (Old Bridge). Sheltered at the end of the Ría Pontevedra, the city was a bustling port, and foreign merchants mingled with local traders, seamen, and fishermen. In the 18th century, the Lérez delta silted up and the busy commerce moved elsewhere. Pontevedra went into decline. The old town, a maze of colonnaded squares and cobbled alleyways, lies between Calle Michelena and Calle del Arzobispo Malvar, stretching to Calle Cobián and the river. The old mansions, called *pazos*, evoke former maritime glory, for the money to build them came from the sea.

Essentials

GETTING THERE   From Santiago de Compostela, 17 **trains** per day make the 1-hour one-way trip to Pontevedra at a cost of 6€ to 7.20€. **RENFE** has an office on Praza Calvo Sotelo s/n (© **90-232-03-20;** www.renfe.com), where you can get information. The rail and bus stations are 0.8km (½ mile) from the town center on Calle Alféreces Provisionales. From Santiago de Compostela in the north, a **bus** leaves every hour during the day for Pontevedra (trip time: 1 hr.); the one-way trip costs 9.50€. For information, call © **98-229-29-00,** or visit www.monbus.es. If you're **driving** from Santiago de Compostela, head south along N-550 to reach Pontevedra.

VISITOR INFORMATION   The **tourist office,** at Casa da Luz, Praza da Verdura (© **98-609-08-90;** www.visit-pontevedra.com/ing), is open Monday to Saturday 10am to 2pm and 4:30 to 7:30pm, and Sunday 10am to 2pm.

Exploring Pontevedra

Pontevedra's **Old Quarter** ★ is almost entirely pedestrian these days, making it a pleasant place to stroll. The major attraction in the old part of the city is the **Basílica de Santa María la Mayor** ★, Calle del Arzobispo Malvar (©**98-686-61-85**), dating from the 16th century. All the metal decoration on the church has taken on an avocado-green patina. Its most remarkable feature is its western facade, carved to resemble an altarpiece, with a depiction of the Crucifixion at the top. The church is open daily 10am to 1pm and 5 to 9pm.

The **Museo de Pontevedra,** Calle Pasantería, 10 (© **98-685-14-55;** www.museo.depontevedra.es), contains a hodgepodge of everything from the Pontevedra civic attic. Displays range from prehistoric artifacts to a still life by Zurbarán. Many of the exhibits are maritime-oriented, and there is a valuable collection of jewelry. The museum is open Tuesday to Saturday 10am to 7pm, Sunday 11am to 2pm. Admission is free. The museum opens onto a major square in the old town, Praza de Leña (Square of Wood).

Iglesia de San Francisco, Praza de la Herrería, is another church of note. Its Gothic facade opens onto gardens. It was founded in the 14th century and contains a sculpture of Don Payo Gómez Charino, noted for his part in the 1248 Reconquest of Seville, when it was wrested from Muslim domination.

Where to Stay in Pontevedra

Hotel Rías Bajas ★   Built in the late 1960s when Pontevedra was a busy business center, the Rías Bajas has switched gears to cater to leisure travelers who have come to see the quaint stone buildings and narrow, pre-modern streets of the Old

Pontevedra's Old Quarter.

Quarter. Although the hotel is on a bustling street corner, it is less than a 5-minute walk from the Old Quarter. The decor of the public areas features lots of stone and paneled wood, and it is frequently used as a backdrop for political press conferences. The guest rooms are simpler and more traditional. They tend to be small (although some triples are available), but all feature a usable work desk.

Calle Daniel de la Sota, 7. ✆ **98-685-51-00**. www.hotelriasbajas.com. 100 rooms. 45€–90€ double; 75€–110€ triple. Parking 12€. **Amenities:** Restaurant; bar; free Wi-Fi.

Parador de Pontevedra ★★   This handsome Renaissance town house, once home to the counts of Maceda, has been beautifully restored, with a carved stone staircase leading from the courtyard to the guest rooms. Quiet and regal, the *parador* makes a perfect base for exploring Pontevedra (the basilica is nearby) and for making day trips to O Grove to the west or to the wine country on the southwest coast.

Calle Barón, 19. ✆ **98-685-58-00**. www.parador.es. 47 units. 85€–155€ double; 200€–260€ suite. Limited free parking. **Amenities:** Restaurant; bar; free Wi-Fi.

Where to Eat in Pontevedra

Alameda 10 ★ GALICIAN ·   A little bit modern, a little bit traditional, Alameda 10 focuses mostly on making good, simple food without a lot of fuss. It has an extensive tapas menu that includes some unusual dishes like a small green salad with duck "ham" and a Portuguese-style cornbread, chicken croquettes, and freshly fried potato chips with Cabrales cream.

Calle Alameda, 10. ✆ **98-685-74-12**. www.restaurantealameda10.com. Reservations recommended. Main courses 15€–30€. Mon–Sat 1–4pm; Mon and Wed–Sat 9–11:30pm.

Casa Román ★ GALICIAN   Calling itself a "restaurant *marisquería,*" Casa Román signals that the menu is really all about the shellfish. Oven-roasted scallops are particularly popular, but the kitchen focuses on crustaceans. Several dishes use the European lobster (somewhat smaller than its American cousin). Depending on what's on display on ice, you can also enjoy the big meaty crabs found all over the rocks along the *rías* (excellent roasted in the oven), steamed

Norway lobster (what the Italians call *langostinos*), and several species of shrimp and prawns. The restaurant is in the new section of town, Praza de Galicia.

Calle Augusto García Sánchez, 12. ℂ 98-684-35-60. www.casaroman.com. Main courses 14€–25€. Tues–Sun 1:30–3:45pm; Tues–Sat 9–11:45pm.

Solla ★★★ GALICIAN   Self-taught chef Pepe Solla is an original, and his embrace of the classic flavors of Galician cuisine is matched only by his determination to make it all new. The old country house where Solla has just nine tables has been a restaurant for many years, but the chef gave it a complete makeover in contemporary Spanish style. Having won one Michelin star already, Solla is a likely contender for another with dishes like a cream of oysters, hake roe, sturgeon caviar, and bluebell flowers. He matches the meatiness of sea bass with braised turnip greens, Galician cabbage (similar to kale), and an orange-lemon sauce. Solla is a prime regional exemplar of the *cocina de autur*. He has caught the "locavore" fever, so almost everything on his menus comes from within a 1-hour radius, and all the fish is caught inshore in sustainable fisheries.

Av. Sineiro 7, Km 2, San Salvador de Poio, 2km (1¼ miles) from the center of town, toward El Grove. ℂ **98-687-28-84.** www.restaurantesolla.com. Reservations recommended. Fixed-price menus 59€–102€. Tues–Wed and Fri–Sat 1:30–4pm and 9–11:30pm; Thurs and Sun 1:30–4pm. Closed Dec 20–Jan 4.

Side Trips from Pontevedra
O GROVE & A TOXA ★

Only 34km (21 miles) west of Pontevedra on the PO-308, O Grove (El Grove in Castilian) is a summer resort and fishing village. It is surrounded by 8km (5 miles) of beaches and some of the most extensive shellfish flats on the Galician coast.

The nominally 45-minute drive from Pontevedra is a pleasure. We say "nominally," because you'll be hard-pressed to drive through without stopping frequently for photographs. The road follows the north coast of the Ría de Pontevedra, part of the famous Rias Baixas wine district. Small vineyards hanging with Albariño wine grapes are on one side of the road, and the rugged coast with scenic vistas on the other.

A quiet beach in O Grove.

When you do reach O Grove, you can get local information at the **tourist information office,** Praza Do Corgo, s/n (ℂ **98-673-14-15;** www.turismo-grove.com), which is open in winter Monday and Wednesday to Friday 10am to 2pm and 4 to 6pm, Tuesday and Sunday 11am to 2pm (closed Monday in summer). Besides feasting on shellfish at **La Posada del Mar,** Calle Castelao, 202 (ℂ **98-673-01-06;** main courses 10€–24€, menus 26€–35€; closed Mon), there are really only two other things to do.

The Eiffel-built bridge, outside of Túi.

The first is to cross the bridge next La Posada del Mar to visit **A Toxa** ★ (La Toja in Castilian), an island holding Galicia's most famous spa and the most fashionable resort. The casino and the golf course are both very popular. The island is covered with pine trees and surrounded by some of the finest scenery in Spain. A Toxa first became known for its health-giving properties when, according to legend, the owner of a sick donkey left it on the island to die. The donkey recovered, and its cure was attributed to the waters of an island spring.

The other principal attraction is the **Acuario de O Grove,** Punta Moreiras (© **98-673-23-27;** www.acuariodeogrove.es). Renovations in 2013 to 2014 altered the exhibits to focus mainly on the immediate coastal zone and converted the facility to being powered entirely by wind and solar cells. In addition to seeing a lot of the tastiest sea life in its natural environment, the aquarium has a few sea otters and other marine mammals. Admission is 10€ adults, 8€ seniors and ages 4 to 14. From mid-June to mid-October it is open daily 10:30am to 8:30pm; from mid-October to mid-June it is open Wednesday to Friday 10am to 6pm and Saturday and Sunday 10am to 7:30pm.

WINE & HISTORY ON GALICIA'S SOUTHWEST COAST ★★

The coastline from the Ría de Vigo to the Río Miño, which forms the border between Spain and Portugal, is steeped in history and blessed with a climate that favors the cultivation of Albariño grapes. It is also an area with some of the greatest fishing ports in the world, and consequently some of the best casual fish restaurants in Spain.

Begin at the village of **Baiona** ★, 57km (36 miles) south of Pontevedra; its moment of enduring fame came on March 1, 1493, when Columbus's vessel, *La Pinta,* made landfall here. The ship's navigator was from Baiona, which became the first place in Europe to learn of the Columbus's discoveries across the Atlantic Ocean. A replica **Carabela *Pinta*** (© **98-638-59-21**) constructed for the quincentennial bobs in the harbor among the recreational sailboats. The ship is open daily 11am to 2pm and 4:30 to 7:30pm. Admission is 2€.

Just above the harbor stand the picket-fence stone walls of Baiona's **Fortaleza de Monterreal** (✆ **98-668-70-67**). The fort was constructed fitfully from the 12th century onward but was completed in the early 1600s. Its 3km (1.9 miles) of walls wrap around the headland above the harbor. It is open daily 10am to 9pm. Admission is 2€.

As you drive south on the PO-552 from Baiona, there are several pull-outs along the road that allow you to enjoy the dramatic views. In 30km (19 miles), the fishing port of **A Guarda** ★ (La Garda in Castilian) nestles in a deep cove at the mouth of the Río Miño. This ancient Celtic port predates the Roman presence and is now home to Europe's most important swordfish fleet. Pastel houses, restaurants, and bars form a Cubist wall around the harbor.

The Paseo Marítimo leads to the breakwater, with a walkway along the top, and to the tiny **Museo do Mar** (✆ **98-661-00-00**) in a replica of the cannon emplacement that once guarded A Guarda. Exhibits include aquarium tanks and good explication of traditional local fishing equipment and vessels. The museum is open mid-September to early June Saturday and Sunday 11am to 2pm and 4 to 7pm; early June to mid-September daily 11am to 2pm and 6 to 9pm. Admission is 1€, 0.50€ under age 14.

If seeing the fishing fleet makes you hungry, head to the road above the harbor for grilled swordfish or rice and shellfish casseroles at **Xeito Restaurante Mariquería** (✆ **98-661-04-74**), Av. Fernández Albor, 19. The restaurant on the rocky headland has outdoor tables for taking in the view. It's open daily for lunch and dinner. Main dishes cost 15€ to 30€.

The highway turns north at A Guarda to follow the Río Miño toward Túi. In about 11km (7miles), you reach the important D.O. wine district known as **O Rosal** (a subdivision of Rías Baixas). The highway suddenly sprouts side roads leading to vineyards. Grapes line the roadside in tracts as small as backyard gardens and as big as fields reaching over the hillside. The dominant grape is Albariño, which makes a fruit-forward, slightly acidic wine with a long finish for which the Rías Baixas region is justifiably famous among wine-lovers. Several winemakers in O Rosal offer tastings, including **Bodegas Terras Gauda,** PO-552 km 55 (✆ **98-662-10-01;** www.terrasgauda.com). The tasting room is open Monday to Saturday 11am to 2pm and 4 to 8pm, Sunday 11am to 2pm. Free winery tours are offered Monday to Saturday at 5:30pm, Sunday at 12:30pm.

About 16 km (10 miles) north, the cathedral city of **Túi** sits right on the border with Portugal near the two-tiered road-and-rail bridge over the Río Miño that links the two countries. The bridge was designed by Alexandre-Gustave Eiffel. (He designed a tower in Paris you may have heard of.)

There is a footpath along the river here that represents the southern Iberian branch of the **Camino de Santiago.** Locals maintain it as a greenway, and fishermen often come to the path to cast a line into the Río Miño. The winding streets of Túi's Old Quarter lead to the **Catedral** ★ (✆ **98-669-05-11**), a national art treasure that dominates the *zona monumental*. The acropolis-like cathedral/fortress, built in 1170, wasn't used for religious purposes until the early 13th century. Later architects respected the original Romanesque and Gothic styles and made few changes in its design. It is usually open daily 9am to 2pm and 4 to 9pm. Admission to the church is free, but 2€ will also get you into the museum, cloister, tower, and gardens.

From Tuí, it is a 40-minute drive north on PO-340/AP-55 to return to Pontevedra.

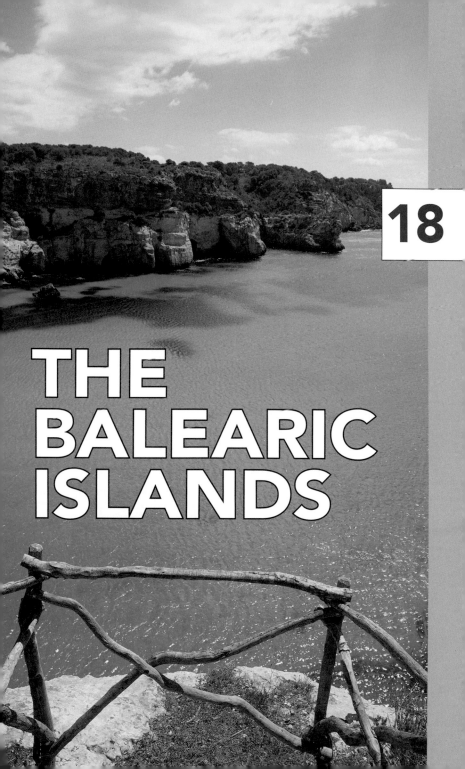

18

THE BALEARIC ISLANDS

T he Balearic Islands (Los Baleares)—an archipelago of the major islands of Mallorca, Menorca, and Ibiza, plus Formentera and other diminutive islands—lie off the coast of Spain between France and the coast of northern Africa. The islands have been ruled and occupied by Carthaginians, Greeks, Romans, Vandals, and Moors. But despite a trove of Bronze Age megaliths and some fine Punic artifacts, the invaders who have left the largest imprint on Balearic culture are the sun-seeking vacationers who descend every year.

After Jaume I expelled the Moors in 1229, the islands flourished as the kingdom of Mallorca, but declined after being integrated into the kingdom of Castilla in the mid–14th century. The 19th century provided a renaissance, as artists such as George Sand, Chopin, and, later, poet Robert Graves established the islands as a haven for musicians, writers, and artists. Gradually the artists' colony attracted tourists of all dispositions.

Very few visitors have time to explore all three major islands, so you'll have to decide early which one is for you. **Mallorca,** the largest, is the most commercial and touristy, with sprawling hotels and fast-food joints in all but the most scenic parts. Freewheeling **Ibiza** attracts the international party crowd, as well as seekers of white-sand beaches and sky-blue waters. The smallest of the major islands, **Menorca,** is the most serene. It is less touristy than Mallorca and Ibiza, and for that reason it is now experiencing an "anti-tourist" tourist boom. The government of the islands has recently safeguarded 35% of the entire island group from further development.

MALLORCA ★★★

Mallorca is the most popular of Spain's Mediterranean islands, drawing millions of visitors each year. About 209km (130 miles) from Barcelona and 145km (90 miles) from Valencia, Mallorca has a coastline 500km (311 miles) long. An explorer's paradise in its interior, it's overbuilt along certain coastal regions. The north is mountainous; the fertile southern flatlands offer olive and almond groves interrupted by windmills. The golden sands of Mallorca are famous, with lovely beaches such as Ca'n Pastilla and El Arenal, but tend to fill with package tourists. Both Cala Mayor and Sant Agustí have good beaches, including Playa Magaluf, the longest beach on the Calvía coast. Cala de San Vicente, 6.5km (4 miles) north of Pollença, is a beautiful beach bordered by a pine grove and towering cliffs. Stretches of golden beach lie between Cala Pi and Cala Murta in Formentor. The main city, Palma, is the financial and political capital of the Balearic Islands.

Island Essentials

GETTING THERE   If you're coming in August, make sure you have a reserved return ticket. There are no empty airplane or ferry seats.

PREVIOUS PAGE: **Cala'n Porter beach on Menorca.**

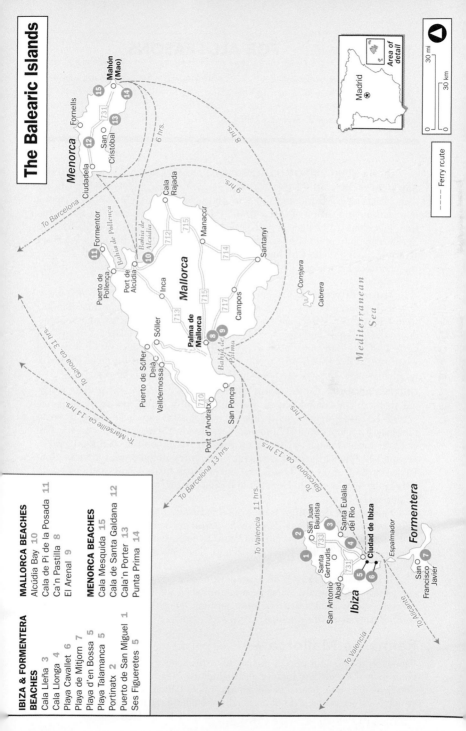

The Balearic Islands

IBIZA & FORMENTERA BEACHES
Cala Lleña 3
Cala Llonga 4
Playa Cavallet 6
Playa de Mitjorn 7
Playa d'en Bossa 5
Playa Talamanca 5
Portinatx 2
Puerto de San Miguel 1
Ses Figueretes 5

MALLORCA BEACHES
Alcúdia Bay 10
Cala de Pi de la Posada 11
Ca'n Pastilla 8
El Arenal 9

MENORCA BEACHES
Cala Mesquida 15
Cala de Santa Galdana 12
Cala'n Porter 13
Punta Prima 14

Ferry route

Area of detail

Madrid

30 mi
30 km

NOT AN island FOR ALL SEASONS

July and August are high season for Mallorca; don't even think of coming then without a reservation. It's possible to swim comfortably from June to October; after that, the water is prohibitively cold and many hotels and restaurants close until May.

Iberia (© 90-240-05-00; www.iberia.com) flies to Palma's **Aeroport Son San Joan** (© 90-240-47-04) from Barcelona, Valencia, and Madrid. There are daily planes from Madrid and Valencia, and several daily flights from Barcelona in summer. **Air Europa** (© 90-240-15-01; www.aireuropa.com) flies to Palma from Barcelona (twice daily in peak season) and less frequently from Madrid and Sevilla. About 30 other airlines also make the trip in season, including **Vueling, Ryanair, EasyJet,** and **Lufthansa.** An airport bus takes you to Plaça Espanya in the center of Palma for 3€. A metered cab costs about 30€ for the 25-minute drive into town.

Trasmediterránea, Estació Marítim in Palma (© 90-245-46-45; www.trasmediterranea.es), operates a daily **ferry** from Barcelona (trip time: 3½ hr.) from 65€ one-way. There are six ferries per week from Valencia (none on Sunday), taking 7 hours and costing 56€ one-way. (A faster boat takes 4–6 hours and costs 130€.) In Barcelona, book tickets at the Trasmediterránea office at Estació Marítim (© 90-245-46-45), and in Valencia at the office at Terminal Trasmediterráneo Muelle Deponiente, Estacio Marítima (© 90-245-46-45).

GETTING AROUND At the tourist office in Palma, you can pick up a bus schedule that explains island routes. Or, call Empresa Municipal de Transportes (© 97-121-44-44; www.emtpalma.es), which runs city buses from its main terminal, Estació Central D'Autobus, Plaça Espanya. The standard one-way fare is 1.50€ within Palma; at the station you can buy a booklet good for 10 rides, costing 10€. One of the most frequented bus routes includes transportation from Palma to the Cuevas del Drach; the one-way trip takes 1 hour and costs 12€. Other popular routes go to Dexa (45 min.; 8€ one-way) and Valldemossa (30 min.; 5€ one-way).

Ferrocarril de Sóller, Carrer Eusebio Estada 1 (© 97-175-20-51; www.trendesoller.com), off Plaça Espanya, has **train** service through majestic mountain scenery to Sóller. Trains go from Palma to Sóller daily from 8am to 7pm, also stopping at Mirador Del Pujol d'en Banya. The ticket costs 13€ one way, 20€ round-trip.

If you plan to stay in Palma, you don't need a car. Otherwise consider such companies as **Europcar,** at the airport terminal (© 90-210-50-55; www.europcar.com), or **Avis,** also at the airport terminal (© 90-211-02-61; www.avis.com). Reservations are essential.

Palma de Mallorca ★★

Palma, on the southern tip of the island, is the seat of government and has the lion's share of hotels, restaurants, and nightclubs. Nearly half the island's population lives in Palma. Islanders call Palma simply Ciutat (City). The Moors constructed Palma in the style of a casbah, or walled city. Its foundations are still visible, although obscured by high-rise hotels. It is the largest of the Balearic

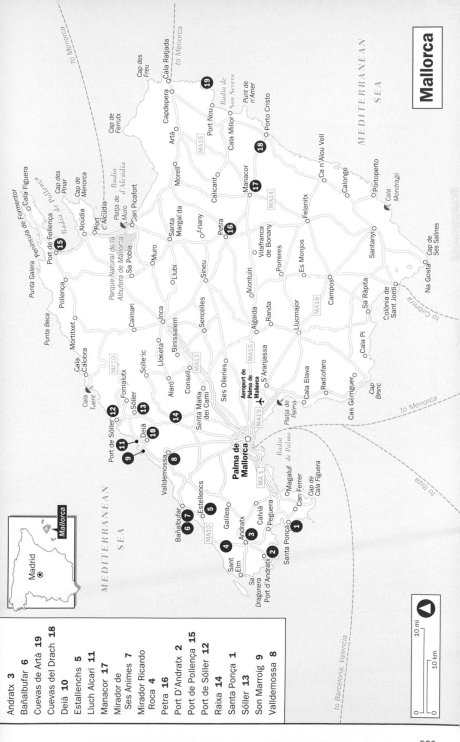

Mallorca

Andratx **3**
Bañalbufar **6**
Cuevas de Artà **19**
Cuevas del Drach **18**
Deià **10**
Estallenchs **5**
Lluch Alcari **11**
Manacor **17**
Mirador de
  Ses Animes **7**
Mirador Ricardo
  Roca **4**
Petra **16**
Port D'Andratx **2**
Port de Pollença **15**
Port de Sóller **12**
Raixa **14**
Santa Ponça **1**
Sóller **13**
Son Marroig **9**
Valldemossa **8**

ports, its bay often filled with yachts. Arrival by sea is the most impressive, with the skyline characterized by Bellver Castle and the cathedral's bulk. The area immediately surrounding the cathedral epitomizes old Palma, with mazes of narrow alleys and cobblestone streets.

ESSENTIALS

VISITOR INFORMATION   The **Tourist Information Office** is at Plaça Reina, 2 (☎ **97-117-39-90;** www.palmademallorca.es). It's open Monday to Friday 9am to 8pm, and Saturday 9am to 2pm.

GETTING AROUND   In Palma, you can get around the Old Town and the Paseo on foot. Otherwise, make limited use of taxis, or take one of the buses that cuts across the city. Out on the island, use buses or a rental car.

FAST FACTS   The **U.S. Consulate,** Edificio Reina Constanza, Porto Pi, B, 9D (☎ **97-140-37-07**), is open Monday to Friday from 10:30am to 1:30pm. The **British Consulate,** Carrer Convent dels Caputxins 4 (☎ **97-171-24-45**), is open Monday to Friday from 8:30am to 1:30pm.

In case of an **emergency,** dial ☎ **112.** If you fall ill, head to **Clínica Rotger,** Calle Santiago Rusiñol, 9 (☎ **97-144-85-00;** www.clinicarotger.es), or **Clínica Juaneda,** Calle Company, 30 (☎ **97-173-16-47;** www.clinicajuaneda. es). Both clinics are open 24 hours.

For **Internet access,** go to **Babaloo Internet Centre,** Calle Verja, 2 (☎ **97-195-77-25;** www.babaloointernet.com), just off Calle Sant Magi. It charges 2€ per hour and is open Monday to Friday 10am to 8pm and Sunday 3 to 8pm. It's closed on Saturday.

WHERE TO STAY IN PALMA

Almost all lodging on Mallorca requires guests to take breakfast. Most strongly encourage half- or full board, which you can decline (it's rarely economical). Prices here reflect room with breakfast.

Expensive

Sheraton Mallorca Arabella Golf Hotel ★★   You don't come to this Sheraton to lounge about on the beach—the hotel doesn't even have a shuttle to the strand. You come to play the Son Vida golf course, where the hotel is set, or the Son Muntanera, Son Quint, and Son Quint (9-hole) executive golf courses where the hotel offers a shuttle. Room rates include a greens fee discount at Son Vida, and staying here guarantees preferential tee times at all four. Spacious rooms have good views of the beautifully landscaped grounds.

Carrer de la Vinagrella, s/n. ☎ **800-325-3535** in the U.S., or 97-178-71-00. www.sheratonmallorcagolfhotel.com. 93 units. 400€–600€ double; from 544€ junior suite. Free parking. Bus: 7. **Amenities:** 2 restaurants; bar; bikes; children's center; concierge; exercise room; 3 18-hole golf courses, 1 9-hole course; 3 pools (1 heated indoor); spa; fitness center; sauna; 3 outdoor tennis courts (lit); Wi-Fi (free in lobby, fee in rooms).

Puro ★★   With the addition of the "Private Wing" in 2014, Puro marked its 10th anniversary as Palma's hippest hotel by expanding the options for luxury travelers. The wing includes 11 guest suites on the upper levels along with lounges, living rooms, a spa, a massage area, and a full kitchen on the ground level. The original wing is no slouch, either. During the expansion, the original Puro got a larger bar and restaurant, and some new furniture in warm-colored leathers and earth-tone fabrics to tone down the dazzling white decor it boasted when it opened. Guest rooms still exhibit an air of whimsy, and they're all fitted

ATTRACTIONS
Banys Arabs **7**
Castell de Bellver **13**
Catedral **9**
Es Baluard Museu d'Art
 Modern i Contemporani
 de Palma **12**
Fundació Pilar i Joan
 Miró a Mallorca **13**
Marineland **13**
Museu Fundación
 Juan March **5**
Palau de l'Almudaina **8**

HOTELS
Dalt Murada **6**
Hotel Bon Sol **14**
Puro **11**
Sheraton Mallorca
 Arabella Golf Hotel **1**
Tres Mallorca **10**

RESTAURANTS
La Bodeguilla **2**
Misa Braserie + Bar **4**
Tast Union **3**

Palma de Mallorca

with 52-inch TVs and Bose surround-sound audio systems. The roof terrace with lounge and plunge pool remains one of the most desirable places to be seen in Palma.

Calle Montenegro, 12. © **97-142-54-50.** www.purohotel.com. 34 units. 159€–299€ double; 219€–359€ junior suite; 334€–474€ suite. **Amenities:** Restaurant; bar; free Wi-Fi.

Tres Mallorca ★★ Located in the midst of Palma's historic center, this superb boutique hotel is entered through the 16th-century mansion that forms its core. Some architectural touches from the original structure are retained, such as the colonnaded balconies and the tile floor on the ground level. But guest rooms are modern and spacious, with a breezy contemporary design that features either hardwood or marble floors and airy furnishings that give every room a spa ambience. There are two roof terraces linked by a bridge; they have excellent views of the city rooftops and the port.

Calle Apuntadores, 3. ✆ **97-171-73-33.** www.hoteltres.com. 41 rooms. 130€–238€ double; 190€–267€ junior suite. **Amenities:** Restaurant; bar; outdoor pool; sauna; free Wi-Fi.

Moderate

Dalt Murada ★ This hotel built into a 16th-century manor in Palma's old Gothic quarter has splendid views of the cathedral from the roof terrace. The rooms feature a mix of parquet wood and tile floors, exposed wooden beams on the ceilings, and dark wooden window frames. Rooms vary a lot in size, with some being quite small, so ask to see the room before moving in. The location is perfect for sightseeing, less ideal for lying on the beach. Breakfast is served beneath lemon trees on the central patio.

Calle Almudaina, 6A. ✆ **97-142-53-00.** www.daltmurada.com. 16 units. 103€–210€ double; 197€–277€ suite. Bus: 3 or 7. **Amenities:** Restaurant; bar; free Wi-Fi in business center.

Hotel Bon Sol ★ Family owned and operated, this charming four-story hotel with a vaguely Moorish tower sits up on a cliff above the sea in Illetes. A walkway of about 200 steps winds through the mature landscaped gardens down to the small beach below. The original hotel complex built in a few stages in the 1950s has about two-thirds of the rooms. Some of the larger rooms and suites are distributed among the outlying villas. The family has gone to great lengths to evoke a medieval Moorish fantasy with antique furniture and decorative elements.

Paseo de Illetas, 30. ✆ **97-140-21-11.** www.hotelbonsol.es. 147 units. 149€–210€ double; 197€–277€ suite. Free parking. Bus: Take bus marked Illetas. Closed Nov 6–Dec 20. **Amenities:** 2 restaurants; bar; children's center; exercise room; 2 pools; spa; 2 outdoor tennis courts (lit); free Wi-Fi.

WHERE TO EAT IN PALMA

Surprisingly for an island, Mallorca's most typical main dish is *lomo,* or pork loin. If you order *lomo con col,* the meat comes enveloped in cabbage leaves and topped with a sauce of tomatoes, grapes, pine nuts, and bay leaf. The local version of *sabrosada* sausage is made with pure pork and red peppers. *Sopas mallorquinas* typically consist of mixed greens in soup flavored with olive oil and thickened with bread. The best-known vegetable dish is *el tumbet,* or lasagna of potato and eggplant with tomato sauce.

Moderate

La Bodeguilla ★★ MALLORCAN/SPANISH Run by two brothers who really know their wines, it can be hard to tell if this is a wine shop, a tapas bar, or a restaurant. Actually, it's all three. Wine-barrel tables with glass tops are arrayed on two stories. Downstairs, where all the hams are hanging, is ostensibly the tapas bar, but you can also get tapas upstairs, and you can ask for the restaurant menu in the bar. Dishes are quite sophisticated for the casual nature of the place—a starter of egg poached in a foie gras *veloute,* for example. The selection of Catalan wines is particularly strong.

Carrer San Jaume 3. ✆ **97-171-82-74.** www.la-bodeguilla.com. Tapas 4€–7€, main courses 12€–36€. Daily noon–midnight. Bus: 2, 3, 7, 15, 20, 25, 46.

Misa Braseria + Bar ★★ MEDITERRANEAN British-born Marc Fosh was the best thing ever to happen to Palma dining. His Simply Fosh remains a posh night out for inventive twists on Mediterranean standards, but this basement brasserie brings simple joy back to dining. Fosh isn't afraid to list a roasted farmhouse chicken or beef filet with truffled potatoes as house specialties, but you can also opt for the comforting pleasures of stewed beef cheeks or roast leg of lamb with creamy polenta. The midday menu is a terrific buy, offering versions with or without dessert. The menu changes every week but is likely to include a choice of soup or fried fish as a starter, then a choice of fish, meat, or rice dish as a main plate.

Carrer Can Maçanet, 1. ✆ **97-159-53-01.** www.misabraseria.com. Main courses 18€–29€; lunch menu 13€–16€. Bus: 3, 7, 15, 20, 25, 46.

Inexpensive

Tast Unión ★★ MALLORCAN You'll have to use your elbows to get in at meal time, but Tast Unión welcomes drinkers and diners at all hours. Like its sister tapas bar **Tast Avenidas** (Av. Comte de Sallent, 11; ✆ **97-110-15-40**), it specializes in creative tapas, crafted by executive chef Patxi Castellano, that use seasonal produce and the catch of the day. His version of squid stuffed with *gulas* (imitation baby eels) and *sabrosada* was a big winner at the national Spanish tapas competition. The meltingly soft pan-fried duck liver is also popular. Don't worry if you can't get to the bar; tapas are also passed on trays, with plates color-coded to indicate the price.

Carrer Unión, 2. ✆ **97-172-98-78.** www.tast.com. Tapas 3€–7€; large plates 12€–25€. Mon–Sat 12:30pm–midnight. Bus: 3, 7, 20, 46.

EXPLORING PALMA

Banys Arabs ★ HISTORIC SITE
These Moorish baths date from the 10th century and are the only intact Moorish-constructed buildings in Palma.

Carrer Serra 7 in the Gothic Quarter. ✆ **97-172-15-49.** Admission 2€. Apr–Nov daily 9:30am–8pm; Dec–Mar daily 9am–7pm. Bus: 15.

Castell de Bellver ★ CASTLE
Erected in 1309, this round hilltop castle was the summer palace of the kings of Mallorca—during the brief period when Mallorca had kings. The castle, which was a fortress with a double moat, is well preserved and now houses the Museu Municipal, which is devoted to archaeological objects and old coins. The chief attraction here is the view—in fact, the name, Bellver, means "beautiful view."

Carrer de Camillo Josè Cela, s/n. ✆ **97-173-06-57.** www.cultura.palma.es. Admission 4€ adults; 2€ children 14–18, students, and seniors; free for children 13 and under. Apr–Sept Mon–Sat 8:30am–8pm, Sun 10am–8pm; Oct–Mar Mon–Sat 8am–6pm, Sun 10am–6pm. Bus: 3, 4, or 20.

The wrought-iron canopy, by Gaudí, at the Catedral.

The sculpture garden at Fundacio Pilar i Joan Miró a Mallorca.

Catedral (La Seu) ★ CATHEDRAL   This Catalan Gothic cathedral stands in the old town overlooking the ocean. Begun during the reign of Jaume II (1276–1311), it was completed in 1601. Its central vault is 43m (141 ft.) high, and its columns rise 20m (66 ft.). There is a wrought-iron *baldachin* (canopy) by Gaudí over the main altar. The treasury contains pieces said to be part of the True Cross, and relics of San Sebastián, patron saint of Palma. Museum and cathedral hours often change, so call ahead.

Plaça de l'Almoina s/n. © **97-172-31-30.** www.catedraldemallorca.info. Free admission to cathedral; museum and treasury 4€. Apr–May and Oct Mon–Fri 10am–5:15pm, Sat 10am–2:15pm; Nov–Mar Mon–Fri 10am–3:15pm, Sat 10am–2:15pm; June–Sept Mon–Fri 10am–6:15pm, Sat 10am–2:15pm. Bus: 15 or 25.

Es Baluard Museu d'Art Modern i Contemporani ★ ART MUSEUM Created to promote Balearic and Mediterranean art from the 20th and 21st centuries, the building gives an impressive panoramic view of the whole Bay of Palma from the site of the 16th-century defensive fortress known as the Baluard de Sant Pere (Bastion of St. Peter). The museum opened in 2004, and has frankly struggled to find an audience for its collections. The best work tends to be the monumental-scale outdoor sculpture, but the galleries have some hidden gems of paintings by the likes of Picasso, Chagall, Miró, and Gustav Klimt.

Plaça Porta de Santa Catalina 10. © **97-190-82-00.** www.esbaluard.org. Admission 6€ adults, 4.50€ seniors and students, free ages 11 and younger. Oct–mid-June Tues–Sun 10am–8pm; mid-June–Sept Tues–Sun 10am–10pm. Bus: 1.

Fundació Pilar i Joan Miró a Mallorca ★★ ART MUSEUM   Joan Miró lived in Palma from 1956 until his death and produced a prodigious amount of art here. After his death in 1983, his widow Pilar Juncosa donated a vast number of his paintings, drawings, and graphic works along with a collection of personal documents. Here at his former estate, you can see rotating exhibitions dealing with his life and work in the beautiful building designed by Rafael Moneo.

Carrer Joan de Saridakis, 29. ☏ **97-170-14-20.** miro.palmademallorca.es Admission 6€ adults, 3€ children and seniors; free to all on Sat. Mid-May to mid-Sept Tues–Sat 10am–7pm, Sun 10am–3pm; off-season Tues–Sat 10am–6pm, Sun 10am–3pm. Bus: 3 or 6.

Museu de Arte Español Contemporaní (Fundación Juan March) ★
ART MUSEUM   Small but select, this museum has 69 works of 20th-century Spanish art representing the first generation of the Spanish avant-garde—Picasso, Miró, Dalí, and Juan Gris—as well as Spanish painters such as Carlos Saura and Antoní Tápies from the mid-century. Temporary exhibitions show contemporary work by Spanish painters as well as representative work from the international avant-garde.

Carrer Sant Miquel, 11. www.march.es. ☏ **97-171-35-15.** Free admission. Mon–Fri 10am–6:30pm; Sat 10:30am–2pm.

Palau de l'Almudaina ★ PALACE   The former Alcázar Real was built first by Muslim rulers in 1281, then significantly modified by the kings of Arágon who held sway here over the next few centuries and made this their royal residence when they came to Mallorca. Opposite the cathedral, it is surrounded by Moorish-style gardens and fountains. The palace museum displays antiques, artwork, suits of armor, and Gobelin tapestries. The grounds have panoramic views of the harbor.

Carrer Palau Reial s/n. ☏ **97-121-41-34.** www.patrimonionacional.es. Admission 9€ adults, 4€ children. Apr–Sept Mon–Fri 10am–5:45pm, Sat 10am–1:15pm; Oct–Mar Tues–Fri 11am–1:15pm and 4–5:15pm, Sat 10am–1:15pm. Bus: 15.

PALMA OUTDOORS

Beaches

You can swim from late June to October; don't believe the promoters who try to sell you on mild Mallorcan winters in January and February—it gets downright cold. There is a beach near the Palma cathedral, but adjacent foul-smelling (covered) sewers make swimming unappealing. The closest public beach to downtown is **Playa Nova,** a 35-minute bus ride. Some hotels, however, have private beaches. If you head east, you reach the excellent beaches of **Ca'n Pastilla.** The golden-sand beaches at **El Arenal** are well equipped with tourist facilities.

Playa Nova.

AN unspoiled MEDITERRANEAN ISLE

Declared a National Reserve in 1991, **Illa de Cabrera ★★** lies off the south coast of Mallorca. It is the largest of the 19 islands that form the Archipelago of Cabrera. With its lush vegetation, dramatic coastline, and abundant animal life, it makes an intriguing day trip. Large colonies of birds and marine animals await visitors. In the 13th and 14th centuries, pirates used Cabrera as a base to attack Mallorca. Ruins of a castle built in the 14th century can be seen at the entrance to the port. **Excursions à Cabrera** (© **97-164-90-34;** www.excursionsacabrera.es) operates 40-minute tours from Colonia de Sant Jordi, 47km (29 miles) southeast of Palma around 10am daily, returning at 5pm; round-trip costs 40€ adults, 25€ ages 3 to 11.

Going to the southwest, you find good but often crowded beaches at **Cala Mayor** and **Sant Agustí.**

Golf

Mallorca is a golfer's dream. The best course is **Arabella Golf Son Vida,** Urbanización Son Vida, about 13km (8 miles) east of Palma along the Andrade Highway. This 18-hole course is shared by two hotels, but the course is open to anyone who calls (© **97-179-12-10;** www.sonvidagolf.com). Greens fees are 55€ to 70€ for guests at the Sheraton hotel (see above) and 75€ to 100€ for non-guests. Cart rentals are also available for 45€. For more on Mallorca golf, contact **Federación Balear de Golf** (© **97-172-27-53;** www.fbgolf.com).

PALMA AFTER DARK

Palma is packed with bars and dance clubs. The island's northern tier has some clubs, but for a laser- and strobe-lit club, boogie in Palma.

Right on the beach by lots of hotels, **Tito's,** Passeig Marítim (© **97-173-00-17;** www.titosmallorca.com), is the most popular disco on the island (it's frequented by an international crowd). Tito's charges a cover of 18€ to 20€, including the first drink. Between June and September, it's open nightly from 11pm to 6am; Thursday to Sunday 11pm to 6am the rest of the year.

Costa Galana, Av. Argentina 45 (© **97-145-46-58**), is a bar with white leather chairs and a sound menu of electric jazz and deep house music. Upstairs is a bustling cafe; the lounge downstairs pulsates at night. Open Monday to Thursday and Sunday 8am to 2am, Friday and Saturday 8am to 4am. Beer costs from 3€, mixed drinks from 7€.

Gran Casino Mallorca lies on the harborfront promenade at Av. Gabriel Roca 4 (© **97-113-00-00;** www.casinodemallorca.com). You'll need a passport (plus a shirt and tie for men) to enter and play table games or slots. The casino is open daily 4pm to 5am. Entry is 4€.

Palma's best beer hall is **Lórien,** Carrer de les Caputxines, 5 (© **97-172-32-02**), with 100 selections from two dozen countries.

Exploring Mallorca by Car: The West Coast

Mountainous Mallorca's dramatic scenery is best appreciated by driving. This daylong circuit of 142km (88 miles) begins and ends in Palma.

Leave Palma heading west on C-719. Just a short distance from the sea rises the Sierra de Tramuntana. The road passes Palma Nova before coming to **Santa**

Ponça, a town with a fishing harbor divided by a promontory. A fortified Gothic tower and a watchtower are evidence of the days when this small harbor suffered repeated raids and attacks. Jaume I's troops landed in a cove here on September 12, 1229, to begin the reconquest of the island from the Muslims.

From Santa Ponça, continue along the highway, passing Paguera, Cala Fornells, and Camp de Mar, all beautiful spots with sandy coves. From Camp de Mar twisting, cliff-top roads lead to **Port D'Andratx.** Summer vacationers mingle with fishermen in this natural port set against a backdrop of pines. The place was once a haven for smugglers.

Continue northeast along C-719 to reach **Andratx,** 5km (3 miles) away. Because of frequent raids by Turkish pirates, this town moved inland. Located 31km (19 miles) west of Palma, Andratx is one of the loveliest towns on the island, surrounded by fortifications and boasting a Gothic parish church.

From Andratx, take C-710 north, a winding road parallel to the island's jagged northwestern coast. Most of the road is perched along the cliff edge and shaded by pine trees. It's hard to drive and pay attention to the scenery, so stop at the **Mirador Ricardo Roca** for a panoramic view of a series of coves that can be reached only from the sea.

The road continues to **Estallenchs,** a town of steep slopes surrounded by pine groves, olive and almond trees, and fruit orchards (especially apricot). Estallenchs sits at the foot of the Galatzo mountain peak. Stop to explore some of its steep, winding streets on foot. From the town, you can walk to Cala de Estallenchs cove, where a spring cascades down the high cliffs.

The road winds on northeast to **Bañalbufar,** 8km (5 miles) from Estallenchs and about 26km (16 miles) northwest from Palma. Set 100m (328 ft.) above sea level, it seems to perch directly over the sea. **Mirador de Ses Animes ★**, a belvedere constructed in the 17th century, offers a panoramic coastal view.

Many small excursions are possible from here. You might want to venture over to **Port d'es Canonge,** reached by a road branching out from the C-710 to the north of Bañalbufar. It has a beach, a simple restaurant, and some old fishermen's houses. The same road takes you inland to **San Granja,** a mansion originally constructed by the Cistercians as a monastery in the 13th century.

Back on C-710, continue to **Valldemossa,** the town where composer Frédéric Chopin and French novelist George Sand spent a now-famous winter (see below). After a visit to the **Cartoixa Reial** (Carthusian monastery) where they lived, wander through the steep streets of the Old Town. The cloister of **Ses Murteres** has a romantic garden. The **Carthusian church** is from the late 18th century. Goya's father-in-law, Bayeu, painted the dome's frescoes.

Beyond Valldemossa, the road runs along cliffs some 395m (1,300 ft.) high until it reaches **Son Marroig,** the former residence of Archduke Lluis Salvador. He erected a small neoclassical temple on a slope overlooking the sea to give visitors a panoramic vista. From a balcony, you can enjoy a view of the famous pierced rock, the Foradada, rising out of the water.

You have now reached **Deià,** where small tile altars in the streets reproduce stations of the cross. This was the home of English writer Robert Graves for many years. He is buried at the **Campo Santo** cemetery.

Continue north along the highway. You come first to **Lluch Alcari,** where Picasso retreated for a short period in the 1950s. The settlement was once the victim of pirate raids, and you can see the ruins of several defense towers.

C-710 continues to **Sóller,** just 10km (6¼ miles) from Deià. The urban center has five 16th-century facades, an 18th-century convent, and a parish church of the 16th and 17th centuries. It lies in a broad basin where citrus and

---

TAKE THE train

If you're not driving, you can still reach Sóller aboard a turn-of-the-20th-century narrow-gauge railroad train from Palma. You can catch the train at the Palma

Terminal on Calle Eusebio Estada, near Plaça d'Espanya. It runs daily from 8am to 7pm; the fare is 10€ one-way. Call ✆ **97-175-20-51** for information.

---

olive trees are abundant. Many painters, including Rusiñol, settled here and found inspiration.

Travel 5km (3 miles) north on C-711 to reach the coast and **Port de Sóller,** perched on a sheltered round bay. A submarine base is here today, but it is also a harbor for pleasure craft and has a lovely beach. The **Sanctuary of Santa Catalina** has one of the best views of the inlet.

After leaving the Sóller area, you face a choice: If you've run out of time, you can cut the tour in half here and head back along C-711 to Palma with two stops along the way. Your other option is to continue north, following the C-710 and local roads, to **Cap de Formentor,** where even more spectacular scenery awaits you. Among the highlights of this coastal detour: **Fornalutx,** a lofty mountain village with steep cobbled streets, Moorish-tiled roofs, and groves of almond trees; the splendid, hair-raising road to the harbor village of **Sa Calobra,** plunging to the sea in one area and then climbing arduously past olive groves, oaks, and jagged boulders in another area; and the 13th-century **Monasterio de Lluch,** some 45km (28 miles) north of Palma, which is home to the Black Virgin of Lluch, the island's patron saint. The well-known "boys' choir of white voices" sings there daily at noon and again at twilight.

Those not taking the coastal detour can head south along C-711 with a stop at **Jardines de Alfàbia,** Carretera Palma–Sóller Km 17 (✆ **97-161-31-23;** www.jardinesdealfabia.com), a former Muslim residence. This foothills estate includes a palace and romantic gardens. You can wander among pergolas, a pavilion, and ponds, or go indoors to see a collection of Mallorcan furniture and an Arabic coffered ceiling. The gardens are open April to October Monday to Saturday 9:30am to 6:30pm, and November to March Monday to Friday 9:30am to 5:30pm and Saturday 9:30am to 1pm. Admission is 5€.

From Alfàbia, the highway becomes straight and Palma is just 18km (11 miles) away. But before reaching the capital, consider a final stop at **Raixa,** a manorial estate and gardens owned by the island government. It was built on the site of an old Muslim hamlet. It stands 1.5km (1 mile) outside the village of Buñola ("Small Vineyard"). The present building was once the estate of Cardinal Despuif and his family, who constructed it in the Italian style near the end of the 1700s. Ruins from Roman excavations are found on the grounds. Rusiñol came here, painting the place several times. Raixa keeps the same hours as Jardines de Alfàbia (see above), and admission is free. The estate, however, is closed for renovations and restorations until sometime in 2016, pending funding. After Raixa, the route leads directly to the northern outskirts of Palma.

Valldemossa & Deià ★★

Valldemossa is the site of the **Cartoixa Reial ★**, Plaça de las Cartujas s/n (✆ **97-161-21-06**), where George Sand and the tubercular Frédéric Chopin wintered in 1838 and 1839, shocking the locals. Fearing they'd catch Chopin's tuberculosis, the peasants burned all but a small painting and a French piano after the couple left. The residential cells where they lived may be visited November to February Monday to Saturday 9:30am to 4:30pm, Sunday 10am to 1:30pm; and March to October Monday to Saturday 9:30am to 6pm. Admission is 8€ adults, 5.60€ students, 3.70€ ages 10 to 14, free ages 9 and under.

During the same hours and on the same ticket, it also possible to visit **Palau del Rei Sancho** ★, next door to the monastery. This Moorish retreat was built by one of the island kings, and a guide in Mallorcan dress leads the tours.

From Valldemossa, continue through the mountains, following the signposts for 11km (6¾ miles) to Deià. Set against a backdrop of olive-green mountains, **Deià** is peaceful and serene, with stone houses and creeping bougainvillea. It has long had a special meaning for artists. Robert Graves, the English poet and novelist (*I, Claudius*), lived in Deià and died here in 1985. He is buried in the local cemetery. It is now possible to visit Graves's home, **Ca N'Alluny** ★, Carretera de Soller Km 1 (© **97-163-61-85;** www.lacasaderobertgraves.com), a 5-minute walk from the center of the town. Graves and Laura Riding built the house in 1932. The poet wrote: "I wanted to go where town was still town; and country, country." The house has been restored to circa 1946, when Graves returned to the island. Visitors can explore the studies of both Laura Riding and Robert Graves, and visit the kitchen and dining room. It is open April to October Monday to Friday 10am to 5pm and Saturday 10am to 3pm. October to April it is open Monday to Friday 9am to 4pm and Saturday 9am to 2pm. Admission is 7€ adults, 5€ students and seniors, 3.50€ ages 12 and under.

Valldemossa lacks basic services, including a tourist office. It is connected to a bus service from Palma, however. **Bus Nort Balear** (© **97-149-06-80**) goes to Valldemossa 13 times daily for a one-way fare of 8€. Buses leave Palma at Plaza España (Calle Eusebio Estrada). To reach Deià by public transportation from Palma, 27km (17 miles) away, stay on the bus that stops in Valldemossa. If you're driving from Palma, take the Carretera Valldemossa–Deià to Valldemossa and continue to Deià.

WHERE TO EAT & STAY IN DEIÀ

El Olivo ★★ CONTEMPORARY SPANISH   The rather rustic nature of the building—a former olive oil mill with stone walls and wicker furniture—belies the sophistication of the contemporary Spanish cuisine. Chef Guillermo Méndez is adept at gilding the lily, serving the sweet Sóller prawns sautéed with pancetta and topped with a purée of Jabugo ham and celery. Even vegetarians can get the full treatment with a house classic of "carpaccio" of zucchini with goat cheese and basil vinaigrette. In La Residencia Hotel, Son Canals. s/n. © **97-163-93-92.** www.hotel-laresidencia. com. Main courses 24€–46€; tasting menus 105€–120€. Winter Wed–Sun 7:30–10:30pm; summer daily 7:30–11pm. Closed Dec–Feb.

Es Racò d'es Teix ★★ MEDITERRANEAN   You're likely to get your best meal on the island at this delightful Michelin-starred and family-run

A courtyard of the Cartoixa Reial.

restaurant in an old stone house with spectacular views of the mountains. The rather rustic dining room has tables on two levels. Chef Josef Sauerschell is an inventive sort who makes the most of local products, offering dishes like lobster ravioli with white peaches and slow-cooked suckling pig stuffed with spicy *sabrosada* sausage and glazed with honey. Make reservations here as far in advance as possible.

Carrer de sa Vinya Veia, 6. ℭ **97-163-95-01.** www.esracodesteix.es. Main courses 37€–40€. Tasting menu without wine 98€, with wine 165€. Wed–Sun 1–3pm and 8–11pm. Closed mid-Nov to mid-Feb.

The peaceful town of Deià.

Hoposa Costa d'Or ★ Fully overhauled in 2013 to bring the rooms up to luxury standards, this adults-only (14+) hotel sits in a pine grove on a hill above the rugged coast on the road to Sóller, about 1.5km (1 mile) north of Deià. It is designed to blend into the landscape. The gardens are filled with citrus trees, date palms, and gnarled old fig trees. A pathway leads through the forest down to a private and secluded cove beach.

Carrer Lluch Alcari, s/n. ℭ **97-163-90-25.** www.hoposa.es. 41 rooms. 164€–284€ double; 230€–305€ suite. Free parking. Closed late-Oct–Mar. **Amenities:** Restaurant; bar; bikes; exercise room; 2 freshwater pools (1 heated indoor); 2 outdoor tennis courts (lit); Wi-Fi (free in lobby).

Hotel Es Molí ★★ Widely considered the most alluring of the larger properties in Deià, Es Molí is built around a 19th-century manor house to which new wings were added in the 1960s to create the current hotel. Unlike many such transformations, the additions did not compromise the original charm. Rooms are spacious and beautifully furnished, and some share a private porch overlooking the gardens. The hotel has a private beach, Sa Muleta, with a shuttle from the hotel four times a day.

Carretera Valldemossa, s/n, Deià. ℭ **97-163-90-00.** www.esmoli.com. 87 units. 225€–274€ double; 360€–395€ junior suite; 425€–475€ suite. Free parking. Closed Nov–Apr. **Amenities:** Restaurant; bar; exercise room; outdoor freshwater heated pool; outdoor tennis court (lit); free Wi-Fi.

Port de Pollença/Formentor ★

Beside a sheltered bay between Cap de Formentor to the north and Cap del Pinar to the south lies Port de Pollença, 65km (40 miles) north of Palma. The town is flanked by two hills: **Calvary** to the west and **Puig** to the east. Calvary Chapel offers the best views of the resort and the bay, which provides excellent water-skiing and sailing. Low-rise hotels, private homes, restaurants, and snack bars line the very attractive beach, which is narrow at its northwestern end but has some of the island's whitest sand and clearest water. Windsurfing, waterskiing, and scuba diving are among the watersports offered in the area.

Wednesday is **market day** in Port de Pollença, so head for the town square between 8am and 1pm to browse through fresh produce, leather goods, embroidered tablecloths, ceramics, and more. Bargaining is part of the fun. Sunday is market day in the town of Pollença.

In the town of Pollença, about 6km (3¾ miles) from Port de Pollença, an 18th-century stairway leads up to an *ermita* (hermitage). Consisting of 365 stairs, it is known as the **Monte Calvario (Calvary),** but you can also reach the top by car via Carrer de las Cruces, which is lined with 3m-high (9¾-ft.) concrete crosses. **Cala San Vicente,** between Pollença and Port de Pollença, is a pleasant, sandy cove with notable surf and several small hotels and restaurants.

Cap de Formentor ★, "the devil's tail," can be reached from Port de Pollença via a spectacular road, twisting along to the lighthouse at the cape's end. Formentor is a dramatic landscape of mountains, pine trees, rocks, and sea, plus some of the best beaches on Mallorca.

ESSENTIALS

GETTING THERE Five **buses** a day leave the Plaça Espanya in Palma, pass through Inca, and continue on to Port de Pollença; a one-way fare costs 7.50€. If you're driving, you can continue on from Deià (see above) along C-710 all the way to Pollença.

VISITOR INFORMATION The **tourist information office,** on Passeig de Saralegui s/n (© **97-186-54-67**), is open Monday to Saturday 8am to 3pm and 5 to 7pm.

WHERE TO EAT & STAY IN PORT DE POLLENÇA

Stay Restaurant ★ MALLORCAN A mainstay on the waterfront since the 1970s, Stay was rebuilt from scratch in 2006 to provide a great harbor experience. Sure, the dining room has panoramic views, but the huge terrace all but

Cap de Formentor.

Parc Natural de S'Albufera.

puts you in the yachts anchored in the marina. Seafood dishes are plentiful and uniformly excellent, ranging from filet of John Dory with caramelized onions to a mixed grill of whatever the fishermen bring in. The best of the meat dishes is roasted leg of Mallorcan lamb.

Muelle Nuevo, Estació Marítim s/n. ℭ **97-186-40-13.** www.stayrestaurant.com. Main courses 15€–40€. Daily menu 35€. Daily noon–4pm and 7:30–10:30pm.

Son Brull ★★★   Probably the best residence in the area for gastronomes, this former 17th-century monastery was transformed into an ultrachic contemporary hotel without losing sight of its rustic roots. Although it's at least a 10-minute drive to the beach, the hillside country setting has its own appeal. The hotel offers cooking classes and dish tastings with chef Rafel Perello at the gastronomic restaurant 3/65.

Carretera Palma-Pollença s/n, ℭ **97-153-53-53.** www.sonbrull.com. 23 units. 281€–519€ double; 455€–697€ junior suite. Restaurant menus 49€, 66€; tasting menu 80€. Free parking. Closed Dec–Mar. **Amenities:** Restaurant; bar; bikes; exercise room; 2 freshwater heated pools (1 indoor); spa; outdoor tennis court; free Wi-Fi.

EXPLORING THE COAST

Mallorca's northwest coast is full of plunging cliffs and rocky coves. The **Mirador de Colomer** provides an expansive view of the California-like coast from Punta de la Nau to Punta de la Troneta and includes El Colomer (Pigeon's Rock). But it is the 20km (12-mile) stretch of winding, at times vertiginous road leading from Port de Pollença to the tip of the **Formentor Peninsula** that delivers the island's most intoxicating views. Cliffs more than 200m (656 ft.) high and rock-rimmed coves embrace turquoise waters. About halfway along this road is **Cala de Pi de la Posada,** with a lovely bathing beach. Continuing on to the end, you'll come to the lighthouse at **Cap de Formentor.**

   Alcúdia Bay is a long stretch of narrow, sandy beach with beautiful water backed by countless hotels, whose crowds rather overwhelm the area in peak season. The nightlife is more abundant and varied here than in Port de Pollença.

   Between Port de Alcúdia and Ca'n Picafort is the **Parc Natural de S'Albufera,** Carretera Alcúdia–Artá Km 27 (ℭ **97-189-22-50**). A wetlands area of lagoons, dunes, and canals covering some 800 hectares (1,977 acres), it attracts nature enthusiasts. More than 200 species of birds have been sighted here, with the largest numbers during spring and fall migrations. The park is open daily (except Christmas) October to March from 9am to 5pm and April to September from 9am to 7pm. Visits are free, but you must get a permit at the reception center, where all motorized vehicles must be left.

Mallorca's East Coast: The Cueva Route

Less dramatic than the west coast, Mallorca's east coast is studded with caves and is often call the *cueva* route. Leave Palma on the freeway, but turn onto Carretera C-715 in the direction of Manacor. About 56km (35 miles) east of Palma, you come to your first stop, Petra.

PETRA

Petra was founded by Jaume II on the ruins of a Roman settlement. Father Junípero Serra (1713–84) was born here, and a statue commemorates the Franciscan who founded California's San Diego, Monterey, and San Francisco missions. **Museo Beato Junípero Serra,** Carrer Barracar (© **97-156-11-49**), gives you an idea of 18th-century island life. The museum, 457m (1,500 ft.) from the center of the village, is open daily, but visits are only by appointment. Admission is free, but donations are encouraged.

CUEVAS DEL DRACH ★★★

After Petra, follow C-715 southeast into Manacor, and take the road east toward the town of **Porto Cristo,** 61km (38 miles) east of Palma. Go 0.8km (½ mile) south of town to **Cuevas del Drach** (**Caves of the Dragon;** © **97-182-07-53;** www.cuevasdeldrach.com). The caves contain a forest of stalactites and stalagmites, as well as five lakes, where you can listen to a concert and later go boating. Martel Lake, 176m (577 ft.) long, is the largest underground lake in the world. From April to October, tours depart daily every hour from 10am to 5pm; from November to March, they depart daily at 10:45am, noon, 2, and 3:30pm. Admission is 14€ adults, 7€ ages 3 to 12. If you don't have a car, four daily buses leave from Palma. Buses pass through Manacor on the way to Porto Cristo.

Cuevas del Drach.

CUEVAS DE ARTÀ ★★★

Near Platja de Canyamel (Playa de Cañamel, on some maps), **Cuevas de Artà** (© **97-184-12-93;** www.cuevasdearta.com) are said to have inspired Jules Verne's 1864 novel *Journey to the Center of the Earth*. Formed by seawater erosion, the caves are about 32m (105 ft.) above sea level, and some chambers rise about 46m (151 ft.). You enter a vestibule where torches once used to light the caves have blackened the walls. The Reina de las Columnas (Queen of the Columns) rises about 22m (72 ft.) and is followed by a lower room called the "Inferno" for its Dante-esque appearance. It is followed by a field of stalagmites and stalactites (the "Purgatory Rooms"), which eventually lead to the "Theater" and "Paradise." The caves were once used by pirates, and centuries ago they provided a haven for Spanish Moors fleeing the persecution of Jaume I. The stairs in the cave were built for Isabel II for her 1860 visit. Tours depart daily May to October every half-hour from 10am to 6pm, off-season 10am to 5pm. Admission is 13€ adults, 7€ ages 7 to 12.

IBIZA ★★

Once virtually unknown and unvisited, Ibiza began to thrive as an art colony in the 1950s and became popular with hippies in the 1960s. Today, it attracts northern European package tourists, ravers, and is a mecca for gay travelers. At 585 sq. km (226 sq. miles), Ibiza is the third largest of the Balearic Islands, with a jagged coastline, some fine beaches, whitewashed houses, secluded bays, cliffs, and hilly terrain dotted with fig and olive trees. Warmer than Mallorca, it's a better choice for winter, but swelters in July and August.

Ciudad de Ibiza boasts **Playa Talamanca** in the north and the white sandy beaches of **Ses Figueretes** and **Playa d'en Bossa** in the south. Las Salinas, in the south, near the old salt flats, offers excellent sands. **Playa Cavallet** and **Aigües Blanques** attract nude sunbathers. The long sandy cove of Cala Llonga, south of Santa Eulalia del Río, and the white sandy beach of El Cana to the north are sacred to Ibiza's sun worshipers. In Formentera, **Playa de Mitjorn** stretches 5km (3 miles) and is relatively uncrowded. Set against a backdrop of pines and dunes, the pure white sand of **Es Pujols** makes it Ibiza's most popular beach.

Both soft drugs and hard sex are available, but there are dangers. Visitors can be deported for *irresponsibilidad económica* (no money) or *conducta antisocial* (drunk and disorderly conduct). Some young travelers have forsaken Ibiza in favor of the tiny island of Formentera, where they find less harassment. Because of limited lodging options, restaurants, and nightlife, Formentera is most often visited on a day trip from Ibiza.

Island Essentials

GETTING THERE   As with Palma, if you come in July and August, be sure you have a return ticket and a reservation.

Iberia (© **90-240-05-00;** www.iberia.com) flies into **Ibiza International Airport** (© **90-240-47-04;** www.aena-aeropuertos.es), 5.5km (3½ miles) from Ciudad de Ibiza. Seven daily flights connect Ibiza with Palma. There are two daily flights from Valencia and three from Madrid. With the exception of charter flights, Iberia is the main carrier servicing Ibiza. Its only other competitor is **Air Europa** (© **90-240-15-01** in Ibiza; www.aireuropa.com), which offers flights to Ibiza from Barcelona (a maximum of two flights a day), as well as from Madrid, at less frequent intervals than Iberia. The price of flights varies considerably because of season and availability.

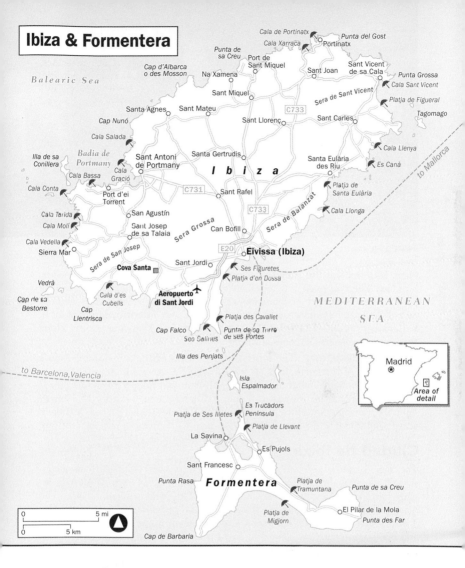

Ibiza & Formentera

Balearic Sea

Cala de Portinatx
Cala Xarraca
Punta del Gost
Portinatx
Punta de sa Creu
Port de Sant Miquel
Sant Joan
Sant Vicent de sa Cala
Punta Grossa
Cala Sant Vicent
Cap d'Albarca o des Mosson
Na Xamena
Sant Miquel
Sera de Sant Vicent
Platja de Figueral
Santa Agnes
Sant Mateu
C733
Tagomago
Cap Nunó
Sant Llorenç
Sant Carles
Cala Salada
Illa de sa Conillera
Badia de Portmany
Sant Antoni de Portmany
Santa Gertrudis
Santa Eulària des Riu
Cala Llenya
Es Canà
Cala Gració
Cala Bassa
I b i z a
Platja de Santa Eulària
Cala Conta
Port d'ei Torrent
C731
Sant Rafel
Sera de Balanzat
to Mallorca
Cala Tarida
Cala Molí
San Agustín
C733
Cala Llonga
Cala Vedella
Sant Josep de sa Talaia
Sera Grossa
Can Bofill
Sierra Mar
Sera de San Josep
E20
Eivissa (Ibiza)
Cova Santa
Sant Jordi
Ses Figueretes
Vedrà
Cala d'es Cubells
Aeropuerto di Sant Jordi
Platja d'on Bossa
Cap de sa Bestorre
Cap Llentrisca
MEDITERRANEAN SEA
Cap Falco
Platja des Cavallet
Ses Salines
Punta de sa Torre de ses Portes
Illa des Penjats
Madrid
Area of detail
to Barcelona, Valencia
Isla Espalmador
Es Trucàdors Peninsula
Platja de Ses Illetes
Platja de Llevant
La Savina
Es Pujols
Sant Francesc
Punta Rasa
Formentera
Platja de Tramuntana
Punta de sa Creu
Platja de Migjorn
El Pilar de la Mola
Punta des Far
Cap de Barbaria

0   5 mi
0   5 km

Trasmediterránea, Estación Marítima, Andenes del Puerto s/n (© **90-245-46-45;** www.trasmediterranea.es), operates **ferry service** from Barcelona at the rate of four per week; a one-way ticket costs 57€. From Valencia to Ibiza, there is one boat per week, costing 57€ one-way. From Palma, there is one boat on Saturday, which costs 49€ one-way. Check with travel agents in Barcelona, Valencia, or Palma for ferry schedules. You can book tickets through any agent.

GETTING AROUND If you land at the airport outside Ciudad de Ibiza, you will find **bus** service for the 5.5km (3½-mile) ride into town. Sometimes taxis are shared. In Ciudad de Ibiza, buses leave for the airport from Av. Isidor Macabich 24 (by the ticket kiosk), every hour on the hour, daily from 7am to 11:30pm.

Ibiza's D'Alt Vila.

Once in Ibiza, you can walk the compact city, but buses travel to the nearby beaches. The two main bus terminals are at Av. Isidor Macabich 20 and 42 (© 97-134-05-10). Mopeds and bicycles are popular, especially in the southern part of the island. Rentals can be made through **Casa Valentín,** corner of Av. B. V. Ramón 19 (© 97-131-08-22). Mopeds cost from 25€ to 35€ per day. Hertz and Avis have car rental offices at the airport.

VISITOR INFORMATION   The **tourist information office** is at Antonio Riquer 2, in the port of Ciudad de Ibiza (© 97-119-19-51; www.ibiza.travel). It's open June to November Monday to Friday 9am to 9pm, Saturday 9:30am to 7:30pm; and December to May Monday to Friday 8:30am to 3pm, Saturday 10:30am to 1pm. There is another office at the airport (© 97-180-91-18), which is open year-round Monday to Saturday 9am to 2 pm and 3 to 8pm, Sunday 9am to 2pm.

Ciudad de Ibiza

The island's capital was founded by the Carthaginians 2,500 years ago. Today it consists of a lively marina district around the harbor and an old town, **D'Alt Vila ★**, with narrow cobblestone streets and flat-roofed, whitewashed houses. The marina district is full of galleries, shops, bars, and restaurants. Much of the Old Town's medieval character has been preserved. Many houses have Gothic styling and open onto courtyards. The Old Town is entered through the Puerta de las Tablas, flanked by Roman statues. Plaça Desamparadors, crowded with open-air restaurants and market stalls, lies at the top of the town. Traffic leaves town through the Portal Nou.

WHERE TO STAY IN CIUDAD DE IBIZA

Cénit ★   These gay-friendly budget rooms and apartments perch on a hillside about a 10-minute walk to the beach (and a 20-minute walk from the beach). Floors are staggered so each room has a terrace, most on top of another room. Studio and 2-bedroom apartments book up fast, but single rooms are also available. All accommodations are on the small side, but the beds are comfortable, and you didn't come to Ibiza to stay in your room.

Carrer Archiduque Lluis Salvador, s/n. © **97-130-14-04.** www.ibiza-spotlight.com/cenit. 63 units. 80€ single, 118€ double, 118€–165€ apt. No parking. Closed mid-Oct to Apr. **Amenities:** Outdoor freshwater pool; no Wi-Fi.

El Pachá ★★   An Ibiza clubbers' legend, El Pachá sits close to the marina and channels an international party style that would be at home on Miami's South Beach. Rooms are spacious, and suites are huge. El Pachá was renovated in 2005 to a Philippe Starck style where the only noticeable color is the tan (or burn) on the guests. Glitterati without a friend's villa stay here when they visit Ibiza. One of the perks is guaranteed access to the Pacha Ibiza Club.

Paseo Marítimo, s/n. © **97-131-59-63.** www.avantgardehotels.com. 55 units. 180€–450€ double; 650€–1,100€ suite. **Amenities:** Restaurant; bar; bikes; outdoor freshwater pool; free Wi-Fi.

WHERE TO EAT IN CIUDAD DE IBIZA

Fresh fish has always been the mainstay of the local diet, though pork is equally important. Some islanders feed figs to these animals to sweeten their meat. The most famous dessert is *flaó*, akin to American cheesecake but flavored with mint and anise. *Greixonera* is a spiced pudding, and *maccarrones de San Juan* is cinnamon- and lemon-flavored milk baked with cheese.

Restaurante S'Ametller ★★ MALLORCAN   It's worth seeking out this slightly out of the way restaurant for good dining at reasonable prices with excellent service. The daily menus include everything available that day, making ordering a little easier and the final price more predictable. It comes down to whether you want both fish and meat at the same meal. If a local fisherman brings in an especially nice fish, there may be an added special. You can always count on grilled dorada (sea bream) or the pork tenderloin with dates, bacon, and red-wine sauce.

Carrer Pere Frances, 12. © **97-131-1780.** www.restaurantsametller.com. Daily three-course menu 22€, four-course menu 35€; tasting menu 36€ plus wine. Oct–May Mon–Sat 1:30–4pm, 8pm–11pm; June–Sept daily 1:30–4pm, 8pm–midnight.

EXPLORING IBIZA

Ibiza is primarily a beach destination, but one attraction is worth visiting.

Museo Monográfico y Necrópolis Púnica de Puig des Molins ★ MUSEUM   The old archaeology museum in the center of town has closed, but this new facility at an excavation site just outside the city walls houses all its artifacts. Most of the objects on display came from burials on Ibiza and Formentara and date back to prehistoric Iberian settlers of the island. They include substantial collections of terra-cotta figurines from Punic (i.e., Carthaginian) burials, Roman artifacts, Muslim graves, and finally 14th- to 16th-century ceramics associated with Christian burials. Outside the museum building, visitors can wander in the Punic necropolis, even entering one tomb with re-created but realistic human remains.

Carrer Via Romana, 31. © **97-130-17-71.** Admission 4€ adults, 2€ students, free for all Sun. Apr–Sept Tues–Sat 10am–2pm and 6:30–9pm, Sun 10am–2pm; Oct–Mar Tues–Sat 9:30am–3pm, Sun 10am–2pm.

BEACHES IN CIUDAD DE IBIZA

The most popular and crowded beaches are **Playa Talamanca** in the north and **Ses Figueretes** (also called Playa Figueretes) in the south. Don't be surprised to find a lot of nudity. The best beaches are connected by boats and buses. More remote ones are accessed by car or private boat. Both Playa Talamanca and Ses Figueretes are near Ciudad de Ibiza, as is another popular beach, **Playa d'en Bossa,** to the south.

To avoid crowds near Ciudad de Ibiza, continue past Playa d'en Bossa to **Las Salinas,** near the old salt flats farther south. Here, beaches include **Playa Cavallet,** one of the officially designated nudist strands.

SHOPPING

Ibiza developed its nonconformist style in the 1960s by combining elements of traditional local attire with more relaxed hippie garb. In recent years, Ibizan designs have become much more sophisticated and complex, but the individualistic spirit has not wavered. At the corner of Conde Rosselón, artisan Pedro Planells creates hand-sewn leather goods at **Pedro's,** Carre Aníbal 8 (✆ **97-131-30-26**). **Sandal Shop,** Plaça de la Vila 2 (✆ **97-130-54-75**), sells high-quality leather goods made by local artisans. One-of-a-kind accessories, including bejeweled belts and leather bags, are designed for individual clients.

Playa Talamanca.

CIUDAD DE IBIZA AFTER DARK

El Divino, Puerto Ibiza Nueva (✆ **97-131-83-38;** www.eldivino-ibiza.com), is the most beautiful disco on Ibiza. Open daily in summer only, it prides itself on attracting supermodels and other celebs. Wear the most hip outfit you packed. The club is open midnight to 6am. Cover ranges from 25€ to 50€.

The crowd at the **Montesol** hotel bar, Vara de Rey 2 (✆ **97-131-01-61**), a short walk from the harbor on the main street, tends to include expats, arriviste social climbers, and Spaniards along for the ride. If you enjoy people-watching, sit at one of the sidewalk tables. Montesol is open daily from 8am to 11pm.

Pachá, Av. 8 de Agosto s/n (✆ **97-193-21-30;** www.pacha.com/ibiza), is one of Ibiza's oldest discos but still has its groove on. Three bar areas and dance floors, open only in the summer, attract the young and not-so-young, the bored, and the jaded. Overheated dancers cool off in a pool. Cover is 40€ to 60€.

Opposite Pachá, everyone from supermodels to soccer stars floods into the **Bombay Lounge,** Av. 8 Agosto 23 (✆ **97-193-12-37;** www.bombay-lounge. com), the top cocktail lounge in the city. Drink *caipirinhas* to a soundtrack of jazz, soul, and house. Light bites as well as burgers and fries are served until 2:30am. The club opens at 10pm, but the A-list comes after midnight. No cover.

The modern **Casino de Ibiza,** Carrettera Ibiza-San Antonio at the Juan XXIII Roundabout (✆ **97-131-33-12;** www.casinoibiza.com), has gaming tables and slot machines; it's open nightly 6pm to 5am. The adjoining nightclub and dining hall offer live cabaret entertainment between May and October, beginning at 11pm. Casino entrance is 6€. A passport is required for admission.

The Northern Coast

Except for a few coves with good swimming—at **Portinatx,** at the very northern tip, and at **Port de Sant Miquel,** north of the small town of Sant Miquel—the north is less traveled by tourists. You'll find some of the island's prettiest countryside, with fields of olive, almond, and carob trees and the occasional *finca* raising melons or grapes.

WHERE TO STAY

Hotel Hacienda Na Xamena ★★★   Located high on a promontory over-looking Na Xamena Bay 23km (14 miles) northwest of Ciudad de Ibiza, this utterly beautiful hotel is precisely what every magazine art director dreams that Ibiza should be like. The rooms are spacious and flooded with light. The sea seems to be all around. Many rooms feature large oval freestanding tubs for soak-ing, and many have a private hot tub or a pool looking out at the ocean. This is CEO and celebrity heaven, where no matter how public your face back home, you can relax in anonymity here with attentive (but not obsequious) personal service.

Na Xamena s/n, San Miquel. © **97-133-45-00.** www.hotelhacienda-ibiza.com. 65 units. 248€–330€ double; 473€–1,895€ suite. Free parking. Closed Nov–Apr. **Amenities:** 4 restaurants; bar; bikes; exercise room; 3 freshwater pools (1 heated indoor); spa; outdoor tennis court (lit); free Wi-Fi.

EXPLORING THE AREA

Off the road leading into Port de Sant Miquel (Puerto de San Miguel) is **Cova de Can Marçà** (© **97-133-47-76;** www.covadecanmarsa.com). After a stun-ning descent down stairs clinging to the cliff's face, you enter a cave that's more than 100,000 years old and forms its stalactites and stalagmites at the rate of about 0.6 centimeter (¼ in.) per 100 years. Once a favored hiding place for smug-glers and their goods, it's now a smartly orchestrated surrealistic experience—including a sound-and-light display. The half-hour tour is conducted in several languages for groups of up to 70. From May to October, tours are offered every half-hour from 10:30am to 1:30pm and 2:30 to 8pm. From November to April, they're offered every 45 minutes from 11am to 5:30pm. Admission is 10€ for adults and 6€ for children.

At the island's northern tip is **Portinatx,** a series of beaches and bays marred by a string of shops and haphazardly built hotels. For a taste of its rugged beauty, go past the construction to the jagged coast along the open sea.

Every Saturday year-round there is a **flea market** just beyond Sant Carles (San Carlos), on the road to Santa Eulalia. Open from about 10am until 8 or 9pm, it offers vintage and new clothing, crafts, and the usual odds and ends. A beautiful drive leads from Sant Carles (San Carlos) along the coast to Cala Sant Vicent (San Vicente).

Santa Eulalia del Río

Santa Eulalia is at the foot of the Puig de Missa, on the estuary of the only river in the Balearics. The principal monument in town is a fortress church standing on a hilltop, or *puig.* Dating from the 16th century, it has an ornate Gothic altar screen.

ESSENTIALS

GETTING THERE   During the day, **buses** run between Ciudad de Ibiza and Santa Eulalia del Río every hour; a one-way fare costs 2€. You catch the bus at Avenida D'Isidor Macabich.

Seven **boats** a day run between Ciudad de Ibiza and Santa Eulalia del Río. The boats run on the hour, and the first leaves Ciudad de Ibiza at 10:30am and Santa Eulalia del Río at 9:30am. The boat ride takes 45 minutes. For informa-tion, call © **61-649-66-06.**

VISITOR INFORMATION   The **tourist information office,** at Marià Riquer Wallis, 4 (© **97-133-07-28;** www.santaeulalia.net), is open Monday to Friday 9am to 2pm. In summer the office is open Sunday to Friday 9:30am to 1:30pm and 5 to 7:30pm, and Saturday 10am to 1pm.

BEACH TIME MINUS THE crowds

If you want to escape to a lovely beach without hotel construction, head for **Playa Benirras,** just north of Port de Sant Miquel. An unpaved but passable road leads out to this small, calm, pretty cove, where lounge chairs are available and pedal boats are for rent. You'll find snack bars and restaurants on the beach.

WHERE TO STAY & EAT

Can Curreu Hotel Rural & Spa ★★★ MALLORCAN   Actually located within the village of Sant Carles on PM-810, this spectacular hotel and spa features one of the best dining rooms on Ibiza. The pastel-decor rooms with soft lighting are romantic and spacious, and each has a balcony with a beautiful vista. Suites also have kitchenettes. The spa and wellness center offers Turkish baths as well as the usual spa and massage treatments. In addition to the dining room, the restaurant serves meals on the outdoor terrace next to a 1,000-year-old olive tree. The menu incorporates just enough international dishes (duck breast in red wine, sea bass in a salt crust) to provide a change from such local fare as grilled red shrimp with gray sea salt, or skewers of grilled vegetables with romesco sauce.

Ctra San Carlos, km. 12. ✆ **97-133-52-80.** www.cancurreu.com. 195€–295€ double, 250€–495€ suite. Main courses 20€–40€; tasting menu 52€. Daily 1:30–3:30pm and 7:30–11:30pm.

EXPLORING THE AREA

You can reach the famous northern beaches from Santa Eulalia by bus or boat, departing from the harbor near the boat basin. **Aigües Blanques,** one of the best beaches, is 10km (6¼ miles) north. (It's legal to go nude here.) There are four buses a day. A long, sandy cove, **Cala Llonga,** is 5km (3 miles) south and is serviced by 12 buses a day. Cala Llonga fronts a bevy of package-tour hotels, so it's often crowded. Boats depart Santa Eulalia for Cala Llonga every 30 minutes, from 9am to 6pm. **Es Caná** is a white-sand beach, 5km (3 miles) north of town;

boats and buses leave every 30 minutes, from 8am to 9pm. Four buses a day depart for **Cala Lleñya** and **Cala Nova.**

FORMENTERA ★

For years, Formentera was known as the "forgotten Balearic." The smallest island of the archipelago, it's a 78-sq.-km (30-sq.-mile) flat limestone plain marked on the east by La Mola, a peak rising 187m (614 ft.), and on the west by Berberia, at 96m (315 ft.). The Romans called it Frumentaria (meaning "wheat granary") when they oversaw it as a booming little agricultural center. But a shortage of water, coupled with strong winds, has allowed only meager vegetation to grow, notably fig trees and fields of wild rosemary. Its year-round population of 5,000 swells in summer. Most visitors come over for the day to enjoy the beaches.

Island Essentials

GETTING THERE   Formentera is serviced by up to 36 **boat** passages a day in summer and about 8 per day in winter. Boats depart from Ciudad de Ibiza, on Ibiza's southern coast, for La Savina, 3km (1¾ miles) north of the island's capital and largest settlement, Sant Francesc. Passage across the 5km (3-mile) channel separating the islands takes between 35 minutes and 1 hour. A round-trip fare costs from 40€. For information, contact **Trasmapi** (𝒞 **90-231-44-33;** www. trasmapi.com), or check at your hotel.

GETTING AROUND   As ferryboats arrive at the quays of La Savina, taxis line up at the pier. One-way passage to such points as Es Pujols and Playa de Mitjorn costs 10€ to 15€; negotiate the fare in advance. To call a taxi in Sant Francesc, dial 𝒞 **97-132-20-16;** in La Savina, 𝒞 **97-132-20-02.**

You can rent bicycles and motor scooters from **MotoRent Migjorn,** in La Savina (𝒞 **97-132-11-11;** www.motorentmigjorn.com), or from **MotoRent Pujols,** in Pujols (𝒞 **97-132-21-38;** www.motorentpujols.com). Motor scooters cost 25€ to 65€ per day, bicycles 8€ to 12€ per day.

VISITOR INFORMATION   The **tourist office** at Calle de Calpe s/n, in Port de La Savina (𝒞 **97-132-20-57;** www.formentera.es), is open Monday to Friday 10am to 2pm and 5 to 7pm, Saturday 10am to 2pm.

HITTING THE BEACH

Beaches, beaches, and more beaches—that's why visitors come. You can see the ocean from any point on the island.

Playa de Mitjorn.

Playa de Mitjorn, on the southern coast, is 5km (3 miles) long and is the principal area for nude sunbathing. A few bars and hotels occupy the relatively undeveloped stretch of sand. You can make **Es Copinyars,** the name of one of the beachfronts, your stop for lunch.

At **Es Calo,** along the northern coast, west of El Pilar, there are some small boardinghouses. From here you can see the lighthouse of La Mola, which was featured in Jules Verne's *Journey Round the Solar System.*

The town of Sant Ferran serves the beach of **Es Pujols,** darling of the package-tour operators. This is the most crowded beach on Formentera, with pure white sand, good windsurfing, and a backdrop of dunes and pine trees.

Westward, **Cala Sahona** is another popular tourist spot, lying near the lighthouse on Cabo Berberia. Often pleasure vessels anchor here on what is the most beautiful cove in Formentera.

MENORCA ★★

Menorca is one of the most beautiful islands in the Mediterranean. Its principal city is **Mahón** (also called Maó; pop. 25,000), set on a rocky bluff overlooking the great port, which was fought over for centuries by the British, French, and Spanish. Although barely 15km (9⅓ miles) wide and less than 52km (32 miles) long, Menorca is the second largest of the Spanish Balearic Islands. It also has more beaches than Mallorca, Ibiza, and Formentera combined. Stretching along 217km (135 miles) of pine-fringed coastline, the beaches are the island's greatest attraction, although many are not connected by roads. Nude bathing is commonplace, though officially illegal. Our favorite beach is **Cala'n Porter,** 11km (6¾ miles) west of Mahón. Towering promontories guard the slender estuary where this spectacular beach is found. Another of Menorca's treasures, **Cala de Santa Galdana,** is 23km (14 miles) south of Ciudadela; its gentle bay and excellent sandy beach afford the most scenic spot on the island.

Menorca has about 60,000 permanent inhabitants and hosts half a million visitors a year. But it is not overrun by tourism. The island has some industry, including leatherwork, costume-jewelry production, dairy farming, and even gin manufacturing. Life here is quiet and relaxed. Some clubs in Ibiza don't even open until 4am, but on Menorca nearly everybody is in bed well before then.

In addition to trips to the beach, there are some fascinating things to do for those interested in history, archaeology, music, and art. Many artists live in Menorca, and exhibitions of their work are listed regularly in the local paper. The Catedral de Santa María in Mahón has one of Europe's great pipe organs, at which world-famous organists have given free concerts. Golf, tennis, and sailing are available at reasonable fees.

Island Essentials

GETTING THERE   Menorca, lying off the eastern coast of Spain and northeast of Mallorca, is reached by air or sea. It is quickest to fly, but you can take a ferry from mainland Spain or from Ibiza or Mallorca. It is always good to arrive with everything arranged in advance—hotel rooms, car rentals, ferry, or airplane tickets.

Menorca International Airport (© **90-240-47-04;** www.aena-aeropuertos.es) is 3km (1¾ miles) outside the city of Mahón. **Air Europa, Vueling, Iberia, Ryanair, Air Nostrum,** and **Air Berlin** all fly to Menorca at least seasonally from Barcelona, Madrid, Palma, San Sebastián, and Valencia in Spain. **Monarch** flies from Gatwick.

Regular **ferry service,** which operates frequently in the summer, connects Menorca with Barcelona and Palma. From Barcelona, the journey takes 9 hours aboard moderately luxurious lines. If you're on a real budget, bunk in a four-person cabin, which is about the same price as a chair in the lounge.

The ferry service is operated by **Trasmediterránea,** whose offices in Mahón are at Estació Marítim, along Moll (Andén) de Ponent (© **97-136-29-50;** www.trasmediterranea.es); it's open Monday to Friday 8am to 1pm and 5 to 7pm. Saturday hours are 7 to 10pm, and Sunday 2:30 to 5pm, but only to receive

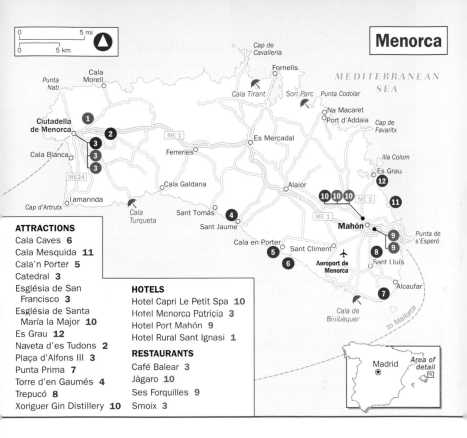

Menorca

MEDITERRANEAN
SEA

Cap de
Cavalleria

Fornells

Cala Morell
Punta Nati

Cala Tirant   Son Parc   Punta Codolar

1 Ciutadella de Menorca

ME 1

Na Macaret
Port d'Addaia   Cap de Favàritx

2

Es Mercadal

Illa Colom

Cala Blanca

3
3
3

Ferreries

Es Grau
12

ME24

Cala Galdana   Alaior

10 **10** **10**   ME 5   **11**

Tamarinda

Cap d'Artrutx

Cala Turqueta

Sant Tomàs   **4**

Sant Jaume   ME 1   **Mahón**

Punta de s'Esperó

Cala en Porter   Sant Climent   **9**

5   **8**
9

6   Aeroport de Menorca   Sant Lluís

Alcaufar

7

Cala de Binibèquer   to Mallorca

ATTRACTIONS

Cala Caves **6**
Cala Mesquida **11**
Cala'n Porter **5**
Catedral **3**
Església de San Francisco **3**
Església de Santa María la Major **10**
Es Grau **12**
Naveta d'es Tudons **2**
Plaça d'Alfons III **3**
Punta Prima **7**
Torre d'en Gaumés **4**
Trepucó **8**
Xoriguer Gin Distillery **10**

HOTELS

Hotel Capri Le Petit Spa **10**
Hotel Menorca Patricia **3**
Hotel Port Mahón **9**
Hotel Rural Sant Ignasi **1**

RESTAURANTS

Café Balear **3**
Jàgaro **10**
Ses Forquilles **9**
Smoix **3**

Madrid   Area of detail

the ferry from Valencia. Any travel agency in Barcelona, Palma, or even Ibiza can book you a ticket.

GETTING AROUND   **Transportes Menorca (TMSA),** Cí Rodees 5, Mahón (🕿 **97-136-04-75;** www.tmsa.es), operates **bus** service around the island. The tourist office (see Mahón's "Visitor Information," below) has complete bus schedules for the island.

The Spanish-owned **Atesa** (🕿 **97-136-62-13;** www.atesa.es) operates a rental-car desk at the airport, charging from 50€ to 117€ for its cheaper models. **Avis** (🕿 **97-136-15-76;** www.avis.com) also operates out of the airport, asking from 58€. Car-rental firms will deliver a vehicle to the airport or to your hotel, but you must specify in advance.

To summon a local taxi, call 🕿 **97-136-71-11.** The taxi stop is at Plaça s'Esplanada in Mahón. A one-way fare from Mahón to the beaches is 18€.

Mahón

With gorgeous Georgian architecture, Mahón (Maó) still shows traces of British occupation. It was built on the site of an old castle on a cliff overlooking one of Europe's finest natural harbors, some 5.5km (3½ miles) long. The castle and the town wall erected to dissuade pirates are long gone, except for the archway of San Roque. The first Christian king from the mainland, Alfonso II, established a base in the harbor in 1287. It became known as **Isla del Rey (Island of the King).** Since 1722, Mahón has been the capital of Menorca.

Boats docked in Mahón.

ESSENTIALS

GETTING THERE & GETTING AROUND

From the airport, a bus goes to central Mahón every half-hour. It costs 2.55€. A taxi is about 40€. Mahón is the **bus** transport depot for the island, with departures from Calle José Anselmo Clave in the heart of town. The most popular run—seven buses daily in summer, four daily in winter—is to Ciudadela, but there are connections to other parts of the island. The tourist office distributes a list of schedules, which is also published in the local newspaper, *Menorca Diario Insular.* Tickets cost 7€ and are purchased once you're aboard. Make sure you carry change.

VISITOR INFORMATION   The **tourist office,** at Carrer del Nord, 4 (© **97-136-23-77**), is open Monday to Friday 9am to 1pm and 5 to 7pm, Saturday 9am to 1pm.

WHERE TO STAY

Hotel Capri Le Petit Spa ★   Simple and modern, every room in this pleasant hotel near the city center has hardwood floors and pale wooden furniture (meant perhaps to evoke a Scandinavian sauna). But each room also has a private balcony, and views of the city are excellent. The spa on the top floor includes a sauna and hot tub. The Artiem group has several hotels on Menorca, but only the Capri is family-friendly.

Carrer Sant Esteve, 8. © **97-136-14-00.** www.artiemhotels.com. 75 units. 80€–142€ double. **Amenities:** Restaurant; bar; exercise room; outdoor freshwater heated pool; spa; free Wi-Fi.

Hotel Port Mahón ★★   A grande dame among Menorca hotels, the Port Mahón has been receiving guests since the 1950s—and some of the first are still returning. Taking advantage of Menorca's mild climate, it's open all year. Rooms can be on the small side, and the furnishings are less grand in the guest rooms than in the lobby. The gardens are quite beautiful, and the hillside location gives sweeping views of the town and harbor. Every room or suite has at least a small private balcony with potted geraniums.

Av. Fort de L'Eau, s/n. © **97-136-26-00.** www.sethotels.com. 82 units. 88€–186€ double; 160€–240€ suite. **Amenities:** Restaurant; 2 bars; outdoor freshwater heated pool; free Wi-Fi.

WHERE TO EAT

Fish and seafood are the basis of the Menorcan diet. The most elegant dish, *caldereta de langosta,* consists of pieces of lobster blended with onion, tomato, pepper, and garlic, and flavored with an anise liqueur. Shellfish paella is also popular, as are the "warty Venus" shellfish, *escupinas.* Wine comes from the mainland, but gin is made on the island, a legacy of the British occupation. It's often drunk with lemon and ice (a *palloza*).

Jàgaro ★ SEAFOOD   With a large outdoor terrace and two indoor dining rooms, this bustling restaurant is one of the largest on Mahón's waterfront. Seafood is the emphasis, and the menu includes such regional dishes as fried lobster with poached egg and a *caldereta de langostina*—a soup studded with large prawns. One of the dining rooms is set up like a wine cellar as a nod to the excellent selection of largely Catalan wines.

Moll de Llevant, 334. ☎ **97-136-23-90.** Main courses 15€–50€. Apr–Sept daily noon–4pm and 8pm–midnight; Oct–Mar Tues–Sun noon–4pm, Tues–Sat 8pm–midnight. Closed Feb.

Ses Forquilles ★★★ MENORCAN   After all the designer dining rooms and frou-frou dinner plates, you owe it to yourself to visit this top-rate but down-to-earth tapas bar with a huge counter, several tables where you can stand and eat, and an upstairs dining room. You can get olives or a plate of *patatas bravas,* but you can also get more creative fare such as fried artichoke chips, mini-cutlets of rabbit loin with aioli, and the house-cured tuna. Great ingredients, imaginative preparation, and reasonable prices.

Rovellada de Dalt, 20. ☎ **97-135-27-11.** Tapas 4€; *raciones* 7€–15€. Daily 1:30pm–midnight.

EXPLORING MAHÓN

The main square of Mahón is **Plaça s'Esplanada.** Locals gather here on Sunday to enjoy ice cream, which some claim is the best in the Balearics. In summer, an artisans' market is held on Tuesday and Saturday 9am to 2pm. The 18th-century Town Hall, constructed in an English Palladian style, sits on **Plaça de la Constitució.** This is where you'll also find **Església de Santa María la Major,** Plaça Constitució (☎ **97-136-39-49**). The church was founded in 1287 by Christian conqueror Alfonso III, and rebuilt by every ruler since. (The major changes came in 1772.) Its celebrated organ with four keyboards and more than 3,000 pipes was constructed by Swiss artisan Johan Kyburz in 1810. A music festival in July and August showcases the organ, which can be heard in nearby cafes. The church is open daily 8am to 1pm and 6 to 8:30pm, and donations are accepted.

The northern boundary of the city is formed by **Puerto de Mahón,** which has many restaurants and shops along Muelle Comercial. Mahón is not a beach town, but it has some hotels and is the shopping and nightlife center. The closest beaches for swimming are at **Es Grau** and **Cala Mesquida.**

The best way to see Mahón's port is to take an hour-long **catamaran tour** offered by **Yellow Catamarans,** Moll de Llevant 12 (☎ **97-135-23-07;** www.yellowcatamarans.com). The cost is 11€ for adults, 5€ for children 10 and under. Part of the sailing craft's hull contains glass windows below the waterline offering views of underwater life. Tours run May to October at 10:30am, and then continue on the hour until 4pm.

You can visit the **Xoriguer Gin Distillery,** on the harbor at Moll de Ponent, 91 (☎ **97-136-21-97;** www.xoriguer.es), to see how the famed Menorcan gin is made in giant copper vats over wood fires. The distillery and a store selling the products are open Monday to Friday 8am to 7pm, and Saturday 9am to 1pm.

SIDE TRIPS BACK IN TIME ★★

From Mahón you can take excursions to some of the prehistoric relics in the area. One of these, marked off the Mahón-Villacarlos highway, is **Trepucó,** where you'll find both a 4m (13-ft.) *taula* (huge T-shaped stone structure) and a *talayot* (circular stone tower). The megalithic monuments stand on the road to Sant Lluís, only about 1.6km (1 mile) from Mahón. Of all the prehistoric remains on the island, this site is the easiest to visit.

Yet another impressive prehistoric monument is **Torre d'en Gaumés,** 15km (9⅓ miles) from Mahón off the route to Son Bou. (The path is signposted.) You can take a bus from Mahón to Son Bou if you don't have a car.

This megalithic settlement spreads over many acres, including both *taulas* and *talayots,* along with ancient caves in which people once lived. The exact location is 3km (1¾ miles) south of Alayor off the road to Son Bou.

The restored **Naveta d'es Tudons** is accessible 5km (3 miles) east of Ciudadela, just to the south of the road to Mahón. This is the best-preserved and most significant collection of prehistoric megalithic monuments on Menorca. Its *naveta* (a boat-shaped monument thought to be a dwelling or a burial chamber) is said to be among the oldest monuments constructed by humans in Europe. Archaeologists have found the remains of many bodies at this site, along with a collection of prehistoric artifacts,

A stone monument in Trepucó.

including pottery and decorative jewelry (now in museums). The site is more easily visited from Ciudadela (see below).

MAHÓN OUTDOORS

BEACHES

Cala'n Porter, 11km (6¾ miles) west of Mahón, is one of the most spectacular beaches on the island. It's a sandy beach at a narrow estuary inlet protected by high promontories. **La Cova d'en Xoroi,** ancient troglodyte habitations over-looking the sea from the upper part of the cliffs, can also be visited. Going around the cliff face, you'll discover more caves at **Cala Caves.** People still live in some of these caves, and there are boat trips to see them from Cala'n Porter.

North of Mahón on the road to Fornells you'll encounter many beachside settlements. Close to Mahón, and already being exploited, is **Cala Mesquida,** one of the best beaches. To reach it, turn off the road to Cala Llonga and follow the signs to playa.

The next fork in the road takes you to **Es Grau,** another fine beach. Along the way you see the salt marshes of S'Albufera, abundant in migrant birds. Reached by bus from Mahón, Es Grau, 8km (5 miles) north of Mahón, opens onto a sandy bay and is crowded in July and August. From Es Grau you can take a boat to **Illa d'en Colom,** an island in the bay with some good beaches.

South of Mahón is the little town of Sant Lluís and the large sandy beach to the east, **Punta Prima.** Favored by local people, this beach is serviced by buses from Mahón, with six departures daily. The same buses will take you to an attractive necklace of beaches, the **Platges de Son Bou,** on the southern shore. Many tourist facilities are found here.

GOLF   Menorca's only course is **Golf Son Parc** (© **97-118-88-75;** www.golfsonparc.com), an 18-hole course.

WINDSURFING & SAILING   The best spots are at Fornells Bay, which is 1.6km (1 mile) wide and several miles long. **WindFornells,** Carrer Nov 33, Es Mercadal (© **97-118-81-50;** www.windfornells.com), supplies gear.

Ciudadela ★

At the western end of the island, the town of Ciudadela (Ciutadella de Menorca) has a classic Mediterranean ambience. The narrow streets of the old city are lined with 17th- and 18th-century mansions and numerous churches. It was the capital until 1722, when the British switched to Mahón for a deeper harbor. The British then built the main island road to link the two cities.

Like Mahón, Ciudadela perches high above its harbor. Known as Medina Minurka under the Muslims, Ciudadela retains Moorish traces despite the 1558 Turkish invasion and destruction of the city. An obelisk in memory of the city's futile defense against that invasion stands in **Plaça d'es Born (Plaza del Born),** the main square overlooking the port.

ESSENTIALS

GETTING THERE   From the airport, you must take a taxi to Ciudadela, as there is no bus link. The cost is approximately 45€ each way. From Mahón, six **buses** go back and forth every day; a one-way fare costs 5€. Departures are from Plaça s'Esplanada in Mahón.

VISITOR INFORMATION   The **tourist office,** Plaça Catedral 5 (☎ **97-138-26-93**), is open June to September daily 9am to 9pm; October to May, hours are Monday to Friday 9am to 1pm and 5 to 7pm, and Saturday 9am to 1pm.

WHERE TO STAY IN CIUDADELA

Hotel Menorca Patricia ★   Centrally located near the main square, Plaça d'es Born, the Patricia is a modern hotel built in the late 1980s to cater to leisure and business travelers alike. (It has good meeting rooms, so Spanish businesses often choose it for small "reward" junket meetings.) The decor is low-key and pleasant, and the rooms are spacious. During the 2014 renovation, the hotel installed all new hardwood floors, upgraded the modern furniture, and brought in new soft bedding and drapes in pale beige and taupe tones. It's about a half-mile to the nearest beach.

Passeig Sant Nicolau, 90–92. ☎ **97-138-55-11.** www.hotelmenorcapatricia.com. 44 units. 61€–123€ double; 110€–150€ junior suite. Closed Nov–Mar. **Amenities:** Bar; outdoor freshwater pool; free Wi-Fi.

Hotel Rural Sant Ignasi ★★   This hacienda-style hotel sits outside of town in a 1777 mansion on beautifully landscaped grounds. Converted to a hotel in 1997, it feels like being invited to a very rich friend's home. Instead of a lobby, there's a living room—although few guests stay indoors. Each ground-level room has a garden, each second-level room a balcony terrace. Bedrooms are amply sized, and the decor is warm and low-key.

Carretera Cala Morell s/n. ☎ **97-138-55-75.** www.santignasi.com. 25 units. 114€–265€ double; 134€–310€ jr. suite; 165€–380€ suite. Free parking. Closed Oct–Mar. **Amenities:** Restaurant; bar; 2 outdoor freshwater pools; free Wi-Fi.

WHERE TO EAT IN CIUDADELA

Café Balear ★ MENORCAN   This is the kind of place every former commercial fisherman looks for in a port: a fish restaurant on the docks with its own boat anchored out front. The menu is flexible—it all depends on what the fishermen catch (it usually includes monkfish, sea bream, rock fish, and John Dory). Other fishermen supply lobster, prawns, and assorted clams. As an indulgence, take the mixed seafood plate with a little of everything.

Pla de Sant Joan, 15. ☎ **97-138-00-05.** www.cafe-balear.com. Main courses 12€–25€. Mon–Sat 1–4pm and 7pm–midnight. Nov–Mar closed Sun–Mon.

Smoix ★★ MENORCAN   Run by a friendly couple, this spot has a romantic garden setting and serves good local food based on seasonal produce and the catch of the day. Unlike many Ciudadela restaurants, many of the house specials are braised meat dishes—lamb trotters, slow-cooked suckling pig. The house "hamburger" is made with freshly ground veal and is presented in a nest of filo with a fried egg on top. When big sardines are in, order one grilled; the waiter will de-bone it before it comes to the table.

Carrer Sant Isidre, 33. 🕿 **97-148-05-16.** www.smoix.com. Main courses 14€–27€. Mon–Sat 1–4pm and 7–11pm.

EXPLORING CIUDADELA: THE CITY

The center of Ciudadela has been **Plaça d'es Born** since the days of Jaume I. Back then Ciudadela was completely walled to protect against pirate incursions, which were a serious threat from the 13th century on. Development stopped in Ciudadela when the capital was transferred to Mahón in 1722. Many buildings now stand that might otherwise have been torn down to make way for progress.

Plaça d'es Born overlooks the port from the north. The square was built around the obelisk that remembers the struggle of the town against the Turks who sacked the city in 1558. The **Ayuntamiento** (Town Hall) anchors the west side of the square. To the southwest of the square stands **Església de San Francisco.** The 14th-century Gothic building has some excellent carved-wood altars. A once-splendid palace, Palacio de Torre-Saura, also opens onto the square. Still owner-occupied, it was constructed in the 1800s.

The fortress-like **cathedral,** Plaça Pío XII, was ordered built by the conquering Alfonso III on the site of the former mosque. The facade of the church, in the neoclassical style, was added in 1813. The church suffered heavy damage during the Spanish Civil War, but it has since been restored.

Ciudadela is at its liveliest at the **port,** with an array of shops, bars, and restaurants. Sailboats and yachts dock here in summer. **Carrer Quadrado,** lined with shops and arcades, is another street worth walking.

The Moorish influence lingers in a block of whitewashed houses in the **Voltes,** off the Plaça s'Esplanada. In Ciudadela, local people still meet at **Plaça d'Alfons III,** the square honoring their long-ago liberator.

Plaça d'es Born.

EXPLORING CIUDADELA: THE BEACHES

Buses depart from Plaça d'Artrutx for most coastal destinations, including the best beaches. **Cala Santandria,** 3km (1¾ miles) to the south, is known for its white sands. This is a sheltered beach near a creek. Nearby rock caves were inhabited in prehistoric times. The coves of **En Forcat, Blanes,** and **Brut** are near Ciudadela.

Cala de Santa Galdana, not reached by public transport, is the most stunning bay in the area, lying 23km (14 miles) south of Ciudadela.

Cala de Santa Galdana.

The tranquil bay is ringed with a beach of fine golden sand. Tall, bare cliffs rise in the background. The road to this beach, unlike so many others on Menorca, is a good one.

Fornells & the Northern Coast

On the northern coast, the tiny town of Fornells snuggles around a bay filled with boats and windsurfers. Built around four fortifications, including the Tower of Fornells at the harbor mouth and the now-ruined Castle of San Jorge, Fornells today is a flourishing fishing village noted for upscale restaurants featuring savory lobster *calderetas.*

West of Fornells is **Platja Binimella,** a beautiful beach (unofficially nudist) easily accessible by car. A snack bar is the sole concession to civilization.

It takes some effort to reach the promontory at **Cap de Cavalleria,** the northernmost tip of the island, marked by a lighthouse. At a bend in the road leading to Platja Binimella, a signpost indicates the turnoff to Cap de Cavalleria through a closed gate heading to a dirt road. The gate is closed to keep in livestock; the custom is to close it after you enter. As you follow the long dirt road, you will encounter several more gates and travel through cultivated fields and scattered grand *fincas.* Park shortly before the lighthouse, then pick your way across the scrub and rocks for the views. The best one is from a circular tower in ruins to the right of the lighthouse. The vista encompasses the whole of Menorca—a symphony of dramatic cliffs and jewel-blue water.

EXTREMADURA

19

S pain's mountainous westernmost region was the wild frontier for more than a millennium. Rome built military outposts here to claim westernmost Europe, and the kings of Castilla fortified the hills against the Moors, then against the Portuguese. Extremadura extends from the Gredos and Gata mountain ranges south to Andalucía, and from Castilla west to the Portuguese frontier. Not to be confused with the Portuguese province of Extremadura, Spanish Extremadura includes the provinces of Badajoz and Cáceres, and has a varied landscape of plains and mountains, meadows with Holm and cork oaks, and fields of boulders and limestone outcrops.

The world knows Extremadura best as the land of the conquistadors. Famous sons include Hernán Cortés and Francisco Pizarro, conquerors of the Aztecs and Incas, respectively; as well as explorers Vasco Núñez de Balboa, Francisco de Orellana, and Hernando de Soto. Driven by economic necessity to find a living far from their sun-parched homeland, they imposed iron wills on peoples half a world away. The riches they sent back to Extremadura financed mansions and public structures that stand today as monuments to Spain's American adventures. Those are hardly Extremadura's only monuments to the past, for you'll also find Roman ruins in Mérida and medieval palaces in Cáceres.

Extremadura is also a popular destination for outdoor vacations. Spaniards come here to hunt, enjoy the fishing and watersports popular in the many reservoirs, and horseback ride along ancient trails. Because summer is intensely hot here, spring and fall are the best times to visit.

GUADALUPE

Guadalupe lies in the province of Cáceres, 450m (1,500 ft.) above sea level. The village has a certain beauty and a lot of local color. Thanks to its famous shrine to the Virgin (known as Our Lady of Guadalupe), it's packed with pilgrims and is a major outlet of the religious souvenir industry. And it's easy to get around—everything of interest lies within a 3-minute walk of the bus drop-off point at Avenida Don Blas Pérez, also known as Carretera de Cáceres.

Around the corner and a few paces downhill is the Plaza Mayor, which contains the Town Hall (where many visitors stop in to ask questions, as there is no tourist office).

The village is best visited in spring, when the balconies of its whitewashed houses burst into bloom with flowers. Wander the twisting, narrow streets, some no more than alleyways. In fact, the buildings are so close together that in summer you can walk in the shade of the steeply pitched sienna-colored tile roofs.

FACING PAGE: **Merida's Teatro Romano.**

The village of Guadalupe lies in a valley at the eastern side of Extremadura.

Getting There

Two **buses** operate every day to and from Madrid (trip time: 3½ hr.). The route through the surrounding regions is full of savage beauty. In Guadalupe the buses park just uphill from the Town Hall. For schedules, contact **Autocares Grupo Samare** (http://samar.es).

One narrow highway goes through Guadalupe. Most maps don't give it a number; look on a map in the direction of the town of Navalmoral de la Mata. From Madrid, follow the A-5 west to exit 171 at Navalmoral de la Mata. Follow signs on EX-118 south to Guadalupe. Driving time from Madrid is about 3 hours outside of rush hour.

Exploring Guadalupe

Except for a handful of basic souvenir shops around the Plaza Mayor, don't expect to find a lot of particularly interesting shopping in Guadalupe. If you are not planning to visit Cáceres, you can purchase Extremadura's famous smoked Spanish paprika at a number of stalls on the Plaza Mayor. You'll pay a pittance compared to what it will cost you at home, and you will have the very best quality.

Real Monasterio de Santa María de Guadalupe ★★ CHURCH   In 1325, a farmer searching for a stray cow reportedly spotted a statue of the Virgin buried in the soil. In time, this statue became venerated throughout the world, honored in Spain by Queen Isabel, Columbus, and Cervantes. Known as the Dark Virgin of Guadalupe, it is said to have been carved by St. Luke. A shrine was built to commemorate the statue, and tributes poured in from all over the world, making the Guadalupe monastery one of the wealthiest in Christendom. The statue is found in the 18th-century chapel, **Camarín ★**, where a treasure-trove of riches surrounds the Virgin, including jasper, marble, and precious woods, plus nine paintings by Luca Giordano.

The church itself is noted for the wrought-iron railings in its naves and a magnificently decorated **sacristy ★★** with eight richly imaginative 17th-century masterpieces by Francisco de Zurbarán. The museum is devoted to ecclesiastical vestments and choir books produced by 16th-century miniaturists. The 16th-century cloister is Flamboyant Gothic in style, but the *pièces de résistance* are the stunning **Mudéjar cloister,** with its brick-and-tile Gothic Mudéjar shrine dating from 1405, and a **Moorish fountain** from the 14th century.

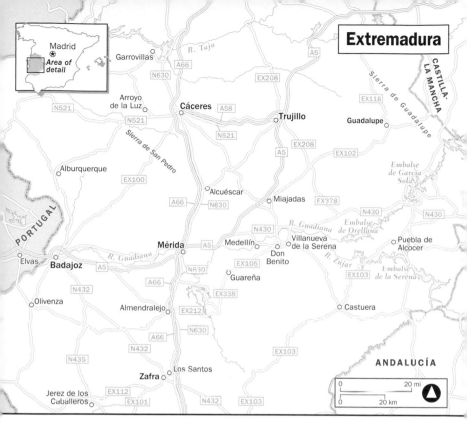

Plaza de Juan Carlos 1. ✆ **92-736-70-00.** www.monasterioguadalupe.com. Admission to museum and sacristy 4€ adults, 1.50€ children 7–14, free for children 6 and under. Daily 9:30am–1pm and 3:30–6:30pm.

Where to Eat & Stay in Guadalupe

Because Guadalupe is remote, even by Extremaduran standards, restaurants are also small inns, and larger hotels have major restaurants.

Hospedería del Real Monasterio ★★★   Attached to a historic monastery, the Hospederia has the ambience of a parador at the prices of a motel. Rooms are high-ceilinged, spacious, and charmingly accoutered, with four-poster beds in some and handsome wooden furnishings in all. Many have Juliet balconies with spectacular views; a favorite are the ones where the former turrets were turned into spa-like showers. You'll need to reserve well in advance as pilgrim groups often lodge here and can book up the entire hotel. The on-site restaurant isn't quite as special, but it's cheery (with its red walls and pink tablecloths) and offers fresh and reasonably priced, if not very exciting, food. We'd recommend the potato soup as a starter and then the stuffed pork tenderloin, sourced from the famed Iberian black-footed pig and filled with dried fruit and foie gras, as your entree.

Plaza Juan Carlos 1. ✆ **92-736-70-00.** www.hotelhospederiamonasterioguadalupe.com. 47 units. Main dishes 10€–14€. Rooms 72€ double; 95€ triple; 108€ quadruple. Closed much of Jan. No parking. **Amenities:** Restaurant; bar.

Hostal-Restaurante Cerezo ★ As you can likely tell from the name, this is another combination hotel and restaurant, and the best deals are reserved for those who choose to eat two meals a day here. That's not a bad idea, as the restaurant is good and serves classic Extremaduran fare. You'll enjoy the food most if you stick with such local specialties as roasted lamb or kid with rosemary, cold tomato soup (like gazpacho, but slightly different), and the dishes that feature pimientos (sweet red peppers). The 18 rooms upstairs are dignified and clean, but lacking in the character that mark our other two choices in town.

Gregorio López 20. ℰ **972-36-73-79.** www.hostalcerezo.com. Diners have a choice of 5 different menus, ranging in price from 8.50€–22€. Rooms 65€–72€ double with two meals, except during Holy Week when the price goes up to 90€. Children under 12 staying in their parent's room pay 50% of the per person price (which is half the double rate quoted above). Daily 1–4pm and 8–11pm.

Parador de Guadalupe ★★★ The most swank rooms in the area are to be had in this converted 16th-century palace, once home to the Marquis de la Romana. You'll be in great company if you stay here: Queen Isabella was once a guest, and the building was the spot where royal representatives and explorers met a number of times to sign their contracts before setting out to conquer the "New World." The location is very pretty, as are the *parador*'s lovely gardens. And rooms are oversized and character-rich, some with four-poster beds, others with balconies, and all with unique pieces of furniture and art on the walls (no two rooms are the same). The dining room here is the best in town, specializing in the meat-heavy Extremaduran cuisine (so get ready for lots of roasts and rich casseroles).

Marqués de la Romana 12. ℰ **92-736-70-75.** www.parador.es. 41 units. Main dishes 16€–29€. Rooms 80€–150€ double. Parking 12€. **Amenities:** Restaurant; bar; outdoor pool; room service; Wi-Fi (free in lobby).

The Real Monasterio de Santa María de Guadalupe dominates the square village.

LAND OF THE conquistadors

It's estimated that some 15,000 Extreme-ños (from a total pop. of 400,000) went to seek their fortunes in the New World. The most fabled of these adventurers were Hernán Cortés (from Medellín), who went to Mexico; Francisco Pizarro (from Trujillo), who went to Peru; Vasco Núñez de Balboa (from Jerez de los Caballeros), who landed in Panama, where he was the first European to sight the Pacific Ocean; Hernando de Soto (from Barcarrota), who discovered the Mississippi River and explored Florida and beyond; and Francisco de Orellana (also from Trujillo), who ventured through Ecuador and the Amazon.

Thanks to these conquistadors, the names of Extremaduran villages are sprinkled through the Americas, as exemplified by the Guadalupe Mountains (Texas), Albuquerque (New Mexico), Trujillo (Peru), Mérida (Mexico), and Medellín (Colombia).

Because Extremeños faced such difficulty making a living in the harsh land of their birth, they often turned elsewhere to seek their fortune. One reason

for the area's extreme poverty was that huge tracts of land, used for ranching, were owned by absentee landlords (as many still are today), in a holdover from the feudal Middle Ages. These ranches are called *latifundios*, and they're often home to tenant farmers and their families, who pay the owners for the privilege of grazing a few goats or growing scanty crops in the dry climate. Worse, a system of *mayorazgo* (still in effect) decreed that all family property must be passed to the eldest son, leaving any younger sons, called *secundinos*, penniless. Not surprisingly, many of *secundinos* set sail for the New World.

Plenty of conquistadors died or stayed in the New World, but others made their fortunes and returned to the land of their birth to build magnificent homes, villas, and ranches, many of which stand today. Bernal Díaz, who fought in 119 battles with the Cortés expedition to Mexico, described the situation very bluntly: "We came here to serve God and the king," he wrote, "and to get rich."

TRUJILLO ★

245km (152 miles) SW of Madrid, 45km (28 miles) E of Cáceres

The walled town of Trujillo as it appears today dates from a Moorish border fort built in the 13th century. But no one remembers the Moors in Trujillo, for the tiny town is known for having conquered or explored half the New World. Among its famous natives are Francisco Pizarro, the conqueror of Peru (whose family palace on the Plaza Mayor was built with gold from the New World), and Francisco de Orellana, the founder of Guayaquil, Ecuador, and the first European to explore the Amazon. Other historical Trujillano notables include Francisco de las Casas, who accompanied Hernán Cortés in his conquest of Mexico and founded the city of Trujillo in Honduras; Diego García de Paredes, who founded Trujillo in Venezuela; Nuño de Chaves, founder of Santa Cruz de la Sierra in Bolivia; and several hundred others whose names are found throughout the Americas. There is a saying that 20 American countries were born here.

Celts, Romans, Moors, and Christians have inhabited Trujillo over the centuries. The original town, lying above today's modern one, was built on a granite ledge on the hillside. It is centered on a lovely Plaza Mayor, encircled by a

View from the bell tower of Trujillo's Iglesia de Santa María la Mayor shows the town's castle in the background.

Moorish castle, a variety of 16th- and 17th-century palaces, as well as several manor houses, towers, churches, and arcades. A bronze equestrian statue of Pizarro by American artists Mary Harriman and Charles Runse rules over the entire scene. Steep, narrow streets and shadowy little corners evoke the bygone times when explorers set out from here on their history-making adventures.

Essentials

GETTING THERE There are 13 **buses** per day to and from Madrid (trip time: 3½–4½ hr.) and six per day to and from Badajoz. A one-way ticket from Madrid costs 20€ to 32€; and from Badajoz, 12€ to 21€. Trujillo's bus station, Calle Marqués Albayda (© **92-732-12-02;** www.avanzabus.com), is on the south side of town, on a side street that intersects with Calle de la Encarnación.

Trujillo lies at a network of large and small roads connecting it to Cáceres via the N-521 and to Lisbon and Madrid via the N-V superhighway. Driving time from Madrid is around 3 hours.

VISITOR INFORMATION The **tourist office,** on Plaza Mayor (© **92-732-26-77;** www.ayto-trujillo.com), is open daily 10am to 2pm and 4 to 7pm.

Exploring Trujillo's Plaza & Beyond

In the heart of Trujillo, **Plaza Mayor ★** is one of the outstanding architectural sights of Extremadura. It's dominated by a statue honoring Francisco Pizarro, whose armies destroyed Peru's Inca civilization. The statue is an exact double of one standing in Lima. Many of the buildings on this square were financed with wealth brought back from the New World.

Each year on the Puente de Mayo (the long weekend closest to May 1), Trujillo hosts the Feria Nacional de Queso, or National Cheese Festival, when small artisanal producers fill the Plaza Mayor offering tastes of their products and selling them at great discounts.

The square's most prominent structure is the **Ayuntamiento Viejo (Old Town Hall),** with three tiers of arches, each tier squatter than the one below.

Iglesia de San Martín stands behind the statue dedicated to Pizarro. This granite church, originally from the 15th century, was reconstructed in the 16th century in Renaissance style. Inside are an impressive nave, several tombs, and a rare 18th-century organ still in working condition.

While you're on the square, observe the unusual facade of **Casa de las Cadenas,** a 12th-century house draped with a heavy chain, a symbol meant to show that Felipe II had granted the Orellana family immunity from heavy taxes.

You can then visit the **Palacio de los Duques de San Carlos,** a 16th-century ducal residence now used as a convent. Ring the bell to gain entry Monday to Saturday 9:30am to 1pm and 4:30 to 6:30pm, and Sunday 10am to 12:30pm. An entrance fee of 1.50€ is required, and a resident will show you around; appropriate dress (no shorts or bare shoulders) is required. Note the Renaissance figures sculpted on the facade. The two-level courtyard inside is even more impressive.

Palacio de la Conquista, also on the square, is one of the most grandiose mansions in Trujillo. Originally constructed by Hernán Pizarro, the present structure was built by his son-in-law to commemorate the exploits of this explorer, who accompanied his half-brother, Francisco, to Peru.

The stores that ring the Plaza Mayor have the town's best **shopping;** they stock stonework, leather, brass, copper, and ironwork.

Casa-Museo de Pizarro ★ MUSEUM Francisco Pizarro was one of Spain's most prolific conquistadors, establishing the first Spanish colony in Peru, founding the city of Lima and, with a relatively small army, bringing the Incan people under the sovereign power of Spain. The museum details the life he lived as a young boy, in this, the house of his grandfather. Interestingly, the upper floor contains information about the Inca culture that Pizarro did his best to end.

C/ Martibés, s/n. no tel. 1.40€ adults, children free. Daily 10am–2pm and 4:30–7:30pm.

The Moorish castle on Trujillo's high ground has a panoramic view of the countryside.

Castillo ★ HISTORIC SITE   Constructed by the Moors on the site of a Roman fortress, this castle stands at the summit of the granite hill (Cabeza del Zorro, or "head of the fox") on which Trujillo was founded. You can climb its battlements and walk along the ramparts, enjoying a panoramic view of Extremadura's austere countryside. Later, you can go below and see the dungeons. It is said that the Virgin Mary appeared here in 1232, giving the Christians renewed courage to free the city from domination by the Moors. *Tip:* Many visitors find it most dramatic at sunset.

Crowning the hilltop. Admission 1.50€. Apr–Sept daily 10am–2pm and 5–8:30pm; Oct–Mar 10am–2pm and 4–8pm.

Iglesia de Santa María la Mayor ★ CHURCH   This Gothic church, with its outstanding Renaissance choir, is the largest in Trujillo, having been built over the ruins of a Moorish mosque. Fernando and Isabel once attended Mass here. The proudest treasure is a *retablo* (altar) with two-dozen panels painted by Fernando Gallego. Also here is the tomb of Diego García de Paredes, the "Samson of Extremadura," who is said to have single-handedly defended a bridge against an attacking French army with only a gigantic sword. To reach the church, go through the gate of Plaza Mayor at Puerta de San Andrés and take Calle de las Palomas through the Old Town. Views from the bell tower are even more magical than from the ramparts of the Castillo.

Calle de Ballesteros. ✆ **92-732-02-11.** Admission 1.40€. Apr–Sept daily 10am–2pm and 5–9pm; Oct–Mar daily 10am–2pm and 4–7pm.

The Feria Nacional de Queso (National Cheese Festival) fills Trujillo's main square on the May Day long weekend each year.

Storks nest on buildings in Trujillo's main square.

Where to Eat in Trujillo

Mesón la Troya ★ EXTREMADURAN   One of the best value restaurants in the region, Meson la Troya serves massive portions of food at reasonable prices. Many go for the 15€ set menu, which buys four courses, and then find they're still full at breakfast the next morning. Best on the menu are the stews, like the *prueba de cerdo* (a garlicky pork casserole) and *carne con tomate* (beef in tomato sauce). We think you'll also like the ambience of the place, which hasn't changed in decades and features lovely ceramic plates against the white walls.

Plaza Mayor 10. ✆ **92-732-13-64.** *Tapas* 3€–15€; fixed-price menu 15€. Daily 1–4:30pm and 8:45–11:30pm.

Where to Stay in Trujillo

Hotel Victoria ★★   This find of a hotel is set in an elegant 19th-century mansion with all the decorative elements of that era—ornate pillars, wrought-iron capitals and balustrades, marble floors, and elaborate decorative tiles. Rooms are oversized, high-ceilinged and—once the shutters are closed—reasonably quiet (if you're sensitive to noise, ask for a room in the back). The only complaints we've ever heard about the Victoria regards the air-conditioning, which can be inadequate (though it varies from room to room; ask to change rooms if you're too hot).

Plaza del Campillo 22. ✆ **92-732-18-19.** www.hotelvictoriatrujillo.es. 27 units. 85€ double; 135€ triple. Parking 10€. **Amenities:** Restaurant; bar; Wi-Fi (free in some rooms).

Izán Trujillo ★★   Another beauty, the Izán is housed in a former 17th-century monastery, complete with atmospheric cloisters. In the central courtyard is a swimming pool—a wonderful perk in a town that can get mighty hot. Guest rooms are quite stylish, ranging from small to quite roomy, all with handsome, terracotta-colored couches and wall treatments, and cherry wood furnishings. Nice touch: The decorative linens are made by the nuns at a nearby convent. The on-site restaurant is good and offers an excellent value prix-fixe dinner for just 11€ for three courses.

Plaza del Campillo 1. ✆ **92-745-89-00.** www.izanhoteles.es. 77 units. 55€–110€ double. Parking 15€. **Amenities:** Restaurant; bar; outdoor pool; room service; free Wi-Fi.

Las Cigüeñas ★ Las Cigüeñas is located east of the town center, so it really only works for those with access to a car. But if you have one, the free parking here can be a real boon. As for the hotel, it's extremely well maintained with good-quality mattresses and modern bathrooms. It's named for the thousands of storks who make this part of Extremadura their nesting grounds.

Av. de Madrid s/n. 📞 **92-732-12-50.** www.hotelascigueñas.com. 44 units. 80€–98€ double; 95€–125€ suite. Free parking. **Amenities:** Restaurant; bar; room service; Wi-Fi (free in lobby).

Parador de Trujillo ★★★ Set in the 1533 Convent of Santa Clara, a building notable for its Trujillo-style medieval and Renaissance architecture, the Parador de Trujillo is a honeymoon-worthy pick. Transformed into a hotel in 1984, it features elegantly decorated rooms (former nuns' cells) with such romantic touches as canopied beds and spacious, marble-clad bathrooms. For relaxation there's a good bar, small pool, and lovely, fruit tree–planted gardens to wander through in the Renaissance cloister. The location is excellent as well; centrally located, just a block south of Avenida de la Coronación.

Calle de Santa Beatriz de Silva 1. 📞 **92-732-13-50.** www.parador.es. 50 units. 70€–150€ double; 160€–214€ double superior; 240€–260€ suite. Free parking. **Amenities:** Restaurant; bar; babysitting; outdoor pool; room service; free Wi-Fi.

CÁCERES ★

298km (185 miles) SW of Madrid, 256km (159 miles) N of Seville

A national landmark and the capital of Extremadura, Cáceres is encircled by old city walls and has several palaces and towers, many financed by gold sent from the Americas by the conquistadors.

One of six cities in Spain designated UNESCO World Heritage Sites, Cáceres was founded in the 1st century B.C. by the Romans as Norba Caesarina. Its present-day name is derived from *alcázares,* an Arab word meaning "fortified citadel." After the Romans, it was settled by all the cultures that have made the south of Spain the cultural melting pot of influences it is today. The contemporary city offers a unique blend of the traces these successive invaders left behind.

Essentials

GETTING THERE There is **rail** service three times a day from Madrid (trip time: 4–5 hr.). A one-way ticket costs 36€. There are also two trains per day from Lisbon (6½ hr.); the fare ranges from 40€ to 136€.

The station in Cáceres is on Avenida Alemania (📞 **90-232-03-20**), near the main highway heading south (Carretera de Sevilla). A green-and-white bus shuttles passengers about once an hour from the railway and bus stations (across the street from one another; board the shuttle outside the bus station) to the busiest traffic junction in the new city, the Plaza de América. From there it's a 10-minute walk to the edge of the old town.

Bus connections to Cáceres are more frequent than railway connections. From the city bus station (📞 **92-723-25-50**) on busy Carretera de Sevilla, about .8km (½ mile) south of the city center, buses arrive and depart for Madrid (trip time: 5 hr.) and Sevilla (4½ hr.) every 2 to 3 hours. There's also bus transport to Guadalupe (1 per day); Trujillo (6 or 7 a day); Mérida (4 a day); Valladolid (2 a day); and Córdoba (2 a day). Many travelers opt to walk the short distance from the Cáceres bus station to the city center.

The old city of Cáceres stands behind fortified walls.

Driving time from Madrid is about 3½ hours. Most people approach Cáceres from eastern Spain via the A-V superhighway until they reach Trujillo. Here they exit onto the A-58, driving another 45km (28 miles) west to Cáceres.

VISITOR INFORMATION   The **tourist office,** Plaza Mayor s/n (✆ **92-701-08-34;** www.turismoextremadura.com), is open Monday to Friday 9am to 2pm and 4 to 6pm, and Saturday and Sunday 9:45am to 2pm. Don't expect efficiency. Things around here are slow.

EVENTS   You'll probably notice literally hundreds of breeding pairs of storks nesting on the rooftops and bell towers in town. Cáceres celebrates them with a weeklong festival in early May. The city is one of the most important stork-breeding sites in Europe.

Exploring the Old Town of Cáceres

The modern city lies southwest of the *barrio antiguo,* **Cáceres Viejo ★★★**, which is enclosed by massive **ramparts.** The heart of the old city lies between Plaza de Santa María and, a few blocks to the south, Plaza San Mateo. **Plaza de Santa María ★** is an irregularly shaped, rather elongated square. On each of its sides are the honey-brown facades of buildings once inhabited by the local nobility. On a casual stroll through the city's cobblestone streets, your attention will surely be drawn to the walls that enclose the old upper town. A mixture of Roman and Arab engineering, they are outstandingly preserved. About 30 towers remain from the city's medieval walls, all of them heavily restored. Originally much taller, the towers reflected the pride and independence of their builders; when Queen Isabel took control, however, she ordered them cut down to size. The largest surviving tower is at Plaza del General Mola. Beside it stands **El Arco de la Estrella (The Arch of the Star),** constructed by Manuel Churriguera in the 18th century. To its right you'll see the Torre del Horno, a mud-brick adobe structure left from the Moorish occupation.

On the far side of Plaza de Santa María rises the **Catedral de Santa María,** a Gothic structure to which many Renaissance embellishments were added when Cáceres became rich. Completed sometime in the 1500s, this is the cathedral of Cáceres and contains the remains of many conquistadors. It has three Gothic aisles of almost equal height and a carved *retablo* at the high altar dating from the 16th century. (Insert coins to light it up.)

La Casa de los Toledo-Montezuma was built by Juan Cano de Saavedra with money from the dowry of his wife, the daughter of Montezuma. The house is set into the northern corner of the medieval ramparts, about a block to the north of Plaza de Santa María. It is now a public-records office.

Plaza Mayor is remarkably free from most of the blemishes and scars that city planning and overregulation have made so common in other historically important sites. Passing through El Arco de la Estrella, you will catch the most advantageous angle at which to view Catedral de Santa María.

Some of the most appealing shops in Cáceres are on the streets radiating from the Plaza Mayor, with a particularly good selection of artifacts along either side of **Calle Pintores.**

Family crests mark all the Renaissance villas in old Cáceres.

Cuesta de la Compañía leads to Plaza San Mateo and the 14th-century **Iglesia de San Mateo,** which has a Plateresque portal and a rather plain nave—except for the Plateresque tombs, which add a decorative touch.

Two adjoining *plazuelas* near here embody the flavor of old Cáceres. The first of them, **Plaza de las Veletas,** on the site of the old Alcázar, has **Casa de las Veletas (Weather Vane House; ✆ 92-701-08-77**), site of a provincial archaeological museum with priceless prehistoric and Roman pieces, along with a famous *aljibe* (Arabic well). Its baroque facade, ancient Moorish cistern, five naves with horseshoe arches, and patio and paneling from the 17th century have been preserved. The museum displays Celtic and Visigothic remains, Roman and Gothic artifacts, and a numismatic collection. Admission is free. The museum is open Tuesday to Saturday 9am to 2:30pm and 4 to 7pm (it stays open until 8pm in summer); on Sunday 10am to 2:30pm. At the second *plazuela,* **San Pablo,** sits **Casa de las Cigüeñas (House of the Storks),** the only palace whose tower remains intact despite the order by Queen Isabel at the turn of the 15th century to reduce the height of all such strategic locations for military reasons. The building holds changing art exhibitions; admission is free.

The **Church of Santiago** was begun in the 12th century and restored in the 16th century. It has a reredos carved in 1557 by Alonso de Berruguete and a 15th-century figure of Christ. The church is outside the ramparts, about a block to the north of Arco de Socorro. To reach it, exit the gate, enter Plaza Socorro, and then walk down Calle Godoy. The church is on your right.

Where to Eat in Cáceres

Atrio ★★★ SPANISH   Considered one of the top chefs in Spain, Toño Pérez single-handedly made Extremadura a foodie destination. He did so by using hyper-local ingredients with great creativity. The now-famous Recinto breed of cattle supplies all the beef, while the pork comes from forest-grazed, acorn-munching Ibérico pigs. As for the vegetables, they're whatever's fresh at the market, meaning that the menu changes almost daily. If it's on offer, be sure to try the *loncheja,* a wonderful mixture of *jamón* with squid, green salad, and curry sauce. The restaurant is also noted for its wine list and has been chosen several times as one the world's best by *Wine Spectator* magazine. (Sommelier José Polo is Pérez's partner.) The setting is as elegant as the fare, a modern room hung with original paintings (by such masters as Andy Warhol and Georg Baselitz) and placed within the shell of a 15th-century palace. The Atrio is part of a luxury hotel (p. 568). Reserve well in advance if you want to dine here.

Av. de España 30. ℂ **92-724-29-28.** www.restauranteatrio.com. Reservations recommended. Fixed-price menus 90€–110€; extra supplement for truffles and percebes. Daily 1:30–4pm; Mon–Sat 9pm–midnight. Closed last 2 weeks in July.

El Figón de Eustaquío ★★ EXTREMADURAN   Since 1947, this family-owned restaurant—you'll see photos of them on the walls, along with all the awards the restaurant has garnered over the years—has been proudly serving the authentic food of Extremadura. It's a remarkably varied oeuvre, ranging from honey soup to *solomillo* (filet of beef) to trout Extremaduran-style (blanketed by ham). For hearty, homemade, and creative food, this mainstay, just west of the western ramparts of the city, is a top pick.

Plaza San Juan 14, near the intersection of Avenida Virgen de Guadelupe and Plaza San Juan. ℂ **92-724-43-62.** www.elfigondeeustaquio.com. Reservations recommended. Main courses 10€–28€; fixed-price menus 19€–25€. Daily 1:30–4pm and 8pm–midnight. Closed July 1–15.

Torre de Sande ★ SPANISH   The views are the key selling point at this restaurant (it's set in a 15th-century palace in Plaza de San Mateo, the town's highest point). To get the full panorama, you'll want to dine in Torre de Sande's lovely terraced garden, if weather permits. As for the food, it's more Spanish than particularly Extremaduran, but it does have some marvelous specialties from the local cuisine, including *boletus con foie* (mushrooms with duck liver), *solomillo de retinto* (succulent local beef), and *perdiz a la cantara con salsa* (partridge stuffed with liver and truffles in a port wine sauce).

Calle de los Condes 3. ℂ **92-721-11-47.** Reservations recommended. Main courses 18€–30€. Tues–Sat noon–4pm and 7pm–midnight. Closed 2 weeks in Jan and 2 weeks in June.

Where to Stay in Cáceres

Alameda Palacete ★★   A mansion, constructed just before the 20th century and with much of its charm intact, is our budget pick for the town. Rarely do you get a place this lovely for these rates. A Venetian architect was in charge, so there are such unusual touches as molded Venetian stucco on the ceilings and staircase, decorative tiles, and lovely chandeliers. Rooms vary in size, but some are marvelously spacious, and all have a real sense of style to them, which plays out in the choice of wall art, the (sometimes) intense blues and reds of the walls themselves, and the drapery that overhangs the beds. No two look alike, but they all have modern bathrooms and good-quality mattresses. The hotel is about a 7-minute stroll from the central square.

Calle General Margallo 45. ℂ **92-721-16-74.** www.alamedapalacete.com. 9 units. 60€–75€ double; 85€–100€ suite. Nearby parking 8€. **Amenities:** Free Wi-Fi.

The Flavor of the Land

The food of Cáceres affords a novel experience to even seasoned travelers. Famous dishes to try here include:

Cuchifrito: Suckling pig stewed in pepper, orange, and vinegar sauce
Caldereta de cordero: Lamb with pepper and almonds
Jabalí a la cacereña: Wild boar marinated in red wine and herbs

You will also find that many dishes are spiced with smoked paprika from Cáceres, the **pimentón de la Vera.** The region was one of the first to receive chili peppers from the expeditions of Cortés in Mexico, and has incorporated them into local cookery since the 1540s. The most characteristic dessert in all of Extremadura is **técula mécula,** an ancient example of the region's marzipan confectionery, which, like most things in Cáceres, has been passed down from one generation to the next for centuries.

Atrio Restaurant Hotel ★★★ With a modern decor, a top-rated restaurant, and a well-trained staff, the Atrio is the Paradore de Cacares' main competitor for high-end travelers, and also its diametric opposite. Here, instead of suits of armor, original works from Andy Warhol stare out as guests wander by. Guest rooms are light and airy, with white plank walls, shiny wood floors (they're lit by floor-to-ceiling windows in some rooms), and groovy, 70s-style lamps. Cushy white duvets cover the beds. To make the experience of staying here more immersive, the hotel sells packages that include meals and personally guided tours of the area.

Plaza de San Mateo 1. ⓒ **927 242 928.** http://restauranteatrio.com/en. 13 units. 240€ double; 350€ junior suite; 400€ deluxe room; 500€ suite. **Amenities:** Restaurant; pool; concierge services; free Wi-Fi.

Casa Don Fernando ★★ The unbeatable location (right on the Plaza Mayor, across from the town hall) is only one of the reasons we like this handsome boutique hotel. The others? The chic decor and roomy layout of the guest rooms, and the high level of service by the friendly, dedicated staff. Best of all, the hotel has a no-smoking policy it actually enforces. The Casa Don Fernando, as you can likely tell from the name, was once a private home, and a stately one at that.

Plaza Mayor 30. ⓒ **92-762-71-76.** www.casadonfernando.com. 36 units. 40€–100€ double; 60€–132€ superior; 89€–145€ family room. Nearby parking 8€. **Amenities:** Cafeteria; bar; babysitting; room service; free Wi-Fi.

Parador de Cáceres ★★★ One of the oldest *paradors* in the system, this state-run beauty is set inside a 15th-century palace. A top-to-bottom renovation in 2011 added LED lighting, modern bathrooms, and much-needed 21st-century heating and air-conditioning. The ambience, however, is still delightfully old-fashioned. How could it not be, with suits of armor standing guard in the lobby and hallways? The rooms are austerely handsome with fine dark-wood furnishings and white walls (very typical of Extremadura decor). Guests love to relax on the plant-and-flower-laden patios.

Calle Ancha 6, 10003 Cáceres. ⓒ **90-254-79-79.** www.parador.es. 33 units. 120€–173€ double; 230€–347€ suite. Garage parking 17€; street parking free. **Amenities:** Restaurant; bar; babysitting; room service; Wi-Fi (free in lobby).

MÉRIDA ★★★

71km (44 miles) S of Cáceres, 56km (35 miles) E of Badajoz

Founded in 25 B.C. to serve as the capital of the Roman Empire's westernmost province of Lusitania, Mérida was once called a miniature Rome. Its monuments, temples, and public works now form some of the finest Roman ruins outside Italy and make it the capital of Extremaduran tourism. The city stands at the intersection of Roman roads linking Toledo with Lisbon and Salamanca with Sevilla. The old town can be covered on foot—in fact, that's the only way to see it. Pay scant attention to the dull modern suburb across the Guadiana River, which skirts the town with its sluggish waters.

Essentials

GETTING THERE **Trains** depart from and arrive at the RENFE station on Calle Cardero (✆ **90-232-03-20;** www.renfe.com), about .8km (½ mile) north of the Plaza de España. Each day there are 6 trains to and from Madrid (5–6 hr.), 6 to and from Seville (3 hr.), and 12 to and from Badajoz (1 hr.). The fare from Madrid to Mérida is 26€ to 37€, varying by time of day and speed of train.

The **bus** station is on Avenida de la Libertad (✆ **92-437-14-04**), near the train station. Every day there are 7 buses to and from Madrid (trip time: 5½ hr.), 6 to 12 buses to and from Seville (3 hr.), 3 buses to and from Cáceres (1 hr.), and 5 to 10 buses to and from Badajoz (1 hr.). From Mérida to Madrid, the fare is 25€ for a local bus, 37€ for an express; Mérida to Sevilla, 13€; Mérida to Cáceres, 11€; and Mérida to Badajoz, 9€.

To drive, take the A-5 superhighway from Madrid or Lisbon. Driving time from Madrid is approximately 5 hours; from Lisbon, about 4½ hours. Park in front of the Roman theater and explore the town on foot.

EVENTS The **Mérida Classical Theater Festival** (✆ **92-400-94-80;** www.festivalmerida.es) is held in July and August. Greek and Roman classic plays are performed in Spanish in the Roman amphitheater and on the stage of the Roman theater, using these ruins from the 1st century B.C. for their original purposes.

Despite the city's Roman ruins, the main square of Mérida is conventionally Spanish.

Exploring Mérida

Walking through Mérida is a study in anachronisms: Modern shops stand cheek-by-jowl with Roman ruins, and no one seems to take much notice except the tourists. The **Roman bridge ★** over the Guadiana was the longest in Roman

Spain—about half a mile—and consisted of 64 arches. It was constructed of granite during the rule of Trajan or Augustus, and then restored by the Visigoths in 686. Felipe II ordered further refurbishment in 1610, and work was also done in the 19th century. The bridge crosses the river south of the center of old Mérida, its length increased because of the way it spans two forks of the river, including an island in midstream. In 1993, it was restored yet again and turned into a pedestrian walkway. A semicircular suspension bridge was built to carry the heavy auto traffic and save the Roman bridge for future generations. Before the restoration and change, this span served as a main access road into Mérida, enduring the evolution of transportation from hooves and feet to trucks and automobiles.

Another site of interest is the old hippodrome, or **Circus Maximus,** which could seat about 30,000 spectators for chariot races. The original Roman masonry was carted off for use in other buildings, and today the site looks more like a parking lot, though excavations have uncovered rooms that may have housed gladiators. The former circus is at the end of Avenida Extremadura on the northeastern outskirts of Old Town, about .8km (½ mile) north of the Roman bridge and a 10-minute walk east of the railway station.

Arco Trajano (Trajan's Arch) lies near the heart of the Old Town beside Calle Trajano, about a block south of the Parador Vía de la Plata. An unadorned triumphal arch, it measures 15m (49 ft.) high and 9m (30 ft.) across.

Acueducto de los Milagros is the most intact of the town's two remaining Roman aqueducts; this one brought water from Proserpina, 5km (3 miles) away. From the aqueducts, water was fed into two artificially created lakes, Cornalvo and Proserpina. The aqueduct is northwest of the Old Town lying to the right of the road to Cáceres, just beyond the railway tracks. Ten arches still stand, and every one of them is covered with nesting storks from February through August.

The most recently excavated monument is the **Temple of Diana** (dedicated to Caesar Augustus). Squeezed between houses on a narrow residential

Built in the 1st century B.C., the Roman bridge in Mérida is the longest extant bridge from antiquity.

The ruins of the Temple of Diana stand on a residential street in Mérida.

street, it was converted in the 17th century into the private residence of a noble-man, who used four of the original Corinthian columns in his architectural plans. The temple lies at the junction of Calle Sagasta and Calle Romero Leal, in the center of town.

While in the area, you can explore the 13th-century **Iglesia de Santa María la Mayor,** Plaza de España, on the west side of the square. It has a 16th-century chapel graced with Romanesque and Plateresque features.

Alcazaba ★ HISTORIC SITE   On the northern bank of the Guadiana River, beside the northern end of the Roman bridge (which it was meant to protect), stands the Alcázar, also known as the Conventual or the Alcazaba. Built in the 9th century by the Moors, who used fragments left from Roman and Visigothic occupations, the square structure was later granted to the Order of Santiago.

Plaza del Rastro, Calle Graciano s/n. ✆ **92-431-73-09.** Admission 12€ for a combo ticket to all the major archaeological sites in town, reduced to 6€ for students and seniors, free for children under 12. Apr–Sept daily 9am–9pm; Oct–Mar daily 9:30am–2pm and 4–7 pm.

Anfiteatro Romano ★ HISTORIC SITE   At the height of its glory in the 1st century B.C., this amphitheater could seat up to 15,000 spectators. Chariot races were held here, along with gladiator combats and mock sea battles, for which the arena would be flooded. Many of the seats were placed dangerously close to the bloodshed. You can visit some of the rooms that housed the wild animals and gladiators waiting to go into battle.

Calle José Ramón Melida s/n. ✆ **92-431-25-30.** Admission 12€ for all the major archaeological sites in town, reduced to 6€ for students and seniors, free for children under 12. Apr–Sept daily 9am–9pm; Oct–Mar daily 9:30am–2pm and 4–7 pm.

Museo Arqueológico de Arte Visigodo ★ MUSEUM   Dedicated to the artifacts left behind by the Visigoths, this tiny museum is set right in front of Trajan's Arch. Though many skip it, folks who enjoy seeing ancient carvings (some are quite beautiful) will enjoy this quick stop.

Calle Santa Julia, Plaza de España. ✆ **92-431-01-16.** Free admission. July–Sept Tues–Sat 10am–2pm and 5–7pm, Sun 10am–2pm; Oct–June Tues–Sat 10am–2pm and 4–6pm, Sun 10am–2pm.

Mérida's Anfiteatro Romano was built in the 1st century B.C. and could seat up to 15,000 spectators.

Museo Nacional de Arte Romano ★★★ MUSEUM   The star attraction in town, this creatively curated museum, in a building by noted architect Rafael Moneo, is Spain's most important repository for Roman artifacts. It holds some 30,000, all from Augusta Emerita, which had been the Roman capital of the province of Lusitania. Part of the excitement of the museum is how it connects with the actual Roman ruins of the town, incorporating a swatch of the Roman road into its design and connecting, by tunnel, with the Roman Amphitheater. Artifacts are beautifully displayed (with excellent wall text, explaining their usage) in glass cases, stacked on different levels around a massive central atrium. Among the treasures displayed here are sculptures from excavations in the Roman theater and amphitheater, pottery, coins, glassware, bronzes, and mosaics.

Calle José Ramón Melida s/n. *Ⓒ* **92-431-16-90.** http://museoarteromano.mcu.es. Admission 3€ adults, 1.50€ for seniors, students, and children 17 and under. Tues–Sat 9:30am–6:30pm, Sun 10am–3pm. In Sept the museum often stays open until 8pm.

Teatro Romano ★★ HISTORIC SITE   This Roman theater, one of the best-preserved Roman ruins in the world, was built by Agrippa (Augustus' son-in-law) in 18 B.C. to house an audience of 6,000 people. Modeled after the great theaters of Rome, it was constructed using dry-stone methods (a remarkable achievement). During the reign of Hadrian (2nd century A.D.), a tall stage wall was adorned with statues and colonnades. Behind the stage, today's visitors can explore excavations of various rooms. From the end of June to early July, you can also enjoy a season of classical plays.

José Ramón Melida s/n. *Ⓒ* **92-431-25-30.** Admission 12€ for all the major archaeological sites in town, reduced to 6€ for students and seniors, free for children under 12. Apr–Sept daily 9am–9pm; Oct–Mar daily 9:30am–2pm and 4–7 pm.

Where to Eat & Stay in Mérida

All the hotels recommended below have good restaurants.

Nova Roma ★   Our value pick, this is a modern hotel meant for business-people, so it's clean, well managed, and with dignified and comfortable decor.

The guest rooms aren't the most spacious, but they're well designed and feature firm beds. The location, not far from the bullring, is also a point in its favor.

Suárez Somonte 42. ☏ **92-431-12-61.** www.novaroma.com. 55 units. 59€–73€ double; 80€–93€ triple. Parking 13€. **Amenities:** Restaurant; bar; room service; free Wi-Fi.

Parador de Mérida ★★ Layers upon layers of history grace this *parador*. The spot where it stands was once a Roman temple, then an 18th-century convent, and next a prison. In 1960, it was the grounds for a meeting between two dictators: Franco of Spain and Salazar of Portugal. Luxurious lodgings come in all different shapes and sizes, but all are splendidly outfitted in quality wood furnishings, coffered ceilings, and fine linens. A salon has been installed in the cloister, and the central garden, lush with flowers and plants, is one of the most tranquil spaces in the town to wander. Though rates spike during the theater festival, the *parador* can be quite reasonable in the off season (hence the wide range of rates below). The restaurant is top-notch, serving roast meats and Extremaduran specialties in a spacious, well-appointed room.

Plaza de la Constitución 3. ☏ **92-431-38-00.** www.parador.es. 82 units. 60€–161€ double; 200€–274€ suite. Parking 19€. **Amenities:** Restaurant; bar; exercise room; small outdoor pool; room service; sauna; Wi-Fi (free in lobby).

Rex Numitor ★★★ A serene dining experience thanks to its beige-on-gold color scheme and the generously spaced tables, Numitor is Merida's special-occasion restaurant. That's partially because the plates of food are as pretty as the decor, with swoops of sauce here and an architectural stack of proteins and vegetables there. But they don't only look good, they taste superb. The menu changes frequently, but some recent standouts have included the crispy sweetbreads in a truffle-mushroom sauce, a cherry gazpacho, and magret of duck sided by pimento ice cream. Along with the restaurant, the owners operate very pretty, short-term vacation apartments next door, complete with concierge service. Their decor is colorful (think peaches and greens), the beds are good quality, and each has a separate living area with a kitchen. Breakfast is included in the nightly cost, as is daily maid service.

Calle de Castelar, 1. ☏ **92-4318.654.** www.apartmentoscapitolina.com. 4 units. 60€–161€ double; 16€ set lunch, 25€ or 30€ set dinner. Apartments are 70€ double, 86€ triple, 106€ for two conjoined apartments housing 4. **Amenities:** Restaurant; kitchen; free Wi-Fi.

TRYP Medea ★ The name doesn't lie: This is rather a trippy hotel, round in shape, with echoes of dance clubs in its decor (think lots of mirrors). In the guest rooms, the postmodern furnishings are made from oxidized wrought iron that's locally crafted (they're bright green and quirky, but in a fun way). Floors are marble, and ceiling-to-floor windows flood the rooms with light. The family rooms come complete with bunk beds your children are sure to love. This being a conference hotel, location isn't its strong point; it's a good 15-minute walk west of the historic center on the opposite bank of the Guadiana River. *Note:* Rooms on the fourth floor have whirlpools and spacious terraces.

Av. de Portugal s/n, 06800 Mérida. ☏ **92-437-24-00.** www.solmelia.com. 126 units. 65€–98€ double. Garage parking 10€; free street parking. **Amenities:** Restaurant; bar; babysitting; outdoor pool; room service; sauna; Wi-Fi (12€ per 24 hr.).

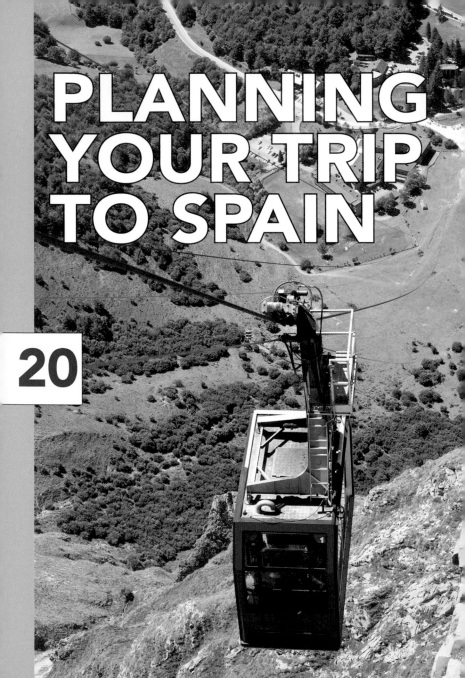

PLANNING YOUR TRIP TO SPAIN

20

G
etting to Spain is relatively easy, especially for those who live in Western Europe or on the East Coast of the United States. If all your documents are in order, you should clear Customs and Immigration smoothly. The staffs of entry ports into Spain usually speak English, and they tend to speed you on your way. In this chapter, you'll find everything you need to plan your trip, from tips on hotels to health care and emergency information.

GETTING THERE
By Plane

FROM NORTH AMERICA   Flights from the U.S. East Coast to Spain take 6 to 7 hours. Spain's national carrier, **Iberia Airlines** (℃ 800-772-4642; www.iberia.com), has more routes into and within Spain than any other airline. It offers daily nonstop service to Madrid from New York all year, and from Chicago, Boston, and Miami seasonally. Iberia flights are often codeshares with **American Airlines** (℃ 800-433-7300; www.aa.com), which offers daily nonstop service to Madrid from New York (JFK) and from Miami. Following completion of the U.S. Airways merger, it may offer nonstops from Philadelphia as well.

Iberia's main Spain-based competitor is **Air Europa** (℃ 011-34-90-240-15-01; www.aireuropa.com), which offers nonstop service from New York to Madrid and seasonal nonstop flights from Miami to Madrid. Air Europe makes connections from other U.S. cities through its codeshare partner **Delta** (℃ 800-221-1212; www.delta.com), which runs daily nonstop service from Atlanta to both Madrid and Barcelona. Direct flights to Madrid depart 5 days a week from New York (JFK). Delta's Dream Vacation department offers independent fly/drive packages, land packages, and escorted bus tours.

FROM THE U.K. AND IRELAND   The airfare market from the U.K. and Ireland is highly volatile. **British Airways** (℃ 0844-493-0787, or 800-247-9297 in the U.S.; www.britishairways.com) and **Iberia** (℃ 0870-609-0500 in London; www.iberia.com) are the two major carriers flying between England and Spain. More than a dozen daily flights, on either British Airways or Iberia, depart from London's Heathrow and Gatwick airports. There are about seven flights a day from London to Madrid and back, and at least six to Barcelona. The Midlands is served by flights from Manchester and Birmingham, two major airports that can also be used by Scottish travelers flying to Spain.

Vueling (℃+44-906-7547-541; www.vueling.com) offers bargain flights between London Gatwick and several points in Spain. **EasyJet** (www.easyjet.com) flies from several U.K. airports to Madrid, Barcelona, Málaga, and the Balearic Islands. **RyanAir** (www.ryanair.com) flies to Madrid, Barcelona, Girona, Valencia, Sevilla, and Málaga from London Stansted, Dublin, and Shannon.

FACING PAGE: **The Fuente Dé teleférico.**

By Car

Highway approaches to Spain are across France on expressways. The most popular border crossing is near Biarritz, but there are 17 other border stations between Spain and France. If you plan to visit the north or west of Spain (Galicia), the Hendaye-Irún border is the most convenient frontier crossing. If you're going to Barcelona or Catalunya and along the Levante coast (Valencia), take the expressway in France to Toulouse, then the A-61 to Narbonne, and then the A-9 toward the border crossing at La Junquera. You can also take the RN-20, with a border station at Puigcerdà.

By Train

If you're already in Europe, you might want to go to Spain by train, especially if you have a Eurailpass. Even without a pass, you'll find that the cost of a train ticket is relatively moderate. Rail passengers who visit from Britain or France should reserve couchettes and sleepers far in advance.

For long journeys on Spanish rails, seat reservations are mandatory. For more information call ✆ **91-631-38-00,** or visit www.renfe.com. Fast and comfortable high-speed trains have superseded most other rail travel in Spain. Both first- and second-class fares are sold on Spanish trains. The Spain Rail Pass (see below) is often a practical option if you're traveling largely by rail.

To go from London to Spain by rail, you'll need to transfer stations in Paris to board an express train to Spain.

By Bus

Bus travel to Spain is possible but not popular—it's quite slow. (Service from London will take 24 hours or more.) But coach services do operate regularly from major capitals of Western Europe and, once they're in Spain, usually head for Madrid or Barcelona. The major bus line from London to Spain is **Eurolines Limited** (✆ **0871-781-8181;** www.nationalexpress.com).

GETTING AROUND

By Plane

By European standards, domestic flights within Spain are relatively inexpensive, and considering the distances within the country, flying between distant points sometimes makes sense. For reservations on Iberia, visit www.iberia.com, or call ✆ **800-772-4642.**

If you plan to travel to a number of cities and regions, the Oneworld Visit Europe Pass can be a good deal. Sold only in conjunction with a transatlantic ticket and valid for most airports in Europe, it requires that you choose up to four different cities in advance in the order you'll visit them. Restrictions forbid flying immediately back to the city of departure. Only one change within the preset itinerary is permitted once the ticket is issued. The dates and departure times of the actual flights, however, can be determined or changed without penalty once you arrive in Europe. Costs depend on what kind of ticket you are issued—consult the folks at your transatlantic carrier if you're interested in a multi-stopover ticket and see what the best deal is at the time of your visit. The ticket is valid for up to 60 days after your initial transatlantic arrival in Europe.

By Car

A car offers the greatest flexibility while you're touring, even if you're just doing day trips from Madrid. But don't plan to drive in the congested cities. Rush hour is every hour.

RENTALS   All the major international rental car firms maintain offices throughout Spain. These include **Avis** (✆ **800-331-1084;** www.avis.com), **Hertz** (✆ **800-654-3001;** www.hertz.com), and **Budget** (✆ **800-472-3325;** www.budget.com). Tax on car rentals is 15%, so factor it into your travel budget. Prepaid rates don't include taxes, which will be collected at the rental kiosk.

Most rental companies require that drivers be at least 25 years of age and, in some cases, not older than 72. To be able to rent a car, you must have a passport and a valid driver's license; you must also have a valid credit card or a prepaid voucher.

DRIVING RULES   Spaniards drive on the right-hand side of the road. Spain's express highways are known as *autopistas,* which charge a toll, and *autovías,* which don't. To exit in Spain, follow the salida (exit) sign, except in Catalunya, where the exit sign says sortida. On most express highways, the speed limit is 120kmph (75 mph). On other roads, speed limits range from 90kmph to 100kmph (56–62 mph). You will see many drivers far exceeding these limits.

If you are fined by the highway patrol (*Guardia Civil de Tráfico*), you must pay on the spot, either to the officer or online using a cellphone and credit card. Penalties for drinking and driving are stiff.

BREAKDOWNS   On a major motorway you'll find strategically placed emergency phone boxes. On secondary roads, call for help by asking the operator for the nearest Guardia Civil. The Spanish affiliate of AAA, **Real Automóvil Club de España** (**RACE;** ✆ **90-240-45-45;** www.race.es), provides limited assistance in the event of a breakdown.

GASOLINE (PETROL)   Service stations abound on the major arteries of Spain and in such big cities as Madrid and Barcelona. They are open 24 hours a day. On secondary roads, most stations open at 7am daily, closing at 11pm or midnight. All gas is unleaded—*gasolina sin plomo.* Many vehicles run on clean diesel fuel called *Gasoleo A* or on more expensive Biodiesel. We generally rent diesel vehicles for much better gas mileage for a given vehicle size. Fuel prices change often. To check prices and available stations, go to http://geoportalgasolineras.es/.

MAPS   For drivers who don't like or trust GPS, there are still old-fashioned paper maps available. Michelin map 990 (folded version) or map 460 (spiral-bound version) cover Spain and Portugal. **Google Maps** (http://maps.google.com) are extremely accurate in metropolitan areas, but the database is somewhat sketchier on rural roads.

By Train

Spain is crisscrossed with a comprehensive network of rail lines on RENFE the national rail line. High-speed AVE, AVANT, ALVIA, and ALTRIA trains have reduced travel time between Madrid and Sevilla and Madrid and Barcelona to only 2½ hours. Trains are now so fast that few hotel trains are offered, apart from those going to Portugal or France. The RENFE website has possibly the world's easiest-to-use online schedule. Pay close attention to prices on the schedule. AVE trains often cost twice as much as other high-speed trains but are not much faster. Reservations are required on all high-speed trains, even with a discount card or pass, and reservation fees vary depending on the class of train.

JUNIOR AND SENIOR DISCOUNT CARDS If you are between 14 and 25, you can purchase the Tarjeta Joven Renfe, which gives you a year of purchasing tickets within Spain for a 30% discount regardless of class, type of train, or day of the week. The pass costs 22€ and must be purchased at a RENFE customer service window. Travelers age 60 and older may purchase a Tarjeta Dorada for 6€ at a customer service window. Also good for a year, it provides 40% discounts on AVE and AVANT tickets Monday to Thursday, 25% Friday to Sunday, and 40% every day on MD (*media distancia*) and *cercanías* (commuter rail) trains.

SPANISH RAIL PASSES RENFE offers discounted rail passes that must be purchased before arriving in Spain. In the U.S. and Canada, contact **Rail Europe** (© **877-272-RAIL** [272-7245]; www.raileurope.com).

The **Eurail Spain Pass** entitles you to unlimited rail travel in Spain. It is available for 3 to 10 days of travel within 2 months in either first or second class. For 3 days within 2 months, the cost for an adult is $314 in first class or $252 in second class; for 10 days within 2 months, the charge is $640 in first class or $513 in second class. Children 4 to 11 pay half-fare on any of these discount passes. *Note:* This pass must be purchased before arriving in Spain.

The pass works most economically for long-distance travel—the kind of routes you might otherwise fly if trains weren't more convenient and faster (Madrid to Barcelona, for example, or Barcelona to Málaga). The **Eurail Select Pass** for travel in adjoining countries no longer includes France. Talk to a Rail Europe representative for pass solutions that allow rail travel in France as well as Spain.

EURAILPASS AND RAIL PASSES The Eurailpass permits unlimited first-class rail travel in any country in western Europe except the British Isles (good in Ireland). Passes are available for purchase online (www.eurail.com). Purchase passes before you leave home as not all passes are available in Europe; also, passes purchased in Europe will cost more.

The **Eurail Global Pass** allows you unlimited travel in 21 Eurail-affiliated countries. You can travel on any of the days within the validity period, which is available for 15 days, 21 days, 1 month, 2 months, 3 months, and some other possibilities as well. Prices for first-class adult travel start at $810 for 15 days and range up to $2,234 for 3 months. Children 4 to 11 pay half-fare; those 3 and under travel for free. A **Eurail Global Pass Saver,** also valid for first-class travel in 21 countries, offers a 15% discount for two or more people traveling together. *Note:* This pass must be purchased before arriving in Spain.

WHERE TO BUY RAIL PASSES The main North American supplier is **Rail Europe** (© **877-272-RAIL** [272-7245]; www.raileurope.com), which can also give you informational brochures and counsel you on which passes work best for your circumstances.

Many different rail passes are available in the United Kingdom for travel in Britain and continental Europe. Stop in at the **International Rail Centre,** Victoria Station, London SW1V 1JY (© **0870-5848-848** in the U.K.). Some of the most popular passes, including Inter-Rail and Euro Youth, are offered only to travelers ages 25 and under; these allow unlimited second-class travel through most European countries.

By Bus

Bus service in Spain is low priced and comfortable enough for short journeys. The efficiency of train travel has cut drastically into available bus routes. Almost every bus schedule in Spain is available on the **Movelia** website (www.movelia. es), which also provides a means for purchasing tickets through the Internet if you have access to a printer.

TIPS ON ACCOMMODATIONS

From castles converted into hotels to modern high-rise resorts overlooking the Mediterranean, Spain has some of the most varied hotel accommodations in the world—with equally varied price ranges. Accommodations are broadly classified as follows:

ONE- TO FIVE-STAR HOTELS   The Spanish government rates hotels by stars, plus the designation "GL" (Grand Luxe) for the most luxurious properties. The star system is not very helpful, since many criteria are based on suitability for business meetings.

HOSTALES   Not to be confused with a youth hostel, a *hostal* is a modest hotel without services. They're often a good buy. You'll know it's a *hostal* if a small s follows the capital letter h on the blue plaque by the door.

YOUTH HOSTELS   Spain has about 140 hostels (*albergues de juventud*) and they are not limited to young people. Some are equipped for persons with disabilities. Many hostels impose an 11pm curfew. For information, contact **Red Española de Alberques Juveniles** (*©* **91-522-70-07**; www.reaj.com).

PARADORES   The Spanish government runs a series of unique state-owned inns called *paradores* that blanket the country. Castles, monasteries, palaces, and other grand buildings have been taken over and converted into hotels. Several newer properties were simply built from scratch to look monumental. To book or learn more contact **Paradores de España** (*©* **90-254-79-79**; www.parador.es). Make reservations directly with the network's website as third-party bookers tend to surcharge reservations. *Paradores* offer good discounts when one of the travelers is under 30 or over 65, or if you purchase 5 nights (which can all be in different *paradores*).

[Fast FACTS] SPAIN

Business Hours   Banks are open Monday to Friday 9:30am to 2pm and Saturday 9:30am to 1pm. Most other offices are open Monday to Friday 9am to 5 or 5:30pm; the longtime practice of early closings in summer seems to be dying out. In restaurants, lunch is usually 1 to 4pm and dinner 9 to 11:30pm or midnight.

There are no set rules for the opening of bars and taverns; many open at 8am, others at noon. Most stay open until 1:30am or later. Major stores are open Monday to Saturday from 9:30am to 8pm; smaller establishments, however, often take a siesta, doing business 9:30am to 1:30pm

and 4:30 to 8pm. Hours can vary from store to store.

Customs   You can bring into Spain most personal effects along with reasonable amounts of alcohol and tobacco products. For sports equipment you are allowed fishing gear, one bicycle, skis, tennis or squash racquets, and golf clubs.

Disabled Travelers

Because of Spain's many hills and endless flights of stairs, visitors with mobility issues may have difficulty getting around the country, but conditions are slowly improving. Newer hotels are more sensitive to the needs of those with disabilities, and the more expensive restaurants, in general, are wheelchair accessible.

Organizations that offer a vast range of resources and assistance to travelers with disabilities include **MossRehab** (✆ **800-CALL-MOSS** [225-5667]; www.mossresourcenet.org); the **American Foundation for the Blind** (**AFB;** ✆ **800-232-5463;** www.afb.org); and **SATH** (Society for Accessible Travel & Hospitality; ✆ **212-447-7284;** www.sath.org). **AirAmbulanceCard.com** (✆ **877-424-7633**) is now partnered with SATH and allows you to preselect top-notch hospitals in case of an emergency.

Many travel agencies offer customized tours and itineraries for travelers with disabilities. Among them are **Flying Wheels Travel** (✆ **877-451-5006** or 507-451-5005; www.flyingwheelstravel.com) and **Accessible Journeys** (✆ **800-846-4537** or 610-521-0339; www.disabilitytravel.com).

Flying with Disability (www.flying-with-disability.org) is a comprehensive information source on airplane travel.

British travelers should contact **Tourism for All** (✆ **0845-124-9971** in the U.K. only; www.tourismforall.org.uk) to access a wide range of travel information and resources for seniors and those with disabilities.

Doctors All hotel front desks keep a list of doctors available in their area; most of them are fluent in English.

Drinking Laws The legal drinking age is 18. Bars, taverns, and cafeterias usually open at 8am, and many serve alcohol to 1:30am or later. Generally, you can purchase alcoholic beverages at almost any market.

Drugstores To find an open pharmacy (*farmacia*) outside normal business hours, check the list of stores posted on the door of any drugstore. The law requires drugstores to operate on a rotating system of hours so that there's always a drugstore open somewhere, even Sunday at midnight.

Electricity The U.S. uses 110-volt electricity, Spain 220-volt. Most low-voltage electronics, such as laptops, iPods, and cellphone chargers, do fine with 220-volt. Spain uses the European standard rounded two-prong plug.

Embassies & Consulates If you lose your passport, fall seriously ill, get into legal trouble, or have some other serious problem, your embassy or consulate can help. These are the Madrid addresses and contact information:

Australia: Torre Espacio, Paseo de la Castellana 259D; ✆ **91-353-66-00;** www.spain.embassy.gov.au; **Canada:** Torre Espacio, Paseo de la Castellana 259D; ✆ **91-382-84-00;** www.canadainternational.gc.ca; **Ireland:** Paseo de la Castellana 46, Ireland House; ✆ **91-436-40-93;** www.irlanda.es; **New Zealand:** Calle Pinar 7, 3rd Floor; ✆ **91-523-02-26;** www.nzembassy.com/spain; **United Kingdom:** Torre Espacio, Paseo de la Castellana 259D; ✆ **91-714-63-00;** www.gov.uk/government/world/organisations/british-embassy-madrid; **United States:** Calle Serrano 75; ✆ **91-587-22-00;** http://madrid.usembassy.gov.

Emergencies Call ✆ **112** for fire, police, and ambulance services.

Health Spain should not pose any major health hazards. Tap water is safe to drink. Sushi and sashimi from Atlantic fish are safe to be eaten raw. During the summer, limit your exposure to the sun. Use a sunscreen with a high sun protection factor (SPF) and apply it liberally.

Insurance For information on traveler's insurance, trip cancellation insurance, and medical insurance while traveling, please visit www.frommers.com/tips.

Internet & Wi-Fi Wi-Fi—pronounced "wee-fee" in Spanish—is becoming ubiquitous in Spain. Most lodgings offer free Wi-Fi, at least in public areas. Some hotels give away basic Wi-Fi but charge for faster access. For Wi-Fi on a phone or tablet, download the GOWEX Free Wi-Fi app from the Apple Store. Internet cafes are vanishing, but if you find one, expect to pay 2€ to 4€ per hour.

Language The official language in Spain is Castilian **Spanish** (or *Castellano*). Although Spanish is spoken in every province of Spain, local tongues reasserted themselves with the restoration of democracy in 1975. After years of being outlawed during the Franco dictatorship, **Catalan** has returned to Barcelona and Catalunya, even appearing on street signs; this language and its derivatives are also spoken in the Valencia area and in the Balearic Islands, including Mallorca (even though natives there will tell you they speak Mallorquín). **Basque** is widely spoken in the Basque region (the northeast, near France). Likewise, **Galego,** which sounds and looks very much like Portuguese, has enjoyed a renaissance in Galicia (the northwest). English is spoken in most hotels, restaurants, and shops.

Legal Aid In case of trouble with the authorities, contact your local embassy or consulate, which will recommend an English-speaking lawyer in your area. You will, of course, be charged a typical attorney's fee for representation.

LGBT Travelers In 1978, Spain legalized homosexuality among consenting adults and in 1995 banned discrimination based on sexual orientation. Madrid and Barcelona are major centers of gay life in Spain. The most popular resorts for gay travelers are Sitges (south of Barcelona), Torremolinos, and Ibiza.

Lost & Found To report a lost credit card, contact the following toll-free in Spain: American Express at ✆ **91-572-03-03;** Diners Club at ✆ **91-547-40-00;** MasterCard at ✆ **90-097-12-31;** or Visa at ✆ **90-099-11-24.**

Mail Sending a postcard or letter to the U.S. starts at 0.90€. To calculate the price, visit http://correos.es. You can also buy stamps at any place that sells tobacco.

Mobile Phones You'll likely not be able to use a North American cellphone in Spain unless it's GSM/GPRS-compatible and unless it operates with a SIM card. Virtually all cellphones in Spain operate with this system, as do AT&T and T-Mobile cellphones from North America. Most mobile phones from the U.K. are compatible.

Many travelers opt to simply buy a pre-paid cell phone on location. **Vodafone** (www.vodafone.com); **Movistar** (aka Telefónica, www.movistar.com); **Orange** (www.orange.es); and **Yoigo** (www.yoigo.com) are the four largest and most reliable mobile phone service

providers in Spain. Movistar is the oldest and most established.

Money & Costs Many prices for children—generally defined as ages 6 to 17—are lower than for adults. Fees for children 5 and under are generally waived. Admission prices for seniors (over 60, 62, or 65, depending on venue) are the same as for children. Exchange enough petty cash to cover airport incidentals, tipping, and transportation to your hotel before you leave home, or withdraw money upon arrival at an airport ATM. Best exchange rates are usually from ATMs. Avoid exchanging money at commercial exchange bureaus and hotels, which generally have the highest transaction fees.

Newspapers & Magazines All cities and towns, of course, have Spanish-language newspapers and magazines. However, in the tourist areas of big cities, many kiosks sell editions of the *International New York Times* along with *Time.*

Safety Spain has not been targeted by jihadists since 2004 and Basque nationalists have foresworn violence. U.S. State Department's Worldwide Caution public announcements are available at http://travel.state.gov, but take them with a grain of salt, as the same conditions that prompt a travel advisory are everyday realities in most American cities and towns.

Spain's crime rate more closely resembles Canada's

than the U.S. That said, muggings and robberies do occur, so be careful. Stay out of dark alleys and don't go off with strangers. Exercise caution by carrying limited cash and credit cards. Leave extra cash, credit cards, passports, and personal documents in a safe location. Don't leave anything visible in a parked car. Loss or theft abroad of a passport should be reported immediately to the local police and your nearest embassy or consulate.

Safety can be a concern for women exploring the world on their own. Avoid deserted streets and do not hitchhike. Dress conservatively, especially in remote towns. If you're a victim of catcalls and vulgar suggestions, look straight ahead and just keep walking. If followed, seek out the nearest police officer.

Senior Travel   Major
discounts are available to seniors in Spain, including reduced rates on most admissions and reduced fares on public conveyances. Special room rates are also available at the national parador network.

Smoking   On January 1,
2006, Spain banned smoking in the workplace, and on January 1, 2011, included restaurants, bars, and nightclubs in the ban. Smoking is also banned on public transportation and in other areas such as cultural centers.

Taxes   The internal sales
tax (known in Spain as IVA) ranges from 8% to 33%, depending on the

commodity being sold. Food, wine, and basic necessities are taxed at 8%; most goods and services (including car rentals), at 18%; luxury items (jewelry, all tobacco, imported liquors), at 33%; and hotels, at 8%.

Telephones   To call
Spain:

1.   Dial the international access code: **011** from the U.S.; 00 from the U.K., Ireland, or New Zealand; or 0011 from Australia.

2.   Dial the country code **34.**

3.   Dial the city code, and then the number.

To make international calls from Spain, first dial 00 and then the country code (U.S. or Canada 1, U.K. 44, Ireland 353, Australia 61, New Zealand 64). Next dial the area code and number. For example, if you wanted to call the British Embassy in Washington, D.C., you would dial 00-1-202-588-7800.

For directory assistance: Dial ℂ **1003** in Spain.

For operator assistance: If you need operator assistance in making an international call, dial ℂ **025.**

Toll-free numbers: Numbers beginning with **900** in Spain are toll-free.

Time   Spain is 6 hours
ahead of Eastern Time in the United States. Daylight saving time is in effect from the last Sunday in March to the last Sunday in September.

Tipping   Don't overtip.
The government requires that restaurant and hotel bills include their service

charges—usually 15% of the bill. However, that doesn't mean you should skip out of a place without dispensing an extra euro or two. Some guidelines:

Your **hotel porter** should get 1€ per bag. **Chambermaids** should be given 1€ per day, more if you're generous. Tip **doormen** 1€ for assisting with baggage and 1€ for calling a cab.

For **cabdrivers,** add about 10% to the fare as shown on the meter. At airports, such as Barajas in Madrid and major terminals, the **porter** who handles your luggage will present you with a fixed-charge bill.

Service is included in restaurant bills, but it is the custom to tip extra—in fact, the **waiter** will expect a tip. **Barbers** and **hairdressers** expect a 10% to 15% tip. **Tour guides** expect 2€, although a tip is not mandatory. Theater and bullfight **ushers** get from 1€.

Toilets   In Spain they're
called *aseos, servicios,* or *lavabos* and are labeled *caballeros* for men and *damas* or *señoras* for women. If you can't find any, go into a bar, but you should order something.

Visas   For visits of less
than 3 months, visas are not needed for citizens of the U.S., Canada, Ireland, Australia, New Zealand, and the U.K. For information on obtaining a visa, see your consulate or embassy.

Visitor Information
The Tourist Office of Spain's official website can be found at **www.spain.info.**

Fast Facts: Spain

PLANNING YOUR TRIP TO SPAIN

TOURS

It would be impossible for us to list all of the tours that are offered for visitors to Spain. We've limited this list to some of the most well-respected and long-established tours. But do your own research as well; even the most long-running company can experience financial difficulties and go out of business. When purchasing a tour, it's often a good idea to purchase travel insurance from a third party, as tours can be expensive. Don't purchase from the company itself; if it goes belly-up, you'll lose your insurance, too.

Art Tours

Heritage Tours (*C* **800-378-4555** or 212-206-8400; htprivatetravel.com) offers customized itineraries focusing on art and architecture. Founded by architect Joel Zack, these tours can be customized and often include guided trips through such art cities as Madrid, Toledo, Granada, Barcelona, and Bilbao.

Featuring groups ranging in size from 15 to 25 participants, **ACE Cultural Tours** (*C* **01223-835055;** www.aceculturaltours.co.uk) in Cambridge, England, offers tours led by an art historian to Moorish Spain or other walking tour options. **Context Travel** (*C* **800/691-6036** or www.contexttravel.com) offers excellent, scholar-led tours of major cities around the globe and has recently added Barcelona and Madrid to its roster.

Biking Tours

A leading U.S.-based outfitter is **Easy Rider Tours** (*C* **800-488-8332** or 978-463-6955; www.easyridertours.com). Their tours average between 48km and 81km (30–50 miles) a day; the most appealing tour follows the route trod by medieval pilgrims on their way to Santiago. The bike tours offered by **Backroads** (*C* **800-462-2848** or 510-527-1555; www.backroads.com), take you through Mallorca or from Barcelona to the Pyrenees. One company that specializes in bike tours of Camino de Santiago is **Saranjan Tours** (*C* **800-858-9594;** www.saranjan.com). **Cyclevents** (www.cyclevents.com) offers a number of affordable, self-guided itineraries throughout the Spanish countryside.

Bravo Bike (*C* **91-758-29-45;** www.bravobike.com) is a travel agency featuring organized cycling tours around Madrid. They have branched out to include other parts of Spain as well, notably the route from Salamanca to Santiago de Compostela. One of the most intriguing bike tours is the *ruta de vino* (the wine route) in La Rioja country.

In England, the **Cyclists' Touring Club** (✆ 0844-736-8450; www.ctc. org.uk), charges 39€ a year for membership; part of the fee covers information and suggested cycling routes through Spain and dozens of other countries.

Hiking & Walking Tours

Several firms offer guided hiking on the Camino de Santiago across the north of Spain, but **Spanish Steps** (✆877-787-WALK [9255]; www.spanishsteps. com) offers the most comprehensive program of walks in terms of number of days and level of difficulty. It also includes some walks in the Picos de Europa combined with a yoga retreat. **Backroads** (see "Biking Tours," above) also offers some deluxe walking tours in Spain.

Food & Wine Trips

Spain Taste offers excellent food and wine tours in Catalunya designed for serious gastronomes. They include dinners at Michelin-starred restaurants, wine tastings, and cooking lessons with famous chefs. Tours are conducted from March to June and from September to October. For more information, contact Spain Taste (✆ 93-847-51-15; www.spaintaste.com).

Catacurian offers 3- to 6-day gastronomic vacations that include cooking classes in Catalan cuisine. Programs also feature olive-picking sessions and 1-day market visits and cooking classes within Barcelona itself. Catacurian is located in a private boutique hotel in the Priorat region of Catalunya. For more information, contact Catacurian (✆ 866-538-3519; www.catacurian.com).

Escorted General-Interest Tours

Escorted tours are structured group tours, with a group leader. The price usually includes everything from airfare to hotels, meals, tours, admission costs, and local transportation. Escorted tours—whether they're navigated by bus, motorcoach, train, or boat—let travelers sit back and enjoy the trip without having to drive or worry about details. They take you to the maximum number of sights in the minimum amount of time with the least amount of hassle. They're convenient for people with limited mobility.

On the downside, you'll have little opportunity for serendipitous interactions with locals and cannot deviate from the schedule and itinerary. The tours can often focus on the heavily visited sites, so you miss out on many lesser-known attractions.

A number of companies are beginning to offer pre-planned tours for individual travelers rather than groups. Some of the most expensive and luxurious independent tours to Spain's major cities are offered by **Abercrombie & Kent** (✆ 888-611-4711; www.abercrombiekent.com). Guests stay in fine hotels and are welcomed by knowledgeable local guides. **Tauck Tours** (www.tauck.com) offers similarly deluxe tours.

Trafalgar Tours (✆ 866-544-4434; www.trafalgartours.com) offers a number of tours of Spain. One of the most popular offerings is a 16-day trip called "The Best of Spain." **Escapade Vacations** (✆ 800-356-24-05; www. escapadevacations.com) sells both escorted and package tours to Spain. It can book you on bus tours as well as land and air packages. It offers some culinary holidays as well as general sightseeing, and can set you up for fly-drive tours on your own. Other companies that offer Spain itineraries include **GoAhead Tours** (www.goaheadtours.com), **Globus** (www.globusjourneys.com), and **Insight Vacations** (www.insightvacations.com).

USEFUL TERMS & PHRASES

Most Spaniards are very patient with foreigners who try to speak their language. That said, you might encounter several difficult regional languages and dialects in Spain: In Catalonia, they speak **Catalan** (the most widely spoken non-national language in Europe); in the Basque Country, they speak **Euskera;** in Galicia, you'll hear **Gallego.** However, Castilian Spanish (**Castellano,** or simply **Español**) is understood everywhere; for that reason, we've included a list of simple words and phrases in Spanish to help you get by.

BASIC WORDS & PHRASES

English	Spanish	Pronunciation
Good day	Buenos días	**bweh-nohs dee-ahs**
How are you?	¿Cómo está?	**koh-moh es-tah**
Very well	Muy bien	**mwee byehn**
Thank you	Gracias	**grah-syahs**
You're welcome	De nada	**deh nah-dah**
Goodbye	Adiós	**ah-dyohs**
Please	Por favor	**pohr fah-vohr**
Yes	Sí	**see**
No	No	**noh**
Excuse me	Perdóneme	**pehr-doh-neh-meh**
Give me	Déme	**deh-meh**

English	Spanish	Pronunciation
Where is . . . ?	¿Dónde está . . . ?	*dohn*-deh es-*tah*
the station	la estación	lah es-tah-*syohn*
a hotel	un hotel	oon oh-*tel*
a gas station	una gasolinera	*oo*-nah gah-so-lee-*neh*-rah
a restaurant	un restaurante	oon res-tow-*rahn*-teh
the toilet	el baño	el *bah*-nyoh
a good doctor	un buen médico	oon bwehn *meh*-dee-coh
the road to . . .	el camino a/hacia . . .	el cah-*mee*-noh ah/*ah*-syah
To the right	A la derecha	ah lah deh-*reh*-chah
To the left	A la izquierda	ah lah ees-*kyehr*-dah
Straight ahead	Derecho	deh-*reh*-choh
I would like	Quisiera	kee-*syeh*-rah
I want . . .	Quiero . . .	*kyeh*-roh
to eat	comer	ko-*mehr*
a room	una habitación	*oo*-nah ah-bee-tah-*syohn*
Do you have . . . ?	¿Tiene usted . . . ?	tyeh-neh oo-*sted*
a book	un libro	oon *lee*-broh
a dictionary	un diccionario	oon deek-syoh-*na*-ryo
How much is it?	¿Cuánto cuesta?	*kwahn*-toh *kwehs*-tah
When?	¿Cuándo?	*kwahn*-doh
What?	¿Qué?	keh
There is (Is there . . . ?)	(¿)Hay (. . . ?)	aye
What is there?	¿Qué hay?	keh aye
Yesterday	Ayer	ah-*yehr*
Today	Hoy	oy
Tomorrow	Mañana	mah-*nyah*-nah
Good	Bueno	*bweh*-noh
Bad	Malo	*mah*-loh
Better (Best)	(Lo) Mejor	(loh) meh-*hor*
More	Más	mahs
Less	Menos	*meh*-nohs
No smoking	Se prohibe fumar	seh proh-*ee*-beh foo-*mahr*
Postcard	Tarjeta postal	tar-*heh*-tah pohs-*tahl*
Insect repellent	Repelente contra insectos	reh-peh-*lehn*-teh *cohn*-trah een-*sehk*-tohs
Do you speak English?	¿Habla usted inglés?	*ah*-blah oo-*sted* een-*glehs*

English	Spanish	Pronunciation
Is there anyone here who speaks English?	¿Hay alguien aquí que hable inglés?	aye **ahl**-gyehn ah-**kee** keh ah-bleh een-**glehs**
I speak a little Spanish.	Hablo un poco de español.	**ah**-bloh oon **poh**-koh deh es-pah-**nyol**
I don't understand Spanish very well.	No (lo) entiendo muy bien el español.	noh (loh) ehn-**tyehn**-doh mwee byehn el es-pah-**nyol**
The meal is good.	Me gusta la comida.	meh **goo**-stah lah koh-**mee**-dah
What time is it?	¿Qué hora es?	keh **oh**-rah es
May I see your menu?	¿Puedo ver el menú (la carta)?	**pweh**-do vehr el meh-**noo** (lah **car**-tah)
The check, please.	La cuenta por favor.	lah **kwehn**-tah pohr fah-**vohr**
What do I owe you?	¿Cuánto le debo?	**kwahn**-toh leh **deh**-boh
What did you say? (Colloquial)	¿Mande?	**mahn**-deh
What did you say? (Formal)	¿Cómo?	**koh**-moh
Do you accept traveler's checks?	¿Acepta usted cheques de viajero?	ah-**sehp**-tah oo-**sted** **cheh**-kehs deh byah-**heh**-roh

NUMBERS

English	Spanish	Pronunciation
1	uno	**oo**-noh
2	dos	**dohs**
3	tres	**trehs**
4	cuatro	**kwah**-troh
5	cinco	**seen**-koh
6	seis	**says**
7	siete	**syeh**-teh
8	ocho	**oh**-choh
9	nueve	**nweh**-beh
10	diez	**dyehs**
11	once	**ohn**-seh
12	doce	**doh**-seh
13	trece	**treh**-seh
14	catorce	kah-**tohr**-seh
15	quince	**keen**-seh
16	dieciséis	dyeh-see-**says**
17	diecisiete	dyeh-see-**syeh**-teh
18	dieciocho	dyeh-see-**oh**-choh

English	Spanish	Pronunciation
19	diecinueve	**dyeh-see-*nweh*-beh**
20	veinte	***bayn*-teh**
30	treinta	***trayn*-tah**
40	cuarenta	**kwah-*rehn*-tah**
50	cincuenta	**seen-*kwehn*-tah**
60	sesenta	**seh-*sehn*-tah**
70	setenta	**seh-*tehn*-tah**
80	ochenta	**oh-*chehn*-tah**
90	noventa	**noh-*behn*-tah**
100	cien	***syehn***
200	doscientos	**doh-*syehn*-tohs**
500	quinientos	**kee-*nyehn*-tos**
1,000	mil	**meel**

TRAVEL TERMS

Aduana Customs
Aeropuerto Airport
Avenida Avenue
Avión Airplane
Aviso Warning
Bus Bus
Calle Street
Cheques de viajeros Traveler's checks
Correo(s) Mail, or post office
Dinero Money
Embajada Embassy
Embarque Boarding
Entrada Entrance

Equipaje Luggage
Este East
Frontera Border
Hospedaje Inn
Norte North
Oeste West
Pasaje Ticket
Pasaporte Passport
Puerta de salida Boarding gate
Salida Exit
Tarjeta de embarque Boarding card
Vuelo Flight

EMERGENCY TERMS

¡Auxilio! Help!
Ambulancia Ambulance
Bomberos Fire brigade
Clínica Clinic
Emergencia Emergency
Enfermo/a Sick
Enfermera Nurse
Farmacia Pharmacy

Fuego/Incendio Fire
Hospital Hospital
Ladrón Thief
Peligroso Dangerous
Policía Police
Médico Doctor
¡Váyase! Go away!

Index

INDEX

Restaurants

PHOTO CREDITS